Law and the
Life Insurance Contract

The Irwin Series in Financial Planning and Insurance
Consulting Editor Jerry S. Rosenbloom *University of Pennsylvania*

Law and the Life Insurance Contract

Muriel L. Crawford

J.D., FLMI, CLU, ChFC
Associate General Counsel and Secretary
Washington National Insurance Company

William T. Beadles

D.B.A., CLU
National Insurance Education Adviser, Emeritus
State Farm Insurance Companies
Senior Educational Consultant, Emeritus
The American College

1989
Sixth Edition

IRWIN
Homewood, IL 60430
Boston, MA 02116

Although lawyers may find this book useful in
gaining a general understanding of life and health
insurance law, the book is intended primarily for
non-lawyers. Non-lawyers are cautioned, however, that
this book is not intended to provide solutions to
individual legal problems, as the law differs from
jurisdiction to jurisdiction and is subject to change
within a jurisdiction. Moreover, slight changes in fact
situations from those presented in the book may require
a material variance in the action to be taken. This book
is intended to educate those who read it to recognize
legal problems, so that they can seek advice from their
own legal counsel.

Sponsoring editor: Michael W. Junior
Project editor: Suzanne Ivester
Production manager: Bette Ittersagen
Compositor: Weimer Typesetting Co., Inc.
Typeface: 10/12 Times Roman
Printer: R. R. Donnelley & Sons Company

LIBRARY OF CONGRESS
Library of Congress Cataloging-in-Publication Data

Crawford, Muriel L.
    Law and the life insurance contract / Muriel L. Crawford, William
T. Beadles.—6th ed.
        p.   cm.
    Rev. ed. of: Law and the life insurance contract / Janice E.
Greider, Muriel L. Crawford, William T. Beadles. 5th ed. 1984.
    Includes indexes.
    ISBN 0-256-06040-1
    1. Insurance, Life—Law and legislation—United States.
2. Insurance, Life—United States—Policies. I. Beadles, William
T. II. Grieder, Janice E. Law and the life insurance contract.
III. Title.
KF1175.G7 1989
346.73'08632—dc 19
[347.3068632]   88–15449
                                                        CIP

Printed in the United States of America

2 3 4 5 6 7 8 9 0 D O 5 4 3 2 1 0

To Eugene Hubbard and Fraser Mills

PREFACE

Law and the Life Insurance Contract has been used to educate students of life insurance law for over a quarter of a century. William T. Beadles labored as coauthor of the first five editions of the book. In honor of his contributions, I have retained his name as coauthor on this sixth edition.

This edition, like the earlier editions, attempts to present the major principles of life insurance law in a manner which can be readily understood by students who do not have legal training. I have tried to define legal terms as they occur and to explain legal concepts in everyday English.

Although the general organization of the earlier editions has been retained, I have incorporated much material not found in the earlier editions. Sections on model laws, criminal law, financial planners, unisex rating, AIDS, universal and variable life insurance laws, long-term care policies, Section 89 of the Internal Revenue Code, COBRA, and wrongful discharge have been added. The rest of the book has been brought up to date. The illustrative case at the end of each chapter has been retained, as I believe that a first-hand introduction to the reasoning of the courts is essential to an understanding of law.

I have had assistance from many people in producing this sixth edition. The lawyers who reviewed parts or all of the manuscript include Patricia Kuehn; Geri Gaughan; Anthony Crement; Harriett Jones, FLMI; Eugene Hubbard, FLMI; and Fraser Mills, FLMI. This edition of the book is dedicated to Eugene Hubbard and Fraser Mills in recognition of their unstinting work on the LOMA 3 Examination Committee, of which I also am a member. Their suggestions have helped enormously in making needed revisions and additions to the book.

Edward E. Graves, CLU, ChFC, associate professor of insurance at the American College, gave me helpful suggestions as did Gale Gran, M.D., medical director of Washington National Insurance Company. Law librarian Joyce Dahlberg did much of the research for this edition. My secretary, Jennifer Donham, expertly typed the revisions and, with the author, proofread the galley proofs and page proofs. Her sense of humor made the many hours of proofreading much less tedious. My sincere thanks to all who have so generously helped me.

Muriel L. Crawford

CONTENTS

1 Insurance and the Law   **1**

Structure and Sources of Law, 2
Common Law, 4
Constitutions, 5
Statutes, 7
Administrative Rules and Regulations, 8
Model Laws, 9
Courts, 9
Court Trials, 13
Civil Law and Criminal Law, 18
Courts of Law and Courts of Equity, 18
Insurance Regulation, 19

2 Contracts   **29**

Two Definitions of *Contract*, 30
Offer, 33
Acceptance, 36
Consideration, 39
Competent Parties, 41
Contract Form, 46
Illegality, 48
Duress and Undue Influence, 50
Rules of Contract Construction, 50
The Parol Evidence Rule, 52
Breach and Materiality, 54
Third-Person Beneficiaries, 54
Liberty of Contract, 54
Constitutional Protection of Existing Contracts, 55
Life and Health Insurance Contract Law, 55

3 Agency   **61**

Power and Authority, 63
Acts and Knowledge of the Agent, 63
Capacity of Principal and Agent, 64

Creation of the Principal-Agent Relationship, 65
Limitations of the Agent's Authority, 70
Principal and Agent, 71
Principal, Agent, and Third Persons, 74
Classification of Agents, 75
Termination of the Agent's Powers, 76
Master and Servant, 77
Employer and Independent Contractor, 78

4 Agency in Life and Health Insurance   **84**

Insurance Agents and Brokers, 85
Consultants, 86
Financial Planners, 87
Licensing of Agents and Brokers, 88
The Contract Between Insurer and Agent, 97
Solicitation of Business, 97
Malpractice Insurance, 107
Collection and Remission of Premiums, 107
Commissions, 109
Records and Reports, 110

5 Waiver and Estoppel   **115**

Waiver and Estoppel Defined, 116
Express and Implied Waivers, 117
Intent to Waive, 119
Knowledge of the Insurer, 120
Authority of the Agent, 123
Forbidden Waivers and Estoppels, 124
Revocation of Waiver, 126
Election of Remedies, 127
Estoppel and the Parol Evidence Rule, 128
Common Waiver and Estoppel Situations, 129

6 Formation of the Life Insurance Contract   **138**

Life Insurance Contract Offer and Acceptance, 139
Delay in Acting on the Application, 141
Premium Receipts, 144
Risk Classification and Selection, 156
Insurable Interest, 160
Consideration, 167
Competent Contracting Parties, 168

Delivery of the Policy, 168
Effective Date of the Policy, 170

7 Structure of the Life Insurance Policy   **175**

Simplified Language, 176
Policy Contents, 177
Policy Face Page, 178
Required Policy Provisions, 179
Optional Policy Provisions, 187
Prohibited Policy Provisions, 189
Universal and Variable Life Insurance Laws, 192
Policy Filing and Approval, 194

8 Added Benefits and Limitations   **199**

Accidental Death Benefit, 200
Disability Benefits, 212
Guaranteed Insurability Option, 216
War Hazard Exclusion, 217
Aviation Hazard Exclusion, 220

9 Property Rights in the Life Insurance Policy   **226**

Property Law, 227
Community Property Rights, 229
Creditors' Rights, 236
Divorce, 244
Killing of the Insured by the Beneficiary, 245

10 Beneficiary Designations and Changes   **251**

The Policyowner's Right to Choose the Beneficiary, 252
Beneficiaries and Their Rights, 253
Beneficiary Designations, 256
Change of Beneficiary, 265

11 Settlement Agreements, Trusts, and Wills   **275**

Settlement Agreements, 276
Trusts, 283
Wills, 289
Will Substitutes, 290

12 Premiums and Dividends   306

The Initial Premium, 307
Renewal Premiums, 309
Time of Payment, 311
Method of Payment, 313
Persons Making Payment, 317
Persons Receiving Payment, 320
Premium Notices, 321
Excuses for Nonpayment, 322
Return of Premiums, 327
Dividends, 328

13 Nonforfeiture Provisions and Policy Loans   335

Cash Values, 335
Nonforfeiture Provisions, 336
Policy Loans, 343

14 Assignments and Other Transfers   355

Absolute Assignments, 356
Collateral Assignments, 357
The Insurer's Role, 361
Requirements for Assignment, 365
Successive Assignees, 368
Assignments by the Beneficiary, 369
Other Transfers, 370

15 Lapse and Reinstatement   377

Lapse and Expiration, 378
Reinstatement Laws, 378
Reinstatement Provisions, 379
Death during the Reinstatement Application Review, 382
Continuation of the Original Contract, 384
Contestability of the Reinstated Policy, 384
Reinstatement and the Suicide Clause, 387
Addition of New Contract Terms, 388
Law Governing the Reinstated Policy, 389

16 Remedies   395

Equitable Principles, 396
Interpleader, 399

Rescission, 402
Reformation, 406
Declaratory Judgment, 410

17   Policy Contests   417

Valid, Void, and Voidable Contracts, 418
Material Misrepresentation, 418
Misrepresentation Statutes, 419
Breach of Conditions, 421
Contest of the Policy, 422
Development of the Incontestable Clause, 423
Conflict with Other Provisions, 425
Contests Not Barred by the Incontestable Clause, 429
Contestability of Disability and Accidental Death Insurance, 432
The Phrase *During the Lifetime of the Insured*, 433
Date from Which the Contestable Period Runs, 436

18   Contract Performance   442

Establishing the Proper Payee, 443
Suicide, 452
Disappearance of the Insured, 456
War or Aviation Hazard Exclusions, 458
Computation of the Benefit Amount, 458
Releases, 458
Compromise Settlements, 459
Unfair Claim Settlement Practices Act, 459
The Reasonable Expectations Doctrine, 460
Claims Litigation, 461

19   Group Insurance   475

History of Group Life Insurance, 476
Group Life Insurance Definitions, 478
Group Life Insurance Standard Provisions, 481
Dependent Group Life Insurance, 489
Group Master Policies and Certificates, 489
The Actively-at-Work Requirement, 490
Termination of Group Insurance, 491
Group Policy Premiums and Dividends, 493
The Policyholder as Agent, 494
Conflict of Laws, 495
Federal Taxation of Group Life Insurance, 497

ERISA and Group Insurance, 497
Section 89 Discrimination Testing, 498
FEGLI and SGLI, 500
Group Health Insurance, 502
Wholesale and Franchise Insurance, 502

20 Health Insurance   **507**

The Uniform Individual Accident and Sickness Policy
   Provisions Law, 508
Definitions of Terms, 516
Preexisting Conditions, 519
Benefit Provisions, 520
Mandated Benefits, 520
Exclusions and Limitations, 521
Cancellation and Renewal Provisions, 522
Medicare and Medicare Supplement Policies, 524
Long-Term Care Policies, 525
Group Health Insurance, 526
Continuation of Group Health Coverage, 528

21 Life and Health Insurance Advertising   **536**

Promotional Literature Presented by Agents, 537
Waiver, Estoppel, and Group Insurance Advertising, 538
Direct Response Insurance Advertising, 538
Regulation by Federal Agencies, 542
State Laws Governing Insurance Advertising, 543

22 Privacy and Insurance   **558**

History of Privacy Law, 559
Federal Privacy Legislation, 560
State Privacy Laws, 562
The NAIC Model Privacy Act, 563
AIDS and Privacy, 568

23 Insurers and Agents as Employers   **578**

Statutory Protection of Employees, 579
Disparate Treatment and Disparate Impact Discrimination, 580
Employment Practices and Decisions, 582
Sexual Harassment, Pregnancy Discrimination, and Reverse
   Discrimination, 588

Affirmative Action, 591
Retaliation by the Employer, 592
Penalties for Employment Discrimination, 593
Wrongful Discharge, 593

Appendixes

Appendix A: Insurance Application Form   **605**

Appendix B: Whole Life Insurance Policy Form   **610**

Appendix C: Dividend Provisions   **633**

Appendix D: War Hazard Rider   **634**

Appendix E: American Bankers Association Assignment Form   **635**

Appendix F: Late Remittance Offer   **637**

Appendix G: Reinstatement Application Form   **638**

Appendix H: Life Insurance Buyer's Guide   **640**

**Appendix I: Adjustable Life Insurance Application and Policy
                Forms**   **646**

Appendix J: Glossary of Legal Terms   **670**

Index of Cases   **679**

Index   **697**

CHAPTER 1

Insurance and the Law

STRUCTURE AND SOURCES OF LAW
    Structure of Law
    Sources of Law

COMMON LAW
    General Principles of Law
    Common Law and Civil Law
    Case Law

CONSTITUTIONS
    A Twofold Purpose
    The Dual Constitutional System of the United States
    The Federal Constitution
    State Constitutions

STATUTES

ADMINISTRATIVE RULES AND REGULATIONS

MODEL LAWS

COURTS
    The Dual Court System of the United States
    Federal Courts
    State Courts
    Jurisdiction
    The Applicable Law

COURT TRIALS
    Pleadings
    Discovery
    Proof of Facts
    Application of Case Law
    Application of Common Law

CIVIL LAW AND CRIMINAL LAW

COURTS OF LAW AND COURTS OF EQUITY
    Law and Equity Today
    Equitable Remedies

INSURANCE REGULATION
The *South-Eastern Underwriters* Decision
The McCarran-Ferguson Act
Federal Regulation Today
State Regulation Today
SUMMARY

The student of life and health insurance needs a basic understanding of the law for four reasons. First, an insurance policy describes a contract, and a contract is an agreement enforceable in a court of law. For this reason, an understanding of contract law is a necessary part of insurance education. Second, a study of contracts leads inevitably to many other areas of law. An acquaintance with the law of agency, property, estates, trusts, community property, creditor-debtor relationships, equitable remedies, and torts is necessary to an understanding of contracts and of the insurance business. Third, insurance is heavily regulated by a body of insurance law which is becoming more complex every day. Insurers must work continually to bring themselves into compliance with these laws. Fourth, insurers must conduct their businesses in accordance with many laws which have nothing to do with insurance. As employers they must deal with employment laws and as issuers of securities with securities laws. The purpose of this chapter is to explain the structure of law and the way the laws governing insurers fit into that structure.

STRUCTURE AND SOURCES OF LAW

When people speak of a "law," they usually mean a statute enacted by a legislature. However, law is a great deal more than a collection of statutes. The structure of law is complex, and its sources manifold.

Structure of Law

Included in the concept of law are the broad philosophies and principles of constitutional law, specific agreements embodied in treaties between nations, congressional enactments and state statutes, decisions of federal and state courts, rules and regulations of numerous administrative departments of federal and state governments, and many general principles of custom and public policy dating back so far that no one can say accurately when they originated. In its broadest sense, law can be defined as a system of rules and principles that comprise an enforceable standard of human conduct.

The laws of a society are shaped by and tailored to the needs of that society. A law appropriate to and necessary for one society might be intolerable in another. Even within a country, different regions require different laws. In the United States, no two states have laws all of which are identical. Moreover, a federal law which applies to the entire country might be readily accepted in some states and not so readily accepted in others. Such was the case with the federal law requiring vehicles to limit their speed to 55 miles per hour. Many people in the western states, where it is often necessary to travel great distances, found this law difficult to accept, while people in small eastern states accepted it more readily. A lack of acceptance of a law will often cause it to be ignored, unenforced, modified, or repealed.

As society changes, some laws lose their acceptance. For example, at one time a state could lawfully deny women the right to practice law.[1] Social changes caused this law to lose its acceptance, and the law was eliminated. Other changes in society make apparent the need for new laws. For example, when computers came into general use, it became necessary for the legislatures and courts to develop a body of computer law.

A society which changes rapidly will have a rapidly changing body of law. The United States with its rapid social and technological change is an example of such a society.

Sources of Law

It is often necessary to consult a number of sources before all the applicable law can be found on any given subject. Constitutions must be examined, as well as pertinent statutes, rules and regulations of administrative bodies, and reports of court decisions. Treaties between nations and executive orders and proclamations might also bear on the question under consideration.

The constitutions and legislative enactments of the federal government and of each state government are compiled and published. Legislative enactments are arranged, or codified, alphabetically by subject matter and indexed so that they can be found easily. Each code has a title indicating its jurisdiction, as *United States Code, Illinois Revised Statutes,* or *Massachusetts General Laws Annotated.*

The decisions of courts of appeals, also called appellate courts, are published in bound volumes called reports or reporters. They occupy many shelves in any law library, and detailed systems have been devised for indexing them. A standard form of reference for these published court decisions has been developed. The title of the case is given thus: *Smith v. Jones.* Then follow the volume number, the abbreviation for the reporter system referred to, the page on which the case begins, and in parentheses, the year in which the case was decided. Thus, the landmark insurance case of *United States v. South-Eastern Underwriters Association,* 322 U.S. 533 (1944), will be found in volume 322 of the United States Reports, beginning at page 533. This case was decided by the United States Supreme Court in 1944.

---

[1]Bradwell v. Illinois, 83 U.S. (16 Wall.) 130 (1872).

Other examples may help in understanding this system. For instance, one famous life insurance case is *Metropolitan Life Insurance Co. v. Conway*, 252 N.Y. 449, 169 N.E. 642 (1930). This means that this case is reported in volume 252 of the Court of Appeals of New York reports on page 449 and in volume 169 of the North Eastern Reporter on page 642. This case was decided in 1930. Similarly, the case of *Monahan v. Metropolitan Life Insurance Co.*, 283 Ill. 136, 119 N.E. 68 (1918) is reported in volume 283 of the Illinois Supreme Court reports on page 136 and in volume 119 of the North Eastern Reporter on page 68. This case was decided in 1918.

Lawyers also make frequent use of various treatises on the law, such as *Restatements of the Law* prepared by the American Law Institute, *Williston on Contracts, Couch on Insurance,* and *Corpus Juris Secundum,* to mention only a few of the general references available. Such treatises help lawyers gain a general understanding of the law. The best treatises have influenced the development of legal principles.

Much of the law has been programmed into computers. LEXIS and WESTLAW are well-known software systems for computer-assisted legal research. Their data bases are large and are being expanded. Thus, lawyers now use computers to assist them to do fast, thorough, accurate legal research.

COMMON LAW

The United States is often said to be a common-law country. The term *common law* has a number of different meanings. Some of the most important meanings are given below.

General Principles of Law

In its broadest meaning, the common law is a heritage of general principles and concepts involving customs, public policy, and ideas of justice that are followed as a matter of legal philosophy by courts of common-law countries, states, and provinces. The traditions of the common law were brought to the United States by the early settlers from England.

Common Law and Civil Law

Common law also means a system of law followed by England and by nations which derive their law from English law. *Common law* is often used in this sense to contrast legal systems based on English law with legal systems based on Roman law. England, Canada (except Quebec), and most of the states in the United States are common-law jurisdictions. By contrast, France, Spain, Italy, Quebec, and some states in the United States derive their legal systems in whole or in part from Roman law. These countries, states, and provinces are said to be civil-law jurisdictions.[2]

Perhaps the most important distinguishing characteristic of the civil law is that it attempts to bring together all the general principles of law and to organize them into a relatively complete code. Court decisions then are made only with reference to principles that have been made a part of that code. In common-law jurisdictions, there is no attempt to write down all the principles that will be used, although such principles often are enacted into statutes or expressed as case law.

Case Law

The term *common law* is sometimes used to distinguish case law (court decisions) from statutory, or legislative, law. In that sense, the common law of a jurisdiction is said to be made up of the decisions of the courts, as contrasted with the enactments of legislatures or written constitutions.

CONSTITUTIONS

A constitution sets forth in general terms the principles that form the legal foundation of a government. Because of its great importance as an instrument of government, the most serious consideration is given to drafting and adopting a constitution. In addition, extensive safeguards are incorporated to prevent frequent or ill-considered amendments. A constitution ordinarily meets the needs of a changing society through interpretation by the courts, rather than by amendment. Its general language makes this flexibility possible. Constitutions tend to be significantly more permanent than statutes.

A Twofold Purpose

A constitution in the United States has a twofold purpose. First, it describes the structure of the government, defining the extent of its powers and outlining the principles on which it is to operate. Thus, it is customary to provide for three branches of government—legislative, executive, and judicial—and to establish a system of checks and balances to guard against any branch becoming too powerful. Second, a constitution establishes a system of safeguards and guarantees of basic human rights, such as freedom of

---

[2]Louisiana comes closest to being a civil-law state. Texas is sometimes said to be a civil-law state. Many states have some laws which have been influenced by civil law. See the discussion on community property law in Chapter 9, "Property Rights in the Life Insurance Policy."

speech, freedom of worship, and the other freedoms enumerated in the Bill of Rights of the federal Constitution.

The Dual Constitutional System of the United States

In the United States, there are two kinds of constitutions: the Constitution of the federal government and the constitutions of the various states. The basic difference between the federal Constitution and the state constitutions is that power is delegated by the federal Constitution to the federal government, whereas the state constitutions define and limit the already existing power of the state governments. The federal government has no power which is not given to it by the federal Constitution. A state government has all powers which are not prohibited to it by the federal Constitution or by the constitution of that state.

The Federal Constitution

Historically, the governing power in the United States was exercised separately by each of the original 13 colonies which had well-defined existences as political units before there was a federal government. When representatives of these colonies met to frame a constitution for a proposed central government, the authority of the new government so formed was delegated to it by the colonies. This idea is summarized in Amendment X of the federal Constitution as follows: "The powers not delegated to the United States by the Constitution, nor prohibited by it to the States, are reserved to the States respectively, or to the people."

The federal government is more than a mere confederation of sovereign states. It has direct authority over the people themselves to the extent of the governing power delegated to it. The United States Supreme Court has the final power to decide whether the federal government has exceeded the limits of its constitutional authority. However, over the years, the Court has tended to broaden the authority of the federal government by holding that many powers not specifically granted to the federal government are implied in the Constitution. Once it has been established that a power is properly exercisable by the federal government, any acts by it in that particular area take precedence over the acts of any state or subdivision of a state with respect to the same subject matter.

The federal Constitution, the laws of the United States that are enacted under its provisions, and all treaties made under the authority of the United States are declared by the federal Constitution to be the "supreme law of the land." Accordingly, any law, whether federal or state, that violates a provision of the federal Constitution is unconstitutional. A court decision, whether federal or state, that violates a right guaranteed by the federal Constitution can be overruled by a higher court. The act of an administrative officer, either federal or state, can be overruled by a court if the act conflicts with the federal Constitution. Nevertheless, there are many areas in which the state constitutions are supreme.

State Constitutions

A state constitution performs some of the same functions for the state that the federal Constitution performs for the United States. That is to say, it outlines the general framework of the government and spells out the guarantees of fundamental human rights. However, a state constitution does not grant the state the power to govern. Instead, it functions as a limitation of the power that is inherent in the state itself. The governing power of a state exists whether there is a state constitution or not. Thus, the state constitution has been called the "mandate of a sovereign people to its servants and representatives."

While the federal Constitution enumerates delegated powers, a state constitution limits powers already acknowledged to exist, powers which in all other respects are unlimited. The practical effects of this concept are significant. For instance, if an act of a state legislature is challenged, it will be considered to be constitutional unless the state constitution or the Constitution of the federal government prohibits it. By contrast, an act of Congress must be based upon some affirmative provision of the federal Constitution and will be constitutional only if it is the exercise of a power delegated to the federal government.

Under the federal Constitution, some of the powers that otherwise would be exercisable by the states were given up and delegated to the federal government. In all other areas, however, the state constitution represents the supreme law of the state. Thus, the Constitution of the United States and the constitutions of the various states—each operative in its own respective sphere—together provide the fundamental principles upon which the government of the United States is based.

STATUTES

A statute is "an act of the legislature declaring, commanding, or prohibiting something; a particular law enacted and established by the will of the legislative department of government; the written will of the legislature, solemnly expressed according to the forms necessary to constitute it the law of the state."[3]

Collections of compiled statutes are often referred to as "revised statutes." A collection of statutes systematically arranged, indexed, revised, and reenacted by the legislature in that form is often referred to as a "code."

---

[3]Black's Law Dictionary 1264–65 (5th ed. 1979).

Thus, an insurance code is a collection of the insurance statutes of a given state, a criminal code is a collection of statutes relating to crimes, and so on.

Both the federal Congress and the state legislatures enact statutes. Statutes are more temporary than provisions found in constitutions, and, ordinarily, statutes are expressed in more specific terms, as rules and standards of conduct. In areas of power granted to the federal government, the Congress of the United States enacts the statutes. In areas that are the concern of the individual states, the legislatures of the respective states enact the statutes. If it is not clear whether Congress or the state legislatures have the power to legislate in a given area, the question can be referred to the courts for decision. In fact, that is how the landmark insurance case, *United States v. South-Eastern Underwriters Association,* arose. The right of the individual states, as opposed to the federal government, to regulate insurance was challenged. The question was decided by the United States Supreme Court.[4]

ADMINISTRATIVE RULES AND REGULATIONS

Theoretically, both state and federal governments in the United States are based upon a separation of powers. A separation of powers means that a government is divided into departments or branches. The legislative branch is empowered to make the laws, the executive branch to carry out the laws, and the judicial branch to interpret the laws and to adjudicate disputes under the laws. One branch must not encroach upon the domain of another.

An administrative officer is part of the executive branch. Under a strict separation-of-powers approach, a rule set down by an administrative officer would not be effective. However, the increasing complexities of modern business have necessitated some overlap among the three branches. Highly technical businesses require that highly technical knowledge be applied to regulate them. Obviously, legislators cannot have the necessary technical knowledge of every business that must be regulated. Consequently, they have adopted the practice of enacting regulatory statutes in general terms. They then authorize the administrative officer having the duty of executing the law to fill in the details by means of administrative rules and regulations that have the force and effect of law. This delegation of rule-making power to administrative officers has been consistently upheld by the courts as constitutional, as long as the rules so made are within the scope of the delegated power, are subject to judicial review, and are surrounded by other safeguards.

Administrative officers also perform judicial functions. They hold hearings, make decisions, and impose penalties. Thus, administrative officers function in all three spheres—executive, legislative, and judicial.

The commissioner, director, or superintendent of insurance is a state administrative officer. Today, most state legislatures have authorized the com-

---

[4]This subject will be discussed more fully in the section below entitled "Insurance Regulation."

missioner, director, or superintendent of insurance to adopt appropriate rules and regulations implementing the provisions of the state insurance statutes. Often such administrative rules and regulations constitute a major part of the regulatory law governing the life and health insurance industry.

MODEL LAWS

A model law is an act or regulation proposed by experts in a particular field for adoption by the states. The National Association of Insurance Commissioners (NAIC) has proposed many model acts and regulations for adoption, some of which are discussed in this book.

A model act or regulation itself is not a law and need not be complied with. It is merely a pattern on which a state legislature might base a statute, or on which an administrative officer, such as an insurance commissioner, might base a regulation. Sometimes statutes or regulations are patterned exactly on model laws, but often various changes are incorporated.

Another name for model laws is *uniform laws*. The latter is probably the preferable term, since an important purpose of the model laws is to promote uniformity among state laws.

COURTS

Courts comprise the judicial branch of government. A court applies laws to resolve controversies brought before it. In so doing, a court interprets laws.

The Dual Court System of the United States

Because there are state and federal governments in the United States, there are two court systems. Each state has its own system of state courts, and there is a national system of federal courts. In matters over which the state courts have authority—that is, in areas where the governing powers have not been delegated to the federal government—the decisions of the state courts are final. In other areas, appeals may be taken to the United States Supreme Court. Many questions can be tried in either a state or federal court as the parties prefer.[5]

Federal Courts

The federal courts are provided for in the federal Constitution. The Supreme Court was established by the Constitution itself. The other federal courts were established by laws enacted by Congress under constitutional authority.

---

[5]See further discussion on this point in the subsection entitled "Where Jurisdictions Overlap," below.

The Federal Court Hierarchy.   There are three levels of federal courts—district courts on the first level, courts of appeals, also called appellate courts, on the intermediate level, and the United States Supreme Court at the top of the hierarchy. Most cases involving subjects over which federal courts have jurisdiction are brought first in one of the United States district courts. Each state has one or more district courts. Next, such a case can be appealed to one of the 13 United States courts of appeals. Lastly, it can be appealed to the United States Supreme Court for a final decision.

The United States Supreme Court.   The Supreme Court of the United States consists of nine judges and is primarily an appellate court. This means that most of the cases it hears come to it on appeal from a lower court. Some cases, however, can be taken directly to the Supreme Court. These include cases affecting foreign ambassadors, ministers, and consuls, and controversies in which a state is a party.

Special Federal Courts.   In addition to the district courts, the courts of appeals, and the United States Supreme Court, there are several federal courts which have limited jurisdiction. These include the United States Court of Claims, the United States Tax Court, and the United States Court of Customs and Patent Appeals.

State Courts

The courts of most states have the same type of three-level organization that the federal courts have. Other states do not have courts on the intermediate appellate level. However, every state has courts of original jurisdiction in which suits can be brought.

Courts of Original Jurisdiction.   All cases begin in a court of original jurisdiction and most end there, as relatively few are appealed to higher courts. There are state courts of general original jurisdiction and state courts of limited original jurisdiction. The courts of general jurisdiction have the authority to decide almost all types of cases, both civil and criminal. These courts usually are called circuit courts, district courts, or superior courts. Courts of limited jurisdiction have authority to decide only certain types of cases. For example, probate courts handle only cases relating to wills and estates. Small claims courts handle only cases where the amount in controversy is small—usually under $1,000 or $1,500.

Appellate and Supreme Courts.   Intermediate courts, often termed appellate courts, are available in about two thirds of the states for appeals from the decisions of the courts of original jurisdiction. Each state has a highest court, usually called a supreme court, whose decisions are final with respect to interpretations of the state constitution and to cases brought under state and local laws. Appeals may be taken from the state supreme courts to the

United States Supreme Court, however, on questions involving the federal Constitution or federal laws and treaties.

Jurisdiction

In a system involving so many different courts, it is obvious that there must be some rules for determining which cases are properly handled by each court. These rules are called "rules of jurisdiction."

Jurisdiction of the Subject Matter. A court has jurisdiction of the subject matter in a case if the constitutional or statutory provisions which establish the court give it the power to hear and make an enforceable decision in that type of case. For example, a tax court has jurisdiction of the subject matter in tax cases, but not in divorce cases.

Often, the amount in controversy will be a governing factor. For example, justice of the peace courts ordinarily do not have jurisdiction in cases involving more than a small amount of money. On the other hand, the United States district courts do not have jurisdiction in some kinds of cases unless the amount involved is in excess of $10,000.

Jurisdiction Over the Person. It is not enough that the court has jurisdiction over the subject matter. In addition, jurisdiction over the person being sued must be obtained by compliance with certain constitutional requirements if that person is to be bound by the decision of the court. To obtain jurisdiction, a summons must be issued by the court and must be served upon the defendant—usually personally—although, in some cases, publication is sufficient. *Publication* means advertising the summons in a newspaper as a means of notifying a defendant who cannot be served with the summons personally.

Where Jurisdictions Overlap. Often, more than one court has jurisdiction in a given kind of case. This is particularly true of insurance cases which frequently involve diversity of citizenship.

Diversity of citizenship means that the parties on opposite sides of a lawsuit are domiciled in different states. Diversity of citizenship is one of the grounds to invoke the jurisdiction of a United States district court, when a controversy also exceeds $10,000 in value. The purpose of diversity of citizenship is to provide out-of-state litigants with an impartial federal court. Alternatively, the lawsuit could be tried in a state court. Thus, many cases involving life or health insurance contracts can be brought either in a state court or in a United States district court.

The Applicable Law

The discussion thus far might seem to imply that state courts always apply the law of their respective states while the federal courts always apply federal law. Such is not the case. A court must often apply the law of another jurisdiction. For example, the activities of persons in one state can become the subject of a lawsuit in another state, requiring the court hearing the case to decide which state's law should apply. Conflict of laws rules are used to resolve this problem.

Conflict of Laws.   Conflict of laws has been defined as "that part of the law of each state or nation which determines whether, in dealing with a legal situation, the law of some other state or nation will be recognized, be given effect, or be applied."[6] Each jurisdiction has its own conflict of laws rules.

In lawsuits on life insurance policies the laws of more than one jurisdiction are often involved, and conflict of laws problems frequently arise. Ordinarily, a life insurance contract must meet the requirements of the state where the applicant has legal residence at the time it is issued and delivered. Often, an applicant-insured lived in one state when the policy was delivered and in another state at the time of death, while the beneficiary brings a court action in still another state. In such instances, the laws of several jurisdictions could be involved in resolving such questions as the rights and obligations of the parties to the contract, interpretation of specific provisions of the policy, and the proper procedure for bringing the action.

In one life insurance case,[7] brought in a Texas state court, the beneficiary's assignees contended that the laws of Texas applied because the beneficiary and the assignees of the policy were Texas residents and the insurer was doing business in Texas. The insurer contended that California law applied because the insured was a resident of California and had applied for and taken delivery of the policy in California. If the Texas court applied Texas law, the assignees would win the lawsuit. If it applied California law, the insurer would win.

The Texas court, applying the Texas conflict of laws rule, determined that California law should apply to the issues in the case. The court stated:

> [N]o part of the transaction leading up to the consummation of the original contract, or to the reinstatement thereof, or to the maturity of any right accruing thereunder, occurred or transpired within the State of Texas . . . . [W]e have concluded that the validity, interpretation, and obligations of the contract in suit must be determined and controlled by the laws of California and not by the laws of Texas, insofar as the laws of the former state may be shown to be different from the laws of the latter.

The insurer, therefore, won the lawsuit.

This case illustrates the application of the traditional conflict of laws rule regarding contracts. This traditional rule is that the validity and effect of a contract is determined by the place where the contract is made, unless the parties have agreed otherwise.

---

[6]BALLENTINE'S LAW DICTIONARY 246 (3d ed. 1969).
[7]Washington Nat'l Ins. Co. v. Shaw, 180 S.W.2d 1003 (Tex. Civ. App. 1944).

A newer conflict of laws rule, used in a few states, is the center of gravity rule. This rule is also called by other names. These are *grouping of contacts*, *principal contacts*, *most significant relationship*, *governmental interest analysis*, and *paramount interest*. States which use this rule apply the law of the state most concerned with the outcome of the litigation.

Application of Law in Federal Courts.   If there is no constitutional provision or statute on a given question, courts ordinarily will apply previous case law on the subject. Case law is law laid down in reported court decisions. In a federal court, the case law of the state in which the court is sitting will be applied where the question involves state law.

The federal courts did not always apply state case law. There has long been a federal statute requiring that, in cases involving diversity of citizenship, a federal court must apply state law. However, in 1842, the United States Supreme Court decided in *Swift v. Tyson*[8] that the word *law* in this federal statute meant state statutory law but not state case law. For almost a hundred years thereafter, each federal court applied the statutory laws of the state in which it was sitting, but if there were no applicable statutory laws, the federal court applied its own version of the common law.[9] In this way, a body of federal case law was built up that was often advantageous to insurers.

The *Swift v. Tyson* decision was followed in the federal courts until 1938. Then, in the case of *Erie Railroad Co. v. Tompkins,*[10] the United States Supreme Court overruled the former decision on this point and held that both the statutory and case law of the state in question must be applied by the federal courts. This is the procedure that is followed today.

COURT TRIALS

Court trials ordinarily occur only when other efforts to settle a dispute have failed. Except for some simplified court actions, such as those in small claims courts, trials are costly in both time and money. Nevertheless, some disputes cannot be resolved in any other way.

The rules for bringing a court action are a part of what is known as procedural law. Rules vary in different jurisdictions and different kinds of courts. They are simple in some courts and for some types of actions and complex in others. The following discussion is in general terms because of the wide variations in terminology and practices from one jurisdiction to another.

---

[8]41 U.S. (16 Pet.) 1 (1842).

[9]Common law was defined and discussed earlier in this chapter. Application of the common law is discussed in a later subsection.

[10]304 U.S. 64 (1938).

Pleadings

Trials usually begin with pleadings. Pleadings are the parties' formal written statements of their respective claims and defenses. Complaints, answers, counterclaims, cross-claims, and third-party complaints are pleadings.

The Complaint.   Ordinarily, a case begins when the person suing, the plaintiff, files a complaint. A complaint is a formal written statement of the plaintiff's cause of action. For example, in a contract case, the plaintiff will set forth the provisions of the contract, allege those respects in which the person being sued, the defendant, has failed to perform a promise, and state the amount of damages sought. The complaint tells the plaintiff's version of the dispute.

When a complaint has been filed, the court issues a summons which is served on the defendant by the sheriff or other designated officer. The summons is a notice to the defendant that an action has been filed against her or him and that a judgment will be granted unless an answer is filed within the specified time. Attached to the summons is a copy of the complaint. The time allowed for answering the complaint is ordinarily 20 to 30 days from the date of service of the summons and complaint. Therefore, the defendant should promptly seek the advice of an attorney. If no answer is filed within the allotted time, the court might grant the plaintiff a default judgment. A default judgment is a judgment, usually in favor of the plaintiff, entered without the defendant's being heard in his or her own defense, because of the defendant's failure to answer the complaint, or to appear at trial.

The Answer.   The defendant answers the complaint in a formal written statement, usually termed an *answer,* in which he or she explains the facts alleged by the plaintiff. The defendant might admit what the plaintiff says, but might contend that the admitted actions still do not constitute a wrong on which a legal action can be based. The defendant might deny the contentions of the plaintiff, or admit them and allege that his or her conduct was excusable under the law.

The Issue.   An issue is a material point which is affirmed by one party and denied by the other. An issue can be deduced by comparing the complaint and the answer.

There are two types of issues—issues of fact and issues of law. If the plaintiff alleges a fact in the complaint, and the defendant denies in the answer that such is a fact, there is an issue of fact to be decided. In a jury trial, the facts are determined by the jury. In a non-jury trial, they are determined by the judge.

In other cases, plaintiff and defendant agree on the facts but disagree on the application of the law to those facts. When this occurs, there is an issue of law for the judge to decide in what is called a summary judgment proceeding. The judge always decides issues of law.

Often there are both issues of fact and issues of law to be decided. When such is the case in a jury trial, the jury will decide issues of fact and the judge will decide issues of law. In a non-jury trial, also called a bench trial, the judge will decide both issues of fact and issues of law.

Discovery

Under modern court procedures, the determination of facts and issues is often done by what is called "discovery." Discovery consists of the pretrial devices used by each party to obtain information from the other party or witnesses. Depositions, interrogatories, subpoenas requiring the production of documents, and medical examinations are discovery devices.

Depositions.   A deposition is the oral testimony under oath of a witness prior to trial. Ordinarily, the plaintiff's attorney, the defendant's attorney, a court reporter, and the witness will be present at the deposition. The court reporter will swear in the witness and record the proceedings. The witness will be examined by the plaintiff's attorney, by the defendant's attorney, or by both.

Interrogatories.   Interrogatories are a series of written questions drawn up by one party and given to the other party, or to a witness, to answer within a fixed period of time. Written answers to the interrogatories are given under oath. The person answering signs a sworn statement, usually before a notary public, that the answers are true.

Subpoenas Duces Tecum.   A subpoena is a command by the court to a witness to appear at a certain time and place to give testimony. A *subpoena duces tecum* requires that the witness bring with him or her documents or other things. Frequently, the appearance of the witness will not be required if the documents or other things themselves are produced. Insurance claim files are sometimes the subject of a *subpoena duces tecum*. For example, a court might subpoena a health insurer to produce a claim file showing payment of medical bills for treatment of its insured's injuries, where the insured has sued a third party whom the insured complains caused the injuries.

Proof of Facts

As stated above, questions of fact are sometimes submitted to a jury for decision, while questions of law are decided by the judge. However, in arriving at its decision, the jury will be instructed by the judge, who is guided by the applicable constitutional, statutory, and case law. This process is governed by a multitude of procedural concepts which are the result of centuries of legal development.

Three procedural concepts—presumptions, the prima facie case, and the burden of proof—are mentioned again and again in court cases. An understanding of the meaning and use of these procedural concepts is essential to an understanding of law.

Presumptions.   A presumption is a conclusion that the law requires to be drawn from a given set of facts. The presumption will stand until adequate evidence to the contrary is presented to the court. For example, every person is presumed to be capable of making a valid, binding contract. Therefore, in a case where the contractual capacity of a person is challenged, there is a presumption that the person has the required capacity. The party challenging the person's contractual capacity has the right to present evidence that the person lacks contractual capacity by reason of minority, mental incompetence, and so on. If the party cannot present adequate evidence of a lack of contractual capacity, the presumption will stand.

The Prima Facie Case.   A prima facie case is a set of facts, established by sufficient evidence, that entitles a person to the relief he or she is asking, in the absence of evidence to dispute those facts. For example, the plaintiff who introduces in evidence the provisions of a contract, and establishes failure on the part of the defendant to carry out the terms of the contract, has presented a prima facie case of breach of contract. It is then the defendant's responsibility to introduce evidence disproving the facts as stated by the plaintiff, or to show that there was an acceptable excuse for nonperformance (for example, that the agreement was not a valid contract, or that the plaintiff made performance impossible). If the defendant produces no contrary proof or presents no excuse, the decision will be in the plaintiff's favor.

Burden of Proof.   The term *burden of proof* has several meanings. We will discuss two of these meanings. First, *burden of proof* means the duty of producing evidence. For example, if a beneficiary sues a life insurer for a death benefit, and the insurer raises the defense that the insured committed suicide, the burden is on the insurer to produce evidence to prove its contention. The beneficiary does not have to prove that there was no suicide. In one case, the court discussed this rule as follows:

> It is the established jurisprudence[11] in this state that, where a defense of suicide is interposed by an insurance company to a suit on a life insurance policy, the insurer must establish the suicide to the exclusion of every other reasonable hypothesis.[12]

In this case, the insured had been shot several times, but there was no evidence to support the insurer's contention that she had shot herself, and

---

[11]Jurisprudence is the science of law.
[12]Brooks v. Louisiana & S. Life Ins. Co., 246 So. 2d 270 (La. Ct. App. 1971).

there had been ample opportunity for someone else to have shot her. The court held, therefore, that the insurer had not sustained its burden of proving that death was the result of suicide, and the decision was for the plaintiff. Thus, the insurer's claim of suicide was denied, and the death benefit was held to be payable.

A second meaning of the term *burden of proof* is the obligation of the plaintiff to present the court with a preponderance of evidence in his or her favor. If the plaintiff fails to sustain this burden, the defendant will win the lawsuit.

Application of Case Law

When an issue reaches a court for decision, constitutional or statutory law will be applied if there is any such law on the subject. If there is none, or if such law is unclear, courts that follow the common-law system—which include most of the courts of the United States—decide cases on the basis of principles established in previous decisions called "precedents."[13] A precedent is a previous decision by that same court, or by a higher court of the same jurisdiction, on the same question, and involving the same general set of facts. If there is such a decision, it will be followed unless there is strong reason to depart from it.

In deciding a question in accordance with precedent, the court is applying what is known as the doctrine of *stare decisis*. *Stare decisis* means the practice of following previous decisions on the same question. *Stare decisis* gives certainty and stability to the law.

Application of Common Law

Sometimes, there is no precedent governing the question. In such instances, the court will decide the question before it in accordance with the common law. In this sense, the common law means a body of general rules, principles, and ideas of justice that have been developed or followed by courts in English-speaking countries.

Authorities differ as to whether there is a common law for every jurisdiction, or one body of common law that includes all common-law jurisdictions. It is generally agreed, however, that the meaning of the term *common law* for any jurisdiction is defined by the courts of that jurisdiction. In deciding a case in accordance with the common law the court is making case law and establishing a new precedent that will be followed in later cases involving essentially the same set of facts.

---

[13]This is possible because appellate courts and some trial courts support their decisions with written opinions that are published and made available to the public. Court decisions are of interest primarily to lawyers and judges, but they are available to anyone who is interested. They form a continuous record of the opinions and decisions of the court.

CIVIL LAW AND CRIMINAL LAW

In the discussion of common law above we defined *civil law* as law derived from Roman law. Another meaning of the term *civil law* is "the body of law which determines private rights and liabilities." In this sense civil law is distinguished from criminal law, which prohibits and punishes conduct causing harm to the public. Thus, civil law is private, while criminal law is public. A private person sues another for the enforcement of rights under civil law, but the state or nation brings criminal proceedings on behalf of the public against a violator of criminal law.

Some violations of rights under civil law are also violations of criminal law. Assault is an example. A person who is assaulted might sue the person who committed the offense and be granted money damages, because assault is a violation of the victim's rights under civil law. The state might also prosecute the offender under the state criminal assault laws. If convicted, the offender might be imprisoned or fined or both. The state would imprison the offender and the fines would go to the state, because assault is a violation of criminal law, or a harm to the public.

The title of a court decision often indicates whether the court was dealing with a civil or a criminal matter. Examples of civil case titles are *Higgins v. McCulloch, Markham Manufacturing Co. v. Johnson Bolt Co.* and *Stillson v. Prudential Insurance Co.* These titles indicate that one private party sued another. Criminal cases, on the other hand, are styled as follows: *People v. Henderson, Stanley v. Georgia, United States v. Robel, Commonwealth v. Root, City of Chicago v. Gregory* or *State v. Lehigh Valley Railroad Co.* In these cases the state or nation prosecuted a person or other entity for violation of the criminal law.

A crime is usually either a felony or a misdemeanor. A felony is a serious crime for which the punishment can be imprisonment in the state or federal penitentiary, or even death. Murder, treason, robbery and larceny are felonies. A misdemeanor is a less serious crime, usually punishable by fine or by imprisonment other than in a penitentiary, as, for example, in a county jail. A parking violation is an example of a misdemeanor.

COURTS OF LAW AND COURTS OF EQUITY

In the early days of the common law, a person seeking justice applied for a royal order, or writ, which authorized the judge to hear his case. During the 13th century, these writs became highly formalized and applicable only to certain kinds of cases. In order to take a problem to court, one had to fit his case into one of the writs that were available. Often, this was not possible, and, as a result, there was no remedy at law. In those situations, special appeals were often made to the king himself. He, in turn, would refer the question to his adviser, the chancellor. By the 15th century, in cases where the remedy at law was not adequate, or where there was none, the chancellor issued special decrees. These remedies were said to be obtained "in chancery" and were known as "equitable remedies."

Law and Equity Today

The distinction between courts of law and courts of equity was preserved in the court systems of the United States for many years. At the present time, however, it has been abolished by statute in most states and in the federal courts. Ordinarily, the same court now has jurisdiction over both legal and equitable matters. Both legal and equitable remedies are available in the same suit. Nevertheless, equitable remedies continue to be distinguished from those available at law, and there has been no change in the basic principles of equity.

Equitable Remedies

Since equity courts arose because of the inadequacy of the ordinary legal remedies, remedies available in equity courts historically have been considered extraordinary in nature. For instance, the legal remedy—that is, the remedy available in a court of law—for breach of contract (failure to perform as promised) is money damages. In situations where money does not adequately compensate the injured person, a remedy known as "specific performance" can be sought as an equitable remedy. If granted, this remedy will require that the contract be carried out as promised. For example, if one person contracts with another to buy land, and the person holding the land refuses to perform the contract by conveying the land, an equity court might decree that the land must be conveyed, and will enforce the specific performance of its decree.

Among other remedies which developed in equity are those of interpleader, rescission, reformation, and declaratory judgment. These remedies are frequently used in connection with problems arising under insurance contracts. They are discussed in Chapter 16, "Remedies."

INSURANCE REGULATION

When the first insurance companies were formed in the United States, the states regulated them, just as they did other corporations. Very little was involved in either instance except the details of incorporation and some taxation. Later, however, as insurance companies began operating in states other than those in which they were organized, the question arose as to whether the transaction of an insurance business across state lines should subject the business to federal regulation as interstate commerce.

The United States Congress has the power to regulate interstate commerce by reason of the Commerce Clause in the federal Constitution. This is found in Article I, Section 8, which reads in part as follows: "The Congress shall have Power . . . To regulate Commerce with foreign Nations, and among the several States, and with the Indian Tribes."

As the result of this provision, the Congress has the sole power to regulate commerce "among the several States." Exactly what constitutes commerce and when it is transacted among, rather than within, the several states are not easy questions. This has been true especially in regard to the business of insurance. Until 1944, however, these questions were consistently resolved in favor of state regulation of insurance on the ground that the business of insurance was not commerce.

In 1868, the question of whether it was proper for the states to regulate the business of insurance reached the United States Supreme Court in the case of *Paul v. Virginia*.[14] In reaching its decision that Virginia had the right to regulate the business of insurance, the court stated the following:

> Issuing a policy of insurance is not a transaction of Commerce . . . in any proper meaning of the word . . . They [insurance policies] are governed by the local law. They do not constitute a part of the commerce between the States.

This view—that issuing contracts of insurance is not commerce and, thus, cannot constitute a part of the commerce among the several states— prevailed for the next 75 years. Other cases presenting essentially the same question followed, but in each of them the court made it clear that insurance was not commerce, and therefore could not be interstate commerce which is subject to federal regulation. The last important case following this reasoning was *New York Life Insurance Co. v. Deer Lodge County,* decided in 1913.[15] After the *Deer Lodge* case, there seemed little reason to question the regulation of insurance by the states.

As a result of this unbroken line of decisions, the states developed extensive systems of laws to regulate the business of insurance, and provided special administrative departments to supervise insurance companies operating within their respective jurisdictions. In some instances, these were separate insurance departments. In others, they were departments combining insurance regulation with supervision over such related businesses as banking. This was the situation in 1944 when the *South-Eastern Underwriters*[16] decision was handed down by the United States Supreme Court.

The *South-Eastern Underwriters* Decision

The facts of the *South-Eastern Underwriters* case were these: the South-Eastern Underwriters Association and its nearly 200 private stock insurance

---

[14]75 U.S. (8 Wall.) 168 (1868).

[15]231 U.S. 495 (1913).

[16]United States v. South-Eastern Underwriters Ass'n, 322 U. S. 533 (1944).

company members had been indicted for alleged violations of the federal Sherman Antitrust Act. Their defense was that the federal act did not apply, because insurance was not commerce and, thus, not a proper subject for regulation by the federal government.

The federal district court had held, in effect, that even though an insurance company conducts a substantial part of its business transactions across state lines, it is not engaged in commerce among the states within the meaning of either the Commerce Clause or the Sherman Antitrust Act. The United States Supreme Court took a different view.

The Supreme Court pointed out that cases prior to *South-Eastern Underwriters* had concerned the power of the states "to regulate and tax specific activities of foreign insurance companies which sell policies within their territories."[17] In *South-Eastern Underwriters*, the Court considered a different question—the effect of an act of Congress on insurance transactions conducted across state lines. In its analysis of prior cases, the Supreme Court stated the following:

> Not one of all these cases, however, has involved an Act of Congress which required the Court to decide the issue of whether the Commerce Clause grants to Congress the power to regulate insurance transactions stretching across state lines. Today for the first time in the history of the Court that issue is squarely presented and must be decided.

In a four-to-three decision, with a strong dissenting opinion by Chief Justice Harlan F. Stone, the Court held that insurance is commerce. Therefore, when insurance business is conducted across state lines, it is interstate commerce, and subject to regulation by the federal government. The gist of the decision is found in the following passage:

> Our basic responsibility in interpreting the Commerce Clause is to make certain that the power to govern intercourse among the states remains where the Constitution placed it. That power, as held by this court from the beginning is vested in the Congress, available to be exercised for the national welfare as Congress shall deem necessary. No commercial enterprise of any kind which conducts its activities across state lines has been held to be wholly beyond the regulatory power of Congress under the Commerce Clause. We cannot make an exception of the business of insurance.

Thus, the landmark *Paul v. Virginia* decision of 1868 was overruled by the United States Supreme Court in 1944 in the *South-Eastern Underwriters* decision. Insurance was subject to regulation by the federal government.

---

[17]A foreign insurance company is a company which is not incorporated in the state. For example, a company incorporated in Illinois is a foreign company in Georgia even though it does business in Georgia.

The McCarran-Ferguson Act

The *South-Eastern Underwriters* decision presented a serious problem for the insurance industry. For 75 years it had been assumed that the question of federal regulation was settled. Insurance had been regulated by the states exclusively, and there were no applicable federal statutes. Because the situation could have become chaotic, Congress almost immediately enacted the McCarran-Ferguson Act.[18] The McCarran-Ferguson Act declared that continued regulation and taxation of insurance by the states "is in the public interest." Under the McCarran-Ferguson Act, acts of Congress are not to be construed to invalidate, impair, or supersede state law regulating insurance, unless the acts of Congress relate specifically to the business of insurance. The Sherman Act, Clayton Act, and Federal Trade Commission Act are applicable to the business of insurance under the McCarran-Ferguson Act, but only "to the extent that such business is not regulated by State law." One exception to this general rule is that the Sherman Act applies to agreements to, or acts of, boycott, coercion, or intimidation.

Immediately after the passage of the McCarran-Ferguson Act, a committee made up of various kinds of insurance companies—property, liability, life, and so on—began the work of drafting model laws designed to guide the state legislatures in their enactment of state laws which would prevent application of the federal antitrust acts. Rate-making laws were the first to be developed and adopted. An unfair trade practices law was enacted by all the states. Most states have also enacted antitrust laws that apply to insurance companies.

In the mid–1980s state regulation of insurance came under attack, as proponents of federal regulation attempted to repeal or amend the McCarran-Ferguson Act. The proponents of federal regulation argue that the federal antitrust law immunity contained in the McCarran-Ferguson Act should be eliminated to enhance competition within the insurance industry. They claim that the availability and affordability of commercial liability insurance has been adversely affected by a lack of competition.

The insurance industry and other proponents of state regulation argue that repealing or restricting the McCarran-Ferguson Act would not enhance competition in the insurance industry, which is already highly competitive, and would not solve the problem of availability and affordability of commercial liability insurance. They cite the unique nature of the insurance industry and the necessity for such cooperative activities as collection of industrywide loss data and pools for jumbo risks, as sound reasons for the McCarran-Ferguson exemption from federal antitrust laws. They also argue that repeal of the McCarran-Ferguson Act would lead to duplicative and conflicting regulation of insurance. As of the time this book went to press, the McCarran-Ferguson Act had not been repealed or modified.

---

[18]15 U.S.C. §§ 1011–1015 (1982).

Federal Regulation Today

The McCarran-Ferguson Act does not entirely exempt insurers from federal regulation. To the extent the insurance business is not regulated by state law, federal law will apply. The Sherman Act will apply to agreements to, or acts of, boycott, coercion, or intimidation. Moreover, other federal laws, notably securities laws, have been held to apply to certain insurance activities. Finally, federal law governs insurers in many areas not specifically related to the insurance business itself.

Interstate Advertising. Since a state cannot regulate beyond its own borders the advertising of insurers domiciled within it, the Federal Trade Commission contended that an area existed that could not be governed effectively by state laws. In 1960, the United States Supreme Court upheld this position.[19] The Court held that the Federal Trade Commission can regulate the interstate mailing of unfair or deceptive advertising material by an insurer for solicitation except in the case of states that have adopted laws sufficient to control the mailing of such material into the state.

Variable Annuities and Variable Life Insurance. In 1956, the Securities and Exchange Commission (SEC) brought an action against two variable annuity companies, contending that their variable annuities must be registered with the SEC. This action was based on the premise that the variable annuity does not resemble a fixed-dollar annuity, which is exempt from SEC regulation as closely as it does a security which is subject to SEC regulation. In *SEC v. Variable Annuity Life Insurance Co.,*[20] the United States Supreme Court upheld this position, conceding that variable annuity contracts contain some insurance features, but pointing out that they also contain "to a very substantial degree" characteristics of investment contracts issued by equity investment trusts (mutual funds). The Court felt, therefore, that the contracts presented regulatory problems of exactly the kind that the Securities Acts of 1933 and 1940 were enacted to resolve, and it held that variable annuities were not included in the exemptions of insurance policies and annuity contracts from the operation of these acts.

When a similar question arose in connection with variable life insurance, insurers sought an SEC ruling that would have exempted variable life insurance contracts meeting certain specified requirements from the Securities Act, the Securities Exchange Act, the Investment Company Act, and the Investment Advisers Act. The SEC ruled that, while variable life insurance would not be as strictly regulated as variable annuities, certain federal securities laws would apply. SEC regulation of variable life insurance has been an

---

[19]FTC v. Travelers Health Ass'n, 362 U.S. 293 (1960).
[20]359 U.S. 65 (1959).

important insurance industry concern in the 1980s. This topic is discussed in Chapter 7, "Structure of the Life Insurance Policy."

Federal Regulation of Non-Insurance Activities.   Federal law governs insurers in many areas not specifically related to the business of insurance. For example, when stock insurance companies offer their securities for sale to the investing public, those companies are regulated by the federal securities laws as are other corporations. As employers, insurers are subject to federal employment laws such as the National Labor Relations Act, the Fair Labor Standards Act of 1938, the Employee Retirement Income Security Act, and the Civil Rights Act of 1964. However, most of the statutes regulating the insurance business itself are state statutes.

State Regulation Today

Insurance is heavily regulated by the states primarily because of the size and importance of the industry. So many people are affected by insurance that the mismanagement or failure of an insurance company has serious social and economic effects. It is for this reason that courts and legislatures speak of insurance as a business "affected with a public interest." This means that insurance is of such importance to so many people that it is in the public interest to enact whatever laws are necessary to assure that the great trust vested in insurers is not abused. As a result, the insurance business is strictly regulated by a detailed system of insurance laws. Safekeeping of funds, company solvency, representation by qualified, ethical agents, and contracts which safeguard the rights of policyowners and beneficiaries—all these and almost every other aspect of the insurance business have been acknowledged as proper subjects for regulation. Thus, every year many new insurance bills are introduced into state legislatures and enacted into law.

The states also regulate insurers in areas not specifically related to insurance. Many state and local laws govern insurers just as such laws govern other businesses.

SUMMARY

The United States is generally said to be a common-law country. In this sense, the term *common law* means the law of countries, states, and provinces which derive their law from English law. Common law also means general principles of law and case law.

Law comes from many sources—constitutions, statutes, rules and regulations of government agencies, and court decisions, among others. Constitutions set forth in general terms the principles that form the legal foundation of a government. Constitutions tend to be permanent and are changed little. In the United States, federal and state constitutions define the extent of governmental powers and outline the principles on which the government is to operate. A constitution provides for an executive, a legislative, and a judicial branch of the government. A constitution also guarantees human rights. The federal and state constitutions in the United States differ in that the federal Constitution delegates power to the federal government, while state constitutions limit the power of the state governments.

Statutes are less permanent and more specific than constitutions. A statute is a law enacted by a legislature. Statutes are arranged in codes so that they can be easily found.

Administrative officers, such as a state's commissioner, director, or superintendant of insurance, also perform legislative functions. That is, they adopt rules and regulations to assist them in executing the laws. They also perform judicial functions when they hold hearings, make decisions, and impose penalties. Thus, although administrative officers are a part of the executive branch of government, they perform legislative and judicial as well as executive functions.

Courts comprise the judicial branch of a government. In the United States, there are two court systems—state and federal. These court systems each have courts of original jurisdiction and a highest court, usually called a supreme court. The federal court system and many of the state court systems have intermediate appellate courts as well.

In order to render a binding decision, a court must have jurisdiction of the subject matter and jurisdiction over the person of the defendant. Often, more than one court has jurisdiction in a case. A court, especially in insurance cases, sometimes must apply the law of another jurisdiction. Conflict of laws rules are used to determine which jurisdiction's law applies.

The rules for bringing a court action are part of procedural law. Court actions usually begin with a complaint filed with the court by the plaintiff. The court then issues a summons to the defendant. The defendant files an answer, and an issue is reached.

In order to discover facts related to the lawsuit, a party might use one or more discovery devices such as a deposition, interrogatories, or a *subpoena duces tecum*. Facts are proved at trial using various procedural concepts. Among these concepts are presumptions, the prima facie case, and burden of proof. In a trial, facts are usually decided by a jury, although in some cases a judge decides the facts. The judge then applies the law to the facts decided.

The judge will apply constitutional or statutory law, and if there is none, or if such law is unclear, the judge will usually apply a precedent. If there is no precedent, the judge will decide the issue in accordance with the common law—that is, in accordance with general principles of law.

Equity courts developed hundreds of years ago in England because of the inadequacy of ordinary legal remedies. For many years, law courts and equity courts were separate. However, modern courts usually have jurisdiction over both legal and equitable matters. Several equitable remedies are important to insurers.

In the early years of the insurance industry, no serious challenge arose to the right of the states to regulate insurance. In 1868, the United States Supreme Court held that insurance was not commerce and hence that the insurance industry was not subject to federal regulation under the Commerce Clause of the federal Constitution. Then, in 1944, the Supreme Court reversed itself and held that insurance is commerce. Congress passed the McCarran-Ferguson Act shortly thereafter. This act declares that state regulation and taxation of insurance is in the public interest. Therefore, most insurance regulation is done by the states.

Insurance is heavily regulated because of the size and importance of the insurance industry. Insurance is so important to so many people that it is said to be a business affected with a public interest.

ILLUSTRATIVE CASE

The following case is included in this introductory chapter because it illustrates the use of presumptions and the prima facie case to arrive at a decision. Explanatory footnotes have been added where the legal terminology may not be clear.

Robinson, as executor of the Creighton estate, brought the suit against the life insurer. In the lower court, therefore, Robinson was the plaintiff and the insurer was the defendant. The decision was in favor of Robinson, and the insurer appealed. In the court of appeals, therefore, the insurer was the appellant and Robinson was the appellee. This information is conveyed in the title of the case by referring to Robinson as "plaintiff-appellee" and the insurer as "defendant-appellant."

WM. HEDGES ROBINSON, JR., EXECUTOR OF THE ESTATE OF
J.R. CREIGHTON, DECEASED, Plaintiff-Appellee
v.
NEW YORK LIFE INSURANCE COMPANY, Defendant-Appellant[21]
Colorado Court of Appeals

COYTE, Judge.

This is an action on the double-indemnity clause of an insurance contract which provides for double recovery of benefits in case of death by accident. However, double recovery is not provided in the policy where death occurs because of suicide. The company claimed the insured committed suicide whereas the estate maintained that his death was accidental, thereby entitling it to recover under the double-indemnity clause. From a jury verdict favoring the estate, the company appeals.

The alleged error is that the verdict is unsupported by the evidence, and that the trial court should have directed a verdict in the company's favor or granted it a new trial.[22]

---

[21]30 Colo. App. 83, 490 P.2d 81 (1971).

[22]Appeals are generally permitted from any decision of a lower court if an error or errors can be shown. In this case the error alleged is that the evidence did not support the verdict. The court is said to "direct the verdict" when it makes the decision for the jury because the evidence is so clear that there is no fact question to be decided by the jury.

The insured in this case was a man in his fifties, suffering from a variety of ailments, including a blood disorder, congestive heart failure, and partial paralysis which affected his speech. He was under medication and was being cared for by a private nurse.

The decedent, together with his wife and nurse, went to Hawaii for a vacation. While there, they rented a suite of rooms on the twentieth floor of a hotel. Adjacent to the suite was an outside balcony, the outer perimeter of which was surrounded by a wall and railing. There was a wooden platform in one corner of the balcony upon which the decedent had stood on occasion to view the scenery.

The following evidence was given concerning the death of decedent. On the night of his death, the decedent and his wife had dinner in the hotel restaurant. Both consumed alcoholic beverages and had been quarreling during dinner. The nurse helped both back to their rooms after dinner. She helped the decedent to bed after giving him his medication and a sleeping pill. Some time after 3:00 A.M., the wife awoke and found her husband had left the bed. She went to the balcony and saw him just before he plunged to his death, but had no other recollection of the event.

The police investigated the occurrence but did not question the wife upon their arrival because she was unresponsive and appeared to be in deep, heavy sleep.

Later in the day, in the afternoon, the wife was questioned concerning her husband's death. The police investigator testified that at that time she stated to him that she went to the balcony and found her husband standing there; that she asked him if he wanted a drink; that he apparently became angry and pushed her away and then went to the platform and began to climb over the wall and railing; that she went to him and attempted to hold him, but again he pushed her away, and went over the side to his death.

This testimony of the officer as to the statement given to him by decedent's wife was the only evidence presented to the jury concerning the precise manner in which the decedent met his death. Whether he accidentally fell or deliberately jumped was the question to be answered by the jury, which found that death was the result of an accident.

The certificate of death, duly authenticated and admitted into evidence, listed death as being "accidental." The certificate showing death to be accidental was prima facie evidence of "accidental death."[23] Defendant maintains that the notation on the death certificate was placed there as a routine matter by the medical officer who signed the certificate and that he had no basis for placing the words "accidental death" on the certificate. The certificate would still be prima facie evidence of its contents, but its weight depends upon the information upon which it is based, the source of that information, and the manner in which it is obtained.

In any event, there is no dispute that defendant met his death as a result of a fall from the balcony. Death by suicide is not a natural occurrence, and is never presumed. The burden is on the company to prove by a preponderance of the evidence that the insured committed suicide.

---

[23]In the case as published in the reporter, the court here referred is to a statute which declares that a death certificate shall be prima facie evidence of the cause of death. Following the statutory reference, a list of cases was cited to support or explain the point just given. In order to simplify this illustrative case, such statutes and cases will be omitted.

It is the contention of the insurance company that the statement made by the wife to the investigator is direct evidence as to how and why the fall occurred and is conclusive proof of the fact the decedent took his own life, and that the court erred in refusing to direct a verdict in the company's favor. We disagree.

After the death certificate was introduced into evidence showing the fact of death to be "accidental," the plaintiff had established a prima facie case and the defendant company then had the burden of proving that death occurred because of suicide. It was for the jury to determine whether the defendant had sustained this burden by producing evidence which outweighed the presumption that decedent had met his death by accident. The presumption has sufficient evidential weight to support the jury verdict.

The only witness to the death of the husband was the wife. There is a conflict between her testimony at the trial when she testified that she did not remember the details of her husband's death and the facts relating to decedent's death as testified to by the investigator, which testimony was received without objections. It was for the jury to hear and weigh the testimony and determine the credibility of the witnesses.

The question as to whether defendant insurance company had sustained the burden of proof as to the manner in which decedent met his death was properly left to the jury. Based on proper instructions, it resolved the matter in favor of the estate.

Judgment affirmed.[24]

QUESTIONS FOR REVIEW

1. In general terms, what is meant by the statement "Insurance is a business affected with a public interest?"

2. List three sources of law.

3. Which of the following statements describes the federal Constitution? Explain.
   a. It establishes a government of delegated powers.
   b. It imposes limitations on the power of the government.

4. What important constitutional question relating to insurance was considered in each of the following cases?
   a. Paul v. Virginia.
   b. South-Eastern Underwriters.

   What was the decision in each case? What effect did each decision have on the regulation of insurance?

5. Briefly summarize the principal provisions of the McCarran-Ferguson Act.

6. Why are administrative rules and regulations considered necessary? What is the legal significance of such rules and regulations?

7. Explain and illustrate the doctrine of *stare decisis*.

8. List three different meanings that are given to the term *common law*.

9. Discuss the development of courts of equity.

10. What is a deposition? What is a *subpoena duces tecum*?

---

[24]That is, the decision of the lower court in favor of the estate was upheld.

CHAPTER 2

Contracts

TWO DEFINITIONS OF *CONTRACT*
    A Binding Promise
    An Agreement Enforceable at Law

OFFER
    A Promise or an Act
    Requirements of a Valid Offer
    Duration of the Offer
    Withdrawal or Revocation
    Rejection and Counteroffer
    Death or Incapacity of Offeror or Offeree

ACCEPTANCE
    Communication of the Acceptance
    Completion of the Contract

CONSIDERATION
    Legally Adequate Consideration
    Inadequate Consideration

COMPETENT PARTIES
    Void and Voidable Contracts
    Minors
    Mentally Infirm Persons
    Intoxicated Persons
    Convicts
    Aliens
    Corporations

CONTRACT FORM
    Oral Informal Contracts
    The Statute of Frauds

ILLEGALITY
    Aleatory Contracts
    Wagering Agreements Versus Insurance Contracts

DURESS AND UNDUE INFLUENCE

RULES OF CONTRACT CONSTRUCTION
    Clear and Unambiguous Language
    Construed as a Whole
    Ordinary Meaning of Words
    Construction in Favor of Validity
    Unclear Language Construed against the Writer
    Printed, Typed, and Handwritten Matter
THE PAROL EVIDENCE RULE
    Formation Defects
    Incomplete Contract
    Interpretation
    Reformation
    Subsequent Modifications
BREACH AND MATERIALITY
THIRD-PERSON BENEFICIARIES
LIBERTY OF CONTRACT
CONSTITUTIONAL PROTECTION OF EXISTING CONTRACTS
LIFE AND HEALTH INSURANCE CONTRACT LAW
SUMMARY

An acquaintance with the basic principles of general contract law gives meaning to the special legal principles applicable to life and health insurance contracts. The purpose of this chapter is to discuss important principles of general contract law with an emphasis on those principles with which life and health insurers are frequently concerned.

TWO DEFINITIONS OF *CONTRACT*

The term *contract* can be defined as "a binding promise" or as "an agreement enforceable at law." Both definitions are helpful in analyzing contract law. These definitions will be examined in the following subsections.

A Binding Promise

The term *contract* has been defined as a "promise or set of promises for breach of which the law gives a remedy or the performance of which the law in some way recognizes as a duty"[1]—that is, a binding promise. There must be a promise or, in some cases, several promises, that create a legal duty of

---

[1] W. Jaeger, Williston on Contracts 1 (1957).

performance on the part of the person, or persons, making the promise in order for a valid contract to be formed.

Life and health insurance contracts illustrate this definition. A typical life insurance policy reads, "The A.B.C. Life Insurance Company agrees to pay. . . ." Health insurance contracts follow a similar pattern.

"Agrees to pay" are promissory words that, when certain other requirements are met, create a legal duty of performance by the insurer. This duty has been affirmed and enforced by court decisions again and again.

Unilateral and Bilateral Contracts.   A person who makes a promise, or promises, under a contract is called a "promisor." A person to whom a promise is made is called a "promisee." Promises may be made by either or both of the persons who are parties to a contract. The word *person* in its legal sense often includes both human beings (natural persons) and organizations such as corporations. *Person* is so used in this discussion.

Contracts under which promises are made by both parties are bilateral contracts—that is, contracts having promises on both sides. Contracts which consist of a promise, or promises, by one party only are called unilateral contracts—that is, contracts having promises on one side only.

Unilateral contracts were recognized and given legal effect at a much earlier date than bilateral contracts. Unilateral contracts continue to be of greater interest to the student of life and health insurance, because the insurance contract is a unilateral contract. The policyowner does not promise to do or to pay anything under today's life or health insurance contract. The contract can be kept in force only if premiums are paid as they become due, but the policyowner does not promise to pay them. If they are not paid, the insurer cannot sue the policyowner for failure to perform the contract.

By contrast, the life insurer makes a legally enforceable promise to pay the amount of insurance specified upon receipt of proof of the death of the insured. Other promises are also included in most life insurance contracts. When required conditions have been met, the insurer must perform its promise, or promises, or the policyowner or beneficiary will have a right to recover damages for breach of contract. A breach of contract is a failure of a party to perform a promise according to its terms without a legal excuse. In other words, the life or health insurance contract contains legally enforceable promises on the part of the insurer, but none on the part of the policyowner. It is an important modern-day unilateral contract.

Formal and Informal Contracts   Merely because a person has promised something does not mean that the promise will be legally enforceable. However, if a contract is intended, there are two ways in which a promise can be made contractually binding. One method concerns the form of the instrument in which the promise is expressed. Negotiable instruments, for example, have legal effect as binding contracts only if they comply with special requirements as to form. For example, a negotiable instrument must be in writing and be signed by the maker or drawer. It must contain an unconditional promise, or order, to pay a definite sum of money on demand or at a definite time to order or to the bearer. A check is one kind of negotiable instrument. It is binding because of its form and is, therefore, called a formal contract.

Other contracts—and the life or health insurance policy is an example—create legal duties because the parties have met requirements that relate to the substance, rather than to the form, of the transaction. Contracts of this kind are called "informal" contracts. Sometimes, they are referred to as "simple" contracts.

An Agreement Enforceable at Law

The term *contract* is often defined as "an agreement enforceable at law." Many agreements cannot be enforced by court action. For example, if one person agrees to go to dinner at another person's house, the law will not enforce the agreement. A contract, therefore, is a special kind of agreement—one that the law will enforce.

Courts sometimes say that there must be a "manifestation of mutual assent" to express this idea of agreement and to make it clear that the law does not try to ascertain the actual state of the minds of the contracting parties. It concerns itself only with their discernible words and actions. This rule is sometimes obscured by statements that a contract requires a "meeting of the minds," but a "meeting of the minds" is not the test the courts use. In many instances, it would be impossible to determine the actual state of mind of any contracting party. State of mind is best evidenced by the words and actions of the persons concerned. Ordinarily, mutual assent, or agreement, is evidenced by the making of an offer by one party and the acceptance of it by another.

A life or health insurance contract is a legally enforceable agreement between an applicant and an insurer. Ordinarily, an insurance agreement is set forth in a policy, but this is not essential. If the actions of the parties and the documents involved otherwise satisfy the legal requirements of an informal contract, an insurance contract may be held to be effective, even though no policy has been issued. Conversely, if the legal requirements of an informal contract have not been met, the insurer might not be legally obligated, even though a policy has been issued and delivered.

The elements that are necessary to form an enforceable informal contract are: (1) an offer; (2) an acceptance; (3) legally adequate consideration; (4) competent parties; (5) a form required by law, if any; (6) no statute or rule of law declaring a contract of that kind void—that is, of no legal effect; and, (7) parties not under duress or undue influence. A large body of law has been developed in connection with each of the elements of an informal contract. Much of this chapter is devoted to a discussion of these elements and of the law pertaining to them.

OFFER

An offer is a proposal that, if accepted by another according to its terms, will create a binding agreement. The person who makes an offer is the offeror, and the person to whom the offer is made is the offeree.

It is impossible for a person to make a binding contract with himself or herself, even though that person may act in a representative capacity. A person acts in a representative capacity when he or she acts as an executor, an agent, a trustee, the officer of a corporation, or in any other capacity where the person is empowered to act for another. For example, an offer made in one's individual capacity to oneself as executor or executrix is void—that is, of no legal effect. The concept of offer and acceptance, therefore, demands that in addition to an offeror who makes the offer or proposal, there must also be an offeree to whom the offer is made.

In considering an offer, the offeree has several choices. The offeree can ignore the offer[2] unless a prior course of conduct would justify the offeror in interpreting the silence as acceptance. If the offeree wishes to reply, these are the choices: (1) the offeree can reject the offer; (2) the offeree can make a counteroffer which is in legal effect a rejection of the original offer and a proposal of a new offer; and, (3) the offeree can accept the offer according to its terms and form a contract.

A Promise or an Act

An offer can be in the form of a promise or an act. It can be in the form of a promise to do or refrain from doing something. For example, it can be in the form of a promise to pay a sum of money on condition that the offeree performs an act or makes a promise requested by the offeror. If the offeror requests the performance of an act in exchange for his or her promise, the contract when completed will be a unilateral contract, as it will involve a promise by the offeror only. If the offeror requests and receives a promise from the offeree in exchange for the offeror's promise, the resulting contract is bilateral.

An act may be offered in exchange for a promise. This is often the case with life and health insurance. The act is submission of the application for insurance and payment of the premium. One authority gave the following example:

A makes written application for life insurance through an agent for B Insurance Company, pays the first premium, and is given a receipt stating

---

[2]As will be explained in a later section, an insurer-offeree might incur liability if it ignores an applicant's offer.

that the insurance "shall take effect as of the date of approval of the application" at B's home office. Approval at the home office in accordance with B's usual practice is an acceptance of A's offer even though no steps are taken to notify A.[3]

Thus, the life or health insurance contract, like any other informal contract, is completed by the making of an offer by one party and its acceptance by the other.

Requirements of a Valid Offer

A valid offer creates a power of acceptance in the offeree. The recipient of a valid offer has the power to create a contract by accepting the offer. A letter or an oral expression of intent to enter into negotiations is not an offer and will not create a power of acceptance in the offeree. However, care must be taken that such an expression of intent does not appear to be an offer, or the court might construe it as one.

A Definite Commitment.   The offeror must manifest a definite commitment to be bound by the offer. Courts are properly reluctant to construe a person's words or acts as an offer unless it would be reasonable to conclude that the person had made a definite commitment. That is to say, they will not determine that the person created a power of acceptance unless he or she clearly manifested an intent to do so. Moreover, an offer must be definite in its material terms (or require such definiteness in the acceptance), so that the terms of the contract can be ascertained.

Communication to the Offeree.   Equally important is the requirement that an offer must be communicated to a person, or persons, with whom the offeror is willing to contract. An offer is made when it is received by an offeree.

Basic in the law of contracts is the principle that one may choose the person, or persons, with whom she or he is willing to contract. For this reason, communication of an offer for contractual purposes requires that the offeror intentionally and actually bring the offer to the notice of a person, or persons, with whom the offeror wishes to contract. If the offer is sent by mail, it must be received by the offeree. If it is published, as with the offer of a reward, the person who performs the act requested and claims the reward must actually have seen the offer and must have performed the act in reliance upon the offer.

---

[3]RESTATEMENT (SECOND) OF CONTRACTS 56 (1981). This is technically a reverse unilateral contract. J. CALAMARI & J. PERILLO, THE LAW OF CONTRACTS 70 (3d ed. 1987).

Duration of the Offer

The offeror can, if he or she wishes, specify the length of time the offer will be held open. The offer will then terminate automatically at the expiration of the stated period without further action on the offeror's part. Any attempt to accept after the offer has expired will be ineffective, because one of the conditions stated in the offer—that it be accepted within the time specified—will not have been met.

If the offer contains no mention of an expiration date, it is presumed to remain open for a reasonable length of time. What constitutes a "reasonable length of time" is a question of fact[4] that depends on the circumstances. An offer to buy stock on the floor of a stock exchange when stock prices are fluctuating rapidly might create a power of acceptance which lasts only a few minutes. On the other hand, an offer of a reward for the capture of a criminal might be held to have a reasonable duration of years.

Withdrawal or Revocation

Unless the offer includes an enforceable promise that it will be kept open for a specified period of time,[5] the offeror has the privilege of withdrawing the offer—that is, revoking it—at any time as long as it has not been accepted. After an offer has been accepted, it cannot be withdrawn.

It is generally considered necessary to notify the offeree of the withdrawal. However, if an offeree knows of acts of the offeror that are inconsistent with a continuance of the offer, the offer is revoked, even though there was no express notice to the offeree. For example, where the offeror sells the property which is the subject of the offer to a third person, and the offeree knows this, the offer is revoked even though the offeree was not notified of the revocation.

Rejection and Counteroffer

The offeree can reject the offer. If this is done, the offer terminates immediately. That particular offer cannot be revived by the offeree, even if the offeree later wishes to accept it in accordance with its original terms.

If the offeree is unwilling to accept the offer as it stands but would be willing to contract on different terms, the offeree can reject the original offer

---

[4]If the question reaches a court of law, it, like all questions of fact, ordinarily will be decided by the jury.

[5]Such an offer is called an option. The optionee (offeree) must have given something of value (consideration) in exchange for the optionor's (offeror's) promise to keep the offer open for a specified period of time, or the offeror will not be bound to his promise to keep the offer open. The option itself is a contract, distinct from the contract it contemplates.

and make a counteroffer. In fact, under such circumstances the offeree need not state specifically that the offer is being rejected. Words or actions that are not in themselves definite rejections, but which reasonably imply that the offeree does not intend to accept, will be considered rejections. Thus, any attempt to substitute new terms or modify the original offer will be considered a rejection of the old offer and the making of a counteroffer.[6]

For example, suppose James Bloch offers to sell his automobile to Thomas Davenport for $4500 and Mr. Davenport replies, "I would pay $4000 for your car if you fix the muffler." Legally, this is a rejection. The offeree has clearly indicated an unwillingness to contract on the terms set forth in the offer. In this situation, therefore, the original offer lapses, and the original offeror becomes, in effect, an offeree. The counteroffer is then subject to acceptance or rejection by the original offeror (now the offeree).

Death or Incapacity of Offeror or Offeree

The death of the offeror prior to acceptance by the offeree terminates the offer. Death of the offeree, assuming there was only one offeree, ordinarily precludes the possibility of acceptance.

At one time, the insanity of either the offeror or offeree was considered to have the same legal effect as death. More recently, the legal capacity of insane persons to create binding contracts under some circumstances has been recognized. However, if the insanity of the offeror or offeree has been established in a court action, the offer is still generally held to terminate. If the insanity has not been judicially established, the person's legal capacity to complete the contract is a question of fact to be decided in the light of all the pertinent circumstances of the particular case.

ACCEPTANCE

The general rule is that an acceptance must be positive, unconditional, and manifest an assent. An acceptance must be sufficiently positive to indicate a clear assent to the exact terms proposed by the offeror. If an act is requested, that act must be performed. If a promise is asked, then that promise, and no other, must be given.[7] Acceptance must be unconditional. As previously pointed out, any attempt to impose new conditions in a purported acceptance will be construed as a counteroffer.

---

[6]Article 2 of the Uniform Commercial Code, which is law in all states except Louisiana, modifies this principle of contract law as to sales of goods. The Uniform Commercial Code states that "additional terms are to be construed as proposals for addition to the contract." U.C.C. § 2–207 (2) (1977).

[7]This rule has been modified as to the sale of goods by the Uniform Commercial Code. See footnote 6 above.

Although it is sometimes said that the offeree must have an intent to accept, the actual intent of the parties is ordinarily not important if there is an adequate manifestation of assent. A secret intent not to be bound, for example, is of no significance if the person's actions or words are such as to justify a reasonable belief that the person has promised to do or refrain from doing something for a valuable consideration.

Any words or actions on the part of the offeree indicating assent to the offer, as made by the offeror, will constitute acceptance. The simple statement "I accept" is sufficient if made with reference to the offer and if the offer requests a promise in return. Performance of the act requested in an offer for a unilateral contract is a legally sufficient acceptance. Is is important, however, that such action be taken or such promise be made with reference to the offer. A manifestation of mutual assent is essential.

Only the person to whom the offer is made can accept it. However, an offer need not be directed to one person only. It may be made to any member of a large group as in the case of an offer of a reward. Regardless of the number of persons who may be eligible to accept, one person must manifest assent to the offer in accordance with its terms, or there will be no contract. For this reason, as a general rule, silence on the part of an offeree will not be construed to be an acceptance.

Despite this general rule of contract law, the majority of courts which have considered the point have held that an insurer must act with reasonable promptness when it receives an application. In those jurisdictions, silence or delay in acting on the application may result in liability for the insurer. Fortunately, the general practice of issuing premium receipts that provide coverage before the policy is issued has made liability for delay less likely. Moreover, courts in a substantial minority of jurisdictions have denied that an insurer has any duty to act promptly on an application.

Communication of the Acceptance

It would seem that a manifestation of mutual assent would require that acceptance, like the offer, be communicated. However, this is not always true. There are some instances in which acceptance does not have to be brought to the attention of the offeror.

Unilateral Contracts.   An offer for a unilateral contract usually contemplates the performance of an act as acceptance. In such cases, unless the offeror specifically requests notification, performance of the requested act is generally held sufficient to complete a binding agreement. In those instances in which the offer is the performance of an act, however, acceptance will be in the form of a promise. The acceptance must then be communicated.

For example, when an applicant for insurance submits an application and the initial premium to an insurer, that act is usually an offer. The insurer communicates its acceptance by delivering the policy applied for to the applicant. The policy contains the insurer's promise.

Bilateral Contracts. An offer for a bilateral contract contemplates acceptance in the form of a return promise. This, of course, implies that the acceptance (i.e., the return promise) will be communicated. However, acceptance does not have to be actually communicated if the offeree uses a means of communication designated by the offeror. The legal theory is that if the offeror requests acceptance by mail, for example, the mail service becomes the agent of the offeror for this purpose. When the offeree mails a letter of acceptance, therefore, a contract is completed, even though the letter is never received by the offeror. By mailing the acceptance, the offeree is delivering it to the agent of the offeror which, legally, is the same as delivering it to the offeror. A similar result is achieved with any other designated means of communication. If the offeror requests an acceptance by telegram, delivery of the acceptance to the telegraph company will be delivery to the offeror. However, if the offeror's requested means of communication is not used in communicating the acceptance, the means of communication selected by the offeree is considered to be the agent of the offeree. In that case, actual delivery of the acceptance to the offeror is required. For example, if an acceptance by telegram is requested and the offeree decides to reply by mail, the mail service is considered to be the agent of the offeree. The letter must then actually reach the offeror for the acceptance to have been communicated.

If the offeror does not specify any particular means of communication, it is presumed that the offeree is expected to reply by the same method that was used in communicating the offer. If the offeror writes a letter, the offeree may accept by letter, and the acceptance is considered to have been communicated the instant the letter is mailed. In any event, if the offeree actually makes his or her acceptance known to the offeror, it will have been communicated effectively.

Completion of the Contract

Assuming that the other requirements are satisfied, the contract is generally considered to be complete and to become effective at the moment there is an overt act by the offeree manifesting assent to the offer. Unless the contract is one required by law to be evidenced by a writing, the oral promises of the parties will usually be held to constitute an effective contract—even though the parties plan to put their contract into writing later. Nevertheless, there are exceptions to this rule. For instance, in some cases, the parties plan to reduce their agreement to writing at a later date and agree not to be bound until this has been done and until the contract has been signed.

CONSIDERATION

Consideration is the thing of value requested and given in exchange for a promise. Consideration involves a bargained-for exchange.

Long before the doctrine of consideration arose, formal contracts were effective by reason of their form alone. Historically, therefore, the doctrine of consideration was not applicable to formal contracts.

With respect to the informal contract, there must be a legally adequate consideration for the promise, or promises, sought to be enforced. This means that the person who seeks to enforce the promise of another must have given something of value for it. This consideration might have been another promise, a sum of money, or something else of value. The person might have performed an act, or refrained from doing something he or she was legally entitled to do. In some way, however, this person must have promised or given something the promisor requested.

Legally Adequate Consideration

As a general principle, the law does not inquire into the adequacy of the consideration agreed upon and given in exchange for a promise. If there was consideration and if it was what the promisor requested, the courts will not substitute their own judgment of value for that of the parties to the contract. The classic statement is to the effect that under such circumstances "even a peppercorn" will be considered legally adequate. After all, adequacy and value are subjective concepts. Something that has great value to one person often has little or no value to another. In the absence of fraud, the courts take the position that the parties knew what they were doing and that the promisor knew what he or she wanted in return for the promise.

One exception to this general rule is found in cases which involve a promise to pay in money a larger sum for a smaller sum at the same time and place. However, if the smaller sum represents more than its nominal value, as with a rare coin, a promise to pay the smaller sum will be sufficient consideration for a promise to pay a larger sum. If there is no such unique value, a promise to pay a smaller sum in money will not be a legally adequate consideration for a promise to pay a larger sum at the same time and place.

A Requested Act or Promise.   There are two generally accepted approaches for determining the adequacy of consideration. One approach, and, perhaps, the one more frequently used by the courts, is that adequate consideration is "any act or promise requested and received by the promisor in exchange for his or her promise." This, it will be noted, is the definition previously given. Thus, if A requests an act on the part of B in exchange for A's promise to pay a specified sum of money, and if B performs the act, the performance of that act is adequate consideration for A's promise. It is what A requested and received in return for A's promise.

A Benefit or Detriment. Consideration is also defined as "any benefit to the promisor or detriment to the promisee." However, these words are not necessarily interpreted literally. For example, a legal detriment need not operate to the promisee's actual disadvantage. The classic illustration of this point concerns an uncle who promises his nephew a sum of money on the nephew's 25th birthday if the nephew refrains from smoking until that date. Here, the consideration for the uncle's promise—abstention from smoking on the part of the nephew—is not physically detrimental to the nephew. However, in legal theory, the voluntary forgoing of a legal right—the right to smoke—is a detriment. In this sense, there is a detriment to the nephew and, thus, a legally adequate consideration for the promise of the uncle.

A Promise for a Promise. Generally speaking, mutual promises constitute adequate consideration for each other. In other words, in a bilateral contract, each promise is consideration for the other, as each is the thing requested and received in exchange for the promise of the other party to the contract.

Conditional Promises. A conditional promise will be adequate consideration for another promise or for an act. For example, a promise to pay an insurance benefit is conditional, as it is conditioned on the occurrence of a loss. Payment will be made only if the loss insured against occurs. Many term life insurance policies expire without the payment of a claim. The insurer promises to pay a death benefit, but only on the condition that the insured dies during the term of the policy. If the insured does not die during the term of the policy, no payment will be made. This does not mean that the contract was not valid or that the promise was not binding. It means only that the specified condition did not occur.

Inadequate Consideration

There are two situations in which courts ordinarily hold that consideration is inadequate. These situations involve past consideration and preexisting legal duty.

Past Consideration. If a promisor says, "In consideration of your not smoking last month, I promise to pay you $500," there is no consideration for the promise and no contract. Past consideration is not valid, because it did not induce the promise and was not given in exchange for the promise. Valid consideration requires a bargained-for exchange.

Preexisting Legal Duty. Ordinarily, the promise to perform or the performance of a preexisting legal duty will not be adequate consideration to create a binding contract. Nor will there be adequate consideration if a party promises to refrain, or refrains, from doing something he or she has no legal right to do.

For example, suppose A has contracted to build B a house for $50,000, but, in the middle of construction, A demands that the contract price be raised to $60,000. B agrees to pay the extra $10,000. B's promise to pay the extra $10,000 will be unenforceable because A has a preexisting legal duty to build the house for $50,000, and there is no consideration for the promise to pay the additional $10,000.

COMPETENT PARTIES

A person of legal age, without mental or other incapacity, is competent to enter into a contract. Such a person is said to have contractual capacity.

Generally speaking, any person is presumed to be capable of entering into a valid and binding contract. The contractual capacity of certain classes of persons is limited, however. These classes include minors, mentally infirm persons, intoxicated persons, convicts, aliens, and corporations. At common law, a married woman had no capacity to contract, but it is doubtful that there is any limitation on the contractual capacity of married women today.

Void and Voidable Contracts

It is said that some contracts of persons with limited contractual capacity are void or voidable. To say that a contract is void is actually a contradiction in terms, as a contract is an agreement enforceable at law. It would be more exact to say that no contract was created. However, the term *void contract* is in general use and will be used in this book.

Where a contract entered into by a legally incompetent person is voidable, that person may disaffirm the contract and avoid the legal relations created by it. If he or she does not disaffirm the contract, however, the contract will remain in effect. The power of some persons of limited contractual capacity to disaffirm—that is, to avoid—a contract after having made it is important to anyone contemplating making a contract with such a person. The competent party will be bound, while the person of limited contractual capacity has the privilege of deciding whether to carry out the contract or disaffirm it.

Minors

At common law, a minor, sometimes referred to as an infant, was any person under the age of 21. However, many states have passed legislation terminating infancy, for contractual purposes, at a younger age—usually 18.

At one time, contracts entered into by a minor were classified as void, voidable, or valid depending upon whether they were harmful, uncertain, or beneficial in their effect upon the minor. This made the courts responsible for determining whether the contract was in fact harmful, uncertain, or beneficial. Today, as a general rule, a few kinds of contracts made by a minor are valid, and all others are voidable, but not void. This means that with respect to most contracts the minor can decide whether continuing with the contract is beneficial and whether he or she wishes to be bound by the contract. If the other party's own contractual capacity is unimpaired, the other party is bound by the contract unless and until the minor decides to disaffirm it.

A minor disaffirms a contract simply by declaring that, thereafter, he or she will not be bound by its terms. Minors are free to disaffirm most contracts at any time during their minority and within a reasonable time after they attain the age of majority.

Disaffirmance of a contract on the ground of infancy requires that the minor return any consideration received if it is still in his or her possession. However, as a general rule, if the minor no longer has the consideration, the minor can still avoid the contract and recover whatever he or she parted with without restoring the other party to the status that person had prior to the making of the contract.

The minor's power of avoiding a contract after it has been made is accorded as a protection from unscrupulous persons who might otherwise seek to take advantage of young people. For this reason, if there is no statute to the contrary, the privilege is almost absolute. It applies to everyone who has not yet attained the age of majority, regardless of how nearly of age he or she may be. Even minors who are engaging in business for themselves or who have married[8] usually retain the power to disaffirm their contracts.

Although it might appear that a minor has only an additional privilege and not a contractual disability, this is not the case. A minor cannot give legal assurance that he or she will not disaffirm a contract. Competent parties, therefore, frequently refuse to contract with a minor. This puts the minor at a practical, as well as a legal, disadvantage.

Contracts Which the Minor Cannot Avoid.   Federal or state statutes relating to banking, military enlistment, educational loans, marriage, and insurance may modify a minor's power to avoid a contract. Also, at common law, there are certain kinds of contracts a minor may not disaffirm. Agreements in fulfillment of a minor's legal duty are binding. For example, a minor's agreement to support the minor's illegitimate child will be binding on the minor, as minors have a legal duty to support their illegitimate children whether or not they contract to do so.

Minors are also liable for the reasonable value of necessaries furnished them or their dependents. Note that they are not liable for the contract price but for the reasonable value of the goods. Necessaries are "those things

---

[8]In a substantial minority of states, marriage will confer contractual capacity upon a minor.

which are reasonably necessary for the proper and suitable maintenance of the infant in view of his social position and situation in life, the customs of the social circle in which he moves, and the fortune possessed by him and his parents."[9] *Necessaries* is a broader word than *necessities,* for *necessaries* includes not only those items essential to subsistence, but also other things which are reasonably required for the minor's maintenance, considering his or her social position and financial status. Food, shelter, clothing, medical services, and education are necessaries. Legal services are often a necessary. Many other articles may be necessaries, such as an automobile needed to transport the minor to his or her place of employment. Questions involving which kinds of food, shelter, clothing, and other goods or services are necessaries for a particular minor are fact questions for the jury. Luxury articles will not usually be found to be necessaries, but an expensive article, such as an automobile, could be a necessary if the minor is in actual need of it.

The Minor as Insurance Applicant.   The courts have held that insurance is not a necessary. In the absence of a special statute, therefore, minors can disaffirm a contract of life insurance. Moreover, the majority rule is that, upon such disaffirmance, the minor can recover all the premiums paid for the insurance. The minor then will have had the insurance protection without cost.

Statutes have been enacted in many states authorizing minors above specified ages to contract for life or health insurance under certain conditions. A typical statute of this kind reads as follows:

> Any minor of the age of fifteen years or more may, notwithstanding such minority, contract for life, health, and accident insurance on his own life for his own benefit or for the benefit of his father, mother, husband, wife, child, brother or sister, and may exercise all such contractual rights and powers with respect to any such contract of insurance as might be exercised by a person of full legal age, and may exercise with like effect all rights and privileges under such contract, including the surrender of his interest therein and the giving of a valid discharge for any benefit accruing or money payable thereunder. Such minor shall not, by reason of his minority, be entitled to rescind, avoid, or repudiate such contract, or any exercise of a right or privilege thereunder.[10]

This statute permits a minor 15 years of age or older to insure "his own life." Note, however, that the beneficiary must be the minor's estate (as indicated by the words "for his own benefit") or a person closely related to the minor. Statutes of this kind sometimes permit the minor to insure the life of a child or spouse, as well as her or his own life.

---

[9]BALLENTINE'S LAW DICTIONARY 836 (3d ed. 1969).
[10]ILL. REV. STAT. ch. 73, ¶ 854 (1987) (Ill. Ins. Code § 242).

Mentally Infirm Persons

A person can be mentally infirm because of insanity, retardation, disease, or advanced age. The contractual capacity of a mentally infirm person depends upon whether or not a court has judged the person incompetent and has appointed a guardian of the person's estate.

Where a Guardian Has Been Appointed.   If a mentally infirm person has been judged incompetent and the court has appointed a guardian of the person's estate, any contract attempted by the incompetent person will usually be void. Such a guardian is appointed to manage the affairs of the incompetent person. The guardian has control of the incompetent person's property, subject to court supervision. The guardianship proceedings are considered public notice of the incompetent person's status.

Where No Guardian Has Been Appointed.   Where no guardian of the estate of a mentally infirm person has been appointed, ordinarily the mentally infirm person can disaffirm a contract he or she has made. After the death of a mentally infirm person, her or his personal representative or heirs can disaffirm a contract made by the mentally infirm person. Ordinarily, an insane person can ratify or disaffirm the contract upon regaining his or her sanity. As with minor's contracts, contracts of the mentally infirm for necessaries will be binding on the mentally infirm person.

Insurance contracts of the mentally infirm are voidable. The mentally infirm person can disaffirm a life insurance contract and receive back the premiums he or she paid.

Intoxicated Persons

A contract is voidable if one of the parties was so much under the influence of alcohol or drugs at the time the contract was made as to be unable to understand the nature and effect of the contract. Upon recovery, the person can affirm or disaffirm the contract. A contract for necessaries will be binding, however.

Convicts

Convicts are under contractual disabilities which vary from state to state. In the absence of a statute to the contrary, a convict is not completely incapacitated to contract. A convict will be liable for necessaries in some states. In some states, a convict can contract with respect to her or his own property.

Aliens

Citizens of different countries frequently make contracts with each other. These contracts are ordinarily valid and enforceable. A person cannot contract with an enemy alien, however. An attempted contract between citizens of two countries at war is void.

Corporations

The contractual capacity of a corporation is determined by the provisions of its charter and the statutes of the state where it was organized—that is, its domiciliary state. A corporation has the express powers granted in its charter and the laws under which it was created. A corporation also has implied and incidental powers when and if such powers are necessary in the exercise of the express powers.

Insurers are ordinarily corporations. The charter of a life and health insurer states that the insurer is authorized to transact life and health insurance business. The insurer's domiciliary state must also issue it a certificate of authority—that is, a license—before it can issue life and health insurance contracts in the domiciliary state. To qualify to do business in another state, the insurer must apply to the proper official of that state for permission to conduct an insurance business there. If the insurer meets the necessary requirements, it will be granted a certificate of authority to do business in that state.

The contractual capacity of an insurance company, therefore, depends upon two things. First, under its charter and the laws under which it was formed, the insurer must have been empowered to issue contracts of insurance of the kind desired—life, health, fire, automobile, and so forth. Second, it must have been authorized to do an insurance business—to issue contracts of insurance of the type desired—in the state where the contract becomes effective. Implied is the power to enter into other contracts incident to the conduct of an insurance business, such as, for example, a contract to purchase a building to house the insurer's corporate headquarters.

The legal effect of a contract of insurance made by a nonlicensed insurer varies with the laws of the different states. Some statutes declare such contracts to be void—creating no rights. Others specify that the contracts will be enforceable by the policyowners according to their terms. In other states, there are no applicable statutes. In the absence of an applicable statute, the majority of courts uphold the rights of the policyowner who has entered into the contract in good faith and without knowledge of the legal incompetency of the insurer. In another group of states, the laws provide for a penalty upon the insurer that does business in the state without being licensed. The prevailing opinion in these states is that a contract made with an unlicensed insurer is valid and enforceable by the policyowner. An agent who sells the policy of an unlicensed insurer can incur severe penalties, however.

CONTRACT FORM

There are a number of practical reasons for expressing informal contracts in writing. Memories are not infallible, and it is convenient for the parties to refer to a written contract. It is also easier to prove the terms of a written contract in the event of the death or incompetency of one of the parties. However, in the absence of a statute to the contrary, an informal contract need not be in writing to be valid.

Oral Informal Contracts

The principal that informal contracts need not be in writing to be valid applies to insurance contracts as well as to other informal contracts. Oral, or partly oral, temporary insurance contracts are commonplace. When a premium receipt incorporating a temporary insurance contract is issued to an applicant, an insurance contract is created which is partly oral and partly written. Some terms of the temporary insurance contract will be in the premium receipt, but many other terms will be governed by a policy which has not yet been issued, and, indeed, will never be issued if the insurer rejects the application, or if the loss occurs before the policy can be issued. Moreover, it has been held that a temporary insurance contract that is entirely oral is enforceable. In one case, the neglect of a life insurance agent to give the applicant a premium receipt incorporating a temporary insurance contract did not make an otherwise valid oral contract of temporary insurance invalid.[11]

Although oral, or partly oral, temporary insurance contracts are enforceable by the applicant or beneficiary, it is highly desirable that the written contract be issued at the earliest possible time. The many and complex terms of an insurance policy make it essential that the policyowner receive the policy and have an opportunity to review those terms.

Oral life insurance contracts, other than those for temporary insurance, are not usually permitted by insurers. Life insurers do not ordinarily grant their soliciting agents the authority to make regular insurance contracts. The applicant wil be on notice of this lack of contractual authority, as a statement to that effect will be in the application. Therefore, except for temporary insurance contracts, the soliciting agent cannot make an oral life insurance contract.

The Statute of Frauds

Some contracts are required by law to be in writing. Formal contracts, such as negotiable instruments, must be written to be valid. In addition, state

---

[11]Overton v. Washington Nat'l Ins. Co., 106 R.I. 387, 260 A.2d 444 (1970).

statutes may require that certain informal contracts be evidenced by a writing. The Statute of Frauds is the most important of these statutes. The Statute of Frauds does not ordinarily apply to life and health insurance contracts, but an explanation of it is, nevertheless, necessary to an understanding of life and health insurance laws.

The Statute of Frauds was originally enacted in England in 1677 and expressed as its purpose the "prevention of many fraudulent practices." Some form of this statute has since been enacted in most states of the United States. In its most usual form, the statute enumerates the following five classes of contracts[12] which must be evidenced by a writing:

1. A promise by an executor, or administrator, to pay a claim against the decedent's estate out of his or her own funds.

2. A promise to be legally responsible for the debt or default of another.

3. A promise made in consideration of marriage.

4. An agreement to sell, or a sale of, any interest in real property.

5. An agreement that cannot be performed within one year after the contract is made.

As enacted in most states, the statute lists these five classes of contracts and provides that any oral agreement falling into one of these classes will be unenforceable unless it is evidenced by some note or memorandum signed by the party to be charged with performance of the contract. This means that a person who sues another for breach of a contract falling into one of these classes can prove the existence of the contract only if it is in writing or if he or she has some note or memorandum identifying the parties, subject matter, and essential terms of the contract signed by the other party to the contract—that is, the party to be charged with performance of the contract. Note that the contract itself does not have to be in writing. A written note or memorandum evidencing the promise is all that is required.

The fifth class of agreements listed in the statute is of significance in a discussion of life insurance contract law—namely, an agreement that cannot be performed within one year after the contract is made. Since many life insurance contracts remain in force for many years, the contention has sometimes been made that life insurance contracts must comply with the Statute of Frauds and that oral contracts of life insurance cannot be proved except by a written note or memorandum. This contention is not supportable under

---

[12]The English Statute of Frauds also included a section dealing with the sale of "goods, wares, or merchandises" for a price in excess of a specified sum. This provision was included in the Statute of Frauds as it was originally adopted by many of the states, but it has since been replaced in many states by provisions of the Uniform Commercial Code. One provision, U.C.C. § 2–201(1), states that a contract for the sale of goods in excess of $500 is not enforceable unless there is a sufficient writing to indicate a contract for sale was made between the parties, and signed by the party, or his or her agent, to be charged with performance.

the statute, as it has been enacted in most states, however, since the insured could die and the life insurance contract therefore could be performed "within one year after the contract is made." Many life insurance contracts are performed within the first year, and an agreement that can be performed within one year from the date it is made is not usually within the Statute of Frauds. Thus, an oral contract of life insurance does not ordinarily have to be proved by a written note or memorandum.

An exception to this general rule is found in the statute enacted in the New York General Obligations Law, Title 7, Section 5–701, which reads in part as follows:

> Agreements required to be in writing. Every agreement, promise or undertaking is void, unless it or some note or memorandum thereof be in writing, and subscribed by the party to be charged therewith, or by his or her lawful agent, if such agreement, promise or undertaking:
>   1. By its terms is not to be performed within one year from the making thereof *or the performance of which is not to be completed before the end of a lifetime.* . . . [Emphasis added.]

As it includes any contract "the performance of which is not to be completed before the end of a lifetime," this New York statute specifically includes life insurance contracts. Therefore, in New York, a life insurance contract does have to be evidenced by a writing under the Statute of Frauds.

ILLEGALITY

A contract is an agreement enforceable in a court of law. As the courts will not enforce an illegal agreement, a contract cannot be illegal.

An agreement may be illegal because it is unconstitutional, forbidden by statute, against an express rule of common law, or against public policy as expressed by the courts.[13] Public policy is the principle of law which holds that no person can lawfully do that which tends to be injurious to the public. Agreements in restraint of trade, usurious agreements, agreements to commit torts[14] or crimes, and wagering agreements are usually illegal.

Ordinarily, the law will not aid either party to an illegal agreement. If the agreement has not been performed, neither party can compel performance or obtain damages. If the agreement has been performed, neither can obtain damages from the other.

Sometimes, however, a statute is written to protect one of the parties and is directed against the other party. In such a case, the protected party can enforce the contract. For example, statutes concerning the validity of life

---

[13]BALLENTINE'S LAW DICTIONARY 1023 (3d ed. 1969).

[14]A tort is the breach of a noncontractual legal duty to another person resulting in injury to that person. Assault, slander, and negligent operation of a motor vehicle resulting in injury to another person are examples of torts.

insurance contracts issued by nonlicensed insurers are meant to protect the citizens of the state. For this reason, these statutes often do not declare such contracts void and unenforceable, but instead permit the owner to enforce them against the insurer at fault.

Aleatory Contracts

In an aleatory contract, the promise by one party is conditioned on the happening of an uncertain event. Some aleatory agreements are illegal, while others are not. Wagering agreements are aleatory agreements which are often illegal. Insurance contracts are also aleatory agreements, but insurance contracts, generally speaking, are legal and will be enforced by the courts.

The uncertain event upon which the promise in a wagering agreement is conditioned could be that of one horse running faster than another in a race or of a certain number of black dots appearing on the tops of dice when they are thrown. One person promises to pay money to another if a certain horse wins the race or a certain number of black dots appear on the tops of dice.

The uncertain event upon which the promise in an insurance contract is conditioned could be a fire, an automobile accident, a death, a sickness, and so forth depending upon the type of insurance contract. The insurer promises to pay money on the happening of the event insured against.

Many contracts are not aleatory. For example, a contract between two people in which one agrees to sell a plot of land to the other, and the other agrees to pay a specified amount for the land, is not conditioned on the happening of an uncertain event and is not an aleatory contract.

Wagering Agreements Versus Insurance Contracts

Wagering agreements are often illegal. In the earliest days of the common law, they were not prohibited, but laws were later enacted declaring certain kinds of wagers to be against public policy. Statutes to this effect are now in force in most states.

Unlike wagering agreements, it is commonly accepted today that insurance contracts are in the interests of society. If issued with proper safeguards, there is no question of their legality, but this question has not always been so clearly settled. A life insurance contract obligates one party to pay another a specific sum of money on the happening of an event that is presumably not within the control of either. Such an agreement bears more than a passing resemblance to a wager. It is obvious that an unscrupulous person standing to gain from the destruction of an insured piece of property or an insured life might feel a strong temptation to implement the whims of chance in his or her own favor. Therefore, if life insurance contracts were issued indiscriminately, they could pose a threat to the public welfare by creating a motive for murder in the minds of the unscrupulous. These problems are avoided by requiring that the beneficiary have an insurable interest in the life of the insured. This is such an essential concept in life insurance law that it will be discussed at some length in Chapter 6, "Formation of the Life Insurance Contract."

DURESS AND UNDUE INFLUENCE

The parties' freedom of will is essential to the validity of a contract. Therefore, duress or undue influence exerted on one of the parties may make the contract unenforceable. Duress occurs when a person is induced to make a contract against her or his will by the wrongful act or threat of another. Undue influence often involves misuse of a position of confidence or dominion by one person to overcome the will of another person. Undue influence also occurs when one person takes advantage of another's weakness of mind, necessity, or distress. Often, it is a combination of a position of confidence or dominion on the part of one person, and weakness of mind, necessity, or distress on the part of the other.

Duress or undue influence may nullify the modification of a contract, as well as its formation. In life insurance, the claim is sometimes made that duress or undue influence was exerted upon the policyowner to make a change of beneficiary. The insurer will not ordinarily be liable if it paid the benefits to the new beneficiary without knowledge of the claim of duress or undue influence. If the insurer receives notice from the original beneficiary of the claim of duress or undue influence before the insurer has paid, an interpleader[15] action may be in order.

RULES OF CONTRACT CONSTRUCTION

There are a number of general rules which will be applied by a court when it interprets a contract. These are called rules of contract construction. The word *construction* comes from the word *construe,* which means to interpret. Rules of contract construction assist the court to interpret a contract. The purpose of the rules is to find the probable intent of the parties. The most important rules of contract construction are discussed below.

Clear and Unambiguous Language

Where the terms of a written contract are clear and unambiguous, there will be no construction by the court. Clear and unambiguous language will

---

[15]Interpleader is an equitable remedy whereby a stakeholder with no claim to the fund he or she holds, and confronted by rival claimants, can pay the money into court and be dismissed from the suit. The court will then decide which claimant is entitled to the money. Interpleader is discussed in Chapter 16, "Remedies."

be given effect. A court is not permitted to rewrite a contract under the guise of interpreting it.[16]

Construed as a Whole

The court will construe the contract as a whole. The meaning will be gathered from the entire context and not from detached portions of the contract. Specific clauses will be subordinated to the contract's general intent.

Ordinary Meaning of Words

Generally, the court will give words their ordinary meaning. However, if it is shown they were meant to be used in a technical sense, words will be given their technical meaning.

Construction in Favor of Validity

If it is possible to do so, the court will give an interpretation which makes a contract valid, rather than an interpretation which makes it invalid. This is because the court presumes the parties intended to make a valid contract, and the court tries to interpret the contract according to the parties' intention.

Unclear Language Construed against the Writer

Where the language in a contract is unclear, the court will interpret that language against the party who selected the language and wrote the contract unless the use of such language is required by law—that is, the unclear language will be interpreted to benefit the other party. This rule applies particularly to the interpretation of insurance policies, which are adhesion contracts written by the insurer.

Adhesion contracts are standard contract forms offered on essentially a "take it or leave it" basis. The other party cannot bargain as to the terms of the contract. Adhesion contracts differ in this respect from contracts in which the terms result from mutual negotiation and concessions of the parties. Thus, when an insurer writes a policy and sells it to a policyowner, if that policy contains unclear or ambiguous terms, the court will interpret those terms in favor of the policyowner or beneficiary and against the insurer.

---

[16]As to insurance contracts, this traditional rule of contract construction has been modified by the reasonable expectations doctrine discussed in Chapter 18, "Contract Performance."

Printed, Typed, and Handwritten Matter

Where there are inconsistencies between printed, typed, or handwritten matter in a contract, the typed or handwritten matter will control. This is because the typed or handwritten terms were selected by the parties themselves, while the printed matter is for general use. The typed or handwritten matter, therefore, will indicate their intent. Where typing and handwriting are inconsistent with each other, the handwriting will control.

THE PAROL EVIDENCE RULE

The term *parole* in French means "speech." French terms are often used in English law, and in laws which derive from English law, because French was used in the English courts after the Norman Conquest of England in 1066.

Parol evidence is oral evidence—that is, testimony given by witnesses in court. Under the parol evidence rule, when parties put their contract into an unambiguous writing, all previous oral agreements merge into the written contract. Parol evidence is not admissible to add to, detract from, or alter the contract as written.

Life insurance policies, as written contracts, are subject to the parol evidence rule. Oral evidence cannot ordinarily be admitted to contradict the provisions of a life insurance policy.

As is true of most legal rules, there are a number of exceptions to the parol evidence rule. Oral evidence can be introduced in the situations described in the following subsections.

Formation Defects

The parol evidence rule does not prohibit testimony for the purpose of showing that no contract was ever formed. This is because the parol evidence rule does not become effective until a binding contract exists. For example, where a party asserts that there was an oral agreement that the contract would not be effective until a certain event occurred, the court can hear oral evidence of such an agreement. Formation defects due to fraud, duress, mistake, lack of consideration, or illegality may also be shown by parol evidence.

Parol evidence was admitted in one life insurance case to show that no contract was ever formed because someone other than the insured took the medical examination. The court noted the general rule that parol evidence cannot be introduced "for the purpose of contradicting, changing, or adding to the terms incorporated into and made a part of a written contract." But it pointed out that this was not the purpose of parol evidence in this case, saying:

In a case such as the instant one, where the defense of fraud is invoked, in that the named insured never knowingly made application for insurance and where a person other than the named insured was substituted for the medical examination, we are of the opinion that the Parol Evidence Rule cannot be invoked to preclude the medical examiner from giving testimony as to the facts and circumstances connected with and surrounding the parties at the time of such examination. The purpose of such testimony is not to vary or contradict a contract, but to show that the alleged contract never came into existence.[17]

Incomplete Contract

If the face of the written contract shows that something remained to be done or another provision was to be incorporated, parol evidence can be used to show those provisions on which the parties had orally agreed, but which they failed to incorporate into the written contract.

Interpretation

If there is ambiguity in a written contract or if the parties disagree as to the meaning of words in the contract, parol evidence will be admissible so that the contract can be interpreted. In addition, where words used in a contract have a special trade meaning or a special meaning by reason of the locality in which the contract was drawn up, parol evidence can be used to explain the meaning.

Reformation

Reformation is an equitable remedy by which a written contract is revised to express the original intent of the parties. Reformation of the contract will be granted when it is proven that the contract as written does not reflect the actual agreement of the parties because of mistake or misrepresentation.[18] The parol evidence rule will not be applied if a party to a written contract alleges facts which would entitle her or him to a reformation of the contract. This is because the writing does not constitute the agreement between the parties.

For example, suppose the purchase price of a painting was agreed to be $1,000. If the person who drafted the contract wrote $100 by mistake, the seller could have the contract reformed to reflect the parties' original intent. The parol evidence rule would not prevent this.

---

[17]Obartuch v. Security Mut. Life Ins. Co., 114 F.2d 873 (7th Cir. 1940).
[18]Reformation is discussed more fully in Chapter 16, "Remedies."

Subsequent Modifications

The parol evidence rule applies only to negotiations occurring prior to the time a written contract becomes effective. Oral modifications of the contract agreed upon after that time may be shown to the court by parol evidence.

BREACH AND MATERIALITY

A breach of contract is a failure of a party to perform a promise according to its terms without a legal excuse. Breach of contract and materiality are discussed together here because only material breach by one party will give the other party a cause of action for money damages, for specific performance, or for cancellation of the contract. Immaterial breach will give the other party the right to a cure of the breach only. An immaterial breach is an unimportant breach. Immaterial breaches frequently occur in the case of building contracts—for example, where a faucet in a newly completed building leaks. The buyer would have a right to a cure of the breach only—that is, repair of the faucet.

A material breach is an important breach. It involves failure of a significant part of the performance. For example, if an insurer paid death benefits where the insured died of an accident but failed to pay the accidental death benefits due the beneficiary, the beneficiary would have a cause of action for damages for material breach. This would be an obvious material breach. Sometimes, it is difficult to tell if a breach is material or immaterial. In those cases, materiality is a fact question to be decided by the jury.

THIRD-PERSON BENEFICIARIES

In the past, there have been conflicting views on whether a third person who is not a party to the contract could maintain an action for breach of contract damages. It is now settled in the United States that when a contract is for the direct benefit of a third person, that person can maintain an action on the contract. Where a life insurance contract is not payable to the policyowner or to his or her estate, it is a contract for the benefit of a third person. The third-person beneficiary of a life insurance contract can, therefore, sue in her or his own name after the insured's death. The beneficiary, rather than the personal representative of the insured, is the proper party to bring the suit. A personal representative of a person is the executor or administrator of that person's estate.

LIBERTY OF CONTRACT

It has been noted in this chapter that an offeror can include what terms he or she wishes in the offer and choose the persons with whom he or she wishes to contract. The offeree can ignore, reject, or accept the offer. The adequacy of the consideration will ordinarily be left to the judgment of the parties. The freedom to contract as one wishes is liberty of contract.

Such liberty of contract prevails unless other laws limit it. Because insurance is affected with a public interest, there are many laws limiting liberty of contract as applied to insurance policies. Nevertheless, the basic principle of liberty of contract should be borne in mind.

CONSTITUTIONAL PROTECTION OF EXISTING CONTRACTS

The Contract Clause of the United States Constitution, found in Article I, Section 10, provides that "No state shall . . . pass any . . . law impairing the Obligation of Contracts." Because of the Contract Clause, states cannot enact statutes which materially change the rights of parties to contracts already in existence at the time the statute is enacted.

In addition, rights under existing contracts are protected by the Due Process Clauses of the 5th and 14th Amendments to the United States Constitution. These amendments prohibit governments from depriving people of property without "due process of law." Contract rights are valuable property, as will be discussed in Chapter 9, "Property Rights in the Life Insurance Policy."

LIFE AND HEALTH INSURANCE CONTRACT LAW

The law of life and health insurance contracts rests upon the general principles of contract law discussed in this chapter. Therefore, in many respects life and health insurance policies are governed by the same rules that apply to any other type of contract.

Nevertheless, for a number of reasons, a large body of special insurance contract law has developed. For example, protective laws are needed to prevent insurance contracts from being used for wagering purposes. The requirement of insurable interest is such a protective law. Legal safeguards are also necessary to prevent the unscrupulous from collecting premiums for many years without observing the necessary accounting and investment practices that will enable them to pay claims as they are presented. Special fair-claims-practices laws were developed to regulate the contract performance of insurers. As a result of the large body of insurance law which has been developed, some general principles of contract law have been modified—either strengthened or weakened—when applied to insurance contracts.

SUMMARY

A contract can be defined as "a binding promise" or as "an agreement enforceable at law." Contracts can be unilateral—that is, with promises by one party only—or bilateral—that is, with promises by both parties. A life or health contract is unilateral, because only the insurer makes a promise.

A contract is either formal or informal. A formal contract is binding because of its form. An informal contract is binding because the parties have met requirements that relate to the substance, rather than to the form, of the transaction. Insurance contracts are informal contracts.

An informal contract is created when an offer by one person, the offeror, is accepted by another person, the offeree. The offer can be in the form of a promise or of an act. The offer must indicate a definite commitment to be bound by the contract. It must be communicated to the offeree.

The offer will last for the period of time the offeror specifies, or for a reasonable period of time if no period is specified. The offeree can reject the offer, in which case it terminates. Or the offeree can make a counteroffer. A counteroffer is a rejection of the offer and a proposal of a new offer. If the offeror or offeree dies, the offer terminates.

Acceptance by the offeree according to the terms of the offer creates the contract. The acceptance must be positive, unconditional, and manifest an assent to enter into the contract. Performance of a requested act is a legally sufficient acceptance in the case of a unilateral contract. Only an offeree can accept the offer.

Consideration is necessary to the formation of a binding informal contract. Consideration is the thing of value requested and given in exchange for a promise. It can also be defined as "any benefit to the promisor or detriment to the promisee." As a general rule, the law does not inquire into the adequacy of the consideration agreed upon. Mutual promises are adequate consideration for each other. A conditional promise is adequate consideration.

A person of legal age and without mental infirmity or other incapacity is competent to contract. Minors, mentally infirm persons, intoxicated persons, convicts, aliens, and corporations have limited or no contractual capacity.

Contracts of those with limited contractual capacity are sometimes void or voidable. Minors' contracts, except for contracts for necessaries, are generally voidable by minors. Contracts for necessaries are valid.

If the minor avoids a contract, the minor can get back the consideration he or she gave. Life insurance contracts are not necessaries and, unless there is a statute to the contrary, are voidable by the minor, allowing the minor to get back the premium she or he paid.

The contractual power of a corporation is determined by the provisions of its charter and the statutes of the state where it was organized. An insurer is ordinarily a corporation. An insurer must have a certificate of authority (license) from each state in which it does business, including its state of domicile.

Informal contracts can be oral unless there is a statute to the contrary. The Statute of Frauds requires some types of informal contracts to be evidenced by a writing, but, in most states, the Statute of Frauds does not apply to insurance contracts.

An illegal agreement will not be enforced by the courts. Some aleatory agreements are illegal. Under an aleatory agreement, the promise of one party is conditioned on the happening of an uncertain event. Wagering agreements are aleatory agreements which are often illegal. Insurance contracts are aleatory agreements which are legal.

Contracts are construed—that is, interpreted—by a court according to certain rules. If the contract language is plain and unambiguous, there will be no construction by the court, but ambiguities will be construed against the writer of the contract. The contract will be construed as a whole, and its words will be given their ordinary meaning. The contract will be given an interpretation which makes it valid rather than invalid. Typed and handwritten matter will control over printed matter.

Parol evidence—that is, oral evidence given by witnesses—will not be admissible to alter the terms of a written contract, as a general rule. However, the parol evidence rule does not apply where there are formation defects, a contract incomplete on its face, ambiguities, or a written contract that does not reflect the original intent of the parties.

A material breach of contract by one party will give the other party a cause of action for money damages, for specific performance, or for cancellation of the contract. A material breach involves failure of a significant part of the performance.

ILLUSTRATIVE CASE

The following case has been selected because it illustrates two important principles, offer and acceptance, in connection with the life insurance contract.

JOHN HANCOCK MUTUAL LIFE INSURANCE COMPANY
v.
DONALD H. DIETLIN et al.[19]
Supreme Court of Rhode Island

JOSLIN, Justice.

This is a bill in equity[20] to declare null and void a policy of life insurance issued by the complainant [the insurer] insuring the lives of Donald H. and Charlotte R. Dietlin, husband and wife, and their minor children, Donna J., Paula R., and Patricia A. Dietlin, all of whom are respondents,[21] as well as the life of Kathleen B. Dietlin, deceased. After appointment of a guardian ad litem[22] to represent the in-

---

[19]97 R.I. 515, 199 A.2d 311 (1964).

[20]A written complaint addressed to a court of equity; the remedy sought is an equitable remedy—rescision (cancellation) of the policy.

[21]Literally, those who respond (to the complaint).

[22]A guardian appointed by the court to represent a minor or minors who are parties to the proceedings.

terests of the minor respondents, the cause was heard on bill, answer and proof[23] by a justice of the superior court who entered a decree declaring the policy to be null and void, ordering the respondents to surrender it to the complainant for cancellation, and granting the complainant other incidental relief. In addition the complainant was directed by the decree to refund to the respondents the sum of $14.60, being the amount of the premium paid at the time of the execution of the application for the policy. From that decree the respondents have appealed to this court.

The material facts are not in dispute. The application for the policy was made by Donald H. Dietlin, hereinafter sometimes referred to as the "insured," and is dated February 28, 1959. Listed therein for inclusion as insured lives in the policy were all of respondents as well as Kathleen, and in reference to the latter the application states that "About 2 months ago Kathleen had pneumonia after which her heart was impaired & has been treated at St Josephs Hosp. Prov R I since then." In the course of the preparation of the application, James R. Lockett, complainant's soliciting agent, questioned whether in the light of her condition Kathleen would be covered in the policy. He told the insured and his wife that Kathleen's name and those of the other minor children were required to be listed on the application, but that he could not assure them that the company would include her as an insured family member.

In the course of the processing of the application by complainant, there was stapled to it a company form designated "Underwriting Data Sheet" on which, under a heading entitled "Company's Action On Application," appear the notations "3–16 Delete Kathleen" and "Deleted Kathleen," the latter having been approved on March 24, 1959.

Thereafter a life insurance policy designating the insured, his wife, and all of their minor children as insured family members was received by Lockett from complainant. Attached to it was a copy of the application and a document designated "Amendment To Application," the former document having been affixed apparently pursuant to clause 19 of the policy which provided in part that "The entire contract between the Company and the applicant consists of the policy and the written application, a copy of which is attached at issue." That amendment, which required the signature of the insured, provided that Kathleen be deleted from the list of the proposed family members on the application and that no coverage should be provided under the policy for her.

Not being able to contact the insured who was not at home when he called, Lockett left the policy and attached documents with the insured's wife and requested that she have her husband execute the amendment. Although the version given by Mrs. Dietlin on this phase of the cause differed slightly from that of Lockett, respondents make no contention that the acceptance by the trial justice of the Lockett version was either clearly wrong or that in accrediting that account he overlooked or misconceived any evidence. In those circumstances in accordance with our well-settled rule his finding on that issue is conclusive.

---

[23]"The cause was heard on bill, answer and proof" means that the case was heard on a basis of the bill in equity filed by the insurer, the answer that was filed by the respondents, and the proof presented in support of the various contentions. Here the decree or decision in the lower court was in favor of the insurer, and the Dietlins appealed.

The amendment had not been signed by the insured when Kathleen died on April 2, 1959 and subsequent refusals so to do resulted in the instant suit being brought.

The only question is whether the insurance policy is in effect.

In the formation of a contract of insurance as in other contracts there must be a manifestation of mutual assent in the form of an offer or proposal by one party and an acceptance thereof by the other. Ordinarily, the application for a policy is the offer and before a contractual relationship can come into being the offer must be unconditionally accepted. An acceptance which is equivocal or upon condition or with a limitation is a counteroffer and requires acceptance by the original offeror before a contractual relationship can exist.

In this case the application or original offer was for a policy insuring the lives of all respondents as well as of Kathleen. The complainant was not required to nor did it accept that offer. Instead it attached the amendment to the contract of insurance, thereby proposing to the insured that there be deleted from the policy one of the lives included in the original application. This constituted a counteroffer and required the unequivocal assent of the insured as a prerequisite to a completed contract. By the terms of such offer that assent could be manifested only by the insured affixing his signature to the amendment. Because that signature was not obtained the counteroffer was not accepted and the policy did not take effect as a contract of insurance.

The respondents' appeal is denied and dismissed, the decree appealed from is affirmed, and the cause is remanded to the superior court for further proceedings.[24]

QUESTIONS FOR REVIEW

1. Briefly explain what a contract is.
2. How do a bilateral and a unilateral contract differ? Explain why the life insurance contract is a unilateral contract.
3. Define an offer. What are the requirements of a valid offer? How may an offer be terminated?
4. What is meant by a counteroffer? What is the legal effect of making a counteroffer?
5. Define and briefly discuss the meaning of consideration as it applies to informal contracts. Would a contract to sell a family heirloom for approximately twice its fair market value be supported by a legally adequate consideration?
6. List three classes of people who have limited contractual capacity. If an insane person makes a contract, what are the possible legal effects?
7. What is meant by the legal term *minor?* What is the common-law rule concerning minority and the capacity to contract? Can a minor disaffirm a contract for necessaries?

---

[24]The case was sent back (remanded) to the superior court for the procedures necessary to carry out the original decision.

8. Many states have statutes relating to the minor as an applicant for insurance. Describe these statutes.

9. Must a life insurance contract always be in writing to be enforceable?

10. Why does the Statute of Frauds, as it is commonly enacted, not apply to the life insurance contract?

11. Briefly summarize the parol evidence rule. Why is this rule important in connection with the life insurance contract? What are some of the exceptions to the parol evidence rule?

CHAPTER 3

Agency

POWER AND AUTHORITY

ACTS AND KNOWLEDGE OF THE AGENT
    Payment to the Agent
    Knowledge of the Agent

CAPACITY OF PRINCIPAL AND AGENT
    Capacity to Be a Principal
    Capacity to Be an Agent

CREATION OF THE PRINCIPAL-AGENT RELATIONSHIP
    Actual Authority
    Apparent Authority
    Ratification
    Subagents

LIMITATIONS OF THE AGENT'S AUTHORITY

PRINCIPAL AND AGENT
    Control by the Principal
    Agent's Duties
    Principal's Remedies
    Principal's Duties
    Agent's Remedies

PRINCIPAL, AGENT, AND THIRD PERSONS
    Principal's Liabilities to Third Persons
    Principal's Rights against Third Persons
    Agent's Liabilities to Third Persons
    Agent's Rights against Third Persons

CLASSIFICATION OF AGENTS

TERMINATION OF THE AGENT'S POWERS
    Termination of Actual Authority
    Termination of Apparent Authority
    Effect of Termination

MASTER AND SERVANT
    Determination of Servant Status
    Respondeat Superior

EMPLOYER AND INDEPENDENT CONTRACTOR
SUMMARY

An insurer's vice presidents, typists, programmers, janitors, soliciting agents, and actuaries are all its agents under the broadest definition of the word *agent*. The term *agent* is broadly defined as a person who acts for another person—the agent's *principal*. The term *person* here includes organizations, such as corporations and partnerships, as well as human beings (natural persons). This definition of agency includes principal-agent, master-servant, and employer-independent contractor relationships.[1]

With few exceptions, a person can appoint an agent to perform any act the person might have performed.[2] A person cannot appoint an agent to vote in a public election, make a statement under oath, or sign a will. Where a contract calls for personal services, such as those of an artist or a surgeon, the artist or surgeon cannot properly delegate the work to an agent. Similarly, a fiduciary cannot delegate to an agent the performance of matters in which the fiduciary must use judgment.[3] Almost everything else can be done by agents.

By its very nature, a corporation must carry on all its business through agents. A corporation is an artificial being—invisible, intangible, and existing only in contemplation of law.[4] It has a legal, but not an actual, existence. It is a legal entity, separate and distinct from its owner, or owners, authorized by law to transact a specific kind of business. An insurer is ordinarily a corporation authorized to transact an insurance business. All the work of a typical insurer is carried on by the natural persons who are its agents.[5]

It has been said that "most of the world's work is performed by agents."[6] This is true under the broad definition of *agency* noted above.

However, *agent* is also defined more narrowly to mean a person who acts for another person, a principal, in contractual dealings with third parties.[7] Thus, an agent is a person who creates, modifies, performs, or terminates contracts for another person. In this sense, the soliciting agent is an agent of

---

[1]Master-servant and employer-independent contractor relationships are discussed later in this chapter.

[2]Although a *contract* to commit a crime or tort is unenforceable, there can be an *agency* to commit a crime or tort. This is because the law wishes to hold the principal liable for a criminal or tortious act the principal directs another to do.

[3]A *fiduciary* is a person who occupies a position of special trust and confidence in handling the affairs or funds of another person.

[4]BALLENTINE'S LAW DICTIONARY 275 (3d ed. 1969).

[5]Such natural persons are subagents in some cases, as where a corporation hires another corporation as its agent.

[6]H. REUSCHLEIN & W. GREGORY, THE LAW OF AGENCY, PARTNERSHIP AND OTHER UNINCORPORATED BUSINESS ASSOCIATIONS 1 (1979).

[7]Unfortunately, terminology in the law of agency is sometimes inconsistent or overlapping.

the insurer, but the typist, programmer, and janitor are not. In this book, we are concerned primarily with contract law. Therefore, the term *agent* will hereafter be confined to this narrower definition unless otherwise noted.

POWER AND AUTHORITY

The essence of agency is power. The agent has the power to subject the principal to contractual liability and to create contractual rights for the principal.

For example, if P appoints A to be her agent to sell corn, and A contracts on P's behalf to sell the corn to T, a contract has been created between P and T. A had the power, and in this case the actual authority, to create a contract for P. P will be bound to the contract and will be entitled to T's performance of the contract exactly as if P herself had negotiated the contract with T.

Although power is sometimes confused with actual authority, power is a broader term. An agent sometimes has power to bind a principal to a contract when the agent has no actual authority to do so. This will be explained below in greater detail in the subsection entitled, "Apparent Authority."

ACTS AND KNOWLEDGE OF THE AGENT

Acts of an agent, within the scope of the agent's power, are acts of the principal. This is the fundamental rule of agency law. It is frequently stated by the courts as the Latin phrase, *Qui facit per alium facit per se,* which means "He who acts through another acts himself."

Payment to the Agent

Payment to an agent, where the agent has express or implied authority to receive payment, is payment to the principal. Express authority is authority expressly granted by a principal to an agent. Implied authority is authority inferred from acts of a principal and an agent. The general rule, however, is that an agent authorized to sell has no implied authority to collect payment for what is sold. Agents sometimes have apparent authority, and, therefore, power to collect payment. Apparent authority is agency authority a person has because another person (the principal) has created the appearance of authority to a third person.

Where a person has made payment to an agent who has express, implied, or apparent authority to receive such payment on behalf of the principal, the person will not be adversely affected if the agent does not turn the money over to the principal. The principal cannot win in a lawsuit against the person for the money. For example, suppose A, an agent, collects money owed to P, the principal, from D, the debtor, with express authority to collect the money. If A then absconds with the money, P cannot recover a second payment from

D. Payment to A is payment to P. The authority of an insurance agent to collect premiums is discussed in Chapter 4, "Agency in Life and Health Insurance."

Knowledge of the Agent

The general rule of agency law is that knowledge of the agent will be considered knowledge of the principal where the agent's knowledge concerns the business transacted by the agent. The principal will be considered to have the knowledge, whether or not the agent actually tells the principal what the agent knows.

Life and health insurance soliciting agents usually fill in the application for the applicant. Moreover, the insurer's medical examiner fills in the medical certificate. These agents of the insurer sometimes write in incorrect statements. Where the insurer's agent has written in an incorrect statement, with knowledge of the truth, courts of some jurisdictions have held that the knowledge of the agent is the knowledge of the insurer. Thus, in these jurisdictions, if the insurer's underwriters issue a policy they would not have issued had they had the actual knowledge of the soliciting agent, the insurer will be bound on the contract. That is, the contract will be valid despite the incorrect statements in the application.

However, it is a rule of contract law that a person who accepts a written contract is presumed to know and assent to its contents. Thus, in most jurisdictions the applicant, upon receiving the policy and attached application, has a duty to read the application and inform the insurer of any incorrect statements. The insurer can then rescind the contract if the incorrect statements are material.

CAPACITY OF PRINCIPAL AND AGENT

The capacity necessary to be a principal differs from that necessary to be an agent. This difference results from the difference in roles of principal and agent.

Capacity to Be a Principal

As a general rule, an agent may be appointed to act on behalf of any person who has the capacity to make a contract. A principal can be a natural person or any organization which is a legal entity. A corporation is a legal entity and can, therefore, appoint agents. However, its capacity to appoint agents is limited. It can appoint agents only for those purposes within its corporate powers.

Partnerships cannot be principals because they are not legal entities. An agent of a partnership is actually the agent of the individual partners.

Persons without capacity to contract cannot be principals. An incompetent person cannot cure his or her incapacity, or enlarge a limited capacity, by appointing someone with contractual capacity to act as an agent. Modern cases hold that minors can contract through agents for necessaries. Other contracts a minor makes through an agent will be voidable by the minor.

Mentally infirm persons who have no contractual capacity cannot appoint agents. A person who is so intoxicated or drugged that his or her reason is suspended cannot appoint an agent, although such a person might do so when not intoxicated or drugged.

Capacity to Be an Agent

Almost any person can be an agent. It is not necessary that an agent have contractual capacity because the contract formed by the agent is the principal's contract. Therefore, a minor, a mentally infirm person, or a person under the influence of alcohol or other drugs can act as an agent if he or she can receive and convey ideas. A contract completed by an agent who is a minor for a principal with contractual capacity cannot be avoided by the principal on the ground that the agent was a minor.

Partnerships and corporations can also act as agents. The general rules of agency law apply whether the agent is a natural person, a partnership, or a corporation.

If the law requires an agent to have a license, the agent cannot act without one. Insurance and real estate agents and brokers, attorneys-at-law, and other agents whose activities involve the public must be licensed before they can represent others.

CREATION OF THE PRINCIPAL-AGENT RELATIONSHIP

An agency relationship can be created in several ways. It can be created by an express or implied grant of authority to the agent by the principal. Apparent authority of an agent can also cause the principal to be bound by the agent's acts. Finally, an agency can be created where there is a ratification by the principal of unauthorized acts by the agent. Ratification is the validation of an unauthorized act.

Actual Authority

Actual authority is that authority to act on the principal's behalf that the agent reasonably believes he or she has been given by the principal. Note that it is what the agent *reasonably believes* that controls and not what the principal may actually have intended. As with offer and acceptance, it is the manifestation of the intent of the parties that the court will examine to determine whether an agency was created.

There are two types of actual authority—express authority and implied authority. A principal may, orally or in writing, appoint an agent to act on the principal's behalf. If this appointment is communicated to the agent, and the agent consents to the agency, the agent will have express actual authority. Consideration is not necessary. An agent can act with or without being paid.

Implied actual authority can arise where there is no express agreement to create an agency relationship but where the relationship can be inferred from the acts of the parties. Again, the agent must reasonably believe he or she has the authority.

Authority may be implied if the principal's failure to object to a series of unauthorized acts by the agent leads the agent to reasonably believe she or he has authority to repeat those acts in the future. For example, in one case[8] an agent who was authorized to make loans also collected money from the debtors which the agent had no express authority to collect. The agent remitted the money to his principal. His principal made no objection to this unauthorized collection of money when the money was remitted to him. This happened repeatedly until the agent died, and it was discovered he had not remitted all the money he had collected. The court held that the agent had implied authority to collect the money and that his principal could not recover the missing money from the debtors.

Implied authority also can be incidental to express authority. An express grant of authority ordinarily cannot spell out every detail of the agent's authority. Authority to use all means reasonably necessary to carry out the purpose of the agency is implied. Moreover, unless the principal directs otherwise, the agent has implied authority to act in accordance with the general customs of the business.

Apparent Authority

As a general rule, a person is not responsible for the acts of another who claims to represent him or her unless the person has consented to the agency relationship. Nevertheless, a person will be responsible if the person by his or her conduct has created the appearance of agency authority to a third person. That is to say, apparent authority and, therefore, agency power, will result from conduct by a principal which causes a third person to reasonably believe that someone who purports to be an agent has authority to contract for the principal. However, third persons cannot maintain that they relied on a purported agent's apparent authority if, in fact, they knew the authority did not exist. Neither can irregularities in the purported agent's behavior be disregarded if the irregularities should have aroused suspicions in the mind of a reasonable person. In other words, the situation must have been such that a

---

[8]Dobbs v. Zink, 290 Pa. 243, 138 A. 758 (1927).

reasonable person actually would have been misled. The third person attempting to establish the apparent authority has the responsibility of proving that she or he did, in fact, believe that the agent was acting within the scope of the agent's authority, and that the facts were such as to justify the third person in that belief.

Apparent authority can arise where the agent has no actual authority or where the agent has some actual authority, but goes beyond the authority given. The agent may be an imposter who, through carelessness on the part of the principal, appears to a third person to be the principal's agent. In one case, a hotel desk was left unattended, and an imposter, posing as the desk clerk, was given money and jewelry by a guest to put into the hotel safe. The imposter gave the guest a receipt and absconded with the money and valuables. Carelessness in leaving the desk unattended made the owner of the hotel liable for the loss the guest suffered.[9] The imposter had apparent authority.

An agent sometimes has some authority but goes beyond that authority. If a principal allows an agent to act beyond the agent's authority, future acts of a similar nature might be done with apparent authority, since a third person could reasonably believe the agent has authority to do them.

In other cases, the agent is forbidden by the principal to exercise the implied authority which is customary in the particular business, but third persons are unaware of this limitation of authority. Apparent authority will be created if the agent exercises the customary implied authority, because a third person could reasonably believe the agent had actual implied authority.

For example, it is customary in the life insurance business for soliciting agents to collect the initial premium. Suppose that a life insurer told its soliciting agent that he or she lacked authority to collect the initial premium, but did not mention this on the application. If an applicant paid the initial premium to a soliciting agent who absconded with it, the applicant would not have to pay again because the agent had apparent authority to collect the premium. Payment to the agent would be payment to the insurer.

An agent whose agency is terminated may still possess lingering apparent authority. Third persons who have dealt with the agent may be justified in believing he or she still retains actual authority. The principal must make certain the third person has notice of the termination of authority, or the agent will have lingering apparent authority. For example, for several years P employs A to purchase supplies for P. A buys the supplies from T. P fires A, terminating A's actual authority. P does not notify T of the termination. After the termination, A wrongfully purchases supplies from T, purporting to be P's agent. P is bound to the contract because A had lingering apparent authority. T reasonably believed A was P's agent.

---

[9]Kanelles v. Lock, 12 Ohio App. 210 (1919).

Lingering apparent authority may result if the agent is permitted to retain indicia of authority. *Indicia of authority* means indications, signs, or evidence of authority. For example, if an insurer discharges an agent, yet permits the agent to retain credentials or documents that had been used in the agency, these credentials or documents may create the appearance of authority to third persons. Thus, if Phyllis Hayes has been the duly authorized soliciting agent of the X.Y.Z. Life Insurance Company, and if she still retains a supply of life insurance application forms and a rate book, there is no compelling reason for a client to doubt that she continues to represent that insurer as an agent. For this reason, insurers require the surrender of all such indicia of authority at the termination of an agent's contract.

Ratification

Sometimes, an agent who is authorized to represent a principal in one line of business makes a contract in the name of that principal in an entirely different business. For example, an agent authorized to sell the principal's automobiles might sell one of the principal's trucks which the agent was not authorized to sell. Sometimes, also, a person who has no agency authority whatever purports to make a contract for another person. In such situations, the contract ordinarily will not have any binding effect upon the purported principal. If the contract proves advantageous, however, the purported principal may wish to adopt it as her or his own by ratifying it.

Ratification is the validation by a purported principal of an unauthorized act done by his or her purported agent. Generally speaking, any acts that can be authorized before they are taken can be ratified after they are taken. The relationship thus established is agency by ratification.

Requirements for Ratification.   Certain requirements must be met if the ratification of an agent's unauthorized act is to be effective. First, the person who performed the act must have purported to have acted on behalf of the principal. The person must have represented himself or herself as an agent. The third person must have thought he or she was dealing with an agent.

Second, no one except the person in whose name the contract was made may ratify the act. Thus, if Fred Petersen purports to make a contract in the name of Harold Osborn, then Frieda Bauer cannot ratify that act as principal. No one except Harold Osborn can ratify that act.

Third, if the ratification is to be effective, the ratifier must know all the material facts about the transaction at the time of ratification. If the ratifier was not made aware of all the material facts, he or she can, upon learning the truth, avoid the ratification.

Fourth, the entire transaction must be ratified. A principal cannot select those parts of a transaction that are beneficial to him or her, ratify them, and reject other parts which are burdensome. Therefore, the principal must either ratify the transaction in its entirety, or not at all.

Fifth, intervening events sometimes nullify the power of ratification. For example, the third person with whom the purported agent dealt is free to withdraw before the ratification. If the third person withdraws, an attempted ratification will be ineffective. Moreover, the death or loss of capacity of the third person will destroy the principal's right to ratify.

A change in the circumstances of the transaction will also nullify the right to ratify. For example, if an agent sells the purported principal's cow to a third party, and the cow dies before the ratification, the purported principal's right to ratify is lost.

The lapse of time can destroy the right to ratify. As with the acceptance of an offer, ratification must be made within a reasonable time.

Form of Ratification. If special formalities (a writing, for example) would have been required to authorize the act in the first place, ratification must be effected in that form also. In the absence of such a requirement, any conduct indicating approval of the act is sufficient to constitute an effective ratification. Thus, ratification can consist of express words, spoken or written, or it can be implied from conduct by the purported principal clearly indicating that he or she ratifies the actions of the purported agent and accepts them as his or her own.

Even if the principal does not intend to ratify the agent's actions, ratification will be the legal effect if the benefits or proceeds of the agent's activities are accepted or retained by the principal. For example, acceptance by a life insurer of the premium for a life insurance contract, with full knowledge of an agent's misconduct in accepting the application and premium, will constitute ratification of the agent's action. One cannot accept the benefits of a transaction while refusing to assume the responsibility it entails.

Silence alone does not indicate ratification. However, a principal will ordinarily be held to have ratified the agent's act if, with full knowledge of the facts, the principal fails to repudiate it within a reasonable time.

Effects of Ratification. An effective ratification binds the principal exactly as if the agent had acted according to the principal's directions. When a person, as principal, ratifies the act of another, as agent, the ratification becomes effective as of the date of the act. In other words, ratification relates back to the time the act was done.

Ratification of an unauthorized contract will usually relieve the agent of liability to the principal for acting without authority. It will also, ordinarily, relieve the agent of liability to the third party. Moreover, the agent will be entitled to the customary commission or other compensation.

Subagents

A subagent is the agent of an agent. Subagents are not simply agents of the principal who were chosen and employed by other agents, but they are agents of the agent. The subagent is employed by the agent to act for the agent in performing transactions for the principal. The agent is responsible to the principal for the subagent's conduct.

In matters requiring discretion, the general rule is that the agent cannot delegate to the subagent. That is, the agent, as a fiduciary, cannot properly delegate the performance of acts which require the skill, knowledge, or judgment for which the agent was chosen by the principal. Only mechanical or ministerial acts can be delegated to the subagent. A mechanical or ministerial act is an act which requires no special skill, knowledge, or judgment. Such mechanical acts would include obtaining signatures or delivering a contract.

There are many exceptions to this general rule, however. For example, a corporation which is employed as an agent must of necessity delegate matters requiring discretion to natural persons. The customs or nature of the business involved can also create exceptions to the general rule. Thus, in the life insurance business, it is customary for the general agent of an insurer to appoint soliciting agents who can bind the insurer by issuing premium receipts evidencing temporary insurance contracts.

LIMITATIONS OF THE AGENT'S AUTHORITY

A principal can limit the authority of his or her agent. Such limitations will be binding on parties with whom the agent deals if the limitations are properly communicated to those parties and if the limitations themselves are proper. Proper limitations are reasonable, legal, and not against public policy.

One improper limitation in a life insurance policy is a statement which attempts to make the soliciting agent the agent of the applicant for the purpose of taking the application. Ordinarily, this limitation will not be effective. Another limitation which is ineffective in some states is one which stipulates that the knowledge of the agent shall not be imputed to the insurer. This limitation goes against the general rule of law that knowledge of the agent is knowledge of the principal.

A statement in an insurance policy that no agent can exercise certain powers except in a manner spelled out in the policy is effective as to some agents but not as to others. This limitation can be effective as to agents with limited contractual powers, such as soliciting agents for life insurers, but ineffective as to agents having full authority to contract, such as senior officers of the insurer. For example, a policy clause may prohibit the waiver of any condition in the policy except in writing by specified officers. However, this clause itself could be struck out by an agent with full contracting authority.

Proper communication to applicants of policy limitations on the agent's authority is essential if those limitations are to be effective. The applicant usually is not on notice of limitations of the agent's authority contained in the policy before the policy has been delivered. The applicant, therefore, is not bound by such policy limitations as to acts of the agent occurring before delivery of the policy if the applicant could reasonably suppose the agent has authority to do such acts. For this reason, insurers often put notice of limitations on their agents' authority in the application. Such notice of limitations is ordinarily binding upon the applicant who signs the application.

PRINCIPAL AND AGENT

In agency relationships, it is the principal's business which is transacted. Therefore, the agent has a duty to respond to the wishes of the principal in regard to that business. The principal has control over the conduct and activities of the agent.

Control by the Principal

The degree of control the principal exercises depends upon whether the agent is an employee-agent or an independent contractor-agent. The principal exercises control over the manner and method of doing the job where the agent is an employee-agent. An independent contractor-agent follows his or her own discretion in carrying out the job. For example, an attorney is ordinarily an independent contractor-agent of her or his client.

Agent's Duties

The agent has duties which spring from the agent's fiduciary role, from the agency relationship, and from any contract between the agent and the principal governing their rights and duties.

Duty of Loyalty.   An agent is a fiduciary. A fiduciary is a person who occupies a position of special trust and confidence in handling the affairs or funds of another person. All fiduciaries have a duty of loyalty. The trustee is a fiduciary with a duty of loyalty toward the trust beneficiary, and the agent is a fiduciary with a duty of loyalty toward the principal. A duty of loyalty means that the agent must act solely for the benefit of the principal in every matter connected with the agency. It means that the utmost good faith and integrity must be exercised by the agent in dealing with the principal.

An agent must not deal for himself or herself where the agent should be dealing for the principal. For example, in a case where an agent was sent to purchase a parcel of land for his principal but took title in his own name, the court held that the agent had breached his duty of loyalty and that the land belonged to the principal.[10]

If the agent has an interest which is adverse to the principal's interest, the agent must reveal his or her interest to the principal. For instance, if the

---

[10]Krzysko v. Gaudynski, 207 Wis. 608, 242 N.W. 186 (1932).

agent's personal dealings with a third person might affect the agent's judgment when dealing for the principal, the agent must tell the principal.

An agent must not serve two principals whose interests are adverse unless both principals consent. A contract negotiated by an agent acting for both parties to the contract is voidable by a party who did not know the agent was also acting for the other party.

The agent must be scrupulously honest in all his or her dealings with the principal. Agency funds or property held by the agent must be used for agency purposes only. Such funds or property are held in trust. Any use of them for a nonagency purpose will subject the agent to liability to the principal for the funds or property and for profits made from their use.

If the agent receives anything of value from a third party with whom the agent is dealing on behalf of the principal, the agent must account for it to the principal. Such profits belong to the principal unless the principal allows the agent to keep them.

Duty of Obedience.   The agent has a duty to follow the principal's lawful and reasonable instructions. Moreover, the agent has a duty to act within the bounds of the authority given by the principal. Even where the principal's termination or limitation of the agent's authority breaches an agency contract, the agent must obey the principal.

Duty of Reasonable Care and Skill.   An agent has a duty to carry out the agency with reasonable care. The agent must exercise the skill ordinarily possessed by persons in the same business. The agent has a duty not to undertake to do business that the agent is incapable of performing properly.

Principal's Remedies

A principal has a variety of legal and equitable remedies against an agent who violates his or her agency duties. For example, if a third person sues the principal as a result of the agent's wrongful acts, and the principal loses the lawsuit, the principal can recover from the agent the money paid to the third person plus the principal's attorney's fees.

The principal can also recover from the agent for conversion of the principal's property. Conversion is an unauthorized act which deprives an owner of his or her property. Conversion is a wrong or tort. A tort is a violation of a duty to another person imposed by law, rather than by contract, for which the person harmed can recover money damages from the person who committed the tort. As in other tort actions, in an action for conversion the plaintiff sues for money damages. The agent may also be liable to the principal for money damages in tort if the agent causes loss to the principal by exceeding the authority given by the principal.

When money belonging to the principal is paid to the agent by a third person, and the agent does not give the money to the principal, the principal can maintain an action against the agent to recover the money. The principal can also maintain an action against the agent for an accounting where the accounts are complicated.

The principal can deny the agent compensation if the agent's services have been improperly performed. Finally, the principal has a right to dismiss the agent before the termination date of their employment contract if the agent has breached the agency duties of loyalty, obedience, or reasonable care.

Principal's Duties

The principal sometimes has a duty to provide the agent with an opportunity to work. This is true in the case of a selling agent who works on a commission basis. The principal must provide the necessary goods to sell.

In most instances, the principal has a duty to compensate the agent. The principal must also reimburse the agent for authorized payments made by the agent and indemnify the agent for liabilities the agent incurred in acting for the principal, unless their contract indicates otherwise. An agent guilty of fraud, misconduct, or disobedience can lose the right to be compensated for services the agent performed for the principal.

The principal has a duty to keep accounts of what the principal owes the agent. The principal sometimes has statutory obligations to deduct various amounts from the agent's compensation for remission to government agencies (for example, income tax payments). In addition, the principal often has other duties toward the agent stemming from worker's compensation laws, unemployment compensation laws, pension laws, and other employment laws.

Agent's Remedies

An agent has the legal and equitable remedies of any party to a contract, except that the agent does not ordinarily have the remedy of specific performance. Specific performance would require that the agency contract be carried out by the principal. Because both principal and agent must consent to the agency relationship, the remedy of specific performance, which would require the principal to continue with the agency relationship against her or his will, would not be appropriate.

In addition, agency contracts are not specifically enforceable by the agent because the principal could not specifically enforce the contract against the agent. To make the agent carry out the contract would be unconstitutional because the constitution forbids involuntary servitude. Generally, specific performance will be granted only where there is "mutuality of remedy," which means that both parties must have the right to performance. The agent, however, can appropriately be given money damages by the court to compensate the agent for the principal's breach of the agency contract.

This rule that specific performance will not be granted for breach of an agency contract by the principal does not always apply where employment discrimination is involved. Moreover, specific performance may at times be available under labor legislation.

The agent sometimes has a right to a lien upon property belonging to the principal which the agent holds. Unless otherwise agreed, an agent in lawful possession of property belonging to the principal has a lien on the property for money due the agent from the principal as a result of the agency relationship. The agent can keep possession of the property until the principal pays the agent the money.

PRINCIPAL, AGENT, AND THIRD PERSONS

A principal becomes a party to an informal contract made for him or her by the principal's agent if such transaction was within the agent's powers. The principal's liability to the third person is spelled out by the contract.

Principal's Liabilities to Third Persons

The principal will be liable on a contract made by an agent just as if the principal had made it personally. The principal will also be liable on a contract formed by the unauthorized act of another if the principal later ratifies the act.

The third person will ordinarily have all the remedies available to any contracting party. If, however, the agent acts with an improper motive, and the third person knows this, the principal will not be bound.

The principal can be liable to third persons for torts committed by the agent in the scope of his or her employment. This subject will be covered in greater detail in the section entitled, "Master and Servant."

Principal's Rights against Third Persons

The principal may enforce a contract made by the agent. The third person with whom the contract was made will be bound by it just as if the principal had negotiated the contract.

The principal has a cause of action against a third person who knowingly induces or assists the agent to violate fiduciary duties to the principal. A third person who bribes, coerces, or fraudulently induces the agent to act contrary to the principal's interests will be liable to the principal for the harm that results.

Agent's Liabilities to Third Persons

A person who represents herself or himself as an agent makes an implied promise to the third person that she or he has authority to act for the principal. If a person purports to act as an agent when the person has no authority, with the result that the principal is not bound and no contract is formed, the purported agent will be liable for the harm caused to the third person.

An agent will also be liable for other misrepresentations made to third persons. Such a misrepresentation is a tort against the third person. The agent has a duty not to injure third persons, regardless of agency status.

Agent's Rights against Third Persons

The agent who negotiates a contract for a principal is not a party to the contract and is, therefore, not entitled to maintain an action on the contract. The causes of action agents have against third persons ordinarily arise from unlawful interference with the agency itself, as where a third person improperly prevents the agent's employment, or causes the agent to be fired.

CLASSIFICATION OF AGENTS

Agents are often classified as "general agents" or "special agents." Unfortunately, these terms have not been precisely defined in either legal or insurance terminology. The legal definitions of *general agent* and *special agent* are inconsistent and often difficult to apply. Moreover, these legal definitions are not necessarily the same as the insurance definitions. Finally, the terms *general agent* and *special agent* are not used consistently throughout the insurance industry. These terms may mean one thing when applied to life or health insurance agents and another when applied to agents for other types of insurance.

Some courts have defined a general agent as an agent who is employed to conduct a series of transactions involving continuity of service, and a special agent as an agent authorized to conduct one or a few transactions only, without continuity of service. Other courts define a general agent as an agent who has authority to perform all acts in connection with the business in which the agent is engaged, whereas a special agent is defined as an agent who is authorized to do only one or more special kinds of acts following particular instructions. According to the latter definition, a medical examiner employed by an insurer is a special agent.

A special agent, such as a medical examiner, has limited powers. Nevertheless, the acts or knowledge of a special agent can be crucial to the principal. Knowledge of the medical examiner with respect to diseases or prior treatment of an applicant which are not disclosed on the application is sometimes imputed to the insurer and can prevent it from asserting an otherwise valid defense or obtaining a rescission based on the applicant's misrepresentation of material facts.

A general agent in life insurance terminology is ordinarily a person holding a franchise to develop an insurer's business within a certain geographical area. The general agent hires soliciting agents and clerical staff to run the general agency. Because final underwriting authority for life insurance is customarily retained in the home office, life insurance general agents do not complete contracts of insurance. For this reason, they have been legally classified as special agents by some courts. Soliciting agents are sometimes called special agents in insurance terminology to contrast them with general agents. Soliciting agents find prospects for insurance sales, determine their needs, and make sales of the insurer's products.

Confusion has arisen because of the imprecision with which the terms *general agent* and *special agent* are used. However, agency authority is not governed by the title of the agent. Rather, the facts of the situation will determine whether the agent has actual or apparent authority to do a particular act.

TERMINATION OF THE AGENT'S POWERS

An agent's powers terminate when the agent's actual and apparent authority terminate. Actual authority terminates by agreement, by act, or by operation of law. Apparent authority ends when third persons no longer have reason to believe the agent has authority to act for the principal.

Termination of Actual Authority

An agent's actual authority can terminate by agreement of principal and agent, by an act of the principal or of the agent, or by operation of law.

Agreement of Principal and Agent. Sometimes, the principal and agent agree that the agency is to last for a specified period of time. In such a case, the agent's actual authority will terminate at the end of this period. In other cases, the agency agreement specifies that the agent will have authority until the accomplishment of some objective. When that objective is accomplished, the agent's actual authority will terminate.

Act of Principal or Agent. Either the principal or agent can terminate the agency relationship. The power to terminate exists even if the one terminating breaches an agency contract by the termination. If there is such a breach, the injured party can recover money damages from the other party.

Operation of Law. If certain events occur, the agent's authority will be terminated by operation of law. *Operation of law* refers to the determination of rights and obligations through the automatic effects of the law, and not by any direct act of an affected party. As a general rule, the death of the principal will cause the agent's authority to terminate by operation of law, even if the agent and third persons with whom the agent is dealing are unaware of the death. Death of the agent also terminates the agency.

The principal's permanent loss of contractual capacity (by insanity, for example) will usually cause the agent's authority to terminate by operation of law. An agent does not need contractual capacity to have authority to act. However, an agent's authority terminates when the agent loses capacity to do the authorized act. For example, in one case an insurance agent's authority was terminated where paralysis made it impossible for the agent to handle the business.[11] If the agent loses his or her license or fails to qualify for a license which is required, the agency will terminate.

A change of circumstances sometimes causes the agency to terminate by operation of law. Bankruptcy of the principal, for example, can cause the agency to terminate. Bankruptcy of the agent will cause the agency to terminate if the agent's financial condition affects the principal to such an extent that, with knowledge of the facts, the principal would have revoked the agent's authority.

War ordinarily suspends commercial activities between citizens of enemy countries. If war makes an agent the enemy of the principal's country, the agency will usually terminate by operation of law.

Termination of Apparent Authority

If a third person knows the agency has terminated, the agent will no longer be able to bind the principal in dealings with that person. However, the agent will have lingering apparent authority, and hence power to bind the principal, if third persons are not aware of the termination. Those who have dealt with the agent must ordinarily be given direct notice of the termination if apparent authority is to be avoided.

If a principal allows an agent whose authority is terminated to keep indicia of authority which cause third persons to reasonably believe the agency is still in effect, the principal will bear the loss if the agent deceives those who deal with her or him. If the principal suffers loss because the agent deceives a third person, the principal can, of course, recover money damages from the agent.

Effect of Termination

When the authority of the agent ends, all rights to act for the principal are lost. However, the agent still has the duty to account to the principal for actions taken prior to termination of the agency.

MASTER AND SERVANT

Under the broadest definition of agency, an agent is a person who acts for another person, the principal. A master is one type of principal under this broad definition. A servant is one type of agent—one who acts for a master. The terms *master* and *servant* are ordinarily used in cases involving torts against third persons committed by one person in the course of acting for another. The terms *employer* and *employee* are sometimes used. The master whose servant commits a tort against a third person may be liable to the third

---

[11]Citizen's Home Ins. Co. v. Glisson, 191 Va. 582, 61 S.E.2d 859 (1950).

person. If, for example, a person driving a company car on business for a corporation negligently runs down a pedestrian, the pedestrian will have a cause of action against the corporation, if the corporation is a master and the driver is its servant. If the driver is an independent contractor, the corporation will not ordinarily be liable.

Determination of Servant Status

It is often difficult to determine when an agent is acting as a servant. An agent may be a servant for some purposes but not for others.

The most important test of servant status is that of physical control. A master has the right to control the physical conduct of a servant in the performance of the servant's duties. A clear example of a servant is a person who works full time for an employer, is paid on a time basis, and is subject to the supervision of the employer as to the details of his or her work.

Respondeat Superior

Respondeat superior means "Let the master answer." This term stands for the principle that the master, as well as the servant, is responsible for a tort of the servant committed in the course of the servant's employment. Ordinarily, the tort involves a lack of care—that is, negligence—on the servant's part. An intentional tort (assault, for example) committed by the servant will usually be considered outside the course of the servant's employment, and hence the master will not be liable.

A person injured by the servant's wrongful act will have grounds to sue the servant, the master, or both. Ordinarily, there will be a better chance of recovery from the master. The master will have grounds to sue the servant where the servant's wrongful act causes liability of the master to an injured person.

EMPLOYER AND INDEPENDENT CONTRACTOR

An employer will not ordinarily be liable to a third party for the torts of an independent contractor.[12] However, it is not always easy to distinguish an independent contractor from a servant. Independent contractors often have some characteristics of servants and vice versa.

A person who has a distinct business, is highly skilled, is hired to do a particular job, is paid for that job rather than on a salary basis, uses his or her own tools, and follows his or her own discretion in carrying out the job is ordinarily an independent contractor. An accountant hired to prepare an annual report for a corporation acts as an independent contractor.

---

[12]An employer may be liable for the torts of an independent contractor the employer has hired where the work of the independent contractor is inherently dangerous (blasting, for example) or where the employer knowingly or negligently selects an incompetent independent contractor.

The important distinction between servants and independent contractors is that the employer does not control the manner and method in which the independent contractor performs the job, as the employer does in the case of the servant. In other words, the employer does not exercise control of the independent contractor's physical conduct in the performance of the job.

SUMMARY

An agent is a person who acts for another in contractual dealings with third persons. The essence of agency is power. The agent has the power to subject the principal to contractual liability and to create contractual rights for the principal. Acts of the agent, within the scope of the agent's power, are acts of the principal. Knowledge of the agent is generally considered to be knowledge of the principal where the knowledge concerns the business transacted by the agent for the principal.

A person must have contractual capacity to be a principal, but an agent need not have contractual capacity. Corporations can be principals or agents. Partnerships can be agents.

An agency relationship can be created by an express or implied grant of authority to the agent by the principal. Apparent authority also creates an agency relationship. Apparent authority results from conduct of the principal which causes a third person to reasonably believe that a purported agent has authority to contract for the principal. Finally, an agency relationship can be created by ratification. Ratification is the validation by the principal of an unauthorized act done by the agent. An effective ratification binds the principal exactly as if the agent had acted according to the principal's directions.

A principal can limit the agent's authority. Proper limitations, properly communicated to third persons, will be binding on the third persons.

The agent is a fiduciary with duties of loyalty and obedience toward the principal. The agent also has a duty to carry out the agency with reasonable care and skill. The principal can take legal action against an agent who violates his or her agency duties.

The principal has a duty to provide the agent with an opportunity to work in some instances. In most instances, the principal has a duty to compensate the agent and to keep accounts of what she or he owes the agent.

The principal is liable to a third person if a contract made by the agent with the third person was within the agent's power. The principal also has the right to enforce the contract against the third person. A principal has a cause of action against a third person who knowingly induces or assists the agent to violate fiduciary duties.

A person who represents that he or she is an agent, when such is not the case, will be liable for harm resulting to a third person to whom the misrepresentation is made. An agent will also be liable for other misrepresentations made to third persons.

An agent's actual authority can terminate by agreement of principal and agent, by an action of the principal or of the agent, or by operation of law. Death of the principal generally terminates the agency. Death of the agent always terminates the agency. The principal's loss of contractual capacity or the agent's loss of a necessary license will cause the agency to terminate. Bankruptcy of principal or agent can also cause the agency to terminate. When the agency terminates, the agent no longer has the right to act for the principal, but the agent has the duty to account to the principal for actions taken prior to the termination.

The terms *master* and *servant* are used in cases involving torts against third persons committed by one person in the course of acting for another. A master whose servant commits a tort against a third person is liable to the third person under the doctrine of *respondeat superior*. The most important test of servant status is that of physical control by the master of the servant in the performance of the servant's duties.

An employer will not ordinarily be liable to a third person for the torts of an independent contractor. The employer does not control the manner and method in which an independent contractor performs the job.

ILLUSTRATIVE CASE

In this case, an insurer, through its chief claims consultant, was held to have ratified an unauthorized act of the insurer's soliciting agent.

THE PRUDENTIAL INSURANCE COMPANY OF AMERICA,
Plaintiff-Appellee
v.
WILLIAM D. (BILL) CLARK and MARGARET CLARK,
Defendants-Appellants[13]
United States Court of Appeals, Fifth Circuit

Before THORNBERRY, MORGAN, and CLARK, Circuit Judges.
CLARK, Circuit Judge.

This appeal requires that we review a case tried to a jury on disputed evidence. . . . We will consider the facts in the light most favorable to the jury's findings.

Steve Clark (Steve), a young single man residing with his parents, who are the defendants and appellants here, enlisted in the Marine Corps in January 1966 and thereafter purchased a 10,000 dollar life insurance policy with the World Service Life Insurance Company (World Life). This policy has no war risk and aviation exclusion clauses. In late 1966, Steve was contacted by Robert Brumell, an agent employed by Prudential Insurance Company of America (Prudential) to sell its insurance policies, who urged Steve to drop the World Life policy and to permit Pru-

---

[13]456 F.2d 932 (1972).

dential to replace it with one of its life insurance policies. Brumell advised Steve that he could obtain a 10,000 dollar policy similar to the World Life policy without any limiting war risk or aviation exclusion clause. An application was completed and mailed to Prudential for approval. Steve, meanwhile, in reliance upon Brumell's representation, dropped his World Life policy. Subsequently, Prudential mailed the application back to Brumell in order to secure some additional, minor information. The jury found that Prudential issued this initial 10,000 dollar policy when the application was returned to Brumell. The policy, however, was never delivered to Steve because when Brumell received the policy and the request for additional information Steve had already left for Marine training in California. Brumell contacted a Prudential agent in California and asked him to go out to the Marine base and secure the requested information from Steve. The California agent balked because he wanted to share in the commission which would be paid to the writing agent. It took six weeks before Brumell and Prudential's California agent could reach an agreement as to how they would divide these funds. By this time, Steve had been shipped to Viet Nam. We have no way of knowing the contents of that first Prudential policy. Presumably it was destroyed pursuant to Prudential's internal procedure of eliminating all records over thirteen months old.

A year later, in early May 1968, Steve returned from Viet Nam and was again contacted by Brumell. Brumell told Steve what had happened and requested that he submit another application. This second application also sought a 10,000 dollar policy without the war risk and aviation exclusion clauses. Brumell explained that he thought it would be possible to obtain such a policy in view of the prior events. Another application was completed and, along with Steve's prepaid premium, mailed to Prudential. The jury found that Brumell wrote an accompanying letter asking that the policy be issued without the exclusion clauses. On May 20, 1968, Steve returned to Viet Nam. Thereafter the policy issued effective June 1, but unfortunately, Prudential did not comply with Brumell's letter request. However, Steve never had a chance to protest. The policy was not delivered to him, and no one told him that it contained war risk and aviation exclusion clauses. Brumell either had no chance to communicate this information, or remained silent in the hope that these exclusions would not become material; but this was not to be.

On July 28, Steve was killed in Viet Nam when his helicopter crashed and burned. Thereafter, Brumell assisted the defendants in preparing a claim against Prudential. He also wrote an accompanying letter asking Prudential to pay the claim despite the fact that the current policy contained the exclusion clauses. He urged this course of action in view of the above described circumstances, the position of the defendants in the community, the impairment of Prudential's image, and the possibility of legal action being taken against Prudential.

The claim was submitted to Raymond Thomas, the Chief Claims Consultant, who had the ultimate authority for approving or rejecting claims. Thomas approved the claim, and 10,000 dollars was disbursed to the defendants. The policy was then sent to the home office of Prudential in New Jersey for actuarial studies and statistical analyses but not for further review. An employee in the actuarial office noticed the exclusion clauses and Thomas was notified that the claim should not have been paid. Demand was then made upon the defendants for the return of the money. When they refused, this suit ensued.

Thomas testified that he paid this claim through oversight and mistake. The jury, however, refused to credit this testimony because it found that Prudential, by paying the face amount of the policy, intentionally waived the exclusionary clauses.

Since the instructions to the jury correctly defined waiver as the voluntary, intentional relinquishment of a known right, and since Thomas was the ultimate authority for approving claims, it follows that the jury must have found that Thomas was cognizant of the exclusion clauses and Steve's war death, but deliberately and knowingly relinquished Prudential's right to rely upon those clauses and paid the claim, not under the policy, but to honor the commitments made to the deceased by the company's representative. There is abundant evidence to support this finding of the jury. First of all, Prudential knew what Brumell knew. He was the company's representative. His "twisting" to further Prudential's business caused Steve to drop the other policy and to prepay a premium to Prudential. Second, the claims department had Brumell's letter detailing all of the circumstances. Their correspondence discloses that they in fact knowingly dealt with this claim as one resulting from the operation of a military aircraft, because they would not accept the burial permit tendered by Steve's parents but insisted on the Marine Corps' Official Casualty Report listing the death. This report showed he met his death as a crew member of a helicopter on a Marine combat supply mission in Viet Nam. Third, Thomas testified that he personally knew a war death was involved when he reviewed the claim. Fourth, a notice that the policy contained the exclusion clauses is conspicuously stamped across the face of the policy.

* * * * *

[T]he non-contract theory of ratification is fully applicable here. When a principal, with full knowledge of the facts, chooses to approve and adopt an unauthorized act of an agent, he is bound by that action as fully as if it had been preauthorized. Assuming *arguendo* that Brumell's promise to obtain a policy of insurance without war risk or aviation exclusion clauses was unauthorized, the act of payment by Prudential constituted a ratification of the agent's promise to obtain the form of policy the deceased applied for rather than the one actually issued. Certainly the jury could have found and did find that Prudential was fully cognizant of the facts and circumstances involved contemporaneously with its payment. Indeed, Prudential not only paid the defendants in accordance with Brumell's representations but, in calculating the amount of their debt to them, deducted a premium to cover the month of July 1968, which had not yet been paid to them by Steve's Marine Corps allotment.

Prudential argues that under no theory may this Court take cognizance of the agent's promise and its inequitable conduct because of the Florida rule that any matters transpiring prior to or contemporaneous with the signing of an application for insurance are waived or merged into the application. This argument highlights the basic error of Prudential's position in the court below and here. The jury's verdict found that Prudential did not part with its monies because of a mistaken supposition that they were owed on the policy of insurance it issued to Steve. Rather, this verdict recognized a duty of Prudential, dehors the writing, to act in an honorable and upright way in accordance with its agent's promise. Thus, application of promissory estoppel in no way trammels upon the parol evidence rule. Involved here is a separate enforceable promise and not a variance or modification of the terms of the policy. Additionally, Prudential's act of payment, which ratified its agent's commitment, and thereby recognized its duty to honor this action which had enriched the company and misled Steve to drop the World Life policy to the detriment of his beneficiaries, could not have been merged into the document since it did not occur until after the instrument was in being. The Florida "merger" rule is wholly inapplicable to either legalism which would support the jury's verdict.

The judgment of the court below is reversed and the cause is remanded with directions to enter judgment on the jury verdict for the defendants, and to include therein an award for attorneys' fees.

Reversed and remanded.

QUESTIONS FOR REVIEW

1. Define agency.
2. Two fundamental rules of agency law relate to acts of the agent and knowledge of the agent. Describe each of these rules.
3. Distinguish between the power of an agent and the authority of an agent. What different kinds of authority can an agent have?
4. Distinguish between the actual authority and the apparent authority of an agent. What is lingering apparent authority?
5. What is ratification? What are the requirements for an effective ratification?
6. What are subagents? Describe the legal relationship between (a) a subagent and the agent, and (b) between a subagent and the agent's principal.
7. Describe the effectiveness of limitations upon the powers of an agent (a) as between the agent and the principal, and (b) as between the agent and a third person.
8. What are the duties which an agent owes to the principal? What are the duties which a principal owes to the agent?
9. How can an agency relationship be terminated?
10. Define the term *respondeat superior*.
11. Describe some characteristics which may indicate that a person is an independent contractor rather than a servant.

CHAPTER 4

Agency in Life and Health Insurance

INSURANCE AGENTS AND BROKERS

CONSULTANTS

FINANCIAL PLANNERS

LICENSING OF AGENTS AND BROKERS
    Persons Who Must Be Licensed
    Doing Business
    Requirements for Licensing
    Nonresident Licenses
    Temporary Licenses
    Limited Licenses
    Licensing Exemptions
    Continuing Education
    Suspension, Revocation, and Refusal of License

THE CONTRACT BETWEEN INSURER AND AGENT

SOLICITATION OF BUSINESS
    Unlicensed Insurers
    Unapproved Policy Forms
    Misrepresentations
    Disclosure
    Replacement
    Rebating
    Defamation
    Forgery
    Timely and Competent Service
    Unauthorized Practice of Law
    Agent's Duty to Inform the Insurer

MALPRACTICE INSURANCE

COLLECTION AND REMISSION OF PREMIUMS
    Duty of the Agent Regarding Premiums Collected
    Premium Payment with the Agent's Own Funds

COMMISSIONS
    Renewal Commissions
    Sharing Commissions
RECORDS AND REPORTS
SUMMARY

Persons who solicit the sale of life and health insurance policies are governed by the general law of agency as described in Chapter 3. They are also subject to laws which govern only them. This chapter is concerned with statutory, regulatory, and case laws governing life and health insurance agents, brokers, and consultants. These laws often vary considerably from state to state. Nevertheless, there are patterns among the state laws and certain general principles which apply in most or all states. These will be discussed in this chapter.

INSURANCE AGENTS AND BROKERS

Insurance agents and brokers are governed by both state and federal laws. As with other aspects of the insurance business, state laws are predominant, although there are some federal laws governing insurance agents and brokers, such as ERISA[1] and the Securities Exchange Act.

An insurance agent is a person or an organization appointed by an insurer to solicit applications for insurance on its behalf. Usually, the agent and insurer have signed a written agency contract. The agent ordinarily must be licensed by the state to solicit applications for the insurer.

In many instances, a person is licensed to sell insurance for more than one insurer. Unfortunately, the term *broker* is sometimes applied to such a person, resulting in confusion. Legally, in most cases, such a person is an agent of each insurer—not a broker.

A broker is a person whose business is to bring buyers and sellers together. An insurance broker is ordinarily a person who procures insurance for those who request this service. An insurance broker is usually the agent of the applicant for purposes of procuring the insurance or of making the application, although the broker may be the agent of the insurer for other purposes, such as collection of the premiums or delivery of the policy. Life insurance brokers sell the policies of a number of life insurers. They often sell other types of insurance as well.

Somewhat more than half the states recognize and license life and health insurance brokers.[2] In those states, an insurer can accept applications from,

---

[1]The federal Employee Retirement Income Security Act of 1974, Public Law No. 93–406, 88 Stat. 829 (codified as amended in scattered sections of 5, 18, 26, 29, 31, and 42 U.S.C.).

[2]Two states, California and Louisiana, recognize and license health insurance brokers but not life insurance brokers.

and pay commissions to, a licensed broker. Before accepting an application from a person claiming to be a broker, an insurer usually requires proof that the person has a valid broker's license. This is necessary because it is unlawful for an insurer to accept an application which was not lawfully solicited.[3]

CONSULTANTS

An insurance consultant is a person who receives fees from clients for rendering advice regarding insurance contracts.[4] Some states require consultants to be licensed.[5]

The National Association of Insurance Commissioners' (NAIC) Agents and Brokers Licensing Model Act also requires insurance consultants to be licensed.[6] A model act is a statute proposed by experts in a particular field for adoption by the states as a uniform law. Under the model act, agents and brokers, attorneys, bank trust officers, actuaries, and public accountants, acting in their professional capacities, do not have to be licensed as consultants. The model act provides that a licensed insurance consultant cannot also hold an agent's or broker's license, or receive remuneration from agents, brokers, or insurers. A written examination is required before a person can be licensed as an insurance consultant. The commissioner of insurance may investigate the other qualifications of an applicant for an insurance consultant's license.

The model act mandates that there be a written agreement between the insurance consultant and his or her client before the consultant can render service. The agreement must be signed by both consultant and client, and must outline the work to be performed and the fee to be charged.

Section 7h of the model act states the following in regard to the duties of a consultant:

> A consultant is obligated under his license, to serve with objectivity and complete loyalty the interests of his client alone; and to render his client such information, counsel, and service as within the knowledge, understanding, and opinion, in good faith of the licensee, best serves the client's insurance needs and interests.

State laws regarding insurance consultants vary considerably from one state to another. The New York law exempts from licensing most of the

---

[3]Some states have licensing exemptions which permit an insurer to accept an application from an agent licensed with another insurer. These will be discussed later in the subsection entitled "Licensing Exemptions."

[4]Insurance consultants are sometimes called insurance analysts, insurance advisors, insurance specialists, policyholders' advisors, or policyholders' counselors.

[5]*See, e.g.,* CAL. INS. CODE §§ 1831–1849 (West 1972 & West Supp. 1987); MASS. GEN. LAWS ANN. ch. 175 § 177A-D (West 1987); MICH. COMP. LAWS ANN. §§ 500.1232–500.1236 (West 1983 & West Supp. 1987); N.Y. INS. LAW §§ 2102, 2107 (McKinney 1985); TEX. INS. CODE ANN. art. 21.07-2 (Vernon 1981 & Vernon Supp. 1987).

[6]AGENTS AND BROKERS LICENSING MODEL ACT §§ 2e, 7 (1974).

classes of persons mentioned in the model act plus salaried officers or employees of an insurer who devote substantially all their services to activities other than consulting while discharging the duties of their employment.[7] In Texas, a licensed agent may also be licensed as an insurance consultant. However, the agent may not receive both commissions as an agent and fees as a consultant for services to the same client.[8] California law makes it a misdemeanor punishable by fine and imprisonment for an unlicensed person to act or offer to act as a life insurance consultant.[9]

FINANCIAL PLANNERS

Many insurance agents and brokers have become financial planners in recent years. The American College, which offers the course of study leading to the Chartered Life Underwriter (CLU) designation, now offers another course of study for financial planners leading to a Chartered Financial Consultant (ChFC) designation.

Financial planning typically involves providing advice to individuals or families regarding management of financial resources based upon an analysis of individual client needs. The financial planner elicits information from the client, develops an overall financial plan, and assists in implementing the plan. The financial planner then periodically reviews the plan to be certain it is still appropriate, making changes where necessary.

Insurance agents and brokers who are also financial planners will often involve the client's attorney and accountant in the implementation of the plan. This is necessary because the insurance agent or broker cannot draft wills or trust documents for the client, or give the client detailed legal or accounting advice. The client's securities broker might also be involved.

An insurance agent or broker who is also a financial planner ordinarily must register under the federal Investment Advisors Act of 1940.[10] A person must register as an investment advisor if he or she "(1) provides advice or issues reports or analyses regarding securities; (2) is in the business of providing such services; and (3) provides such services for compensation."

The SEC has asserted that a financial planner who provides even nonspecific advice which concerns securities is an investment advisor under the act. This is true even if the financial planner merely discusses the relative advantages and disadvantages of investing in securities in general, as compared to other investment media.

---

[7]N.Y. INS. LAW §§ 2102,2107 (McKinney 1985).
[8]TEX. INS. CODE ANN. art. 21.07–2 § 4(a) (Vernon 1981).
[9]CAL. INS. CODE § 1844 (West Supp. 1987).
[10]15 U.S.C.A. § 806–1, et seq. (West 1981 & Supp. 1987); Applicability of Investment Advisors Act to Financial Planners, Investment Advisors Release No. 1092, 52 Fed. Reg. 38,400 (Oct. 8, 1987).

Investment advice need not constitute the financial planner's principal business or any particular portion of it, but need only be done on a regular basis for the financial planner to be considered an investment advisor.

The financial planner does not have to receive a separate fee for investment advice as long as the advice is considered part of the total services rendered. Moreover, the compensation does not have to come from the financial planner's client. The SEC has stated that "a person providing a variety of services to a client, including investment advisory services, for which the person receives any economic benefit, for example, by receipt of . . . commissions upon the sale to the client of insurance products . . . would be performing such advisory services 'for compensation'. . . ."

Once the financial planner has registered under the Investment Advisors Act, he or she must comply with the duties of registered investment advisors set out in the act. These duties involve delivery of disclosure statements to clients, recordkeeping, compliance with advertising and fee restrictions, compliance with restrictions on assignment or transfer of investment advisory contracts, and fiduciary responsibilities.[11] In addition, a financial planner is not permitted to use the initials RIA after his or her name, although the financial planner can use the words "registered investment advisor."[12] There are also restrictions on the use of the term "investment counsel" under the act.

There are state investment advisor statutes also. Thus, financial planners must register in some states, as well as under the federal act. There has been much discussion in the press of additional federal and state regulation of financial planners.

LICENSING OF AGENTS AND BROKERS

The power of a state to regulate the insurance business includes the power to license and control persons who solicit the sale of insurance. All states and the District of Columbia have licensing laws. As with other laws regulating agents and brokers, these laws are not uniform. The NAIC adopted the Agents and Brokers Licensing Model Act in 1973, but only four states have based their licensing laws on it. The other states already had licensing laws which they have not as yet seen fit to change.

A new model act designed to streamline agent and broker licensing laws was introduced by the NAIC in 1987. It is a "one license" model act. Under the new model act agents and brokers (producers) would no longer have to secure separate licenses for each type of insurance they sell and for each

---

[11]Kelvin, *Post RIA Registration Responsibilities Facing the Financial Services Professional,* J. AM Soc'y CLU & ChFC 76 (Nov. 1987).

[12]Securities & Syndication Review, SEC No-Action Letter [1984 Transfer Binder] Fed. Sec. L. Rep. (CCH) Par. 77,602 at 77,813 (Jan. 17, 1984).

insurer they represent, nor would they have to maintain separate agent and broker licenses. A single license would be issued listing the types of insurance the producer was authorized to sell. Under this producer concept, the contractual relationship between the insurer and the producer—rather than the license—would determine whether the producer was acting as an agent or as a broker.

There are, of course, patterns among the licensing laws currently in force. Some idea of their diversity and similarities can be obtained from the following comparison.

The Texas statute defining *life insurance agent* reads as follows:

> The term "life insurance agent" for the purpose of this Act means any person or corporation that is an authorized agent of a legal reserve life insurance company, and any person who is a sub-agent of such agent, who acts as such in the solicitation of, negotiation for, or procurement of, or collection of premiums on, an insurance or annuity contract with a legal reserve life insurance company.[13]

This definition goes on to exclude home office or agency employees who do not receive commissions, persons operating employee benefit programs who do not receive compensation from the insurer, banks involved in collecting and remitting premiums, ticket agents selling travel accident insurance, and certain credit insurance agents. In Texas, the term *broker* is not used. Subagents must have regular agent licenses.

The NAIC Agents and Brokers Licensing Model Act, on which the licensing laws of Colorado, Massachusetts, North Dakota, and Oklahoma are based, defines the term *agent* as follows:

> An individual, partnership or corporation appointed by an insurer to solicit applications for a policy of insurance or to negotiate a policy of insurance on its behalf.[14]

The model act defines the term *broker* as follows:

> Any individual, partnership or corporation who, for compensation, not being a licensed agent for the company in which a policy of insurance is placed, acts or aids in any manner in negotiating contracts for insurance or placing risks or effecting insurance for a party other than himself or itself.[15]

Excluded from these definitions and, therefore, from the licensing requirements, are regularly salaried officers and employees of insurers or insurance agencies if such officers' duties do not include the negotiation or solicitation of insurance. Also excluded are persons involved in the administration of employee benefit plans, group creditor policies, or other group

---

[13]TEX. INS. CODE ANN. art. 21.07–1 § 1(b) (Vernon 1981).
[14]AGENTS AND BROKERS LICENSING MODEL ACT § 2a.
[15]*Id.* § 2b.

plans if they receive no commissions or compensation from the insurer, and certain persons representing fraternal organizations. Note that, unlike the Texas statute, the model act does not mention banks or ticket agents. Moreover, under the model act, home office employees are exempt from licensing only if they do not solicit or negotiate contracts of insurance; whereas, under Texas law, receipt of commissions is the test of which persons are exempt from licensing. The model act further provides for the licensing of limited insurance representatives. These persons can sell certain types of insurance, such as limited travel accident insurance, which do not require the professional competency of a licensed agent or broker. No examination is required of limited insurance representatives.

Persons Who Must Be Licensed

All persons soliciting the sale of insurance contracts must be licensed in the state, or states, where they do business, as a general rule. As was noted above, consultants who merely advise on insurance purchases without selling insurance or receiving commissions are also required to be licensed in some states. A person who sells variable annuities or variable life insurance must have two licenses—a license to sell insurance from the state and a license to sell securities from the National Association of Securities Dealers. Both licenses are required because variable annuities and variable life insurance policies are considered to be securities as well as insurance. Moreover, in some states a person must have a special type of insurance license in order to sell variable annuities or variable life insurance.[16]

Doing Business

As stated above, agents and brokers must be licensed in each state where they do business. However, it is not always readily apparent where an agent or broker is doing business. Obviously, if an agent is a resident of a state selling to other residents of the same state, the agent is doing business there and must be licensed in his or her state of residency. However, other selling situations are not so clear-cut. For example, an agent selling in New York may have clients who live in Connecticut or New Jersey. Or, an agent who sells a group contract may wish to issue the master contract in a state other than the state where he or she ordinarily does business. Credit life and health insurance sales by banks, loan companies, and companies engaged in consumer financing has been a troublesome area.

A state sometimes makes an extraterritorial application of its licensing statute. That is, it might require an agent selling to a state resident to be

---

[16]*E.g.*, TEX. INS. CODE ANN. art. 3.75 § 7 (Vernon Supp. 1987).

licensed in the state, even though the contract is sold and delivered in another state. For example, a Kansas statute reads in part as follows:

> [I]t shall be unlawful for any insurance company to effect contracts of insurance in this State on the life or person of residents of this State or on property located in this State except through persons duly licensed and certified in accordance with the insurance laws of this State.[17]

The Kansas Department of Insurance takes the position that an insurer may not effect insurance contracts on the life or health of Kansas residents except through persons duly licensed in Kansas. If a Kansas resident travels to another state, meets with an insurance agent, fills out an application for insurance on his or her own life, pays the premium, and returns to Kansas, the Department most likely would hold that the out-of-state agent selling the policy to a Kansas resident must have a Kansas license. The Department puts more emphasis on the involvement of a Kansas resident than on the place of contracting. Court cases uphold the right of a state to regulate contracts which are made outside its borders if the risk insured is located within the state.

Because state laws are so diverse, the question of when and where an agent or broker is doing business cannot be answered without careful scrutiny of the laws of the states involved. However, generally speaking, an insurance agent or broker will be subject to licensing in all states where he or she solicits or negotiates insurance sales, delivers contracts, collects premiums, or has an office for the conduct of an insurance business. Where there is a doubt, prudent agents and brokers obtain nonresident licenses.

Requirements for Licensing

A natural person can, of course, be licensed as an agent. State statutes also list various organizations which may be licensed. These include partnerships, corporations, and associations.

A natural person who applies for a license often must be over a certain age, usually 18. Ordinarily, the person must meet required educational standards. A certain number of hours of classroom instruction in insurance-related subjects are required in many instances. For example, a New Jersey statute provides "[t]hat the applicant shall be required to have taken, and successfully completed, a program of studies established by regulation of the commissioner. . . ."[18] An examination conducted by the insurance commissioner is ordinarily mandated. The course of study or the examination is not always required, however, if the applicant has previously been licensed to sell

---

[17]KAN. STAT. ANN.§ 40–214 (1986). Enrollment of individuals under a group policy and the inclusion of insurance in a credit transaction are excepted.

[18]N.J. STAT. ANN.§ 17B:22–9(a) (West 1985).

insurance; is a Chartered Life Underwriter;[19] has worked for an agent, broker, or insurer; or intends to sell only certain types of limited insurance, such as travel insurance.[20]

An applicant for an agent's or broker's license must be of good character. In California, for example, an agent who has been convicted of a felony or of certain misdemeanors will be denied a license, as will an applicant who has had a license denied, suspended, or revoked within the prior five years.[21] New Jersey requires the applicant to state whether or not she or he "has ever been convicted of a crime involving moral turpitude."[22] The model act stipulates that an applicant "must be deemed by the Commissioner to be competent, trustworthy, financially responsible, and of good personal and business reputation."[23] An insurer which is endeavoring to have an applicant for a license represent it as an agent must state that it has satisfied itself that the applicant is trustworthy and competent, and that the insurer will appoint the applicant its agent.

Some states have a requirement that an applicant for a license is to be actively engaged in the insurance business. In Illinois "[n]o insurance producer license shall be granted . . . if the Director has reasonable cause to believe . . . that during the 12 month period following the issuance . . . of the license . . . the aggregate amount of premiums on controlled business would exceed the aggregate amount of premiums on all other insurance business of the applicant . . ." "Controlled business" is insurance procured by a person on his own "life, person, property or risks, or those of his spouse" or of "his employer or his own business."[24] In other words, the applicant for a license in Illinois must intend to sell insurance to the public, not merely to procure insurance for himself or herself, or his or her associates.

Nonresident Licenses

Nonresident licenses are issued by a state to an agent who is a resident of another state to authorize the agent to sell insurance in the licensing state.

---

[19]*See, e.g.,* MASS. GEN. LAWS ANN. ch. 175, § 163A (West 1987); N.J. STAT. ANN. § 17B:22–12(h) (West 1985); TEX. INS. CODE ANN. art.21.07–1 § 5(a)(3) (Vernon 1981). The Agents and Brokers Licensing Model Act, § 6, exempts persons previously licensed and CLUs from examination, except that CLUs must study the laws of the licensing state.

[20]CAL. INS. CODE § 1755 (West 1972 & West Supp. 1987).

[21]*Id.* § 1669.

[22]N.J. STAT. ANN. § 17B:22–9 (West 1985). *Moral turpitude* is defined as "baseness, vileness or depravity in the private or social duties which a man owes to his fellowmen or to society in general." BALLENTINE'S LAW DICTIONARY 815 (3d ed. 1969).

[23]AGENTS AND BROKERS LICENSING MODEL ACT § 5(4).

[24]ILL. REV. STAT. ch. 73 ¶1065.51–1 (1985) (Ill. Ins. Code § 504.1).

The agent must represent an insurer which is authorized to do business in the licensing state.

The states differ in their treatment of nonresident applicants. In Illinois, a nonresident agent can be licensed only if her or his state of residence grants nonresident licenses to Illinois producers. Examinations may be waived if the other state waives examinations for Illinois residents.[25]

Massachusetts requires nonresident agents of foreign companies to "transact business in the commonwealth only through the lawfully constituted and licensed resident agents of such company in the commonwealth."[26] Some states will license natural persons who are nonresidents but not foreign corporations.

Nonresident agents and brokers can be sued in the licensing state. Sometimes, the state law provides that an agent or broker, by receiving a license, is deemed to have appointed the commissioner of insurance as agent to receive the summons and complaint.[27]

Countersignatures of a resident agent are required in some states. A countersignature is an additional signature required to be put on the application or policy. West Virginia requires that all life, accident, and sickness policies issued as a result of solicitation by nonresident agents "shall be reported, placed, countersigned and consummated by and through a duly licensed resident agent of the issuing insurer."[28] In Wyoming, accident and health policies, but not life policies and annuity contracts, must be signed by resident agents. The amount of commission which must be paid to the countersigning resident agent is spelled out in the Wyoming statutes.[29]

Most states do not have countersignature requirements. The only purpose of a countersignature requirement seems to be to guarantee that a local agent will share in the commission on a policy sold by a licensed nonresident agent. The trend is toward elimination of countersignature requirements. The Agents and Brokers Licensing Model Act specifically provides that:

> Notwithstanding the provisions of this chapter, or any other laws of this state, there shall be no requirement that a licensed resident agent or broker must countersign, solicit, transact, take, accept, deliver, record, or process in any manner an application, policy, contract, or any other form or insurance on behalf of a non-resident agent or broker and/or an authorized insurer; or share in the payment of commissions, if any, related to such business.[30]

---

[25]ILL. REV. STAT. ch. 73, ¶1065.44–1(1985) (Ill. Ins. Code § 497.1).
[26]MASS. GEN. LAWS ANN. ch. 175, § 163 (West 1987).
[27]N.J. STAT. ANN. § 17B:22–24 (West 1985).
[28]W. VA. CODE § 33–12–8(a) (1982).
[29]WYO. STAT.§§ 26–3–127, –128 (Supp. 1983).
[30]AGENTS AND BROKERS LICENSING MODEL ACT § 13 (1986).

Temporary Licenses

Temporary licenses are issued for several purposes.[31] A temporary license can be issued in some states to allow an applicant for a permanent license to sell insurance while the applicant is pursuing the required course of study for the permanent license.[32] Some states allow a temporary license to be issued to a relative, guardian, or personal representative of a disabled or deceased agent or broker[33] or to a person designated by an agent who is entering military service.[34] These temporary licensees are allowed to renew the business of the absent agent or broker and perform other acts necessary to assure continued operation of the agent's or broker's business. Such temporary licensees do not have to pass an examination. In addition, some states allow temporary licenses to be issued to a person to enable him or her to collect home service insurance premiums pending permanent licensing.[35]

The statutes usually specify the maximum time that a temporary license will remain in effect. Ninety days is the time specified in the Agents and Brokers Licensing Model Act,[36] and this period is frequently found in state statutes.

Limited Licenses

Licenses for limited purposes are available in some states. The Agents and Brokers Licensing Model Act reads as follows:

Limited Insurance Representative. A limited insurance representative is an individual, partnership or corporation who is authorized by the Commissioner to solicit or negotiate contracts for a particular line of insurance which the Commissioner may by regulation deem essential for the transaction of business in this state and which does not require the professional competency demanded for an insurance agent's or insurance broker's license.[37]

In California, a person may be licensed to sell travel insurance only.[38]

---

[31]Temporary licenses are sometimes called certificates of convenience.

[32]*See, e.g.,* TEX. INS. CODE ANN. art. 21.07–1 § 10(b) (Vernon Supp. 1987); CAL. INS. CODE §§ 1685, 1689 (West 1972 & West Supp. 1987).

[33]*See, e.g.,* CAL. INS. CODE § 1685 (West 1972 & West Supp. 1987); MASS. GEN. LAWS ANN. ch. 175, § 174D (West 1987); N.Y. INS. LAW § 2109 (McKinney 1985).

[34]*See, e.g.,* CAL. INS. CODE § 1685 (b) (West 1972 & West Supp. 1987); N.Y. INS. LAW § 2109 (McKinney 1985).

[35]*See, e.g.,* CAL. INS. CODE §§ 1685, 1688 (West 1972 & West Supp. 1987).

[36]AGENTS AND BROKERS LICENSING MODEL ACT § 14(b).

[37]*Id.* § 2(d).

[38]CAL. INS. CODE § 1752 (West 1972).

Other types of selling for which a limited license is available in some states include the sale of burial insurance by undertakers and the sale of credit life and disability insurance by the employees of financial institutions. Under some state laws, a person need not pass an examination in order to receive a limited license.[39]

Solicitor licenses are available in some states. The solicitor works for a licensed agent or broker. Under New Jersey law, an applicant for a solicitor's license must complete a program of studies and take an examination unless the commissioner is satisfied that the applicant, because of previous experience, already possesses sufficient knowledge of insurance.[40] The New Jersey statute further provides:

> Any licensed solicitor shall solicit or negotiate insurance only in the name of or for the account of his employer and shall only be authorized to write the same kinds of insurance his employer is authorized to write.[41]

Licensing Exemptions

About one third of the states have licensing exemptions which permit an insurer to accept an application from an agent licensed with another insurer or insurers if certain conditions are met. Some of these states permit such solicitation if the agent knows the application would not be accepted by any insurer with which the agent is licensed. Some states will permit solicitation if an application for appointment as agent for the insurer which is being asked to issue the policy accompanies the application for the policy.

Continuing Education

Insurance agents, like other professionals, need to keep abreast of the changes in their field. In recognition of the need for continuing education, in the 1970s the states began to pass laws requiring licensed agents and brokers to take a certain minimum number of insurance-related courses each year.

In 1978, the NAIC drafted an Agents Continuing Education Model Regulation. This model regulation applies to resident agents or brokers engaged in the sale of those lines of insurance which require the agent or broker to take an examination in order to be licensed. Under the model regulation, new licensees must "satisfactorily complete courses or programs of instruction equivalent to a minimum of 25 classroom hours of instruction" each year for four years. Thereafter, 15 classroom hours of instruction are required each

---

[39]*Id.* § 1755 (West Supp. 1987).
[40]N.J. STAT. ANN. § 17B:22–21(b) (West 1985).
[41]*Id.* § 17B:22–21(c).

year. Among the courses which can be used to satisfy the requirement are Chartered Life Underwriter courses, Life Underwriter Training Council life courses, Certified Insurance Counselor Program courses, and college or university insurance courses. A certificate of compliance with the education requirement must be furnished to the commissioner.

About one third of the states have continuing education laws. Unfortunately, no two states agree on the standards for continuing education. This has created a difficult situation for nonresident agents, who must comply with the continuing education requirements of two or more states.

Suspension, Revocation, and Refusal of License

An agent's or broker's license can be suspended, revoked, or refused for many reasons. Felony convictions or violations of the insurance code can result in denial or removal of a license.

Agents and brokers are, of course, subject to the general body of criminal law applicable to all persons. Crimes such as embezzlement of funds, larceny, theft, fraud, forgery, and conspiracy are punishable by imprisonment or fine under the general criminal laws, and will ordinarily cause forfeiture of the license as well.

In addition to the general criminal laws, there are criminal laws specifically relating to insurance agents and brokers. For example, the Massachusetts statutes provide as follows:

> An insurance agent or broker . . . who receives any money or substitute for money as premium for . . . a policy or contract from the insured or holder thereof, shall be deemed to hold such premium in trust for the company. If he fails to pay the same over to the company after written demand made upon him therefor, less his commission and any deductions to which, by the written consent of the company, he may be entitled, such failure shall be prima facie evidence that he has used or applied the said premium for a purpose other than paying the same over to the said company and upon conviction thereof he shall be guilty of larceny.[42]

Among the insurance code violations which can result in loss of a license are rebating,[43] twisting,[44] solicitation made without authority from the insurer, solicitation for an unlicensed insurer, delinquency in premium remission, and misrepresentation in the license application. These violations may also be punishable as misdemeanors or felonies.

---

[42]MASS. GEN. LAWS ANN. ch. 175, § 176 (West 1987).

[43]Rebating occurs when an agent gives something of value to a prospect to induce the purchase of insurance.

[44]Twisting is the effort of an agent to induce a person to drop his or her existing insurance and buy insurance the agent is selling when such effort is characterized by misrepresentation.

THE CONTRACT BETWEEN INSURER AND AGENT

An agency relationship between an insurer and a selling agent is created in the same way that other agency relationships are created. The grant of authority by the principal to the agent can be express or implied, or the agency can exist because of apparent authority.

The agency contract between the insurer and the agent can be oral if no law, corporate charter, or by-law forbids an oral contract. However, an agent almost always has a written agency contract with an insurer or with a general agent. The agency contract describes the agent's compensation and, in some instances, grants exclusive rights to represent the insurer in a certain geographic area. The agent might or might not agree to work for the insurer exclusively. The agent's duties and authority will be spelled out in the agency contract.

It is the agency contract which controls the extent of the agent's authority to act for the insurer—not the license (although the agent must not act in areas where he or she is not licensed). For example, if an agent is licensed to sell both life and health insurance, but the agency contract gives authority to sell life insurance only, the license itself does not confer the further agency authority to sell health insurance. Authority from the state under the license and agency authority from the insurer under the agency contract are both necessary.

The agency contract will usually specify the manner in which the contract will terminate. Generally speaking, unless the agency contract says otherwise, either insurer or agent can terminate the contract without breaching it. If the agent is discharged in violation of the terms of the agency contract, the agent has a right to an action for the wrongful discharge. The insurer can, however, rightfully discharge an agent who has breached a duty to the insurer, lost his or her license, or committed a crime.

SOLICITATION OF BUSINESS

Having studied insurance, passed an examination, entered into an agency contract, and received a license or licenses, the typical life or health insurance agent begins soliciting insurance business from the public. The general rules of agency law apply to the agent's actions. In addition, there are laws which apply specifically to solicitation of business by insurance agents. Indeed, there is a large body of statutory, regulatory, and case law which applies to the agent's role in the making of insurance contracts. This section will deal with some of the most significant of these laws.

Unlicensed Insurers

An agent or broker must make certain that the insurer which is to issue the policy has a certificate of authority—that is, a license—admitting it to do business in the state where the solicitation is made. An insurer must comply with detailed requirements bearing on many phases of its business before it will be licensed to do business in a state. An insurer can be licensed to do business in one state, a number of states, or all states.

It could be a serious matter for an agent to solicit insurance applications for an insurer which has not been licensed to do business in the state of solicitation. In *Robertson v. California*,[45] the United States Supreme Court upheld the conviction of an agent who violated a provision of the California Insurance Code prohibiting a person from acting as an agent for an unlicensed insurer except under specified conditions. Other states have similar laws. The South Carolina statute reads as follows:

> No person shall in this State act as agent for any insurer not authorized to transact business in this State or negotiate for or place or aid in placing insurance coverage in this State for another with any such insurer.[46]

Unapproved Policy Forms

The policy form which the agent or broker sells must be approved by the state insurance department in the state where it is sold. If a policy form has not been approved, the insurer which issues such a policy could be fined or have its license revoked. Therefore, the insurer would ordinarily refuse to issue such a policy. In cases where an insurer has issued an unapproved policy, the policy is usually enforceable by the policyowner or beneficiary as long as there was no intent on the applicant's part to circumvent the law.

Misrepresentations

The coverage provided by a policy must be truthfully presented by the agent who sells the policy. The states have statutes providing penalties for false statements by an agent about the insurance she or he is selling. For example, in California, the statutes provide that an agent who misrepresents the terms, benefits, or dividends of a policy is "guilty of a misdemeanor and punishable by a fine not exceeding two hundred dollars or by imprisonment not exceeding six months."[47] In addition, the agent's license may be suspended for up to three years.[48] Misrepresentation by an agent to an insurer to induce issuance of a policy can also be illegal under the statutes of some states,[49] as well as a breach of the agent's fiduciary duty.

---

[45]328 U.S. 440 (1946).

[46]S.C. CODE § 38–52–10 (Law. Co-op 1976).

[47]CAL. INS. CODE § 780–82 (West 1972 & West Supp. 1987).

[48]*Id.* § 783 (West 1972).

[49]PA. CONS. STAT. ANN. tit. 40, § 518 (Purdon Supp. 1987).

Disclosure

In recent years, there has been a growing concern among insurance regulatory officers and other interested persons about the consumer's lack of understanding of the technicalities of life insurance. This concern has lead to the requirement in a number of states that the policyowner be given a period of time, usually 10 days, in which to examine the policy and, if not satisfied, to return it for a refund of premium. The laws requiring a 10-day free examination period (often called a "free look" period) are discussed in a later chapter.

Concern over the consumer's lack of understanding has led also to requirements in many states that the life insurance applicant be provided with a buyer's guide[50] and a policy summary to help the applicant make an informed choice of policies. A buyer's guide contains simple descriptions of term insurance, whole life insurance, and endowment insurance. It also explains the use of costs indexes. Cost indexes were developed to assist those purchasing life insurance to compare the costs of similar policies.

A policy summary discloses detailed financial data with respect to a particular policy. These data include a listing of premiums payable, death benefit, additional benefits, cash surrender values, estimated cash dividends, guaranteed endowment amounts, and loan interest information. Cost indexes are also included.[51]

The NAIC has encouraged the states to require that buyer's guides and policy summaries be provided to applicants. In the 1970s, the NAIC adopted model regulations concerning deceptive practices and life insurance cost comparison requirements. In 1984, those regulations were superseded by a Life Insurance Disclosure Model Regulation. The stated purpose of this model regulation is to require insurers to deliver to buyers of life insurance information which will improve the buyers' ability to select the plan of life insurance most appropriate for their needs, to evaluate the relative costs of similar plans of life insurance, and to improve the buyers' understanding of the basic features of the policy which has been purchased, or which is under consideration. Most of the states now have statutes or regulations requiring that this type of disclosure be made to prospective purchasers of life insurance, although not all of these laws are based on the NAIC Life Insurance Disclosure Model Regulation.

Replacement

Replacement of one policy with another is sometimes in the best interests of the policyowner, but often it is not. Policy replacement which is induced by misrepresentations on the part of the agent is called "twisting." The

---

[50]A life insurance buyer's guide is shown in Appendix H.
[51]The illustrative policy form in Appendix B contains a policy summary with cost indexes.

NAIC has adopted a Replacement of Life Insurance and Annuities Model Regulation. The purpose of this model regulation is to protect the interests of life insurance and annuity purchasers by assuring that they receive information with which a replacement decision can be made that is in the purchasers' best interests.

Most of the states have adopted regulations governing replacement of one life insurance policy by another. These regulations require elaborate disclosure to the policyowner who is considering replacing a policy. In addition, the existing and replacing insurers must both be made aware of the intended replacement. The policyowner is encouraged to confer with representatives of the existing insurer.

Certain types of policies ordinarily do not fall under the state replacement regulations. These include most group policies, conversion policies, and nonconvertible, nonrenewable term policies expiring in five years or less.

Rebating

Rebating occurs when an agent gives part of the commission or some other thing of value to a prospect to induce the purchase of insurance, or when an insurer makes a deduction from the stipulated premium to induce such a purchase. Rebating was widely practiced early in this century, but now is forbidden by law in all states except Florida.

There is a widespread debate over whether or not rebating should be allowed.[52] Generally speaking, the insurance industry opposes rebating; some consumer groups and agents favor it.

Opponents of rebating argue that the practice would harm policyowners, agents, and insurers. They say that owners of small policies might pay more per $1000 of face value for their life insurance because owners of large policies could negotiate lower prices. They argue that rebating can encourage frequent replacement of existing policies with new policies, with a consequent rise in price for all policyowners. They say that commissions would have to increase if rebating by agents were allowed, with a resulting increase in insurance costs to the public. They argue that rebating would make accurate cost comparisons among policies most difficult for the prospective purchaser of insurance.

Opponents of rebating also argue that newer agents would not be able to compete against agents with a large, established clientele if rebating were allowed, and that this would lead to monopolistic domination by a few large

---

[52]Arndt, *Rebating Will Result in Serious Industry Problems, Panel Warns*, NAT'L UNDER-WRITER, LIFE & HEALTH INS. EDITION, Oct. 20, 1986 at 1; Benham, *Rebating: Poultice or Poison?*, BEST'S REV., Sept. 1986 at 38; Moyse, *Legalized Rebating—A Marketing View*, J. AM. SOC'Y CLU, Sept. 1986 at 56; Comment, *Insurance Anti-Rebate Statutes and Dade County Consumer Advocates v. Department of Insurance: Can a 19th Century Idea Protect Modern Consumers?*, 9 U. PUGET SOUND L. REV. 499 (1986).

agencies. Some oppose rebating because they fear it would create an undignified insurance marketing atmosphere in which agents would give away television sets and food mixers in order to induce a sale.

Insurer solvency is another concern of opponents of rebating. They argue that policyowners would replace their policies more frequently in order to obtain the rebate. Because the first-year life insurance commission of an agent is often 100 percent of the first year's premium, a policy must stay in force for several years before the insurer can generate a profit. Thus, opponents of rebating argue, frequent replacement could threaten insurer solvency.

The major argument of those who favor rebating is that it would drive down insurance prices by permitting more competition. Those who favor rebating also argue that a policyowner should be made aware of the charge made for the agent's services (the commission), and be allowed to negotiate that charge.

There have been efforts at the state and federal levels to repeal state antirebate laws; it is likely that such efforts will continue. In 1986, the Florida Supreme Court declared the Florida antirebate statute unconstitutional under the state's constitution.[53] However, over a year later, there was little evidence of rebating activity in Florida.[54]

In 1986, a Georgia life insurance agent filed a lawsuit challenging the Georgia antirebate statute on grounds that it is in violation of the Fifth and Fourteenth Amendments to the United States Constitution. There have also been efforts to legalize rebating in California, Louisiana, Michigan, South Carolina, and Tennessee.[55]

Defamation

Defamations by insurance agents, or against insurance agents by other persons, occur occasionally. A defamation is a false communication which tends to harm the reputation of a person so as to lower that person in the estimation of others and deter others from associating or dealing with the defamed person. Corporations, as well as natural persons, can be defamed. Slander is spoken defamation. Other types of defamation, such as written or pictorial defamation, are called libel.

Defamation is a tort. A tort is a violation of a duty to another person imposed by law, rather than by contract. It is a civil wrong for which the

---

[53]Department of Insurance v. Dade County Consumer Advocate's Office, 492 So. 2d 1032 (Fla. 1986).

[54]Van Aartrijk, *No Sign of Rebating Taking Hold,* NAT'L UNDERWRITER, LIFE & HEALTH INS. EDITION, Aug. 10, 1987 at 19; Diamond, *Anti-Rebate Law in Florida Has No Domino Effect,* NAT'L UNDERWRITER, LIFE & HEALTH INS. EDITION, July 6, 1987 at 1.

[55]Knowles, *Georgia's Anti-Rebate Case Most Threatening of All?,* NAT'L UNDERWRITER, LIFE & HEALTH INS. EDITION, Dec. 14, 1987 at 1; Burger, *Insurance Rebating Suits Multiply,* Fin. Services Week, June 20, 1988, at 1, col. 1.

person harmed can recover money damages, as opposed to a crime which is punished by the state (although some torts, such as assault, are also crimes).

Note that a statement is not defamatory unless it is false. If a person accused of defamation can prove that the statement he or she made is true, there is an absolute defense, and the person will not be liable for defamation.

There are circumstances under which defamations can be made with impunity. Persons involved in judicial proceedings have absolute immunity from liability for defamation. Judges, lawyers, plaintiffs, defendants, jurors, and witnesses involved in judicial proceedings have such absolute immunity. Legislators and executive officers of the government in the performance of their duties also have absolute immunity in most instances.[56]

In certain instances persons who make defamatory statements are protected by a qualified privilege. For example, in *Pierce v. Northwestern Mutual Life Insurance Co.*[57] an insurer made allegedly defamatory statements about an agent in a required report to an insurance department. The insurer was held to have a qualified privilege to do so, as the insurer had acted without ill will or malice.

Many states have a statute which provides that certain required communications regarding agents' activities made by insurers to the state insurance department shall be privileged. Even if such a statement is defamatory, the statute will protect the insurer from a defamation lawsuit by the agent. Some of these statutes provide that the statement cannot be used as evidence in a court action. Others simply state that such statements are privileged or absolutely privileged. The Connecticut statute provides that the agent shall not have a cause of action against the insurer unless the required statement "is false and was known to such company to be false when made."[58] Under any of these statutes, the insurer would be protected in making the required report unless it acts in bad faith.

Because defamation is a tort, an insurer could be liable for money damages for its agent's defamation under the doctrine of *respondeat superior*.[59] The insurer's liability will usually depend on whether or not the defamation was made within the course of the agent's employment.[60] There have been cases in which an insurance agent, an insurer, or both were held liable for the agent's defamation.[61] These cases ordinarily involve defamation of a rival agent or insurer. In some instances, as in the *Pierce* case mentioned above, an insurer has been sued by an agent for defamation.

---

[56]W. PROSSER & W. KEETON, THE LAW OF TORTS 816–23 (5th ed. 1984).

[57]444 F. Supp. 1098 (D.C.S.C. 1978).

[58]CONN. GEN. STAT. ANN. § 38–76a (West 1987).

[59]*Respondeat superior* (i.e., "Let the master answer") stands for the principle that an employer is responsible for the wrongful act (tort) of an employee committed in the course of employment.

[60]Annot., 55 A.L.R. 2d 828 § 3 (1957).

[61]*Id.*

Some states have insurance statutes forbidding defamation. Louisiana's statute reads as follows:

> The following are declared to be unfair methods of competition and unfair or deceptive acts and practices in the business of insurance:
>
> * * * * *
>
> Defamation. Making, publishing, disseminating, or circulating, directly or indirectly, or aiding, abetting of encouraging the making, publishing, disseminating or circulating or any oral or written statement or any pamphlet, circular, article or literature which is false, or maliciously critical of or derogatory to the financial condition of an insurer, and which is calculated to injure any person engaged in the business of insurance.[62]

Forgery

Forgery is ordinarily committed by signing another person's name to a document with the intention of deceitfully and fraudulently presenting the signature as genuine.[63] Forgery is a crime punishable by fines and imprisonment. It is, therefore, extremely inadvisable to sign another person's name unless that person's permission to sign the document in question can be clearly established.

Some agents have signed an applicant's name to an application where the original application has been lost or improperly completed. This is a practice which can create serious problems, even if the issue of forgery does not arise. For example, the policyowner might recognize that the application does not contain his or her signature and demand that the premium be returned. Or, the agent might be blamed for misrepresentations made by the applicant on the original application.

False signatures on change of beneficiary forms or assignment forms can also create serious problems. If a former beneficiary can prove that the signature on a change of beneficiary form is not genuine, the change would likely be held to be ineffective. A policyowner-insured's wishes might then be frustrated, and the intended beneficiary could take legal action against the person who made the signature. A false signature on an absolute assignment of a policy could result in serious adverse tax consequences to an insured's estate and result in liability to the person who made the false signature.

Timely and Competent Service

A life or health insurance agent or broker can be liable to an applicant for the breach of an implied contract to procure insurance. For example, an insurance agent who takes an application might be liable to the applicant if

---

[62]LA. REV. STAT. ANN. § 22:1214(3) (West 1978).
[63]BLACK'S LAW DICTIONARY 585 (5th ed. 1979).

the agent unreasonably delays in taking further action on the application.[64] The proposed insured could become uninsurable or die before the insurance is obtained if the agent does not act promptly. The agent also has a duty to notify the applicant promptly when the application has been rejected so that the applicant can try to obtain insurance elsewhere. The agent can be held liable to the applicant for harm to the applicant resulting from a breach of this duty.[65]

In giving advice to a client, an agent or broker has a duty not to harm the client. Numerous cases hold agents and brokers liable to policyowners or beneficiaries for improper advice. An agent or broker who holds himself or herself out as an expert will be bound to exercise the expertise claimed.

Clients and beneficiaries can be harmed in many ways by carelessness, incompetence, or bad faith of agents and brokers on whom they must rely. Agents and brokers have been held liable for convincing a client to adopt an insurance plan which the agent knew to be completely inappropriate to the client's needs,[66] for improper advice or conduct regarding the preparation of an application which resulted in lack of coverage,[67] and for failure to point out that a suicide period would run anew under a new policy which replaced a policy the client already owned.[68]

A supposed agent who lacks authority can also be liable to the applicant.[69] An agent who acts for an insurer where the insurer has no capacity to contract will be personally liable for harm caused to the applicant in some states.

An agent or broker might be liable for damages to a beneficiary or intended beneficiary, or cause the insurer to have liability, because of the agent's or broker's careless acts. In one case, an agent who failed to include on the application all the intended beneficiaries named by the policyowner caused the insurer to be liable to those not included.[70]

Unauthorized Practice of Law

The professionals who may be involved in planning a person's estate are accountants, trust officers, lawyers, and insurance agents. Only the lawyers are permitted to practice law. There are serious sanctions against the unauthorized practice of law by nonlawyers. The problem arises in determining

---

[64]Talbot v. Country Life Ins. Co., 8 Ill. App. 3d 1062, 291 N.E.2d 830 (1973).

[65]Annot., 64 A.L.R. 3d 398 (1975).

[66]Anderson v. Knox, 297 F.2d 702 (9th Cir. 1961), *cert. denied,* 370 U.S. 915 (1962).

[67]Miller v. Union Cent. Life Ins. Co., 33 N.Y.S. 112 (1895).

[68]Larson v. Transamerica Life and Annuity Ins. Co., 41 Or. App. 311, 597 P.2d 1292 (1979).

[69]Brawner v. Welfare Finance Corp., 61 Ohio L. Abs. 329, 104 N.E.2d 203 (Ohio Ct. App. 1950).

[70]Sovereign Camp, W.O.W. v. Nash, 36 S.W.2d 284 (Tex. Civ. App. 1931).

exactly what constitutes the practice of law. The drafting of wills, trust agreements, and pleadings for others is clearly the practice of law. So is the representation of others in court or before administrative bodies.[71] At the other end of the spectrum, it is not practicing law to remind someone of a generally known legal principle. A parent who reminds a child to drive under the speed limit to avoid breaking the law, or a life insurance agent who points out that death benefits are not taxed to beneficiaries under the federal income tax law, is not practicing law. In between those two extremes lies a gray area in which it can be difficult to ascertain whether the act in question is the practice of law. However, whenever legal knowledge, skill, and judgment are involved in giving advice, and the advice is applied to specific factual situations or is a substantial part of the service rendered, there can be an unauthorized practice of law. An act calling for the skill and learning of an attorney will be regarded as the practice of law.[72]

A leading case involving the unauthorized practice of law by insurance brokers involved in estate planning is *Oregon State Bar v. John H. Miller & Co.*[73] In that case, the Oregon Supreme Court enjoined the defendant insurance brokers from "preparing estate plans embodying legal analysis either as a separate service or as an incident to carrying on the business of selling insurance."

The court held that the brokers were engaged in the unauthorized practice of law when they performed the following activities:

a. Suggesting, recommending or advising on the form or contents, in whole or in part, of legal documents, and particularly wills and trusts.

b. Directly or indirectly preparing, construing or drafting legal documents, including wills and trusts.

c. Rendering any legal opinion or advice, particularly as to the tax consequences of any activity or asset except life insurance or annuity plans.

d. Preparing any estate plan except that part of the plan which directly concerns life insurance or annuities.

e. Holding themselves out as persons who prepare legal documents, give legal advice or prepare estate plans whether by use of business names or otherwise.

f. Employing any person, firm or corporation to give legal advice to customers of defendants.

---

[71]Haberkorn v. Sears, Roebuck & Co., 5 Ariz. App. 397, 427 P.2d 378 (1967); *In re* Unauthorized Practice of Law, 175 Ohio St. 149, 192 N.E.2d 54 (1963), *cert. denied,* 376 U.S. 970 (1964), *reh'g denied,* 377 U.S. 940 (1964).

[72]*In re* Baker, 8 N.J. 321, 85 A.2d 505 (1951).

[73]235 Or. 341, 385 P.2d 181 (1963).

The court further held that the defendant brokers were not engaged in the unauthorized practice of law when they performed these activities:

a. Collecting information on customer or potential customer's financial affairs, including kind and value of assets.

b. Questioning customers as to the customer's desires as to the amount of estate to be left in the case of death.

* * * * *

e. Preparing the policies of insurance.

The court went on to say that "an insurance salesman can explain to his prospective customer alternative methods of disposing of assets, including life insurance which are available to taxpayers *generally* . . . [and] may inform his prospect in general terms that life insurance may be an effective means of minimizing his taxes." An insurance agent would be prohibited from giving advice with respect to a prospective purchaser's "*specific* need for life insurance as against some other form of disposition of his estate unless the advice can be given without drawing upon the law to explain the basis for making the choice of alternatives." This Oregon case has been cited with approval by the courts of several other states.

In another case, an advertisement by an insurance agency which mentioned "Trusts" and "Wills" was held to violate a statute prohibiting nonlawyers from advertising legal services.[74] The defendants in this case asserted that they did not prepare trusts or wills but only intended to advise clients to seek the services of a lawyer. This argument did not prevail.

The federal Employee Retirement Income Security Act (ERISA) enacted in 1974 has created further problems for insurance agents in avoiding the unauthorized practice of law. ERISA is a complex law administered by multiple agencies. Agents who wish to sell insurance to employee benefit plans need a good grasp of the basic features of the law so that they can serve their clients competently. On the other hand, such agents must be wary of the unauthorized practice of law in this area.

Agent's Duty to Inform the Insurer

An insurance agent, like any agent, has a fiduciary duty to act in the best interests of the principal. Part of this duty consists of the full disclosure by the agent to the principal of facts known to the agent that the principal needs to know to protect itself. For example, a life or health insurance agent has a duty to inform the insurer of facts regarding the proposed insured's health which are material to the risk. A fact which is material to the risk is a fact which would influence the insurer's decision as to whether to issue the

---

[74]Burch v. Mellor, 43 Pa. D. & C. 597 (1942).

applied-for policy. A negligent failure to inform the insurer of a material fact could result in a lawsuit by the insurer against the agent. An intentional concealment of such a material fact can be a criminal matter as well.

The agent also has a duty to the insurer to relay applications promptly and to advise the insurer of the issuance of premium receipts. Where an application is not acted upon promptly, the insurer, the agent, or both may be liable for the resulting loss to the applicant. The insurer must be promptly informed when a premium receipt has been issued, so that it can take the appropriate underwriting action. This is especially important where a binding receipt is issued, as the insurer has the risk upon issuance of the receipt.[75]

MALPRACTICE INSURANCE

Malpractice insurance coverage for life and health insurance agents and brokers has become commonplace, as the complexities of selling insurance, and the number of lawsuits against agents and brokers, have increased. These policies are similar to those covering physicians, lawyers, accountants, dentists, and other professionals.

Malpractice policies ordinarily cover the agent or broker for negligence, error, or omission in performing professional services. They are often called errors and omissions policies. Ordinarily, the malpractice insurer will have an obligation to defend an agent or broker who is sued for negligence, error, or omission and to pay the damages if the suit is lost. The malpractice insurer will not have a duty to defend or pay damages for an agent's or broker's intentional torts or criminal acts. The policy will usually provide for a deductible that must first be met by the agent or broker. A body of case law interpreting these policies has begun to build up, the first reported case being decided in 1961.[76]

COLLECTION AND REMISSION OF PREMIUMS

An insurer may authorize its agent to collect the initial premium or to collect initial and renewal premiums. Authorized collection of premiums by the agent is payment to the insurer, because payment to an agent within the scope of the agent's power is payment to the principal. Ordinarily, brokers who collect premiums are agents of the insurer for this purpose.[77]

Often, a life insurance agent has authority to collect only the initial premium. If the policy states that renewal premiums are to be paid only at the

---

[75]Annot., 35 A.L.R. 3d 821 (1971).

[76]Otteman v. Interstate Fire and Casualty Co., 172 Neb. 574, 111 N.W.2d 97 (1961).

[77]Johnson v. Schrapferman, 67 Ind. App. 606, 119 N.E. 494 (1918); Aetna Life Ins. Co. v. Harris & Reichard Fur Dyers, 270 N.Y.S. 543 (1934).

home office or to an authorized agent in exchange for a special receipt, payment to an unauthorized agent is not payment to the insurer.[78] Payment to an unauthorized agent is payment to the insurer if the insurer accepts and retains the payment from the agent or if the insurer has done so in the past and, thus, conferred apparent authority to receive renewal premiums upon the agent.[79]

Duty of the Agent Regarding Premiums Collected

An insurance agent has a duty to account to the insurer for premiums collected. In some instances, such money is held by the agent as debtor of the insurer. In other instances, the agency contract or a state statute declares that the money is held in trust. A trust is a fiduciary relationship in which one person, the trustee, holds legal title to property subject to a duty to manage the property for the benefit of another person. Missouri law states that:

> Any person who shall be appointed or who shall act as agent for any insurance company within this state, or who shall, as agent, solicit applications, deliver policies or renewal receipts and collect premiums thereon, or who shall receive or collect moneys from any source or on any account whatsoever, as agent, for any insurance company doing business in this state, shall be held responsible in a trust or fiduciary capacity to the company for any money so collected or received by him for such company.[80]

Premium Payment with the Agent's Own Funds

An agent sometimes has an agreement with the insurer, the policyowner, or both regarding premium payment with the agent's own funds. The rights and liabilities of the agent, insurer, and policyowner will depend upon their agreements.

In some instances, the agent and insurer agree on conditional payment of the premium by the agent. Conditional payment means that the agent will be charged with the premium by the insurer, but if the policyowner or applicant does not pay, the agent will then be credited with the amount. The insurer will not be bound on the policy where the policyowner or applicant does not pay unless there was an agreement between the agent and the policyowner or applicant for payment of the premium by the agent.

As a general rule, an agent or broker has no duty to pay or loan money for premiums. However, agents and brokers do sometimes pay premiums with their own funds. The agent sometimes pays the premium and takes back a promissory note from the policyowner. The premium will then be paid, so far

---

[78]Gordon v. New York Life Ins. Co., 187 Ark. 515, 60 S.W.2d 907 (1933).

[79]Huber v. New York Life Ins. Co., 18 Cal. App. 2d 269, 63 P.2d 318 (1936); Annot., 42 A.L.R. 3d 751 (1972).

[80]Mo. ANN. STAT. § 375.051 (Vernon 1968).

as the insurer is concerned, and the agent can collect or sue on the promissory note.

Where the agent pays the premium under an agreement between agent and policyowner that the agent will loan the premium money, the agent is entitled to repayment and can maintain an action against the policyowner if the policyowner does not pay.[81] However, the agent must be able to prove that there was such an agreement. If the court deems the agent a volunteer—that is, one who paid the premium without being requested or authorized to do so—the agent might not be allowed to recover the premium payment.[82]

COMMISSIONS

Commissions are calculated as a percentage of the premium paid to the insurer. As a general rule, only the licensed agent or broker who produces a signed application and a premium can receive commissions. Most states have statutes forbidding payment of commissions to unlicensed persons. The Texas statute reads as follows:

> No insurer or licensed insurance agent doing business in this State shall pay directly or indirectly any commission, or other valuable consideration, to any person or corporation for services as an insurance agent within this State, unless such person or corporation shall hold a currently valid license to act as an insurance agent as required by the laws of this State; nor shall any person or corporation other than a duly licensed insurance agent, accept any such commission or other valuable consideration; provided, however, that the provisions of this Section shall not prevent the payment or receipt of renewal or other deferred commissions to or by any person solely because such person or corporation has ceased to hold a license to act as an insurance agent.[83]

The agent or broker who is recognized by the insurer as the person to whom the commission is payable is called the agent or broker of record. Where more than one agent or broker dealt with the client, the client's designation of one of them as agent or broker of record is usually the deciding factor.

Commission arrangements are spelled out in the agency contract. An agent who has faithfully performed the duties required by the contract is entitled to the compensation the contract provides.[84] An agent can lose the right to commissions, however, if the agent breaches any of his or her duties as an agent.

---

[81]Annot., 90 A.L.R. 2d 1291 (1963).
[82]Parsons v. John Hancock Mut. Life Ins. Co., 20 App. D.C. 263 (1902).
[83]Tex. Ins. Code Ann. § 21.07(1) (b) (Vernon 1981).
[84]44 Corpus Juris Secundum *Insurance* § 162 (1945 & Supp. 1987).

Renewal Commissions

An agent's right to commissions on renewal premiums is also determined by the agency contract. Some agency contracts provide that renewal premium commissions cease upon termination of the contract. Other agency contracts provide that the renewal premiums will belong to the agent who obtained the business unless he or she is terminated for cause.[85] Usually, the contract specifies that either the agent or the insurer can terminate the contract on notice to the other. These contract provisions are ordinarily upheld by the courts.

Sharing Commissions

In some states, it is specifically permitted by statute for licensed agents to share commissions. For example, the statutes of South Carolina provide that:

> [A]gents licensed under this Title may write insurance at the request of other licensed agents or licensed brokers or licensed nonresident brokers and allow such licensed agents or licensed brokers or licensed nonresident brokers not exceeding one half of the commissions which they receive on the business written.[86]

An agent is ordinarily entitled under the agency contract to commissions on insurance placed by her or his subagents. These commissions are called overrides.

RECORDS AND REPORTS

Agents and brokers must keep careful records of their business. State statutes and regulations sometimes spell out in detail exactly how records are to be kept and bank accounts set up.[87] Commingling of premiums with personal funds in such accounts is sometimes explicitly forbidden by statute[88] or regulation.[89]

Reports regarding agents and brokers must be filed with the insurance department by insurers and by the agents and brokers themselves. Each state has its own requirements. Most require notification of address changes of agents and brokers and agent appointments or terminations. Some require that agents selling variable life insurance or annuity contracts report discipli-

---

[85]*Terminated for misconduct* is the usual meaning of *terminated for cause*.

[86]S.C. CODE ANN. § 38-51-230(1985).

[87]*E.g.,* CAL. INS. CODE § 1727 (West 1972 & West Supp. 1987); Ill. Admin. Code tit. 50 §§ 3113.40–3113.50 (1985).

[88]IDAHO CODE § 41–1064 (1977).

[89]Ill. Admin. Code tit. 50 §§3113.40–3113.50 (1985).

nary actions taken against them by securities agencies.[90] Various records sometimes have to be kept and made available to the insurance department upon request. Agents and brokers must carefully comply with state statutes regarding recordkeeping to avoid loss of license or other sanctions provided by these statutes.

SUMMARY

Although persons who solicit life and health insurance are governed by the general laws of agency, there are laws in each state which specifically apply to these persons. State laws governing life and health insurance agents and brokers vary from state to state, but there are certain similarities. All the states have licensing laws which govern life and health insurance agents. Some states recognize and license brokers also. Insurance consultants must be licensed in some states.

Generally speaking, persons soliciting life and health insurance must be licensed in states where they do business. An agent who does business in a state where he or she is not a resident must obtain a nonresident license. Temporary licenses are issued in some states for certain purposes spelled out in the state's statutes. Limited licenses are issued in some states to permit certain types of solicitation, such as the sale of travel accident policies, or employment as a solicitor by a licensed agent or broker. In some states, an agent licensed with one insurer may submit an application for insurance to another insurer with which he or she is not licensed.

Solicitation of insurance requires that an agent be licensed and have an agency contract with an admitted insurer. The policy form sold must have been filed or approved by the state insurance department. It is illegal for the agent to misrepresent coverage. In most states it is illegal to give rebates. Laws regarding disclosure, replacement, and timely and competent service must also be observed. Agents and brokers must avoid the unauthorized practice of law. Accurate records must be kept in accordance with state laws. Malpractice insurance protects agents and brokers in a selling environment which has become increasingly complex.

The agent or broker of record is entitled to commissions on sales. The commission arrangement is usually spelled out in the agency contract. Commissions are sometimes shared between agents.

ILLUSTRATIVE CASE

The following was an action by a named beneficiary against a life insurer and its soliciting agent where the agent failed to take action on the insurance application within a reasonable time. The court decided the case in favor of the beneficiary.

---

[90]La. Ins. Dept. Reg. 28 (1969). There are also recordkeeping requirements under ERISA in accordance with Prohibited Transaction Exemption 77–9.

SUZANNE TALBOT, Plaintiff-Appellant
v.
COUNTRY LIFE INSURANCE COMPANY and ROY MELODY,
Defendants-Appellees[91]
Appellate Court of Illinois, Third District

DIXON, Justice.

This is an appeal from a judgment of the Circuit Court of Rock Island County dismissing, for failure to state a cause of action, an amended complaint filed by Suzanne Talbot, the plaintiff, against Country Life Insurance Company, the defendant in Count I and against Roy Melody, the defendant in Count II.

Count I of the amended complaint alleges in substance that; on September 13, 1969 Larry L. Talbot the husband of plaintiff applied in writing to the company's agent, Roy Melody for a life insurance policy in the amount of $15,000.00 on his own life, designating plaintiff as beneficiary; a first premium was then and there paid; on Feb. 19, 1970 Larry Talbot died; defendant retained the first premium and made no attempt to return it until Feb. 21, 1970; between the time of application and death Larry L. Talbot was in good health, his life was an insurable risk; he would have been able to obtain and would have obtained a policy from another company if it had not been for the representations of defendant; that defendant failed to take action on the application within a reasonable time; failed to issue a policy in accordance with the application and; failed to give notice of the action, if any, taken on the application and; that as a direct and proximate result the plaintiff was damaged.

One of the steps necessary to effecting an insurance policy is the filing of an application by the prospective insured; the application, being a mere offer or proposal for a contract of insurance, is not a contract. The existence of a contractual relationship between the parties (absent a binder) depends upon the acceptance by the insurer of the application. In the instant case the appellant concedes that she has no action ex contractu[92] (the original complaint was on that theory). Neither the application nor the premium receipt provisions, if any, were pleaded, no binder is claimed; so the issue (Count I) is whether an insurer may be liable in tort for damage resulting from unreasonable delay in passing on an application for insurance.

There are divergent views on the question. On the one hand, it has been said that the failure of an insurer to act upon an application for insurance within a reasonable time, with resultant damage is a breach of the insurer's duty subjecting the company to liability for negligence. On the other hand, it has been said that an application for insurance is a mere offer and the insurer is under no duty to act on the offer.

* * * * *

Appleman[93] . . . states in Sec. 7232, "The better rule is to the effect that where application was made for a life policy with a beneficiary being designated to receive

---

[91]8 Ill. App. 3d 1062, 291 N.E.2d 830 (1973).

[92]*Ex contractu* means arising from or out of a contract.

[93]*Insurance Law and Practice* by John Alan Appleman and Jean Appleman is a multi-volume treatise on insurance law.

the proceeds, a cause of action lodges in such beneficiary, upon the applicant's death, for unreasonable delay on the part of the insurer, in accepting or rejecting such application."

Count II charges the agent Roy Melody with having failed to take action on said application within a reasonable time and failing to give notice of any action taken on the application. The complaint clearly alleges that Roy Melody was the agent of Country Life Insurance Company (as distinguished from being a broker). Brokers as distinguished from soliciting agents have long been held liable in tort. The agent here is not the agent of the applicant. He is the agent of the company and his primary responsibility is to the company.

It has been suggested that the duty of an agent to use care in dealing with the application may be based on the principle, familiar in negligence cases, that one who enters upon an affirmative undertaking, to perform a service for another, is required to exercise reasonable care in performing it, to avoid injury to the beneficiary of the undertaking. Insurance agents who take applications, particularly where they receive premiums, may be said to have entered definitely upon a course of affirmative conduct, and be liable for misfeasance if they unreasonably delay. This appears to us to be a salutory rule. The thought it stands for is that the agent or company owes an applicant for insurance what amounts to be a legal obligation to act with reasonable promptness on the application, either by providing the desirable coverage or by notifying the applicant of the rejection of the risk so that he may not be lulled into a feeling of security or put to prejudicial delay in seeking protection elsewhere.

Those engaged in the insurance business understand perfectly the peculiar urgency of the need for prompt attention in these matters, and in fact many premium receipts provide for delay by inserting an express provision that if the application is not accepted within a definite time it shall be deemed to have been rejected; others provide for a definite termination date (where conditional [sic] insurance is expressly given from the date of the application provided the applicant is then insurable for the plan and amount and at the premium rate applied for).

For the above reasons the judgment of the Circuit Court of Rock Island is reversed.

Reversed.

QUESTIONS FOR REVIEW

1. What are some of the objective evidences that a life or health insurance agent is doing business in a given state? Why is it necessary to determine the states in which such an agent is doing business?

2. What are the usual requirements for one to be licensed as a life insurance agent?

3. What are countersignature laws? What appears to be their chief purpose?

4. What are some of the grounds on which an agent's license can be suspended or revoked?

5. What is defamation? Under what conditions might an insurer be held liable for defamatory statements of an agent?

6. What are the probable legal effects of a life insurance agent collecting a renewal premium without the authority to do so?

7. What is meant by the term *agent of record?*
8. Why is the subject of unauthorized practice of law so important to life insurance agents?
9. What are some of the grounds on which a life or health insurance agent can become liable to the applicant? To the principal (insurer)?
10. What is rebating? Twisting?

CHAPTER 5

Waiver and Estoppel

WAIVER AND ESTOPPEL DEFINED

EXPRESS AND IMPLIED WAIVERS
   Express Waivers
   Implied Waivers
   Waiver by Silence

INTENT TO WAIVE

KNOWLEDGE OF THE INSURER
   Knowledge of an Agent Imputed to the Insurer
   Collusion Between Agent and Applicant

AUTHORITY OF THE AGENT

FORBIDDEN WAIVERS AND ESTOPPELS
   Rights Which Are Partly for the Public Benefit
   Creation of Coverage
   Releases

REVOCATION OF WAIVER

ELECTION OF REMEDIES

ESTOPPEL AND THE PAROL EVIDENCE RULE

COMMON WAIVER AND ESTOPPEL SITUATIONS
   Application Submission
   Premium Payment
   Claim Adjustment

SUMMARY

The words or actions of insurers' agents sometimes give rise to waivers or estoppels. For this reason, an understanding of the legal doctrines of waiver and estoppel is necessary to an understanding of agency and contract law. In this chapter, waiver and estoppel will be defined, compared, and illustrated.

Unfortunately, the rules governing waiver and estoppel are not always consistent from jurisdiction to jurisdiction. Therefore, the authors have dealt primarily with the most important rules which have been recognized by the majority of jurisdictions.

WAIVER AND ESTOPPEL DEFINED

A waiver is the voluntary and intentional giving up of a known right. Thus, waiver requires a knowledge of one's right coupled with an intention not to assert the right. For example, an insurer knows that if it does not receive the renewal premium by the end of the grace period, it has a right to declare the policy lapsed. If the insurer tells the policyowner at the end of the grace period that it will not declare the lapse at that time, but will give the policyowner an additional 10 days to pay the premium, the insurer has waived its right to declare the lapse at the end of the grace period. It will, however, be able to declare the lapse at the end of the additional 10 days.

The word *estoppel* has a number of meanings. There is estoppel by record, estoppel by deed, and equitable estoppel. An estoppel by record precludes a person from denying the truth of matters set forth in a judicial or legislative record.[1] Estoppel by deed bars a party to a deed from denying the truth of material facts set forth in the deed.[2] In this book, we will be concerned only with the third kind of estoppel, equitable estoppel, as this is the kind of estoppel found in insurance cases. Whenever the word *estoppel* is used in this book, therefore, it will mean equitable estoppel. As its name implies, equitable estoppel developed in the equity courts. Equitable estoppel has, however, been adopted by courts of law. For this reason, equitable estoppel is frequently invoked in legal actions based on contracts.

Equitable estoppel rests on words or conduct of one party which misleads a second party to act so that harm results to the second party. For example, in order for Michael Gold to establish an estoppel in a court action against Otis Black, Mr. Gold must prove the following: (1) that words or conduct of Mr. Black misled Mr. Gold into believing that certain facts existed when they did not exist; (2) that Mr. Gold was ignorant of the facts; and (3) that Mr. Gold, relying reasonably and in good faith on the words or conduct of Mr. Black, acted to Mr. Gold's harm. If Mr. Gold can establish an estoppel against Mr. Black, Mr. Black will not be able to use the facts—that is, the truth—in his own defense.

For example, in *Boggio v. California-Western States Life Insurance Co.*,[3] an insurer, through its agent, told an applicant that the applicant's head injury, incurred while in military service, did not have to be disclosed on the application. The evidence showed that, at the time the application was filled out, the applicant discussed this with the agent who said, "Well, as long as you do not have a medical discharge they don't care about all this. As long as you have an honorable discharge and not a medical discharge you can sign this application." The head injury, therefore, was not mentioned in the application, and the insurer denied the death claim for that reason. The insurer

---

[1]28 AM. JUR. 2D *Estoppel and Waiver* § 2 (1966).

[2]*Id.* § 4.

[3]108 Cal. App. 2d 597, 239 P. 2d 144 (1952).

stated, in essence, that it did "care about all this" and that the head injury should have been mentioned in the application. In the lawsuit that followed, the court said:

> The question presented is whether a binding insurance contract arises when the application of the insured contains misstatements of fact occurring because a soliciting agent of the insurer wrongfully represents to the applicant that certain facts (which were fully disclosed to the agent) need not be included in the application and the application is signed in good faith by the applicant who relies on the agent's superior knowledge of insurance matters. . . .
>
> To allow the insurer under these circumstances to place the responsibility upon the insured would not only be manifestly unjust but would allow it to profit by its own wrong. In such cases the courts have uniformly held the insurance company to be estopped to assert the defense of material misrepresentations.

Thus, the insurer, through its agent, misled the applicant into believing that information revealing his head injury was not required in the application when, in fact, the insurer did require such information. The insurer was, therefore, estopped to assert the defense of material misrepresentation, even though, in fact, there had been a material misrepresentation. That is, the insurer was not allowed to use the fact that there had been a material misrepresentation in its defense. It was estopped from doing so by the court to protect the applicant, because if the applicant had known that he would not be covered, he could have sought other, valid, insurance—perhaps at substandard rates. Had the insurer not been estopped, the applicant would have been misled by the insurer into relying on this insurance to the applicant's harm.

EXPRESS AND IMPLIED WAIVERS

A waiver can be expressly made by the waiving party. It can also be implied from words, from conduct, or in some instances, from the silence of the waiving party. This section contains a comparison of express and implied waivers. It also contains an explanation of why some courts have equated implied waivers with estoppels. Finally, it describes those situations in which silence can result in an implied waiver.

Express Waivers

Express waivers can be either oral or written. An oral express waiver would occur if an insurer's authorized agent told a policyowner or beneficiary that the insurer was willing to waive a right. For example, if an authorized agent of the insurer told a beneficiary over the telephone that the beneficiary need not submit proof of loss within the time specified in the policy, the insurer would have made an oral express waiver of its right to require timely submission of proof of loss. The insurer could not then deny liability for payment of the policy proceeds based on the beneficiary's failure to submit proof of loss within the time specified in the policy.

A written express waiver can occur in the policy itself or in a writing outside the policy. When incontestable clauses were first included in life insurance policies, they were waivers written in the policy. The incontestable clause stated that the insurer waived its right, after a specified period of time, to contest the validity of the policy because of a material misrepresentation in the application. As incontestable clauses are no longer voluntary on the insurer's part, but are required by statute, they are not true waivers today.

Express written waivers can also be made outside the policy. For example, if an insurer expressly states in a letter to the policyowner its intention to accept a premium after the expiration of the grace period, the insurer creates an express written waiver, outside the policy, of the insurer's contractual right to timely payment of the renewal premium.

Implied Waivers

An implied waiver can be created when there is an unexpressed intention to waive a right and that intention can be clearly inferred from the words or conduct of the waiving party. For example, if an insurer repeatedly accepts premium payments from a policyowner 60 days after the end of the grace period, the insurer will usually be held to have waived its right to timely payment of premium. If the insured should die 30 days after the grace period has expired and before the premium has been paid, a court would likely hold that the contract was in effect at the time of death and that the death benefit is payable.[4] The only reasonable explanation that could be given for the insurer's act of repeatedly accepting late premiums is that the insurer wished to waive its right to declare the policy forfeited because the premium had not been paid on time.

According to the courts of some jurisdictions, an implied waiver can also be created in a second, quite different, situation. These courts hold that an implied waiver can be created where there is, in fact, no actual intention to waive a right, but the conduct of one party has led the other party into acting on a reasonable belief that the first party has waived a right. This second type of implied waiver is inconsistent with the usual definition of waiver which is based on the intent of the waiving party to make the waiver. Furthermore, this definition of implied waiver is so similar to the definition of estoppel that it has caused the courts of some jurisdictions to declare that there is no difference between a waiver and an estoppel.[5] However, the courts of other jurisdictions have said that waiver and estoppel are different con-

---

[4]Hoffman v. Aetna Life Ins. Co., 60 Ohio App. 497, 22 N.E.2d 88 (1938).
[5]*E.g.,* Liberty Mut. Ins. Co. v. Cleveland, 127 Vt. 98, 241 A.2d 60 (1968).

cepts.[6] This is the better view in the authors' opinion. Among the myriad of fact situations where waiver or estoppel can be applied, there are some fact situations which can best be dealt with by a waiver analysis and others which can best be dealt with by an estoppel analysis, as well as borderline cases where either a waiver or an estoppel analysis can be made by a court.

Waiver by Silence

A person's silence will not create an implied waiver of his or her rights unless the person has a legal duty to speak. For example, if, before a loss occurs, an insurer learns of a ground, other than nonpayment of a premium, on which the policy can be forfeited, the insurer has a duty to notify the policyowner within a reasonable time that it intends to rescind the policy. If the insurer does not do this, it can be held to have waived its right to declare the policy forfeited.[7] The insurer must notify the policyowner that it declares the policy forfeited, so that the policyowner will have an opportunity to procure other insurance.

For example, suppose an insurer learns, three months after the issuance of a policy, that the policyowner-insured made a material misrepresentation in the application regarding her health. If the insurer makes no attempt to rescind the policy, and the insured dies six months later, the insurer will probably be held to have waived its right to rescind. The courts in a majority of jurisdictions have held that it would be unfair to allow the insurer to lull the policyowner into a false sense of security, rather than to inform the policyowner of the intent to rescind the policy so that the policyowner could obtain valid insurance elsewhere. However, some courts have disagreed with this view and have held that a waiver will not be inferred if the insurer remains silent after learning of a breach which would cause a forfeiture of the insurance.[8]

INTENT TO WAIVE

One of the key elements in the definition of waiver is the intent on the part of the waiving party that there be a waiver. Even where the intent to waive a right is expressed in the policy, difficult legal questions can be presented. The legal questions which have arisen in connection with waiver of premium because of disability constitute one example. Some of these questions are discussed in Chapter 8, "Added Benefits and Limitations."

However, the greatest number of problems as to the insurer's intent arise in connection with implied waivers. Some acts clearly create implied waivers.

---

[6]*E.g.*, American Ins. Co. v. Nationwide Mut. Ins. Co., 110 N.H. 192, 270 A.2d 907 (1970).
[7]Swedish-American Ins. Co. v. Knutson, 67 Kan. 71, 72 P. 526 (1903).
[8]44 AM. JUR. 2D *Insurance* § 1640 (1982).

For example, the repeated acceptance of overdue premiums creates an implied waiver of the right to require timely payment of the premiums. Many other acts have an uncertain meaning, however, and the courts often must determine whether the insurer intended to waive a right. In one case, an insurer was notified of the insured's death, but rather than sending proof of loss forms, the insurer requested a newspaper account of the accident causing the death. The insurer was held to have waived the requirement that the proof of loss forms be submitted. The court stated that:

> The receipt and retention by the company of informal notice and proofs, without objection, or demand for further or more definite notice and proofs, constitute a waiver of objections as to their regularity.[9]

The intent of the insurer to accept the newspaper account, in lieu of formal proofs, was implied by its actions.

KNOWLEDGE OF THE INSURER

A party to a written contract is ordinarily presumed to know and assent to its contents. The insurer is the party which drafts the policy, and the insurer will be held to have a knowledge of its rights under the policy form.

However, sometimes the insurer does not know of a situation which would give it the right under the policy form to avoid a particular contract. The insurer's acts will not create a waiver or estoppel where it does not know the pertinent facts.[10] For example, suppose an insurer, not knowing of a misrepresentation in the application for the policy which would allow it to declare the policy forfeited, accepted a premium payment. The insurer's acceptance of the premium payment would not create an implied waiver of its right to declare the policy forfeited, because it did not know of its right. The decisions in many of the cases in this area hinge on whether or not the insurer knew the material facts.

Knowledge of an Agent Imputed to the Insurer

Often a soliciting agent or medical examiner has knowledge which is imputed to the insurer under the general rule of agency law that knowledge of an agent, acquired while in the performance of the agent's duties, is knowledge of the principal. Soliciting agents or medical examiners, who are agents of the insurer, frequently fill in questions on the application for the applicant. If such an agent is told the truth about a proposed insured's health but fills in answers which are false, without the applicant's knowledge or consent, the

---

[9]Barstow v. Federal Life Ins. Co., 259 Mich. 125, 242 N.W. 862 (1932).
[10]Gardner v. North State Mut. Life Ins. Co., 163 N.C. 367, 79 S.E. 806 (1913).

agent's knowledge is imputed to the insurer in a minority of jurisdictions.[11] In these jurisdictions, if the insurer issues a policy, it will be bound by the knowledge of its agent and cannot rely upon the falsity of the answers in the application in seeking to avoid liability under the contract. In some of these cases, the courts have held that the insurer waived its right to avoid such liability. In others, the courts have held that the insurer was estopped to assert a material misrepresentation.

However, in the majority of jurisdictions, the courts have held that the applicant is responsible for the truth of statements in an application he or she signs. In those jurisdictions, the applicant must read the application to be certain the questions have been correctly answered. If those answers are false, the insurer can avoid liability on the contract within the contestable period.[12]

This rule is summarized in the case of *Theros v. Metropolitan Life Insurance Co.,*[13] as follows:

> It is also the majority rule that an insured is under a duty to read his application before signing it, and will be considered bound by a knowledge of the contents of his signed application. This is merely an application of fundamental contract law. While courts generally are inclined to treat insurance contracts as special and do not always vigorously apply all the principles of contract law, that tendency should not be allowed to overrun the bounds of legitimate exception.

The court noted that there was no evidence to show that the insured was

> by fraud, accident, misrepresentation, imposition, illiteracy, artifice or device reasonably prevented from reading the application before signing it. Therefore, he is, by law, conclusively presumed to have read the application and his beneficiary is bound by the contents thereof.

In other words, the applicant is presumed to have knowledge of a misstatement in an application he or she has signed, and that is made a part of the policy that was delivered. Thus, the insurer is not estopped to deny the truth of the answers recorded by its own agent, since the applicant is presumed to have known of the false answers and yet did not inform the insurer.

Sometimes, however, the special facts of the case will overcome the presumption that the applicant has read the application. In one case,[14] the evidence showed that the applicant gave correct information concerning the

---

[11]Pannunzio v. Monumental Life Ins. Co., 168 Ohio St. 95, 151 N.E.2d 545 (1958); Progressive Life Ins. Co. v. Dooley, 209 Ark. 608, 192 S.W.2d 128 (1946).

[12]*See*, generally, INTERNATIONAL CLAIM ASSOCIATION, KNOWLEDGE OF THE AGENT IMPUTED TO THE COMPANY (1962).

[13]17 Utah 2d 205, 407 P.2d 685 (1965).

[14]Hart v. Prudential Ins. Co., 47 Cal. App. 2d 298, 117 P.2d 930 (1941).

diabetic condition of her daughter (the proposed insured), but the agent recorded incorrect answers which made it appear that the daughter's health was good. After the daughter's death, the company denied the claim on grounds of misrepresentation of material facts in the application. The insurer contended that even if the agent inserted false answers, the applicant was presumed to have knowledge of the false statements, since the application was attached to the policy. The mother testified that there was no copy of the application attached to the policy, however, and that was the finding of the court. The holding, therefore, was against the insurer.

In another case (*Boggio v. California-Western States Life Insurance Co.*, cited above), the soliciting agent told the applicant that the applicant's military service head injury did not have to be disclosed on the application because the applicant had an honorable, rather than a medical, discharge from military service. Of the insured's duty to read the application under these circumstances, the court said:

> Defendant correctly states that when the insured has a copy of the application in his possession he is presumed to have read it and to be aware of any misstatements therein even though they were not due to his own fault . . . .
>
> The rule would not apply here to charge Boggio with knowledge he did not have when he signed the application unless he could have ascertained that his statements were false in the sense that they withheld information sought to be elicited by the questions contained in the application. This was not the case. He relied on Angelino's [the soliciting agent's] statement that the questions did not call for information as to the injury received in the service unless it had led to medical discharge. Having had the question interpreted for him in this manner, repeated reading of the questions and answers would not have led him to believe that his service injury was material. He knew at all times that his answers were literally untrue but not that they would be deemed untrue by the company in determining whether he was an insurable risk.[15]

Collusion Between Agent and Applicant

Collusion is a secret agreement between two or more persons to do some act in order to defraud a third person. Where an applicant and an agent agree to write false answers in an application in order to defraud the insurer, there is collusion between the applicant and agent. Neither the applicant nor the beneficiary will be allowed by a court to benefit from the collusion. Where there is collusion, the rule that knowledge of the agent is knowledge of the principal is not applicable.[16] The insurer will not be estopped from asserting

---

[15]108 Cal. App. 2d 597, 239 P.2d 144 (1952).

[16]Gardner v. North State Mut. Life Ins. Co., 163 N.C. 367, 79 S.E. 806 (1913); Commonwealth Life Ins. Co. v. Spears, 219 Ky. 681, 294 S.W. 138 (1927); Aetna Life Ins. Co. v. Routon, 207 Ark. 132, 179 S.W.2d 862 (1944).

the material misrepresentation in the application in defending a lawsuit for the death benefits.

In one case, the soliciting agent knew of the applicant's diabetic condition and recent hospitalization. The agent inserted false answers in the application for insurance on the applicant's life with respect to the diabetes and hospitalization. The applicant knew that false answers had been inserted. The court held that the insurer had properly canceled the policy under these circumstances. The court said:

> As to the question of waiver and estoppel appellant [the beneficiary] earnestly contends that the knowledge of Jones [the agent] concerning the status of Gardner's [the insured's] health was imputed to appellee insurance company and therefore it, with such knowledge, issued the policy and can now not be heard to complain or assert the defenses presented. Such is not the law.[17]

AUTHORITY OF THE AGENT

The princpal's rights can be waived by an authorized agent. In the case of a corporate insurer, waiver is always by agent, as all of a corporation's acts must be by an agent. The term *agent* is used here to include not only soliciting agents but also officers, medical examiners, underwriters, and others whose actions affect the insurer's contractual relationships.

In many waiver cases, the authority of the agent to make the waiver is in question. Waiver by an agent of the conditions of an insurance policy becomes binding upon the insurer only if the agent has power to make the waiver. If the applicant or policyowner knows that the agent lacks authority to make a waiver, there can be no claim of apparent authority to waive. The applicant or policyowner is bound by the limitations on the authority of the agent of which the applicant or policyowner has notice.

Notice to applicants of limitations on the agent's authority is usually contained in the application, as well as in the policy. This notice is often called a "nonwaiver clause." The nonwaiver clause in the application form which appears in Appendix A reads in part as follows:

> No agent is authorized to make or modify contracts, to waive any of the Company's rights or requirements or to bind the Company by making or receiving any promise, representation or information, unless the same be in writing, submitted to the Company, and made a part of such contract.

The word *agent* in this clause pertains to soliciting agents. Other agents of the insurer at the home office will determine whether to permit a waiver which is submitted in written form by the soliciting agent.

---

[17]Bennett v. National Life & Acci. Ins. Co., 438 S.W.2d 438 (Tex. Civ. App. 1969).

The policy itself contains the following nonwaiver provision:

> Only our President, one of our Vice Presidents, our Secretary or our Actuary has the authority to modify or waive any provision in this policy, and then only in writing. No Agent or other person has the authority to change or waive any provision of this Policy.

The court decisions regarding the effectiveness of nonwaiver clauses are conflicting. There is, first of all, the rule stated above that the applicant or policyowner is bound by limitations on the authority of an agent, if the applicant or policyowner has notice of those limitations. Moreover, the applicant or policyowner is deemed to have notice of the nonwaiver provision, especially where it appears in the application, as well as in the policy.

On the other hand, there are decisions which limit the effectiveness of the nonwaiver clause. First, the nonwaiver clause itself can be waived. The clause will not prevent an agent who has full authority to make contracts, such as a senior officer of the insurer, from effecting a waiver or creating an estoppel.

Second, several jurisdictions follow a rule that nonwaiver provisions apply only to waivers made after issuance of the policy. The reasoning here is that the policyowner cannot be bound by a policy provision he or she has not seen. For this reason, insurers frequently also put a nonwaiver clause in the application.

Finally, there is a rule in the majority of jurisdictions that a nonwaiver clause does not apply to conditions which must be fulfilled by a beneficiary after a loss has occurred. That is, waivers of policy provisions, such as provisions requiring notice or proof of loss, are not affected by a nonwaiver clause. Agents of the insurer can waive such provisions despite the nonwaiver clause.

FORBIDDEN WAIVERS AND ESTOPPELS

The general rule is that a party to a contract can waive any right which was inserted in the contract solely for that party's benefit. Some rights under insurance policies cannot be waived, however, because they are not solely for the benefit of one party, but are partly for the benefit of the public. Other rights cannot be waived because such a waiver would create coverage which the policy does not provide. Moreover, an estoppel cannot be invoked to create such coverage. Finally, a legal right to receive a sum of money may be released, but it cannot be waived.

Rights Which Are Partly for the Public Benefit

Rights which are partly for the public benefit cannot be waived. For example, in some jurisdictions, the doctrine of waiver cannot be invoked to validate a policy where the applicant had no insurable interest in the life of the proposed insured. This is because public policy requires that an applicant have such an insurable interest. The right to require insurable interest is not for the insurer's sole benefit, but is also for the benefit of the public.

The policyowner may also be prevented from waiving certain rights. For example, rights under statutes which require notice of premium due cannot be waived by a policyowner, because they are for the benefit of the public, as well as for the policyowner's benefit.[18]

Rights under nonforfeiture statutes ordinarily cannot be waived by the policyowner, again because these statutes have been enacted for the benefit of the public. One court said the following in regard to nonforfeiture statutes:

> The benefits conferred by these statutes cannot be abrogated, waived, or contracted away, either by agreement in the policy or by agreement made between the parties prior to default . . . The public policy involved overrides the freedom of contract of the parties.[19]

Creation of Coverage

The rule in the majority of jurisdictions is that neither waiver nor estoppel can be invoked to create coverage.[20] If a risk is not included in the coverage or is specifically excluded from it, waiver or estoppel will not bring the risk within the coverage.

For example, in *Pierce v. Homesteaders Life Association*[21] the policy provided that the death benefit would be paid only if the insured died prior to attaining age 60. The insured attained age 60 on March 3 and died on March 11, but the premium had been paid through September. After the insured's death, the insurer tendered back the excess premium. The beneficiary argued in a lawsuit for the benefits that, because the insurer had accepted premium payment for a period beyond the insured's 60th birthday and beyond her death, the insurer had waived the expiration of the insurance. The court held that the insurer did not owe the benefits. The court stated the following: "It has been repeatedly held that while a forfeiture of benefits contracted for may be waived, the doctrine of waiver or estoppel cannot be successfully invoked to create a liability for benefits not contracted for at all." There are, however, exceptions to this general rule, as will be shown in the illustrative case at the end of this chapter.

Releases

If one person has a right to receive a sum of money from another person, this right can be released, but it cannot be waived. A release is the giving up of a right or claim, and it is, therefore, similar to a waiver. However, a release

---

[18]Reynolds v. Metropolitan Life Ins. Co., 105 Kan. 669, 185 P. 1051 (1919).

[19]Fayman v. Franklin Life Ins. Co., 386 S.W.2d 52 (Mo. Sup. Ct. 1965).

[20]Kaminer v. Franklin Life Ins. Co., 472 F.2d 1073 (5th Cir. 1973), *cert. denied*, 414 U.S. 840 (1973); Garland v. Jefferson Standard Life Ins. Co., 179 N.C. 67, 101 S.E. 616 (1919).

[21]223 Iowa 211, 272 N.W. 543 (1937).

ordinarily requires that consideration be given by the person receiving the release. For example, an insurer gives the death benefit, as consideration, in exchange for a release from the beneficiary of the beneficiary's right to receive the death benefit.

A written release under seal, without consideration, will also be effective in some states. A seal is an impression on wax or a gummed wafer affixed to a document, or an impression in the paper of the document, made to authenticate the document. The seal developed in medieval England, because widespread illiteracy made signatures impractical. In most states, the seal has been abolished for most purposes, but there are some states where it is still effective for releases. A few states by statute give an unsealed release the effect of a sealed release. In those states, an unsealed release will be effective without consideration being given by the person receiving the release.

A release is usually made in the form of a written statement by a creditor that the debt owed is discharged. This writing is delivered to the debtor and provides the debtor a defense to a later claim of legal liability for the debt. Insurers often include a release on the back of a draft made in payment of a claim. When the beneficiary endorses the draft, he or she is also signing the release.

REVOCATION OF WAIVER

If an insurer acquires a right to rescind a contract or to set up a defense to payment of benefits because a condition of the contract has been breached, the insurer usually can waive its right if it wishes to do so. Once it waives its right, however, it cannot revoke the waiver. The contract is as binding as before the breach of the condition.[22]

For example, suppose a policyowner breached a condition of the contract by failing to pay the premium before the end of the grace period. If the insurer told the policyowner it would not lapse the policy but would allow an extra 10 days for payment of the premium, it would have waived its right to declare the policy lapsed as of the end of the grace period. If the insured died five days after the end of the grace period, the insurer could not then revoke the waiver and declare the policy lapsed as of the end of the grace period.

Nevertheless, an insurer may give express notice that it will, in the future, insist that the contract conditions be fulfilled, even where it has waived strict compliance with those conditions in the past. For example, suppose an insurer has repeatedly accepted late payment of premiums. Its actions can give rise to an implied waiver of timely payment of premiums. However, if the insurer notifies the policyowner before a premium due date that it will no longer accept late payment, the implied waiver of the insurer's right to timely payment of premium will be revoked. In that case, the policy will lapse if the policyowner does not pay the premium on time.

---

[22]State Life Ins. Co. v. Finney, 216 Ala. 562, 114 So. 132 (1927).

ELECTION OF REMEDIES

The doctrine of election of remedies has elements of both waiver and estoppel. It is sometimes called estoppel by election. The doctrine of election of remedies is applied by the courts when a person has two or more inconsistent remedies available for the redress of a single wrong. The person must elect one of the remedies. This necessarily means she or he must forgo, or waive, the other inconsistent remedies.

For example, in one case, an insurer took action to cancel an insurance contract which provided disability income benefits.[23] The policyowner-insured, Rhame, sued the insurer for fraudulent breach of contract and was awarded money damages. Later, Rhame claimed continuing disability benefits. The insurer filed a suit for declaratory judgment asking the court to rule on whether or not Rhame had a right to sue for the disability benefits.[24] The court held that Rhame had already chosen his remedy and that the courts could not "permit repeated actions of a nature inconsistent with that already adopted by the insured with reference to the contract in question." Quoting from another case the court noted that:

By the weight of authority, where an insurer wrongfully cancels, repudiates, or terminates the contract of insurance, the insured may at once pursue either of three courses: (1) He may elect to treat the policy as still in force, and let the test of the validity of the cancellation or repudiation await until the policy is payable and is sued on; (2) he may sue in equity to set aside the cancellation, and to have the policy declared to be valid and in force; or (3) he may maintain an action at law to recover damages for the wrongful cancellation or repudiation.[25]

The court pointed out that in the *Rhame* case

Rhame unquestionably chose as his remedy the alternative of treating the contract at an end and instituting an action at law to recover damages for its wrongful cancellation or repudiation. The allegations of his complaint, which has been exhibited, do not in any manner indicate that he regarded the policy as still in force, or seek to base recovery on the provisions of the contract.

The court further said, quoting from yet another case:

The doctrine of election of remedies is regarded as being an application of the law of estoppel, upon the theory that a party cannot in the assertion of his right occupy inconsistent positions in relation to the facts which form the basis of his respective remedies; it is based on the

---

[23]Pacific Mut. Life Ins. Co. v. Rhame, 32 F. Supp. 59 (E.D.S.C. 1940).

[24]A declaratory judgment is an action in which one party asks the court to declare the rights and duties of the parties to the action, but involves no relief by the court as a consequence of the judgment.

[25]Schuler v. Equitable Life Assur. Soc., 184 S.C. 485, 193 S.E. 46 (1937).

proposition that, when a party has two remedies proceeding upon opposite and irreconcilable claims of right, the one adopted excludes the other.[26]

Thus, Rhame was bound by his first choice of remedy, the award of money damages for wrongful cancellation of the contract, and could not proceed with the second suit for the payment of disability benefits. In other words, he could not treat the contract as canceled in one suit and later sue for disability benefits as if the contract were still in force. If a person carries an action for one remedy through to judgment, he or she cannot, therefore, elect to pursue a second, inconsistent remedy. The doctrine of election prevents this. As one authority has pointed out, election is "a legal version of the idea that one can't have his cake and eat it too."[27]

ESTOPPEL AND THE PAROL EVIDENCE RULE

Estoppels were originally equitable remedies, applied only in courts of equity. When they were adopted by the common-law courts, they did not fit in well with all of the common-law rules.

Conflict between estoppel and the parol evidence rule of the common-law courts was almost inevitable. The parol evidence rule forbids the introduction into court proceedings of oral testimony of words or actions of the parties before the contract was signed when that testimony would contradict the written contract. If a lawsuit was brought in which an alleged estoppel was based on words or actions of the parties after the contract became effective, it did not conflict with the parol evidence rule. However, lawsuits involving alleged estoppels based on words or actions of a party before the policy was in force did conflict with the parol evidence rule.

In 1872, in the leading case in this area, *Union Mutual Insurance Co. v. Wilkinson*,[28] the United States Supreme Court held that such evidence was admissible to establish an estoppel. In the *Wilkinson* case, an application for a life insurance contract was signed by the proposed insured. By the terms of the policy, the policy became void if any of the representations in the application proved to be untrue. The statement in question concerned the age of the mother of the insured at the time of the mother's death. Alleging the untruth of the age represented, the insurer denied the claim for the death benefit.

At the trial that followed, evidence was offered by the beneficiary to show what actually took place at the time the application was taken. Witnesses testified that the agent asked the insured the age of her mother at the mother's death, and the insured said she did not know. Someone else who

---

[26]McMahan v. McMahan, 122 S.C. 336, 115 S.E. 293 (1922).

[27]D.B. Dobbs, Remedies 14 (1973).

[28]80 U.S. (13 Wall.) 222 (1872).

was present volunteered an answer, and the agent inserted it in the application. The answer was later found to be incorrect. If admitted in the trial, this evidence would support an equitable estoppel against the insurer. The issue was whether oral testimony could be admitted under such circumstances or whether the parol evidence rule would preclude its admission.

The Court held that the oral testimony was admissible to establish an estoppel and that the insurer was estopped to plead the misrepresentation. The Court said:

> It is in precisely such cases as this that courts of law in modern times have introduced the doctrine of equitable estoppels, or, as it is sometimes called, estoppels *in pais*. The principle is, that where one party has by his representations or his conduct induced the other party to a transaction to give him an advantage which it would be against equity and good conscience for him to assert, he would not in a court of justice be permitted to avail himself of that advantage. And although the cases to which this principle is to be applied are not as well defined as could be wished, the general doctrine is well understood and is applied by courts of law as well as equity where the technical advantage thus obtained is set up and relied on to defeat the ends of justice or establish a dishonest claim.
>
> . . . This principle does not admit oral testimony to vary or contradict that which is in writing, but it goes upon the idea that the writing offered in evidence was not the instrument of the party whose name is signed to it; that it was procured under such circumstances by the other side as estops that side from using it or relying on its contents; not that it may be contradicted by oral testimony, but that it may be shown by such testimony that it cannot be lawfully used against the party whose name is signed to it.

This holding has been followed by the courts of most states, although there have been exceptions.

COMMON WAIVER AND ESTOPPEL SITUATIONS

There are a number of common situations in the insurance business which can result in a waiver or an estoppel. This section is divided into subsections dealing with waivers and estoppels which are apt to occur in connection with application submission, premium payment, and claim adjustment.

Application Submission

Many waivers and estoppels have resulted from the application process. Some of these have resulted from words or actions of the soliciting agent or the medical examiner. Others have resulted from words or actions of other agents in the home office, such as underwriters.

Fraud, Misconduct, or Negligence of an Agent.   Collusion between an agent of the insurer and the applicant to insert false answers in the application will not result in an estoppel of the insurer to defend on basis of the misrepresentation. However, where the applicant gives the insurer's agent true answers, but the agent writes in false answers, the courts of a minority of jurisdictions hold that the agent's knowledge is imputed to the insurer. If the insurer issues a policy, the insurer will be held to have waived the incorrect answers. If a court holds that an insurer waived a false answer written in the application by its agent who was told the true answer by the applicant, the insurer will have a cause of action against the agent for breach of the agent's fiduciary duty.

Where the soliciting agent, while preparing an application, suggests an answer to a question to the applicant, or interprets the meaning of the question, a false answer is binding upon the insurer unless the applicant should reasonably suspect the agent's interpretation is incorrect. For example, where an applicant tells an agent of a health problem, but the agent assures him it need not be included in the application, the insurer might be estopped if it tries to deny benefits on the ground that the information was not included. The *Boggio* case cited above is an example of this principle.

Insurer's Failure to Inquire About Incomplete Answers.   Where an insurer receives at its home office an application that has a missing or incomplete answer, but it does not make further inquiry of the applicant before issuing the policy, the insurer will have waived its requirement that the answer be complete. The insurer cannot afterward rely upon the incomplete application to deny benefits.[29]

Premium Payment

The insurer, eager to keep the policy in force, frequently does not insist that the policyowner strictly abide by the terms of the policy in paying the premium. As a result, waivers and estoppels are often invoked in connection with premium payments.

Waiver of Timely Payment of the Premium.   An insurer that accepts an overdue premium payment before a loss occurs has waived its right to require timely payment of that premium. As pointed out above, if the insurer repeatedly accepts overdue premiums, this can create an implied waiver of timely payment. The insurer cannot insist that the policy is lapsed if there is a delay in payment similar in length to past delays, if it has not notified the policyowner beforehand that it will insist upon timely payment. If an insured dies shortly after the end of the grace period and before the premium is paid, the

---

[29]Franklin Life Ins. Co. v. Bieniek, 312 F.2d 365 (3rd Cir. 1962).

benefits will be payable in such a case. Moreover, if the insurer knows the insured has died and accepts late payment after the insured's death, this will also create a waiver of timely payment.

Acceptance of a Check Rather Than Cash.   An insurer which has an established practice of accepting checks, rather than cash, in payment of premiums cannot declare a policy forfeited if the policyowner submits a check in payment. This is true even when the policy requires payment in cash. The insurer will be held to have waived its right to receive payment in cash.

Dishonored Checks.   A check given to an insurer in payment of a premium is ordinarily accepted by the insurer upon condition that it be paid upon presentation for payment.[30] If an insurer returns a dishonored check to the policyowner, the insurer will not have waived its right to declare the policy forfeited. However, if the insurer attempts to collect on the dishonored check, it might be held to have waived its right to declare the policy forfeited.[31] This is because an attempt to collect on the check is inconsistent with the position that the check had been accepted on condition that it be paid upon presentation. If the insured dies while the insurer is attempting to collect on the check, and the court holds that the insurer has waived its right to declare the policy forfeited, the death benefit, minus the unpaid premium, will be payable to the beneficiary.

Premium Due Notices.   Often, the policyowner comes to rely on premium due notices sent by the insurer to remind the policyowner to pay the premium. When the insurer, without notifying the policyowner that it intends to cease sending such notices, fails to send a premium due notice, the policy will not be forfeited if the policyowner does not pay on time. The insurer will be estopped from asserting such a forfeiture because it has misled the policyowner into believing that a premium due notice would be sent.

Moreover, where an insurer has customarily sent an agent to collect renewal premiums, the policyowner has a right to rely upon this kind of notice, also. If the insurer stops sending an agent to collect the premiums but does not notify the policyowner that it intends to stop, the policy will not be forfeited if the premium is not paid on time.

Claim Adjustment

There are many cases in which the words or actions of an insurer during adjustment of a claim have resulted in a waiver or an estoppel. Some of the most common of these are described in this subsection.

---

[30]Kansas City Life Ins. Co. v. Davis, 95 F.2d 952 (9th Cir. 1938).
[31]Stewart v. Union Mut. Life Ins. Co., 155 N.Y. 257, 49 N.E. 876 (1898).

The general rule here is that if the insurer knows of the breach of a condition which will cause a forfeiture of benefits but, nevertheless, enters into negotiations with the beneficiary which cause the beneficiary to incur trouble or expense in the belief that the benefits will be paid, the breach of condition will be waived or the insurer will be estopped to assert the breach.

Proof of Loss.   If an insurer furnishes proof of loss forms to a beneficiary without a specific request that they be completed and returned, a court will not infer that the insurer has waived a breach of condition known to it. On the other hand, if the insurer requires the beneficiary to submit the completed proof of loss forms without informing the beneficiary that the claim is disputed, the courts of many jurisdictions will infer a waiver. To avoid the possibility of a waiver being inferred, the insurer must notify the beneficiary of the breach of condition and that the insurer does not intend to waive the breach. The insurer can insert a specific nonwaiver clause in the policy or in the proof of loss forms saying that the insurer does not waive the breach of a condition by the adjustment of a loss. It can also obtain an agreement with the beneficiary that the beneficiary's submission of proof of loss will not constitute a waiver by the insurer of the breach of a condition.

If an insurer receives defective proofs of loss but does not object to the defect in a timely manner, the insurer will be held to have waived the defect. It cannot then base a forfeiture of benefits on the defect.

If a beneficiary notifies the insurer of loss and requests proof of loss forms, but the insurer does not promptly send the forms, the insurer will have waived its right to require the timely submission by the beneficiary of the completed forms. Moreover, as previously pointed out, if the insurer fails to send proof of loss forms when requested but instead asks for other information, such as a newspaper account, submission of proof of loss forms is waived.

Delay of Claims Investigation.   If an insurer asks for additional time for claims investigation, and the investigation goes beyond the time in which the beneficiary is allowed to bring suit under the terms of the contract, the insurer will have waived the limitation of time in which the beneficiary can sue. The beneficiary will have a reasonable additional time in which to bring suit.

Promise to Pay.   The majority rule is that if the insurer promises to pay a claim where it knows of the breach of a condition which could result in a forfeiture of benefits, it has waived the breach of condition. On the other hand, an offer to compromise coupled with a denial of liability will not ordinarily result in such a waiver. An actual payment in full of the claim, where the insurer knows of the breach of a condition, implies a waiver of the breach.

Denial of Liability on One of Several Known Grounds.   In most jurisdictions, the courts apply the principle that an insurer which denies liability on less than all grounds for denial known to it will be deemed to have waived any ground it has not specified. This is true especially when the beneficiary was put to trouble and expense in trying to collect the benefits before he or she knew of the additional grounds for denial. Therefore, an insurer which has more than one ground for denying liability under a contract should state all grounds in its denial. If it fails to do so, and the beneficiary files suit to recover the benefit, the insurer's unstated grounds for denial will be deemed to have been waived.[32]

Note that the insurer will be deemed to have waived only those defenses it knew of at the time of its denial of liability. Where the insurer does not know of its right to defend a suit for benefits on a certain ground, the courts will not infer a waiver if the insurer did not specify that ground in its denial of liability.

SUMMARY

A waiver is an intentional and voluntary giving up of a known right. An estoppel, on the other hand, will be invoked in a situation where one person, A, has by words or conduct caused another person, B, in reasonable reliance on those words or conduct, to act so that harm results to B. A will be estopped—that is, forbidden—by a court to use the facts (the truth) in A's own defense. Waivers may be express, implied, or even, in some cases, implied by silence. Implied waivers are said by the courts of some jurisdictions to be the same thing as estoppels. The better view is that implied waivers do differ from estoppels.

A waiver requires an intent to waive—express or implied—and requires that the waiving party have knowledge of the pertinent facts. Estoppel also requires knowledge of the pertinent facts. Only an authorized agent may waive a condition of a policy. However, knowledge of an insurer's agent often can be imputed to the insurer. Such imputation of knowledge has resulted in waivers by, or estoppels against, insurers.

Some waivers are forbidden. A person cannot waive a right which is partly for the public benefit. Waivers cannot create coverage for which the parties did not contract. The right to receive a sum of money can be released, but the right cannot be waived.

The legal doctrine of election of remedies is a special application of waiver and estoppel. Election of remedies means that a person, having chosen one remedy for the redress of a wrong, cannot later choose another, inconsistent remedy to redress the same wrong. The person has waived the inconsistent remedy and will be estopped to assert it.

The doctrine of estoppel, which had developed in courts of equity, conflicted with the parol evidence rule of the common-law courts when estoppel

---

[32]Craddock v. Fidelity Life Ass'n, 226 Iowa 744, 285 N.W. 169 (1939).

was adopted by the common-law courts. Most common-law courts have held that parol evidence is admissible to establish an estoppel.

ILLUSTRATIVE CASE

In the following case, the court pointed out the general rule that waiver and estoppel cannot create coverage beyond that stipulated in the contract. The court then decided that, under the extreme circumstances of this case, a decision contrary to the general rule was equitable.

MARGARET B. PITTS, Respondent

v.

NEW YORK LIFE INSURANCE COMPANY,
Appellant[33]

Supreme Court of South Carolina

LEGGE, Acting Justice.

Action by the beneficiary of a policy of insurance on the life of her husband to recover double indemnity by reason of his accidental death. The case was tried before the Honorable Clarence E. Singletary, Presiding Judge, without a jury; appeal is from his judgment in favor of the plaintiff.

On July 1, 1920, appellant insured the life of Reuben B. Pitts under a ten-year term policy for $10,000, or $20,000 in the event that his death should result from accident. On July 30, 1925, this policy was converted into an ordinary life policy, with like provision for double indemnity in case of death by accident, and with provision for payment of disability benefit of $100.00 per month if the insured should become disabled before age sixty. As so converted, its annual premium was $405.20, of which $10.00 was stated to be for the double indemnity coverage and $28.20 for the disability coverage, with the provision that after the insured should reach the age of sixty years the premiums to become due would be reduced by the amount of the premium charged for the disability coverage. It excluded the double indemnity coverage in case of death resulting from certain causes, among them "engaging, as a passenger or otherwise, in submarine or aeronautic operations."

On January 27, 1933, pursuant to application by the insured and the beneficiary, the double indemnity provision was amended by endorsement reading as follows:

> "In accordance with the request of the insured, the double indemnity benefit is hereby modified to permit the double indemnity provision to apply if the insured's death occurs as the result of riding as a fare-paying passenger in a licensed passenger aircraft provided by an incorporated passenger carrier and operated by a licensed pilot on a regular passenger route between definitely established airports.

---

[33]247 S.C. 545, 148 S.E.2d 369 (1966).

"It is also understood and agreed that the entire provisions for double indemnity as included in the policy will apply only if death occurs prior to the anniversary of the policy on which the insured's age at nearest birthday is 65.

"Any premium due on and after the anniversary on which the age of the insured at nearest birthday is 65 will be reduced by the amount of premium charged for the double indemnity benefit."

In 1942, when the insured reached age sixty, appellant reduced the annual premium by $28.20, the amount charged for the disability coverage. The insured became sixty-five years of age in 1947, but in that year and each year thereafter appellant continued to bill him without reduction of the premium by the amount ($10.00) charged for the double indemnity benefit; and the insured continued to pay the premiums as thus billed until his death, at the age of eighty-one, on March 25, 1963.

That the insured's death resulted from accident is not disputed. Appellant paid the face amount of the policy, $10,000 but refused to pay under the double indemnity provision. Its offer to refund the double indemnity premiums paid subsequent to August 1, 1947, together with interest on each such payment, was rejected.

In her complaint respondent [the beneficiary] alleged that appellant, having failed and neglected, after the insured had reached the age of sixty-five, to reduce the premium by the amount charged for the double indemnity benefit as it was obligated to do by the terms of the 1933 endorsement before mentioned, "has waived its right to rely upon the provisions of the said endorsement and is now estopped" to deny liability for such benefit. In its answer appellant alleged that its failure to note that the premium should be reduced in 1947 was the result of a clerical error, and that the continued payment by the insured and acceptance by it of the unreduced premium after the insured had reached the age of sixty-five were the result of inadvertence and mutual mistake and were contrary to the express terms and conditions of the policy.

It appears undisputed that appellant did not discover the error in its records, and the resulting erroneous billing of premiums, until after the insured's death.

The trial judge held that by having billed the insured for the full premium and accepted payment of the same each year for sixteen years after the insured had reached the age of sixty-five years appellant had waived a right to deny coverage under the double indemnity provision of the 1933 endorsement; and he accordingly ordered judgment for the plaintiff for $10,000.00, with interest from the date on which the face amount of the policy was paid to the beneficiary. That ruling is here challenged by several exceptions.

Policy provisions under which an insurer may assert non-coverage fall into two classes: (1) those providing for forfeiture; and (2) those limiting or excluding coverage. The former may be waived; with regard to the latter, the weight of authority is said to support the view expressed in 29A Am. Jur., Insurance, Section 1135, Page 289, as follows:

The rule is well established that the doctrines of implied waiver and of estoppel, based upon the conduct or action of the insurer, are not available to bring within the coverage of a policy risks not covered by its terms, or risks expressly excluded therefrom, and the application of the doctrines in this respect is therefore to be distinguished from the waiver of, or estoppel to assert, grounds of forfeiture. Thus, while an insurer may be estopped by its conduct or its knowledge from insisting upon a forfeiture of a policy, the coverage, or restrictions on the coverage, cannot be extended by the doctrine of waiver or estoppel.

To the same effect is the following, from 16 Appleman, Insurance Law and Practice, Section 9090, page 629:

> It has been broadly stated that the doctrines of waiver and estoppel cannot be used to extend the coverage of an insurance policy or create a primary liability, but may only affect rights reserved therein. While an insurer may be estopped, by its conduct or its knowledge or by statute, from insisting on a forfeiture of a policy, under no conditions can the coverage or restrictions on coverage be extended by waiver or estoppel.

* * * * *

The essential elements of equitable estoppel are: (1) ignorance of the party invoking it of the truth as to the facts in question; (2) representations or conduct of the party estopped which mislead; (3) reliance upon such representations or conduct; and (4) prejudicial change of position as the result of such reliance. The presence of these elements is not essential to the establishment of implied waiver, which results merely from conduct of the party against whom the doctrine is invoked from which voluntary relinquishment of his known right is reasonably inferable. But the two doctrines are related, and have this in common: that the applicability of each in a particular situation results from conduct of the party against whom it is invoked which has rendered it inequitable that he assert a right to which, in the absence of such conduct, he would be entitled.

Whether an insurer, by accepting and retaining the premium for a coverage that by the terms of the policy is excluded or terminated, may be estopped to deny such coverage, must of course depend upon the circumstances of the particular case. For estoppel is an equitable doctrine, essentially flexible, and therefore to be applied or denied as the equities between the parties may preponderate . . . Where the insurer over a long period of time after the date prescribed by it for the termination of a particular coverage has continued to demand, accept and retain the premium fixed by it for that coverage, it may reasonably be inferred that the insured, who in the normal course of things relies upon the insurer's billing, has been misled by such conduct to believe that the insurer has continued to accept the coverage. Upon the same premise, excusable ignorance on the part of the insured as to the true fact, i.e., that the insurer has made a mistake in its billing, may likewise be inferred.

In the present case, as has been noted, the premium for the double indemnity coverage, $10.00, was separate and distinct from, and in addition to, that charged for the normal coverage, $367.00. Although by the terms of the policy the double indemnity coverage was to expire in 1947, when the insured became sixty-five, the undisputed fact that appellant continued for sixteen years thereafter to bill him for such coverage, and to collect and retain it, in our opinion furnished sound and adequate basis for the three elements of estoppel,—ignorance, misleading, and reliance—before mentioned. The fourth element, prejudicial change of position, is also present. For not only did the insured expend the amount of such premium, in response to the erroneous billing, during each of the sixteen years between 1947 and 1963, but the insurer's claim for relief from the consequences of its error comes not until after the death of the insured and therefore, we think, too late.

We need not, and do not, decide whether the rule of non-waiver is applicable in the present case, for we think that under the facts apparent in the record here the insurer is estopped to deny the coverage in question. The issue of estoppel was before the Court; it was one of law, the essential facts being undisputed; and the result reached was the just and correct one. Affirmance in that result is proper in such case[34] . . . .

Affirmed in result.

QUESTIONS FOR REVIEW

1. Define the term *waiver*.
2. Discuss revocation of waiver.
3. Under what conditions will an attempted waiver be ineffective? What are some policy provisions which cannot be waived by the policyowner?
4. What is the nonwaiver clause in an application or policy? Discuss its effectiveness.
5. Describe the doctrine of election of remedies.
6. Define the term *equitable estoppel*.
7. Discuss the conflict between equitable estoppel and the parol evidence rule.
8. Describe some situations involving insurance transactions in which an insurer might be held to have waived a right or be estopped to assert the truth.

---

[34]The appeals court affirmed the decision of the trial court, which was in favor of the beneficiary.

CHAPTER 6

Formation of the Life Insurance Contract

LIFE INSURANCE CONTRACT OFFER AND ACCEPTANCE
    Offer and Acceptance
    Counteroffers
    Withdrawal of the Application
    Rejection of the Application
    Signature on the Application

DELAY IN ACTING ON THE APPLICATION
    Contract Liability for Unreasonable Delay
    Tort Liability for Unreasonable Delay

PREMIUM RECEIPTS
    Conditions Precedent and Conditions Subsequent
    Approval Premium Receipts
    Insurability Premium Receipts
    Binding Premium Receipts
    Premium Receipts in the Courts
    Statutes and Regulations Governing Premium Receipts

RISK CLASSIFICATION AND SELECTION
    Discrimination
    Limitations on Liberty of Contract
    Nonsmoker Premium Discounts

INSURABLE INTEREST
    Insurable Interest in a Person's Own Life
    Insurable Interest in Another Person's Life

CONSIDERATION

COMPETENT CONTRACTING PARTIES

DELIVERY OF THE POLICY
    Constructive Delivery
    Delivery for Inspection

EFFECTIVE DATE OF THE POLICY

SUMMARY

The formation of the life insurance contract is governed by many of the same rules which govern the formation of any informal contract, plus rules specific to life insurance contracts. These rules specific to life insurance contract formation are the subject of this chapter.

LIFE INSURANCE CONTRACT OFFER AND ACCEPTANCE

As with other informal contracts, life insurance contracts are completed by the making of an offer by one party and its acceptance by the other. Under some circumstances, the offer is made by the life insurance applicant and, under other circumstances, by the insurer.

Offer and Acceptance

The traditional life insurance offer and acceptance theory is that the applicant makes the offer, and the insurer accepts the offer. This is true in many instances but, in many others, it is not. The wording of the application usually governs. Usually, too, the initial premium must accompany the application if there is to be an offer by the applicant. If the initial premium does not accompany the application, submission of the application is ordinarily an invitation to the insurer to make an offer. The insurer can make the offer by issuing and delivering the policy. The applicant can then accept the insurer's offer by paying the premium.

A direct-response insurance advertisement for accidental death insurance, with application attached, was held in one case to be a complete offer by the insurer.[1] Direct response insurance solicitation is done by direct mail or media advertisement, without the involvement of a soliciting agent. Thus, no agent was available to discuss the coverage with the applicant. The advertisement contained all the information needed by the applicant to make a decision regarding purchase of the insurance. No medical questions had to be answered by the applicant and rejection of the application was highly unlikely. The advertisement indicated that the insurance would be issued upon receipt of an application and the premium from any member of a certain automobile club. When the applicant sent in the application and the premium, she accepted the insurer's offer.

In the case of insurance marketed by a soliciting agent, ordinarily, when the applicant submits an application and the required initial premium, the insurer can accept the applicant's offer by issuance of a policy in accordance with the terms of the application. If such acceptance occurs during the lifetime of the proposed insured, an effective contract results.

---

[1]Riordan v. Automobile Club, 100 Misc. 2d 638, 422 N.Y.S.2d 811 (1979).

Counteroffers

If, in the situation just described, the insurer chooses to issue a policy with different terms than the policy applied for, it is rejecting the applicant's offer and making a counteroffer. The general rule of contract law regarding acceptances is that they must be in accordance with the offer. A purported acceptance which differs from the offer is actually a rejection and counteroffer. For example, if an applicant applies for a policy with a standard premium, and the insurer issues the policy with a higher-than-standard premium,[2] the insurer has rejected the applicant's offer and made a counteroffer.

The insurer's counteroffer must be accepted by the applicant before there will be a contract. Therefore, if the proposed insured dies before the counteroffer has been accepted, there is no contract, and no death benefits will be payable.

The law in counteroffer situations is summarized in one case as follows:

The company reserved the right to accept or reject the proposition contained in the application.

"The application being a mere proposal to the company, it can either accept the proposal, decline it altogether or impose such conditions as to the making of the contract, as it may choose." McCully's Admr. v. Phoenix Mutual Life Insurance Co., 18 W. Va. 782 . . .

In this case the insurance company's reply to the application was the sending of a policy, differing in essential terms from that applied for, to the Wheeling Branch Office. This amounted to a counter-proposition and there was no contract, no meeting of the minds of the parties on the new terms, without acceptance thereof by [the applicant].[3]

Withdrawal of the Application

Until there has been an acceptance of the offer, an offeror has a right to withdraw the offer. Therefore, if, before the insurer has accepted an applicant's offer, the applicant tells the insurer that he or she withdraws the application, the offer terminates. It will not matter that the premium has been submitted.[4] The insurer must return it.

Rejection of the Application

An insurance contract, like other contracts, rests on the assent of the parties. An insurer does not ordinarily have a duty to accept an application.

---

[2]A rated policy, in insurance terminology.
[3]Kronjaeger v. Travelers Ins. Co., 124 W. Va. 730, 22 S.E.2d 689 (1942).
[4]Wheelock v. Clark, 21 Wyo. 300, 131 P. 35 (1913).

It can reject the application for any reason or even without a reason.[5] As with most general rules, this rule has exceptions. Statutes or regulations may prohibit denial of insurance on the basis of mental or physical impairment, sex, marital status, or sexual preference.

Signature on the Application

Generally, the insurer requires that the application be signed by the applicant. When this is so, failure to sign the application precludes the making of a contract. Ordinarily, the applicant must sign personally. However, if the application has been signed by another person at the direction of the applicant, and the insurer's agent knows this, it will usually result in a contract binding on the insurer.[6]

DELAY IN ACTING ON THE APPLICATION

The general rule is that silence on the part of an offeree will not be interpreted as an acceptance. Nevertheless, as to insurers, the majority of courts which have considered the point have held that an insurer must act with reasonable promptness when it receives an application.[7] In a few states, contract liability will be imposed if the insurer does not act promptly. In nearly one third of the states, tort liability will be imposed.

Contract Liability for Unreasonable Delay

The weight of authority is that silence and inaction by the insurer do not result in an acceptance of the applicant's offer. Some courts have stated that where there is a delay, the applicant should infer a rejection and act accordingly.

A few courts, however, have held that an unreasonable delay in passing upon an application gives rise to an implied acceptance by the insurer. A few others have held that where the initial premium is submitted along with the application, and there is such a delay, retention of the premium is inconsistent with rejection of the risk. For this reason, there will be an implied acceptance.

---

[5]Mutual Life Ins. Co. v. Young's Adm'r, 90 U.S. (23 Wall.) 85 (1874); Reynolds v. Guarantee Reserve Life Ins. Co., 44 Ill. App. 3d 764, 358 N.E.2d 940 (1976); Kimbro v. New York Life Ins. Co., 134 Iowa 84, 108 N.W. 1025 (1906); Lechler v. Montana Life Ins. Co., 48 N.D. 644, 186 N.W. 271 (1921).

[6]Thornburg v. Farmers Life Ass'n, 122 Iowa 260, 98 N.W. 105 (1904); Somers v. Kansas Protective Union, 42 Kan. 619, 22 P. 702 (1889).

[7]Annot., 32 A.L.R. 2d 487 (1953).

Illustrative of this point of view is the discussion of the Michigan Supreme Court in the case of *Wadsworth v. New York Life Insurance Co.*[8] That case dealt with an application for life insurance by a captain in the United States Air Force who paid the first full premium in cash at the time of application. He was lost in action in the Korean War before the application was approved. The court discusses the effect of delay in considering the application as follows:

> Appellant [the beneficiary] contends in her second issue that a contract arose as a matter of law through defendant's [the insurer's] unreasonable delay in acceptance or rejection of the application filed by the deceased. . . .
>
> Michigan, it appears, is among the minority of States in holding that there is a duty on the part of the insurance company to act with reasonable promptness. In Robinson v. United States Benevolent Society, 132 Mich. 695, at page 699, 94 N.W. 211, at page 212, this Court stated:
>
> "In insurance contracts of this character it is the duty of the company to act with reasonable promptness. Failing to reject within reasonable time, the law implies an acceptance . . ."
>
> We do not know what other facts may be shown on retrial but where, as currently shown in the record before us, substantial delay in accepting or rejecting is coupled with retention of the first and succeeding premiums, the question of whether or not there was such unreasonable delay on the part of the defendant or its agent as to imply acceptance would be a question of fact for the jury.

Although this discussion is phrased primarily in terms of contract law, the statement that there is a duty on the part of the insurer to act with reasonable promptness brings an element of tort liability into the analysis.

Since delay can mislead the applicant to his or her harm, the insurer has been estopped to deny acceptance in a few cases. For example, if an insured had been induced to believe that his application would be accepted and in reliance on the representations made to him refrained from obtaining other insurance, the insurer might be estopped to deny that it had accepted the application.[9]

Tort Liability for Unreasonable Delay

An unreasonable delay in acting on an application can subject the insurer to tort damages for negligence in some jurisdictions.[10] A tort is a wrongful act

---

[8] 349 Mich. 240, 84 N.W.2d 513 (1957).

[9] Zielinski v. General Am. Life Ins. Co., 96 S.W.2d 1059 (Mo. Ct. App. 1936).

[10] Duffy v. Banker's Life Ass'n, 160 Iowa 19, 139 N.W. 1087 (1913); Continental Life & Acci. Co. v. Songer, 124 Ariz. 294, 603 P.2d 921 (Ariz. Ct. App. 1979); Smith v. Minnesota Mut. Life Ins. Co., 86 Cal. App. 2d 581, 195 P.2d 457 (1948); Boyer v. State Farmers' Mut. Hail Ins. Co., 86 Kan. 442, 121 P. 329 (1912); Witten v. Beacon Life Ass'n, 225 Mo. App. 110, 33 S.W.2d 989 (1931); Fox v. Volunteer State Life Ins. Co., 185 N.C. 121, 116 S.E. 266 (1923),

or omission, not arising out of a contractual relationship, causing harm to another person and giving the other person a cause of action for money damages. A suit of this kind is called an action in tort. It is based on a legal duty of the defendant, the defendant's violation of that duty (usually through negligence), and resulting harm to the plaintiff. For example, where A negligently operates an automobile and collides with an automobile driven by B, A can be liable in tort for any harm to B's car or person. A has a legal duty to drive with reasonable care.

A tort liability doctrine for an insurer's unreasonable delay in acting on an application has developed in nearly one third of the states. This doctrine is based on the premise that when an insurer receives an application, it has a duty to act on the application with reasonable promptness. If the insurer fails to do so, it can be liable in tort damages up to the amount that would have been recoverable under the policy. Courts which take this position concede that most business organizations have no comparable duty but maintain that, because insurance is affected with a public interest and insurers operate under a state franchise, an insurer has a duty to accept or reject an application within a reasonable length of time.

A nearly equal number of states have rejected this tort liability doctrine on the grounds that insurers are not public utilities and that a duty to consider applications promptly should not be imposed upon them. One of the earliest rejections of the tort liability doctrine was voiced in 1929 by the Supreme Court of Mississippi in the case of *Savage v. Prudential Life Insurance Co.*[11] There the court said:

> The fact that the insurance companies are granted a franchise to do business in this state does not and should not impose upon them the duty to consider promptly all who offer to them the risk of insuring their lives, no more than would be required of a bank to lend money promptly to all who should make application and suffer loss while the bank was negligent in determining whether or not it would accept the offer and enter into a contract.

A discussion of the tort liability doctrine by the North Dakota Supreme Court reads as follows:

> Insurance is a contract, which, like other contracts, results only from an offer and acceptance of the offer. There is a conflict in the authorities as to whether legal obligations arise only after a contract of insurance has been made, or whether in certain circumstances a legal duty arises, from the relationship created during the negotiations between an applicant for insurance and the insurance company, to act promptly upon the application, and to inform the applicant whether the offer is accepted or re-

---

later appealed, 186 N.C. 763, 119 S.E. 172 (1923); Peddicord v. Prudential Ins. Co. of Am., 498 P.2d 1388 (Okla. 1972).

[11]154 Miss. 89, 121 So. 487 (1929).

jected. Generally speaking, there are two main lines of decisions dealing with these questions. According to one view, the legal relations between an applicant and the insurance company "are fundamentally the same as those between parties negotiating any other contract, and are 'purely contractual'"; that "mere delay, mere inaction by an insurance company in passing on an application does not constitute an acceptance or establish the relationship of insurer and insured," and that such delay or inaction does not constitute any breach of duty by the insurance company. . . . According to this view, no duty arises unless, and until, a contract has been created; if there is no contract, there is no duty, and consequently there is no liability on the part of the insurer because of any delay or inaction on its part in passing upon the application, or in issuing or delivering the policy.

* * * * *

The other line of decisions holds that an insurance company that has solicited and received a completed application for insurance is under a legal duty to take prompt action on the application, and give prompt notice to the applicant of its action; and that consequently such insurance company is liable in tort for negligent delay in acting upon the application and notifying the applicant in case the application is rejected. . . .[12]

The theory that imposes tort liability has been severely criticized by many insurance spokesmen and lawyers. Although the tort theory became popular in the 1920s, this popularity has since diminished, and, in the recent years, there has been little change in the number of states in which the doctrine has been adopted or rejected. The widespread use of premium receipts providing temporary insurance has no doubt played an important part in slowing what once appeared to be a popular trend. Nevertheless, where there is a conditional premium receipt, but the insurer rejects the application after death of the insured, if there has been delay there can be tort liability in some states. Moreover, in 1979, an Arizona appellate court said that damages for negligent delay in passing on an insurance application need not be restricted to the amount which would have been paid if the contract had existed, but could include damages for emotional distress and punitive damages.[13] Because of these various theories of liability, insurers are well advised to act on applications with reasonable promptness.

PREMIUM RECEIPTS

A premium receipt is given to an applicant when the applicant submits the initial premium along with the application. Usually, such a receipt includes a contract providing temporary insurance. This section contains a de-

---

[12]Bekken v. Equitable Life Assur. Soc'y of the United States, 70 N.D. 122, 293 N.W. 200 (1940).

[13]Continental Life & Acci. Co. v. Songer, 124 Ariz. 294, 603 P.2d 921 (Ariz. App. 1979).

scription of various types of contracts included in premium receipts, and the law governing these contracts.

There is nearly always some time between the date the application is submitted and the date the policy is effective. During this period, the death of the proposed insured will not ordinarily be covered without a premium receipt providing temporary insurance, even if the initial premium has been paid. Therefore, it is apparent that it would be to the advantage of the applicant and beneficiary if insurance could be provided during the period in which the underwriting procedures were being completed. It is just as clearly to the advantage of the agent and the insurer to provide such insurance. Without it, there is no compelling reason for the applicant to pay the initial premium before the policy is delivered. If the premium is not prepaid, the agent frequently has to make the sale twice—once when the application is taken and later when the policy is delivered. Often, it is difficult or impossible to make the sale the second time. Moreover, when the premium has been submitted, the applicant is less likely to continue to shop around for life insurance. The use of a premium receipt providing temporary insurance gives the soliciting agent a strong argument in his or her attempt to persuade the applicant to pay the initial premium at the time the application is completed.

Without a premium receipt providing temporary insurance, a difficult situation for the agent arises if the applicant pays the initial premium with the application, and the proposed insured dies before the policy becomes effective. The agent is then in the unhappy position of having to tell the beneficiary that, although the insurer had the premium in its possession during the intervening period, no insurance was in force.

For these reasons, life insurers began at an early date to experiment with ways to provide insurance during the period that an application was being considered. This made life insurance practices more consistent with practices followed in other lines of insurance where coverage often is made effective immediately, subject to the insurer's right to cancel later if the application is found not to be acceptable.

Where there is a premium receipt providing temporary insurance, the agent is authorized to extend the insurer's offer to make the insurance effective on a date prior to the issuance or delivery of a policy, if conditions specified in the premium receipt are met. The applicant accepts this offer by performing the act requested by the insurer—paying the premium at the time the application is submitted—and thereby creates a contract. The performance of the temporary insurance contract by the insurer—that is, the payment of benefits—will depend on whether the conditions in the premium receipt have been fulfilled.

Ordinarily, a premium receipt states that the temporary insurance contract is subject to the terms of the applied-for policy. Thus, for example, if there were a suicide exclusion in the applied-for policy, and the proposed insured committed suicide while the temporary insurance contract was in effect, no benefits would be payable. A material misrepresentation in the application will allow the insurer to avoid liability under the temporary insurance contract, just as it will under the policy itself.

Where there is a difference between the terms of the temporary insurance contract and the terms of the policy, however, the terms of the temporary insurance contract control. For example, if the temporary insurance contract limits the benefits to $50,000, and the insured dies while the temporary insurance contract is in effect, no more than $50,000 will be payable. It will not matter that the applied-for policy provides higher benefits.

Although the wording of temporary insurance contracts in premium receipts varies a great deal, three distinct types of premium receipts have been recognized: the approval premium receipt, the insurability premium receipt, and the binding premium receipt. The approval premium receipt and the insurability premium receipt are often called conditional premium receipts. That is, they will not provide temporary insurance unless certain conditions occur. Two types of conditions—conditions precedent and conditions subsequent—are discussed below. All premium receipts providing temporary insurance involve one or the other.

Conditions Precedent and Conditions Subsequent

The word *precedent* means "coming before." A condition precedent is an uncertain event which must occur before a right arises. For example, the death of an insured is an uncertain event which must occur before the beneficiary's right to the death benefit arises. Other uncertain events (conditions) also must occur before the beneficiary has a right to the death benefit. The life insurance policy must be in force on the date of the insured's death. Notice and proof of death must be provided to the insurer.

Another way to view a condition precedent is that it is an uncertain event which must occur before the duty to perform a promise arises. Thus, the death of the insured is a condition precedent to the duty of the insurer to pay the death benefit.

The word *subsequent* means "following after." A condition subsequent is an event which cancels an existing right. For example, if a policy contains a provision that the beneficiary cannot bring suit on the policy after two years from the date of loss, the expiration of the two-year period will ordinarily cancel the beneficiary's right to maintain an action on the policy. The expiration of the two-year period is the occurrence of a condition subsequent.

Simply stated, the occurrence of a condition precedent gives rise to a right; the occurrence of a condition subsequent cancels an existing right. The relationship of conditions precedent and conditions subsequent to premium receipts will be explained in the following analyses of conditional and binding premium receipts.

Approval Premium Receipts

The approval premium receipt is one type of conditional premium receipt. Where an approval premium receipt is issued, if the proposed insured dies after the receipt is given, but before the insurer approves the risk, there is no insurance. The temporary insurance contract in this type of premium receipt gives the applicant very little protection, as it provides temporary insurance only from the date of approval of the risk until the date the policy is issued or delivered. At one time, the approval premium receipt was probably the most commonly used conditional premium receipt, but because it unnecessarily restricts temporary insurance, it has largely been replaced by the insurability premium receipt.

The effectiveness of temporary insurance under the approval premium receipt is subject to the occurrence of a condition precedent. That is, before the right to receive the death benefit arises, the risk must be approved by the insurer.

Insurability Premium Receipts

A typical insurability premium receipt provides that temporary insurance will become effective on the later of the date of the receipt, or of any required investigation or medical examination, on condition that the proposed insured is found to have been insurable on the date of the receipt. There is usually a limitation as to the amount which will be payable under the agreement in the receipt. An illustrative insurability premium receipt is found in Figure 6–1.

Where an insurability premium receipt is given and the proposed insured dies before the policy itself is effective, insurability as of the date of death can be determined after the death. Therefore, the insured does have significantly more coverage than if there were no temporary insurance.

To illustrate, suppose James Diebold completes and signs an application for a $50,000 policy from the Ajax Life Insurance Company and submits the initial premium along with the application. Ellen Ludlum, the soliciting agent, issues an insurability premium receipt and forwards the application to the home office.

By completing the application and paying the initial premium, Mr. Diebold has accepted the offer of temporary life insurance from the Ajax Life Insurance Company made by agent Ludlum. Insurance will become effective under the temporary life insurance contract if Mr. Diebold is found to have been insurable. The condition—that the proposed insured be found to have been insurable—is a condition precedent. It must have occurred before insurance becomes effective. That is, the condition must have occurred before the right to death benefits arises under the temporary insurance contract.

FIGURE 6–1   Insurability Premium Receipt

A. The face of the receipt

RECEIVED FROM _____ , Applicant,
Name of Proposed Insured
if other than Applicant _____

$\left(\begin{matrix}\text{Amount of cash}\\\text{settlement received}\end{matrix}\right)$ $ .... in connection with the initial
premium for the proposed insurance for which an application is this day made
to the Ajax Life Insurance Company.

   Life Insurance and any additional benefits in the amount applied for (but
not exceeding a maximum liability of $50,000, including all additional benefits
on all pending applications to the company combined) shall be deemed to
take effect as of the date of this receipt, subject to the terms and conditions
printed on the reverse side hereof.

   The amount of settlement received shall be refunded if the application is
declined or if a policy is issued other than as applied for and is not accepted.
Any check, draft, or moneyorder is received subject to collection.

_____   _____

   Date of Receipt   Signature of Agent

B. The back of the receipt

   Subject to the limitations of this receipt and the terms and conditions of
the policy that may be issued by the company on the basis of the application,
the life insurance and any additional benefits applied for shall not be deemed
to take effect unless the company, after investigation and such medical examination, if any, as it may require, shall be satisfied that on the date of this
receipt each person proposed for insurance was insurable for the *amount* of
life insurance and any additional benefits applied for according to the company's rules and practice of selection; provided, however, that approval by
the company of the insurability of the Proposed Insured for a plan of insurance other than that applied for, or the denial of any particular additional
benefit applied for, shall not invalidate the terms and conditions for this receipt relating to life insurance and any other additional benefit applied for.

(Not to be detached unless issued under the requirements for using Conditional Receipt)

   Where the Condition Has Occurred.   Suppose risk appraisal personnel
in the issuing office of the insurer review the application, the inspection report, and the medical examiner's report and find that Mr. Diebold does, in
fact, meet their risk appraisal requirements. An authorized officer then approves the issuance of a policy on the exact plan and in the same amount

applied for by Mr. Diebold. Suppose that this officer has just approved and initialed the application when the telephone rings.

It is agent Ludlum calling long distance to say that on the previous day Mr. Diebold was struck by a hit-and-run driver while crossing the street. Mr. Diebold died in the ambulance on his way to the hospital. Was he insured? The determination of Mr. Diebold's insurability and the decision on the part of the appropriate officer, even after Mr. Diebold's death, that a policy can be issued will put the temporary insurance contract into effect. The condition has occurred, and Mr. Diebold was insured under the temporary insurance contract as of a date prior to his death.

Generally, under insurability receipts, if the insurability of the proposed insured has not been evaluated at the time of death, the insurer is required to evaluate it afterwards. This evaluation must be made in good faith and in accordance with the insurer's own insurability rules.

Where the Condition Has Not Occurred.   Suppose now that agent Ludlum mails the application and the premium check to the insurer, orders an inspection report, and arranges for a medical examination. Suppose also that the risk appraiser reviews the documents and finds that Mr. Diebold does not meet the insurer's requirements in accordance with its standard practices of risk selection. The risk appraiser has just made that notation on the application file when the telephone rings, and agent Ludlum reports Mr. Diebold's fatal accident.

It seems clear that in this instance Mr. Diebold is not insured under the terms of the temporary insurance contract. The condition of insurability has not occurred. Even though no notice of disapproval has yet been sent, this can follow the death of the proposed insured. However, the insurer must be prepared to support its decision as to the proposed insured's lack of insurability and to set forth the controlling language of the insurability premium receipt in a court of law if necessary. Even if it succeeds in doing this, the insurer's liability will depend upon the jurisdiction involved, as an increasing number of jurisdictions find that there is coverage, even where the proposed insured was not eligible for the applied-for insurance. This topic will be discussed in the subsection below entitled "Premium Receipts in the Courts."

Binding Premium Receipts

Some insurers use what is appropriately termed a "binding premium receipt." Under a binding premium receipt, temporary insurance becomes effective on the date the receipt is given. Typically, as with conditional premium receipts, there is a limitation as to the amount which will be payable under the contract in the receipt.

The temporary insurance continues for a maximum period of time specified in the receipt or until the insurer acts on the application if this happens earlier. An illustrative binding premium receipt is shown in Figure 6–2.

FIGURE 6–2   Binding Premium Receipt

A. The face of the receipt

Received $_____ (amount) from the Applicant in connection with the life application made this day to the Ajax Life Insurance Company for insurance on the life of _____ (proposed insured) and any others named in the application. Any check or draft is received subject to collection, and, if it is not honored when presented for payment, this receipt is void.

Effective with the date of the application and subject to the terms and conditions on the front and reverse of this receipt, all death benefits applied for shall take effect for death as a result of accidental or natural causes originating after the date of the application. HOWEVER, THE TOTAL DEATH BENEFIT FOR ANY PERSON INSURED UNDER THIS AND ALL OTHER BINDING RECEIPTS AND PENDING APPLICATIONS COMBINED SHALL NOT EXCEED $100,000. IF SUCH PERSON IS UNDER THE AGE OF 15 DAYS AT DEATH, THE TOTAL DEATH BENEFIT SHALL NOT EXCEED $1,000.

Signature

Date of application _____ of agent _____

B. The back of the receipt

Coverage under this receipt shall continue until terminated by the earliest of *(a)* approval of the application, *(b)* notification of disapproval of the application, or *(c)* expiration of a 60–day period beginning with the date of the application. The company reserves the absolute right to disapprove the application by offering to issue a policy with an extra rating or other than as applied for, or by declining to issue a policy. Notification of disapproval of the application shall be given to the proposed insured or to the applicant, if other than the proposed insured, by either *(a)* personal notification or *(b)* mailing of such notification to the last known address, in which case the termination of coverage is effective upon mailing.

Monies received with the application will be refunded if a policy is offered and is not accepted or if the coverage under this receipt is terminated by either *(a)* notification of disapproval without offer of any policy or *(b)* the expiration of the 60-day period beginning with the date of the application.

Coverage under this receipt shall be void if the application contains any material misrepresentation.

NO AGENT OR OTHER COMPANY REPRESENTATIVE MAY WAIVE OR MODIFY THE ANSWER TO ANY QUESTION IN THE APPLICATION OR MODIFY THE TERMS OR CONDITIONS OF THIS RECEIPT.

A binding premium receipt is subject to a condition subsequent. That is, there is an existing right to receive the death benefit which arose at the time the applicant submitted the application and initial premium in exchange for the premium receipt. This right to receive the benefit will be canceled if the proposed insured is found uninsurable.

Binding premium receipts are more to the advantage of the applicant than are conditional receipts, as the coverage under binding receipts is effective immediately on payment of the initial premium. The courts of some jurisdictions have interpreted premium receipts that were meant by insurers to be conditional as if they were binding receipts. For this reason, some insurers have abandoned conditional receipts and now use binding receipts instead. This avoids the legal problems that are continuing to develop for insurers who use conditional receipts. It also has the advantage that binding receipts are easier to explain and more appealing to applicants. The following subsection contains a discussion of court cases interpreting premium receipts.

Premium Receipts in the Courts

Binding premium receipts have not presented the significant legal problems for life insurers that conditional premium receipts have presented. This is true because binding receipts make insurance effective immediately upon payment of the initial premium and, thus, some insurance is usually in effect if the proposed insured dies prior to issuance of the policy.

Binding receipts are subject to a condition subsequent. That is, they provide that the right to receive a death benefit, which is effective on issuance of the receipt, will be canceled after a specified period of time or when action is taken on the application if that happens earlier. Conditional receipts, on the other hand, are subject to a condition precedent. The right to a death benefit arises only on the occurrence of a condition—approval of the application in the case of an approval premium receipt and insurability of the insured in the case of an insurability premium receipt.

Sometimes, an insurer intends a premium receipt to be subject to a condition precedent, but a court interprets the receipt to be subject to a condition subsequent instead. In other words, sometimes a court interprets a receipt as binding when the insurer meant it to be conditional. This requires the payment of a death benefit, even though the application was not approved, or the proposed insured was not insurable.

Until recently, a clear majority of the courts that had considered questions involving conditional receipts had upheld the conditions intended by the insurer. Unless the wording was definitely ambiguous, it was usually held to express a condition precedent with the result that no insurance was effective unless the condition had occurred.

Indeed, many courts still take this position. For example, in a 1971 Maryland case, the court held that an applicant must meet the insurer's objective test of insurability in order to have coverage under a conditional premium receipt.[14]

There is, however, a strong trend in the courts toward interpreting conditional receipts as if they were binding. The courts that have done so have based their decisions on ambiguity in the premium receipt in some instances. In other instances, they have based the decision on the doctrine that the reasonable expectations of the applicant must be honored and that an average applicant would expect temporary insurance to be immediate and unconditional. In still others, the decision has been based on unconscionability or public policy.

The leading case interpreting a conditional receipt as if it were binding is *Gaunt v. John Hancock Mutual Life Insurance Co.*[15] This case was decided by a federal court of appeals in 1947. An approval premium receipt was involved. The proposed insured was insurable, but the application was not approved before he died. A famous judge, Learned Hand, stated the following in the *Gaunt* opinion:

> [T]he application was not to be submitted to underwriters; it was to go to persons [applicants] utterly unacquainted with the niceties of life insurance, who would read it colloquially. It is the understanding of such persons that counts . . .
>
> [T]he ordinary applicant who has paid his first premium and has successfully passed his physical examination, would not by the remotest chance understand the clause as leaving him uncovered until the insurer at its leisure approved the risk; he would assume that he was getting immediate coverage for his money. . . .
>
> [I]nsurers who seek to impose upon words of common speech an esoteric significance intelligible only to their craft, must bear the burden of any resulting confusion. We can think of few situations where that canon is more appropriate than in such a case as this.

Another important conditional receipt case, decided in 1954 by the California Supreme Court, is *Ransom v. Penn Mutual Life Insurance Co.*[16] *Ransom* was the first of the California line of cases construing conditional receipts as binding. The premium receipt involved was an insurability receipt. The court stated the following in the *Ransom* opinion:

> We must determine whether a contract of insurance arose immediately upon receipt by defendant [the insurer] of the completed application with the premium payment, subject to the right of defendant to terminate the agreement if it subsequently concluded that Ransom was not acceptable, or whether, as defendant contends, its satisfaction as to Ransom's ac-

---

[14]Cannon v. Southland Life Ins. Co., 263 Md. 463, 283 A.2d 404 (Md. 1971).

[15]160 F.2d 599 (2d Cir. 1947), *cert. denied*, 331 U.S. 849 (1947).

[16]43 Cal. 2d 420, 274 P.2d 633 (1954).

ceptability for insurance was a condition precedent to the existence of any contract.

* * * * *

> We are of the view that a contract of insurance arose upon defendant's receipt of the completed application and the first premium payment. The clause quoted above is subject to the interpretation that the applicant is offered a choice of either paying his first premium when he signs the application, in which event "the insurance shall be in force . . . from the date . . . of the application," or of paying upon receipt of the policy," in which event "no insurance shall be in force until . . . the policy is delivered." The understanding of an ordinary person is the standard which must be used in construing the contract, and such a person upon reading the application would believe that he would secure the benefit of immediate coverage by paying the premium in advance of delivery of the policy. There is an obvious advantage to the company in obtaining payment of the premium when the application is made, and it would be unconscionable to permit the company, after using language to induce payment of the premium at that time, to escape the obligation which an ordinary applicant would reasonably believe had been undertaken by the insurer. Moreover, defendant drafted the clause, and had it wished to make clear that its satisfaction was a condition precedent to a contract, it could easily have done so by using unequivocal terms. While some of the language tends to support the company's position, it does no more than produce an ambiguity, and the ambiguity must be resolved against defendant.

Thus, ambiguity, the applicant's reasonable expectations, and unconscionability were all bases used by the court to interpret the *Ransom* premium receipt as binding rather than conditional.

In 1975, the California Supreme Court, in *Smith v. Westland Life Insurance Co.*,[17] held that where the insurer has received an application and initial premium, there is a contract of insurance created immediately. Again, a conditional premium receipt was involved. The applicant had been rejected as a standard risk, and a substandard policy had been issued. The applicant refused to accept this policy. He was killed before the insurer returned the initial premium. The *Smith* court stated that the contract of insurance which had arisen could only be terminated by actual rejection of the application and notice of that rejection to the applicant, and refund of the initial premium. The benefits were, therefore, payable.

The supreme courts of some other states have interpreted conditional receipts to be binding. In 1965, the New Jersey Supreme Court decided *Allen v. Metropolitan Life Insurance Co.*[18] Again, a conditional premium receipt had been issued. The court held that the receipt was binding because of ambiguity, because of the applicant's reasonable expectations, and because of public policy. The court said:

---

[17]15 Cal. 3d 111, 123 Cal. Rptr. 649, 539 P.2d 433 (1975).
[18]44 N.J. 294, 208 A.2d 638 (1965).

In the life insurance field premium receipts have presented considerable difficulty and have been dealt with by the courts throughout the country in varying fashions. . . .

Much of the difficulty may be laid at the doorstep of the life insurance industry itself for, despite repeated cautions from the courts, it has persisted in using language which is obscure to the layman and in tolerating agency practices which are calculated to lead the layman to believe that he has coverage beyond which may be called for by a literal reading. The reports are replete with instances where company agents, as here, obtained payment of the full annual premium in advance on the broad representation that there would be interim coverage pending the company's investigation of the application and its action thereon. . . . Indeed, the very acceptance of the premium in advance tends naturally towards the understanding of immediate coverage though it be temporary and terminable; any collateral advantage other than interim coverage is insubstantial and is not what the lay applicant is generally seeking by his advance payment.

The Nevada Supreme Court took a harsh view of conditional receipts in a 1967 case.[19] There the court said:

A conditional receipt tends to encourage deception. We do not mean to imply affirmative misconduct by the soliciting insurance agent. We suggest only that if nothing is said about the complicated and legalistic phrasing of the receipt, and the agent accepts an application for insurance together with the first premium payment, the applicant has reason to believe that he is insured. Otherwise, he is deceived.

In 1971, the Idaho Supreme Court declared that the use of conditional premium receipts "borders on the unconscionable."[20] The Kansas Supreme Court in 1972 declared that:

[W]hen an application for life insurance is made and the company receives the initial premium and issues a receipt therefor, a policy of temporary insurance is created and said policy of temporary insurance continues in effect until the insurance company declines the application, notifies the insured, and returns the premium, notwithstanding the provisions of the application and the receipt to the contrary.[21]

Finally, in 1978, the Pennsylvania Supreme Court implied that conditional receipts are against the public policy of Pennsylvania.[22] There the court said:

---

[19]Prudential Ins. Co. of Am. v. Lamme, 83 Nev. 146, 425 P.2d 346 (1967).

[20]Toevs v. Western Farm Bureau Life Ins. Co., 94 Idaho 151, 483 P.2d 682 (1971).

[21]Tripp v. Reliable Life Ins. Co., 210 Kan. 33, 499 P.2d 1155 (1972).

[22]Collister v. Nationwide Life Ins. Co., 479 Pa. 579, 388 A.2d 1346 (1978), *cert. denied,* 439 U.S. 1089 (1979).

The insurance industry is regulated by the Commonwealth in order to provide protection to the insurance buying public. . . . If . . . the insurer wishes to enjoy the substantial benefits it receives by securing the customer's cash at the time of the taking of the application, it must return what the customer can reasonably expect that the insurer is selling: i.e., immediate coverage. Alternatively, the insurer could inform the prospective applicant, *before any money changes hands,* that it does not intend to give the customer anything in return for advance payment, and that the customer is actually paying money now for nothing because no insurance will take effect until approval. Such notification would have to be given *before* the consumer paid the initial premium in order to avoid placing that consumer at the psychological disadvantage of having to ask for a return of the premium if he or she is dissatisfied with such terms. Furthermore, any such notice must be made in a manner calculated to bring the facts of the transaction—that the customer is paying money now, but getting nothing until later—to the customer's attention in no uncertain terms. As such, the notice could not be printed on a receipt.

There was a vigorous dissent in this case. The dissenting judge stated the following:

I must confess that the strained argument of the majority strikes me as a complete tour de force. While the doctrine of "reasonable expectations" has found acceptance and indeed has validity in some situations in insurance litigation, it has no place in the case at bar. The idea of recognizing "reasonable expectations" of an applicant or an insured does not mean that a claimant on a policy is entitled to every benefit imaginable within a contractual framework. Rather, the approach is an equitable one, meant to guard against the use of complex and confusing qualifications and exceptions by insurers to defeat the reasonable expectations of the average layman entering into an insurance transaction.

Thus, the dispute over the propriety of conditional premium receipts continues. The uncertainty this has created for insurers has led some to use binding receipts. Another possible solution to the dilemma is for the insurer to collect the initial premium only when the policy is delivered. This, of course, has the disadvantage that the agent often must resell the policy.

A number of other legal problems can arise in connection with conditional premium receipts. There have been instances where a soliciting agent did not deliver a conditional premium receipt to the applicant, because the agent preferred to have the receipt in his or her possession in the event the application was declined or a rated policy issued. The legal effect of this practice might be to leave the applicant without temporary insurance, even though the proposed insured was insurable, and the policy was approved. However, some life insurers in a situation of this kind treat the temporary insurance as if the receipt had been issued. Their theory is that, merely because the agent did not follow instructions, the applicant or beneficiary should not be penalized for that failure.

Another situation which can cause problems occurs where a medical examination has not been required at the time of application, is later requested by the underwriter, but has not been performed prior to the proposed insured's death. In some cases, the courts have held that the medical examination was a condition precedent that did not occur, and the temporary insurance, therefore, did not become effective. In other instances, the requirement has been held not to be a condition precedent, and the temporary insurance was, therefore, effective.

Statutes and Regulations Governing Premium Receipts

A few states have statutes or regulations governing premium receipts. California has sought to reduce conditional premium receipt problems by enacting a statute requiring that the claim be paid where the proposed insured dies prior to the date the application is approved, if he or she was insurable and if the initial premium was submitted with the application. It does not matter whether or not a premium receipt was issued.[23]

RISK CLASSIFICATION AND SELECTION

Risk classification means the insurer's identification of people with similar loss potential and placement of those people in the same risk group for the purpose of setting premium rates. Age, sex, health, occupation, and hobbies are criteria used in risk classification.

Risk selection means the insurer's choice from among its proposed insureds those persons it is willing to insure. Selection of life insurance risks is ordinarily done by underwriters in the insurer's home office. Soliciting agents do not have the authority to pass upon the insurability of a proposed insured. The reason for this is that the life insurance contract, unlike most other types of insurance contracts, cannot ordinarily be canceled by the insurer. Therefore, life insurance risks must be selected with great care.

Discrimination

One meaning of the word *discriminate* is "to note differences." All risk classification involves discrimination in this sense of the word. Young people are charged less for insurance on their lives than older people. Healthy people pay less than those with impaired health, and those few with very impaired health may not be insurable at all. Persons in hazardous occupations pay more than persons in safe occupations. Women—who as a group live seven years longer than men—pay less than men for insurance on their lives, but

---

[23]CAL. INS. CODE § 10,115 (West 1972).

more for annuities. Each person pays according to the risk he or she presents. Classifying and pricing risks is the very essence of insurance.

The states have passed laws prohibiting unfair discrimination. For example, the New York insurance law, which is typical, provides that no life insurer "shall make or permit any unfair discrimination between individuals of the same class and of equal expectation of life" in premiums, terms, benefits, or dividends.[24] Note that this law prohibits *unfair* discrimination, not discrimination itself. Under these laws, fairness means equal treatment for equal risk.

Unfair Handicap Discrimination.   Unfair discrimination among applicants on the basis of handicap has been a concern of legislators and regulators. In 1979 the National Association of Insurance Commissioners (NAIC) adopted a Model Regulation on Unfair Discrimination in Life and Health Insurance on the Basis of Physical or Mental Impairment. The purpose of this model regulation is to prohibit refusal or limitation of coverage or rate differences based solely on physical or mental impairment unless the refusal, limitation, or rate difference is based on sound actuarial principles or on experience. About one half of the states now have statutes or regulations prohibiting discrimination against handicapped persons.

Unfair Sex Discrimination.   In 1976, the NAIC adopted a Model Regulation to Eliminate Unfair Sex Discrimination. Some states have patterned their regulations after this model regulation, while others already had regulations similar to the model. The majority of states now have regulations, insurance laws, or equal rights provisions in their constitutions which prohibit unfair discrimination because of sex.

Limitations on Liberty of Contract

Under the general law of contracts, each person has the right to choose the contracts she or he is willing to enter into, and the persons with whom she or he is willing to contract. Generally speaking, therefore, an insurer has the right to accept or reject an applicant's offer to contract, and the right to insure a proposed insured at a standard rate, a substandard rate, or not at all. However, there are limitations on this general rule of liberty of contract as it applies to insurers. These limitations have increased in recent years.

Two limitations on insurers' liberty of contract which have been of particular concern to the insurance industry are mandatory unisex insurance rates and restrictions on the right of insurers to determine if a proposed insured has been infected with the AIDS virus. These limitations will be discussed below.

---

[24]N.Y. Ins. Law § 4224(a) (McKinney 1983).

Mandatory Unisex Rates. In 1983, the United States Supreme Court in *Arizona Governing Committee v. Norris*[25] ruled that the use of gender-based actuarial tables in a life annuity option of an employer's pension plan violates the federal Civil Rights Act of 1964. Title VII of the Civil Rights Act of 1964 forbids discrimination in employment. Natalie Norris, an employee of the state of Arizona, received a smaller life annuity upon retirement than a male would have received in identical circumstances. Arizona pointed out that all insurers through which it could offer a life annuity used gender-based actuarial tables, and that the state did not intend to discriminate. Nevertheless, the United States Supreme Court ruled in favor of Natalie Norris.

The *Norris* case involved only an employment practice. It does not prevent insurers from using gender-based annuity tables. However, insurers did begin to provide products with unisex rates to enable their employer-clients to comply with the *Norris* decision. The NAIC designed a regulation which permits insurers to use sex-blended tables and most states have adopted this regulation.

Prior to the *Norris* decision, a few states mandated that automobile insurance be priced the same for men and women. After *Norris,* Congress and legislatures of many states considered mandatory unisex rates for all insurance lines, but only Montana has actually enacted such a statute.[26] A 1987 Massachusetts insurance department regulation and a 1988 Pennsylvania lower court decision which would result in unisex rates for all insurance lines were being contested as this book went to press.

Most insurers have steadfastly opposed unisex insurance rates. Insurance industry spokespersons argue that the use of gender for classifying insureds is not unfair discrimination, but rather allows insurance costs to more accurately reflect risks. Statistical and actuarial data have clearly established that, as a group, women live significantly longer than men. A mortality table is a display of death rates by age. It can be much refined by taking gender into consideration also.

Underwriting for AIDS. Health is one of the principal risk factors insurers take into account in pricing individual life insurance. The life insurance application ordinarily contains questions about the proposed insured's history of such illnesses as cancer, heart disease, hypertension, diabetes, and strokes. The insurer also might require an attending physician's statement, hospital records, a physical examination, various blood and urine tests, and an electrocardiogram.

Persons with the AIDS antibody are uninsurable because of the high risk of morbidity and early mortality that they present. Moreover, those who learn that they have the AIDS antibody are apt to seek insurance. If insurers can-

---

[25]463 U.S. 1073 (1983).
[26]MONT. CODE ANN. § 49–2–309 (1987).

not test for the AIDS antibody, and ask questions aimed at determining if the applicant has been infected with the AIDS virus, antiselection will occur, resulting in a dramatic rise in premiums for all insureds.

In most states, such tests and questions are permitted, but in some they have been restricted or even forbidden. In the District of Columbia all tests for the AIDS antibody are forbidden, and, as a result, most life insurers have ceased to issue new policies there. California has a law which forbids the use of AIDS antibody tests. The New York and Massachusetts Insurance Departments have attempted to restrict AIDS antibody testing by regulation. There has been a great deal of lobbying both by those who oppose and those who favor AIDS antibody testing by insurers, and there have been numerous lawsuits involving testing issues. This struggle will almost certainly continue.

Nonsmoker Premium Discounts

There is proof that cigarette smoking substantially increases the risk of early death—by as much as eight years for young people who smoke two packages of cigarettes a day. Therefore, many life insurers offer nonsmoker premium discounts to persons who have not smoked for some period of time, usually a year. The lower premium charged nonsmokers may tempt some proposed insureds to deny their smoking habit. For this reason, some insurers are testing for byproducts of smoking—often by measuring nicotine in urine—in addition to asking about smoking on the application.

In 1988, the United States Court of Appeals for the Second Circuit ruled in *Mutual Benefit Life Insurance Co. v. JMR Electronics Corp.*[27] that a misrepresentation concerning the proposed insured's history of cigarette smoking, made in an application for a nonsmoker policy, was material as a matter of law and entitled the insurer to rescind the policy. In 1985, JMR Electronics Corp. (JMR) applied for a key man life insurance policy on the life of its president, Joseph Gaon. Mr. Gaon represented in the application that he had never smoked cigarettes, and the insurer issued a life policy at nonsmoker rates. Mr. Gaon died within the policy's contestable period. In the course of investigating the claim for the death benefits, the insurer discovered that Mr. Gaon had smoked half a pack of cigarettes a day for at least 10 years. The district court ordered rescission of the policy and the return of the premiums paid by JMR, with interest.

In affirming the district court's decision, the court of appeals rejected the contention of the beneficiary, JMR, that the proper remedy would have been to allow JMR to recover the amount of benefits the premiums would have purchased at the smoker rate. The court stated the following:

> There is no doubt that Mutual was induced to issue the non-smoker, discounted-premium policy to JMR precisely as a result of the misrepresen-

---

[27]848 F.2d 30 (2d Cir. 1988).

tations made by Gaon concerning his smoking history. That Mutual might not have refused the risk on *any* terms had it known the undisclosed facts is irrelevant. Most risks are insurable at some price. The purpose of the materiality inquiry is not to permit the jury to rewrite the terms of the insurance agreement to conform to the newly disclosed facts but to make certain that the risk insured was the risk covered by the policy agreed upon. If a fact is material to the risk, the insurer may avoid liability under a policy if that fact was misrepresented in an application for that policy whether or not the parties might have agreed to some other contractual arrangement had the critical fact been disclosed. As observed by Judge Sweet, a contrary result would reward the practice of misrepresenting facts critical to the underwriter's task because the unscrupulous (or merely negligent) applicant "would have everything to gain and nothing to lose" from making material misrepresentations in his application for insurance. Such a claimant could rest assured not only that he may demand full coverage should he survive the contestability period, . . . , but that even in the event of a contested claim, he would be entitled to the coverage that he might have contracted for had the necessary information been accurately disclosed at the outset. New York law does not permit this anomalous result.

INSURABLE INTEREST

The requirement of an insurable interest goes back to the early 18th century in England. At that time, life insurance policies were not applied for by, and issued to, the persons whose lives were to be insured. Rather, they were applied for by, and issued to, third persons. The insureds were merely subjects of the insurance. Often, an insured did not know the person who had obtained the insurance or that insurance had been effected on his or her life.

Naturally, this arrangement was subject to abuses. At one time, it was a sport to wager that public figures would or would not live for even a few days. Thus, persons in public life were made the subjects of life insurance contracts by people who were not even acquainted with them. The vicious nature of this wagering shocked the conscience of an 18th century public not noted for its squeamishness, because such wagering provided an inducement to the murder of the insured.

In 1774, the English parliament took action to end such "a mischievous kind of gaming." It enacted a statute which made null and void all life insurance policies "wherein the person or persons for whose use, benefit, or on whose account such policy or policies shall be made, shall have no interest, or by way of gaming or wagering."[28] Thus, the objective of the insurable interest requirement is to prevent people from profiting from insurance on the lives of others.

---

[28]14 GEO. III, ch. 48.

The insurable interest requirement was adopted early in the United States. In most states, it has been enacted into statutory law and, in others, expressed as case law. All states require that there be an insurable interest at the inception of a life insurance contract.

Today, most life insurance is taken out by the applicant on her or his own life. The insurable interest rules which apply when the proposed insured is the applicant differ from those which apply to third-party insurance contracts. Third-party contracts will, therefore, be discussed separately.

Insurable Interest in a Person's Own Life

Generally speaking, a person has an unlimited insurable interest in his or her own life. A person can apply for as much insurance on his or her own life as the insurer is willing to issue and can name anyone as beneficiary. In most states, the beneficiary of such a policy need not have an insurable interest. The reason for this rule is that the insured presumably will not name as beneficiary anyone who would be more interested in the insured's destruction than in her or his continuing to live. Thus, persons who apply for insurance on their own lives ordinarily do not need to be concerned with the question of insurable interest.

United States Supreme Court Justice Oliver Wendell Holmes described the reasoning behind this rule in a famous case, *Grigsby v. Russell*,[29] as follows:

> The danger that might arise from a general license to all to insure whom they like does not exist. Obviously, it is a very different thing from granting such a general license, to allow the holder of a valid insurance upon his own life to transfer it to one whom he, the party most concerned, is not afraid to trust.

A life insurance contract taken out by the insured and naming as beneficiary one without insurable interest must be made in good faith, however. Such a contract will be void if it can be shown that the contract was made for the purpose of wagering. For example, in one case,[30] a man took out a policy on his life naming his wife as beneficiary. He shortly thereafter changed the beneficiary designation and named a person with no insurable interest. This person paid the premiums. The court held the policy void for lack of an insurable interest.

Statutes in a few states prohibit life insurance in favor of a beneficiary who has no insurable interest in the insured's life. Such a statute can preclude an applicant-insured from naming someone without an insurable interest as beneficiary.

---

[29]222 U.S. 149 (1911).
[30]Lakin v. Postal Life & Cas. Co., 316 S.W.2d 542 (Mo. 1958).

Insurable Interest in Another Person's Life

An insurable interest in another person's life has been defined as "any reasonable expectation of benefit or advantage from the continued life of another person."[31] Such a benefit or advantage need not be monetary. It may also arise from natural affection or dependence.

The Maine Insurance Code, quoted below, contains language typical of insurable interest statutes.

> "Insurable interest" means that every individual has an insurable interest in the life, body, and health of himself, and of other persons as follows:
>
> A. In the case of individuals related closely by blood or by law, a substantial interest engendered by love and affection;
>
> B. In the case of other persons, a lawful and substantial economic interest in having the life, health or bodily safety of the individual insured continue, as distinguished from an interest which would arise only by, or would be enhanced in value by, the death, disablement or injury of the individual insured; and
>
> C. An individual heretofore or hereafter party to a contract or option for the purchase or sale of an interest in a business proprietorship, partnership or firm, or of shares of stock of a closed corporation or of an interest in such shares, has an insurable interest in the life, body and health of each individual party to such contract and for the purposes of such contract only, in addition to any insurable interest which may otherwise exist as to such individual.[32]

The courts have tried to identify the relationships that create an insurable interest, but the list is incomplete and sometimes inconsistent. In some states there are no court decisions regarding insurable interest.

The United States Supreme Court has described insurable interest in another's life as follows:

> It is not easy to define with precision what will in all cases constitute an insurable interest, so as to take the contract out of the class of wager policies. It may be stated generally, however, to be such an interest, arising from the relations of the party obtaining the insurance, either as creditor of or surety for the assured, or from ties of blood or marriage to him, as will justify a reasonable expectation of advantage or benefit from the continuance of his life. It is not necessary that the expectation of advantage or benefit should always be capable of pecuniary estimation, for a parent has an insurable interest in the life of his child, and a child in the life of his parent; a husband in the life of his wife, and a wife in the life of her husband. The natural affection in cases of this kind is considered as more powerful, as operating more efficaciously, to protect the life of the insured than any other consideration. But in all cases there

---

[31]BALLENTINE'S LAW DICTIONARY 642 (3d ed. 1969).
[32]ME. REV. STAT. ANN. tit. 27, § 2404(3) (1974).

must be a reasonable ground, founded upon the relations of the parties to each other, either pecuniary or of blood or affinity, to expect some benefit or advantage from the continuance of the life of the assured. Otherwise the contract is a mere wager, by which the party taking the policy is directly interested in the early death of the assured. Such policies have a tendency to create a desire for the event. They are, therefore, independently of any statute on the subject, condemned, as being against public policy.[33]

An applicant for insurance on another's life can name himself or herself as beneficiary, or name another person as beneficiary. Usually, an applicant for insurance on another's life names himself or herself as beneficiary. For example, a wife might apply for insurance on her husband's life, naming herself as beneficiary. Sometimes in modern practice, however, the applicant names someone else as beneficiary. A wife might apply for insurance on her husband's life and name their children as beneficiaries. Some states have, therefore, enacted statutes which make it clear that, in such a situation, it is the beneficiary who must have an insurable interest in the life of the insured. The New York Insurance Law states the requirement as follows:

No person shall procure or cause to be procured, directly or by assignment or otherwise any contract of insurance upon the person of another unless the benefits under such contract are payable to the person insured or his personal representatives, or to a person having, at the time when such contract is made, an insurable interest in the person insured.[34]

Ordinarily, one person has an insurable interest in the life of another if they are closely related by blood or marriage, or if they have a business relationship which will cause the beneficiary to profit from the continuance of the life insured or to suffer a loss upon the premature termination of that life.

Relationships by Blood.   According to the majority rule, a parent has an insurable interest in his or her child's life, and the child has an insurable interest in the life of the parent. It is also the majority rule that a grandchild has an insurable interest in the life of a grandparent. Although there are no cases on the subject, it seems reasonable that grandparents have an insurable interest in the lives of their grandchildren.

The modern cases support the position that brothers and sisters have an insurable interest in each other's lives because of their close blood relationship.[35] An uncle or aunt and niece or nephew do not have an insurable interest in each other's lives arising out of their relationship alone, according to the majority rule. The same is true of cousins. However, a dependency or business relationship can confer an insurable interest upon such relatives.

---

[33]Warnock v. Davis, 104 U.S. 775 (1882).
[34]N.Y. INS. LAW § 3205 (b)(2) (McKinney 1985).
[35]Annot., 60 A.L.R. 3d 98 (1974).

Relationships by Marriage.   A husband and wife have an insurable interest in each other's lives. Moreover, some courts hold that a person has an insurable interest in the life of another whom she or he is engaged to marry.[36] Relatives by marriage, other than spouses, ordinarily have no insurable interest merely because of the relationship. For example, a stepchild has no insurable interest in the life of a stepparent, or vice versa, unless there is dependency. Where a stepson is dependent on his stepfather for support, the stepson will have an insurable interest in his stepfather's life. This would be true, however, whether or not there was a relationship by marriage. Foster children and other dependents have an insurable interest in the life of a person who supports them, by reason of the dependency.[37]

Business Relationships.   There are many business relationships which, if severed by the premature death of one of the parties, could mean serious financial loss to the survivor. In such a situation, the person who would suffer a financial loss by the death of the other has an insurable interest in the other's life.[38] Thus, for example, an employer has an insurable interest in the life of a key employee. An application of this principle is found in *Theatre Guild Productions v. Insurance Corporation of Ireland.*[39] The Theatre Guild had procured five policies providing that the insurer would pay $1500 for each performance that the star of its play, Gertrude Berg, missed by reason of death or disability. Miss Berg became ill, and the show closed 11 days later. The court said that the Theatre Guild's "insurable interest derived from its employment of Gertrude Berg as the star of its production. . . . The economic success of the production depended on the effective appearance and performance of Gertrude Berg."

A corporation ordinarily has an insurable interest in the lives of its directors, officers, and managers. This is because the success of the business is usually dependent upon the continued existence of these persons.

A partner who expects economic benefit from the continued life of his or her partner has an insurable interest in that life.[40] The partnership also has an insurable interest in the life of a partner if it would be expected to realize economic benefit from the partner's continued life. In *Connecticut Mutual Life Insurance Co. v. Luchs,*[41] the United States Supreme Court said:

> Certainly Luchs had a pecuniary interest in the life of Dillenberg on two grounds: because he was his creditor and because he was his partner. The continuance of the partnership, and, of course, a continuance of Dillenberg's life, furnished a reasonable expectation of advantage to himself.

---

[36]Annot., 17 A.L.R. 580 (1922).
[37]Annot., 25 A.L.R. 1547 (1923).
[38]Annot., 125 A.L.R. 408 (1940).
[39]25 A.D. 2d 109, 267 N.Y.S.2d 297 (1966), *aff'd.* 19 N.Y.2d 656, 225 N.E.2d 216 (1967).
[40]Annot., 70 A.L.R. 2d 577 (1960).
[41]108 U.S. 498 (1883).

It was in the expectation of such advantage that the partnership was formed and, of course, for the like expectation, was continued.

A creditor has an insurable interest in the life of his or her debtor. The amount of insurance must bear a reasonable relationship to the amount of the debt plus the insurance premium. If the amount of insurance taken out by a creditor is disproportionately higher than the amount of the debt, the contract will be a wagering contract and, therefore, void.

Creditor policies fall into two classes. In one class are policies taken out by the creditor on the debtor's life, and in the other class are policies taken out by the debtor, with the creditor made beneficiary or assignee. Where the debtor applies for the insurance, the excess over the amount of the debt will be paid to a contingent beneficiary named by the debtor or to the debtor's estate. However, where the creditor takes out the policy, the courts often hold that the creditor is entitled to the proceeds in full, even if they are greater than the amount of the debt.

Consent of the Insured.   As a general rule, a policy taken out on the life of another person is void without the consent of that person, even though the beneficiary has an insurable interest in the proposed insured's life. One court pointed out that

> [i]t is certainly against public policy for one to procure a policy of insurance on the life of another without such one's knowledge or consent. The wife has an insurable interest in the life of the husband; yet she could not obtain insurance upon his life without his knowledge and consent. Neither should the husband be allowed to procure a policy of insurance on the life of the wife without her knowledge and consent. If such practice was indulged, it might be a fruitful source of crime.[42]

Moreover, if, in such a situation, the premiums were paid with the insured's money without his or her knowledge and consent, the insured can recover those premiums.

An exception to the consent rule is ordinarily made for minor children. A parent can insure a minor child's life without the child's consent, since a minor child does not have capacity to give consent.

Insurable Interest—a Question of Fact.   The basic rules concerning insurable interest are always subject to exceptions, especially where the facts show there was not a good faith application for the insurance. For instance, it is often stated that partners have an insurable interest in each other's lives. This general rule is ordinarily borne out by the facts, but not always. In one case, two partners were involved in a hunting accident. The victim was insured for $25,000 in favor of his partner. The court decided the beneficiary did not have an insurable interest. The court said, in part:

---

[42]Metropolitan Life Ins. Co. v. Monohan, 102 Ky. 13, 42 S.W. 924 (1897).

While it is true that partners usually, and perhaps in most cases, have an insurable interest in the life of a copartner, it is the existence of circumstances which arise out of or by reason of the partnership, and not the mere existence of the partnership itself, that give rise to an insurable interest. The legal relationship of one partner to the other does not, and should not, necessarily create an insurable interest as does the relationship of husband and wife.

* * * * *

The better rule, and the one based on sound reasoning, is that an insurable interest does not necessarily arise by virtue of the mere partner relationship alone. Therefore, the showing by appellant [the surviving partner] that he and Hankinson were partners did not of itself establish the existence in him of an insurable interest in the life of Hankinson. We must therefore look to the circumstances arising out of or by reason of the partnership to determine whether an insurable interest existed in this case.

Appellant's evidence conclusively establishes that Hankinson made absolutely no financial or capital contribution whatever to the alleged partnership, and that he did not in any way obligate himself to do so; that he had no technical knowledge, skill or ability as a worker or manager to add to the partnership; that he did not have any experience in the type of work he was to do or in the business of the alleged partnership; that appellant had no legal claim for his continued services; and that Hankinson did not purchase or acquire an interest in the business or the tools and equipment used in the business. Also there is nothing to indicate that Hankinson brought or could be expected to bring any business to the partnership, or that his presence as a partner increased or favorably affected the partnership good will.

* * * * *

Therefore, we are constrained to and do conclude that appellant's evidence affirmatively establishes that as a matter of law he had no insurable interest in the life of Hankinson.[43]

Insurer's Tort Liability.   An insurer has a legal duty to use reasonable care to determine whether the requisite insurable interest exists and to procure the consent of the insured. If this duty is breached, the insurer will be liable for tort damages for any resulting harm. The leading case in this area is *Liberty National Life Insurance Co. v. Weldon*.[44]

The applicant in the *Weldon* case was a nurse working in a small Alabama town. One afternoon in 1952, she visited her brother-in-law and his family and gave his two-year-old daughter a soft drink in a cup. The child died before evening. An investigation showed arsenic in the cup, in the child's body in a sufficient quantity to cause her death, and in the clothes of the child and her

---

[43]Lakin v. Postal Life & Cas. Co., 316 S.W.2d 542 (Mo. 1958).
[44]267 Ala. 171, 100 So. 2d 696 (1957).

aunt-in-law, the nurse. The aunt-in-law was charged with murder, convicted, and executed.

In the course of the murder trial, it was revealed that three life insurers had issued policies on the applications of the aunt-in-law, insuring the life of the child and designating the aunt-in-law as beneficiary. These policies had face amounts of $500, $5,000, and $1,000. The child's parents had not given their consent to the issuance of any of these policies.

The parents brought suit against the life insurers under a wrongful death statute. A wrongful death statute gives the executor, administrator, or heirs of a deceased person a cause of action for injuries to the deceased that resulted from the wrongful acts of another. The plaintiffs' theory in the *Weldon* suit was that the insurers were under a duty to use reasonable care not to issue a life insurance policy in favor of a beneficiary who had no interest in the continuation of the insured's life and that issuance of the policies was a breach of that duty which resulted in the child's death by murder.

The verdict was for the parents. The Alabama Supreme Court quoted a basic rule of tort law that every person has a duty to exercise reasonable care not to injure another. It said that a life insurer has a duty to use reasonable care not to issue a life insurance policy to someone who has no interest in the continuation of the insured's life. "Policies in violation of the insurable interest rule are not dangerous because they are illegal," the court said, "they are illegal because they are dangerous." The opinion continued:

> We cannot agree with the defendants [the insurers] in their assertion that we should hold as a matter of law that the murder of the young girl was not reasonably foreseeable. This created a situation of a kind which this court and others have consistently said affords temptation to a recognizable percentage of humanity to commit murder.

The jury had held that the issuance of the policies was the proximate cause of the murder of the child and awarded damages to the parents in the amount of $100,000. The reviewing court reduced the award to $75,000, but even so it was the largest wrongful death verdict ever to come out of that court. This case illustrates the importance of the insurable interest requirement.

Conscientious life insurers carefully examine every application to make certain that the legally required insurable interest standards have been met. Moreover, many life insurers impose stricter insurable interest standards than are required by law.

CONSIDERATION

In the case of an informal contract, the promise or promises to be enforced must always be supported by a legally sufficient consideration. Consideration can take the form of an act or a promise. It is the value requested and given in exchange for the promise or promises sought to be enforced. It can also be defined as a benefit to the promisor or a detriment to the promisee.

Most life insurance policies specifically state that the insurance shall not be effective until the first premium is paid. The validity of this stipulation has been uniformly upheld. The initial premium and application constitute the consideration which makes the insurer's promises enforceable.

COMPETENT CONTRACTING PARTIES

The parties to an insurance contract are the insurer and the applicant. The offer is always made by either the insurer or the applicant and accepted by the other, thus creating the contract.

A life insurer is considered competent to issue life insurance contracts if it has been authorized to do so by the terms of its charter or articles of incorporation, and if it has a certificate of authority in the state in which the contract is made. The competency of an insurer is certified each year in the various states in which it does business.

The applicant is the other party to the insurance contract, and, therefore, the applicant must have contractual capacity. Of course, as was discussed in Chapter 2, "Contracts," a minor, or a mentally infirm person with limited contractual capacity, can enter into an insurance contract which will be binding on the insurer and voidable by the minor or mentally infirm person.

The beneficiary, as such, is not a party to the contract and need not have contractual capacity. In many instances, a beneficiary does not know of the existence of the contract. If a beneficiary without full contractual capacity, such as a minor, is made irrevocable beneficiary, however, the policyowner will ordinarily be unable to exercise ownership rights because the beneficiary cannot give consent to their exercise.

The insured, as such, is not a party to the contract, either. Where one person takes out insurance on the life of another, the insured's consent will be required, but the insured is not thereby made a party. For example, a wife may apply for insurance on the life of her husband who gives his consent to the contract. The insurer and the wife are the parties to the contract. The husband, who is the insured, is not a party. An insured must have the capacity to give consent to the contract, however, unless the insured is a minor child and a parent gives consent.

DELIVERY OF THE POLICY

Most life insurance applications expressly provide that the policy shall not become effective until (1) the application is approved, (2) a policy is issued, and (3) the policy is delivered and the initial premium is paid during the continued good health of the proposed insured. If there is no agreement to the contrary, each of these conditions must be fulfilled before the policy becomes effective. Thus, all of these are conditions precedent.

The effectiveness of the policy itself should not be confused with the effectiveness of temporary insurance under a premium receipt. Issuance and delivery of the policy are not conditions precedent to temporary insurance under a premium receipt.

Once the initial premium has been paid, the contract is completed when the agent delivers the policy. Of course, the policy can be delivered by handing it to the applicant. This is actual delivery.

Constructive Delivery

The policy does not actually have to be placed in the hands of the applicant for there to be delivery, however. There are situations where a court will say there has been a delivery even though the applicant was not actually handed the policy. Such delivery is called "constructive delivery."

A policy is ordinarily constructively delivered when the insurer has parted with control of it with intention to be bound by it as a completed instrument.[45] That is, the courts will construe the policy to be delivered the moment the insurer relinquishes possession of the policy by mailing it to the agent if nothing further remains to be done but the ministerial act of seeing that the applicant receives the policy.[46] For example, suppose the applicant pays the initial premium at the time application is made, and the insurer accepts the application, issues the policy, and puts it in the mail to the agent with the intention that it be delivered to the applicant. If the insured dies while the policy is in the mail or in the hands of the agent, most courts would hold that there was constructive delivery and that the benefits are payable under the policy.

Delivery to an agent of the applicant will ordinarily constitute constructive delivery, also. For example, a policy might be delivered to an applicant's home in the applicant's absence and given to his or her spouse in exchange for the initial premium. The spouse would act as the applicant's agent for receipt of the policy. Delivery to an agent of the applicant is, in legal effect, delivery to the applicant.

Delivery for Inspection

Occasionally, a policy is delivered to the applicant for inspection. That is, the applicant is permitted to keep the policy for a few days for inspection without the insurance being in force. There is no intention by either party to be bound by the contract at that time.

In such cases, it is customary to have the applicant sign an inspection receipt, specifying the conditions under which the policy was left with her or him. If there were no inspection receipt, and the proposed insured died while

---

[45] Annot., 53 A.L.R. 492 (1928).

[46] A ministerial act is an act that does not require discretion on the part of the person performing the act.

the policy was in the applicant's possession, it could be difficult for the insurer to establish that no binding obligation was intended. The inspection receipt makes it clear that the insurance is not in force and that there has been no delivery, in the legal sense of the word.

Delivery for inspection should not be confused with the free examination period (free look) provision mandated by the laws of many states. In the case of the free examination period provision, the policy is in full force at the time of delivery, but the policyowner has the right to cancel it and have the initial premium returned by the insurer.

EFFECTIVE DATE OF THE POLICY

There are a number of factors which can affect the date when a policy becomes effective. These are (1) an effective date agreed upon by the insurer and policyowner; (2) backdating; (3) date of payment of initial premium; (4) delivery date; and, (5) a rider providing coverage at an earlier date than the date stipulated in the policy itself.

Generally, an effective date agreed upon between the insurer and policyowner will be binding. This will be the case even though the initial premium was paid on a different date.

The parties can agree on an effective date sometime in the past. Thus, backdating a policy is permissible if done within limits established by state law. Six months is the usual limit on the length of time a policy can be backdated.

Life policies often require that there be payment of the initial premium and delivery of the policy before there is coverage. This sometimes conflicts with another policy provision regarding the date from which the premium due date will be calculated. The majority rule is that the premium due date will be calculated from the date stipulated in the policy. A minority of cases have held that the premium due date will be calculated from the date coverage began.

Sometimes a policy has a rider which provides preliminary coverage until the policy becomes effective. In such cases, the courts have held that the policy is effective from the date stipulated in the rider, rather than the date stipulated in the policy itself. In one such case,[47] the insured committed suicide on December 10, 1928. The death would have been within the one-year suicide exclusion period if the main policy effective date of February 28, 1928, was controlling. Hence, no benefits would have been payable. There was, however, a rider providing preliminary coverage beginning on November 28, 1927, for a small additional premium. The insurer contended that the rider was a separate contract. The court disagreed, holding that the rider formed a part of the main contract. The main contract was, therefore, in force from

---

[47]Narver v. California State Life Ins. Co., 211 Cal. 176, 294 P. 393 (1930).

the earlier date, November 28, 1927, and the suicide on December 10, 1928, occurred after the one-year exclusion period. Thus, the benefits were payable. This case represents the law on this point.

SUMMARY

The formation of the life insurance contract is governed by the general rules of contract law and also by special rules which apply to life insurance. The offer to contract can be made by either the applicant or the insurer, depending on the circumstances. An offer by an applicant may evoke an acceptance, rejection, or counteroffer from the insurer. Generally, the insurer must act on an application with reasonable promptness, or it might incur contract or tort liability.

Premium receipts, given to the applicant when the initial premium is submitted with the application, usually contain a contract providing temporary insurance coverage. There are three types of premium receipts: approval premium receipts, insurability premium receipts, and binding premium receipts. Approval premium receipts and insurability premium receipts are conditional premium receipts requiring certain conditions to be met before they become binding. The binding premium receipt is binding at the time it is given to the applicant in exchange for the initial premium. There is a strong trend in the courts to treat conditional receipts as if they were binding.

Risk classification means the insurer's identification of people with similar loss potential and placement of those people in the same risk group for the purpose of setting premium rates. *Risk selection* means the insurer's choice from among proposed insureds those persons it is willing to insure. Life insurance risk selection is ordinarily done by underwriters at the insurer's home office, rather than by the soliciting agent.

Many states have laws prohibiting unfair discrimination in insurance. Some have laws prohibiting unfair handicap or sex discrimination. Laws mandating unisex insurance rates and laws restricting insurers' ability to test for the antibody to the AIDS virus have been a concern of the life insurance industry during the 1980s.

Insurable interest is required for public policy reasons to prevent people from profiting from insurance taken out on the lives of others. As a person usually has an unlimited insurable interest in his or her own life, insurable interest is ordinarily of concern only when the applicant applies for insurance on the life of another. Ordinarily, one party has an insurable interest in the life of another if they are closely related by blood or marriage, or if they have a business relationship in which the applicant expects economic benefit from the continued life of the insured. An insurer must use reasonable care not to issue a policy to one with no insurable interest, or it may incur tort liability.

A life contract, like any informal contract, requires consideration and competent contracting parties. The consideration given by the applicant, in exchange for the insurer's promise, is the application and initial premium.

The applicant is one party to the contract, and the insurer is the other. The insured and the beneficiary, as such, are not parties to the contract. The applicant must have contractual capacity.

Delivery of the policy is ordinarily required before the policy becomes effective. Actual delivery by placing the policy in the applicant's hands is not necessary, however. Constructive delivery is sufficient. The policy is ordinarily constructively delivered when the insurer has parted with control of it with the intention to be bound by it as a completed instrument, or when it is delivered to the applicant's agent.

ILLUSTRATIVE CASE

This case deals with the insurable interest of a father in the life of his son. The court held that the father had such an insurable interest. A question of material misrepresentation in the application for the life insurance policy was also raised by the insurer and decided in favor of the father (the plaintiff-appellee). Material misrepresentation is discussed in Chapter 16, "Remedies," and in Chapter 17, "Policy Contests."

T.J. BOWMAN, FATHER OF JAMES BOWMAN, DECEASED, Plaintiff-Appellee
v.
ZENITH LIFE INSURANCE COMPANY, Defendant-Appellant[48]
Appellate Court of Illinois, First District, Third Division

McNAMARA, Justice.

Plaintiff, T. J. Bowman, commenced this action to recover as the beneficiary under an insurance policy purchased by him on the life of his son, James Bowman. After a trial without a jury, the court entered a judgment in favor of plaintiff for $3,000, the face value of the policy. Defendant appeals. Its principal contention in the trial court and in this court is that plaintiff had no insurable interest in the life of his son and, therefore, that the policy was void at its inception.

On February 4, 1974, plaintiff applied to defendant for the policy in question through one of defendant's agents, and the policy was issued. The son was unaware that plaintiff had applied for the insurance. The son lived with his mother most of his life and not with plaintiff. Plaintiff did not know if his son was working prior to his death which occurred on March 3, 1974.

The trial court specifically found that "[t]he defense urged by the defendant that the plaintiff had no insurable interest in the life of his son is without merit in that the father had a reasonable expectation of receiving financial support from his son in his declining years, if needed."

Defendant argues that the trial court erred in holding that plaintiff had an insurable interest in the life of his son. The requirement that one obtaining a policy

---

[48]67 Ill. App. 3d 393, 384 N.E.2d 949 (1978).

of insurance upon the life of another must have an insurable interest therein is founded upon a public policy which "forbids one person who has no interest in the continuance of the life of another from speculating on that life by procuring a policy of insurance." The lack of an insurable interest renders the policy "a pure wager that gives the insured a sinister counter interest in having the life come to an end." (*Grigsby v. Russell* (1911), 222 U.S. 149, 154, 32 S.Ct. 58, 56 L.Ed. 133). In the present case, we cannot say that the policy of insurance procured by plaintiff upon the life of his son was a pure wager. We believe the face amount of the policy is not grossly disproportionate to the extent of plaintiff's interest. This factor is an indication that plaintiff acted in good faith in obtaining the policy. The trial court correctly held that plaintiff did have an insurable interest in his son's life.

Defendant further argues that certain statements in connection with the policy were not answered truthfully by plaintiff and thereby the policy was voided. Defendant's agent came to plaintiff's home to prepare the latter's application for the insurance policy. At that time, plaintiff was asked the following questions, the answers to which the agent recorded on the application:

1. Are you now in good health and free from impairment or disease? Answer—Yes.
2. Are you now receiving or contemplating any medical attention or surgical treatment? Answer—No.
3. Have you during the past five years consulted any physician or other practitioner or been confined to any hospital, sanitarium or similar institution? Answer—No.

At trial, it was stipulated that plaintiff's son had a pre-existing diabetic condition. Defendant's claims manager testified that defendant would not have issued the policy had it known this fact at the time the application was made.

Defendant maintains that the foregoing answers were not truthful. It urges further that, even if the answers were given in good faith, such conduct amounted to a misrepresentation which materially affected defendant's decision to issue the policy. Plaintiff's testimony, which is uncontradicted by any other evidence, was that he believed defendant's agent was inquiring into his own health due to the manner in which the questions were phrased. Since plaintiff himself signed the application, the completed application supports plaintiff's belief. In completing the application, plaintiff was required to disclose only such facts as were responsive to the questions asked.

The trial court correctly found that plaintiff was not guilty of any misrepresentation which would entitle defendant to void the policy.

For the foregoing reasons, the judgment of the circuit court of Cook County awarding judgment to plaintiff in the amount of $3,000 is affirmed.

Judgment affirmed.

SIMON, P.J., and JIGANTI, J., concur.

QUESTIONS FOR REVIEW

1. Under what conditions is the applicant considered to be making an offer to the insurer? When the conditions are such that the applicant is not considered to be making the offer, what is the legal significance of the application?

2. How does offer and acceptance in relation to life insurance contracts differ from that in relation to most other business contracts with regard to a delay in acting upon the application?

3. Explain the difference between a condition precedent and a condition subsequent. What are some conditions precedent in relation to the life insurance contract?

4. The applicant does not have to pay the initial premium until after the policy has been issued. Describe how the applicant may benefit from paying the premium in advance.

5. What are the two types of conditional premium receipts? How do binding premium receipts differ from conditional premium receipts? Why are more insurers issuing binding premium receipts now?

6. Why do life insurers not give their soliciting agents power to complete a contract for life insurance?

7. In relation to life insurance:
    a. How is insurable interest defined?
    b. When must the required insurable interest exist?
    c. What is meant by the statement "A person has an unlimited insurable interest in his or her own life"?
    d. Who must have the required insurable interest in the life of the insured?

8. What is meant by constructive delivery?

9. Describe the conditions under which an inspection receipt is used and tell why it is used.

CHAPTER 7

Structure of the Life Insurance Policy

SIMPLIFIED LANGUAGE

POLICY CONTENTS

POLICY FACE PAGE
  Officers' Signatures
  Policy Description
  Free Examination Period Provision

REQUIRED POLICY PROVISIONS
  Introductory Statutory Language
  Settlement Options Tables
  Nonforfeiture Provisions
  Grace Period Provision
  Incontestable Clause
  Entire Contract Provision
  Misstatement of Age Provision
  Divisible Surplus Provision
  Policy Loan Provision
  Reinstatement Provision

OPTIONAL POLICY PROVISIONS
  Ownership Provision
  Assignment Provision
  Suicide Provision
  Contract Change Provision

PROHIBITED POLICY PROVISIONS
  Time Limit on Legal or Equitable Actions
  Dating Back Provision
  Less Value Statutes
  Forfeiture for Failure to Repay a Policy Loan
  Agent of the Insured

UNIVERSAL AND VARIABLE LIFE
INSURANCE LAWS
   Universal Life Insurance Regulations
   Variable Life Insurance Laws
   Variable Universal Life Insurance Laws
POLICY FILING AND APPROVAL
SUMMARY

The life insurance policy is drafted by the insurer. The insurer cannot write the policy in any manner it wishes, however. There are many legal constraints on the form and content of life insurance policies. Policies must be written in simplified language in many jurisdictions. They must contain certain specified provisions and are forbidden to contain other provisions. The policy forms must be filed with and approved by the departments of insurance in the states where the policy will be sold. Finally, legally-required provisions which are omitted from a policy form will be considered by the courts to be part of the contract exactly as if they were written in the policy. This chapter contains a review of the form and content of life policies and a discussion of the required insurance department filing or approval of policy forms.

SIMPLIFIED LANGUAGE

The consumerist movement of recent years has resulted in laws requiring that the language of many types of legal documents be simplified so that consumers can more readily understand them. Most of the states now have laws or regulations requiring that life and health insurance policies be written in simplified language. Some of these laws or regulations are patterned on the National Association of Insurance Commissioners (NAIC) Life and Health Insurance Policy Language Simplification Model Act, which was adopted by the NAIC in 1977. More states can be expected to adopt such simplified language laws.

Simplified language laws often require policies to meet a particular minimum Flesch scale readability score. The Flesch scale was invented by psychologist Rudolph Flesch and is explained in his book, *The Art of Readable Writing*.[1]

The Flesch scale is based on the relationship between reading ease and the length of words and sentences. Shorter words and sentences are more easily understood. To compute a Flesch readability score for a policy clause, a person counts the sentences, words, and syllables in the clause and runs the totals through a formula. The higher the score, the more easily under-

---

[1]R. FLESCH, THE ART OF READABLE WRITING (rev. 1974).

stood the clause. The NAIC Policy Language Simplification Model Act requires that a policy have a minimum score of 40. Some state laws require other minimum scores. Medical terms, words which are defined in the policy, policy language required by law, the insurer's name and address, the policy title, and certain other printed matter do not have to be scored. Other reading ease tests which are comparable to the Flesch test can be permitted by the commissioner of insurance under the model act.

In addition to meeting a readability ease test, the NAIC Policy Language Simplification Model Act requires that policies be "printed, except for specification pages, schedules and tables, in not less than ten point type, one point leaded." This eliminates fine print which makes policies difficult to read. This book is printed in 10 point type, one point leaded.

The style, arrangement, and overall appearance of the policy must "give no undue prominence to any portion of the text of the policy or to any endorsements or riders." The policy must contain a table of contents or an index of its principal sections if the policy has more than 3,000 words, or more than three pages.

The drafters of the NAIC Policy Language Simplification Model Act were aware that technical terms cannot be completely eliminated from insurance policies. In a drafting note, they stated the following:

> In establishing minimum standards, it is recognized that certain terminology used in policies is difficult or impossible to restate in simplified language. This is because there are no suitable alternatives to necessary medical terminology, other insurance words of art, and statutory or regulatory language requirements. It is not the intention of this Act to preclude the use of such terminology or to penalize insurance companies for its continued use.

A whole life policy written in simplified language is shown in Appendix B.

POLICY CONTENTS

The typical life policy contains a face page followed by numerous provisions, both required and optional. A modern policy probably will contain a table of contents and a section containing definitions of technical terms used in the policy. There will be a section providing for designations and changes of beneficiary. A settlement options section will spell out the various options and provide tables showing monthly amounts payable under each option. A policy providing cash values will contain a nonforfeiture section which describes the options available if the policyowner decides to discontinue paying premiums before the policy is paid up.

Other provisions which are ordinarily required include the free examination provision, the grace period provision, the incontestable clause, the entire contract provision, the misstatement of age provision, the divisible surplus provision (required in participating policies), the policy loan provision, and the reinstatement clause. The policy may also contain optional provisions dealing with ownership, suicide, assignment, or contract change. These required and optional provisions will be discussed in this chapter.

There are certain provisions which are prohibited from inclusion in life policies. Provisions severely limiting the time in which legal actions can be brought are sometimes prohibited. Dating back the policy more than a specified period of time prior to the submission of the application is unlawful in some states. Provisions which curtail payment of the face amount are forbidden under less value statutes in some states. Forfeiture of the policy for failure to repay a policy loan is specifically forbidden under the laws of some states. Finally, a statement that the insurer's agent shall be the agent of the applicant or policyowner is sometimes expressly forbidden by statute. These prohibited provisions will also be discussed in this chapter.

Additional benefits or limitations are often included in the policy or added by rider. These include accidental death benefits, disability benefits, guaranteed insurability benefits, and war and aviation hazard exclusions. These benefits and limitations will be discussed in the next chapter.

POLICY FACE PAGE

The face page of an illustrative life insurance policy is reproduced in Appendix B. The face page contains the insurer's basic promise. This promise can be stated in various ways. The illustrative policy, which is written in simplified language, contains the following promise:

> If the Insured dies while this Policy is in force, we will pay the Sum
> Insured to the Beneficiary, when we receive at our Home Office due proof
> of the Insured's death, subject to the provisions of this Policy.

In most older policies, as well as some newer ones, the basic promise is in the form of a statement that in consideration of the application and the payment of premiums as they become due, the insurer promises to pay the face amount to the beneficiary upon receipt of satisfactory proof of the insured's death. Legally, however, the application and payment of the initial premium constitute the consideration for the insurer's promise. The promise will remain in effect only if a required condition—the payment of renewal premiums—occurs.

Officers' Signatures

Below the insurer's promise are the signatures of company officers—usually, the president and secretary. These signatures may be personally written on each policy by these officers, but usually facsimile signatures are preprinted on the policy form for convenience. Whether signed by hand or preprinted, the signatures are evidence that the policy has been put into force by the insurer. Thus, the signatures are essential to the completion of a written contract of insurance.[2]

Policy Description

At the bottom of the face page will be found a brief policy description. One of the objectives of legislation on life insurance policy provisions is to assure that the policyowner understands the coverage provided by the policy. For that reason, state statutes commonly require that a brief description of the coverage be included on the face page of every policy. For example, one insurer describes its whole life policy as follows:

WHOLE LIFE INSURANCE POLICY
Premium Payable for a Stated Period
or Until Prior Death of Insured
Sum Insured Payable at Death
Non-Participating

Free Examination Period Provision

Many states have adopted a statute or regulation requiring insurers to include a provision on the face page of a life insurance policy permitting the policyowner to return the policy within some period of time (usually 10 days) after receiving it and obtain a full refund of the premium paid. The policy will then be deemed void from the beginning. These provisions are called free examination provisions, trial examination period provisions, free look provisions, or 10-day free look provisions.

An illustrative policy provision reads as follows:

RIGHT TO EXAMINE AND RETURN POLICY WITHIN 10 DAYS

You may, at any time within 10 days after receipt of this Policy, return it to us at our Home Office or to the Agent through whom it was purchased, and we will cancel it. The return of the Policy will void it from the beginning and any premium paid will be refunded to the owner.

Required provisions which do not appear on the face page are analyzed in the next section.

REQUIRED POLICY PROVISIONS

The insurance laws enacted in New York in 1906, as the result of the Armstrong Investigation of insurance practices, prescribed uniform policy

---

[2]Coen v. American Surety Co., 120 F.2d 393 (8th Cir. 1941), *cert. denied,* 314 U.S. 667 (1941); Prudential Ins. Co. v. Connallon, 108 N.J. Eq. 316, 154 A. 729 (1931).

forms for straight (ordinary),[3] limited pay, endowment, and term life insurance policies. Life insurers were required to issue policies in exactly those forms. When this legislation proved too rigid, it was replaced in 1910 by a law which specified certain provisions that must be included in life insurance policies, but permitted the insurers to use their own wording, as long as the substance was essentially the same as that prescribed in the law, and the language used was not less liberal to the policyowner and the beneficiary. This is the New York standard policy provisions law. Similar laws have been adopted by considerably more than half the states, including most of the states that have the largest insurance companies. Accordingly, most life insurance policies now being issued include such provisions. The following is an analysis of these required provisions.

Introductory Statutory Language

A state's standard policy provisions law is usually introduced with a paragraph similar to the following excerpt from the New York law:

> All life insurance policies, except as otherwise stated herein, delivered or issued for delivery in this state, shall contain in substance the following provisions, or provisions which the superintendent deems to be more favorable to policyholders.[4]

The phrase *in substance* indicates that a policy provision need not be stated in the exact words of the statute. Whether the policy provisions actually used are more favorable to policyowners than the provisions outlined in the statute is left to the opinion of the superintendent of insurance.[5]

The New York law excludes from the requirements such policies as single-premium policies, nonparticipating policies, and term policies, to the extent that any of the required provisions are not applicable. Thus, a nonparticipating policy would not be required to include dividend provisions, and a single-premium policy would not be required to contain provisions relating to the payment of renewal premiums. The standard policy provisions law does not apply to group life insurance.

Settlement Options Tables

The New York standard policy provisions law, and the standard policy provisions laws of other states, require settlement options tables to be in-

---

[3]Straight life insurance is whole life insurance with premiums payable until death, or until some advanced age such as 100, if the insured is still living at that age.

[4]N.Y. INS. LAW § 3203(a) (McKinney 1985 & Supp. 1988).

[5]*Superintendent* is a title given to the head of the New York Insurance Department. In other states, this official is referred to as "director" or "commissioner."

cluded if the policy provides settlement options. The New York statute requires the following:

> [A] table showing the amounts of the applicable installment or annuity payments, if the policy proceeds are payable in installments or as an annuity.[6]

The illustrative policy in Appendix B shows several settlement options tables.

Nonforfeiture Provisions

Nonforfeiture provisions result from the level premium system. Because of the level premium system, the owner of a whole life or endowment policy, or a level term policy for any of the longer terms, contributes more in the early years than is required to meet his or her proportionate share of the current mortality cost to the insurer.

The standard policy provisions laws require that in the case of lapse of a whole life insurance contract that has been in effect for a minimum stated period (usually three years), the insurer must provide a cash surrender value. Alternatively, either paid-up insurance for a reduced amount or extended term insurance for the net face amount, or both, must be offered in whatever amounts could be purchased by the net cash surrender value of the policy.

Nonforfeiture laws and policy provisions are discussed at length in Chapter 13, "Nonforfeiture Provisions and Policy Loans." An illustrative nonforfeiture section will be found in the specimen policy included in Appendix B.

Grace Period Provision

A grace period provision usually is required in statutory language such as the following:

> [A life policy shall contain a provision]
>
> (1) that, after payment of the first premium, the policyholder is entitled to a thirty-one day grace period or of one month following any subsequent premium due date within which to make payment of the premium then due. During such grace period, the policy shall continue in full force; [and]
>
> (2) that if the death of the insured occurs within the grace period provided in the policy, the insurer may deduct from the policy proceeds the portion of any unpaid premium applicable to the period ending with the last day of the policy month in which such death occurred, and if the death of the insured occurs during a period for which the premium has been paid, the insurer shall add to the policy proceeds a refund of any premium actually paid for any period

---

[6]N.Y. Ins. Law § 3203(a)(9) (McKinney 1985).

beyond the end of the policy month in which such death occurred, provided such premium was not waived under any policy provision for waiver of premiums benefit. This paragraph shall not apply to single premium or paid-up policies.[7]

A grace period provision from the illustrative life insurance policy in Appendix B reads as follows:

GRACE PERIOD

We will allow a period of 31 days after the premium due date for payment of each premium after the first. This is the grace period. If the Insured dies during the grace period before the premium is paid, we will deduct one month's premium from the death proceeds of this policy.

If any premium is not paid on or before its due date, that premium is in default. If that premium is still unpaid at the expiration of the grace period, this Policy terminates except for any nonforfeiture benefits.

Like many other standard provisions, the grace period provision was first included in life insurance policies by insurers on a voluntary basis. By the time of the Armstrong Investigation, such provisions were widely used. Thus, the standard policy provisions law required all insurers to follow a practice already adopted by many insurers.

The grace period provision gives the policyowner an additional period of time in which to pay a premium after it has become due. During that period, the policy continues in force, and the premium continues to be payable. If the insured dies during the grace period and prior to payment of the premium, therefore, the premium will be deducted from the proceeds of the policy. If the insured does not die during the grace period, and the premium is not paid by the end of the period, the policy lapses, but the policyowner owes nothing for the additional days of protection.

Length of the period.   Most life insurance policies provide a grace period of 31 days. If the last day of grace falls on a nonbusiness day, the premium ordinarily is payable on the following business day.

The grace period is not extended by a late remittance offer. A late remittance offer is sometimes made by an insurer after a policy has lapsed. It allows the policyowner a limited period of time after the expiration of the grace period in which to reinstate the policy without providing evidence of insurability, as long as the insured is alive when payment is tendered. A late remittance offer form is illustrated in Appendix F.

Interest charge.   If premiums are paid at the end instead of at the beginning of the grace period, the insurer will have lost the investment value of the

---

[7]*Id.* § 3203(a)(1)(2).

premium for one month. For this reason, the statute quoted above permits the insurer to deduct the amount of overdue premium, plus interest, from policy benefits if the insured dies during the grace period. For competitive reasons, and because such losses are not significant, most insurers do not make this interest charge, as illustrated by the policy provision quoted above.

Incontestable Clause

Most standard policy provisions laws require a provision making the life insurance policy incontestable after it has been in force for two years. In the absence of this clause, the life insurer could, at any time, have the policy rescinded, or defend a lawsuit for benefits, if it had issued the policy in reliance on material misstatements of the applicant.

A thorough explanation of the incontestable clause, its history, and its relationship to other policy provisions would be too lengthy for this chapter. This will be covered in Chapter 17, "Policy Contests."

Entire Contract Provision

Entire contract statutes vary from state to state. Some statutes require that an entire contract policy provision state that the policy, together with the application if attached, constitutes the entire contract. Other statutes state directly that the policy and the application constitute the entire contract.

The requirement that an entire contract provision be included in life policies grew out of the practice of incorporation by reference. Incorporation by reference is a rule of contract law that permits contracting parties to incorporate into a written contract any other document they wish simply by referring to it in the contract. A document so incorporated must be in existence at the time the contract is made. The reference to the document must be express and made in such a way that the document can be identified. Incorporation by reference greatly simplifies contract drafting in many instances.

As applied to the life insurance contract, however, incorporation by reference can be subject to abuse. Provisions in the insurer's charter and by-laws, for example, could be made an effective part of every life insurance contract an insurer issued simply by adequate reference to them in the contract. The privileges and benefits under the contract could be limited in that way, yet the policyowner might never see the charter or by-laws and, in most instances, would be unaware of their provisions.

The application could also be incorporated into the policy by reference if there were no entire contract provision. An important purpose of the entire contract statutes is to require the insurer to provide the policyowner with a copy of the application, rather than allowing the insurer to hold it and incorporate it into the policy by reference. This eliminates uncertainties for the policyowner about the contents of the application and allows the policyowner to inform the insurer of necessary corrections.

The entire contract provision assures the policyowner that the policy includes every document affecting the privileges and benefits, as well as the duties and conditions, of the contract. It also prevents the policyowner from contending that he or she was not aware of statements made in the application. A copy of the application is almost always attached to the policy. If a copy is not attached, any misstatements in the application ordinarily cannot be used to contest the validity of the policy.

The entire contract provision of the illustrative policy reads in part as follows:

ENTIRE CONTRACT

We have issued this Policy in consideration of the application and payment of the premiums. A copy of the application is attached and is a part of this Policy. The Policy with the application makes the entire contract. All statements made by or for the Insured will be considered representations and not warranties. We will not use any statement in defense of a claim unless it is made in the application and a copy of the application is attached to this Policy when issued.

Two further points should be noted in regard to entire contract statutes. First, entire contract statutes do not prevent inclusion of a legally-required policy provision which has been omitted. If any legally required provision has not been included in a policy, the contract will be interpreted by a court as if such a provision were included in it.

Second, an entire contract statute or clause refers to the contract at the time it is made. It does not ordinarily prevent later agreements relating to the contract. For example, an insurer can enter into a valid written agreement with the policyowner to extend the time for premium payment, upon condition that failure to comply with the terms of the agreement shall lapse the policy without further action on the part of the insurer.[8]

Misstatement of Age Provision

The age of the proposed insured is of such importance with respect to the degree of risk assumed that a misstatement of age can make a significant difference in the amount of premiums that should have been paid. In other words, a statement of the age of a proposed insured is a material representation. Yet misstatements of the age of the proposed insured were common from the outset of the life insurance business. Thus, some equitable method of adjusting the amount of premium paid or the amount of insurance payable has been necessary from an early date. The problem was resolved in the New York standard policy provisions law by a requirement that life policies contain a provision stating

---

[8]Lincoln Nat'l Life Ins. Co. v. Hammer, 41 F.2d 12 (8th Cir. 1930); Keller v. North Am. Life Ins. Co., 301 Ill. 198, 133 N.E. 726 (1921).

that if the age of the insured has been misstated, any amount payable or benefit accruing under the policy shall be such as the premium would have purchased at the correct age.[9]

A majority of states have a similar misstatement of age statute.

The misstatement of age provision assures the policyowner that all death claims will be adjusted uniformly where the insured's age has been misstated, and the misstatement is discovered after the insured's death. In the absence of such a provision, it would be possible to adjust either the amount of the benefit or the amount of premiums paid. There could be certain inequities in allowing premium adjustments, rather than benefit adjustments. For example, if the age of the insured had been understated, the beneficiary could pay the difference in premium after the insured's death and, in effect, buy more insurance than would have been provided by the premium paid before death.

If an error as to age is discovered *before* the insured's death, however, there can be an adjustment in either premiums or coverage. If the insured's age was understated, the policyowner can be issued a policy for a reduced amount, or allowed to pay the difference in premiums with interest and keep the original policy. If the insured's age was overstated, the insurer will usually refund the excess premiums paid.

The misstatement of age provision generally applies only where there is an innocent mistake and not where there is fraud or collusion.[10] In one case, where the insurer's agent and the beneficiary had collusively represented the insured to be about 30 years younger than her actual age, the court allowed the insurer to deny payment of the death benefit.[11]

In policies for which lower premium rates are charged for women than for men, the misstatement of age provision sometimes includes a reference to misstatement of sex. A reference to misstatement of sex is required by the statutes of a minority of states. Such a reference is found in the illustrative policy in Appendix B as follows:

INCORRECT AGE OR SEX

This Policy is issued at the age shown on page three, which should be the age attained by the Insured on the last birthday prior to the Policy Date. If the Policy Date falls on the Insured's birthday, the age should be the Insured's attained age on the Policy Date.

If the Insured's age or sex is incorrectly shown on page three, we will adjust the proceeds payable under this Policy to the proceeds the premium would have purchased at the correct age and sex based upon our rates in effect when this Policy was issued.

---

[9]N.Y. INS. LAW § 3203(a)(5) (McKinney 1985).

[10]Lucas v. American Bankers' Ins. Co., 141 So. 394 (La. Ct. App. 1932). *See also* dicta in Smith v. National Life & Acci. Ins. Co., 183 Ark. 852, 39 S.W.2d 319 (1931).

[11]Lucas v. American Bankers' Ins. Co., 141 So. 394 (La. Ct. App. 1932).

Divisible Surplus Provision

The 1905 Armstrong Investigation of insurance practices included an investigation of the dividend practices of some of the large mutual life insurance companies. Instead of paying policyowner dividends each year under participating life insurance policies, as is done today, it was then customary for life insurers to accumulate surplus funds for long periods of time—often 20 years or more. Only those policyowners whose policies were still in force at the end of the period shared in the funds so accumulated. The others forfeited their shares. The amounts paid to those who did receive dividends were increased by the forfeitures.[12]

Legislation resulting from the Armstrong Investigation made it mandatory, under participating policies, for insurers to ascertain and apportion divisible surplus to the policyowners at frequent intervals and required this to be expressed as a policy provision. Accordingly, the present New York Insurance Law requires participating policies to include a provision stating

> that the insurer shall annually ascertain and apportion any divisible surplus accruing on the policy.[13]

About one third of the states have laws requiring frequent apportionment of divisible surplus. One such policy provision reads as follows:

> Annual dividends such as the company may apportion shall be payable at the end of each policy year after the first while this policy is in force other than as extended term insurance.

Note that no divisible surplus provision appears in the illustrative policy in Appendix B. This is because it is a nonparticipating policy which does not provide for the payment of dividends. A dividend section from a participating policy is included in Appendix C.

A few states specify optional methods of applying dividends and require that these options be included in the contract. These requirements will be discussed in Chapter 12, "Premiums and Dividends."

Policy Loan Provision

The policy loan provision, like the nonforfeiture provisions, grew out of the legal reserve, level premium system. The nonforfeiture provisions guarantee to the policyowner an equitable share of the values he or she has helped to accumulate, but only if the policy is surrendered for cash or permitted to lapse. The policy loan provision benefits the policyowner who does not wish to lapse the policy and yet has a present need for cash. Policy loans were first made available on a voluntary basis and later by statutory requirement.

---

[12]This is the tontine system, so called because it was devised by Lorenzo Tonti.
[13]N.Y. INS. LAW § 3203(a)(6) (McKinney 1985).

Policy loans are not actually loans from a legal standpoint. That is, a policy loan does not create a debtor-creditor relationship between the policyowner and the insurer, as in the case of a true loan. Policy loans are actually advances. An advance is money paid before the stipulated time of payment. A policy loan is an advance of the cash surrender value payment or of the death benefit. It will be deducted from the cash surrender value if the policy is surrendered before the loan is repaid, or from the death benefit if the loan is not repaid prior to the insured's death.

Policy loans and automatic premium loans will be discussed at length in Chapter 13, "Nonforfeiture Provisions and Policy Loans."

Reinstatement Provision

Reinstatement provisions came into general use in life insurance policies in this country during the final decade of the last century. Until 1905, however, there were no laws requiring them. At the present time, more than half the states have laws requiring that any policy issued, or issued for delivery, in the state must include a reinstatement provision.

A reinstatement provision allows the policyowner to reinstate a lapsed policy. Such a provision ordinarily requires that the application for reinstatement be made within three years from the date of policy lapse. The policyowner must produce satisfactory evidence of the insurability of the insured. Unpaid premiums must be paid with interest. Policy loans must be paid with interest or reinstated. The policy must not have been surrendered for cash, nor any extended term insurance exhausted.

Reinstatement provisions provide a valuable contractual right to the policyowner. They will be discussed at length in Chapter 15, "Lapse and Reinstatement."

OPTIONAL POLICY PROVISIONS

In addition to those policy provisions required by law, policies ordinarily contain a number of provisions which are permitted but not required. Among these are the ownership, assignment, suicide, and change of plan provisions.

Ownership Provision

Most policies are issued on the application of the insured who names a revocable beneficiary. Thus, the insured has full ownership and control over the policy. However, most insurers also sell policies which are applied for and issued to persons other than the insured.[14] The insured has no ownership

---

[14]Policies owned by someone other than the insured are not new. The first policy issued by the Mutual Life of New York was applied for by a woman on the life of her husband. She was both the owner and the beneficiary, but not the insured.

rights under such policies. Most policies owned by a person other than the insured are for business purposes. Personal insurance is usually issued on the application of the proposed insured.

The ownership provision indicates the owner of the policy and describes ownership rights. There is an ownership provision in the illustrative policy in Appendix B.

Assignment Provision

An assignment of a life insurance policy is a transfer by the policyowner of some or all of the rights of ownership. Unless the policy states that assignment is restricted or prohibited, the policyowner has a right to assign the policy as a matter of law. A policy provision permitting assignment is not required. Assignment provisions, therefore, do not legally grant the right to assign the policy, although they may state that the policyowner has this right. They do define the insurer's rights and responsibilities in the event that the policyowner elects to exercise the right to assign.

The assignment provision can prohibit or restrict assignment of the policy. The insurer will not be bound by an assignment if the policy prohibits assignment. If the policy restricts assignment, the terms of the assignment provision must be complied with, or the insurer will not be bound.

The assignment provision in the illustrative policy in Appendix B reads as follows:

COLLATERAL ASSIGNMENT

You may assign this Policy as collateral for a loan without the consent of any revocable beneficiary. We are not bound by any assignment unless it is in writing and recorded at our Home Office. We are not responsible for the validity of any assignment. The rights of an assignee will at all times be subject to any indebtedness to us at the time the assignment is recorded by us, and, if applicable, to loans granted at any time by us under the automatic premium loan provision of the Policy.

Assignments are discussed in detail in Chapter 14, "Assignments and Other Transfers."

Suicide Provision

If the policy has no provision declaring that suicide is not a risk assumed under the policy, the death of the insured by suicide is generally held by the courts to be covered. However, nearly all modern life policies do contain a provision excluding deaths by suicide. The exclusion will usually be for a specified period of time. Two years is typical. Some states limit by statute the period of time during which suicide can be excluded. This is reasonable, as most people who commit suicide do not plan the act far in advance. On the other hand, it is also reasonable to exclude suicide for some period of time immediately after the application is submitted. A person who is planning suicide is not an insurable risk, as the event insured against is within the applicant's control.

The typical suicide provision establishes a compromise between the requirement that there be an insurable risk, on the one hand, and the needs of the suicide's beneficiaries, on the other. The provision protects the insurer from persons who would take out life insurance intending suicide, while also protecting beneficiaries of persons who die by suicide after the policy has been in effect for a while. A typical provision is that in the illustrative policy in Appendix B which reads as follows:

SUICIDE

If the Insured dies by suicide, while sane or insane, within two years from the Policy Date, our liability will be limited to the amount of the premiums paid, less any indebtedness.[15]

Contract Change Provision

The parties to any contract can, by mutual consent, change their agreement. They can incorporate new terms or effect an entirely new contract. This is true of a life insurance policy, as well as of other contracts. A contract change provision is often included in the policy to make this clear. The provision does not give the parties any rights they would not otherwise have under the law, however. The provision in the illustrative policy in Appendix B reads as follows:

POLICY EXCHANGE PRIVILEGE

While this Policy is in force with no premium in default, you may exchange the Policy for another form of Policy. Our approval is needed. An additional payment and evidence the Insured is then insurable under our underwriting rules then in effect may be required.

PROHIBITED POLICY PROVISIONS

In addition to requiring that certain provisions be included in life policies, the insurance laws of most states also specify some provisions that cannot be included in policies issued or delivered in the state. These prohibited provisions are considered to be against the public interest. The most important of these prohibitions are discussed in this section.

---

[15]The phrase *while sane or insane* is explained in the section concerning suicide in Chapter 18, "Contract Performance."

Time Limit on Legal or Equitable Actions

The Illinois law mandating a time limit on legal or equitable actions is typical of many states. The Illinois Insurance Code states the following:

> After the effective date of this Code no policy of life insurance may be issued or delivered in this State if it includes . . . [a] provision limiting the time within which any action may be commenced to less than 3 years after the cause of action accrues.[16]

The purpose of this prohibition is to prevent insurers from including a provision in the policy allowing the policyowner or beneficiary an unreasonably short time period in which to initiate a legal or equitable action against the insurer. The statute does not prohibit such time limitation policy provisions, but merely those which are too restrictive.

Without a provision for a time limit on legal or equitable actions, the policyowner or beneficiary would be limited only by the state statute of limitations for contract actions. Sometimes, such state statutes of limitation allow a long period of time in which to initiate contract actions. Illinois, for example, requires that an action on a written contract be brought within ten years of the date when the cause of action arose.[17] However, if the policy contains a provision restricting the time for initiation of contract actions to three years, as is allowed in Illinois, the time period for initiating an action would be reduced by seven years.

A delay of many years in the initiation of a contract action could create hardship for the insurer. Key witnesses might die or disappear, and other circumstances could change so much that it would be difficult or impossible for the insurer to support its position with convincing evidence. It is, therefore, permissible in the majority of states to include a provision in the policy that will shorten the time allowed for initiation of contract actions, but not by more than a specified period. The periods specified in state statutes range from one to six years. Periods of three and five years are common. There are states which do not allow such policy provisions at all.

A contractual limitation of the time in which a suit must be brought generally will be upheld by the courts unless there is a statute forbidding such a provision. Insurers do not have to include a provision limiting the time in which suit can be brought, however, and many do not. The illustrative policy contains no such limitation.

Dating Back Provision

Occasionally, an applicant wishes the policy dated back to "save age." This means that the applicant wants the policy to be dated back to a time when the applicant was at a younger age, so that he or she gets the benefit of

---

[16]ILL. REV. STAT. ch. 73 ¶ 837(1)(a)(1985) (Ill. Ins. Code § 225(1)).
[17]ILL. REV. STAT. ch. 110, ¶ 13-206 (1985).

a lower premium. Within limits there is no objection to this procedure. However, when a policy is dated back, a premium will be payable for a period in which no insurance was in force. In addition, the contestable and suicide periods are shortened by the period for which the policy has been dated back. For example, if the two-year contestable and suicide periods begin on the policy date, a policy issued July 1, 1988, but dated back to January 1, 1987, would be contestable for only six months from policy issuance. The suicide period would also run for only six months. The insured's suicide seven months after policy issuance would be beyond the suicide exclusion period. To prevent such results, many states have enacted statutes making it unlawful for insurers to date back policies beyond a stipulated period, usually six months prior to the date of the original application. The Illinois law accomplishes this by prohibiting:

> A provision by which the policy purports to be issued or take effect more than six months before the original application for the insurance was made.[18]

The New York version of this prohibition forbids dating any policy more than six months before the application was made if that reduces the premium below the premium that would be payable as determined by the nearest birthday of the insured on the application date.[19]

Less Value Statutes

The less value statutes enacted by many states are intended to prevent the insurer from promising benefits on the face of the policy that are curtailed or extinguished in the body of the policy. The practice of excluding the hazards of war, aviation, and suicide has created a direct conflict with less value statutes, as has the misstatement of age provision.

The Illinois law partially avoids the problem by prohibiting:

> A provision for any mode of settlement at maturity after the expiration of the contestable period of the policy of less value than the amount insured plus dividend additions, if any, less any indebtedness to the company on or secured by the policy, and less any premium that may by the terms of the policy be deducted, except as permitted by clause (c) of subsection (1) of Section 224.[20]

Clause (c) of subsection (1) of section 224, referred to in the statute, permits war and aviation hazard exclusions. In the less value statutes of some states, there is no phrase referring to hazards which can be excluded in the policy, but, usually, the state will have other statutes relating to war and aviation

---

[18]ILL. REV. STAT. ch. 73, ¶ 837(1)(b) (1985) (Ill. Ins. Code § 225(1)(b)).
[19]N.Y. INS. LAW § 3208(a)(McKinney 1985).
[20]ILL. REV. STAT. ch. 73, ¶ 837(1)(c) (1985) (Ill. Ins. Code § 225(1)(c)).

hazard exclusions, and to suicide, contestability, or misstatement of age provisions. The courts can take those statutes into consideration in interpreting the state's less value statute.

Forfeiture for Failure to Repay a Policy Loan

Illinois law forbids:

> A provision for forfeiture of the policy for failure to repay any loan on the policy, or to pay interest on such loan, while the total indebtedness on the policy, including interest, is less than the loan value thereof.[21]

This prohibition implements the required policy loan standard provision. One fourth of the states have such a prohibition.

Agent of the Insured

Courts generally have held legally ineffective an attempt by an insurer to make the insurer's soliciting agent, by policy provision, the agent of the insured for the purpose of taking the application. The Illinois legislature has enacted this into statutory law by prohibiting:

> A provision to the effect that the agent soliciting the insurance is the agent of the person insured under the policy, or making the acts or representations of such agent binding upon the person so insured under the policy.[22]

UNIVERSAL AND VARIABLE LIFE INSURANCE LAWS

Universal, variable, and universal variable life insurance policies were developed to counter the trend to "buy term insurance and invest the difference." Sales of these policies increased rapidly during the 1980s. The laws governing universal and variable life insurance are so varied and complex that only a brief outline of these laws can be given in this book.

Universal Life Insurance Regulations

There are three basic types of life insurance policies: whole life insurance, term insurance, and endowment insurance. Universal life insurance is a type of whole life insurance. It was developed during the early 1980s to capitalize on current interest rates, which were then high. Under a universal life

---

[21]*Id.* ¶ 837(1)(d).

[22]*Id.* ¶ 837(1)(e). Note the use of the word *insured* in this statute. Legislators sometimes say "insured" when "applicant" or "policyowner" is what they really mean. It is to be hoped that insurance lobbyists and others knowledgeable about insurance will persuade them to use correct terminology in statutes.

insurance contract, mortality and expense charges are first deducted from the premium, and then the remainder of the premium is put into the cash value portion of the policy where it earns current interest rates. The insurer holds different investment portfolios for universal life policies than for its other whole life policies. The policyowner shares some of the risks of lower current interest rates. There is usually a low guaranteed rate of interest, such as 3.5 percent.

Although the structure of universal life policies differs from insurer to insurer, some features frequently found are death benefits which are level or increasing—at the policyowner's option—and flexibility in the amount and timing of premiums the policyowner must pay.

In 1984 the NAIC adopted a Universal Life Insurance Model Regulation. The purpose of regulations based on the model regulation is to supplement existing life insurance regulations. In the model regulation a universal life insurance policy is defined as "any individual life insurance policy under the provisions of which separately identified interest credits and mortality and expense charges are made to the policy." The model regulation has sections governing valuation, nonforfeiture values, policy provisions, disclosure to policyowners and prospective policyowners, and filing with the state insurance department. About one third of the states have adopted universal life insurance regulations based on the model regulation. Most of the others have various guidelines which apply to universal life insurance policies.

Variable Life Insurance Laws

Variable life insurance was first developed in the 1960s, but real interest in variable life insurance began in the 1980s. Generally speaking, variable life insurance is a level premium, cash value, whole life insurance contract with premiums which go into investment accounts separate from the insurer's other investment accounts. The policyowner has two or more investment accounts to choose from. One of these accounts might contain growth stocks, another long-term corporate bonds, another intermediate-term government bonds, and so forth. The policyowner is credited with the actual return on the money in the accounts chosen. There is no guarantee of principal or interest. The cash value may increase or decrease on a daily basis. Likewise, the death benefit will increase or decrease depending on the performance of the investment accounts. Most variable life insurance policies guarantee that the face amount will not fall below a specified minimum. The insurer adjusts the death benefit annually.

Variable life insurance is considered a security, as well as an insurance contract. Those selling variable life insurance must obey federal and state securities laws as well as life insurance laws. Variable life insurance policies must be registered under the federal Securities Act. Those selling variable life insurance policies have to register as broker-dealers under the federal Securities Exchange Act. The insurer or other entity providing investment advisory services to the separate accounts must comply with the Investment Advisors Act. State securities laws also apply to variable life insurance policies.

More than half the states have regulations based on the NAIC's Model Variable Contract Law. About one third have other variable contract regulations or statutes. The model law provides for the establishment of separate accounts by insurers domiciled in the state.

The NAIC's Variable Life Insurance Model Regulation contains detailed provisions governing insurers' qualifications, policy content and filing, reserves, separate accounts, information to be given applicants and policyowners, and agent qualifications. More than half the states have regulations based on this model.

Variable Universal Life Insurance Laws

Variable universal life insurance policies are similar to universal life policies, except that with variable universal policies the amount in the policy account can go up and down with the investment experience of the separate account. By contrast, under a universal life insurance policy, a minimum guaranteed interest rate is credited to the policy account and the insurer can declare higher rates periodically. Insurers issuing variable universal life insurance policies are subject to federal and state securities laws and insurance laws.

POLICY FILING AND APPROVAL

To assure compliance with the policy provisions laws, every insurance commissioner is given responsibility for policy forms, although the nature of this responsibility varies from state to state. Insurers are prohibited from issuing or delivering a policy within the state until the form has been filed with and approved by the commissioner. In some states, the commissioner is required to notify the company within a stated period, usually 30 days, if the policy form does not comply with the statutory requirements. If such notice is not received, the insurer can assume that the form has been approved. In other states, the insurer must wait until actual approval is received before the form can be used.

If a policy is issued without the required approval of the commissioner, it is generally held to evidence a valid contract, enforceable by the policyowner or beneficiary. The statutory requirements are for their benefit, and, therefore, such contracts are usually considered binding on the insurer. These contracts are construed as if they included any required provisions that are more favorable to the policyowner or beneficiary than those actually included in the policy.

Usually, there is a penalty which can be imposed on an insurer for issuing a policy that has not been approved by the commissioner as required by the statute. The penalty can be a fine, or even the revocation of the insurer's license to do business in that state.

SUMMARY

A life insurance policy is required by law to be written in simplified language in many jurisdictions. It is also ordinarily required by law to contain certain standard policy provisions, such as settlement options tables, nonforfeiture provisions, a grace period provision, an incontestable clause, an entire contract provision, a misstatement of age provision, a divisible surplus provision (if it is a participating policy), a policy loan provision, and a reinstatement provision.

Certain optional provisions may be included in the life policy. Among these are the ownership provision, assignment provision, suicide provision, and contract change provision.

The law prohibits certain other provisions. A policy cannot contain a clause which too severely limits the time during which legal or equitable actions may be brought. Backdating to save age may not be done beyond a certain time period, usually six months. Less value statutes prohibit insurers from reducing benefits promised on the face of the policy. Statutes in some states prohibit an insurer from stating in the policy that the soliciting agent is the agent of the applicant.

Universal life insurance policies have special regulations which govern them. Those selling variable life insurance policies must obey state and federal securities laws and state insurance laws, including special insurance laws governing variable contracts.

A life policy form must be approved by the insurance commissioner of the state where the policy will be sold. Usually, there is a penalty that can be imposed on the insurer for issuing a policy that has not been approved by the commissioner.

ILLUSTRATIVE CASE

The following case illustrates the interpretation of the provisions of a life insurance policy by a court.

GRACE L. SUGGS

v.

THE LIFE INSURANCE COMPANY OF VIRGINIA[23]
Supreme Court of Appeals of Virginia

EGGLESTON, Chief Justice.

* * * * *

These are the material facts: On July 1, 1955 the Company issued its policy insuring the life of William Durwood Suggs, III, who was born on February 16, 1942, became twenty-one years of age on February 16, 1963, and died on April 16, 1963. The plaintiff was named as beneficiary in the policy and at the time of the death of the insured all of the premiums had been paid.

---

[23]207 Va. 7, 147 S.E.2d 707 (1966).

Under the terms of the policy the Company contracted to pay $3,000 as "Initial Insurance" "in the event of the death of the Insured during the initial insurance period," or to pay $15,000 as "Ultimate Insurance" "in the event of the death of the Insured after the initial insurance period." The policy defined the "Initial Insurance Period" as "the period between the policy date and the policy anniversary nearest the Insured's 21st birthday excluding such policy anniversary."

On the back of the policy and at the bottom of the first page the following was printed:

"JUNIOR ESTATE BUILDER
"Insurance Payable at Death of Insured—Increased After Age 21
"Premiums Payable to Age 65 or Until Prior Death
"—Non-Participating—"

It is agreed that these notations are printed on the policy pursuant to Code, Section 38.1-403, which provides: "On the face and on the back of each such policy there shall be placed a title which shall briefly and accurately describe the nature and form of the policy."

The question presented is whether the plaintiff is entitled to the initial insurance of $3,000, payable during the initial insurance period as defined in the policy, or the ultimate insurance of $15,000 payable after the initial insurance period.

The plaintiff does not question that under the policy definition of the initial insurance period, standing alone, she is entitled to recover only $3,000. It is clear that the death of the insured on April 16, 1963 occurred within the initial insurance period which is defined as "the period between the policy date [July 1, 1955] and the policy anniversary nearest the Insured's 21st birthday [February 16, 1963]." But she contends that the Junior Estate Builder endorsement is a part of the insurance contract; that since the death of the insured occurred after he had reached 21 years of age, under the provision in the endorsement—"Insurance Payable at Death of Insured—Increased After Age 21"—she became entitled to the increased amount of insurance, or $15,000. She further contends that there is an inconsistency as to when the ultimate insurance is payable under this language in the endorsement and that in the body of the policy, and that this inconsistency creates an ambiguity which under familiar principles should be resolved against the Company and in her favor.

The lower court held that the Junior Estate Builder endorsement, which it characterized as a "Title" description, is not a part of the insurance contract, nor is it the purpose and intent of the statute . . . to make it a part of the contract. It further held that if such endorsement be deemed a part of the insurance contract, the language therein is not inconsistent with the provisions in the policy fixing the time for the payment of the initial insurance and the ultimate insurance, respectively, and that the plaintiff was entitled to recover the initial insurance of $3,000.

There is a conflict of authority as to whether an endorsement on an insurance policy, designating its kind and type, is a part of the insurance contract.

The obvious purpose of Section 38.1-403 is to require an insurance company to display on the face and on the back of a policy a description of its nature and form in order that a prospective purchaser may know what type of insurance he is purchasing. Such requirement is for the benefit of the prospective purchaser and he is entitled to rely on it. While it may not be strictly accurate to say that such an endorsement is a part of the contract of insurance, in construing the contract the policy must be considered as a whole and the endorsement read in connection with the remainder thereof, as an aid in arriving at the intention of the parties.

The contention of the plaintiff that she is entitled to increased amount of insurance under the language of the endorsement is based upon the premise that the word "After" in the phrase "Increased After Age 21" means "immediately after," "upon," or "as soon as." She argues that as soon as such event occurred she became entitled to the increased amount of the insurance—$15,000. We do not agree with this contention.

When the contractual terms and the provisions of the policy including those in the endorsement, are read in their entirety it is clear that the word "After" as used in the phrase "Increased After Age 21" means "subsequent in point of time" to, or "later in time" than, the insured's attainment of his 21st birthday. This is in accord with the commonly accepted definition of the word after. The language indicating that the amount of insurance payable at the death of the insured is "Increased After Age 21" obviously refers to the provision in the policy that upon the happening of that event the amount of the insurance is increased as therein provided.

Such interpretation removes any question as to the inconsistency between the language of the endorsement and that of the other provisions of the policy and brings them into complete harmony. It accords with the principle that all of the provisions of a contract of insurance should be considered and construed together and seemingly conflicting provisions harmonized when that can be reasonably done, so as to effectuate the intention of the parties as expressed therein. . . . Thus, while the insured's death was "After Age 21," it was also within the initial insurance period.

We agree with the holding of the lower court that there is no inconsistency or ambiguity in the provisions of the policy and that since the insured died "After Age 21" but within the initial insurance period the plaintiff was entitled to recover the amount of the initial insurance—$3,000.

Affirmed.

QUESTIONS FOR REVIEW

1. Generally speaking, what is the legal status of an oral contract for life insurance? Why are life insurance contracts nearly always expressed in writing?

2. List the different provisions which usually are required to be in a life insurance policy. What is the significance of the words *in substance* in relation to these required provisions?

3. What is the purpose of the free examination provision?

4. Describe the grace period provision in life insurance policies and the way in which it operates if the insured dies during the grace period.

5. Show the relationship between the principle of incorporation by reference and the entire contract provision in a life insurance policy.

6. Within recent years, the word *sex* has been incorporated into the misstatement of age provision of some policies. Tell how this change affects the operation of the provision.

7. Describe three optional life policy provisions.

8. Describe the provisions of a typical suicide clause.

9. Among the usually prohibited policy provisions are those relating to (a) dating back, and (b) agent of the insured. Describe each of these prohibited provisions.

10. Suppose a policy is issued without the required approval of the commissioner of insurance. What is the legal status of such a contract?

CHAPTER 8

Added Benefits and Limitations

ACCIDENTAL DEATH BENEFIT
  Accident and *Accidental* Defined
  Proximate Cause
  Accidental Means and Accidental Result
  Accidental Means Defined
  Accidental Means Cases
  External and Violent Means
  Voluntary Assumption of a Known Risk
  Suicide
  Harm Inflicted by Another
  Accident and Disease
  Time Limitation Clauses
  Risks Not Covered
  Burden of Proof
DISABILITY BENEFITS
  Total Disability
  General and Occupational Disability
  Permanent Disability
  Risks Not Covered
GUARANTEED INSURABILITY OPTION
WAR HAZARD EXCLUSION
  Status and Result Clauses
  Military Service
  Military Activities
  Existence of War
AVIATION HAZARD EXCLUSION
SUMMARY

The traditional life insurance contract provided one benefit, payable at the death of the insured. Today, it is common practice to make additional benefits available—sometimes as an integral part of the policy and sometimes by means of separate, added sections called riders. The practice of adding benefits by appropriate riders permits flexibility in adapting basic plans to indi-

199

vidual needs. Clauses or riders can also be added to the policy to limit coverage under certain circumstances.

Benefits often added to the traditional death benefit are the accidental death benefit, disability benefits (waiver of premium and disability income), and the guaranteed insurability option. Coverage is sometimes limited by war or aviation hazard exclusions. These added benefits and limitations will be discussed in this chapter, along with the more important legal problems associated with their use.

ACCIDENTAL DEATH BENEFIT

The accidental death benefit is a frequently-added benefit.[1] It is an integral part of some policies. As a general rule, however, the accidental death benefit is available only on application and for an additional premium and is added by rider. The proposed insured ordinarily must meet some underwriting requirements.

Typically, the accidental death benefit is provided in an amount equal to the amount of insurance provided by the life policy. Thus, if the policy provides $50,000 of insurance, the accidental death benefit will provide an additional $50,000. For this reason, the accidental death benefit is often referred to as double indemnity. Triple or quadruple the amount of insurance provided by the life policy is offered by some insurers for losses due to certain types of accidental deaths.

Accident and Accidental Defined

The courts will interpret the terms *accident* or *accidental* according to their ordinary definitions unless a statute or policy provision requires otherwise. According to the ordinary definition, an accident is an unusual event which the insured does not foresee. The event happens suddenly, unexpectedly, and without the insured's intent. There is usually an element of force or violence in an accident. The term *accidental* means occurring by accident.

Proximate Cause

The accident must be the proximate cause of the death if an accidental death benefit is to be payable. *Proximate cause* means a cause that is either directly responsible for the death or that initiates an unbroken chain of events, each causing the next, which leads to and brings about the death. The

---

[1]Although this is a discussion of accidental death benefits in life insurance policies, most of the principles stated will also apply to other types of policies insuring against accidental death, as, for example, health insurance policies with accidental death and dismemberment provisions, or travel accident insurance policies. Many of the principles will apply as well to coverage of accidental injury in health insurance policies.

proximate cause of a death is the primary cause. Without the proximate cause, the death would not have occurred.

Proximate cause is an especially important concept where accident and disease combine to cause an insured's death. This topic will be discussed later in this chapter.

Accidental Means and Accidental Result

We have used the term *accidental death benefit* as a generic term encompassing all types of life policy clauses allowing an additional benefit where the insured's death involves an accident. Actually, two categories of clauses have been recognized by some of the courts—accidental means clauses on the one hand and accidental result clauses on the other. Both accidental means clauses and accidental result clauses have many variations in wording. Some patterns do recur, however.

Under one fairly typical accidental means clause, the insurer promises to pay the specified amount

> upon receipt of due proof that death of the insured resulted from bodily injury effected directly and independently of all other causes by violent, external, and accidental means.

One insurer's accidental result clause reads in part as follows:

> The Company agrees to pay an Accidental Death Benefit upon receipt at its Home Office of due proof that the death of the Insured resulted, directly and independently of all other causes, from accidental bodily injury.

Under an accidental result clause, only the result must be accidental, while under an accidental means clause, both means and result must be accidental if benefits are to be payable. Coverage under an accidental result clause is, therefore, broader than that under an accidental means clause. For this reason, a distinction between the two can mean the difference between payment or nonpayment of benefits.

In recent years, the courts of many states have rejected the distinction between accidental means and accidental result. These courts treat accidental means clauses as if they were accidental result clauses. They have said that the distinction is unduly technical and not readily understood by policyowners.

The movement to reject the distinction was given impetus by a dissenting opinion of United States Supreme Court Justice Benjamin Cardozo in *Landress v. Phoenix Mutual Life Insurance Co.* in 1934.[2] There, Justice Cardozo asserted that "[t]he attempted distinction between accidental results and ac-

---

[2]291 U.S. 491.

cidental means will plunge this branch of the law into a Serbonian Bog."[3] Moreover, most insurers now use accidental result policy language.

Although the distinction between accidental means and accidental result clauses has ceased to be recognized in many jurisdictions, and although most insurers use clauses which do not mention accidental means, the distinction is still important in many instances. It has been upheld in recent cases in several jurisdictions.[4] It is, therefore, necessary for the student of life and health insurance law to understand the distinction the courts have made.

Accidental Means **Defined**

Means is the same as *cause.* The difference between accidental means clauses and accidental result clauses is the difference between cause and effect. Death is not caused by accidental means merely because the effect or result is accidental in the sense that it is unforeseen, unintended, and unusual. The means or cause itself must also be accidental if benefits are to be payable under an accidental means clause, in a state recognizing such clauses. The accidental means test is, thus, more difficult to meet than the accidental result test. Deaths which would be accidental under an accidental result clause have been held not covered where there was an accidental means clause in the policy. One court expressed the distinction between accidental means and accidental result as follows:

> [A]ccidental death is an unintended and undesigned result, arising from acts done; death by accidental means is where the result arises from acts unintentionally done.[5]

Thus, where there is an accidental means clause, courts have often held that no benefits are payable where the acts of the insured leading up to the death took place as intended and expected by him or her, though the resulting death was unintended and unexpected. In other words, the cause itself must be accidental.

This principal is easy to state, but, unfortunately, it is difficult to apply. One court said:

---

[3]Referring to Lake Serbonis in Egypt in which, according to Herodotus, whole armies were engulfed. The Supreme Court of Colorado, citing Justice Cardozo's reasoning with approval, said "Whatever kind of bog that is, we concur." Equitable Life Assur. Soc'y v. Hemenover, 100 Colo. 231, 67 P.2d 80 (1937).

[4]Nicholas v. Mutual Benefit Life Ins. Co., 451 F.2d 252 (6th Cir. 1971); Chelly v. Home Ins. Co., 285 A.2d 810 (Del. Super. Ct. 1971), aff'd, 293 A.2d 295 (Del. 1972); Mozingo v. Mid-South Ins. Co., 28 N.C. App. 352, 224 S.E.2d 208 (1976); Praetorian Mut. Life Ins. Co. v. Humphrys, 484 S.W.2d 413 (Tex. Civ. App. 1972). In two of these cases, *Nicholas v. Mutual Benefit Life Ins. Co.* and *Chelly v. Home Ins. Co.,* the policy language did not mention accidental means, but the courts, nevertheless, construed the clauses involved to be accidental means clauses.

[5]Pledger v. Business Men's Acci. Ass'n., 197 S.W. 889 (Tex. Civ. App. 1917).

A consideration of the literally hundreds of cases where the courts have sought to construe such provisions in policies of insurance and interpret "accidental means" brings one to the sharp realization of the great truth in Justice Cardozo's warning, "The attempted distinction between accidental results and accidental means will plunge this branch of the law into a Serbonian Bog." The cases are in irreconcilable conflict.[6]

Some examples of the way in which the courts have dealt with accidental means clauses may help the reader to grasp the difficulty the courts have had in trying to develop a coherent body of law in this area.

Accidental Means Cases

In *United States Mutual Accident Association v. Barry*,[7] the insured, a doctor, died from internal injuries after jumping from a platform four feet high. Another doctor who had made the same jump testified that the insured made a heavy, inert sound when he landed. The United States Supreme Court upheld, as correct, the following instructions given by the trial court to the jury:

> [I]f a result is such as follows from ordinary means voluntarily employed in a not unusual or unexpected way, then, I suppose it cannot be called a result effected by accidental means . . . you must go further and inquire . . . was there or not any unexpected or unforeseen or involuntary movement of the body, from the time Dr. Barry left the platform, until he reached the ground, or in the act of alighting? . . . Did he accomplish just what he intended to in the way he intended to?

The Court further said:

> [I]f, in the act which precedes the injury, something unforeseen, unexpected, unusual occurs which produces the injury, then the injury has resulted through accidental means.

This case is frequently relied upon by the courts. It is notable, because it has been cited as supporting authority both by courts adhering to a strict interpretation of the term accidental means and by those using a moderate approach.

In *Avent v. National Life and Accident Insurance Co.*,[8] the Supreme Court of Tennessee took a strict approach to interpretation of an accidental means clause. There, the insured was receiving treatment for a stiff neck. The treatment was administered while the patient lay on a table and consisted mainly of manipulating the insured's head and neck. At the conclusion of one treatment session, the insured was unable to move. Subsequent surgery revealed a chipped bone in his neck, and he died 36 hours later.

---

[6]Thompson v. Prudential Ins. Co. of Am., 84 Ga. App. 214, 66 S.E.2d 119 (1951).
[7]131 U.S. 100 (1889).
[8]Life, Health & Acci. Ins. Cas. 2d (CCH) ¶ 506,422 (Tenn. 1954).

The insurer took the position that death was the result of a voluntary and intended act and, thus, was not caused by accidental means as required by the policy. The beneficiary contended that "excessive force and pressure was unintentionally and accidentally applied . . . and, as a result, a bone in the neck was accidentally broken." The court held that the benefit was not payable, saying:

> It is not sufficient that the injury be unusual and unexpected, but the cause itself must have been unexpected and accidental . . .
> The cause of the injury which resulted in the death of Avent was the aforesaid manipulation of his neck. That manipulation was not unexpected or accidental. It was intended by both Avent and the doctor. The means, therefore, producing the injury were not accidental under the rule followed in this State.

The reader likely has a mixed reaction to this case. Is it what the policyowner would reasonably have expected? Could the case not as logically have been decided the opposite way? The difficulty of separating cause and effect which was pointed out by Justice Cardozo is evident here.

Consider also an Alabama case where the policy contained an accidental means clause.[9] There, a gash was cut in the insured's lip while he was shaving himself or being shaved. The gash became infected, the infection spread to other parts of his body, and he died. The Alabama Supreme Court stated:

> There was no evidence whatever to show that the insured, or any other person, intentionally cut the gash; but all the evidence shows that the scar, cut, or gash was an accident, and within the risk of the policy.

The facts of this case and the policy language were similar to those in *Avent,* but, here, the court looked to the intent of the insured or of whoever was shaving him and concluded that the means were accidental and that the benefit was payable.

The court also examined the insured's intent in a Missouri case where the insured took an overdose of a prescription drug (paraldehyde) and died. There the court said:

> In poison cases, where the poison is mistaken for a harmless substance, there is lack of knowledge of, and intent to take, poison. There is thus unexpectedness with reference to the means. But in the instant case the insured knew he was taking paraldehyde, and the only thing unexpected was the result.[10]

The court, therefore, held that the means were not accidental, because the insured had done exactly what he intended to do, stating:

---

[9]National Life & Acci. Ins. Co. v. Singleton, 193 Ala. 84, 69 So. 80 (1915).
[10]Murphy v. Western & S. Life Ins. Co., 262 S.W.2d 340 (Mo. Ct. App. 1953).

If it had been shown that when insured was in the act of drinking from the bottle of paraldehyde, intending to take the dose prescribed, his foot slipped causing him to gulp down an excessive amount, the requirement of accidental means would have been satisfied.

In other words, the court said that if there is a slip or mishap in the action causing the injury, the cause would be accidental, as required by the accidental means provision. In this case, the court held that taking an overdose of the prescription drug was not such a "slip or mishap," as to make the means accidental.

By contrast, a Kansas court has held that taking an overdose of barbituates was accidental means, and the insured's death, therefore, was death by accidental means. The court said:

There is no evidence that the insured was aware of what amount of the drug would produce death. Without repeating all the evidence as to dosages taken by the insured, we think it such the jury could properly infer that insured was in ignorance that the amount she took was a lethal dose and that her death was by accidental means.[11]

Therefore, whether taking an overdose of a prescription drug does or does not constitute accidental means depends on the jurisdiction in which the question is presented.

However, the courts generally agree that death results from accidental means where it is caused by taking poison by mistake. This view is illustrated in a case where the insured took an arsenic preparation thinking it was a vitamin tonic. There, the court held that because of the mistake, the means were accidental, saying, "When death or injury results from taking poison by mistake, the injury or death results from external, violent or accidental means within the terms of a policy of insurance."[12]

As was noted earlier, the courts of some states have concluded that accidental means clauses should not be distinguished from accidental result clauses. This position was discussed in *Burr v. Commercial Travelers Mutual Accident Association*[13] as follows:

In this State [New York] there is no longer any distinction made between accidental death and death by accidental means, nor between accidental means and accidental results . . . insurance policies upon which the public relies for security in case of accident should be plainly written in understandable English "free from fine distinctions which few can understand until pointed out by lawyers and judges." A distinction between "accidental means" and "accidental results" is certainly not understood by the average man and he is the one for whom the policy is written.

---

[11]Hawkins v. New York Life Ins. Co., 176 Kan. 24, 269 P.2d 389 (1954).
[12]National Life & Acci. Ins. Co. v. Karasek, 240 Ala. 660, 200 So. 873 (1941).
[13]295 N.Y. 294, 67 N.E.2d 248 (1946).

The number of states which have abolished the distinction between accidental means and accidental result continues to increase. For example, in 1978, the Oregon Supreme Court abolished the distinction, saying:

> We have previously expressed doubts as to whether the ordinary purchaser would expect the concept of "accident" to have a different meaning depending upon whether the policy purports to require accidental means or accidental results. . . . We are convinced that no distinction would be expected.[14]

In states where the courts have abolished the distinction, even though the insurer has used accidental means language in its policies the court will treat it no differently from accidental result language. This, of course, is the most favorable interpretation from the policyowner's or beneficiary's viewpoint, as only the result must be accidental, rather than both means and result.

External and Violent Means

Accidental means clauses often state that benefits will be paid

> upon receipt of due proof that the death of the insured resulted directly and independently of all other causes from bodily injuries effected solely through *external, violent,* and accidental means evidenced by a visible contusion on the exterior of the body, except in the case of drowning or of internal injuries revealed by an autopsy [emphasis added].

The term *external means* refers to an agency external to the person. The agency may act internally, however. Poison is an example of an external agency which acts internally.

Violent means signifies a physical force producing a harmful result. The degree of force is unimportant. A very slight force will ordinarily satisfy the policy requirement.

Note that in the clause quoted above the "external, violent, and accidental means" must be "evidenced by a visible contusion on the exterior of the body, except in the case of drowning or of internal injuries revealed by an autopsy." Thus, the provision requires some abnormal bodily manifestation which can be ascertained by observation. The purpose of this requirement is to protect insurers from sham claims. However, the courts have generally been liberal toward the beneficiary in construing the visible contusion requirement. Discoloration of the skin, pallor, or slight abrasions have sufficed to meet the policy requirement.[15]

---

[14]Botts v. Hartford Acci. & Indem. Co., 284 Or. 95, 585 P.2d 657 (1978).
[15]Annot., 28 A.L.R. 3d 413 (1969).

Voluntary Assumption of a Known Risk

Generally speaking, if death is the natural and probable result of the insured's voluntary act, there is neither an accident nor accidental means. It is a basic legal principle that a person is presumed to have intended the natural and probable consequences of his or her own actions. Thus, if a person deliberately exposes himself or herself to what he or she knows are dangerous circumstances which will probably cause death, it cannot be maintained that a resulting death is either accidental or from accidental means.

For example, where an insured stated that she was going to jump from a car which was being driven around a turn at night at 25 miles per hour, and did leave the car immediately after making the statement, her ensuing death from head injuries was not accidental. Even if she did not intend to die, death was a natural and probable result of her action.[16]

The cases where the insured voluntarily assumed a risk often turn on whether death was foreseeable. In one case, the insured's death was held foreseeable by him where he had suggested playing Russian roulette and died a short time after, as a result of a gunshot wound in the head. The death was held not accidental and the insurer, therefore, was not liable for accidental death benefits.[17]

In another case, where the insured died of a gunshot wound in the head, but evidence showed he had thought the safety was in place when he put the gun to his head, the death was held accidental. The court held that the insured did not foresee his death under these circumstances.[18]

Suicide

Where the insured, while sane, intentionally takes her or his own life, the death is not accidental or by accidental means. This is because suicide is an intentional act. However, where an insured is insane at the time of her or his death by self-destruction and unconscious of the nature or result of the act, the death is by accident or accidental means.

Suicide is a risk which is frequently excepted in an accidental death benefit provision or rider. The accidental death benefit rider in the illustrative policy in Appendix B states the following:

> Certain risks are not covered. We will not pay the Accidental Death Benefit if the Insured's death results from any of the following causes: (1) Intentionally self-inflicted injury while sane; (2) Self-inflicted injury while insane; or . . . (10) Suicide, whether sane or insane . . .

---

[16]Zuliskey v. Prudential Ins. Co., 159 Pa. Super. 363, 48 A.2d 141 (1946).

[17]Koger v. Mutual of Omaha Ins. Co., 152 W. Va. 274, 163 S.E.2d 672 (1968). Russian roulette is an act of bravado where a person places one cartridge in a revolver, spins the cylinder, points the gun at his or her head, and pulls the trigger without looking to see where the cylinder has stopped.

[18]New York Life Ins. Co. v. Harrington, 299 F.2d 803 (9th Cir. 1962).

Harm Inflicted by Another

In the absence of a policy provision on the subject, the general rule is that injury to an insured inflicted by another person results from accident or accidental means if the insured did not foresee the injury. Whether or not the death is unforeseeable, and hence accidental, is determined from the viewpoint of the insured and not that of the other person.[19]

For example, in one case, where the insured was waylaid and killed by a robber, the death was held to be accidental.[20] In another case, the insured was hanged by a mob, and, again, the death was held accidental.[21]

On the other hand, where the insured provoked an assault or was the aggressor, the insured's resulting death will not be accidental if it was foreseeable and a natural and probable result of his or her actions. For example, where an insured used a deadly weapon to attack police officers, the insured's death at the hands of the officers should have been foreseen by the insured and was, therefore, not an accident.[22]

Where the insured assaults a spouse or other family member, the courts are more likely to hold that the death was accidental, particularly where there was a pattern of family fights. This is because, often, the insured could not foresee that death would result from such an altercation. In one case, where an insured husband had beaten his wife many times in the past, but she had never violently resisted the beatings, his death was held not foreseeable by him when the wife shot him as he was attempting to beat her. His death was, therefore, accidental, and the insurer was liable for the accidental death benefit.[23]

Accident and Disease

The accidental death benefit will not be payable if disease is the cause of the death, as ordinarily the risk insured against is loss resulting solely or independently from accident or accidental means. There are many instances where accident and disease are both present, however. In those cases, the courts will usually look to see whether the accident or the disease was the proximate—that is, primary—cause of the loss.

If the injury would have caused the death regardless of the insured's state of health, the accidental death benefit will be payable. If, for example, an insured who had a potentially fatal cancer failed to see a fast-moving train and was struck and killed, the insurer would be liable. Moreover, where the

---

[19]Annot., 49 A.L.R. 3d 673 (1973).

[20]Hutchcraft's Ex'r v. Travelers' Ins. Co., 87 Ky. 300, 8 S.W. 570 (1888). *See also* Allen v. Travelers' Protective Ass'n, 163 Iowa 217, 143 N.W. 574 (1913).

[21]Fidelity & Cas. Co. v. Johnson, 72 Miss. 333, 17 So. 2 (1895).

[22]Price v. Business Men's Assur. Co., 188 Ark. 637, 67 S.W.2d 186 (1934). *See also* Bernhard v. Prudential Ins. Co., 134 Neb. 402, 278 N.W. 846 (1938).

[23]Atlantic Am. Life Ins. Co. v. White, 332 So. 2d 389 (Ala. Civ. App. 1976).

accident is the primary cause of the death, there will ordinarily be liability, even if the insured is weakened by disease. For example, in one case, an insured had severe cirrhosis of the liver. He fell from a high platform, ruptured his weakened liver, and died from internal bleeding. Even though his chances of survival would have been better if he had had a healthy liver, the court held that the death was caused by the accident, and the accidental death benefit was payable. Here, the accident, not the disease, was held to be the proximate cause of the death.[24]

Conversely, where the disease, rather than the accident, is the primary cause of death, there will be no liability for the accidental death benefit. That is, if no considerable injury would have resulted from an accident had the insured not been afflicted with an existing disease, then the accident is not the proximate cause of the resulting harm. For example, in one case, where the insured had a severely diseased heart, death caused by a heart attack was held not to be the result of an accident, although death followed the excitement and exertion generated by a minor incident involving locked car bumpers. The court said the insured was in such bad health that she could have died without there being any noticeable stimulus.[25]

In many cases involving the combined effects of accident and disease, it is difficult to ascertain which was the primary cause of death. These cases are often conflicting.

The courts do agree that if an accidental injury causes a disease and death results from the disease, the accident will be held to be the proximate cause of death. There will be coverage under accidental means clauses if the disease was proximately caused by injury occasioned by accidental means. For example, in one case, where death resulted from blood poisoning following an accidental cut on the insured's finger, the accidental death benefits were held payable.[26]

Time Limitation Clauses

Policies containing either an accidental result or an accidental means clause ordinarily include a requirement that death must occur within 90 days of the injury if the accidental death benefit is to be payable.[27] This requirement is intended primarily to reduce problems that arise when the intervening time lapse makes it difficult or impossible to ascertain whether the injury was the proximate cause of death.

---

[24]Lindemann v. General Am. Life Ins. Co., 485 S.W.2d 477 (Mo. Ct. App. 1972).

[25]Tix v. Employers Cas. Co., 368 S.W.2d 105 (Tex. Civ. App. 1963).

[26]Central Acci. Ins. Co. v. Rembe, 220 Ill. 151, 77 N.E. 123 (1906).

[27]Ninety days is the most common time limitation, but other periods, such as 30, 60, 120, or 180 days have been used. For a discussion of accident insurance time limitations, *see* Annot., 39 A.L.R. 3d 1311 (1971).

When this requirement originated, medical science was not as far advanced as it is today. The requirement, therefore, causes problems now that it did not cause even a few decades ago. For example, it is not uncommon now for an injured insured to lie in a coma for more than 90 days before dying. Is a 90-day limit realistic, then, in this day of medical skill in prolonging life? Policies currently issued by several insurers indicate that some thought has been given to this question in that the time period has been lengthened to 120, 180, or 365 days.

Moreover, when it is clear from the circumstances that death resulted from the accident and that only medical skill prolonged the insured's life beyond the specified limit, should the death benefit be denied simply because the death did not occur within the time limit specified? Some insurers waive the time limit requirement under these circumstances. Others waive it if the insured dies within a few days after the time limit has expired.

Prior to 1973, it was well settled that the time limit requirement was enforceable. In 1973, the Pennsylvania Supreme Court held that the time limit requirement is against public policy and void in Pennsylvania.[28] Lower courts in New Jersey and California have since declared the requirement to be arbitrary and unreasonable where the accident was clearly the cause of the death.[29] However, courts in several other states have affirmed the majority position, stating that the requirement is enforceable.

Risks Not Covered

Insurers customarily list in their accidental death benefit provisions certain risks which are not covered. A reference source lists 100 different exclusions which are currently in use. Most insurers use only a small fraction of these, however. The accidental death benefit rider attached to the illustrative policy in Appendix B contains a typical list of risks not covered. The rider states the following:

> Certain risks are not covered. We will not pay the Accidental Death Benefit if the Insured's death results from any of the following causes:
>
> 1. Intentionally self-inflicted injury while sane; or
>
> 2. Self-inflicted injury while insane; or
>
> 3. Participation in an assault; or

---

[28]Burne v. Franklin Life Ins. Co., 451 Pa. 218, 301 A.2d 799 (1973).

[29]Karl v. New York Life Ins. Co., 154 N.J. Super. 182, 381 A.2d 62 (1977); National Life & Acci. Ins. Co. v. Edwards, 119 Cal. App. 3d 326, 174 Cal. Rptr. 31 (1981). The California case extended what is termed "the process of nature rule" from disability cases to accidental death cases in California. Under the process of nature rule, where the death clearly results from the accident, but the processes of nature take more than the specified time to cause the death, the accidental death benefit will be payable.

4. Participation in a felony; or

5. Travel or flight in or descent from any kind of aircraft; (a) on which the Insured is a pilot, officer or member of the crew; or (b) on which the Insured has duties aboard; or (c) which is being operated for any training or instructional purpose; or (d) on which the Insured is being flown for the purpose of descent while in flight; or

6. Any bodily or mental infirmity existing before or beginning after the accident; or

7. Any infection or disease existing before or beginning after the accident, except a disease or infection as provided in the definition of "accidental death"; or

8. Any drug, medication or sedative voluntarily taken unless; (a) administered by a licensed physician; or (b) taken as prescribed by a licensed physician; or

9. Alcohol in combination with any drug, medication or sedative; or

10. Suicide, whether sane or insane; or

11. Any poison, gas or fumes voluntarily taken, absorbed or inhaled; or

12. War or any act of war, whether or not the Insured is in military service. The term "war" includes war declared or undeclared. It also includes armed aggression resisted by: (a) the armed forces of any country; and (b) any international organization or combination of countries.

Burden of Proof

A plaintiff suing for an accidental death benefit has the burden of proving that the death was caused by accident or by accidental means. If the policy requires that the death result from external, violent, and accidental means, the plaintiff must prove that the means were external and violent, as well as accidental.

Where the plaintiff has established the accidental character of the death, there is a split of authority as to whether the plaintiff has to prove that the death was not proximately caused by disease. Some courts have held that the burden of proof is on the plaintiff. Other courts have held that the insurer has the burden of proving that the death was proximately caused by disease if it wishes to avoid liability on that ground.

As a general rule, the insurer has the burden of proving that the loss resulted from a risk which was excepted from coverage. Thus, an insurer might have to prove that an accidental death resulted from participation in a felony and that this risk was not covered by the accidental death policy provision.

Where plaintiff alleges that the insured's death was accidental, and the insurer alleges that the insured's death resulted from suicide, the majority view is that the burden is on the insurer to prove the suicide. However, a minority of courts have held that under accident provisions the plaintiff's burden of proving death by accident includes proving that the death was not by suicide.

DISABILITY BENEFITS

Disability benefits in life insurance contracts were first offered before the beginning of the century. A waiver of premium for disability was the first disability benefit offered. A disability income benefit was added not long afterward. The disability income benefit provided at first for payment of the face amount of the policy in annual installments. Later, the face amount was left intact to be paid as a death benefit, and disability income installment payments were made in addition to the death benefit. It was at first customary to provide installments of $10 per month for each $1,000 of face value. The premiums were waived as long as the disability continued.

In offering disability benefits, life insurers were embarking on uncharted seas, for ordinarily disability does not involve the clear-cut and ascertainable set of facts that death presents. On the contrary, disability is usually a highly subjective risk. Moreover, the only disability statistics available to the early life insurers were derived from the experience of the fraternal orders. The fraternal orders had been providing disability benefits for some time, but their business was conducted in a different way from that of the commercial insurers. To complicate the situation further, competition soon caused the companies to increase the benefits they offered, although they had no assurance that their rates were adequate.

By the middle 1920s, it was generally recognized that premiums for disability income coverages were inadequate. Before the situation could be corrected, the depression of the 1930s had struck. With it came some of the most unfavorable experience ever suffered in this or any other field by the life insurance industry. So disastrous was the experience that the majority of the larger life insurance companies ceased issuing disability income coverages entirely. After the end of World War II, a number of life insurers resumed offering disability income coverages. Their rates were then based on much more adequate statistics.

Today disability income benefits are offered by many life and health insurers. Generally, such benefits are offered as a monthly income payable in the event the insured becomes disabled as defined in the policy. The coverage can be short-term or long-term. Under short-term coverages, disability income benefits are ordinarily payable for not more than two to five years, depending on the provisions of the policy. A long-term disability income benefit will typically be payable during the continuance of disability, as defined in the policy, until the insured is 65 years old.

Disability income coverages are, of course, offered in other forms than as a part of a life insurance policy. Many insurers offer individual disability income insurance contracts, group or franchise disability income insurance, or health insurance contracts covering loss of income along with reimbursement for medical expenses.

As part of a life insurance policy, the waiver of premium for disability benefit is more extensively sold than is the disability income benefit. The waiver of premium for disability benefit provision ordinarily states that if the insured becomes disabled, as defined in the life insurance policy, the insurer will waive the payment of premiums which become due on the policy during the continuance of disability, however long disability may last.[30] The benefit is usually not granted, however, if the disability begins after the insured has reached a specified age such as 60 or 65.

Total Disability

Most policies or riders issued today require that an insured be totally disabled in order to receive disability benefits. Total disability is ordinarily defined in terms of the insured's inability to work and earn an income. This is true for both waiver of premium and disability income coverages.

For example, a definition of total disability used by some insurers is that the insured is totally disabled when he or she is "wholly prevented from performing any work, following any occupation or engaging in any business for remuneration or profit." A literal view of this definition—that if the insured is able to work at anything, he or she is not totally disabled—has been taken by some courts, although not many. By far the majority of courts today take the position that total disability does not mean a state of absolute helplessness as would be true under the literal interpretation. Their reasoning is that benefits payable only if the insured is literally "wholly prevented from performing any work, following any occupation or engaging in any business for remuneration or profit" would be of limited value. Under this interpretation, an almost complete paralysis would not be disabling, since a person with sufficient gifts and spirit could presumably work at something even under those circumstances.

On the basis that a reasonable interpretation is intended, therefore, the great majority of courts have taken the position that the insurers could not have intended to require a state of complete helplessness, as would be true if the definition were applied literally. Instead, the definition above is interpreted by the majority of courts to mean a disability of such a nature as to prevent the insured from performing the substantial and material acts of her or his own occupation or of any other occupation for which the insured's experience, education, or training might fit her or him. This is the interpretation followed by most insurers which have used or still use this definition.

---

[30]In some convertible term policies, if the disability occurs while the policy is still convertible, the insurer will waive payment of premiums until the end of the conversion period and continue the waiver after the conversion to whole life as long as the disability lasts.

There have been court holdings yet more liberal to the insured where the position is taken that if the insured is unable to work at his or her customary occupation, the insured is totally disabled within the meaning of this definition. In effect, this rewrites the policy provision. However, most courts do not go this far in their interpretation.

Many companies today use a policy definition of total disability that incorporates the interpretation followed by the majority of the courts. Illustrative of this type of definition is the following:

> Total disability is disability of the insured as a result of bodily injury or disease which causes the insured to be wholly and continuously prevented thereby from engaging in any gainful occupation for which he or she is reasonably fitted by reason of education, training or experience.

Still another definition is used by some insurers in which the insured will be considered totally disabled if unable to work at any occupation for which he or she is fitted by training or experience or if the income he or she is able to earn is reduced to a specified fraction of the income earned before the disability began. Illustrative of this approach is the following policy definition:

> The insured will be deemed to become totally disabled on the Total Disability Date, which is the day when for a period of four consecutive months because of accidental bodily injury or sickness, either (a) he or she has been unable to engage in his or her former occupation or in any other occupation for which he or she is suited by education, training or experience; or (b) his or her average monthly Earned Income has been reduced to one-fourth or less of his or her former monthly income.

A clause frequently added to disability provisions or riders defines total disability as the total loss of the use of both legs or both arms or one leg and one arm or the total loss of the sight of both eyes. Usually this definition has no reference to whether the insured is able to work or to the amount of earnings. This clause appears in addition to the clause defining total disability in relation to occupation. The following is typical:

> The total and irrecoverable loss of the sight of both eyes or of the use of both hands or of both feet or of one hand and one foot shall be considered total disability even if the insured shall engage in an occupation.

The disability benefit rider in Appendix B contains a similar clause.

General and Occupational Disability

Some disability clauses, such as that first mentioned above, require that the insured be unable to engage in any work, occupation, or business. These are general disability clauses. By contrast, occupational disability clauses require only that the insured be disabled from his or her own occupation.

There are also combination clauses which require the insured to be disabled from her or his own occupation for a specified period of time and, thereafter, from any occupation. The following is an example:

Total disability is incapacity as the result of bodily injury or disease, to engage in an occupation for remuneration or profit. During the first 24 months of disability, occupation means the occupation of the insured at the time such disability began; thereafter it means any occupation for which he or she is or becomes reasonably fitted by education, training, or experience.

Permanent Disability

At one time, it was customary to require that disability be both total and permanent. It is now uncommon to require that disability be permanent, although many policies still in effect do contain this language.

It seems relatively certain that, in the early days, the insurers intended, by a permanent disability, to indicate a disability of long-term duration. But how long, and what of the disability from which the insured has already recovered at the time suit is brought for the disability benefits? The literal meaning of *permanent disability,* obviously, is disability that continues until the death of the insured. However, this cannot be what the insurers meant. They have long included in their policies provisions relating to the cessation of benefits upon recovery of the insured. Obviously, under these circumstances, they cannot have contemplated only disability that continues until the death of the insured. This ambiguity has created the necessity of interpretation by the courts.

The courts have been divided on the meaning of permanent disability. Some courts have given the words *permanent disability* their literal meaning—that is, that disability must continue until the end of the insured's lifetime. This interpretation creates the practical problem that the insured would either have to die or recover before it could be known whether benefits were payable.

The majority of courts have, therefore, taken a more moderate approach. They have interpreted *permanent disability* to mean disability expected to last for an indefinite, continuous period of time, without any present indication of recovery.

Insurers require that disability must have continued for at least six months[31] before it will be considered permanent. Insureds have sometimes made efforts to have this six-month period construed by a court to mean that disability that had continued for the six-month period would be presumed to be permanent in the literal sense of the word. As a general rule, however, the

---

[31]Sometimes four months is the time period specified.

courts have interpreted the six-month period to be a mere waiting period, included in the policy for the purpose of relieving the insurer of the expense of having to consider and investigate numerous premature claims.

In permanent disability provisions, insurers usually emphasize that the six-month waiting period is not to be interpreted to mean that the disability is considered for all purposes permanent by using language such as the following:

> If, and only if, total disability as herein defined has existed uninterrupt- edly during the lifetime of the Insured for at least six months, it shall be deemed to have been and to be permanent, but only for the purpose of determining the commencement of liability hereunder.

Risks Not Covered

As with the accidental death benefit provision, insurers usually specify some risks not covered with respect to the disability of the insured. Most insurers use only two or three exclusions. Intentionally self-inflicted injury and war hazard exclusions are the most common. Other exclusions which are sometimes used are "committing or attempting to commit a felony" and "par- ticipation in parachute jumping, skydiving or skin or scuba diving." The waiver of premium disability benefit rider in the illustrative policy in Appen- dix B has the following clause:

> Certain risks are not covered. They are as follows. We will not waive premiums if total disability results from:
>
> (1) intentionally self-inflicted injury while sane; or
> (2) self-inflicted injury while insane; or
> (3) war, or any act of war, whether or not the Insured is in military service. The term "war" includes armed aggression resisted by:
>   (a) the armed forces of any country; or
>   (b) any international organization; or
>   (c) any combination of countries.

GUARANTEED INSURABILITY OPTION

The guaranteed insurability option provides insurance against the risk of becoming uninsurable. It offers the option of purchasing, on specified dates in the future, additional policies on the insured's life without evidence of in- surability. The maximum amount of insurance which can be purchased is stated in the guaranteed insurability option.

Until the development of the guaranteed insurability option, a person's only hedge against the risk of becoming uninsurable was to purchase as much insurance as possible as soon as possible. In the 1950s, however, this risk was recognized as insurable. Insurers did not accept the idea quickly, but now it is a coverage which is offered by many insurers. The policy in Appendix B has a guaranteed insurability rider.

Because this is a relatively new type of coverage, legal problems have not had much time to develop. Nevertheless, the New York legislature has anticipated the possibility of one type of problem. This is the operation of the contestability and suicide provisions under each new policy issued under such options. The legislature has, therefore, enacted a statute which would preclude a policy issued under a guaranteed insurability option from having new contestable and suicide periods.[32] The contestable and suicide periods of the new policy must run from the policy date of the original policy—that is, the policy containing the guaranteed insurability option. Thus, the insured not only purchases a new policy without evidence of insurability, but also purchases an incontestable policy without a suicide period on each option date after the expiration of two years from the date the original policy was issued.

WAR HAZARD EXCLUSION

A war hazard exclusion section or rider is a part of a life insurance policy which limits the liability of the insurer in the event that the insured dies as a result of war or while in the military services. It is included only in policies issued during periods when war exists or is imminent, and only when the proposed insured is in an age group that is particularly subject to call to military duty.[33]

It is generally acknowledged that the hazard of war cannot be accurately predicted. It is impossible to predict when a war will occur, and equally impossible to predict the death toll of a war. Thus, statistical studies on which life insurance rates are based generally do not include war deaths. Some underwriting limitations are, therefore, necessary with respect to war hazards.

Acceptable solutions have not been easy. Refusal to insure persons who are subject to war hazards is one possible solution. Some insurers have followed this practice to some extent. Limitation of the amount of coverage that will be offered to such persons is a second approach. A third approach is issuance of life insurance as applied for, but with a war hazard exclusion.

The war hazard exclusion provides a way to issue coverage that would otherwise not be available to a large number of young persons in time of war or when war is imminent. Without the exclusion, the insurer might be unwilling to issue any coverage at all. With the exclusion, the insured can be covered for all risks other than those excluded in the war hazard section or rider.

---

[32]N.Y. INS. LAW § 3203(d)(2) (McKinney 1985 & Supp. 1988).

[33]The modern policy in Appendix B does not have a war hazard exclusion section or rider, because war has not been existent or imminent since it was written. A war hazard exclusion from another older policy has, therefore, been included in Appendix D.

In 1951, the NAIC adopted a Model War Risk Exclusion Provision Law. To date, no states have enacted this model law verbatim, although nearly one half have laws regulating war hazard exclusions. There are many court cases interpreting war hazard exclusions, however.

Status and Result Clauses

War hazard exclusion clauses have a great variety of wording. Nevertheless, two general types of clauses have been recognized by the courts—status clauses and result clauses. Status clauses exclude from coverage any death that occurred while the insured was in military service in time of war, regardless of the cause of death. The insured's status as a member of the armed forces is the determining factor. Result clauses, by contrast, exclude from coverage only deaths resulting from the insured's military activities.

Where the status of the insured, and not the cause of death, clearly furnishes the basis of exclusion, the courts have usually held that the insurer is not liable if the insured is in the military service in time of war, even though the death did not result from any hazard peculiar to war. Therefore, with a status clause, the insured has no life insurance protection while in the military service in time of war.

Use of the status clause has the disadvantage of creating poor public relations by overcompensating for the added risk created by the insured's military service. For example, assume that two young men, aged 22, are killed in an automobile accident near their homes. One is on leave from the army. The other is a civilian. They have identical life insurance contracts with the same insurer, and each contract contains a status war hazard exclusion clause. Only the civilian's beneficiary would receive the full proceeds. The soldier's beneficiary would receive some lesser amount, ordinarily the amount of premiums paid or the reserve, whichever is greater. This outcome is difficult to justify to beneficiaries. For this reason, among others, most insurers have elected to use result clauses.

Some courts have interpreted status clauses as if they were result clauses because the clauses were not clearly written, and the unclear writing created an ambiguity which the court resolved in favor of the beneficiary. A few courts have indicated that status clauses may be against public policy. In some instances, a statute will control the interpretation.

The status clause does have the advantage that it is simpler to administer than the result clause. Ordinarily, under a result clause, both the status of the insured and the cause of death must be determined, whereas, under the status clause, only the status of the insured must be determined.

Under a policy with a result war hazard exclusion clause, if the insured is in the military service in time of war and dies as a result of military activities, the death will not be covered. Ordinarily, the insurer will be liable for either the amount of premiums paid or the policy reserve, but not the death benefit. Three questions can arise where there is a result clause. First, was the insured in military service? Second, did the death result from military activities? Third, did the death occur in time of war?

Military Service

Both status and result clauses are ordinarily worded so that persons serving in any of the armed forces are included. The term *in military service* applies to conscripts and volunteers, officers and enlisted men and women alike. An army nurse[34] and a member of the military police[35] have been held to be in military service. On the other hand, persons in the national guard or naval reserve when not on active duty are not in military service, according to some cases.[36]

Under the wording of some result war hazard exclusion clauses, the status of the insured will not matter, so long as her or his death resulted from war. The death from war of a civilian insured will not be covered if the policy excluded death as a result of war, but did not mention military service.

Military Activities

The insured's death as a result of military activities is excluded by result war hazard exclusion clauses. Therefore, if the insured dies in combat, the death will not be covered. Even where the insured does not die in combat but dies as a result of military training or maneuvers or other causes peculiar to military service, the death ordinarily will not be covered. By contrast, death from disease or accidents not related to war or military service will ordinarily be covered where there is a result clause.

Existence of War

Since 1941, the definition of war has caused problems in regard to war hazard exclusion clauses. On December 7, 1941, some 3,000 persons serving in the United States Armed Forces were killed at Pearl Harbor in a surprise attack by the Japanese. War was not officially declared by Congress until the next day. Most courts ruling on the question later held that war, as that term was used in life insurance policies with war hazard exclusions, did not exist until officially declared by Congress on December 8, 1941. The beneficiaries were, therefore, entitled to the benefits.

The Korean and Vietnam conflicts presented an even more difficult question, for, in those instances, war was never officially declared. The majority of the courts took a position opposite to that usually taken in regard to the

---

[34]New York Life Ins. Co. v. White, 190 F.2d 424 (5th Cir. 1951).

[35]Jorgenson v. Metropolitan Life Ins. Co., 24 N.J. Misc. 22, 55 A.2d 2 (N.J. Sup. Ct. 1947), *aff'g* 136 N.J.L. 148, 44 A.2d 907 (N.J. Ct. Com. Pleas 1945).

[36]Feick v. Prudential Ins. Co., 1 N.J. Super. 88, 62 A.2d 485 (1948).

Pearl Harbor cases. The majority held that war meant any actual hostilities between the armed forces of two or more countries. Therefore, even though the war was undeclared, it was war within the meaning of a war hazard exclusion. Many companies have changed the wording of their war hazard exclusions to include war "declared or undeclared."

Where there has been a cessation of actual hostilities, the courts have held that war no longer exists, even though a peace treaty has not yet been signed. Conversely, where there has been a formal surrender, but active hostilities nonetheless continue, a state of war still exists.

AVIATION HAZARD EXCLUSION

The risk of death as a result of certain aviation activities is sometimes excluded from the coverage provided by a life insurance contract. As with war hazard exclusions, an aviation hazard exclusion may appear in the policy itself or be added to the policy by rider. An aviation hazard exclusion appears in a rider attached to the illustrative policy in Appendix B.

In the early days of aviation, when there were no statistics to measure the added risk, it was common to exclude aviation deaths in most policy forms. As insurers gained experience, it became possible to measure with reasonable accuracy the added risks of flying under various circumstances. As the safety of flying increased, it became possible to demonstrate that the added risks were minimal for fare-paying passengers on regularly-scheduled commercial airlines. This type of risk is rarely excluded from coverage in policies issued today.

Insurers often insure those engaged in more hazardous aviation activities for an extra premium. In other instances, coverage will be provided if there is an exclusion from the accidental death benefit for aviation deaths. Insurers still use exclusions in life policies for especially hazardous aviation activities, such as military flying, crop-dusting, or sports piloting, where an extra premium or exclusion from the accidental death benefit are not practical solutions.

The wording of aviation hazard exclusion clauses is extremely varied. Such a clause will be carefully examined by the court, and the wording given paramount importance, although, as with other insurance policy clauses, ambiguities will be interpreted in favor of the insured.

Most of the court cases deal with the interpretation of specific terms or phrases in the aviation hazard exclusion. For example, a glider,[37] a seaplane,[38] and a hang kite[39] have been held to be aircraft within the meaning of aviation hazard exclusion clauses. A parachute, on the other hand, has been held not

---

[37]Spychala v. Metropolitan Life Ins. Co., 339 Pa. 237, 13 A.2d 32 (1940).
[38]Wendorff v. Missouri State Life Ins. Co., 318 Mo. 363, 1 S.W.2d 99 (1927).
[39]Wilson v. Insurance Co. of N. Am., 453 F. Supp. 732 (N.D. Cal. 1978).

to be an aircraft.[40] The term *fare-paying passenger* has been held not to include a stewardess[41] or a person traveling on a pass.[42] As the use of the aviation hazard exclusion has been reduced, so have the legal problems associated with it.

SUMMARY

Accidental death benefits, disability benefits, and guaranteed insurability options are often added to traditional life insurance policy benefits. Coverage is sometimes limited by war or aviation hazard exclusions.

Accidental death benefits provide additional payments when the death is accidental. The two types of accidental death clauses are accidental result clauses and accidental means clauses. In order for benefits to be payable under accidental means clauses, both the cause and the result of the death must be accidental, whereas accidental result clauses require that only the result be accidental.

Accidental death is ordinarily death that was not foreseeable by the insured. The death must have been proximately or directly caused by an accident—not by disease. Suicide is not accidental. Death inflicted by another person upon the insured will ordinarily be accidental if not foreseeable by the insured.

Waiver of premium for disability and disability income benefits are often included in life insurance policies. Most policies issued today require that the insured be totally disabled either from his or her own occupation or from any occupation for which the insured has education, training, or experience. Permanent disability is now rarely required.

War hazard exclusions limit the liability of the insurer in the event the insured dies as a result of war or while in the military services. The two major categories of war hazard exclusion clauses are result clauses and status clauses. A result clause—the type more commonly used—excludes from coverage death resulting from the insured's military activities. A status clause excludes death occurring while the insured is in the military service.

Aviation hazard clauses exclude the risk of death from certain hazardous aviation activities. Ordinarily, today, death while flying as a fare-paying passenger on a regularly scheduled commercial airline will not be excluded.

ILLUSTRATIVE CASE

In this case, the insured died from a gunshot wound after he was discovered in the act of adultery with his assailant's wife. The question before the court was whether or not the insured died as the result of an accident.

---

[40]Clark v. Lone Star Life Ins. Co., 347 S.W.2d 290 (Tex. Civ. App. 1961).

[41]State *ex rel.* Mutual Life Ins. Co. v. Shain, 344 Mo. 276, 126 S.W.2d 181 (1939).

[42]Krause v. Pacific Mut. Life Ins. Co., 141 Neb. 844, 5 N.W.2d 299 (1942).

GREAT AMERICAN RESERVE INSURANCE COMPANY,
Appellant
v.
TINA ELIZABETH SUMNER, Appellee[43]
Court of Civil Appeals of Texas, Tyler

MOORE, Justice.

This is a suit for the recovery of proceeds of an insurance policy insuring against accidental death. The policy was issued by appellant Great American Reserve Insurance Company upon the life of Hoyt V. Sumner, deceased. His wife, Tina Elizabeth Sumner, appellee, was named as beneficiary. The policy was in the principal sum of $5,000.00 and provided such sum would be paid to the beneficiary if "(1) loss or disability resulting solely, directly and independently of all other causes from accidental bodily injury sustained during the term of this policy." Section VI of the policy provided: "If such injury shall independently of all other causes and within ninety (90) days from date of accident solely result in any one of the following specific losses, the Company will pay in lieu of any other indemnity payable under this policy: . . . Life—The Principal Sum."

The insurance company pleaded that the insured died as the result of a gun shot wound to the head when he was confronted by his assailant, David Smith, while the insured was allegedly engaged in an act of sexual intercourse with the assailant's wife. The company denied appellee's claim under the policy on the ground that the deceased should have anticipated death by reason of his adulterous act and did not die as the result of accidental bodily injuries. After a trial before the court sitting without a jury, the trial court entered judgment in favor of the beneficiary-appellee, from which the insurance company perfected this appeal.

The policy in question does not contain any provision which would limit or destroy the insurer's liability for death or injury to the insured as a result of an intentional act of another, nor is there any provision in the policy excluding liability where death or injury results to insured while engaged in the violation of law.

The parties are in basic agreement that the sole question presented by the case in the trial court was whether or not the insured died as a result of an accident. They both further agree that the prevailing law was correctly stated in the case of Releford v. Reserve Life Insurance Company, 154 Tex. 228, 276 S.W.2d 517, at page 518 (1955), wherein the rule is stated:

> As stated in the *Hutcherson* case, the test of whether the killing is accidental within the terms of an insurance policy is not to be determined from the viewpoint of the one who does the killing, but rather from the viewpoint of the insured. If from his viewpoint his conduct was such that he should have anticipated that in all reasonable probability his wife would kill him, his death was not accidental; if from his viewpoint his conduct was not such as to cause him reasonably to believe that she would probably kill him, then his death was accidental.

It seems to be the well settled law in this state that death by gun shot, or by any form of homicide, at the hands of a third person is deemed to be an "accident",

---

[43]464 S.W.2d 212 (Tex. Civ. App. 1971).

even though death was intended by the person doing the shooting. This rule, however is not without exception. If the deceased, prior to death, engaged in some conduct toward his assailant from which he did know, or should have known, the assailant would kill him by violent means, then the death is deemed not to be an "accident".

By its first point as we understand it appellant challenges the legal sufficiency of the evidence to support findings of fact numbers 6 through 8 made by the trial court, whereby the court found that the death was a result of an accident as viewed from the standpoint of the deceased/insured that the deceased/insured had not entered into an affray with his assailant immediately prior to the shooting, and that from the information available to him, the deceased/insured could not reasonably foresee that he would be killed by his assailant. By his third point, appellant says that the deceased, by reason of his adulterous conduct, should have anticipated death and therefore his death did not constitute an accident. Both points will be discussed together.

Under the first point of error it becomes our duty to examine the record and determine whether or not there is any evidence of probative force to support the fact findings of the trial court. No rule is better settled than the one to the effect that if there is any evidence of probative force to sustain the findings of the trier of the fact, the appellate court is bound by such findings. In determining this question we must view the evidence in a light most favorable to the appellee, rejecting all evidence favorable to the appellant. The findings challenged by appellant as being without support in the evidence are as follows:

(6) Viewed from the standpoint of the deceased, it was not reasonably foreseeable to the deceased that by reason of his illicit meeting in a secluded place with assailant's wife that he, the deceased, would encounter the armed assailant, DAVID SMITH, at the place and upon the occasion in question.

(7) After being surprised and confronted by the armed assailant, the deceased did not enter into an affray with the assailant nor engage in any further conduct calculated to invite or provoke the shot which killed him.

(8) Viewed from the deceased's standpoint, with the information available to him at each step of the transaction, it was not reasonably foreseeable to the deceased that any act of the deceased would bring about a fatal gun shot wound.

The only testimony as to what actually occurred at the time and place of the killing was given by the assailant, David Smith; his wife, Birdie Smith, having died prior to trial, there were no other witnesses to the incident. When viewed in a light most favorable to the findings, the evidence shows that the deceased had been acquainted with Smith and his wife, Birdie, for approximately one year prior to his death. During this time he testified that all of his dealings with the deceased had been friendly. On the occasion in question, Smith testified that he became suspicious of his wife when he saw his granddaughter driving his wife's automobile. He testified that immediately thereafter he drove down the Bellview Road, stopped his automobile, took out his 12-gauge shotgun, and walked across the pasture about 300 feet where he discovered his wife and the deceased engaged in sexual intercourse. His purpose, he testified, in taking the gun was to kill his wife. He testified that upon discovering her, he told her "Birdie, haven't I told you I was going to walk up on you." At this point Birdie got up and came toward him attempting to talk to him and he told her not to come any closer. As she continued to approach him, he testified he cocked his gun and threw it on her. At this point the deceased said "Don't shoot her." To which he replied, "I'm not talking to you. I'm talking to my wife." Commencing at this point his testimony appears to be in conflict. On one occasion he testified that the deceased was walking toward him while he had his gun pointed toward his wife and that he shot the deceased. On another occasion he testified that he could not remember just what happened. He also testified that he could not deny the fact that while he was holding the gun on his wife Birdie, it went off and struck the deceased in the head while he was standing some 25 to 30 feet away. He further testified that the deceased was only partially clothed at the time and admitted that he could see that he was not armed with any type of weapon.

The test of whether death is accidental, within the terms of the policy supplement, is a fact question to be determined by the trier of the fact and is to be determined from the viewpoint of the insured and not from the viewpoint of the one that does the killing.

In Hanna v. Rio Grande Nat. Life Ins. Co., 181 S.W.2d 908 (Tex. Civ. App., Dallas, 1944, err. ref.), the court states: " 'Where the effect is not the natural and probable consequence of the means which produce it—an effect which does not ordinarily follow and cannot be reasonably anticipated from the use of the means, or an effect which the actor did not intend to produce, and which he cannot be charged with a design of producing—it is produced by accidental means.' "

Even though we recognize that the act of adultery is morally reprehensible, yet we do not believe death is the usual or expected result of it. In other words, participation in an adulterous affair does not naturally lead to a violent and fatal ending. To hold to the contrary would be to say that the killing of an adulterer, in the absence of any other aggravating circumstances, follows his offense in the ordinary cause of events. Such a holding would appear to be contrary to the relatively few reported cases on the subject. Other than the act of adultery, the deceased did nothing, except taking a few steps toward his assailant, to provoke the deadly assault. He made no threats or threatening gesture and his assailant admitted he could see that he was unarmed. Thus when the evidence is viewed in a light most favorable to the finding, the killing of deceased cannot be said to be the natural and probable consequence of the means which produced it. There is nothing in the crime of adultery, although a violation of the law of the land and a great moral wrong, which in its essence is calculated to produce the death of the adulterer. Under some circumstances it may be the occasion of the death of the adulterer, but his death is not the natural and legitimate consequence of the adultery itself.

The mere fact that Article 1220, Vernon's Annotated Penal Code provides that homicide is justifiable when committed by the husband upon one taken in the act of adultery with the wife does not necessarily mean that every adulterer is bound to anticipate death as the inevitable result of his act. Ordinarily most husbands do not undertake to vindicate such wrongs by homicide but rather lay their problem in the lap of the divorce courts. Therefore we do not believe it can be said that the deceased should have reasonably anticipated such violent consequence by reason of his conduct. As we view the record there is at least some evidence of probative force in support of the trial court's finding that the deceased met death solely as a result of an accident.

* * * * *

The judgment of the trial court is affirmed.

QUESTIONS FOR REVIEW

1. What is meant by the term *proximate cause?* How does proximate cause relate to the accidental death benefit?
2. Upon what grounds have the courts in many states rejected the distinction between accidental means and accidental result?
3. Explain which policy language, accidental means or accidental result, is more favorable to the insured person.
4. Describe the typical time limitation clause included in most provisions for accidental death benefits. What is its intended function? Why does this clause cause problems today that it did not cause a few decades ago?
5. With regard to accidental death, tell how each of the following is treated:
    a. Voluntary assumption of a known risk.
    b. Suicide.
    c. Harm inflicted by another.
6. Tell where the burden of proof lies when the majority of courts are asked to settle an accidental death claim: (a) if there is no agreement as to the accidental nature of the death, and (b) when it is claimed that accidental death resulted from an excluded risk?
7. What are the different types of disability benefits which are available under life insurance policies?
8. Contrast, from the viewpoint of the insured, the most liberal and the most restrictive definitions of the term *total disability.*
9. Describe the different approaches the courts have taken to determine what is meant by the term *permanent disability.*
10. What is a guaranteed insurability option?
11. Contrast war hazard exclusion result clauses with status clauses.

CHAPTER 9

Property Rights in the Life Insurance Policy

PROPERTY LAW
>   Real Property
>   Personal Property
>   Rights Under Life Insurance Policy Terms
>   Rights by Operation of Law

COMMUNITY PROPERTY RIGHTS
>   General Rules of Community Property Law
>   The Policy or Proceeds as Community Property
>   A Third Person as Beneficiary
>   Termination of the Community by Divorce
>   Settlement Agreements
>   Exoneration Statutes

CREDITORS' RIGHTS
>   Creditors' Rights Under the Policy
>   Creditors' Rights to Property of the Debtor
>   Exemptions from Creditors' Claims
>   Insurance Exemptions
>   Creditors of the Policyowner-Insured
>   Creditors of the Beneficiary
>   The Spendthrift Clause

DIVORCE

KILLING OF THE INSURED BY THE BENEFICIARY

SUMMARY

In order to understand property rights in a life insurance policy it is necessary to understand property law. This chapter contains a brief outline of property law. It also contains a discussion of rights under policy terms. Finally, it contains a discussion of rights in the policy by operation of the law.

PROPERTY LAW

The term *property* is popularly associated with anything over which rights of possession, use, control, and disposition are exercised, such as land, buildings, automobiles, jewelry, and shares of corporate stock. The term is used in this nontechnical sense in modern legal writing and will be so used in many places in this book. The term *property* will, however, be used in its strict legal sense in this section explaining property law.

In the strict legal sense, *property* does not mean a thing over which rights of possession, use, control, and disposition are exercised, but rather these ownership rights themselves. To illustrate the meaning of *property*, or *ownership rights*, if you own a chair, you can keep it in your house and sit on it. Or, you can lend it to a friend, give it as a birthday gift to your mother, will it to your sister, or sell it to a second-hand store. You can put it in storage, or chop it up and use it as kindling wood. You can rent it to someone who needs a chair, or pledge it as security for a loan. It is your chair, and you have the rights of possession, use, control, and disposition of it. You may use or dispose of it in any legal manner. Your right to do so is protected by the government.

There are two main classes of property—real property and personal property. The terms *real* and *personal* are derived from the forms of legal action which were used in the early days of the common law to enforce ownership rights. Laws applying to these two types of property differ in many ways. Real property and personal property will, therefore, be discussed separately.

Real Property

Real property consists of rights over land and that which is attached to the land. *Real estate* is often used as a synonym for real property. Suppose, for example, there is a plot of land with a house erected on it, a tree growing on it, a ball lying on the lawn, and an automobile parked in the driveway. A right over the land itself, the house, and the tree is real property. A right over the ball or the automobile is not real property, as they are not attached to the land. If the tree is cut down and sawed into firewood, it is no longer attached to the land. A right over the firewood is personal property.

Real property law began to develop in England at the time of William the Conqueror—nearly a thousand years ago. At that time, and for many centuries thereafter, land was the most important thing a person could own. Through the years, a vast and complex body of real property law has evolved. Real property law includes laws relating to landlords and tenants, deeds, mortgages, easements, fixtures, condominiums, and water rights, among many other subjects.

Personal Property

A right over that which is not land or something attached to the land is personal property. A right over a chair, a bracelet, a racehorse, or money is personal property. A contract right or a debt is also personal property.

The chair, bracelet, racehorse, and money are choses in possession. The word *chose* is French for "thing." A chose in possession is something tangible of which one has actual possession.

A contract right or a debt, on the other hand, is a chose in action. A chose in action is a right that can be enforced by legal action or by a suit in equity. If, for example, an insurer breaches an insurance contract, the policyowner or beneficiary will have a right to recover money damages from the insurer. This right is a chose in action. The terms *chose in possession* and *chose in action* are used only in connection with personal property, not with real property.

Rights Under Life Insurance Policy Terms

The whole life insurance policy ordinarily confers on its owner a number of valuable rights. Among these are the rights to obtain a policy loan, to withdraw or direct the application of dividends, and to surrender the policy for its cash value.

It is sometimes advantageous to transfer these valuable prematurity rights. As with a chose in possession, such as a chair, there are many ways in which these rights can be transferred. They can be transferred gratuitously as a gift. They can be transferred for value in a sale. They can be pledged as security for a loan. In cases of divorce, life insurance owned by either spouse will often become part of the property settlement. Policies owned by someone other than the insured will pass at the policyowner's death to his or her personal representative for distribution to heirs or to those named in the policyowner's will.

The beneficiary may also have prematurity rights in the policy. The consent of an irrevocable beneficiary often must be obtained if the policyowner is to surrender a life policy for cash or to take out a policy loan. Whether an irrevocable beneficiary's consent must be obtained will depend on the policy provisions and on the laws of the jurisdiction.

At the death of the insured person, the beneficiary has a chose in action. That is, the beneficiary has a right that can be enforced by legal action. The beneficiary can transfer this chose in action to another person. A chose in action is usually transferred by an assignment. Assignments will be discussed in Chapter 14, "Assignments and Other Transfers."

Rights by Operation of Law

People other than the policyowner or beneficiary sometimes obtain rights in the insurance contract by operation of law, rather than by the terms of the contract. Wives or husbands in community property states, creditors of the policyowner or beneficiary, trustees in bankruptcy, divorced spouses, and others can sometimes assert rights not expressly provided in the life insurance policy itself. Indeed, these rights are often contrary to policy provisions. The following sections contain a discussion of contract rights by operation of law.

COMMUNITY PROPERTY RIGHTS

The settlers of the United States on the east coast took their ideas of law mainly from England. Thus, in the United States, the life insurance contract had its origin and most of its development in a legal climate based upon English common law.

The early explorers of the South and West, however, brought their ideas of law from the countries of their origin—France and Spain. For that reason, the legal systems of many southern and western states have been influenced by the legal systems of these two countries. Community property is a legal concept which derives from French and Spanish law. Today, the states which have community property laws are Arizona, California, Idaho, Louisiana, Nevada, New Mexico, Texas, Washington, and Wisconsin.

Community property is a concept foreign to the English common law. Community property rights are, therefore, based on state statutes.

An understanding of community property law is necessary to students of life insurance because of the rights in life policies which may be conferred by it.

General Rules of Community Property Law

In a community property state, a husband and wife constitute a community. Community property is property owned by a husband and wife residing in a community property state. Each has an undivided one-half interest in the community property because of their marital status. Usually, all property acquired by the husband and wife during the marriage is community property, except property acquired by one of the spouses through gift, inheritance, or under a will.

When the community is dissolved by the death of a spouse, the surviving spouse has a right to one half of the community property. The deceased spouse's half usually becomes the property of his or her estate.

Property owned before the marriage is ordinarily the separate property of the spouse who owned it. It remains separate property during the marriage. Property acquired during the marriage by one spouse by gift, inheritance, or under a will is also the separate property of that spouse and remains separate property.

Property acquired with community funds is ordinarily community property, even if title is taken in the name of one spouse only. Property acquired during the marriage with separate funds is separate property. Ordinarily, if both community and separate funds are used in acquiring property, the property so acquired is owned by the husband and wife, as community property and separate property, in the same proportion as the funds that were used to acquire it.

Until recently, the husband has had the right to manage community property, subject to certain limitations. For instance, the husband has traditionally had the right to control or sell community property. He could not ordinarily make a gift of community property without the wife's consent, however. Moreover, the husband could not use his management power to defraud his wife.

In recent years, statutes have been enacted in community property states mandating equal management. That is, the management of the community property is now shared by the husband and wife. Illustrative of such statutes is the following from the California Civil Code:

(a) . . . either spouse has the management and control of the community personal property, . . . with like absolute power of disposition, other than testamentary, as the spouse has of the separate estate of the spouse.

(b) A spouse may not make a gift of community personal property, or dispose of community personal property without a valuable consideration, without the written consent of the other spouse.

(c) A spouse may not sell, convey, or encumber community personal property used as the family dwelling, or the furniture, furnishings, or fittings of the home, or the clothing or wearing apparel of the other spouse or minor children which is community personal property, without the written consent of the other spouse.

* * * * *

(e) Each spouse shall act in good faith with respect to the other spouse in the management and control of the community property in accordance with the general rules which control the actions of persons having relationships of personal confidence, . . . until such time as the property has been divided by the parties or by a court. This duty includes the obligation to make full disclosure to the other spouse of the existence of assets in which the community has an interest and debts for which the community may be liable, upon request.[1]

Note that paragraph (a) provides that either spouse has the right to manage and control the community property, including the right to dispose of it. The remaining paragraphs impose certain restrictions on that right. Thus, paragraph (b) forbids either husband or wife from making a gift of community property without the written consent of the other. Paragraph (e) should be

---

[1]CAL. CIVIL CODE § 5125 (West Cum. Supp. 1988).

especially noted, for it summarizes an important rule of community property management: "Each spouse shall act in good faith with respect to the other spouse in the management and control of the community property. . . ."

Most of the cases that are mentioned in the following discussion of community property and life insurance were decided at a time when only the husband had rights of management. Therefore, they concern actions taken by the husband as manager which were challenged by the wife. Under present-day statutes, similar actions could be taken by the wife and challenged by the husband.

Community property laws vary from state to state. In the following discussion of community property laws, as applied to life insurance, it should be borne in mind that the rules stated will not always apply in every state.

The Policy or Proceeds as Community Property

A life policy can be either separate property or community property. Likewise, the proceeds can be either separate property or community property.[2]

When a person applies for and is issued a life policy before marriage, the policy is separate property when it is issued. In most community property states, it remains separate property, even though premiums are paid on it after marriage out of community funds.[3] At the death of the insured, if the spouse is not the beneficiary, in some states the community is entitled to part of the proceeds if community funds were used to pay premiums.[4]

When a person applies for and is issued a policy of life insurance on his or her life during marriage, and the premiums are paid for with community funds, the policy is community property. The proceeds also are community property where the estate of the insured is the beneficiary. Where the insured's spouse is the beneficiary, however, the proceeds are ordinarily the spouse's separate property. The theory behind this rule is that a gift of the proceeds was made to the beneficiary-spouse.

A Third Person as Beneficiary

A policyowner in a community property state sometimes names someone other than her or his spouse as beneficiary. This is the same as making a gift to that person if no consideration is given by the beneficiary. If the policyowner's

---

[2]Annot., 114 A.L.R. 545 (1938), supp. 168 A.L.R. 342 (1947).
[3]Aetna Life Ins. Co. v. Schmitt, 404 F. Supp. 189 (D.C. Fla. 1975).
[4]McCurdy v. McCurdy, 372 S.W.2d 381 (Tex. Civ. App. 1963).

spouse does not consent to the gift, the spouse could be entitled to one half of the proceeds[5] or, in some cases, to all of the proceeds.[6]

The policyowner is sometimes held to have acted in fraud of the spouse's rights in these cases. For example, in an Arizona case, the insured husband had changed his life insurance beneficiary designation from his wife to his niece without the wife's knowledge or consent. The insurance had been obtained after marriage, and the premiums were paid with community funds. The husband died, and the wife and niece both claimed the proceeds. The court ruled that the actions of the husband in changing the beneficiary without the consent of the wife "worked as a constructive fraud" upon her community property right to one half of the proceeds.[7]

If, however, the policyowner owes a legal duty to provide for a third person who is named beneficiary, such as a child of a prior marriage, in some jurisdictions the policyowner's spouse will not have a right to the proceeds.[8]

Where a beneficiary change from the spouse to a third person is made in exchange for a valuable consideration, there is no gift involved. In such a case, the third person might be entitled to the full proceeds.[9] For example, in a California case, the insured owed a sum of money to his sister. He changed the beneficiary designation from his wife to his sister in payment of the debt. The court held that the sister was entitled to the full proceeds.[10]

Where the beneficiary-spouse gives his or her consent to the beneficiary change, it will be valid if the state's law so provides.[11] In some states, this consent must be in writing. In other states, a spouse might be held to have released her or his community property rights in the policy proceeds by failing to assert those rights. For example, in a California case, the policy owner-insured named his sister beneficiary of the policy. His wife failed to assert her right to one half of the proceeds. Indeed, her attorneys told the insurer they believed she had no such right. The court held that the designation of the sister was voidable by the wife as to one half of the proceeds, but as the wife did not act to avoid the designation before the proceeds were paid to the sister, the designation became valid.[12]

Termination of the Community by Divorce

The husband-wife community is terminated by death, divorce, or annulment of the marriage. The community property belonging to the husband and

---

[5]Tyre v. Aetna Life Ins. Co., 54 Cal. 2d 399, 6 Cal. Rptr. 13, 353 P.2d 725 (1960).

[6]Guerrero v. Guerrero, 18 Ariz. App. 400, 502 P.2d 1077 (1972); Moore v. California-Western States Life Ins. Co., 67 S.W.2d 932 (Tex. Civ. App. 1934).

[7]Guerrero v. Guerrero, 18 Ariz. App. 400, 502 P.2d 1077 (1972).

[8]Great Am. Reserve Ins. Co. v. Sanders, 525 S.W.2d 956 (Tex. 1975); Rowlett v. Mitchell, 114 S.W. 845 (Tex. Civ. App. 1908).

[9]Johnson v. Johnson, 182 Wash. 573, 47 P.2d 1048 (1935).

[10]Union Mut. Life Ins. Co. v. Broderick, 196 Cal. 497, 238 P. 1034 (1925).

[11]Pacific Mut. Life Ins. Co. v. Cleverdon, 16 Cal.2d 788, 108 P.2d 405 (1940).

[12]Blethen v. Pacific Mut. Life Ins. Co., 198 Cal. 91, 243 P. 431 (1926).

wife will be divided upon divorce—either by agreement of the parties or by the court. The question of whether the cash value of a life insurance policy is community property has arisen in connection with divorce. The courts of several states have ruled that the cash surrender value of a life insurance policy is community property if premiums were paid with community funds.[13]

For example, the Supreme Court of Texas held that the cash surrender value of four life insurance policies purchased with community property funds was community property to be divided between the spouses. Three of the policies insured the life of the husband and had a total cash surrender value of $1,542.84. The other policy insured the life of the wife and had a cash surrender value of $252. The spouses divided the other property between them, but the legal question as to whether the cash surrender value of the policies constituted community property was left open for later determination by the court. The trial court and Court of Civil Appeals ruled that the cash value was community property. The Texas Supreme Court affirmed the decisions of those courts stating the following:

> Article 4619, Vernon's Annotated Civil Statutes, as amended in 1927, defines community property as follows:
>
> "All property acquired by either the husband or wife during marriage, except that which is the separate property of either, shall be deemed the common property of the husband and wife; and all the effects which the husband and wife possess at the time the marriage may be dissolved shall be regarded as common effects or gains, unless the contrary be satisfactorily proved."
>
> The word "property" has been frequently defined and its meaning determined by many decisions of the courts. In the case of *Titus v. Terkelsen,* 302 Mass. 84, 18 N.E.2d 444, 445, the court, in discussing the word "property," said:
>
> "It is a word of comprehensive meaning . . . In its ordinary legal signification it 'extends to every species of valuable right and interest, and includes real and personal property. . . .' "
>
> . . . It is true that in the early decisions of the courts of this country, including the decisions of the courts of this State, it was held in some of them that policies of life insurance were not property . . . Many of the modern decisions hold that a life insurance policy is property. In the case of *Grigsby v. Russell,* 222 U.S. 149, . . . Mr. Justice Holmes, speaking for the Supreme Court of the United States, said: "Life insurance has become in our days one of the best recognized forms of investment and self-compelled saving. So far as reasonable safety permits, it is desirable to give life policies the ordinary characteristics of property . . ."
>
> The word "property" in our bankruptcy laws is construed to include the "cash surrender value" of life insurance policies, and such property rights pass to the creditors of the insured. The courts recognize the right

---

[13]*E.g.,* Estate of Mendenhall, 182 Cal. App. 2d 441, 6 Cal. Rptr. 45 (1960); Estate of Leuthold, 52 Wash. 299, 324 P.2d 1103 (1958).

of the insured to pay his creditors the "cash surrender value" of his policy and retain the policy. . . . The courts of this State have held that the "cash surrender value" of a policy is property, and may be considered and treated as community property. . . .

. . . The trial court and Court of Civil Appeals correctly held that the cash surrender value of the policies was community property, and that respondent was entitled to judgment for one-half thereof.

The rule announced in the case of *Whitesell v. Northwestern Mutual Life Insurance Company, supra* as well as in any other cases holding contrary to the rule announced herein, is expressly overruled.[14]

Settlement Agreements

A spouse in a community property state may defeat a settlement agreement entered into by the other spouse as to one half of the policy proceeds, according to a case decided in 1960 by the Supreme Court of California.[15] In that case, the wife was the named beneficiary. Originally, the proceeds were to be paid to her in a lump sum, but the insured husband changed the method of payment to a life income with a 10-year period certain. The contingent payees, in the event the wife did not live for 10 years, were the couple's three grown daughters. The wife did not know of or consent to the change in the method of payment. After the husband's death, she disavowed his choice and requested payment in a lump sum.

The court held that the wife could receive one half of the lump sum amount, or $10,000. The three daughters received one half of the life income amount for the wife's lifetime or 10 years, whichever was longer. The court stated:

A policy of insurance on the husband's life is community property when the premiums have been paid with community funds . . . During the existence of the marriage the respective interests of the husband and wife in community property are present, existing, and equal, but "the husband has the management and control of the community personal property, with like absolute power of disposition, other than testamentary, as he has of his separate estate; provided, however, that he cannot make a gift of such community personal property, or dispose of the same without a valuable consideration, . . . without the written consent of the wife." When the community is dissolved by death, "one-half of the community property belongs to the surviving spouse; the other half is subject to the testamentary disposition of the decedent."

. . .[I]t is settled that even though the insurance contract provides that the insured husband has the right to change the beneficiary without the wife's consent when she is named as such, any such change of beneficiary without her consent and without a valuable consideration other than sub-

---

[14]Womack v. Womack, 141 Tex. 299, 172 S.W.2d 307 (1943).
[15]Tyre v. Aetna Life Ins. Co., 54 Cal. 2d 399, 6 Cal. Rptr. 13, 353 P.2d 725 (1960).

stitution of beneficiaries is voidable, and after the death of the husband the wife may maintain an action for her community share in the proceeds of the policy.

. . . Just as the husband cannot deprive his wife of her community interest by exceeding his testamentary powers to make gifts of more than half the community property to third persons, so he cannot defeat her interest by making a testamentary gift to her under conditions that restrict her management and control of the property. Her remedy in both situations is to disavow the gift and stand on her community rights. . . . If the primary beneficiary of a life insurance policy disqualifies himself, the proceeds are payable to the alternate beneficiary and not to the insured's estate even though the alternate beneficiary's interest was conditioned upon surviving the primary beneficiary as well as the insured.

Therefore, the court held that the wife could take one half of the proceeds as a lump sum but that the other half was payable to the daughters under the settlement agreement entered into by the husband.

Exoneration Statutes

Fortunately for insurers, the community property states have statutes which make payment of the death benefit to the named beneficiary, in good faith and without knowledge of an adverse claim, sufficient to discharge the insurer of liability. These are called exoneration statutes. They exonerate—that is, excuse—the insurer from liability if a spouse should make a claim to proceeds already paid to a third party. The Idaho exoneration statute reads as follows:

Whenever the proceeds of or payments under a life or disability insurance policy or annuity contract heretofore or hereafter issued become payable in accordance with the terms of such policy or contract, or the exercise of any right or privilege thereunder, and the insurer makes payment thereof in accordance with the terms of the policy or contract or in accordance with any written assignment thereof, the person then designated in the policy or contract or by such assignment as being entitled thereto shall be entitled to receive such proceeds or payments and to give full acquittance therefor, and such payments shall fully discharge the insurer from all claims under the policy or contract unless, before payment is made, the insurer has received at its home office written notice by or on behalf of some other person that such other person claims to be entitled to such payment or some interest in the policy or contract.[16]

Ordinarily, such a statute will protect the insurer. If there is any doubt as to whom payment should be made, the insurer can obtain the surviving spouse's consent or file an interpleader action.[17]

---

[16]Idaho Code § 41–1828(1) (1977).

[17]Interpleader actions are discussed in detail in Chapter 16, "Remedies."

CREDITORS' RIGHTS

A creditor is a person to whom money is owed by another person who is called the debtor. Creditors can have rights in life insurance policies in two ways. First, if the creditor is the policyowner, assignee, or beneficiary of the policy, the creditor has rights derived directly from the contract. Second, a creditor with no rights under the contract terms sometimes has rights to the contract values as property of the debtor. State statutes provide that a creditor can obtain a judgment in court against his or her debtor and seize the debtor's property. Just as a debtor's car or house can be seized, life policy values belonging to a debtor can sometimes be seized, although life policy values are often protected from creditors' claims by exemption laws.

Creditors' Rights Under the Policy

Creditors who have had the foresight to protect themselves against possible loss by insuring their debtors' lives in their own favor are entitled to repayment from the policy proceeds of the debt and of any premiums paid by the creditor.[18] Courts often hold that the creditor is entitled to the entire proceeds, even though the amount of the insurance is greater than the amount of the debt, as long as the difference is not so great as to suggest that the insurance was secured for wagering purposes.[19]

A debtor may transfer some of the rights in a policy she or he owns to a creditor as security for a loan. This is called a collateral assignment. The creditor is called a collateral assignee. A collateral assignee usually has a right to share in the insurance proceeds only to the extent of the debt remaining unpaid at the death of the insured debtor, plus any premiums paid by the creditor. Assignments are discussed in greater detail in Chapter 14, "Assignments and Other Transfers."

In some instances, a debtor who owns a policy insuring his or her own life names the creditor as beneficiary to secure a loan. This method of securing a loan is not as popular with creditors as is the collateral assignment, because prematurity values cannot be reached by the creditor. Usually, the creditor will be entitled only to the amount of the unpaid debt, plus any premiums paid by the creditor, from the proceeds.

Creditors' Rights to Property of the Debtor

Every state has its own procedures that a creditor can employ to sue a debtor, obtain a judgment, and have property of the debtor applied to satisfy the judgment. Some types of property are specified by state constitution or

---

[18]Sachs v. United States, 412 F.2d 357 (8th Cir. 1969), *cert. denied,* 396 U.S. 906 (1969).

[19]Rittler v. Smith, 70 Md. 261, 16 A. 890 (1889); Ulrich v. Reinoehl, 143 Pa. 238, 22 A. 862 (1891); Annot., 115 A.L.R. 741 (1938).

statute to be exempt from creditors' claims. Life insurance values are often exempt from creditors' claims.

Exemptions from Creditors' Claims

An exemption is a right given by law to a debtor to retain certain property free from seizure by her or his creditors. It is a right created by constitution or statute. It does not exist at common law.

The purpose of exemption laws is to protect an unfortunate debtor and the debtor's family, as well as the public. Granting an insolvent debtor the right to retain a homestead, household goods, wearing apparel, the tools of the debtor's trade, and part of his or her wages allows the debtor to remain self-supporting. It keeps the debtor and the debtor's family from becoming a burden upon the public.

Exemption of life insurance values from creditors' claims protects the debtor's family from destitution. Proponents of generous exemption statutes take the position that, while people should, perhaps, be "just before they are generous," they should also be encouraged to make reasonable provision for the support of their dependents. Laws exempting life insurance values from creditors' claims encourage people to provide for their dependents through the purchase of life insurance.

Insurance Exemptions

There must be a positive constitutional or statutory provision for the exemption of insurance moneys from the claims of creditors, or such an exemption will not exist. Most states have laws protecting insurance moneys from seizure. Types of insurance moneys which are protected under various state exemption laws include life insurance proceeds, cash values, accrued dividends and interest, health insurance benefits, disability income benefits, and payments under annuity contracts.

Each state's exemption law governs exactly which insurance moneys will be protected, but these laws differ widely from state to state. Some derive from statutes which enabled a married woman to apply for and own insurance on her husband's life and, incidentally, included a provision exempting such insurance from the claims of her husband's creditors. Several states have statutes that establish a liberal exemption in favor of life insurance, but limit the exemption to the amount of insurance which can be purchased by a stated maximum amount of premiums annually. Others follow the lead of an early New York exemption statute and establish a broad exemption in favor of life policies insuring the life of the debtor, or of life policies owned by the debtor and insuring the life of another. In addition, there are numerous miscellaneous insurance exemption laws in effect.

A model law, the Uniform Exemptions Act, was drafted by the National Conference of Commissioners on Uniform State Laws in 1976. The purpose of this model law is to encourage the states to adopt uniform exemption statutes. The commission has stated that the present laws are mostly archaic and that some of them are unduly generous while others are exceedingly nigardly.[20]

Several sections of the Uniform Exemptions Act refer to insurance. The act exempts "proceeds or benefits paid or payable on the death of an insured if the individual was the spouse or a dependent of the insured" to the extent reasonably necessary for support. "Benefits paid or payable by reason of disability [or] illness" are also exempt to the extent reasonably necessary for support. Annuity contracts "providing benefits by reason of age, illness, disability or length of service" are similarly exempt. "Benefits paid or payable for medical, surgical or hospital care, to the extent they are or will be used to pay for the care" are exempt without limitation.

The Uniform Exemptions Act also provides an exemption for a debtor's unmatured life insurance contracts. Loan values, accrued dividends, and interest up to $5,000 are exempt for all contracts of a single debtor. As to values in excess of $5,000, the creditor can reach these by obtaining a court order authorizing that these be paid to the debtor.

It remains to be seen whether the states will reform their exemption laws, and pattern them on the Uniform Exemptions Act.

Creditors of the Policyowner-Insured

Whether or not a creditor of the policyowner-insured can obtain the policy values depends on a number of factors—the applicable state law, the beneficiary named, the creditor's identity, and whether the creditor is trying to reach cash values or death benefit proceeds.

Cash Values. The policyowner's right to surrender the life insurance policy for cash ordinarily cannot be seized by the policyowner's creditors where the exemption law protects the proceeds. If the cash surrender value could be seized, it would defeat the purpose of the statute, which is to protect the beneficiary.

Although, in the majority of cases, the cash value of life insurance policies have been unavailable to creditors of the policyowner, this is not always true. In some states, the courts have held that creditors may reach the cash surrender value of a policy where the statute exempts only the proceeds.[21] Policy loan values actually received by the policyowner are not exempt from the claims of the policyowner's creditors once the policyowner has the money.[22]

---

[20]Quoted in the Prefatory Note to the UNIF. EXEMPTIONS ACT, 13 U.L.A. 207 (1986).

[21]Brown v. Gordon, 90 F.2d 583 (2d Cir. 1937); Hilliard v. Wisconsin Life Ins. Co., 137 Wis. 208, 117 N.W. 999 (1908).

[22]Kuhn v. Wolf, 59 Ohio App. 15, 12 Ohio Op. 339, 16 N.E.2d 1017 (1938).

Where the federal government is the policyowner's creditor because the policyowner has not paid federal income taxes, a federal tax lien attaches to the loan value of the policy up to the amount of the tax.[23] The federal tax lien applies despite a state exemption statute to the contrary. If the policyowner has not made other arrangements to pay the government, the insurer must pay the government the loan value, up to the amount of the unpaid tax, 90 days after notice of levy. The policy will remain in force, however.

An insurer can make policy loans without regard to possible federal tax liens if the insurer has been given no actual notice of a federal tax lien at the time the loan is made. Automatic premium loans may be made by the insurer even after the insurer has received notice of a federal tax lien, as long as the insurer had no notice of the lien at the time the automatic premium loan agreement was made.

Proceeds of the Life Policy.   Exemption laws commonly provide that the proceeds of a life insurance policy owned by the insured, and where a spouse or children are named as beneficiary, shall be exempt from the claims of creditors of the policyowner. Some provide merely that the policy must be payable to a third person—that is, someone other than the policyowner or the policyowner's estate.

A typical example is Oklahoma's statute which reads in part as follows:

> When a policy of life insurance is effected by any person on his own life or another life in favor of some person other than himself having an insurable interest therein, or made payable by assignment, change of beneficiary or other means to a third person, the lawful beneficiary thereof or such third person, other than the person effecting the insurance or his legal representatives, shall be entitled to its proceeds against the creditors and representatives of the person effecting the same.[24]

Where the federal government is the creditor because of income taxes owed by the policyowner-insured, the state exemption laws apply to the proceeds payable after the insured's death, just as they do in the case of other creditors.[25] The exception to this rule occurs where a federal tax lien has attached to the cash values of the policy before the policyowner-insured's death. In that case, the beneficiary must pay the federal government the tax up to the amount of the cash values out of the proceeds.[26]

Life insurance benefits payable to the estate of the insured are paid to the executor or administrator of the estate. The executor or administrator has certain duties as a matter of law, and one of these duties is to pay the debts

---

[23]Federal Tax Lien Act of 1966, 26 U.S.C.A. §§ 6321, 6332(b) (West 1967 & Supp. 1988).
[24]OKLA. STAT. ANN. tit. 36, § 3631 (West 1976).
[25]Commissioner v. Stern, 357 U.S. 39 (1958).
[26]United States v. Bess, 357 U.S. 51 (1958).

of the decedent.[27] In the absence of a statute to the contrary, life insurance proceeds paid to the insured's estate are used for this purpose exactly as are any other moneys or property belonging to the estate.

Bankruptcy of the Policyowner-Insured.   Under the federal Constitution, Congress is authorized to make "uniform laws on the subject of Bankruptcies throughout the United States."[28] Nevertheless, in the Bankruptcy Act of 1893, Congress mandated that the state exemption statutes should govern in bankruptcy cases, even though this has resulted in a lack of uniformity.

The Bankruptcy Reform Act of 1978 made important changes in bankruptcy law. Under the Bankruptcy Reform Act of 1978, a debtor is given a choice between the exemptions granted by state statute or federal exemptions created under the act, unless the state passes a law prohibiting selection of the federal exemptions.

The federal exemptions cover life insurance values. A debtor is allowed to keep unmatured life insurance policies he or she owns.[29] That is, the bankruptcy trustee cannot surrender the policies for their cash value.[30] Loan values and accrued dividends and interest are exempt to the extent of $4,000.[31] In addition, the federal exemptions apply to a life insurance benefit payable to the debtor at the death of a person on whom the debtor was dependent for support.[32] Thus, a bankrupt dependent spouse could keep insurance proceeds paid at the death of the other spouse to the extent reasonably necessary for the support of the bankrupt spouse and the bankrupt's dependents.

If the debtor chooses his or her state's exemption statute, rather than the federal statute, the exemptions vary widely from state to state. In determining whether an insurance policy will pass to the trustee in bankruptcy, one first rules out unmatured policies which have no cash surrender value. In those cases, there is no property to which the trustee can take title. Those policies which do have a cash surrender value will then be viewed in the light of the applicable state statute. Policies that are exempt from the claims of the insured's creditors will not pass to the trustee in bankruptcy.

Payment of Premiums in Fraud of Creditors.   An insolvent policyowner who pays insurance premiums ordinarily will not lose her or his exemptions from creditors' claims, so long as there was no intent to defraud the creditors. Statutes exempting life insurance values cannot be used as a means of intentionally defrauding creditors, however.

---

[27]A *decedent* is a dead person. This term is commonly used in legal contexts.

[28]U.S. CONST. art. I, § 8, cl. 4.

[29]11 U.S.C.A. § 522(d)(7) (West 1979). This rule does not apply to credit life insurance contracts.

[30]A bankruptcy trustee is the representative of the estate in bankruptcy. Among many other duties, the bankruptcy trustee collects property of the estate, sells it to pay creditors, investigates the financial affairs of the debtor, and makes reports to the court.

[31]11 U.S.C.A. § 522(d)(8) (West 1979).

[32]*Id.* § 522(d)(11)(C).

Intent to defraud must be proved if the creditors are to defeat the exemption. In one case, for example, intent to defraud was established because an insolvent debtor bought an unreasonably large amount of insurance.[33]

Premiums Paid from Wrongfully Taken Funds. Where the funds of one person have been wrongfully taken by another person who uses them to pay life insurance premiums, the courts usually hold that the person whose money was wrongfully taken is entitled to receive at least part of the proceeds.[34] Exemption statutes generally do not apply where a person whose funds were wrongfully taken and used to pay premiums is seeking relief. The courts ordinarily will hold that the proceeds in such a case are "impressed with a constructive trust" in favor of the person whose funds were wrongfully taken. That is, the court will construe, or interpret, the situation as if the proceeds were held in trust for the person whose funds were taken. A few courts have reached the same result by stating that the wronged person is entitled to a lien against the proceeds.

The principal question arises in connection with the amount of money the wronged person is entitled to recover out of the proceeds. As a general rule, if all the premiums were paid out of wrongfully taken funds, then all the proceeds are payable to the person whose funds were taken. However, if only part of the premiums were paid from funds wrongfully taken, then the person from whom the funds were taken is generally held to have a right to a proportionate share of the proceeds. A minority of courts have held that the wronged person is entitled to recover only the amount of the premiums wrongfully taken.

One case illustrating the majority rule involved the president of a bank who misappropriated the bank's funds and used them to pay three fourths of the premiums of several policies insuring his life. His wife and children were the named beneficiaries. After his death, the court ruled that three fourths of the proceeds belonged to the bank and only one fourth to the insured's wife and children.[35]

Creditors of the Beneficiary

Whether creditors of the beneficiary can reach the insurance proceeds depends on a number of factors—the wording of the state exemption statute, whether the proceeds are paid in a lump sum or are left with the insurer for deferred settlement, and whether there is a clause in the policy protecting the proceeds from claims of the beneficiary's creditors.[36]

---

[33]Hise v. Hartford Life Ins. Co., 90 Ky. 101, 13 S.W. 367 (1890).
[34]Annot., 24 A.L.R. 2d 672 (1952).
[35]Vorlander v. Keyes, 1 F.2d 67 (8th Cir. 1924).
[36]Annot., 164 A.L.R. 914 (1946).

Under some exemption statutes, the insurance proceeds are protected from claims of the insured's creditors, but not from claims of the beneficiary's creditors. In other states, the statute exempts the proceeds from the claims of creditors of both the insured and the beneficiary.

If the proceeds are not protected by the exemption statute from the beneficiary's creditors, they can be garnished while in the hands of the insurer as soon as the beneficiary has a right to receive them. Garnishment is a court proceeding by a creditor to obtain property of his or her debtor which is in the hands of a third person. If the proceeds are protected from the beneficiary's creditors, the proceeds cannot be garnished while the insurer holds them. Once they are paid to the beneficiary they are still protected under the exemption statutes of some states, while under the exemption statutes of other states they become subject to the claims of the beneficiary's creditors.

In some instances, the policyowner can protect the proceeds of an insurance policy from the creditors of the beneficiary by setting up a "spendthrift" clause in the policy.

The Spendthrift Clause

A spendthrift clause in a life insurance policy prevents the creditors of a beneficiary from claiming benefits payable to the beneficiary while those benefits are in the insurer's hands. Spendthrift clauses derive from spendthrift trusts.

A trust is an arrangement whereby property is transferred to a trustee with the intention that the property be administered for the benefit of someone other than the trustee. Thus, a trust requires at least two parties—a trustee and a trust beneficiary.

When a trust is created, a grantor transfers the property into the trust. In some instances, the grantor is also the trustee or the trust beneficiary. Trusts will be described in greater detail in Chapter 11, "Settlement Agreements, Trusts, and Wills."

A spendthrift trust is a special type of trust. It provides a fund for the benefit of a person other than the grantor, secures the fund against the improvidence of the trust beneficiary, and places it beyond the reach of the trust beneficiary's creditors. Most states permit spendthrift trust provisions that prohibit creditors from seizing property in a spendthrift trust.

The theory behind the spendthrift trust is that creditors of the trust beneficiary are not harmed by this arrangement. Prior to the creation of the trust, they had no rights in the property. If after the creation of the trust they have no rights, they have lost nothing. Thus, they are not harmed by such a provision.

This would not be true of creditors of the grantor, who do have rights in the property of the grantor. Therefore, a grantor cannot put property in trust for himself or herself and, thus, exempt the property from the claims of his or her creditors.

In regard to life insurance proceeds held by an insurer for deferred payment under a settlement option, a true spendthrift trust is not possible. This is because a life insurer and an insurance beneficiary have a debtor-creditor relationship, rather than a relationship of trustee and trust beneficiary. Nevertheless, in view of the emphasis in the law upon protection of life insurance values from the claims of creditors, it was natural that persons responsible for drafting settlement agreements would think of the spendthrift trust as a means of protecting insurance proceeds from the claims of the insurance beneficiary's creditors. However, since the life insurer's relationship with the insurance beneficiary is not one of trustee and trust beneficiary, special statutes were required before this could be done. Such statutes have now been enacted in well over one half of the states.

Illustrative of this type of statute is the following provision of the Illinois Insurance Code:

> Trust Settlements. Any domestic life company shall have the power to hold the proceeds of any policy issued by it under a trust or other agreement upon such terms and restrictions as to revocation by the policyholder and control by beneficiaries, and with such exemptions from the claims of creditors of beneficiaries other than the policyholder as shall have been agreed to in writing by such company and the policyholder. Upon maturity of a policy in the event the policyholder has made no such agreement, the company shall have power to hold the proceeds of the policy under an agreement with the beneficiaries. Such company shall not be required to segregate funds so held but may hold them as part of its general company assets. A foreign or alien company, when authorized by its charter or the laws of its domicile, may exercise any such powers in this State.[37]

Thus, the insurer is given the power to hold policy proceeds under an agreement which provides for exemptions from the claims of creditors of the beneficiary but not those of the policyowner. This means that a policyowner who is the payee under a settlement agreement providing for settlement of funds payable on surrender for cash or the maturity of an endowment cannot make an agreement with the insurer which will preclude the policyowner's own creditors from any rights in those funds. This is in accord with the previously mentioned point regarding grantors. Just as a grantor cannot protect herself or himself from the claims of creditors through a spendthrift clause in a trust document, neither can a policyowner protect herself or himself from claims of creditors through a spendthrift clause in a policy or settlement agreement.

When the policyowner attempts to leave cash surrender proceeds or endowment proceeds with an insurer for his or her own benefit but exempt from his or her own creditors, the policyowner is attempting to deprive the credi-

---

[37]ILL. REV. STAT. ch. 73, ¶ 853 (1985) (Ill. Ins. Code § 241).

tors of rights they otherwise would have had. The Illinois statute, and similar statutes in other states, do not permit this.

Spendthrift clauses included in policies or settlement agreements are drafted in many different forms. One such clause reads as follows:

> No payee other than the policyowner under settlement agreement elected by the policyowner shall have any right in advance of actual receipt of payment from the company, to transfer, assign, alienate, encumber, anticipate, or commute any installment or payments, or to make any change in the provisions elected; and, except as otherwise prescribed by law, no payment of the interest or principal shall, in advance of actual payment of the company to payee, be subject to the debts, contracts, or engagements of any payee, nor to any judicial process to levy upon or attach the same for the payment thereof.

DIVORCE

In most states, a divorce between the policyowner and the beneficiary will not affect their respective rights in the life insurance policy in the absence of a policy provision, property settlement agreement, or divorce decree clause to the contrary.[38] A small minority of states have laws which will cause an irrevocable beneficiary designation to become revocable, or will cause the beneficiary designation to become void, upon divorce.

In many instances, a divorce decree contains a clause providing for the disposition of insurance policies upon the life of one of the spouses.[39] Frequently, the policyowner-spouse is required to maintain the insurance and keep the other spouse or the minor children as beneficiaries. Sometimes, this has been agreed to between the spouses in a property settlement and incorporated into the divorce decree.

A number of problems can arise in connection with clauses disposing of life insurance policies in divorce decrees. If, contrary to the requirements of the divorce decree, the policyowner names a second spouse or some other person as beneficiary, both the first spouse (or the children) and the named beneficiary might claim the proceeds. The insurer often will be forced to interplead in that instance, assuming the insurer learns of the claim of the first spouse before paying benefits. If the insurer pays benefits before learning of the divorce decree, however, it probably will not be liable a second time.

Divorce decree clauses disposing of life insurance policies are not always so clearly written that the insurer can be certain which policies were meant. An interpleader action might be necessary in these instances also.

Where the policyowner-spouse must maintain the policy for the benefit of the ex-spouse or the children, the policyowner cannot obtain a loan on the policy in order to pay the premiums, according to those courts which have

---

[38]Annot., 175 A.L.R. 1220 (1948).
[39]Annot., 59 A.L.R. 3d 9 (1974).

considered the question. One court pointed out that it violated the purpose of the divorce decree for the policyowner to pay the premiums by reducing the value of the insurance.[40]

KILLING OF THE INSURED BY THE BENEFICIARY

If the beneficiary wrongfully kills the insured, the law will not permit the beneficiary to receive the policy proceeds. If the policy was taken out by the beneficiary with the intention of killing the insured for the insurance money, some courts have declared the policy void.

In the more usual situation, the policy was taken out by the insured, and later the beneficiary (often the spouse of the insured) kills the insured. In this instance, the proceeds will be payable. The legal question then becomes "To whom shall the benefits be paid?"

The beneficiary could be entitled to the proceeds if the killing was not wrongful. For example, if it was clearly established that the beneficiary killed the insured in self-defense, the beneficiary ordinarily would not be disqualified from receiving the proceeds.

If the beneficiary wrongfully killed the insured, and is therefore disqualified from receiving the proceeds, usually a secondary beneficiary or the insured's estate will be entitled to the proceeds.

SUMMARY

Property, in the strict legal sense, means rights of possession, use, control and disposition—that is, ownership rights. The term *property* is popularly associated, however, with the things over which ownership rights are exercised.

There are two main classes of property—real property and personal property. Real property consists of a right over land and that which is attached to the land. A right over that which is not land or something attached to land, such as a chair, a bracelet, or a contract, is personal property. The chair and bracelet are choses in possession. A chose in possession is something tangible of which one has actual possession. The contract right is a chose in action. A chose in action is a right that can be enforced by legal action, or by a suit in equity.

The policyowner and the beneficiary have rights under the life insurance contract terms. Other people sometimes acquire life insurance contract rights by operation of law. Wives or husbands in community property states, creditors of the policyowner or beneficiary, trustees in bankruptcy, and divorced spouses sometimes acquire such rights. The estate of the insured or a secondary beneficiary might acquire such rights if the primary beneficiary wrongfully kills the insured.

---

[40]Hart v. Hart, 239 Iowa 142, 30 N.W.2d 748 (1948).

In the community property states, a husband and wife each has an undivided one-half interest in property acquired during the marriage, except for property acquired by either spouse by gift, inheritance, or under a will. When premiums are paid with community property funds, and the spouse is the beneficiary, the proceeds are ordinarily the beneficiary's separate property. If a policyowner makes a third person the beneficiary of such a policy, the policyowner's spouse could have an interest in the proceeds unless the spouse consents to the designation. Exoneration statutes in the community property states ordinarily will protect an insurer which pays proceeds without notice of an adverse claim by the spouse.

A creditor has rights under the policy terms where the creditor is a policyowner, assignee, or beneficiary. Creditors sometimes have rights to the policy as property of a debtor-policyowner or debtor-beneficiary. However, state exemption statutes, which vary greatly from state to state, often protect life insurance policy values from creditors. If premiums have been paid in fraud of creditors or from wrongfully taken funds, this protection usually will not be available, however.

Divorce between the policyowner and beneficiary usually will not affect their rights in the policy in the absence of a property settlement, divorce decree, or policy provision to the contrary. A small minority of states have laws which will cause an irrevocable beneficiary designation to become revocable, or will cause the beneficiary designation to become void, upon divorce.

ILLUSTRATIVE CASE

This case involved the community property rights of the common-law wife of the insured in the proceeds of a life insurance policy.

BETTY JACKSON, Appellant,

v.

ELIZABETH SMITH, Appellee[41]

Court of Appeals of Texas,

Dallas

Before STEPHENS, ALLEN and GUILLOT, JJ.

ALLEN, Justice.

Betty Jackson ("Betty") appeals from the judgment on an interpleader action brought by Massachusetts Indemnity and Life Insurance Company ("MILICO") to determine who was entitled to the proceeds from a life insurance policy issued to Sylvester Jackson. Betty, the sister of Sylvester Jackson and the designated beneficiary of the policy, claimed that she was entitled to the $70,000 proceeds. Eliza Smith ("Eliza") claimed that, as the alleged common-law wife of Sylvester Jackson,

---

[41]703 S.W. 2d 791 (Tex. App. 1985).

she was entitled to all, or alternatively, one-half of the proceeds because Sylvester Jackson perpetrated a fraud on the community by designating his sister, rather than Eliza, as beneficiary of the life insurance policy which was purchased with community funds. The trial court rendered judgment awarding $34,250 to Eliza, $34,250 to the estate of Sylvester Jackson, and $1,500 to MILICO for attorneys' fees on its interpleader action. Betty presents five points of error . . . contesting the trial court's judgment. We hold that the trial court erred in awarding $34,250 to Sylvester Jackson's estate. Therefore, we affirm that part of the judgment awarding $34,250 to Eliza Smith and $1,500 to MILICO, and render judgment awarding $34,250 to Betty Jackson.

The case was tried to the court without a jury. The record shows that Eliza and Sylvester Jackson lived together for approximately five years, during which time Sylvester Jackson took out the policy in issue. Sylvester Jackson obtained the policy from Ahmed Kadry and his trainee, Carl Wynn, all of whom worked together for the city of Dallas. Kadry testified that Sylvester Jackson instructed him to designate Betty as the beneficiary of the policy on the insurance application form. Wynn testified that, although he was present when Sylvester Jackson allegedly instructed Kadry to fill in Betty's name on the application, Wynn believed that Eliza was the beneficiary.

The only exhibit at trial was the application form for the policy. The beneficiary is designated as Betty Jackson on page one. On page three, the signature of Sylvester Jackson and Eliza Smith appear as "proposed insured" and "spouse (if to be insured)," respectively.

Wynn presented the insurance application form to Sylvester Jackson and Eliza for their signatures. Kadry was not present. Eliza testified that she did not read the application before signing it and that she relied on Sylvester Jackson's representations that she "would be taken care of." Wynn testified that Eliza did not read the application before signing it. Kadry testified that all three pages of the application form were attached together at the time Eliza signed it. Kadry and Wynn testified that the policy was a "joint" life insurance policy for both Sylvester Jackson and Eliza Smith; that Sylvester Jackson was automatically Eliza's beneficiary, but that Sylvester Jackson could designate a beneficiary for himself other than Eliza. Apparently both Sylvester Jackson and Eliza "turned in" other insurance policies when they took out the MILICO policy.

The trial court found that community funds were used to purchase the policy. This finding is undisputed, except insofar as Betty contends that Eliza failed to prove she was the common-law wife of Sylvester Jackson. Neither party contests the trial court's award of attorneys' fees to MILICO. In her first point of error, Betty contends the trial court's finding that Betty was designated as the beneficiary of the MILICO policy without the knowledge of Eliza was so contrary to the great weight and preponderance of the evidence as to be clearly wrong. Betty argues that Eliza's testimony that she did not read the application should have been discounted because she was an interested witness and that the corroborating testimony of Wynn was inherently unreliable because he was "evasive" and was impeached during cross-examination. We disagree with Betty's assertions.

In reviewing a factual sufficiency point of error, we must consider all the evidence presented at trial. We may set aside the trial court's finding only if it is so against the great weight and preponderance of the evidence as to be manifestly unjust.

Where the trial court is the trier of fact, it is the exclusive judge of the credibility of the witnesses and the weight to be given their testimony. The trial court is authorized to accept or reject some, all, or none of the disputed evidence.

Guided by these principles, we have read the statement of facts before us, and we conclude that the trial court's finding is not so contrary to the weight of the evidence as to be manifestly unjust. Eliza testified that she did not see the first page which carried the beneficiary designation at the time she signed the application. Wynn testified that he did not recall if the first page was attached at the time Eliza signed the application; that Eliza did not read the application after Sylvester Jackson showed signs of impatience at the time Eliza signed the application; and that Wynn himself believed Eliza was the designated beneficiary on the application. Eliza also testified that Sylvester Jackson had told Eliza that she "would be taken care of," and that she was his beneficiary on the MILICO policy.

Betty's evidence consisted entirely of the testimony of Kadry, who was not present when Eliza signed the application. Kadry testified as to MILICO's general policies and as to the prudent conduct of a hypothetical insurance agent trainee. Kadry stated that all three pages of the application form were connected as one continuous page, front and back, and that MILICO would not accept an application form which had been separated into separate pages. Kadry also testified that it was "very possible" for the application to have been folded in a manner that the person signing the application would not see the first page and the beneficiary designation. Kadry stated that a trainee, such as Wynn, should make sure that persons signing insurance application forms read and understand the application before signing. Clearly, none of Kadry's testimony goes to show whether Eliza, in fact, knew that Betty was the beneficiary. Betty's first point of error is overruled.

Betty next asserts that the trial court erred, as a matter of law, in finding that Betty was designated as beneficiary of the policy without the knowledge of Eliza. Betty argues that one who signs an instrument is presumed to have read it and is charged with knowledge of its contents.

Betty correctly states the general rule that one who voluntarily signs an agreement is obligated to protect himself by reading what he signs and, *absent fraud,* may not excuse himself from the consequences of failing to read what he signs. The exception to the rule is that where a person signs an instrument without reading it, in reliance upon misrepresentations made by another, he is not barred from seeking equitable relief.

In this case, Eliza presented evidence, through her own testimony, that she was induced to sign the insurance application by Sylvester Jackson's misrepresentations. The evidence met all of the elements of actionable fraud. Although the trial court did not make a specific finding of fraud, per se, the trial court's finding that "fraud on the community existed when Sylvester Jackson advised Eliza Smith 'she was taken care of' when, in fact, she did not know . . . that Betty Ann Jackson . . . were beneficiaries [sic] of the policy in question," is tantamount to a finding of fraud. We hold that Eliza is not barred from seeking equitable relief. We overrule Betty's second point of error.

In her fifth point of error, Betty asserts that the trial court erred in finding that Sylvester Jackson and Eliza were husband and wife because no evidence of their common-law marriage was presented at trial. We disagree.

The three elements of a common-law marriage in Texas are (1) an agreement to be married; (2) living together as husband and wife; and (3) holding each other out to the public as such. Signing a document in the capacity of husband and wife constitutes some evidence of holding out to the public as husband and wife. An implied agreement to become husband and wife may be inferred from the evidence which establishes that the two lived together and represented to the public that they were married.

In reviewing a "no evidence" point, we consider only the evidence and reasonable inferences which, viewed in their most favorable light, support the trial court's judgment, and we disregard all evidence and inferences to the contrary.

In this case, it is undisputed that Sylvester Jackson and Eliza lived together for approximately five years. Sylvester Jackson had Eliza sign the MILICO insurance application form as his "spouse." Carl Wynn believed Eliza's name was Eliza Jackson. We hold that there was some evidence presented at trial to support the trial court's finding that a common-law marriage existed between Sylvester Jackson and Eliza Smith. Betty's fifth point of error is overruled.

In her third point of error, Betty contests the trial court's finding that fraud on the community existed because the finding was against the weight of the evidence. Betty argues that she, as Sylvester Jackson's sister, was "the natural object of Sylvester Jackson's bounty"; that Sylvester Jackson designated Betty as beneficiary in order to provide for his children; and Eliza was adequately provided for by Sylvester Jackson's estate distribution.

We may set aside the trial court's finding only if it is so contrary to the great weight of the evidence as to be manifestly unjust. We have reviewed all of the evidence presented at trial, and we conclude that the trial court's finding of fraud on the community is not manifestly unjust.

The "fraud on the community" or "fraud on the spouse" doctrine is a judicially created concept based on the theory of constructive fraud. Constructive fraud is the breach of a legal or equitable duty which violates a fiduciary relationship, as exists between spouses. A presumption of constructive fraud arises where one spouse disposes of the other spouse's one-half interest in community property without the other's knowledge or consent. The burden of proof is then on the disposing spouse or his donee to prove the fairness of the disposition of the other spouse's one-half community ownership. Where the donee or beneficiary is related to the disposing spouse or decedent, the courts look to three factors in determining the fairness of the disposition: (1) the relationship of the beneficiary to the decedent; (2) whether special circumstances tend to justify the gift; and (3) whether the community funds used were reasonable in proportion to the remaining community assets. We hold that the disposing spouse or his donee has the burden to prove these three factors in order to rebut the presumption of constructive fraud.

The record shows that Betty proved that she was the sister of Sylvester Jackson, and that she was caring for Sylvester Jackson's minor children by a previous marriage. The record also reflects, however, that Betty did not carry her burden of proof on whether the community funds life insurance proceeds were a reasonable gift, considering the size of the total community estate. The evidence shows that, in the declaration of heirship proceeding, Eliza was awarded a 1979 Ford pick-up truck, a one-half interest in Sylvester Jackson's home and household possessions, and a one-half interest in two parcels of real estate in East Texas. The record does not establish whether these items were obtained during the common-law marriage of Eliza and Sylvester Jackson; if so, Eliza would be entitled to her one-half community interest as a matter of law upon dissolution of the community estate.

The record also shows that Betty was the designated beneficiary on two other policies insuring the life of Sylvester Jackson. One policy, which was purchased during the marriage of Eliza and Sylvester Jackson, had already paid off the $60,000 proceeds to Betty. The record does not show the time of purchase or the amount of the other policy.

On this state of the record, we cannot say that the trial court erred in finding fraud on the community. Betty failed to introduce evidence as to the total value of the community estate and the proportionate value of the proceeds at issue. She thus failed to carry her burden to prove that Eliza was adequately provided for by the remainder of the community assets.

We hold that the trial court's implied finding, that the size of the gift in relation to the total size of the community was a fraud on Eliza Smith's rights, is not manifestly unjust. Betty's third point of error is overruled.

Betty next contends that the trial court erred in awarding one-half of the insurance proceeds to Eliza and one-half to Sylvester Jackson's estate. We agree.

It is axiomatic that Eliza's community property interest in the life insurance proceeds extends to only one-half of those proceeds. The insured may dispose of his one-half interest, or one-half the amount of the proceeds as he pleases. Thus, where the surviving spouse establishes fraud on the community, that spouse may recover the one half of the proceeds which represents that spouse's one-half interest in the community property. The other half of the proceeds, representing the disposing spouse's community interest, is a gift to the designated beneficiary and is unaffected by constructive fraud.

The trial court's finding of fraud on the community affected only Eliza's half of the proceeds. The other half goes to the designated beneficiary. Accordingly, we modify the trial court's judgment to award $34,250 to Eliza Smith and $34,250 to Betty Jackson. The estate of Sylvester Jackson takes nothing.

Accordingly, the judgment of the trial court is affirmed in part and reversed and rendered in part.

QUESTIONS FOR REVIEW

1. Define the term *property*.
2. What is meant by *real property? Personal property?*
3. With regard to community property:
   a. What is the community?
   b. Under what conditions is property considered separate property? Community property?
   c. Under what conditions is the community terminated?
4. What is the function of exoneration statutes?
5. What is meant by the term *exemption statute* with respect to the rights of creditors to life insurance values?
6. Tell how federal tax liens can relate to life insurance. How are they affected by the state exemption statutes?
7. Describe the operation of a spendthrift clause in a life insurance policy or settlement agreement. Tell why such an arrangement is not a true spendthrift trust.
8. As a general rule, if all premiums paid on a life insurance policy are paid out of embezzled funds, what are the rights of the person from whom the money was embezzled?

CHAPTER 10

Beneficiary Designations
and Changes

THE POLICYOWNER'S RIGHT TO CHOOSE
THE BENEFICIARY
    The Right Provided by the Policy
    Limitations on the Right to Choose the Beneficiary
BENEFICIARIES AND THEIR RIGHTS
    Revocable and Irrevocable Beneficiaries
    Primary and Contingent Beneficiaries
    Donee and Creditor Beneficiaries
    Intended and Incidental Beneficiaries
BENEFICIARY DESIGNATIONS
    Designation of a Spouse or Fiancee
    Designation of Children
    Designation of the Insured's Personal Representative
    Designation of a Trustee
    Designation of a Sole Proprietorship or a Partnership
    Designation of a Corporation
    Designations of Multiple Beneficiaries
    Where No Beneficiary is Designated
    Facility-of-Payment Clauses
    Designation of the Policyowner
CHANGE OF BENEFICIARY
    Limitations on the Right to Change the Beneficiary
    Methods of Beneficiary Change
SUMMARY

The beneficiary is the person named (designated) by the policyowner to receive the benefits payable when the insured dies. The right to designate the beneficiary is, perhaps, the most important right the policyowner has. The right to change the beneficiary, granted under most policies, is also an important right. In this chapter, the legal aspects of beneficiary designations and changes will be discussed.

THE POLICYOWNER'S RIGHT TO CHOOSE THE BENEFICIARY

Generally speaking, a person who applies for insurance on his or her own life can name anyone as beneficiary. This right is granted by the contract itself. The right can be subject to limitations, however, some of which are discussed below.

The Right Provided by the Policy

The illustrative policy in Appendix B provides the following:

Beneficiary. The beneficiary named in the application will receive the death proceeds unless you name a new beneficiary.

The owner of a life insurance contract has many rights under the contract, but these rights do not include ownership of the death benefit. The policyowner does have the right to appoint the person who will own the death benefit. Typically, the policyowner insures her or his own life and appoints another person beneficiary. In cases where the policyowner insures the life of another person, the policyowner can appoint himself or herself beneficiary, but, as policyowner, he or she does not own the death benefit.

Limitations on the Right to Choose the Beneficiary

The right of the policyowner to choose any beneficiary she or he wishes is sometimes limited by insurable interest requirements, community property rights, the policyowner's minority, or statutory restrictions on group insurance.

Insurable Interest.   In cases where the policyowner has insured the life of another, the beneficiary must have an insurable interest in the life of the insured. Therefore, the policyowner will be restricted in his or her choice of beneficiaries to those persons with an insurable interest. This will not be the case where the policyowner insures his or her own life, because a person has an unlimited insurable interest in his or her own life and, from a legal standpoint, usually can name anyone as beneficiary.

As a matter of company policy, however, an insurer's issuing office will probably inquire into the reasons for naming as beneficiary a person who appears to have no insurable interest in the life of the proposed insured, even if the proposed insured is the applicant. Insurers routinely follow this practice to avoid any possibility that the insurance is being taken out for speculative purposes.

Community Property Rights.   A spouse living in a community property state has an undivided one-half interest in property acquired by the couple during the marriage except property acquired by the other spouse by gift, by inheritance, or under a will. If premiums are paid with community funds, each spouse has rights in the policy. A beneficiary designation by one spouse of a third person without the consent of the other spouse will often be effective as to only one half of the proceeds.

Minor Policyowners.   At common law, minors have limited contractual capacity. A minor's contracts are ordinarily voidable by the minor. For this reason, insurers usually will not contract with minors unless a statute makes the minor's insurance contract binding upon the minor. Most states have statutes allowing minors above a certain age to enter into contracts for life insurance which are binding upon the minors. These statutes usually limit the classes of persons who may be beneficiary under the minor's contract. The New York Statute is illustrative. It reads as follows:

> A minor above the age of fourteen years and six months shall be deemed competent to enter into a contract for, be the owner of, and exercise all rights relating to, a policy of life insurance upon the life of the minor or upon the life of any person in whom the minor has an insurable interest, but the beneficiary of such policy may be only the minor or the parent, spouse, brother, sister, child or grandparent of the minor.[1]

Group Life Insurance Restrictions.   Although a person insured under a group policy has most of the rights to name or change the beneficiary that an individual policyowner has, there is ordinarily one special restriction on this right. A person insured under a group policy cannot name the group policyholder as the beneficiary. This restriction is found in most state statutes regulating group insurance.

BENEFICIARIES AND THEIR RIGHTS

The earliest life insurance contracts were applied for and owned by the beneficiary, and the insured was involved only as the subject of the insurance. Even when the insured was the policyowner, the beneficiary was considered to have ownership rights, and the insured had no power to alter the interest of the beneficiary.

Revocable and Irrevocable Beneficiaries

About 1900, however, some life insurers began to include in their policies a provision permitting a policyowner-insured to reserve the right to change the beneficiary whenever the policyowner wished to do so. Such a beneficiary is called a revocable beneficiary.

---

[1]N.Y. Ins. Law § 3207(a) (McKinney 1985).

At first, there was some doubt about the legality of this kind of provision, but its legality gained acceptance when the standard policy provisions law, enacted in New York following the 1905 Armstrong Investigation, included a change of beneficiary provision.

Once the right to change the beneficiary had been reserved, the beneficiary had no rights under the policy that could not be terminated by actions of the policyowner. Nevertheless, there followed a period during which a revocable beneficiary was considered to have a qualified interest in the policy. This interest is called a vested right, subject to being divested. A revocable beneficiary's consent was, therefore, necessary if the policyowner was to exercise ownership rights, such as the right to take out a policy loan, change the dividend option election, surrender the policy for cash, or assign the policy. The states have now rejected the view that such consent of a revocable beneficiary is necessary.

Because the rights of a revocable beneficiary can be terminated whenever the policyowner wishes, a revocable beneficiary is usually said to have a mere expectancy to the policy proceeds. That is, the revocable beneficiary can expect to receive the proceeds at the insured's death, but there is no guarantee this expectation will be realized. The policyowner need not obtain the consent of a revocable beneficiary to exercise policy rights in most jurisdictions. At the moment of the insured's death, however, the right of the revocable beneficiary to the death benefit becomes completely vested.

An applicant or policyowner can name a beneficiary irrevocably if she or he wishes. If this is done, the beneficiary immediately has a vested right to the death benefit. This vested right cannot be reduced or destroyed by the policyowner without the beneficiary's consent, as, for example, by the taking of a policy loan.

An irrevocable beneficiary's vested right is subject to termination, however, if the policy is no longer in force at the time of the insured's death. In that case, there is no benefit to which anyone will have a right. Also, most present-day policies terminate the rights of a beneficiary, whether revocable or irrevocable, if the beneficiary dies before the insured dies. Usually, if an irrevocable beneficiary dies before the insured, the policyowner will again have a right to name a beneficiary—either revocable or irrevocable.

Primary and Contingent Beneficiaries

The primary beneficiary is the person who will receive the death benefit if he or she is living at the time of the insured's death.[2] The primary beneficiary is sometimes called the "first beneficiary" or the "direct beneficiary."

---

[2]If there is a time clause (survivorship clause) in the policy, the rights of the primary beneficiary will be extinguished if the primary beneficiary dies within a specified number of days after the insured's death. Time clauses are discussed in Chapter 18, "Contract Performance."

There can be more than one primary beneficiary. In that case, the benefit is shared by the primary beneficiaries equally or in other proportions specified by the policyowner.

If no primary beneficiary is living at the insured's death, the death benefit will be paid to the contingent beneficiary if one has been named. There can be more than one level of contingent beneficiaries. There can also be more than one contingent beneficiary on each level.

The first level of contingent beneficiary is called a "secondary beneficiary" or a "first contingent beneficiary." The secondary beneficiary will receive the benefit if there is no primary beneficiary living at the insured's death.

The second level of contingent beneficiary is called a "tertiary beneficiary" or a "second contingent beneficiary." The tertiary beneficiary will receive the death proceeds if no primary or secondary beneficiary is alive at the death of the insured.

If, at the death of the insured, one or more primary beneficiaries are living, the expectancy of all contingent beneficiaries is automatically extinguished. The primary beneficiary receives the full benefit. If the primary beneficiary dies before the death benefit is paid, payment will be made to the primary beneficiary's personal representative (estate), unless a settlement agreement provides for a contingent payee. No contingent beneficiary will have a right to any of the proceeds. On the other hand, if no primary beneficiary is living at the insured's death, but a secondary beneficiary is living, the secondary beneficiary becomes entitled to the proceeds, and any tertiary beneficiary's expectancy will be extinguished.

Donee and Creditor Beneficiaries

A donee is a person to whom a gift is given. A donee beneficiary is a person whom the policyowner names beneficiary but who gives no consideration to the policyowner in return. The donee beneficiary is the most common type of beneficiary in life insurance contracts. For example, if a husband purchases insurance on his life and names his wife beneficiary, the wife is ordinarily a donee beneficiary.

A creditor beneficiary is a person the policyowner names beneficiary because the policyowner owes a debt to that person. When the benefits are paid to the creditor beneficiary, the debt will be extinguished to the extent of the proceeds. There is no gift to the creditor beneficiary, but rather an exchange of values.

Intended and Incidental Beneficiaries

An intended beneficiary is a person whom the parties to the contract intended would benefit from performance of the contract. Donee beneficiaries and creditor beneficiaries are intended beneficiaries. An intended beneficiary acquires rights under the contract and can sue to enforce those rights.

An incidental beneficiary is a person who benefits from the contract but who has no rights under it. The parties to the contract did not make the contract for the purpose of benefiting the incidental beneficiary. For example, suppose Julia Rossi is the owner of a life insurance policy payable to her estate and that the policy is the estate's only asset. Suppose also that Ms. Rossi owes Sophia Adamski money and that the debt is unsecured.[3] If Ms. Rossi dies, her personal representative has a right to collect the proceeds. The personal representative also has a duty to pay Ms. Rossi's debt to Ms. Adamski. Ms. Adamski will, therefore, benefit if the insurer pays Ms. Rossi's personal representative the proceeds. But Ms. Adamski cannot maintain an action against the insurer to force the insurer to pay the proceeds to the personal representative. Ms. Adamski is an incidental beneficiary. The insurance contract was not intended for her benefit.

BENEFICIARY DESIGNATIONS

A clear, current beneficiary designation is extremely important to the policyowner, the beneficiary, and the insurer. It is important to the policyowner, because she or he purchased the insurance primarily to benefit a certain person, or persons. A beneficiary designation that is clear and current will allow the insurer to carry out the policyowner's intent. The insurer can readily ascertain who is the proper beneficiary, pay that person without delay, and obtain a valid release. Neither the beneficiary nor the insurer will have to resort to costly and time-consuming court action to determine the proper payee. While improper beneficiary designations cause much trouble and expense, it is easy to draft a beneficiary designation properly, once certain principles are understood.

The policyowner should review the beneficiary designation frequently enough to be certain that it reflects his or her current circumstances. The instances are numerous in which, for example, a long-divorced spouse has collected insurance proceeds merely because the policyowner neglected to change the beneficiary designation. In the absence of law to the contrary, the insurer is contractually bound to pay the named beneficiary, no matter how unjust this may appear. Some insurers periodically send notices to their policyowners urging that they review their beneficiary designations and make desired changes.

It is also desirable that a contingent beneficiary (or beneficiaries) be named. If a policyowner-insured and the primary beneficiary die at the same time, the policyowner will not have an opportunity to name another primary beneficiary. Even if the primary beneficiary dies long before the insured, the policyowner might forget to name another primary beneficiary.

---

[3]An unsecured debt is a debt for which no property of the debtor has been pledged to the creditor so that the creditor can be certain of payment.

Most beneficiary designations are simple. The insurance application contains a section in which the names of primary and contingent beneficiaries are to be written. Often, the beneficiaries' names are not written on the policy itself, although many insurers do follow this practice.

When the insurer writes the beneficiary designation on the policy, it is responsible for drafting the designation so that the wishes of the policyowner, as expressed in the application, will be carried out. A beneficiary designation is often not acted upon for many years. By then, all persons involved in the phrasing of the designation might be dead. The wishes of the applicant must, therefore, be clearly expressed.

The person who is to receive the benefits should be named or described in enough detail so that she or he can be readily identified. For example, if a policyowner-insured wishes to name her husband as primary beneficiary and her mother as secondary beneficiary, the designation can read as follows: "To William Henry Smith, husband of the insured, if living at the death of the insured; otherwise to Jane Elizabeth Martin, mother of the insured." If the policyowner-insured wishes to name her estate, the designation can read: "To the executors, administrators, or assigns of the insured." In the second instance, the designation does not name the person to whom the proceeds are to be paid, since the identity of the executors or administrators cannot be known until after the insured's death. It does describe the person with sufficient clarity so that she or he can be readily identified. Payment made to the person so described will discharge the insurer of its obligations under the policy.

Designation of a Spouse or Fiancee

If an applicant designates his or her spouse as beneficiary, the spouse is usually so described, as, for example, "Daniel Allen Janecek, husband of the insured." A wife should be designated by her given names—"Pauline Marie Jackson, wife of the insured," not "Mrs. James Charles Jackson." This type of designation, if kept current, will ordinarily carry out the wishes of the policyowner, as it indicates with certainty the person to whom the benefits are to be paid.

The courts have held, almost unanimously, that words such as "wife of the insured" are descriptive only. The name itself is controlling. For example, if a policyowner-insured names as beneficiary "Joanne Ellen Harrison, wife of the insured," when Mary Alicia Harrison is actually his legal wife, the benefits will ordinarily be payable to Joanne Ellen, even though the description, "wife of the insured," is incorrect.

The same will be true of a description such as "fiancee." One case[4] involved the following beneficiary designation: "To Mariam Amelia Tatum,

---

[4]Scherer v. Wahlstrom, 318 S.W.2d 456 (Tex. Civ. App. 1958).

Fiancee, if living, otherwise to William George Scherer, Father." The policyowner-insured was killed while in military service. About six months before his death, his fiancee wrote to him saying she was going to marry another man. The former fiancee did marry the other man, but the insured did not change the beneficiary designation, although he expressed his intent to do so and sent for a change-of-beneficiary request form. At the insured's death, both the former fiancee and the father claimed the proceeds. The insurer paid the money into court, asking the court to decide who was rightfully entitled to it. The court said:

> In Simmons v. Simmons, 272 S.W.2d 913, we held that where a beneficiary is named or can otherwise be definitely identified, her designation as wife is descriptive only. The rule applies in this case to appellee. Her name as beneficiary is followed in the policy by the word "Fiancee," and it may well be that insured would not have named her beneficiary except for his engagement to her, yet the fact remains that from February, when the engagement was broken, until July 13, when he was killed, he did not change the beneficiary nor did he do all he could have reasonably done to change the beneficiary.

The court, therefore, held that the proceeds were payable to the former fiancee, rather than to the insured's father.

Where a beneficiary designation of "wife" is made without a name, the lawful wife will be entitled to the benefits. A wife in a valid common-law marriage[5] will be entitled to the benefits just as will any other lawful wife.

A designation, such as "wife," "husband," or "fiancee," without naming the beneficiary, should be avoided, however. Such designations can result in ambiguity if the marital status changes or is questionable.

Designation of Children

Children may be designated either by name or as a class. There are advantages and disadvantages to both of these methods of designation.

When children are designated by name, the identity of the beneficiaries is clear. However, children born after the designation is made will not be included unless the policyowner remembers to change the designation to include them. The results of such an oversight can be avoided by designating children as a class.

Class Designations.   A class beneficiary designation is a designation that names several people as a group, without listing them individually. "Children of the insured," "nieces and nephews of the insured," and so forth are class

---

[5]A common-law marriage is created by an agreement to marry, followed by cohabitation, but without a wedding ceremony. In most states, valid common-law marriages cannot be contracted.

designations. Most insurers will allow class beneficiary designations to be made, but some will not because of the problems which can arise with this type of designation. One problem is that of locating all members of the class after the insured's death. The insured's death can occur many years after the designation was made, and the members of the class are sometimes widely scattered. Some may have died, in which case their deaths must be verified. All must be accounted for, for each, if living, has a claim to a share of the proceeds.

Another problem with designating children as a class is that the courts are not agreed on the exact meaning of the term *children*. Some courts have held that the term *children* includes illegitimate children, but others have held that it does not. The trend is to include illegitimate children. Children born after the designation is made are usually included, but there are cases where they have not been. The same is true of a child born after the insured's death, where the children of the insured were designated.

The courts are generally agreed that adopted children, legitimated children,[6] children who have reached majority, and children of a prior marriage are included in the term *children* unless specifically excluded in the designation. The courts are also generally agreed that the term *children* does not include grandchildren and stepchildren.

The policyowner should make it clear in the designation which children are to be included and which are to be excluded. If, for example, children of a prior marriage are to be excluded, this must be clearly spelled out. In one case, where the policyowner-insured had designated as beneficiary his second wife or, if she was not living, "their children," the court held that the insured's children by a prior marriage were also included.[7]

Issue and Heirs. In drafting designations of children as a class, the terms should be chosen carefully, and with knowledge of their meaning. Ordinarily, the term *children* should be used. People sometimes use the terms *issue* or *heirs* when they mean *children*.

The term *issue* includes all lineal descendants—no matter how remote the relationship. That is, it includes grandchildren, great-grandchildren, and so on. *Issue* should be avoided unless the intent is to include all lineal descendants.

The term *heirs* should be avoided because of the uncertainties associated with its meaning. *Heirs* usually means those persons entitled to inherit the property of a person who has no will. Each state has a statute spelling out who these persons are. These statutes differ and are subject to change. A typical statute of this type will specify as heirs the spouse and children, if living; the children, if no spouse is living; the parents, if no spouse or child

---

[6] A legitimated child is a child born out of wedlock whose parents later marry.
[7] Pape v. Pape, 67 Ind. App. 153, 119 N.E. 11 (1918).

is living; the brothers and sisters, if no spouse, child, or parent is living; and so forth.

A legal maxim, often repeated, is that "a living person has no heirs." That is to say, it is impossible to know who will be a person's heirs until that person is dead. For example, on Monday, a person might have as heirs apparent[8] a husband and children. If, however, the person were to die on Tuesday in a common accident one hour after the deaths of her husband and children, her actual heirs might be her parents or, if they were not living, her brothers and sisters, and so on down the line in accordance with the law of her state of residence.

Per Capita and Per Stirpes Designations.   *Per capita* and *per stirpes* are terms which derive from the law of wills and intestate distribution. They also have application in life insurance beneficiary designations.

Per capita means by head or by individual. It also means to share equally. Most beneficiary designations are on a per capita basis. If three primary beneficiaries are named, unless the policyowner specifies a different apportionment, each will receive one third of the proceeds. If only two survive the insured, those two will each receive one half.

Sometimes a policyowner-insured wishes to provide for descendants of a deceased child by making a per stirpes beneficiary designation. Per stirpes means "by family branches." A per stirpes beneficiary designation is a method of dividing the benefits among the living members of a class of beneficiaries (such as the children of the insured) and the descendants of deceased members of the class. Children of a deceased member share their parent's portion of the benefit equally, as representatives of their deceased parent. Grandchildren of a deceased member share their deceased grandparent's share equally if no child of the deceased member is living, and so forth. A per stirpes designation might read as follows:

> In equal shares to the children of the insured who survive the insured, except that if any of said children shall predecease the insured leaving issue who survive the insured, then the share of such deceased child to his or her issue in equal shares, per stirpes.

For example, suppose a policyowner-insured with three children, Thomas, Janet and Frederick, made the beneficiary designation indicated above. If at the insured's death all three children were living, each would get one third of the death benefit. Assume, however, that Thomas and Janet survived the insured, but that Frederick died before the insured, leaving two children who were living at the insured's death. In this case, Thomas and Janet would each receive one third of the death benefit, and each of Frederick's two children would receive one sixth. In other words, each of Freder-

---

[8]An heir apparent is someone who will inherit the estate of another person if the heir apparent outlives the other person, and the other person makes no will.

ick's two children would share Frederick's third as representatives of their deceased parent.

Suppose, however, that at the insured's death Frederick and Janet were living, but Thomas had died leaving no descendants. In that case, Frederick and Janet would each receive one half of the death benefit.

As a final example, suppose Frederick and Janet were living at the insured's death, but Thomas was deceased. Suppose, also, that Thomas left no living children but did leave three grandchildren who were living at the insured's death. In that case, Frederick and Janet would each receive one third of the death benefit. Thomas' three grandchildren would each receive one ninth.

Note that the beneficiary designation quoted above is specific as to who is to receive the benefits. This is desirable because the courts in different jurisdictions have interpreted the per stirpes principle differently where all members of the class most closely related to the insured (the children) have predeceased the insured. The majority view is that the grandchildren then move up into the place of the children, sharing equally; great-grandchildren receive the share of a deceased grandchild. The minority view is that the grandchildren take their parents' shares by representation.

Irrevocable Designations of Minors. It is not generally advisable to designate minors as irrevocable beneficiaries. A policyowner often needs the consent of an irrevocable beneficiary to assign the policy, take out a policy loan, change the beneficiary, or exercise other ownership rights. A minor cannot give consent, nor can consent be given by any other person on behalf of the minor. If the policyowner needs an irrevocable beneficiary's consent, the policyowner would have to wait to exercise ownership rights until a minor irrevocable beneficiary reaches majority and gives the necessary consent.

Guardians. If life insurance benefits become payable to a beneficiary who is a minor, the insurer usually cannot pay the minor directly, as a minor cannot give a binding release. The benefits can be held at interest by the insurer until the minor has reached majority—usually age 18. Alternatively, a guardian of the minor's estate can be appointed by the court. The guardian can receive the benefits and give a binding release.

Parents sometimes wish to name as beneficiary of a life insurance policy a person whom they desire to be guardian of their minor children in the event that both parents die while their children are minors. Naming a guardian beneficiary can cause problems, however. First, there is no certainty that the person chosen will be living at the time of the death of the last parent to die. Second, even if a person is named guardian in the parents' wills, there is no certainty that the court will appoint that person guardian. Finally, there is the possibility that when the proceeds become payable, the children will have reached majority and be competent to receive the proceeds. For all these reasons, if the policyowner wishes his or her children to receive life insurance proceeds, the children themselves should be named, or a trust should be established for their benefit during their minority.

Designation of the Insured's Personal Representative

A policyowner-insured sometimes desires to have life insurance benefits paid to his or her personal representative. A personal representative is the executor of an estate, if there is a will naming an executor, or the administrator of an estate which has no executor. A personal representative manages the estate of a decedent until the decedent's debts have been paid and the remaining assets in the estate have been distributed. Payment of insurance proceeds to the personal representative of the insured is payment into the insured's estate. Inclusion of insurance proceeds in the estate provides money for the personal representative to use to pay funeral expenses, taxes, and other debts of the insured. A beneficiary designation of a personal representative might read: "To the executors, administrators, or assigns of the insured."

Designation of a Trustee

If the policyowner desires that the life insurance proceeds be paid into a trust, the trustee will be named beneficiary. A trustee is sometimes a natural person, but more often is a corporation, such as a bank and trust company. The designation of a corporate trustee has certain advantages. First, the continued existence and qualification of a corporation is more certain than that of a natural person. Second, a trust agreement with a corporate trustee ordinarily will have been prepared with the advice of legal counsel.

There are two types of trusts—the inter vivos trust and the testamentary trust. Each of these trusts presents special problems in drafting the beneficiary designation.

Inter vivos trusts. An inter vivos trust takes effect during the lifetime of the grantor. That is, the trust agreement is executed and the trust is set up during the grantor's lifetime. Ordinarily, where the trustee of an inter vivos trust is the primary beneficiary of life insurance, the estate of the policyowner-insured should be named contingent beneficiary. This is good practice because the trust is sometimes terminated before the insured's death and the usual policy provision makes the benefit payable to the insured's estate if there is no primary or contingent beneficiary *living*. In the case of a trust which has terminated this language creates an ambiguity because the designated beneficiary is not dead, but rather has been disqualified.

The wording of a beneficiary designation of a natural person as trustee might read as follows:

William Kaufmann, as Trustee, or his successor or successors in trust, under trust agreement, between Marian Appleton and William Kaufmann, dated May 23, 1989, and supplements or amendments thereto, if said agreement shall then be in force and, if not, to the executors, administrators or assigns of the insured.

From the insurer's point of view, it is advisable to add a second paragraph to such a designation, absolving the insurer of any responsibility if the insurance proceeds are not disposed of according to the provisions of the trust, thus:

In no event shall the Ajax Life Insurance Company be responsible for the application or disposition by the Trustee of the sum payable. The payment to and receipt by the Trustee shall be a full discharge of the liability of the Ajax Life Insurance Company for any amount paid to such Trustee.

A designation of a corporate trustee might be worded as follows:

The Reliable Bank and Trust Company of Chicago, Illinois, an Illinois corporation, or its successors in trust, under trust agreement between John Garcia and the Reliable Bank and Trust Company dated August 14, 1989, and supplements or amendments thereto, if said agreement shall be in force and, if not, to the executors, administrators, or assigns of the insured.

Testamentary Trusts.   A testamentary trust is created by will and takes effect at the testator's death. Again, it is advisable to name the executors or administrators as contingent beneficiaries, as the will might be changed or might not be valid. A beneficiary designation of a testamentary trustee might read as follows:

The trustee named in the Last Will of the insured; PROVIDED, HOWEVER, that if no will of the insured has been admitted to probate within ninety (90) days after the date of death of the insured, or if the will admitted to probate within such ninety (90) days fails to name a trustee, or if the will admitted to probate within such ninety (90) days names a trustee but no trustee shall have qualified within one (1) year after the date of death of the insured, payment of said sum payable shall be made in one sum to the executors, administrators, or assigns of the insured.

The Ajax Life Insurance Company shall not be obliged to inquire into the terms of any trust affecting this policy or its sum payable and shall not be chargeable with knowledge of the terms thereof. Payment to and receipt by the trustee, or payment to and receipt by the insured's executors, administrators, or assigns, as hereinabove provided, shall fully discharge all liability of the company to the extent of such payment.

Designation of a Sole Proprietorship or a Partnership

Business firms of various types are often the beneficiaries of life insurance. A sole proprietorship is an unincorporated business owned by one person. The business and the person are legally the same. Therefore, if a policyowner-insured designates his or her sole proprietorship as beneficiary, the benefits will be paid to his or her estate.

A partnership is an association of two or more persons to carry on an unincorporated business. A partnership is not always or for all purposes considered a distinct legal entity. Therefore, ordinarily the partners themselves, as well as the partnership, should be named when a partnership is designated beneficiary. Such a designation might read as follows:

> Forsyte and Company, a partnership composed of Maryanne Elizabeth Forsyte and Marvin Lee Thompson.

Designation of a Corporation

A corporation is a legal entity, authorized by law to carry on a business of a specified nature. It can and should be designated as beneficiary of a life insurance policy by its corporate name. One form of such a designation would read as follows:

> The Rawlings Company of Chicago, Illinois, an Illinois corporation, its successors or assigns.

This designation contains its own contingent beneficiary—the corporation's successors or assigns. For this reason, when a designation of this kind is used, no other contingent beneficiary should be named.

Designation of Multiple Beneficiaries

More than one person may be named primary beneficiary, secondary beneficiary, or tertiary beneficiary, and the proceeds can be apportioned in any manner the policyowner desires, as long as the insurer agrees to the arrangement. For example, it would be legally permissible to designate multiple primary and contingent beneficiaries and provide that each would get a different portion of the proceeds. If no provision is made as to which beneficiary gets which portion of the proceeds, the beneficiaries will share equally.

Where No Beneficiary is Designated

Where no beneficiary is designated, or where all primary and contingent beneficiaries die before the insured, the policy usually provides who will be beneficiary. Often, this will be the executors or administrators of a policyowner-insured's estate.

Some policies include a list of classes of persons who will receive the benefits if no named beneficiary survives. For example, the eligible beneficiaries in such an instance might be, in order of preference, the policyowner-insured's widow or widower, child or children, parent or parents, and executors or administrators. This is called a succession beneficiary designation provision.

Facility-of-Payment Clauses

Many home service life insurance policies[9] have a facility-of-payment clause permitting the insurer to choose as beneficiary a person appearing to the insurer to be equitably entitled to part or all of the proceeds because that person has incurred expenses of the last illness or burial of the insured. Facility-of-payment clauses have been upheld by the courts, as they enable the insurer to pay out quickly for these expenses. Because home service life insurance policies are often purchased with provision for expenses of the insured's last illness and burial in mind, this is a reasonable policy provision.

Some group policies also include such a facility-of-payment clause with a limit on the amount which can be paid out under the clause. This limit is sometimes required by statute.

Designation of the Policyowner

If a policyowner insures the life of another person, usually the policyowner is designated beneficiary. For example, a husband might buy insurance on his wife's life and name himself beneficiary. A person other than the policyowner is sometimes named beneficiary, as where a wife buys insurance on her husband's life and names their children as beneficiaries. In either case, the beneficiary must have an insurable interest in the proposed insured's life.

CHANGE OF BENEFICIARY

Most modern life insurance contracts define the rights of a policyowner to designate and change the beneficiary in a policy provision similar to the following:

> You may name a new beneficiary by filing a written request with us. The written consent of any irrevocable beneficiary will be required. Your change-of-beneficiary request will not be effective until recorded by us at our Home Office. Once recorded, the change will be effective as of the date you signed the request whether or not you or the Insured is alive when we record the change. However, the change will be subject to any payments made or other action taken by us before your request was recorded in our Home Office.

Without a clause granting the right to change the beneficiary, no such right exists.

---

[9]A home service life insurance policy is a policy serviced by an agent who collects premiums weekly or monthly. These policies are usually for relatively small amounts. Home service life insurance is also called industrial, debit, or district insurance.

Limitations on the Right to Change the Beneficiary

Even though there is a policy clause reserving the right to change the beneficiary, that right can be limited for a number of reasons. For example, divorce decrees or property settlements can limit the right to change the beneficiary. Community property laws can also limit the right. There can be limitations on the right of an incompetent policyowner to make further beneficiary changes.

Divorce of the Policyowner and Beneficiary.   In the absence of a special statute, the divorce of the policyowner and the beneficiary does not, in itself, affect the beneficiary designation or the policyowner's right to change the beneficiary designation. However, applicable law is in effect in a few states. Under Michigan law, for example, a wife's interest as beneficiary is automatically terminated by a divorce decree unless the decree itself provides differently.[10] Under Kentucky law, the wife's rights are sometimes terminated by divorce, even though she was designated irrevocably.[11] Minnesota has a statute permitting the policyowner to change the beneficiary designation after divorce, even if the designation is irrevocable.[12] In New York, if a divorce is obtained on grounds of adultery, and the beneficiary is the guilty party, the beneficiary loses his or her right to the proceeds except for an amount equal to the premiums he or she paid.[13]

Even where no applicable law is in effect, the right to change the beneficiary can be affected by the property settlement agreement or the divorce decree. Often, such a property settlement agreement or divorce decree will require that the policyowner maintain the policy in force and keep the policyowner's spouse or child as beneficiary.

For example, in one case,[14] the policyowner had taken out policies on his life in 1919, naming his wife, Coral, beneficiary. Two years later, the policyowner and the beneficiary executed a property settlement agreement in which the policyowner promised to name his wife the sole irrevocable beneficiary of the policies, and the policies were delivered to her. The policyowner and the beneficiary were subsequently divorced. The divorce decree repeated the requirement that the wife be named sole irrevocable beneficiary and required that the policyowner continue to pay the premiums on the policies.

---

[10]Mich. Comp. Laws Ann. § 552.101 (West Supp. 1987); Minnesota Mut. Life Ins. Co. v. Hendrick, 316 Mich. 253, 25 N.W.2d 189 (1946); Starbuck v. City Bank & Trust Co., 384 Mich. 295, 181 N.W.2d 904 (1970).

[11]Ky. Rev. Stat. § 403.190(1) (Michie/Bobbs-Merrill (1985)); Sea v. Conrad, 155 Ky. 51, 159 S.W. 622 (1913); Kentucky Central Life Ins. Co. v. Willett, 557 S.W.2d 222 (Ky. Ct. App. 1977) *cf*. Ping v. Denton, 562 S.W.2d 314 (Ky. 1978).

[12]Minn. Stat. Ann. § 61A.12 Subd. 4 (West 1986).

[13]N.Y. Dom. Rel. Law § 177 (McKinney 1977); Wilcox v. Mutual Life Ins. Co., 235 N.Y. 590, 139 N.E. 746 (1923).

[14]Mutual Life Ins. Co. v. Franck, 9 Cal. App.2d 528, 50 P.2d 480 (1935).

In 1923, the policyowner purported to make his estate the beneficiary. Later that year, he borrowed from one Beulah Wheeler the money to pay the premiums then due. The next year he and Beulah Wheeler married. The policyowner again purported to change the beneficiary designation, this time naming his second wife, Beulah, as beneficiary. He also wrongfully procured the policies and gave them to Beulah.

In 1931, when the policyowner died, both the first and second wives claimed the proceeds of the policies. The insurer paid the proceeds into court, asking the court to decide who was rightfully entitled to the money. The second wife was awarded the amount of the premium which she had loaned the policyowner, but the court held that the first wife had an equitable interest as beneficiary that could not be terminated without her consent. The pertinent part of the decision reads as follows:

> It has been determined that while a named beneficiary of a policy which provides for a change thereof by the [policyowner], secures only a contingent interest therein, a subsequent agreement of the [policyowner] in consideration of a settlement of property rights in contemplation of a divorce by the terms of which he covenants to make her sole, irrevocable beneficiary of the policy, vests her with an equitable interest therein which may not be defeated without her consent.

Sometimes, the policyowner will regain the right to change the beneficiary when the ex-spouse is no longer entitled to the policyowner's support. This could be the case if the spouse remarries. Also, a minor child who reaches majority might no longer be entitled to be maintained as beneficiary.[15]

Community Property Rights.   Where a spouse in a community property state is the beneficiary of a policy which was bought with community funds, the other spouse cannot change the beneficiary without the first spouse's consent, according to some cases.[16] In other cases, it has been held that the beneficiary designation can be changed, but the spouse who was beneficiary will be entitled to part of the proceeds.[17]

Incompetency.   Generally, a minor who is a policyowner has a right to change a revocable beneficiary designation, but that change is voidable by the minor. The competency of a minor policyowner to make a beneficiary change is limited in some states by statutes which provide that a minor can name only certain classes of persons as beneficiary.

The competency of an adult policyowner to make a valid beneficiary change is sometimes called into question because of mental infirmity due to advanced age, accident, or illness. A mentally incompetent policyowner does not have the power to make an effective change of beneficiary. The test of mental competency to make a beneficiary change is similar to the test of

---

[15]Cooper v. Cooper, 49 Cal. 2d 30, 314 P.2d 1 (1957).
[16]Metropolitan Life Ins. Co. v. Skov, 51 F. Supp. 470 (D. Ore. 1943).
[17]McBride v. McBride, 11 Cal. App. 2d 521, 54 P.2d 480 (1936).

competency to make a will or execute a deed. It has been summarized by one court as follows:

> The test to be applied in determining the mental competency of deceased at the time the change in beneficiary was attempted is: Did he have sufficient mental capacity to understand the extent of his property and how he wanted to dispose of it, and who were dependent upon him.[18]

When the mental competency of the policyowner to make a beneficiary change is questioned, ordinarily it is questioned by the person standing to lose because of the purported change—that is, the beneficiary previously designated. The burden then would be on that person to prove that the policyowner did not have the competency to make a valid beneficiary change at the time he or she attempted to make the change.

The guardian of an incompetent or minor policyowner cannot make a valid change of beneficiary on behalf of the ward, as a general rule. Occasional cases have held that this can be done if supported by an appropriate court order, however.

As a general rule, an insurance company which pays the proceeds of a policy to a beneficiary designated by an incompetent policyowner will be protected from having to pay again if the incompetency of the policyowner was unknown to the insurer. In the absence of any facts that would suggest incompetency, the insurer is not required to inquire into the competence of the policyowner to make a change of beneficiary. The rule is quoted in a leading case as follows:

> [I]f the insured was insane when a change of beneficiary was made by him, and the insurer without notice of such insanity, acted in good faith upon the paper as genuine, indorsed the policy accordingly, and on his death, still in ignorance of his insanity, paid the money in good faith to the beneficiary as changed, the company would have been protected.[19]

Methods of Beneficiary Change

Generally, the manner in which the beneficiary change must be made is governed by the terms of the policy. If no specific method is required by the policy, any manner in which the policyowner clearly indicates his or her intent to change the beneficiary will suffice. There are several methods of beneficiary change commonly specified in insurance policies. These are the filing method, the endorsement method, and the endorsement at the insurer's option method.

---

[18]Harris v. Copeland, 337 Mich. 30, 59 N.W.2d 70 (1953).

[19]New York Life Ins. Co. v. Federal Nat'l Bank of Shawnee, Okla., 151 F.2d 537 (10th Cir. 1945), *cert. denied,* Federal Nat'l Bank of Shawnee, Okla. v. New York Life Ins. Co., 327 U.S. 778(1946).

Filing. The great majority of modern life insurance policies require that the policyowner file a written request with the insurer for a change of beneficiary. This is commonly called the filing, or recording, method of beneficiary change. The insurer retains a record of the new designation in its files and returns a copy to the policyowner. The advantage of this method over the older endorsement method is that the policy does not have to be submitted to the insurer. The illustrative policy in Appendix B requires filing of the beneficiary change request.

Endorsement. The endorsement method of beneficiary change was relatively standard at one time but is falling out of favor with insurers. Under the endorsement method, the policy must be submitted to the insurer. The insurer types (endorses) the new beneficiary designation on the policy before the designation becomes effective. Those policies which require that the insurer give consent to the change of beneficiary ordinarily also require endorsement to indicate the insurer's consent. As with endorsement, such consent is now required by few insurers.

Endorsement at the Insurer's Option. A third method of beneficiary change, used by some insurers, is endorsement at the insurer's option. This method is a compromise between the filing and endorsement methods. Insurers using the endorsement at the insurer's option method ordinarily allow a beneficiary change to be made by filing a written request, but reserve the right to require that the policy be submitted for endorsement of the change if the insurer deems it advisable. Usually, endorsement would not be required unless the requested designation suggested a possible problem that could be resolved by a review of the policy.

Substantial Compliance. The courts usually hold that the policyowner cannot change the beneficiary by any method other than that required by the policy. There is, however, a well-established exception known as the substantial compliance rule.

Under the substantial compliance rule, if the policyowner has done everything possible to comply with the beneficiary change procedure set forth in the policy but has failed because of circumstances beyond her or his control, the courts of most jurisdictions will hold that the change of beneficiary is effective. The substantial compliance rule rests on a common equitable principle that a court of equity does not demand impossible things. The substantial compliance rule has often been applied in cases where the beneficiary deliberately withholds the policy from the policyowner to prevent the policyowner from having a new beneficiary designation endorsed on it as required by the insurer. If the policyowner has executed a request for a change of beneficiary, has sent it to the insurer, and has otherwise done everything in her or his power to comply with the policy requirements, the change will be effective in most jurisdictions, even though the policy cannot be sent to the insurer for endorsement.

In one case,[20] a policyowner-insured became estranged from his wife who was the revocable beneficiary. The policyowner wished to change the beneficiary designation to his sister, but his wife had possession of the policy and would not give it to the policyowner so that he could send it to the insurer for the endorsement required by the policy. The policy provided that the policyowner could designate a new beneficiary "by filing written notice thereof at the Home Office of the Company accompanied by the Policy for suitable indorsement thereon" and that the change would "take effect when indorsed on the policy by the Company and not before." The policyowner filed two written notices at the home office of the insurer, each directing the insurer to change the beneficiary from his wife to his sister.

The court held that the change of beneficiary was effective because the policyowner did all he could to change the beneficiary, even though he could not submit the policy for endorsement. The court said:

> . . . The insured's intent that the proceeds of the policy in suit should be payable to his sister, and should not be payable to his wife, was clear. In attempting to effect a change of beneficiary in substantial compliance with the terms of the policy, the insured did all that it was practicable for him to do, in view of the fact that he did not have the policy, that his wife had it, and was holding it in order to prevent a change of beneficiary. It is a reasonable inference that a demand upon her for the policy would have been futile, and we do not believe that the insured was required to sue her for its possession. We think that the right of the appellee [the sister] to the proceeds of the policy, under the facts as found by the District Court, was, in equity, superior to the claim of the appellant [the wife]. The appellant was in no position to take advantage of the failure of the insured and the insurer to bring about an indorsement upon the policy of the change of beneficiary.

The courts ordinarily require that a significant degree of compliance be shown if the substantial compliance rule is to apply. It is generally agreed that a policyowner's mere statement of intention to change the beneficiary is not enough to effect the change. Nor is it enough that the policyowner requested a change of beneficiary form, or even completed a written request, if the request was not delivered or mailed to the insurer. If the policyowner is required to submit the policy to the insurer for endorsement and neglects to do so, the attempted beneficiary change will usually be ineffective. However, if the policyowner is prevented from submitting the policy, because it has been lost, destroyed, stolen, or is being withheld from him or her, compliance with all the other requirements will usually be held to satisfy the substantial compliance rule.

It has been said that the facts of substantial compliance cases weigh more heavily than the facts of cases in any other area of life insurance law.

---

[20]Doering v. Buechler, 146 F.2d 784 (8th Cir. 1945).

This is illustrated by one case in which the policyowner-insured, a member of the armed forces, was imprisoned in the Phillipines by the Japanese during World War II.[21] He was allowed to write only to members of his family. He twice sent postcards to his mother in which he stated his intention that the beneficiary designation on his life insurance policy was to be changed to name the mother.

The policy provided that a change of beneficiary must be made in the following manner:

> By filing written request therefor at the home office, in such form as the company may require, such change to take effect only when endorsed hereon by the company at its home office during the lifetime of the insured.

The policy was in the hands of the policyowner's lawyer in Manila, however, and the policyowner could, therefore, neither submit a change form to the insurer nor submit the policy for endorsement. He died while still in prison.

The court held that the policyowner had made an effective change of beneficiary. His intent was clear and under the circumstances, he had done all he could possibly do to change the beneficiary. Hence, the substantial compliance rule applied.

Change by Will.   If a definite procedure for making beneficiary changes is specified in the policy—and this is usually the case today—the general rule is that the procedure must be followed, or the change will not be effective. In such a case, if the policy does not provide for a change by will, an attempted change by will is ineffective.

However, if a life insurance policy does not require that a beneficiary change be made in any specific manner—as is true of some policies issued many years ago—a beneficiary change can generally be made by will. In addition, a beneficiary change by will can usually be made if the method of beneficiary change required by the policy is not an exclusive method.

Courts of some jurisdictions have held that a change of beneficiary by will of a policyowner-insured cannot be valid, since the rights of a beneficiary vest at the moment of the insured's death, and the will is not valid until that time. In one case,[22] where the policyowner-insured attempted to change the beneficiary in his will, the court said:

> A will does not become operative until death; prior to death it is revocable at the whim of the testator, and the objects of the testator's bounty have no vested rights. In that respect it is very similar to the rights of a beneficiary under a life insurance policy in which the insured reserves the right to change the beneficiary such as we have in the instant case.

---

[21]Finnerty v. Cook, 118 Colo. 310, 195 P.2d 973 (1948).
[22]Cook v. Cook, 17 Cal. 2d 639, 111 P.2d 322 (1941).

However, upon death the beneficiary's right becomes vested, and that being the case, no expression in the insured's will purporting to assign his life insurance policy or change the beneficiary can be effective. At death he no longer has a policy to assign. It has passed to his heirs, if no beneficiary was designated; if a beneficiary is named it passes to such beneficiary. He cannot then change the beneficiary because the right of the named beneficiary has vested.

The court, therefore, held the attempted change by will to be ineffective.

SUMMARY

Ordinarily, a person who applies for life insurance can name whomever she or he wishes as beneficiary. The right to name the beneficiary can be limited by insurable interest requirements, community property rights, the policyowner's minority, or group insurance statutory restrictions.

Beneficiaries can ordinarily be designated revocably or irrevocably. A revocable beneficiary is usually considered to have a mere expectancy—but no rights—in the policy, while an irrevocable beneficiary has such rights. Primary and contingent beneficiaries can be designated. The primary beneficiary will receive the death benefit if living at the insured's death. Otherwise, the contingent beneficiary will receive the benefit. A beneficiary is either a donee beneficiary—that is, one who gives no consideration to the policyholder in return for being named beneficiary—or a creditor beneficiary, who gives such consideration. A beneficiary is also either intended or incidental. Only intended beneficiaries have rights under the contract.

Beneficiary designations should be carefully drafted and frequently reviewed. Beneficiaries can be specifically named or merely described. Class designations, such as "children of the insured," are allowed by most insurers. Class designations will usually include members of the class born after the designation is made, but it may be difficult for the insurer to locate all members of the class. Personal representatives, trustees, proprietorships, partnerships, or corporations can be named as beneficiaries, just as individuals can.

The right to change the beneficiary must be granted in the policy, or no such right exists. Even if such a right is granted—and most modern policies do grant the right to change the beneficiary—there can be limitations on the right because of divorce decrees or property settlements, community property rights, or the incompetency of the policyowner.

Most modern policies specify the procedure which must be used to change the beneficiary. Ordinarily, the procedure specified must be followed or the change will be ineffective. The filing method is most common today, but some insurers require endorsement of the policy, or endorsement at the insurer's option. If, because of circumstances beyond the policyowner's control, he or she is unable to strictly comply with the required change-of-beneficiary procedure prescribed in the policy, the courts usually hold the change effective if the policyowner's intent was clear, and he or she did everything possible to comply with the required procedure. Beneficiary changes can be made by will in some jurisdictions if the policy does not specify a procedure to be followed, or if the specified procedure is not exclusive.

ILLUSTRATIVE CASE

The following case is included here to illustrate the mechanics of beneficiary designations and principles of insurable interest.

WESLEY D. CORDER, Plaintiff

v.

PRUDENTIAL INSURANCE COMPANY, Defendant [23]

MATTHEW J. JASEN, Justice.

This is a motion by plaintiff for summary judgment.[24]

An insurance policy was issued to deceased Anna M. Corder in the amount of $5,000.00 on April 27th, 1960. The beneficiaries listed in said policy were Wesley D. Corder, husband of the insured, if living, otherwise Willa Eakman, mother of the insured. On April 15th, 1963 the named insured died. Subsequently, the plaintiff brought action to collect said proceeds from the insurance company who in turn interpleaded Willa Eakman as Administratrix of the Estate of Anna M. Corder. The administratrix answered the complaint herein and interposed a counterclaim that the proceeds of the insurance policy in question be paid to her. . . . [T]his court on December 30th, 1963 permitted the insurance company to deposit the proceeds of said policy with the Treasurer of the County of Erie, to be disposed of in accordance with the direction of this court.[25] . . .

It is the contention of the plaintiff that he is the named beneficiary and therefore entitled to the proceeds.

The mother-administratrix in opposing this motion proceeds upon two theories. First, by reason of fraud of the plaintiff the proceeds of the policy belong to the estate of the insured, and secondly, that plaintiff was not the husband of the insured and that therefore the insurance contract is void by virtue of the deceased's breach of warranty in representing him as her husband.

As to the contention of fraud, the administratrix fails to set forth any evidentiary facts sufficient to raise a question of fact.

The remaining argument of the administratrix is that inasmuch as the plaintiff was not the husband of the insured he has no insurable interest and therefore no valid right to the benefits under the policy.

---

[23]42 Misc.2d 424, 248 N.Y.S. 2d 265 (1964).

[24]Summary judgment is an immediate judgment granted by the court without further proceedings, generally on the basis of the documents filed with the court and without the oral testimony of witnesses.

[25]This means that the named beneficiary sued to collect the proceeds and the insurer filed an interpleader action, asking the court to decide between the named beneficiary and the administratrix of the insured's estate. The administratrix interposed a counteraction and the court permitted the insurer to pay the proceeds into court and have the court decide who was entitled to payment.

It is conceded that the Wesley D. Corder, who brings this action is the Wesley D. Corder named as beneficiary by the deceased in the insurance policy, and that he is the particular person intended by the insured to be the beneficiary of said proceeds.

Where the deceased effects the insurance upon her own life, it is well-established law that she can designate any beneficiary she desires without regard to relationship or consanguinity.

Section 146 of the Insurance Law provides in part that:

1. Any person of lawful age may on his own initiative procure or effect a contract of insurance upon his own person for the benefit of *any person*. . . . (emphasis supplied).

Since the undisputed proof shows that the application for the policy was made by the insured deceased, there is no issue of insurable interest on the part of the plaintiff.

The use of the term "husband" in this connection, was merely descriptive of the relationship which the assured claimed existed between her and the beneficiary. Even though the named beneficiary was not actually the insured's husband, it does not alter the basic fact that the plaintiff is the person to whom the deceased had intended that the proceeds of the policy be paid. . . .

For the reasons stated, motion for summary judgment granted.

QUESTIONS FOR REVIEW

1. Define the word *beneficiary*.
2. Distinguish between a revocable and an irrevocable beneficiary.
3. Why is a revocable beneficiary said to have a mere expectancy prior to the death of the insured? What is the nature of such a beneficiary's right after the insured's death?
4. What are the rights of a contingent beneficiary if:
    a. The primary beneficiary survives the insured?
    b. The primary beneficiary does not survive the insured?
5. Briefly summarize some of the possible problems that can result from:
    a. Designating minor children as beneficiaries irrevocably.
    b. Class beneficiary designations.
6. Explain what is meant by a per stirpes beneficiary designation.
7. Why is it not advisable to designate a guardian by name as a beneficiary under a life insurance policy?
8. What is the general rule concerning an insurer's liability if it pays the proceeds of a life insurance contract to a beneficiary who was designated by a mentally incompetent policyowner?
9. Distinguish between the endorsement and the filing methods of beneficiary change.
10. Briefly summarize the rule of substantial compliance with respect to beneficiary changes.
11. Why are most attempts to change a beneficiary by will held to be ineffective?

CHAPTER 11

Settlement Agreements, Trusts, and Wills

SETTLEMENT AGREEMENTS
  Settlement Agreement Versus Lump Sum
  Choice by Policyowner or Beneficiary
  The Four Types of Settlement Options
  Limitations on Settlement Agreements
  Contingent Beneficiaries and Contingent Payees
  Short-Term Survivorship and Settlement Agreements

TRUSTS
  Trustees, Trust Beneficiaries, and Grantors
  Life Insurance Trusts
  Responsibilities of the Insurer
  Testamentary Trusts
  Rules of Law Bearing on Trusts
  Settlement Agreements and Trusts Contrasted

WILLS

WILL SUBSTITUTES
  Joint Tenancy
  Gifts *Causa Mortis*
  Contracts
  Trusts

SUMMARY

Applicants for life insurance often prefer to have the policy proceeds distributed to the beneficiary over a period of time, rather than in a lump sum. The applicant can accomplish this by choosing a settlement option provided by the policy and entering into a settlement agreement with the insurer, or by arranging for the proceeds to be put into a trust. This chapter contains a discussion of settlement agreements and trusts. It also contains a discussion of the law of wills, as it bears on settlement agreements and trusts. Finally, it contains a discussion of will substitutes, of which the life insurance contract is an example.

SETTLEMENT AGREEMENTS

If the applicant wishes to provide an income to the beneficiary, rather than payment in a lump sum, one way to accomplish this is to choose a settlement option, or options. The applicant's wishes will then be set forth in a settlement agreement which usually will be included in the policy. The settlement agreement states the person, or persons, to receive the benefit payable and which optional method, or methods, of settlement are elected.

The first statute expressly permitting life policies to have settlement option provisions was enacted in New York in 1906, but prior to that date, insurers had issued policies providing for settlement in installments. Other states have enacted statutes similar to New York's. Most modern policies include a settlement options provision.

Typically, the applicant is permitted to elect one or more settlement options for each beneficiary designated. If no settlement option is in effect at the insured's death, the beneficiary can ordinarily choose a settlement option and enter into a settlement agreement with the insurer. The beneficiary can usually designate contingent payees also.

The term *payee,* rather than the term *beneficiary,* is ordinarily used to denote a person receiving life insurance proceeds under a settlement agreement. Often, a person who is a payee under a settlement agreement will not have been a beneficiary under the policy. For example, a beneficiary entitled to a lump sum settlement might elect to receive the proceeds over a period of time under a settlement agreement and name another person to receive any benefits that remain payable at the beneficiary's death. The other person is a contingent payee, but she or he would not necessarily have been a contingent beneficiary under the policy.

The illustrative policy in Appendix B has the following provision:

ELECTION OF OPTIONS

You may elect to have all or part of the proceeds of this Policy applied under one of the following settlement options. You may cancel or change a previous election, but only if you do so prior to the death of the Insured or the endowment maturity date of the policy, if applicable. If you do not elect a settlement option prior to the Insured's death, the beneficiary may do so provided the election is made within one year after the date of death of the Insured. Any settlement option election will be subject to the limitations and conditions set forth [in the policy].

Settlement Agreement Versus Lump Sum

There are several reasons that an applicant might enter into a settlement agreement rather than have the benefits paid to the beneficiary in a lump sum. Beneficiaries often have little experience in managing large sums of money. An inexperienced beneficiary might invest the insurance proceeds imprudently or dissipate the proceeds in other ways. Unscrupulous persons might take advantage of an inexperienced beneficiary. The policyowner can prevent this by entering into a settlement agreement. Moreover, if the policyowner leaves the proceeds in the insurer's hands to be distributed under a settlement agreement, a spendthrift clause generally can be included in the agreement. Such a clause will protect the proceeds from the beneficiary's creditors.

The policyowner or beneficiary can provide for payment of part of the proceeds to a contingent payee if a settlement agreement is chosen. This provides more planning flexibility. It also assists in solving the problems which occur when the insured and primary payee die at the same time. This last point will be discussed later in this chapter.

Choice by Policyowner or Beneficiary

If the policyowner does not enter into a settlement agreement, many policies provide that the beneficiary can do so after the insured's death. Careful thought should be given to whether the policyowner or beneficiary should choose the settlement option. If the policyowner is much more experienced than the beneficiary at managing money, the policyowner probably should make the choice. Moreover, if the policyowner makes the choice, it can be done unemotionally. The beneficiary, on the other hand, will have to make the choice shortly after the insured's death—a time when rational thought about money matters can be difficult.

There are, however, reasons why it is sometimes best to leave the choice of settlement option to the beneficiary. A choice made by the policyowner many years before the proceeds become payable can become entirely inappropriate. The family configuration could have changed greatly due to births, deaths, marriages, divorces, illnesses, retirements, or the maturing of children. Inflation can cause income amounts chosen years before to be inadequate for the beneficiary's needs. If the policyowner chooses the settlement option, he or she should review the settlement agreement frequently.

The Four Types of Settlement Options

There are four basic types of settlement options—interest income, income for a fixed period, income of a fixed amount, and income for life. Each of these options has its variations. Often, two or more options are combined in one settlement agreement.

Interest Income Option. Under the interest income option, the proceeds are left with the insurer. The insurer pays interest of at least a guaranteed rate at intervals agreed on between the insurer and the policyowner (or the beneficiary if the beneficiary chooses the option). If the policy permits, the policyowner can give the primary payee a limited or unlimited right to withdraw part or all of the principal, or no withdrawal rights at all. The primary payee also can be given the right to change to another settlement option, if the policy permits. Usually, a contingent payee, or payees, is named to receive any amount remaining unpaid at the death of the primary payee.

The interest income option section of the illustrative policy in Appendix B reads as follows:

> We will hold the proceeds on deposit and pay or credit interest at the rate of 2½ percent per annum. Payment of interest will be at such times and for such periods as are agreeable to you and us.

This policy guarantees interest at a rate of 2½ percent per year. Most insurers pay interest in excess of the guaranteed amount if earned, however. This is called a dividend, extra interest, or surplus interest. The illustrative policy states the following: "We pay or credit excess interest of such amount and in such manner as we determine."

Use of the interest income option is sometimes indicated when the beneficiary will be employed for a period of time and earning his or her own living, after which time the beneficiary can have the principal paid out under another option. Use of the interest option might also be indicated if the interest alone is sufficient to provide needed income to the beneficiary. After the beneficiary's death, the principal could be paid to successor payees. For example, a policyowner could have the interest paid to his wife during her lifetime and make his children successor payees. The children are called successor, rather than contingent, payees because, in this situation, they are certain to succeed to the principal. Their receipt of the principal is not contingent on anything.

Income for a Fixed Period. Under the income for a fixed period option, the insurer agrees to retain the proceeds and make regular payments in equal amounts for a period of time decided upon by the policyowner. The income for a fixed period option clause in the illustrative policy reads as follows:

> We will pay the proceeds in equal installments over a period of from one to thirty years. The amount of each installment will be based upon the period and the frequency of the installments selected from [the income for a fixed period table].

The income for a fixed period table in the illustrative policy is as shown on the next page.

The proceeds will be paid for the period of time selected by the policyowner, whether or not the primary payee lives for the duration of that period. If the primary payee does not live, the contingent payee will receive the remainder of the money. Dividends, or surplus interest, will increase the amount of income but have no effect on the period during which income will be paid.

Monthly Income for a Fixed Period per $1,000 of Proceeds, at 2½ Percent Annual Interest, Compounded Annually

Years	Monthly Installment	Years	Monthly Installment	Years	Monthly Installment
1	$84.28	11	$8.64	21	$5.08
2	42.66	12	8.02	22	4.90
3	28.79	13	7.49	23	4.74
4	21.86	14	7.03	24	4.60
5	17.70	15	6.64	25	4.46
6	14.93	16	6.30	26	4.34
7	12.95	17	6.00	27	4.22
8	11.47	18	5.73	28	4.12
9	10.32	19	5.49	29	4.02
10	9.39	20	5.27	30	3.93

Note: Annual, semiannual, or quarterly installments may be determined by multiplying the monthly installment by 11.865, 5.969, or 2.994 respectively.

Income of a Fixed Amount. Under the income of a fixed amount option, the insurer retains the proceeds and pays them out in regular payments of a specified amount until the fund is exhausted. Extra interest payments extend the period, but do not change the amount of each payment. A provision from the illustrative policy in Appendix B follows:

> We will pay the proceeds in equal installments in the amount and at the intervals agreed upon until the proceeds applied under this option, with interest at 2½ percent per annum, are exhausted. The final installment will be for the then remaining balance only.

Income for Life. Under the income for life option, the insurer retains the proceeds and pays them out to a named payee in an income of a guaranteed amount for the entire lifetime of that payee. The option can take several forms.

First, the option can take the form of a straight life income. This is the same as a straight life annuity. It will provide the highest periodic payments of any form of income for life option, but nothing further will be payable by the insurer after the payee dies. As there is always a possibility the payee will die soon after the insured, many people prefer other forms of the income for life option.

A life income with period certain is another form of income for life option. If the primary payee of a life income with period certain dies before the end of a designated period—usually 5, 10, or 20 years—the insurer will continue the payments to a contingent payee until the end of the designated period.

Often, another variation of the life income option is available. Under this variation, payments are made to two people for as long as they both live, with payments continued to the survivor for that person's lifetime as well. This is called a joint and survivor annuity. Payments can be reduced at the first death, or continued to the survivor in the original amount.

The privilege of having guaranteed payments made for the remainder of the payee's lifetime, no matter how long the payee might live, is unique to life insurance. This privilege creates a security for the payee not otherwise available and makes the income for life option desirable in many situations.

Limitations on Settlement Options

There are two limitations set forth in the illustrative policy in Appendix B which should be noted at this point. One of these reads as follows:

> The amount applied under any Settlement Option must be at least $2,000 and must provide a periodic installment or interest payment of at least $20.

The insurer has included this limitation because it is inefficient to make payments of small amounts over long periods of time. Moreover, such payments are of limited value to the recipient.

The second limitation in the illustrative policy concerns payment under a settlement option to a beneficiary who is not a "natural person receiving for his or her own benefit." Such a settlement option is available only with the insurer's consent. Beneficiaries in this category are trustees, guardians, executors, partnerships, and corporations.

Some policies provide that the payee can withdraw the proceeds under certain options. Withdrawal of part, rather than all, of the proceeds is sometimes not permitted, however. The right of withdrawal will usually not apply to the life income option.

Contingent Beneficiaries and Contingent Payees

The rights of a contingent beneficiary under a life policy and those of a contingent payee under a settlement agreement are not the same. If the primary beneficiary is living at the time of the insured's death, the contingent beneficiary's expectancy is extinguished. The contingent beneficiary has no right to any of the proceeds.

By contrast, a contingent payee's expectancy is not extinguished at the death of the insured. On the contrary, settlement agreements customarily are drafted so that the contingent payee will receive amounts unpaid at the primary payee's death.

Let us take two fact situations. Herbert Stark is a policyowner-insured with a wife and three minor children. Mr. Stark has designated his wife as primary beneficiary of the life policy and his children as secondary beneficiaries. The benefit is to be paid in a lump sum.

If Mr. Stark dies before Mrs. Stark, the proceeds belong to Mrs. Stark. The children's expectancy will be extinguished. Mrs. Stark can receive the proceeds in a lump sum if she desires, or she can select a settlement option. In the settlement agreement, she can name as contingent payees the children, someone else, or no one. The proceeds are hers, and she is free to name anyone she wishes. Only if she names the children as contingent payees will they acquire the right to receive any guaranteed payments unpaid at her death.

Now suppose Mr. Stark enters into a settlement agreement. If he names Mrs. Stark as primary payee and the children as contingent payees, any payments undistributed at Mrs. Stark's death would be paid to the children.

A contingent payee has a right to enforce payment from the insurer after the death of the primary payee. This right derives from the policy itself if the policyowner entered into the settlement agreement. If, on the other hand, the beneficiary entered into the settlement agreement, the right has been held by some courts to derive from the agreement between the insurer and the beneficiary.

Short-Term Survivorship and Settlement Agreements

Use of a settlement agreement can eliminate problems which can occur when the insured and the primary beneficiary die in a common disaster. A common disaster is any disaster common to two or more people in which they lose their lives. As an insured and primary beneficiary are often spouses or business partners who are together when an automobile accident, fire, flood, or other disaster occurs, it is not unusual for them to lose their lives in a common disaster.

If the insured and beneficiary die simultaneously, the state's simultaneous death act will provide a reasonably satisfactory solution. A simultaneous death act provides that where the deaths are simultaneous or where it is impossible to determine which person died first, the insured shall be deemed to have outlived the beneficiary unless there is a clause in the policy to the contrary. Thus, a contingent beneficiary will receive the proceeds if one has been named. If one has not been named, the policy usually provides who will receive the proceeds.

However, if the beneficiary survives the insured even for a short time, the right to the proceeds will vest in the beneficiary. The proceeds will then pass into the beneficiary's estate on the beneficiary's death. This result might not be in accordance with the intention of the policyowner-insured.

For example, suppose that Alice Bennett was Jim Bennett's second wife, and that Mr. Bennett had three grown children of his first marriage and no children of his second marriage. His insurance was payable to "Alice Margaret Bennett, wife of the insured, if living, otherwise to the children of the insured, equally or to survivor." He wanted Alice to have the insurance proceeds if she survived him, but if she did not survive him, he wanted his children to have the proceeds.

Now suppose that Mr. and Mrs. Bennett were driving home one night when their car went off the road and crashed into a tree. Assume that Mr. Bennett was killed instantly but that Alice lived to talk to the first people on the scene, although she was dead on arrival at the hospital. Assume she had no will. The proceeds vested in Alice because she was living at Mr. Bennett's death. The administrator of Alice's estate will claim the proceeds. The proceeds will be used to pay Alice's debts, and the remainder will be distributed to her relatives under the applicable state law. Mr. Bennett's children will not receive the proceeds, even though this was almost certainly his intent.

Time Clauses.   Now suppose Mr. Bennett had made his beneficiary designation as follows:

> Alice Margaret Bennett, wife of the insured, if living on the thirtieth day after the death of the insured; otherwise equally to the children of the insured who are living on the thirtieth day after the death of the insured, if any; otherwise to the executors, administrators, or assigns of the insured.

In this case, Mr. Bennett's children would have received the benefits if any of them were living on the 30th day after his death. If none was living, Mr. Bennett's estate would have received the proceeds.

This type of beneficiary designation includes what is called a time clause, a survivorship clause, or a delay clause. Such a clause might be found in the beneficiary designation or in the policy itself. A time clause requires that the beneficiary survive the insured for a specified length of time before becoming entitled to the insurance proceeds. This clause takes care of many short-term survivorship problems. But now suppose Alice survived Mr. Bennett by 31 days but then died of her injuries. Again, Alice's creditors and relatives would receive the proceeds, rather than Mr. Bennett's children.

Settlement Options.   Choice of a settlement option, rather than a lump sum payment, can solve the short-term survivorship problem. If Mr. Bennett named Alice as primary payee, if living, and his children as contingent payees, the children's rights would not have terminated at the insured's death. Instead, they would have been entitled to receive any guaranteed payments that had not been paid at Alice's death. Mr. Bennett's wishes would have been carried out, regardless of the order of his and Alice's deaths or of Alice's outliving the period indicated in a time clause.

A properly drafted life insurance trust could also solve the short-term survivorship problem. Trusts will be discussed in the following section.

TRUSTS

In certain situations, use of a trust is preferable to use of a settlement agreement. This section contains a brief description of the law of trusts and a discussion of the ways trusts can be used to distribute insurance proceeds.

Trustees, Trust Beneficiaries, and Grantors

A trust is a fiduciary relationship in which one person—the trustee—holds legal title to property,[1] subject to an obligation to manage the property for the benefit of another person—the trust beneficiary—who has equitable title.

A trust is created when a person who owns property, called the grantor,[2] transfers the property to a trustee (or trustees) to manage for the benefit of the trust beneficiary (or beneficiaries). Ordinarily, the rights of all parties to the trust are spelled out in a trust document, sometimes called a trust agreement, trust instrument, or deed of trust.

The grantor can also be the trustee or the beneficiary. Therefore, three parties are not necessary for a trust to exist. There must be at least two parties, however, as the same party cannot be grantor, trustee, and trust beneficiary. The trustee and trust beneficiary must be different persons.

Trusts can be created by the grantor to take effect during the grantor's lifetime. Such a trust is called an inter vivos trust, or living trust. The grantor can also create a trust in her or his will. This trust will become effective only at the grantor's death. It is called a testamentary trust.

Trusts developed early in English law. They were not introduced into civil law countries until recently. Under the early English common law, the interests of trust beneficiaries were not protected. When the English courts of equity began to develop, trust beneficiaries started to look to those courts for protection of their interests. In the 15th century, the courts of equity began to protect the interests of trust beneficiaries. In modern times, trust beneficiaries continue to enforce their interests in equitable actions. For this reason, it is said that they have "equitable title" in the trust property. The trustee has legal title. Legal title is title enforceable in a court of law. Legal title allows the trustee to manage the trust property, but not to benefit from it.

Life Insurance Trusts

Life insurance trusts have life insurance policies or proceeds as trust property. Life insurance trusts are a type of inter vivos trust. Life insurance

---

[1]Also called the trust res, trust corpus, trust principal, or the subject matter of the trust.

[2]Also called the settlor, trustor, donor, or creator of the trust.

trusts can be revocable or irrevocable. In creating a revocable life insurance trust, the policyowner usually deposits the policy, or policies, with the trustee. The trustee is made beneficiary, but the policyowner retains ownership of the policies and all ownership rights. The policyowner can revoke or change the trust or change the beneficiary. The policyowner has complete control.

A revocable life insurance trust can be funded or unfunded. If money or income-producing property, sufficient to pay the premiums, is conveyed to the trustee along with the policies, the trust is funded. If only the life insurance policies are conveyed to the trustee, the trust is unfunded. The policyowner will pay the premiums if the trust is unfunded.

To create an irrevocable life insurance trust, the policyowner irrevocably assigns ownership of the policies to the trustee. The trustee is made beneficiary of the insurance. As its name implies, this type of trust cannot be revoked. An irrevocable insurance trust can be funded or unfunded.

An irrevocable life insurance trust can have certain tax advantages over the revocable trust. On the other hand, the policyowner retains control of the policies where the trust is revocable.

A type of life insurance trust which is useful in certain situations is the contingent life insurance trust. This trust provides protection for minor children if both of their parents should die.

In setting up a contingent life insurance trust, ordinarily one parent is made primary beneficiary of the other parent's life insurance. The children are named secondary beneficiaries, except that the contingent trust would be substituted as policy beneficiary for those children who had not yet reached majority. The minor children are beneficiaries of the trust. The trust could be substituted as contingent payee where there is a settlement agreement in effect.

Responsibilities of the Insurer

The insurer is not a party to a life insurance trust. The insurer has no responsibility for determining that such a trust is valid, although the insurer should verify the existence of a trust document.

Most insurers allow a trustee to be named as policy beneficiary if the trust is an inter vivos trust and a trust document is in existence at the time the beneficiary designation is made. The insurer will usually request the date of the trust and the names of the parties to the trust in order to verify that a trust document actually exists. If the insurer did not do this, an applicant for insurance might name a trustee as policy beneficiary, but never get around to creating the trust. The insurer has a responsibility to avoid recording a beneficiary designation of a beneficiary that does not exist. If no trust was ever created, but a trustee was named policy beneficiary, settlement would be made in accordance with the policy beneficiary provision for settlement in the absence of a beneficiary designation. However, the task of establishing that no trust was ever created would delay settlement and might be difficult to accomplish.

Although the insurer will ask for verification that a trust document exists, some insurers prefer not to review the trust document itself. These insurers are concerned that they might be charged with responsibilities of administering the trust if they had a copy of the trust document. Insurance trust documents usually contain a clause relieving the insurer of any such responsibility, however. In addition, the insurer can require a clause in the beneficiary designation relieving the insurer of such responsibility.

Testamentary Trusts

Life insurance proceeds are sometimes made payable to the executors or administrators of the policyowner-insured with a provision in the policyowner-insured's will that the proceeds will be held in trust. These arrangements are not, strictly speaking, insurance trusts.

A testamentary trust is more likely to prove invalid than an inter vivos trust, as the validity of the testamentary trust depends on the successful probate of the will. Wills are sometimes lost, revoked, or declared invalid by the probate court. An insurer that permits an applicant to designate a testamentary trustee as beneficiary must take care to see that the designation provides for these possibilities. A suggested beneficiary designation of a trustee named in the last will of the insured appears in Chapter 10, "Beneficiary Designations and Changes."

Rules of Law Bearing on Trusts

Two rules of law which lawyers must take into account when drafting trust documents are the rule against perpetuities and the rule against accumulations. These rules are aimed at preventing what is termed "remoteness of vesting."

The Rule Against Perpetuities. For the public good, the law tries to keep property in the channels of commerce. To this end, there has long been a rule of law known as the rule against perpetuities which prevents tying up property for too long a time.

The rule against perpetuities developed at common law in England. It has been adopted in the United States in a similar form. The common law rule is in force in a majority of states. In some states, it has been modified by statute. The rule against perpetuities applies to deeds and wills as well as to trusts. The rule in all its applications is highly complex. The following is a simplified explanation.

The rule against perpetuities safeguards against property being tied up indefinitely by remote contingent interests in the property. For example, suppose a grantor attempted to put her property in trust. She wanted the income from the trust property to be paid to her children, then to her grandchildren, then to her great-grandchildren, and on down the line of her descendants—in perpetuity. Complete title to the property would never vest in anyone as long as the grantor had descendants. The property could not be sold or otherwise transferred, because unborn persons with future rights in the property could not give their consent to the transfer. This arrangement could keep the property out of the channels of commerce forever.

The rule against perpetuities prevents this from happening. The rule is often stated as follows: "No interest is good unless it must vest, if at all, not later than 21 years after some life in being at the creation of the interest." The period, thus, begins at the creation of the interest. Any interests, or rights, created by a trust, for example, must vest during the period of time measured by the lifetime of a person living at the time the trust is created, plus 21 years. If there is any possibility an interest created by the trust will not vest within the time prescribed by the rule against perpetuities, the interest is void.

The following is an example of a trust which does not violate the rule against perpetuities. Suppose that, in his will, Bruce Sanders created a trust to begin at his death. The income from the trust property is to be paid to his granddaughter, Nancy Murphy, if she is living at his death. On Nancy Murphy's death, the income from the trust property is to be paid to her descendants for 21 years. At the end of the 21 years, legal title to the property is to be transferred by the trustee to Nancy Murphy's descendants, and the trust will end. Nancy Murphy's descendants can then sell or otherwise transfer the property if they desire. It will again be in the channels of commerce. This trust does not violate the rule against perpetuities, because no interest in the trust property will vest after the end of a life in being at the creation of the interest (Nancy Murphy's life) plus 21 years.

If Nancy Murphy is two years old at the time of Bruce Sanders' death, and she lives to be 94, the property could remain in trust for 92 years (her remaining lifetime) plus 21 years, or a total of 113 years. Thus, the rule against perpetuities does not prevent an interest in property from vesting over 100 years from the creation of the interest if the measuring life lasts long after the interest is created. As human beings rarely live past 100, however, there is a definite limit on the time the property will be kept out of the channels of commerce.

The rule against perpetuities applies to both testamentary and inter vivos trusts. It applies to insurance trusts just as to other inter vivos trusts. The policyowner who elects to have the insurance benefits paid to a trustee, therefore, must avoid violation of the rule against perpetuities in the trust document.

Although there is little law on the subject, the rule against perpetuities appears not to apply to life insurance settlement agreements, as a general rule. This is because the beneficiary's interest in the insurance proceeds has already vested. The proceeds are a debt owed by the insurer to the beneficiary. For example, in *Holmes v. John Hancock Mutual Life Insurance Co.*,[3] the court said that the New York rule against perpetuities did not apply to a settlement agreement, although an identical provision in a trust document would have violated the New York rule. A contrary opinion has been expressed in at least one case.[4]

Because the law disfavors devices which tend to keep property out of the channels of commerce, life insurers usually limit settlement plans to a period which accords with the rule against perpetuities. A settlement agreement naming the policyowner-insured's spouse as primary payee and the children as contingent payees ordinarily fulfills the wishes of the policyowner and runs no risk of violating the rule against perpetuities.

The Rule Against Accumulations. The rule against accumulations prohibits one person from leaving property to another person to accumulate income for the other person too far into the future. For example, suppose an accumulation provision in a trust requires the trustee to add the income of the trust to the trust principal, instead of giving it to the trust beneficiary. At common law, there is no rule limiting the time in which the income can be accumulated except that the rule against perpetuities requires ownership of the accumulation to be vested within the period measured by a life in being plus 21 years. A few states have passed statutes, based on the English Thellusson Act of 1800, which specify other periods of time in which it is permissible to accumulate income. One of these periods is the minority of an infant living at the time the interest was created. In other words, it is permissible to accumulate interest for a minor beneficiary until he or she becomes of age.

Because this is a simple and practical rule, many life insurers, as a matter of company policy, do not permit interest on proceeds left under the interest option to be accumulated except during the minority of a beneficiary. Other insurers permit interest to be accumulated, in special situations, for longer periods.

Settlement Agreements and Trusts Contrasted

The policyowner who does not wish to place on his or her beneficiary the responsibility of investing and managing life insurance proceeds can either enter into a settlement agreement or establish a life insurance trust. The functions of settlement agreements and life insurance trusts are similar in many respects. The proceeds are held and invested by the insurer or trustee and paid out to the payee or trust beneficiary according to the policyowner's or grantor's directions. Nevertheless, there are many differences

---

[3]288 N.Y. 106, 41 N.E.2d 909 (1942).
[4]First Nat'l Bank and Trust Co. v. Purcell, 244 S.W.2d 458 (Ky. 1951).

between settlement agreements and trusts which must be taken into account in choosing which to use. The most significant of these are discussed below.

Discretion.   A trustee can exercise a considerable amount of discretion in carrying out the terms of the trust if the grantor directs the trustee to do so. Settlement agreements, on the other hand, will be administered strictly in accordance with the provisions of the policy and settlement agreement. This is one of the most significant considerations in deciding between a trust and a settlement agreement.

If the needs of the beneficiary are difficult to anticipate or if different beneficiaries will have different needs, a trust might be the preferable way to handle the proceeds. A trustee can be given the power to increase or decrease payments made to various beneficiaries in accordance with their needs as determined by the trustee. The life insurer cannot assume any responsibility for exercising discretion in any payments it makes.

Flexibility.   Generally speaking, a trust is more flexible than a settlement agreement. Frequent changes in amounts paid to the beneficiary are possible under a trust. However, some flexibility can be built into a settlement agreement also. For example, the policyowner can elect the interest option and give the beneficiary full rights of withdrawal, as well as the right to elect one or more other options if and when that seems desirable. Nevertheless, under a settlement agreement these variations must be specified in advance and cannot be determined during the payout period solely on the basis of the beneficiary's needs.

Safety of Proceeds.   If safety of the insurance proceeds is important, as in the case of a small estate, the policyowner will favor a settlement agreement, rather than a trust. The safety of the insurance proceeds is guaranteed under a settlement agreement. A minimum rate of interest is also guaranteed. A trust, on the other hand, offers no guarantees whatsoever, either as to principal or income.

Return on Investments.   A grantor of a trust can free the trustee from many restrictions otherwise imposed on investment of trust funds and provide that the trust property can also be invested in stocks and other types of equities. This can considerably enhance the prospects of gain, although the prospects of loss are also enhanced. The investment possibilities open to the insurer are limited and conservative by law.

Life Income.   A life income can be guaranteed if the proceeds are left with the insurer. A life income can be specified in a trust, but neither the amount nor the duration can be guaranteed.

Expense.   A corporate trustee charges a fee for the administration of a trust, while the settlement services of an insurer are offered at no additional cost. Therefore, a trust might not be advisable if the amount of the proceeds is small. Even where the amount of the proceeds is large, a settlement agreement is adequate for the needs of many beneficiaries. If the policyowner-insured's estate is large and made up of much property other than life insurance proceeds, however, a trust for the unified administration of all the property might be desirable. In that case, the trustee would be designated beneficiary of the life insurance.

Counseling.   A trustee can act as a personal counselor to the trust beneficiary. The trustee can advise the trust beneficiary as to the management of the beneficiary's property. An insurer will not function as a personal counselor.

Title.   A trustee has legal title to the proceeds, and the trust beneficiary has equitable title. An insurer and payee, on the other hand, usually have a debtor-creditor relationship, although, in some states, statutes permit a life insurer to act as a trustee with respect to policy proceeds it retains. In either case, however, a payee under a settlement agreement or a trust beneficiary can enforce her or his rights against the insurer or trustee.

Segregation of Funds.   Property of an individual trust is usually segregated from the property of other trusts. It is ordinarily invested, managed, and accounted for separately, although the enactment of common trust fund laws in some states allows the commingling of the funds of small trusts for investment purposes.

Proceeds of insurance retained by a life insurer under a settlement agreement are not segregated. They are commingled for investment purposes with the insurer's other funds. Income and losses are, thus, shared by the smallest unit on the same terms as the largest.

WILLS

A will, like a trust or settlement agreement, is an instrument for the disposition of property. This section contains a discussion of the law of wills and its relationship to trusts and settlement agreements.

Historically, a will was an instrument that directed the disposition of real property after the death of the owner. A testament directed the disposition of personal property. The document that directed the disposition of both real and personal property was called a last will and testament. The term *will* is now applied to what was formerly called a last will and testament. In other words, now a person's real and personal property can both be disposed of by will.

If the will is to be valid, it must be executed in accordance with the statute of wills of the relevant state. Usually, this will be the last state of residence of the testator. If a person dies with a valid will, he or she dies testate. Generally speaking, a testate person's property passes to other persons according to the terms of the will

If a person dies without a valid will, he or she dies intestate. The word *intestate* also means the person himself or herself. An intestate's property will pass to other persons according to the intestate statute of the relevant state. An intestate statute provides that the intestate's spouse will get most or all of the property if there are no children of the intestate. If there are children, ordinarily the spouse will get one half or one third and the children the remainder. If there is no spouse, the children or other descendants take all of the estate. If there is no spouse or children, the intestate's parents take all or share with his or her brothers and sisters. Next in line will be the intestate's nieces and nephews or next of kin. Each state has its own intestate statute which can vary from this scheme.

A will has several important characteristics. First, it is revocable at the whim of the person who made the will—the testator. Second, a will can be changed whenever the testator desires. Third, during his or her life, a testator has control over property he or she owns which is mentioned in the will. The testator can dispose of such property as he or she sees fit. Fourth, a will can be kept secret or highly confidential. This assists a testator to feel free to name whomever he or she wishes as beneficiary under the will. Finally, a will is not effective until the testator's death, regardless of when it was executed.

The prescribed formalities of execution for making a valid will are spelled out in the statute of wills of each state. These formalities vary somewhat from state to state. They involve the form of the will, the number of witnesses, and so forth. A person wishing to pass property by will must comply with the prescribed formalities of execution, or the will will not be valid. The state requires these formalities of execution in order to prevent fraudulent or coerced wills from being probated. To probate a will is to prove its validity in court.

If the instrument purporting to be a will is not executed in accordance with the statute of wills of the proper jurisdiction, the person executing it will be held to have died intestate. The person's property will then be distributed according to the state's intestate statute.

WILL SUBSTITUTES

The law regarding testamentary disposition of property is quite strict. Nevertheless, there are some ways to pass property after one's death without a will. These will substitutes are discussed in the following subsections.

The use of will substitutes does not preclude the use of a will also. It would rarely be advisable to dispense with a will merely because will substitutes were being used.

Joint Tenancy

Property can be passed at death from one person to another without a will if the property is in joint tenancy. If two or more persons hold property with equal rights to share in its enjoyment during their lives and rights of survivorship, they are said to be joint tenants. *Rights of survivorship* means that, on the death of one joint tenant, the deceased tenant's share of the estate automatically goes to the survivor, or survivors. No will is necessary. Thus, joint tenancy is a valid will substitute.

Gifts *Causa Mortis*

Another method of transferring property at death without a will is a gift *causa mortis*. A gift *causa mortis* is a gift made by a person in apprehension of his or her death, when death seems imminent. It is made on condition that if death does not occur as anticipated from the illness or injury then suffered, ownership of the property will return to the giver.

Contracts

A contract which creates a present interest in the parties will not be void for lack of formalities of a will, even though an obligation under the contract is due at one party's death. A contract differs from a will in that, with a contract, consideration is exchanged between the parties. No consideration is given for property passing under a will. Therefore, the dangers of fraud or coercion which make strict execution requirements necessary for wills are not as apt to be present in the case of contracts.

Life Insurance Contracts.   A life insurance contract is unquestionably a valid will substitute. Investment in life insurance is never considered an attempted testamentary disposition in violation of the statute of wills.

A life insurance contract has many of the advantages of a will. For example, the policyowner can keep the beneficiary and the amount of the benefits secret. Secrecy is one of the advantages of a will. Just as a living testator has control of property he or she has willed, the policyowner-insured has control of the insurance contract until his or her death. The policyowner can ordinarily change the beneficiary, can borrow on or assign the policy, or can cancel the policy and receive the cash value.

An insurance contract has advantages that a will does not have. The life insurance beneficiary can receive the proceeds without a court proceeding. The life insurance proceeds are frequently exempt from the claims of the policyowner-insured's creditors, unlike property passing through the estate under a will.

Settlement Agreements.   The designation by a policyowner-insured of a payee, or payees, in a settlement agreement is a valid will substitute. As in the case of the life insurance contract itself, a settlement agreement elected by the policyowner-insured is not considered an attempted testamentary disposition in violation of the statute of wills. One rationale for this is that the policyowner-insured does not own the proceeds and, therefore, does not pass them to others at her or his death. However, where a beneficiary entitled to receive a lump sum instead elects a settlement option and chooses a contingent payee to receive the proceeds at the beneficiary's death, the question of whether this is an attempted testamentary disposition in violation of the statute of wills has arisen.

For example, suppose Howard Brenner owns a life insurance policy insuring his life for $100,000. His wife is the beneficiary. The proceeds are payable to Mrs. Brenner in a lump sum. Following Mr. Brenner's death, Mrs. Brenner elects to leave the proceeds under the interest option with full right of withdrawal. She elects to have the settlement agreement drawn so that any sum remaining at her death shall be payable equally to her children who are then living and to the children of any deceased child per stirpes.

It is clear that Mrs. Brenner owns the proceeds. She has a complete right to the proceeds just as if the money were on deposit in her bank. She agrees with the insurer that any sums it holds at her death are to be paid to contingent payees. This arrangement has been claimed by certain litigants to be an attempted testamentary disposition that violates the statute of wills.

Similar arrangements involving bank deposits have been held ineffective to pass an interest to the persons named to receive the money at the death of the depositor. These arrangements have been held invalid as attempted testamentary dispositions not executed in accordance with the statute of wills. How, then, does the settlement agreement entered into by the beneficiary differ?

Several court decisions have upheld the validity of a settlement agreement entered into by a beneficiary and naming other persons to receive sums remaining at the beneficiary's death. Moreover, some states have enacted statutes allowing proceeds to pass to a contingent payee named by a beneficiary.

Some persons in the life insurance industry have feared that by proposing such legislation the industry is conceding that there is a problem. It is their position that, since so few cases are litigated, it is wiser to simply assume that the practice of allowing beneficiaries to choose contingent payees is valid. Those who favor legislation point out that an adverse court holding would throw in doubt the rights of many thousands of contingent payees.

Trusts

A grantor can create a revocable inter vivos trust under which the trust income is payable to the grantor during the grantor's lifetime and the principal is payable to a trust beneficiary after the grantor's death. Such a trust will not be invalid as an attempted testamentary disposition made without a will, as long as administration is in the hands of the trustee and a present interest is created in the trust beneficiary. Thus, trusts can be valid will substitutes.

Life insurance trusts are also valid will substitutes. Because of the strong public policy favoring life insurance, these trusts have been sustained by the courts as non-testamentary transactions, even though the policyowner reserves many rights of control over the policies and the trusts.

SUMMARY

A policyowner can provide for deferred payout of life insurance proceeds to the beneficiary by entering into a settlement agreement or by making the proceeds payable to a trustee. If the proceeds are payable in a lump sum, the beneficiary ordinarily can elect a settlement option. The four types of settlement options are the interest income option, the income for a fixed period option, the income of a fixed amount option, and the income for life option. The income for life option can be in the form of a straight life income, a life income with period certain, a refund life annuity, or a joint and survivor annuity. Often two or more settlement options are combined in a settlement agreement.

The rights of a contingent beneficiary differ from the rights of a contingent payee. A contingent beneficiary's rights are extinguished if the primary beneficiary is alive at the time of the insured's death. A contingent payee's rights are not extinguished under these circumstances. At the death of the primary payee, a contingent payee will become entitled to any remaining amounts payable.

It is sometimes preferable to have the proceeds payable to a trustee, rather than have them paid under a settlement agreement. A trust is a fiduciary arrangement in which one person—the trustee—holds property for the benefit of another person—the trust beneficiary. Trusts can be either inter vivos (created during the grantor's lifetime) or testamentary (created by the grantor's will). A life insurance trust is an inter vivos trust which has life insurance policies or proceeds as trust property. Life insurance trusts can be revocable or irrevocable. Either revocable or irrevocable life insurance trusts can be funded or unfunded. Funded life insurance trusts contain money or income-producing property which is used to pay policy premiums. Two rules of law bearing on all trusts are the rule against perpetuities and the rule against accumulations.

Trusts allow more discretion and flexibility than do settlement agreements. With a trust, there is a possibility of a greater return on investment. The trustee can act as a counselor to the trust beneficiary. The settlement agreement, on the other hand, can guarantee safety of the proceeds and a life income, which a trust cannot. There usually is a greater expense involved if a trust, rather than a settlement agreement, is chosen.

Like a trust or settlement agreement, a will provides for the disposition of property. It is an instrument directing disposition of property after the owner's death. To be valid, a will must be executed in accordance with the statute of wills of the relevant jurisdiction. If the will is invalid, the owner's property will pass under the relevant state intestate statute, unless it passes by a valid will substitute.

Joint tenancy, gifts *causa mortis,* certain trusts, and certain contracts, including life insurance contracts, are valid will substitutes. A settlement agreement entered into by the policyowner is a valid will substitute. However, where the beneficiary enters into a settlement agreement naming a contingent payee to receive the proceeds remaining at the beneficiary's death, the question has arisen as to whether or not this is an attempted testamentary disposition in violation of the statute of wills. The cases decided so far have upheld the validity of this arrangement. Nevertheless, this question remains a possible concern to the insurance industry.

ILLUSTRATIVE CASE

In the following case, the proceeds of an endowment policy became payable to the insured, who elected to leave the proceeds with the insurer with a right to withdraw them on demand. He then named his nieces and nephew contingent payees in the event there were still proceeds in the hands of the insurer at his death. A majority of five justices of the Washington Supreme Court held that there was a valid third-party donee-beneficiary contract and not an invalid testamantary disposition. Note that four justices dissented.

TOULOUSE v. NEW YORK LIFE INS. CO.[5]
Supreme Court of Washington, en Banc

HILL, Justice.

This appeal presents a challenge to the validity of an agreement between an insurer and an insured, where the insured, exercising one of the optional methods of settlement offered by an endowment policy on maturity of the policy, elected to leave the proceeds of the policy with the insurer, subject to withdrawal on demand, any amount remaining in the insured's possession at the insured's death to be distributed to designated third parties.

In this case the executor of the insured's estate contends that the portion of the agreement which relates to distribution to the designated third parties on the death of the insured is void as an attempted testamentary disposition in violation of the statute of wills. He sues to recover the proceeds of the policy still in the possession of the insurer.

The insurance company takes the position that the agreement between the insurer and the insured constitutes a supplementary insurance contract and is a valid third-party donee-beneficiary contract.

* * * * *

---

[5]40 Wash. 2d 538, 245 P.2d 205 (1952).

The material facts are that December 1, 1923, the New York Life Insurance Company, hereinafter called "the company," entered into a contract of insurance with Robert Sherlock, the same being a twenty-year endowment policy, No. 8 618 424. The beneficiaries named in the policy when it matured (December 1, 1943) were four nieces and a nephew of Mr. Sherlock; however, the policy was by its terms payable to Mr. Sherlock if he was alive on that date, and he therefore became entitled to the proceeds thereof.

Mr. Sherlock wrote a letter to the company, dated December 31, 1943, and headed "Re Pol # 8 618 424," requesting "that $6000.00 of my maturity check be left with the Company under option 1," and indicating his desire that each of the four nieces and the nephew named as beneficiaries in the policy have a one-fifth interest in any amount remaining with the company at his death. Option 1 of the policy was as follows:

"The proceeds may be left with the Company subject to withdrawal in whole or in part at any time on demand in sums of not less than one hundred dollars. The Company will credit interest annually on the proceeds so left with it at such rate as it may each year declare on such funds and guarantees that the rate of interest shall never be less than three per cent."

After a statement of options 2 and 3 (with which we are not concerned) the policy provided:

"In the event of the death of a payee *any unpaid sum left with the Company under Option 1 shall be paid in one sum;* any unpaid instalments payable under Option 2, or any instalments for the fixed period of twenty years only under Option 3 which shall not then have been paid, shall be commuted at three per cent compound interest, *and unless otherwise agreed in writing shall be paid in one sum to the executors or administrators of such payee."* (Italics ours.)

(We can appropriately at this point discuss an issue not raised by appellant but raised *sponte sua* by members of the court, *i.e.,* whether, under Option 1, Mr. Sherlock and the company could agree in writing to the disposition to be made of any unpaid sum remaining in the possession of the company on his death. It seems to us that the concluding italicized phrase, beginning "and unless otherwise agreed in writing," applied to Option 1 as well as to Options 2 and 3. Unless it applied to Option 1, there was nothing to indicate to whom the "unpaid sum" left with the company under that option should be paid on the death of the payee. In any event, the parties to the agreement placed their own interpretation on Option 1. If there be any ambiguity in a contract, the interpretation which the parties have placed upon it is entitled to great, if not controlling, weight in determining its meaning. And that rule is applicable to contracts of insurance. We therefore proceed with further discussion of the case on the assumption that, in making the supplementary contract hereinafter referred to, the company and Mr. Sherlock proceeded under a right given Mr. Sherlock by the original policy of insurance.)

Pursuant to Mr. Sherlock's election to leave six thousand dollars with the company under Option 1, the company issued to Mr. Sherlock a document captioned

"Supplementary Contract No. 100 891," dated January 7, 1944, by the terms of which it acknowledged that it was holding and agreed

" * * * to continue to hold as a part of its general funds the sum of Six Thousand and 00/100 Dollars being part of the proceeds of Policy No 8 618 424 issued by said Company on the life of Robert Sherlock."

By that document the company further agreed to pay interest at a rate of not less than three per cent per annum; "to pay said sum with interest as aforesaid to Robert Sherlock (herein called the payee) on demand in sums of not less than $100 each"; and to pay the unpaid balance, if any, remaining in its possession at the death of Mr. Sherlock, as follows:

"Agnes Tooley, niece, ⅕, daughter of Mary Sherlock, sister of Robert Sherlock, Dominick Sherlock, nephew, son of Dominick Sherlock, brother of Robert Sherlock ⅕, Bridget McCauley niece, daughter of Madge Sherlock, sister of Robert Sherlock, ⅕ Bridget Sherlock, niece, daughter of Dominick Sherlock, brother of Robert Sherlock ⅕, and Margaret McCauley niece, daughter of Madge Sherlock, sister of Robert Sherlock, ⅕, if living, otherwise to the executors or administrators of said Robert Sherlock, upon receipt and approval of satisfactory evidence of their appointment and qualifications."

This document remained in Mr. Sherlock's possession, except when surrendered to have interest credited. At the time it was first forwarded to him, the company also forwarded to him for signature a form letter labeled "Form No. 1," referred to by the company and found by the trial court to be an "acceptance certificate." This letter was addressed to the company and was captioned

"Supplementary Contract No. 100 891
"Re:—Policy No. 8 618 424."

In it the desire of Mr. Sherlock that the company "hold $6000.00 of the proceeds of this policy" was expressed; also, his understanding of the conditions under which the money might be withdrawn and of the manner of calculating the interest was set forth in substantially the same language as in the document of January 7, 1944, with the addition of the following significant words: "It is understood and agreed that once your Supplementary Contract has been issued no change can be made in its terms." These words, and all the rest of the body of the letter except the amount "$6000.00" in the first line and the concluding paragraph, are part of the form acceptance certificate prepared by the company. The concluding paragraph is as follows:

"I further request that in the event of my death any balance remaining in the company's possession is to be paid as follows, Agnes Tooley, niece ⅕, daughter of Mary Sherlock, my sister, Dominick Sherlock, nephew, son of Dominick Sherlock, my brother, ⅕, Bridget McCauley, niece, daughter of Dominick Sherlock, my brother, ⅕, and Margaret McCauley, niece, daughter of Madge Sherlock, my sister ⅕, otherwise to the executors or administrators of my estate."

This form letter or acceptance certificate was dated, in ink, "1/21/1944," and was signed by Robert Sherlock and witnessed. It is stamped as having been received in the office of the company January 26, 1944.

Mr. Sherlock made no withdrawals, and the accumulated funds in the possession of the company on January 7, 1950, after Mr. Sherlock's death and before the commencement of this proceeding, amounted to $7,164.31. The executor of Mr. Sherlock's estate brought this action to recover that amount from the company.

The trial court concluded, as do we, that the original insurance policy (exhibit No. 3), supplementary contract No. 100 891 (exhibit No. 6), and the form letter or acceptance certificate of January 21, 1944 (exhibit No. 5) constitute the agreement between Mr. Sherlock and the company. (Inasmuch as one of the documents which we hold constitute the agreement between Mr. Sherlock and the company is captioned "Supplementary Contract," we will, to avoid confusion, refer to that document as "exhibit No. 6," and to the agreement between Mr. Sherlock and the company as evidenced by exhibits Nos. 3, 5 and 6 as "the supplementary insurance contract.")

The trial court also concluded that the supplementary insurance contract is a valid agreement and that each of the five beneficiaries designated therein is entitled to one fifth of the amount in the possession of the company when Mr. Sherlock died. It therefore dismissed the action of the executor, and he prosecutes this appeal.

The right to take advantage of optional methods of settlement provided in an insurance policy is a valuable one and will be protected. The beneficiary (or, as in this case, the insured) acquires a vested interest in the company's performance of that part of its contract of insurance. Such an interest is in the nature of a property right. The species of property is neither money nor real property, but a contractual obligation. Our insurance code specifically recognizes the right of insurance companies to make such policy settlement agreements:

> "Any life insurer shall have the power to hold under agreement the proceeds of any policy issued by it, upon such terms and restrictions as to revocation by the policyholder and control by beneficiaries, and with such exemptions from the claims of creditors of beneficiaries other than the policyholder as set forth in the policy or as agreed to in writing by the insurer and the policyholder. Upon maturity of a policy in the event the policyholder has made no such agreement, the insurer shall have the power to hold the proceeds of the policy under an agreement with the beneficiaries. The insurer shall not be required to segregate funds so held but may hold them as part of its general assets."

While this statute does not specifically provide that contracts such as the one here under consideration need not comply with the statute of wills, it seems to be implied.

The validity of supplementary insurance contracts by the terms of which insurance companies distribute the proceeds of insurance policies under optional methods of settlement, where the supplementary insurance contracts have provided for payment to designated third parties of any amounts remaining in the companies' hands after the death of the payees, has seldom been passed upon by the courts. The validity of such provisions was assumed without question in Aetna Life Ins.

Co. v. Bartlett, D.C.1944, 53 F.Supp. 1005; New England Mut. Life Ins. Co. v. Harvey, D.C.1949, 82 F.Supp 702; Smith v. Smith, 8 Cir., 1949, 172 F.2d 399.

In the opinion (written by Justice Augustus N. Hand) in Mutual Ben. Life Ins. Co. v. Ellis, 2 Cir., 1942, 125 F.2d 127, 130, 138 A.L.R. 1478, it was recognized that such a supplementary insurance contract would be valid but, going much further, the court stated that, although the contract before it in that case was not a supplementary insurance contract, because the beneficiary of the insurance policy had accepted none of the options offered by the company, it would be upheld as a third-party donee-beneficiary contract. In that case the insurer and the beneficiary had entered into what the court described as an entirely new agreement providing for certain payments to the beneficiary during her lifetime, any amount remaining at her death to be paid to three sisters of her deceased husband. The court there said that the rights of the sisters "would not be derived from the policies or through the exercise of the options but from the new agreement." In the present case, the rights of the four nieces and the nephew in the supplementary insurance contract are derived from the original insurance policy through the exercise of Option 1.

Appellant has cited no cases and we have found none holding that supplementary insurance contracts such as the one in the present case are void, as testamentary dispositions in violation of the statute of wills. The cases on which the appellant relies deal, for the most part, with the requisites of gifts *causa mortis* and are not contract cases.

* * * * *

We are not here concerned with the law of gifts, *inter vivos* or *causa mortis;* but with the question of whether or not the supplementary insurance contract between the insurance company and Mr. Sherlock confers any rights on Mr. Sherlock's nieces and nephew named therein, to whom the company promised to pay any of the proceeds of the original insurance policy (plus accumulated interest) which might be in its possession when Mr. Sherlock died. Their rights under that contract are based upon the contractual obligation of the company to do what it agreed with Mr. Sherlock it would do. Mr. Sherlock might have defeated their rights by withdrawing all the money, but he had no right under the agreement to substitute someone else in their stead as the third-party donee-beneficiary; he could make no change in exhibit No. 6, in which the insurance company's obligations were set forth. By analogy to insurance policy cases, the supplementary insurance contract gave the named nieces and nephew a vested interest, not in any specific property or to any amount of money, but in the performance of the contract by the insurance company.

The mere fact that the death of one of the parties to a contract is designated as a contingency upon which a promise to deliver property to a third-party donee-beneficiary turns, is not alone sufficient to make such a contract a testamentary disposition and subject it to the statute of wills.

As was said in [Mutual Ben. Life Ins. Co. v. Ellis, *supra*] "their right to enforce is based upon a contractual obligation and not on any interest in the property of the decedent."

Deciding, as we do, that the supplementary insurance contract between Mr. Sherlock and the company is evidenced by exhibits Nos. 3, 5 and 6 and flows from and is the result of an exercise by Mr. Sherlock of Option 1 contained in the insurance policy, and that the supplementary insurance contract, like the original contract of insurance, constitutes a valid third-party donee-beneficiary contract and is not a testamentary disposition, we conclude that the trial court's action in dismissing the complaint of the executor, appellant here, should be, and it hereby is, affirmed.

FINLEY and GRADY, JJ., concur.

OLSON, Justice (concurring specially).

In my opinion, the decision of this case should rest solely upon the conclusion that the contract described by the majority is a valid third-party donee-beneficiary contract. The insurance company is the promisor, and the deceased is the promisee, for the benefit of named third parties. The fact that such a contract is conditional, as in this case in which the promisee could have withdrawn the funds, does not render it invalid. The rights of the donee-beneficiaries under it are subject to that limitation. The conditional event not having occurred, the beneficiaries are entitled to the funds under the contract.

HAMLEY, Justice.
I agree with the views expressed by Judge OLSON.

DONWORTH, Justice (dissenting).
The majority opinion sanctions, for the first time in this state, a transaction whereby one person deposits money with another upon an agreement that the depositor may withdraw during his lifetime all or any part of the money so deposited and that the depositary will upon his death pay any balance then remaining to certain designated parties. This transaction is upheld upon the ground that it is based upon a contract of life insurance. In my opinion, the supplementary contract here involved is not in any way connected with life insurance and is an attempt to circumvent the statute of wills and constitutes an invalid testamentary disposition. The far-reaching consequences of the majority opinion impel me to register my dissent.

The endowment policy issued to Mr. Sherlock matured December 1, 1943, while he was still living. By its terms the company obligated itself to pay him on that date (if then living) the sum of five thousand dollars (plus accrued dividends not previously withdrawn). The optional methods of settlement included the following:

> "Option 1—The proceeds may be left with the Company subject to withdrawal in whole or in part at any time on demand in sums of not less than one hundred dollars. The Company will credit interest annually on the proceeds so left with it at such rate as it may each year declare on such funds and guarantees that the rate of interest shall never be less than three per cent."

After describing options 2 and 3 (with which we are not concerned), the policy provided:

> "*In the event of the death of a payee any unpaid sum left with the Company under Option 1 shall be paid in one sum;* any unpaid instalments payable under Option 2, or any instalments for the fixed period of twenty years only under Option 3 which shall not then have been paid, shall be commuted at three per cent compound interest, and unless otherwise agreed in writing shall be paid in one sum to the executors or administrators of such payee." (Italics mine.)

The majority opinion interpret the italicized portion of the quoted provision as being modified by the phrase "unless otherwise agreed in writing" which appears in the latter part thereof. In my opinion, the provision is not ambiguous in any degree and is not susceptible to the interpretation placed upon it by the majority, which seems to me to be a strained and unreasonable interpretation.

Had the life insurance company in drafting this policy intended that the phrase "unless otherwise agreed in writing" apply to option 1, it would not have placed a semicolon after the words "shall be paid in one sum" appearing in the first part of the provision. We have confessed, in the recent case of Peters v. Watson Co., Wash., 241 P.2d 441, to a very high regard, in interpretation of a contract, for the position of a comma. A semicolon, it appears to me, is entitled to at least the same regard in interpreting a provision as free from ambiguity as the one under consideration here.

We also, in the Peters case, recognized and applied, without stating it in so many words, the rule that, unless the intention of the parties appears to be otherwise, a relative word or phrase will be interpreted as referring to, or modifying only its nearest antecedent.

Option 1 does not purport to give Mr. Sherlock any right to name beneficiaries to receive at his death any balance of the proceeds left with the company under that option. Since no right to designate any person or persons to whom such payment should be made was reserved to Mr. Sherlock in the endowment policy, the intention of the parties must have been that such proceeds were to be paid to his legal representative. It is the statutory duty of an executor or administrator to collect all debts due the deceased which, in this case, would include any balance remaining in the fund upon Mr. Sherlock's death.

By his letter of December 31, 1943, Mr. Sherlock requested the company to retain a portion of the proceeds under option 1 and requested that payment thereof be made (presumably at his death) to five named nephews and nieces.

On January 21, 1944, he signed a letter addressed to the company (evidently prepared for his signature by its agent) referring to a certain supplementary contract which was dated January 7, 1944, but which evidently had not been delivered to him. This letter stated in detail certain conditions as to the manner of exercising the right of withdrawal and also specified the method of computing interest on the deposit. It concluded as follows:

> "It is understood and agreed that once your Supplementary Contract has been issued no change can be made in its terms.
>
> "I further request that in the event of my death any balance remaining in the company's possession is to be paid as follows [Here are listed the names of the five nephews and nieces.] otherwise to the executors or administrators of my estate."

The supplementary contract referred to in this letter made no reference to its irrevocability. It contained the following provision:

> "If at the death of said payee there shall remain any unpaid balance to the credit of said account, the amount of said balance remaining in the Company's possession shall be payable in one sum, upon receipt of due proof of the death of the payee and surrender of this agreement, to as follows [Here are listed the names of the five nephews and nieces.] if

living, otherwise to the executors or administrators of said Robert Sherlock. * * *

"This agreement is not negotiable nor assignable and must be submitted with each demand for any part of said sum for proper entry herein, and shall be surrendered to the Company whenever the sum so held is paid in full. All payments hereunder are payable at the Home Office of the Company in the City and State of New York."

It is very plain to me that this so-called supplementary contract is an entirely new contract between the parties which is not supplementary to, nor in anywise connected with, option 1 of the endowment policy in so far as it purports to designate substitute payees upon Mr. Sherlock's death. There is nothing in the endowment policy relating to the payment of the proceeds to any person other than Mr. Sherlock *after the close of the endowment period.*

When the endowment policy matured by the lapse of twenty years on December 1, 1943, Mr. Sherlock was alive and the proceeds were payable solely to him. Under option 1 he could and did elect to leave a portion of the proceeds with the company, but the endowment policy (as I construe it) gave him no right to designate to whom the proceeds should be paid at his death.

This supplementary contract is a new contract having nothing whatever to do with life insurance. The fact that the depository of the proceeds was a life insurance company is immaterial. It might have been a bank or an individual. A deposit in a bank with instructions to pay any balance remaining at the depositor's death to certain designated beneficiaries would clearly, in my opinion, be void as an attempt at testamentary disposition.

The majority appear to hold that the supplementary contract was a third party donee beneficiary contract by which the nieces and nephew acquired a vested interest in the fund during Mr. Sherlock's lifetime. The supplementary contract reserved to Mr. Sherlock the right to withdraw and use any or all of the principal and/or accrued interest during his lifetime as he should see fit. Furthermore, any creditors of Mr. Sherlock could have reached this money by garnishment or otherwise. He had not parted with any incidents of ownership in, nor control over, the money. The interests of the nieces and nephew in this deposit cannot be considered as having vested at any time prior to Mr. Sherlock's death.

The majority, in support of their conclusion that the nieces and nephew of Mr. Sherlock acquired vested interests under the supplementary contract, attempt to draw an analogy between the interest of a beneficiary under a life insurance contract wherein the insured has surrendered his right to change the beneficiary, and the interests of the nieces and nephew under this contract, which was issued pursuant to an agreement that "no change can be made in its terms."

There can be no question that the interest of a beneficiary under a contract of life insurance wherein the insured has surrendered, or has failed to retain, his right to change the beneficiary is a vested one. In such event the beneficiary takes a vested interest which cannot be impaired or extinguished by the acts of the insured. But here Mr. Sherlock expressly reserved the right to extinguish the alleged interests of the named nieces and nephew by withdrawing all of the fund at any time. The rule is that if an insured retains the power to extinguish the rights or interest of a beneficiary, even though he cannot change his designation of the beneficiary, then the beneficiary has a mere expectancy or contingent interest.

It cannot, therefore, be maintained that even by analogy to the law of life insurance the named nieces and nephew acquired at any time prior to Mr. Sherlock's death vested rights to the balance of the fund.

The majority opinion cites, in support of its holding, the decision of the Circuit Court of Appeals, 2d Cir., in Mutual Benefit Life Ins. Co. v. Ellis, 1942, 125 F.2d 127, 138 A. L.R. 1478, which upheld a similar contract. The court in that case applied what it conceived to be the applicable law of Colorado because the policies involved were payable there.

The basis upon which that case was decided (if such ever was the law in Colorado) has been swept away by the recent decision of the supreme court of Colorado in Urbancich v. Jersin, 123 Colo. 88, 226 P.2d 316, 318, which was decided in December, 1950. There the deceased (one Novak) and the defendant opened joint accounts in two banks in which the deceased made all the deposits. It was agreed between them that during Novak's life the defendant should have no right to withdraw any funds. It was further agreed that upon Novak's death the defendant should withdraw the entire balance and send it to Novak's nieces and nephews. This arrangement was held to be an abortive attempt to make a testamentary disposition of the money without compliance with the statute of wills. The supreme court also held that the arrangement did not constitute an *inter vivos* gift to the nieces and nephews because the deceased did not surrender dominion and control over the money during his lifetime.

The court made it clear that it would not countenance such a contract as was involved in the Ellis case, supra, when it said:

> "The money in question belonged to Novak at the time the joint accounts were created. There is no claim that defendant contributed in any way to the fund. It is undisputed that at the time the joint accounts were created, Novak and defendant expressly agreed that *upon Novak's death* defendant would withdraw the money and send it to Novak's nieces and nephews. These nieces and nephews were the sole beneficiaries named in Novak's will, which was attested prior to the arrangement with defendant. The sole purpose of the transaction resulting in the creation of the joint accounts, was to avoid the probate of the will.
>
> "The agreement between Novak and defendant vested no interest whatever in the nieces and nephews of Novak upon creation of the joint accounts. There was no gift inter vivos. The gifts, channeled through the defendant by the agreement, were to take effect *only upon Novak's death.* Novak kept complete and unrestricted control over all the money so long as he lived, and could have withdrawn all of it and made disposition thereof in any manner he desired. Under the agreement, defendant had no right whatever to withdraw any of the money for any purpose during the lifetime of Novak, and upon Novak's death he could only do so for the purpose of transmittal to the nieces and nephews.
>
> * * * * * *
>
> "We are fully satisfied that the transaction from the beginning was an abortive attempt to make a testamentary disposition of property without compliance with the statutory law which governs such transactions. It is fundamental that any testamentary disposition of property made other-

wise than by compliance with the statute cannot be enforced, and gives rise to no enforceable rights whatever."

* * * * *

The result of the majority opinion will be to permit a contract between a bank and its depositor to the effect that, if the depositor dies before his account is closed, the bank shall pay the balance to X, Y and Z.

In Stevenson v. Earl, 65 N.J.Eq. 721, 55 A. 1091, 1093, a husband had a savings account in which he had made periodic deposits and withdrawals. He delivered the pass book to his wife, stating that if he should die the money in the account should go to her. The court held that there was no gift *inter vivos* because he had no intention of parting with complete dominion and control over the money during his lifetime but that it was an attempt to transfer the savings account to his wife at his death. In holding that this arrangement violated the statute of wills, the court stated:

> "But, in order to legalize such a gift, there must be not only a donative intention, but also, in conjunction with it, a complete stripping of the donor of all dominion or control over the thing given. Cook v. Lum [26 Vr. 375, 376], 55 N.J.L. 375, 376, 26 A. 803. As was said in the case cited, this is the crucial test; and if it be applied to the present case the gift is not to be sustained, *for neither by force of his contract with the company nor by the delivery of the passbook did he intend to, nor did he in fact, part with his complete dominion over any part of the moneys deposited by him.* The expressed intention of the deceased was only to bestow upon his wife so much of his deposit as should remain undrawn by him at his death. Such a gift, it seems to us, is purely testamentary in its character. If it is not, then it is a perfectly easy thing for a person to retain the absolute control and dominion over his moneys and personal securities during his life, and transfer that dominion to another at his death, with total disregard of the requirements contained in the statute of wills, by the simple device of depositing such moneys and securities under an agreement with the depository that he shall have the right to use them or deal with them as he pleases during his life, and that at his death so much of them as may remain shall be delivered to such person as is named in the agreement, who shall then become the owner thereof, and then delivering the agreement to the beneficiary with a statement of the same purport as that made by the deceased to his wife when he gave the passbook to her. To hold that such a method of disposing of property by the owner at his death is valid *would be to practically repeal the statute of wills in its operation upon personal property,* so far as its mandatory provisions are concerned." (Italics mine.)

I think that the principles enunciated in this decision and in those referred to above are applicable to the case at bar and that, since Mr. Sherlock retained possession of the supplementary contract and control over the funds during his lifetime, no interest therein vested in his nieces and nephew. Their claim to the money could only arise *by reason of his death* and, not being based upon his will, nothing was transmitted to them by the supplementary contract.

Let us examine the nature of a third party donee beneficiary contract. The very word "donee" connotes a gift. A third party donee beneficiary contract is one means of effecting a gift. It cannot be used as a vehicle for passing property at death, without regard for the requirements of the statute of wills. There is no authority, to my knowledge, which attempts to divorce such type contracts from all other fields of law, or which holds that they shall be given effect regardless of whether or not a contract interest vests during the lifetime of the donor.

It is fundamental that a valid gift *inter vivos* can be completed by delivery to another person for the benefit of the donee. But it is equally fundamental that in such a case the donor must irrevocably divest himself of dominion and control over the subject matter of the gift. In the present case, Mr. Sherlock expressly retained control and dominion over the funds during his lifetime, and the transaction must, then, fail both as an abortive attempt to make a gift *inter vivos* as well as an abortive attempt to make a testamentary disposition of the funds.

By the decision in this case, it is held for the first time that the owner of personal property may avoid probate proceedings and the expense of administering his estate by the simple expedient of reducing his assets to cash and entering into a contract with a bank, insurance company or individual (similar in form to the supplementary contract here involved), while still retaining control over the money during his lifetime.

If such a revolutionary change is to be made in this state in the method of transmitting property at death, which has heretofore been recognized as exclusive, only the legislature should make it effective. It surely did not amend or repeal the statute of wills by enacting the section of the insurance code which is quoted in the majority opinion.

I think that the judgment should be reversed with instructions to direct the payment of this money to appellant as executor of Mr. Sherlock's estate.

SCHWELLENBACH, C. J., and WEAVER, J., concur.

MALLERY, Justice (dissenting).

I concur with Judge DONWORTH, but desire to add the following: The majority opinion rests on the proposition that "the rights of the four nieces and the nephew in the supplementary *insurance* contract are derived from the original insurance policy through the exercise of Option 1." (Italics mine.)

This premise is unsound. No present rights reach back of the supplementary contract. The original insurance policy was fully executed. It has no significance now, other than being merely the consideration for the option.

The supplementary contract is not a contract of *Insurance* within the purview of RCW 48.01.040, which reads:

"Insurance" defined. Insurance is a contract whereby one undertakes to indemnify another or pay a specified amount upon *determinable contingencies.*" (Italics mine.)

The existence of a *determinable contingency* in the supplemental contract is negatived by the right to withdraw any or all of the "deposit" at will. Since the supplementary contract is not insurance, the insurance code does not apply to the exclusion of the probate code.

QUESTIONS FOR REVIEW

1. Distinguish between beneficiaries and payees of life insurance benefits.

2. Contrast the position of a contingent beneficiary when the primary beneficiary survives the insured with that of a contingent payee when the primary payee survives the insured.

3. What is the problem when the insured and the beneficiary die under conditions where it is not possible to prove who died first? How is this problem handled today under the state simultaneous death acts?

4. What is the potential problem if the primary beneficiary dies shortly after the death of the insured? Suppose a contingent beneficiary is named in the policy. Tell why this cannot be relied upon to solve the problem of short-term survivorship. How does a time clause attempt to solve the problem? What are the weaknesses of this proposed solution?

5. Contrast the relative advantages and disadvantages of using a settlement agreement, as opposed to a trust, to distribute death proceeds to the beneficiary.

6. Distinguish between an inter vivos and a testamentary trust.

7. Describe the rule against perpetuities. The rule against accumulations.

8. *a.* What is intestacy?
   b. How does it affect the distribution of the property of the deceased?

9. What is meant by an attempted (unsuccessful) testamentary disposition of property?

10. There are several ways to pass property to another after one's death without a will. Describe these will substitutes.

CHAPTER 12

Premiums and Dividends

THE INITIAL PREMIUM
Presumption of Payment
Waiver of Timely Payment

RENEWAL PREMIUMS

TIME OF PAYMENT
Renewal Premium Due Date
Backdated Policies
Grace Period
Extension of Time
Premiums Paid in Advance

METHOD OF PAYMENT
Payment by Personal Check
Payment by Promissory Note
Payment by Credit
Payment by Premium Loan
Payment by Dividends

PERSONS MAKING PAYMENT
Payment by Order on a Bank or Employer
Payment by the Beneficiary
Payment by the Assignee
Payment by Agent or Broker

PERSONS RECEIVING PAYMENT

PREMIUM NOTICES

EXCUSES FOR NONPAYMENT
Agreement by the Insurer
Implied Waiver of Timely Payment
Refusal of Tender by the Insurer
Failure of the Insurer's Agent to Collect the Premium
Failure to Send a Premium Notice
Failure of the Post Office to Deliver a Premium
Failure to Pay Premiums Due to War

RETURN OF PREMIUMS
Risk Assumed
Risk Not Assumed

DIVIDENDS
  Right to Dividends
  Dividend Options
  Automatic Dividend Option
SUMMARY

The operation of an insurer turns upon the regular collection of premiums, their investment, and the payment of claims. The premium is the agreed price paid to the insurer for assuming and carrying the risk. The purpose of this chapter is to discuss legal problems which can occur in connection with premium payments and premium abatements (dividends).

THE INITIAL PREMIUM

The initial premium and the application constitute the consideration given by the life insurance applicant in exchange for the insurer's promises. This consideration is necessary to put the policy in force. Most insurance policies are expressly declared not to be effective unless the initial premium is paid and the policy is delivered during the lifetime and continued insurability of the proposed insured. Thus, the promises of the life insurer become binding at the time of delivery of the policy and payment of the initial premium.[1]

Conversely, no premium is due unless the insurer assumes the risk. Where the insurer declines the risk, the initial premium must be returned to the applicant. A great deal of life insurance law centers around the initial premium because of the essential role it plays in the formation of the life insurance contract.

Presumption of Payment

Most policies provide that the insurance will not become effective until the initial premium is paid. Nevertheless, possession of the policy by the beneficiary at the time of the insured's death creates a presumption that the policy is in force. This presumption will be either rebuttable or conclusive, depending upon the wording of the policy and the law of the state involved. A rebuttable presumption is a presumption that can be overturned upon the showing to the court of proof to the contrary. A conclusive presumption is a presumption which cannot be rebutted. That is, no proof contrary to the presumption will be allowed to be shown to the court.

---

[1]If a premium receipt has been issued to the applicant, promises of the insurer made in the receipt will become binding before the policy is delivered.

Many policies, particularly older policies, contain a clause referring to the "initial premium, receipt of which is hereby acknowledged," or similar language. The majority of courts have held that where a policy containing such a clause has been unconditionally delivered, there is a conclusive presumption that the policy is in force.[2] This rule has been enacted into statutory law by the legislatures of some states. For example, the California Insurance Code contains the following language:

> An acknowledgment in a policy of the receipt of premium is conclusive evidence of its payment so far as to make the policy binding.[3]

Note that this statute says that the acknowledgment is conclusive evidence of receipt of the premium *so far as to make the policy binding.* If the initial premium has not been paid, and the insurer can prove this, the insurer can recover the premium under both statutory and case law. In the usual case, the insurer would deduct the initial premium from the death benefits before paying them to the beneficiary.

In a minority of states, policy language acknowledging receipt of the initial premium will raise a rebuttable, rather than a conclusive, presumption that the policy is in force. Also, if the policy does not acknowledge receipt of the initial premium, possession of the policy by the beneficiary ordinarily creates a rebuttable presumption that the policy is in force. For example, in *Woloshin v. Guardian Life Insurance Co. of America,*[4] the policy was in the possession of the insured at the time of his death, which occurred one month after the policy was issued. The insurer refused to pay the death benefit, contending the initial premium was never paid. The question was whether possession of the policy by the beneficiary after the insured's death creates a presumption that the policy was delivered with intent on the part of the insurer to be bound. The court said:

> The evidence does not support the contention of defendant [the insurer] that the policy was delivered to Woloshin for inspection merely and that the delivery, therefore, was not absolute. The agent mailed the policy to him with a bill for the premium. No interim receipt[5] was taken pending payment. Delivery of the policy was made on the credit of the assured and resulted in a contract between the parties conditioned only by its terms. But assuming that the question of conditional delivery were in issue, that question, clearly, was for the jury. "The beneficiary's lawful possession of a life insurance policy after the death of the insured, and especially when, as here, there is no allegation of fraud, accident, artifice, or mistake, to impeach this possession, *prima facie* sustains the burden of proof resting on the plaintiff, by raising a strong presumption that

---

[2]Annot., 44 A.L.R. 3d 1361 (1972).

[3]CAL. INS. CODE § 484 (West 1972). Conclusive evidence of payment means that the law will not permit such evidence to be challenged by the insurer.

[4]146 Pa. Super. 152, 22 A.2d 54 (1941).

[5]A receipt showing that the policy was held for inspection only.

the policy was not only manually delivered but was also *legally* delivered to the insured, and puts the defendant in a position where, to avoid an adverse verdict, it must offer evidence of the conditional delivery alleged, sufficiently convincing to countervail the strong presumption of legal delivery arising from the lawful possession of the policy by the beneficiary."

If, however, the applicant is put on notice by language in the application that the agent has no authority to extend credit, the insurer often will not be bound in a similar situation.

Waiver of Timely Payment

An insurer is sometimes said to have waived timely payment of the initial premium in situations as described above in *Woloshin*. In *Henderson v. Capital Life & Health Insurance Co.*,[6] for example, a mother applied for a policy on the life of a minor child. The policy was delivered while the mother was away from home. The father of the insured testified that the agent left the policy and said that he would collect the initial premium on his next visit. The agent assured the father that the policy was then in force. Before the agent's next visit, the insured died.

Upon learning of the death, the agent went to the client's house and picked up the policy, saying he would do everything he could to obtain the proceeds for the beneficiary. However, the proceeds were not paid, and the agent refused to return the policy. In the lawsuit that followed, the lower court held that the insurer had waived timely payment of the premium. On appeal, the Supreme Court of South Carolina agreed, stating:

> Under the well-settled rule, the company may waive the time and method of the payment of premium. . . . It has been repeatedly held in this State that the manner and method of the payment of the initial premium may be waived and that credit may be extended for the initial premium.

RENEWAL PREMIUMS

All premiums paid after the initial premium are renewal premiums. The payment of the renewal premium is usually considered a condition precedent[7] to continued coverage under a life or health insurance policy. This is the position of the majority of courts.

Ordinarily, the policyowner does not promise to pay the renewal premium. Therefore, the renewal premium is not a debt the policyowner owes,

---

[6]199 S.C. 100, 18 S.E.2d 605 (1942).

[7]Pierce v. Massachusetts Acci. Co., 303 Mass. 506, 22 N.E.2d 78 (1939); Browne v. John Hancock Mut. Life Ins. Co., 119 Pa. Super. 222, 180 A. 746 (1935). See the discussion of conditions precedent and conditions subsequent in Chapter 6, "Formation of the Life Insurance Contract."

and the insurer cannot sue the policyowner to recover the renewal premium if the policyowner refuses to pay it. Nonpayment of the renewal premium by the end of the grace period will simply cause the policy to lapse. Thus, nonpayment of the renewal premium has been held by a minority of courts to be a condition subsequent, cutting off the rights of the policyowner.[8]

Whole life insurance renewal premiums are usually paid once a year during the lifetime of the insured. Alternatively, these premiums can be paid over shorter time periods. For example, a policyowner might wish to pay for the entire contract in annual installments over 5, 10, or 20 years. Sometimes, a policyowner pays for the entire contract with a single premium.

Courts in some early cases took the view that a whole life annual renewal premium paid for two things. First, it paid for the cost of insurance for the year in question; and, second, it paid for the right to renew the insurance for another year.[9] By the weight of authority today, however, the annual whole life renewal premium is part-payment of the whole contract, not simply payment for the year in question. This view squares with single premium and 5-, 10-, or 20-pay whole life insurance.

A United States Supreme Court opinion discussing whole life insurance renewal premiums was written by an actuary-lawyer turned judge. Justice Joseph P. Bradley had served as consulting mathematician for a leading life insurer before becoming a member of the United States Supreme Court. With this background, he was well-equipped to write the opinion in *New York Life Insurance Co. v. Statham*.[10] This opinion reads in part as follows:

> We agree with the court below [the court from which the appeal was taken], that the contract is not an assurance for a single year, with a privilege of renewal from year to year by paying the annual premium, but that it is an entire contract of assurance for life, subject to discontinuance and forfeiture for nonpayment of any of the stipulated premiums. Such is the form of the contract, and such is its character. It has been contended that the payment of each premium is the consideration for insurance during the next following year, as in fire policies. But the position is untenable. It often happens that the assured pays the entire premium in advance, or in five, ten, or twenty annual installments. Such installments are clearly not intended as the consideration for the respective years in which they are paid; for, after they are all paid, the policy stands good for the balance of the life insured, without any further payment. Each installment is, in fact, part consideration of the entire insurance for life. It is the same thing, where the annual premiums are spread over the whole life. The value of assurance for one year of a man's life when he is young, strong and healthy, is manifestly not the same when he is old and decrepit. There is no proper relation between the annual premium and

---

[8]Thomas v. Northwestern Mut. Life Ins. Co., 142 Cal. 79, 75 P. 665 (1904); Masonic Relief Ass'n. v. Hicks, 47 Ga. App. 499, 171 S.E. 215 (1933).

[9]*See, e.g.,* Worthington v. Charter Oak Life Ins. Co., 41 Conn. 372 (1874).

[10]93 U.S. 24 (1876).

the risk of assurance for the year in which it is paid. This idea of assurance from year to year is the suggestion of ingenious counsel. The annual premiums are an annuity, the present value of which is calculated to correspond with the present value of the amount assured, a reasonable percentage being added to the premiums to cover expenses and contingencies. The whole premiums are balanced against the whole insurance.

This case represents the prevailing view of the courts today.

TIME OF PAYMENT

Renewal premiums must be paid on or before a date specified in the policy unless an extension of time is given by the insurer. In this respect, it is said that "time is of the essence," which means that if June 20 is the specified date, and no extension has been given, payment on June 21 is too late. However, payment can be made at any time prior to midnight on the specified date. If a premium is due on a nonbusiness day, payment on the following business day will usually be sufficient.

Renewal Premium Due Date

As life insurance policies usually stipulate that the insurance will not become effective unless the initial premium is paid and the policy delivered during the continued good health of the proposed insured, a number of days will ordinarily elapse between the date written on the policy—the policy date (which is usually either the date of the application or the date the insurer issued the policy)—and the date the insurance becomes effective—the effective date. For example, the policy might be issued and dated November 15, 1988, with the insurance becoming effective December 5, 1988, the date the policy was delivered, and the initial premium was paid. The question then arises, "From which date should the renewal premium due date be computed, the policy date or the effective date?"

According to the majority of courts, if a renewal premium due date is specified in the policy, that date will govern, even though the policyowner receives insurance for a period slightly shorter than the period stated in the policy. These courts take the position that there is no ambiguity, and that the contract must be enforced as written. This reasoning is followed in *D. & P. Terminal, Inc. v. Western Life Insurance Co.*[11] That decision reads in part as follows:

> The only question is the date premiums were to be paid to avoid a lapse in coverage. These dates were specifically decided and clearly set out in the insurance contract. We cannot write another contract for the parties

---

[11]368 F.2d 743 (8th Cir. 1966).

. . . expressing dates contrary to those established by the parties. When the intention of the parties is clear and unambiguous, as it is here, the Court may not assume an ambiguity. It is the duty of the Court to give effect to this intention. . . According to the contract, the premiums were due November 5, February 5, May 5, and August 5. Failure to pay on these dates, plus any grace period, would cause a lapse in coverage.

Where there is no renewal premium due date specified in the policy, and delivery of the policy is not required to make the policy effective, the renewal premium due date will usually be held to run from the policy date.[12] Where delivery of the policy is required to make it effective, the renewal premium due date will generally run from the delivery date.[13]

Backdated Policies

Where the policy is backdated at the applicant's request to give the benefit of a lower premium, the renewal premium due date runs from the policy date, regardless of when the policy was delivered. This is true even though backdating results in payment for a period of time when there was no coverage. However, some states have laws limiting the length of time a policy can be backdated. The most typical limit is six months.

Grace Period

The insurance laws of most states require that policies issued or delivered in the state must include a grace period of a month or 31 days within which renewal premium can be paid without default. Payment can be made at anytime prior to midnight of the last day of grace, or on the following business day if the last day of grace falls on a nonbusiness day.

The grace period runs from the due date of the renewal premium in default. However, the renewal premium due date depends on the wording of the policy and the laws of the jurisdiction.

There is no grace period for the initial premium because the contract is ineffective, for lack of consideration, until the initial premium has been paid.

Extension of Time

As prompt payment of the premium is for the insurer's benefit, the insurer can waive prompt payment and grant extensions of time for payment. Such extensions are not unusual. A grace period does not follow the extension period. For example, if the premium is due on June 10, the grace period ends on July 11, and the insurer grants a two-week extension of time (until

---

[12]Rose v. Mutual Life Ins. Co., 240 Ill. 45, 88 N.E. 204 (1909); Wolford v. National Life Ins. Co. of the United States, 114 Kan. 411, 219 P. 263 (1923).

[13]Annot., 44 A.L.R. 2d 472 (1955).

July 25) in which to pay the premium, no grace period will follow the extension. Moreover, usually the insurance is not in force if the insured dies before the premium has been paid during the extension period, unless it is in force under a nonforfeiture option.

Premiums Paid in Advance

Although most policyowners pay their premiums as they fall due, some policyowners are concerned that they might not be able to meet future payments. Persons whose incomes are irregular, for example, sometimes wish to pay premiums in advance. Or, an older person might wish to make a gift to a grandchild of a policy on the grandchild's life and pay premiums in advance, so that no more premiums need be paid until the child is grown.

To accommodate such needs, most insurers allow premiums to be paid in advance for a specified period of time. As a general rule, premiums paid in advance are accepted on a discounted basis for not longer than 20 years. A receipt is given to the payor that specifies the circumstances under which the money so paid can be withdrawn and the disposition of any premiums that remain unearned at the death of the insured.

Generally speaking, it is within the authority of a life insurer to accept advance premium payments, as this is an activity reasonably related to the insurer's business. However, when such sums are subject to withdrawal at the request of the payor, the insurer is providing a service which resembles that provided by banks. An insurer does not have the legal power to operate a banking business. In order to distinguish the advance premium from a bank deposit, insurers limit the payor's right to withdraw the unapplied portion of the fund. Sometimes, there is a limitation as to the date on which withdrawal can be made. In other instances, only the entire unapplied amount can be withdrawn. In still others, the request to withdraw is subject to deferral at the insurer's option.

Advance premiums which are unearned at the insured's death will be paid according to the terms of the receipt given the payor. Ordinarily, the receipt will provide that these funds will be paid to the beneficiary, to the payor, or to the payor's estate.

METHOD OF PAYMENT

The insurer can make whatever terms it wishes with respect to the method by which the premium must be paid. It has the right to demand payment in cash. Alternatively, it can accept another method of payment such as a personal check, a promissory note, a bank draft, or a money order. The insurer can also extend credit for a premium payment. Acceptance of these other methods of payment can create legal problems which are discussed in this section. Legal problems associated with premium payment by policy loan or by application of policy dividends are also discussed.

Payment by Personal Check

It is customary today to pay a premium by personal check. When the insurer has received the check, the premium has been paid, even though some time will elapse before the insurer receives the actual cash. Ordinarily, however, the courts assume that payment of a premium by check is conditioned upon the check's being honored upon proper presentation to the bank, unless the insurer has agreed to unconditional payment by check. That is, there is an implied condition that the check must be honored.

If a check is dishonored, the insurer can either lapse the policy for non-payment of the premium or attempt to collect on the dishonored check. If it elects to lapse the policy, it should act promptly, return the check, request the return of the premium receipt, and declare the policy forfeited. If the insurer attempts to collect on the dishonored check, and then the insured dies, the insurer might be held to have waived its right to lapse the policy and have to pay the benefits.

The effect of electing to rely on a dishonored check is illustrated in *Sjoberg v. State Automobile Insurance Association.*[14] This was a suit brought on a $5,000 insurance policy after the insured was killed in an automobile accident. The insurer contended that the policy had lapsed prior to the date of death because of nonpayment of the last premium. The facts showed that the death occurred on August 5 and that the last quarterly renewal premium, due July 1, was paid by personal check on July 8, well within the grace period. The check was returned to the insurer, however, with the notation "insufficient funds." The insurer did not return the check, rescind the receipt, and declare the policy forfeited, as it had the right to do. Instead, it requested the local agency to contact the insured and secure a "bankable check or other remittance." This had not been accomplished at the date of death.

The court noted the general rule that, if there is no agreement to the contrary, payment by check is conditioned upon the check's being honored. However, here the court said that the insurer's failure to declare a forfeiture after the check was dishonored indicated its intention to keep the policy in force. The court said:

> On the occasion in question [the insurer] gave the insured a full receipt of the premium upon receiving his check. There was some delay in the presentation of the check for payment but when it was returned dishonored defendant did not repudiate the transaction but wrote his agents to contact insured to get "bankable check or other remittance." The agent notified the insured thereof. Neither the letter nor the conversation between defendant's agent and the insured referred to a forfeiture of the policy. Instead the whole tenor of both was to effect the collection of the check. Such negotiations indicate an intention to keep the policy in force. . . . They indicate defendant's election to rely upon the check rather than

---

[14]78 N.D. 179, 48 N.W.2d 452 (1951).

upon forfeiture and reinstatement. . . . The District court held that the defendant waived its right to forfeit the policy and elected to keep the policy in force. We agree with this holding of the court.

An insurer must promptly present a check in payment of premium for collection. Retention of the check for an unreasonably long time might cause the insurer to be estopped from declaring a forfeiture of the policy if the insured dies and the check is dishonored after the last day of grace.

Where the insurer accepts a postdated check, the check is payment of the premium as of the date of the receipt given for it, if it is honored on the date it bears. This is the view of the majority of courts.[15]

A minority of courts take the view that acceptance of a postdated check is equal to an extension of credit by the insurer. Thus, if the insured dies after the check is given, and the check is dishonored after the insured's death, the benefits will be payable because the insurer extended credit to the policyowner by accepting the check.[16]

Payment by Promissory Note

An insurer can waive the requirement that a premium be paid by cash or check and accept a promissory note if it wishes. A promissory note is a written promise to pay a stated sum of money.

In legal effect, the unconditional acceptance of a promissory note for an insurance premium constitutes payment of the premium.[17] If the policyowner defaults on payment of the note, the insurer's remedy is to sue for payment of the note. The insurer cannot declare the policy lapsed for nonpayment of the premium.

Insurers do not usually accept a promissory note unconditionally, however. A promissory note is usually accepted by the insurer upon the express condition that it will not operate as payment of the premium if the note is not paid when due. The policy, the note, or both, ordinarily will contain a provision that the policy will be forfeited if the note is not paid when due.

Payment by Credit

Credit can be extended by the insurer for the payment of either the initial premium or a renewal premium. Such credit binds the insurer as fully as a cash payment. For example, if the insurer extends credit for a renewal premium, and the insured dies after the grace period but during the period credit is extended, the benefits will be payable.

---

[15]Annot., 50 A.L.R. 2d 630 (1956).

[16]John Hancock Mut. Life Ins. Co. v. Mann, 86 F.2d 783 (7th Cir. 1936).

[17]Narver v. California State Life Ins. Co., 211 Cal. 176, 294 P. 393 (1930); Raney v. Piedmont S. Life Ins. Co., 387 F.2d 75 (8th Cir. 1967).

The period of the extension of credit can be specified by the insurer. If the policyowner does not pay by the end of the specified period, the insurer can lapse the policy. If the insurer does not specify a period, the period will be for a reasonable time.

The insurer's agent can pay the premium and extend credit to the policyowner on the agent's own behalf. If the insured dies before the agent is paid, the benefits will nevertheless be payable.

If the agent extends credit on behalf of the insurer itself, however, the agent must have authority from the insurer to do so. That authority can be express, implied, or apparent. The insurer will not be bound if the policyowner knows the agent exceeded his or her authority to extend credit.[18]

Payment by Premium Loan

The automatic premium loan provision, if elected by the policyowner, permits the insurer to establish a policy loan to pay a premium which remains unpaid at the end of the grace period. Most life insurance policies with cash values include an automatic premium loan provision. Such a provision appears in the illustrative policy in Appendix B.

An automatic premium loan will be established only if necessary to prevent lapse and only if the policy has a loan value. It is customary to notify the policyowner that the loan has been made.

The automatic premium loan has advantages and disadvantages for the policyowner and the insurer. Among the advantages are that the automatic premium loan prevents an inadvertent lapse. Furthermore, it maintains accidental death and disability benefits in force. These benefits would not remain in force if the policy lapsed and continued under a nonforfeiture option. The automatic premium loan prevents the necessity of reinstatement and protects against the danger that the policyowner will not be able to reinstate the policy because the insured has become uninsurable.

One of its disadvantages is that, if used indiscriminately, the automatic premium loan can give the policyowner a false sense of security. Often, the establishment of the first loan is the beginning of a process which ultimately results in lapse. The continued use of the loan drains away cash values so that, at the time of lapse, there can be little, if any, value to be applied under the nonforfeiture options. In addition, if the insured dies while the policy is in force, there will be a smaller death benefit if policy values were used to pay premiums.

According to the majority of courts, the payment of a premium by an automatic premium loan enhances the cash value of the policy, just as payment of the premium by the policyowner would.[19] That is, the cash value will

---

[18]Hill v. Philadelphia Life Ins. Co., 35 F.2d 132 (4th Cir. 1929).

[19]Sovereign Camp, W.O.W. v. Harris, 195 Ark. 820, 114 S.W.2d 449 (1938); Balyeat v. American Nat'l Ins. Co., 274 Mich. 694, 265 N.W. 774 (1936).

be decreased by the amount of the loan but increased due to payment of the premium. A minority of courts have held that the cash value is not enhanced by payment of a premium by automatic premium loan.[20]

The insurer is under no duty to notify the policyowner that the loan value is insufficient to pay the premium due[21] unless there is a statute requiring such notice.[22] Likewise, the insurer does not have to notify the policyowner of the length of time the policy will be kept in force by the available loan value.[23]

Payment by Dividends

The general rule is that an insurer cannot declare a life insurance policy forfeited for nonpayment of a premium if it has in its possession dividends belonging to the policyowner sufficient to pay the premium, and the policyowner has not elected to have the dividends applied in some other manner.[24] Ordinarily, the policyowner elects a dividend option when she or he fills out the application. Where the policyowner chooses an option other than the payment of premiums, the insurer will have neither the duty nor the right to apply the dividends to pay the premium.

If the dividends are not sufficient to pay the whole premium, the insurer is not obliged to make a partial payment unless it has agreed to do so, according to the majority rule. However, the insurer has a duty to notify the policyowner of the additional amount needed to pay the premium.[25] The policyowner would not know the additional amount to pay if such a notice is not sent, as he or she cannot know the dividend amount unless told by the insurer. If the insurer does not notify the policyowner of the additional amount, the insurer cannot lapse the policy for nonpayment of the premium.

PERSONS MAKING PAYMENT

From the insurer's standpoint, ordinarily it is irrelevant who pays the premium. The insurer will accept the premium from whoever tenders it.

Payment of the premium, by itself, does not usually give the payor any right to insurance proceeds. Thus, a person with no interest in the policy who voluntarily paid the premium would ordinarily have no right to any of the proceeds.

Usually, the policyowner pays the premium or authorizes someone else to do so. The beneficiary, an assignee, a trustee, an agent or broker, or some

---

[20]de Almada v. Sovereign Camp, W.O.W., 49 Ariz. 433, 67 P.2d 474 (1937).

[21]General Am. Life Ins. Co. v. Butts, 193 Ga. 350, 18 S.E.2d 542 (1942).

[22]Lester v. Aetna Life Ins. Co., 433 F.2d 884 (1970), *cert. denied*, 402 U.S. 909 (1971).

[23]General Am. Life Ins. Co. v. Butts, 193 Ga. 350, 18 S.E.2d 542 (1942).

[24]The dividends referred to in this subsection are policyowners' dividends, not stockholders' dividends. For an explanation of the difference between these two types of dividends, see the section entitled "Dividends," below.

[25]Mau v. Union Labor Life Ins. Co., 31 N.J. Super. 362, 106 A.2d 748 (1954).

other person sometimes pays the premium. The legal questions which can arise when someone other than the policyowner pays the premium are discussed in this section.

Payment by Order on a Bank or Employer

Sometimes, the policyowner authorizes his or her bank or employer to pay the premium. Preauthorized check plans, electronic funds transfers, and salary allotment plans help the policyowner keep the policy in force.

Preauthorized Check Plans.   Under a preauthorized check plan, the policyowner authorizes the insurer to draw checks to the insurer's own order from the policyowner's bank account to pay the premiums.[26] Usually, this is done monthly. The policyowner, in addition to authorizing the insurer to draw checks, also authorizes the bank to accept and process the checks.

A separate agreement between the insurer and the bank provides that the insurer will indemnify the bank for any liability the bank might incur by reason of participating in the plan. Preauthorized check plans were opposed by some bankers in the past on the grounds that, as the policyowner is not notified each time the insurer forwards a check, overdrafts could occur. The indemnity agreements between the insurer and the bank help to counter such objections.

Preauthorized check plans help policyowners who are already paying many bills monthly by also putting insurance premium payments on a monthly basis. In addition, such plans free the policyowner from having to remember to pay the premium, thus helping to prevent inadvertent lapse.

Generally speaking, if the check clears through regular banking channels, the premium is paid just as effectively as if the policyowner had drawn it personally. If the check does not clear, the insurer ordinarily will take the same action it would take when any other check is returned. However, the insurer must promptly draw and present the check. If the insurer fails to do this, it cannot claim nonpayment of the premium.[27]

Preauthorized Electronic Funds Transfers.   Modern banks have computers which are programmed to transfer funds from one account to another electronically. Thus, funds can be transferred from the policyowner's account to the account of the insurer without a check being written. This is a preauthorized electronic funds transfer.

In 1978, Congress passed the Electronic Funds Transfer Act[28] which governs electronic funds transfers. The act requires that a policyowner-depositor

---

[26]Annot., 45 A.L.R. 3d 1349 (1972).

[27]Pacific Mutual Life Ins. Co. v. Watson, 223 Ala. 571, 137 So. 414 (1931).

[28]15 U.S.C.A. § 1693 *et. seq.* (West 1982 & Supp. 1987).

having his or her funds electronically transferred to the insurer sign an authorization permitting the transfers. There are also state laws governing electronic funds transfers.

Allotment Plans.   Under a salary allotment plan, a policyowner authorizes her or his employer to withhold the premium from the policyowner's salary and forward it directly to the insurer. This is usually done monthly.

The federal government also has a salary allotment plan for members of the military service. These deductions are made monthly. Once initiated, the deductions will continue to be made until the policyowner authorizes their discontinuance.

Payment by the Beneficiary

Sometimes, the beneficiary pays the premiums. Assume, for example, that Arnold Wallace owns a policy on his life and has named his wife as revocable beneficiary. Mr. Wallace takes no interest in his family or the policy. His wife, Margaret, keeps the premiums paid as they fall due. Several years later, there is a divorce, and Mr. Wallace remarries. He then wishes to change the beneficiary designation to his new wife, Paulette. The general rule is that payment of the premium by the beneficiary will not prevent the policyowner from changing the beneficiary designation in accordance with the policy provisions. Of course, if Margaret had been named irrevocable beneficiary, Mr. Wallace could not have changed the beneficiary designation without her consent, under the laws of most states.

Thus, a revocable beneficiary might pay the premiums of a life insurance policy for many years without having his or her mere expectancy enlarged by such payment. However, if a revocable beneficiary who pays the premiums has been promised the proceeds by the policyowner, the courts frequently award the beneficiary the amount of the premiums he or she paid.[29] A person who pays premiums under the mistaken impression that he or she is beneficiary might also be entitled to recover the amount of the premiums he or she paid.[30]

A life insurance beneficiary who is the trustee of a funded life insurance trust has a duty to pay insurance premiums under the terms of the trust. Failure to pay the premiums is a breach of the trustee's fiduciary duty. The trust beneficiary can sue the trustee for such a breach.

---

[29]Leal v. Leal, 401 S.W.2d 293 (Tex. Civ. App. 1966); New York Life Ins. Co. v. Walls, 124 F. Supp. 38 (N.D. W. Va. 1954); Perry v. Perry, 484 S.W.2d 257 (Mo. 1972); Walsh v. John Hancock Mut. Life Ins. Co., 221 Pa. Super. 484, 293 A.2d 71 (1972). *See* Annot., 92 A.L.R. 3d 1330 (1979).

[30]Fendler v. Roy, 331 Mo. 1083, 58 S.W.2d 459 (1932); Metropolitan Life Ins. Co. v. Tesauro, 94 N.J. Eq. 637, 120 A. 918 (1923).

Payment by the Assignee

Under the usual collateral assignment, the assignee is under no duty to pay the premium. If the collateral assignee does pay the premium, however, the assignee has a right to recover the premium paid, in addition to any unpaid debt for which the assignment was made.

An absolute assignee is in the same position with respect to paying the premium as was the original policyowner. That is, an absolute assignee ordinarily has no duty to pay the premium, but payment must be made by someone as a condition of keeping the policy in force.

Payment by Agent or Broker

If the insurer's agent (or a broker) extends credit to the policyowner and pays the premium, the policy will be in force, even if the policyowner fails to repay the agent.[31] The agent's recourse would be to sue the policyowner on the debt.

PERSONS RECEIVING PAYMENT

Most life insurance policies today provide that renewal premiums shall be paid to the insurer at its home office, or to an authorized agent in exchange for an official receipt signed by the secretary and countersigned by the agent. Where payment is made to the home office few problems result. Nor does payment to an agent usually present any problem if the agent promptly remits the payment to the home office.[32]

Payment made to an agent authorized to receive payment is payment to the insurer. If the agent fails to remit the money to the insurer, the insurer can sue the agent to collect it, but, as far as the policyowner is concerned, the premium has been paid.

If the agent was not actually authorized to collect the premium but promptly remits it to the insurer, there will be no problem. Where an unauthorized agent collects the premium and fails to remit it, however, a question might arise as to whether the agent had apparent authority. If the policyowner can establish the agent's apparent authority to collect premiums, the legal effect is that the insurer was paid when the agent received the payment, whether or not the agent remits the money to the insurer.

Payment by the policyowner to his or her own agent is not payment to the insurer where the agent fails to remit the payment to the insurer. Payment to a broker will be payment to the insurer if the broker is the insurer's agent for collection of premiums. If the broker is the policyowner's agent to remit

---

[31]Markel v. Travelers Ins. Co., 510 F.2d 1202 (10th Cir. 1975).
[32]Annot., 42 A.L.R. 3d 751 (1972).

premiums, payment to the broker is not payment to the insurer. The actions of the parties will usually govern whether the broker is the agent of the policyowner or of the insurer when collecting premiums.

PREMIUM NOTICES

A life insurer ordinarily has no legal duty to send a notice that premium payment is due unless there is a statute or a policy provision requiring such notice. Nevertheless, insurers routinely send premium notices, because premium notices are an effective means of keeping life insurance contracts in force.

When an insurer has consistently sent premium notices over an extended period of time, even though not required to do so, it will be estopped from lapsing the policy if it discontinues the practice without warning and the premium is not paid when due, according to the majority of courts. If the insurer informs the policyowner beforehand of its intention to stop sending premium notices, however, there will not be an estoppel.

The insurer also has a duty to send a premium notice where the policyowner cannot know the amount due without one. For example, where dividends are to be applied to reduce the premium, the insurer knows the amount of the dividends, but the policyowner does not. The insurer must send the policyowner a premium notice stating the amount remaining to be paid on the premium or the insurer cannot lapse the policy for nonpayment of the premium when due.

Some states have statutes which require that the insurer send a premium notice to the policyowner. These states limit the right of an insurer to lapse the policy for nonpayment of the premium when due if the notice has not been sent. The Illinois statute reads as follows:

> No life company doing business in this State shall declare any policy forfeited or lapsed within six months after default in payment of any premium installment or interest or any portion thereof, nor shall any such policy be forfeited or lapsed by reason of nonpayment when due of any premium, installment or interest, or any portion thereof, required by the terms of the policy to be paid, within six months from the default in payment of such premium, installment or interest, unless a written or printed notice stating the amount of such premium, installment, interest or portion thereof due on such policy, the place where it shall be paid and the person to whom the same is payable, shall have been duly addressed and mailed with the required postage affixed, to the person whose life is insured, or the assignee of the policy, (if notice of the assignment has been given to the company) at his last known post office address, at least fifteen days and not more than forty-five days prior to the day when the same is due and payable, before the beginning of the period of grace, except that in any case in which a parent insures the life of his minor child, the company may send notice of premium due to the parent. Such notice shall also state that unless such premium or other

sums due shall be paid to the company or its agents the policy and all payments thereon will become forfeited and void, except as to the right to a surrender value or paid-up policy as provided for by the policy.[33]

EXCUSES FOR NONPAYMENT

There is almost no excuse for nonpayment of premium relating to circumstances involving only the policyowner. Thus, the policyowner's illness, accident, poverty, illiteracy, incapacity, or disappearance are generally held not to excuse her or his failure to pay the premium. Nearly all of the valid excuses relate to some agreement or act of the insurer, or to conditions of war which made timely payment impossible.

This is a sound proposition of law, as payment of the premium is a condition precedent to the insurer's duty to perform its promises. Nonpayment of premium is, therefore, a defense the insurer has for its nonperformance. Nevertheless, many circumstances arise where the insurer has made some agreement or done some act that results in the insurer being unable to declare the policy lapsed for nonpayment of premium.

Agreement by the Insurer

The insurer might agree not to lapse the policy in certain situations for nonpayment of the premium. For example, if the insurer has agreed to apply the loan value to pay the premium, it cannot declare the policy lapsed if the policy has a sufficient cash value to pay the premium then due. As another example, if the policy has a waiver-of-premium clause or rider, the insurer cannot declare the policy lapsed for nonpayment if the insured becomes disabled and, hence, has a right to have premium payment waived.

Insurers often expressly waive timely payment. An agreement to extend the time for the payment of a premium which is overdue is an express waiver of timely payment. Such an agreement, called a late remittance offer, is found in Appendix F. Note that the waiver of timely payment offer is made on strict conditions—the insured must be alive, the offer is for a limited period, and the protection is not in force from the end of the grace period until the overdue premium is paid.

Implied Waiver of Timely Payment

Where the insurer has repeatedly accepted late payment, it usually will be held to have waived timely payment by implication. For example, in *Gleed v. Lincoln National Life Insurance Co.*,[34] the insurer had habitually accepted premiums beyond the grace period. The insured died while the premium was

---

[33]ILL. REV. STAT. ch. 73, ¶ 846 (1985) (Ill. Ins. Code § 234).
[34]65 Cal. App. 2d 213, 150 P.2d 484 (1944).

in default. The insurer was estopped to declare a forfeiture of the policy. The court said:

> On the issue of waiver and estoppel the evidence is that for a period of six years all premiums had been paid by Mrs. Boggs to Hansen [the agent of the insurer], either in cash or by her personal check, and that no one of these payments was exchanged for the company's receipt signed by the president or secretary as required in the policy. It is also in evidence that each and all of these payments were made in this manner while the insured was in default, and in many cases after the period of grace had expired. During this period of six years, eighteen separate premiums became due. Fourteen of these were accepted by appellant [the insurer] after the period of grace had expired. In only one instance—September, 1940—the appellant demanded and received an application for reinstatement.
>   . . . [W]e conclude that the course of conduct in relation to the payments of premiums running over a period of six years was such that the respondents [the beneficiaries] were entitled to assume that the terms of the policy need not be adhered to strictly, and that the appellant was estopped from insisting upon a strict compliance with those terms until it had given the respondents reasonable notice of its change in policy.

The insurer can protect itself from such implied waivers by expressly providing in a notice of default, such as that in Appendix F, that a late premium will be effective only if paid during the lifetime of the insured. This is illustrated by *Hutchinson v. Equitable Life Assurance Society of the United States*[35] as follows:

> The plaintiff [the beneficiary] contends that Florida applies a blend of waiver and estoppel to an insurer who follows a course of dealing with the payment of premiums so as to induce the insured to believe that a delay in his premium payment will not give rise to a forfeiture. Plaintiff then concludes that this principle applies to the instant case.
>   The fallacy of plaintiff's argument is that the default notices expressly stated that there would be no reinstatement if the insured died prior to receipt of the defaulted premium; thus there was no course of conduct by the insurer which in any way could have led the insured to believe that a default payment would be accepted after his death or that the policy had not lapsed. Accordingly there can be no waiver or estoppel.

Refusal of Tender by the Insurer

A tender of payment which is refused by the insurer is generally an excuse for nonpayment. *Tender* means an unconditional and timely offer to pay the full sum due in a medium of payment (cash, check, and so forth) acceptable to the insurer. If the insurer refuses a tender, it cannot forfeit the policy

---

[35]335 F.2d 592 (5th Cir. 1964).

for nonpayment of premium. A tender preserves the policyowner's rights as much as payment.[36] For example, in *Harms v. John Hancock Mutual Life Insurance Co.,*[37] the beneficiary tendered the premium payment to the insurer's collecting agent two days before the grace period expired. The collecting agent refused the money, saying he would collect it 20 days later. The insured died 13 days after the grace period had expired. The death benefits were payable, as the tender acted to prevent the policy from lapsing. The court discussed the case as follows:

> The insurance in this case was solicited by an agent of the defendant insurer named Balistreiri who collected the first two premiums and called at plaintiff's house on June 20, 1945 to collect the last quarterly premium. This was two days before the expiration of the grace period. Defendant's agent informed Mrs. Hatch that he had come to collect her son's insurance. She told him that the son was sick and would not have a paycheck until July 5th and that she would have to pay the premium herself although she wished that the youngster would pay for his own insurance. She extracted three ten dollar bills from her pocketbook and told the agent that he might as well take it. The agent declined and said that he would hold the matter open until the 10th of July so that the boy would have a chance to pay it. As he left plaintiff said, "Well, Mr. Balistreiri, it's right here," and the agent said, "It's all right, Mrs. Hatch. I will hold it open until the 10th of July."
>
> The jury found that plaintiff Josephine Hatch offered to pay and that the agent put off the matter as above indicated.
>
> It is contended by appellant [the insurer] that the agent having no authority to issue policies could not grant an extension of time for the payment of a premium. This contention misses the point and the case is governed adversely to appellant by *Baumann v. Metropolitan Life Ins. Co.,* 144 Wis. 206, 128 N.W. 864. The point is that the amount of the premium was offered to a collecting agent of the company who declined to take the money and under those circumstances it must be held that plaintiff was "deterred from making such payment by conduct or statements on the part of such agent which induced in her an honest belief that a failure to then make the payment or tender would not then be relied upon by the company to work a failure or forfeiture of the policy."

Even though a tender acts as payment to prevent lapse of the policy, the insurer will still be entitled to recover the amount of the premium. It will have a right to deduct this amount plus interest from the death benefits if the insured has died.

A wrongful cancellation of the policy by the insurer is considered tantamount to a declaration that it will refuse a tender of premium. Such an act by

---

[36]Beatty v. Mutual Reserve Fund Life Ass'n, 75 F.65 (C.C.A.Cal. 1896); Kincaid v. New York Life Ins. Co., 66 F.2d 268 (5th Cir. 1933).

[37]253 Wis. 448, 34 N.W.2d 687 (1948).

the insurer will excuse the tender itself.[38] For example, *Western & Southern Life Insurance Co. v. Giltnane*[39] involved a weekly premium policy with a four-week grace period. The premiums on the policy had been paid regularly until the insured applied for additional insurance and was found at that time to be an uninsurable risk. The insurer then wrongfully canceled the original policy, stating that it refused to receive any more premiums. Seven months later, the insured died. The court held that the benefits were payable, saying:

> When the insurance company notified the insured that it would not receive from her any further premiums, this dispensed with the necessity of making a tender of the premiums thereafter. It would be a rather curious rule, to say the least of it, that would allow an insurance company to defeat the payment of a policy upon the ground that the premiums had not been regularly paid, when it declined to receive them, insisting that it had canceled the policy.

Failure of the Insurer's Agent to Collect the Premium

If the insurer has designated an agent to collect the premium, the failure of the agent to collect might excuse the nonpayment. For example, in *Standard Life Insurance Co. v. Grigsby*,[40] the beneficiary had been instructed by the insurer to pay the collecting agent at the agent's office. The beneficiary did this until the November premium was due. In November, and again in December, the beneficiary tried repeatedly to locate the collecting agent so as to pay the premium on time. When the beneficiary did locate the agent, he told her the policy had been canceled for failure to pay the premium due in November. The beneficiary then tendered the November and December premiums, but these were refused. The insured died a few months later. The court held that the insurer had wrongfully canceled the policy and that the nonpayment was excused. The benefits were, therefore, payable.

Failure to Send a Premium Notice

As pointed out above, the insurer's failure to send a premium notice can serve as an excuse for nonpayment of the premium. Although the general rule is that the insurer has no duty to send such a notice, a statute or the insurance contract sometimes imposes such a duty. In addition, the insurer has a duty to send a premium notice if the policyowner has no other way to know how much to pay. Finally, an insurer that has consistently sent premium notices over an extended period of time will ordinarily be estopped from lapsing the policy if it discontinues the practice without warning and the premium is not paid when due.

---

[38] Annot., 160 A.L.R. 629 (1946), supp. 122 A.L.R. 385 (1939).
[39] 157 Ky. 275, 163 S.W. 192 (1914).
[40] 80 Ind. App. 231, 140 N.E. 457 (1923).

Failure of the Post Office to Deliver a Premium

If the insurer regularly accepts premiums by mail, and the policyowner mails a premium in what would ordinarily be sufficient time to reach the insurer before the end of the grace period, the insurer cannot lapse the policy because the mail was delayed and the premium arrived late.[41] Even if the premium is lost in the mail, the insurer will not be allowed to lapse the policy if the policyowner or beneficiary can establish that the premium was mailed on time.[42] This will not be true, however, if the insurer has not sanctioned use of the mail to transmit premiums.[43]

Failure to Pay Premiums Due to War

When communications between the policyowner and the insurer are cut off because their respective countries are at war, payment of the premium is, of course, impossible. The legal effect of nonpayment of premiums during war has been decided differently in different states. After the Civil War, the courts of some states held that war merely suspends the contract. After the war, back premiums can be paid, and the contract revived. The courts of other states held that the contract terminates according to its terms if premiums are not paid, regardless of the reason for nonpayment.

The United States Supreme Court in *New York Life Insurance Co. v. Statham*[44] held that the contract terminates, but that the policyowner is entitled to the equitable value of the policy arising from the premiums already paid. The equitable value as defined in *Statham* is approximately the reserve value. The Court in *Statham* construed federal common law which was abolished after the *Erie Railway Co. v. Tompkins*[45] decision. *Statham,* therefore, does not have the weight at the present time that it had prior to the *Erie* decision.

After World War I, the Treaty of Versailles provided that where the war prevented the payment of premiums, contracts which had lapsed could be surrendered for cash as of the date of lapse, or be restored within three months following the date of the treaty upon payment of arrearages of pre-

---

[41]Mutual Reserve Fund Life Ass'n v. Tuchfeld, 159 F. 833 (C.C.A. Tenn. 1908); Travelers Ins. Co. v. Brown, 138 Ala. 526, 35 So. 463 (1903); Minnick v. State Farm Mut. Auto Ins. Co., 54 Del. 125, 174 A.2d 706 (Del.Super.Ct. 1961); Hartford Life & Annuity Ins. Co. v. Eastman, 54 Neb. 90, 74 N.W. 394 (1898); Kenyon v. Knights Templar & M. Mut. Aid Ass'n, 122 N.Y. 247, 25 N.E. 299 (1890); Coile v. Order of United Commercial Travelers of Am., 161 N.C. 104, 76 S.E. 622 (1912).

[42]Annot., 1 A.L.R. 677 (1919).

[43]Rice v. Grand Lodge of A.O.U.W., 103 Iowa 643, 72 N.W. 770 (1897); Beeman v. Supreme Lodge, Shield of Honor, 215 Pa. 627, 64 A. 792 (1906).

[44]93 U.S. 24 (1876).

[45]304 U.S. 64 (1933), *cert. denied* 305 U.S. 637 (1938). This case is discussed in Chapter 1, "Insurance and the Law."

mium, plus interest. Of the numerous treaties signed at the close of World War II, none repeated the provisions of the Treaty of Versailles. Generally speaking, after World War II, American insurers took the position that, because many of their contracts contained automatic nonforfeiture provisions, an equitable course of action was simply to carry out the contracts according to their terms.

RETURN OF PREMIUM

As a general rule, once the risk has attached, the whole premium paid is earned. In other words, if the insurer has assumed the risk, the insurer has a right to keep the whole premium paid. There are, however, exceptions to the general rule which will be discussed in this section.

If the insurer has not assumed the risk, the premium is unearned and must be returned. There are also exceptions to this rule which will be discussed in this section.

Risk Assumed

There are several exceptions to the general rule that when the insurer has assumed the risk, it can keep the premium. As one example, in the absence of a statute to the contrary, ordinarily a minor-policyowner who disaffirms the insurance contract is entitled to a return of the premiums he or she paid. In some jurisdictions, however, the insurer will have a right to deduct the cost of the coverage the minor received.

Premiums which are paid under a mistake of fact must be returned by the insurer. For example, if the premium payor believes the insured to be alive when the insured is actually dead, premiums paid after the insured's death must be returned. This sometimes happens in cases where the insured has disappeared.

Premiums paid in advance must be returned if the insured dies before the premiums have been earned. Suppose, for example, a grandmother were to purchase a life insurance policy on the life of her one-year-old grandchild and were to pay 20 annual premiums in advance at the time she bought the policy. If the child died at age 16, the four annual premiums which were unearned would be returned by the insurer according to the terms of the premium receipt.

Often the policy itself contains provisions which require return of premiums under certain circumstances. The illustrative policy in Appendix B contains several such provisions. One of these is in the free examination (free look) clause. This clause states that the policyowner has a right to return the policy at any time within a certain number of days after receiving it, and "any premium paid will be refunded to the owner."

Another policy clause providing for return of premiums is the suicide clause. This clause provides that, if the insured dies by suicide within the suicide period, the insurer's "liability will be limited to the amount of the premiums paid, less any indebtedness."

If the insurer wishes to rescind the contract for misrepresentation in the application, ordinarily the premiums paid must be returned. Failure to promptly tender back the premiums to the policyowner after discovery of the misrepresentation could jeopardize the insurer's right to rescind the policy.

Some persons have a right to have premium payments they have made refunded to them out of the proceeds. For example, if a named revocable beneficiary who has been promised the proceeds pays the premiums, and later the policyowner names someone else beneficiary, the courts frequently award the original beneficiary the amount she or he paid.[46] A collateral assignee can also recover from the policy proceeds the premiums the assignee has paid.

Risk Not Assumed

If the risk has not been assumed, the insurer ordinarily must return the premium. For example, if an insurer receives an application and the initial premium but finds the applicant uninsurable, it must return the premium when it rejects the application. The insurer has not assumed the risk and has no right to the premium. The same is true if the insurer issues a policy which differs from that applied for, and the applicant rejects the policy issued. Again, the risk has not been assumed, and the insurer must return the premium.

Premiums paid upon policies which are void *ab initio*—that is, void from the beginning—because of a lack of insurable interest must be returned according to the majority of courts, unless there was fraud by the applicant. The premium must also be returned, according to the majority of courts, where the policy is void *ab initio* because it was issued without the knowledge or consent of the insured. For example, in *Magers v. Western & Southern Life Insurance Co.,*[47] the applicant took out policies on the lives of her two brothers who did not know about the policies. The policies were void from the beginning because they were not consented to by the brothers. The applicant was allowed to recover the premiums she paid.

DIVIDENDS

It is unfortunate that the term *dividends* is used for both stockholders' dividends and policyowners' dividends, as this frequently results in confusion. Stockholders' dividends are paid to the owners of corporate stock. Such dividends are usually paid out of the accumulated earnings of the corporation by resolution of the corporation's board of directors. Policyowners' dividends,

---

[46]Annot., 92 A.L.R. 3d 1330 (1979).

[47]344 S.W.2d 312 (Mo. Ct. App. 1961).

on the other hand, are paid to the owners of participating insurance policies. Whenever the term *dividends* is used in this book, it will refer to policyowners' dividends, unless otherwise indicated.

Usually, mutual insurers issue participating policies, whereas stock insurers issue nonparticipating policies.[48] This is not always true, however. Some mutual insurers issue both participating and nonparticipating policies. Some stock insurers issue participating policies or both participating and nonparticipating policies.

Nonparticipating policies are issued at a fixed premium. The policyowner has no right to a return of premium. The premium of a nonparticipating policy must be calculated with great care, as there can be no later adjustment for experience.

Participating policies are issued at a premium high enough to cover all likely future experience. The insurer expects to be able to operate on a smaller amount. The difference is a margin of safety. The insurer refunds any excess premium if the experience of that class of policy warrants such a refund. This refund is the dividend. The dividend is a premium abatement. The policyowner does not pay income tax on this dividend because he or she is simply having part of the premium returned. By contrast, stockholders' dividends are taxed as income to the stockholder receiving them.

Right to Dividends

The insurer does not have to pay a dividend unless it has sufficient earned surplus. Moreover, the insurer has a right to keep surplus for contingencies, as it deems necessary, as long as it acts in good faith.[49]

The insurer must treat policyowners equitably in distributing dividends. Policies can be divided into classes based on the type of policy or other criteria, but the policyowners in any one class must be treated alike.

The policyowner owns the dividends. When a policyowner-insured dies, accumulated dividends pass to his or her estate, unless there is a contrary policy provision. The beneficiary has no right to the dividends unless the policy provides such a right.

When, as is usual, the dividends belong to the policyowner, the policyowner can assign them to another person. In addition, the creditors of the policyowner can attach the dividends unless the state statute exempts them from attachment.

The right to elect the way in which dividends are to be applied is one of the valuable rights a policyowner has under a participating life insurance policy. Carrying out the policyowner's wishes as to dividends is an important responsibility of the insurer.

---

[48]Both mutual and stock insurers are corporations. The difference between them lies in their ownership. Mutual insurers are owned by their policyowners who are both owners and customers, whereas stock insurers are owned by their stockholders.

[49]Royal Highlanders v. Wiseman, 140 Neb. 28, 299 N.W. 459 (1941).

Dividend Options

Most states have statutes regulating the distribution of dividends. Typically, such statutes specify the rights of the owners of participating policies to participate in the insurer's surplus, and the methods of surplus distribution. The Illinois statute,[50] for example, requires that a participating policy include "[a] provision that the policy shall participate annually in the surplus of the company beginning not later than the end of the third policy year . . ." The statute also provides that

> the insured under any annual dividend policy shall have the right each year to have the dividend arising from such participation either paid in cash, or applied in reduction of premiums, or applied to the purchase of paid-up additional insurance, or be left to accumulate to the credit of the policy, with interest at such rate as may be determined from time to time by the company.

As in Illinois, the statutes in many other states require annual participation in the earned surplus of the insurer. Some states, notably Illinois and New York, specify the optional methods that must be provided in the policy for the application of dividends. This does not prevent the insurer from offering additional options, however.

Most participating life insurance contracts provide four dividend options. The policyowner can elect to have the dividend applied in one of the following ways:

1. Paid to the policyowner in cash;
2. Applied to reduce premium;
3. Applied to purchase paid-up additions to the policy; or
4. Accumulated with interest.

One-Year Term Insurance Dividend Option.   Many insurers provide a special option in some policies that permits the dividend to be used to purchase term insurance for one year. This is often called the "fifth dividend option." This option permits the policyowner to have the dividend (or part of it) used to purchase one-year term insurance that will be payable in addition to the face amount of the policy. This insurance is, of course, payable only if the insured dies during the one-year term. New term insurance can be bought with each year's dividends, however.

The amount of additional insurance permitted under this option is sometimes limited to the amount of the cash surrender value of the policy. Excess dividends not needed to purchase this amount of term insurance will be applied under another option. If the one-year term insurance dividend option is elected, the policyowner can usually take out a maximum policy loan and the

---

[50]ILL. REV. STAT. ch. 73, ¶ 836(1)(e) (1985) (Ill. Ins. Code § 224(1)(e)).

beneficiary will still receive the full face amount of the policy. Typically, the one-year term insurance which can be purchased under this option will replace a maximum policy loan until the insured is quite old.

Other Dividend Privileges. It is fairly standard practice to include a policy provision permitting the application of accumulated dividends to pay up the policy or to mature it as an endowment if the policyowner wishes.

Automatic Dividend Option

State laws regulating dividends often provide that, if dividend options are offered, the insurer shall specify which option will take effect if the insured does not elect an option. A review of the participating policies of various insurers indicates that most insurers choose the paid-up additions option as the automatic dividend option.

A few states specify which option shall take effect automatically if there is no election by the policyowner. Unfortunately, these states do not all specify the same option. For example, one state provides that dividends shall be paid in cash, while another requires that the paid-up additions option be put into effect. Some insurers deal with these differing state requirements by providing in their policies that, if no option is elected by the policyowner, the dividend shall be applied to purchase a paid-up addition or as may be required by the laws of the state in which the policy is delivered.

SUMMARY

The initial premium, along with the application, is the consideration which puts the insurance contract in force. Nevertheless, possession of the policy by the beneficiary at the insured's death creates a presumption that the policy was in force. If the policy contains a clause acknowledging receipt of the premium, the majority view is that this presumption is conclusive, at least to make the policy binding.

Payment of a renewal premium is usually considered a condition precedent to continued coverage under an insurance policy. The policyowner does not owe the insurer the renewal premium, however. Failure to pay a renewal premium will simply cause the policy to lapse. A renewal premium must be paid before the end of the grace period or the policy will lapse unless the insurer waives timely payment expressly or by implication. If a date for payment of the renewal premium is specified in the policy, usually that date will govern. If a payment date is not specified, the renewal date will usually run from the policy date or, if delivery is required to make the policy effective, from the delivery date. Renewal premium due dates of backdated policies run from the policy date.

The insurer has a right to be paid in cash but can accept checks, promissory notes, or other methods of payment. Payment by personal check is, by implication, conditioned upon the check's being honored. Acceptance of a promissory note, on the other hand, constitutes premium payment whether or not the promissory note is honored, unless there is an express condition that the note must be paid when due. Credit extended by the insurer for payment of a renewal premium binds the insurer as fully as cash payment. Renewal premiums also can be paid by premium loans or by accumulated policyowner dividends.

Persons other than the policyowner often pay the renewal premiums. Sometimes, the policyowner's bank or employer pays premiums out of the policyowner's funds. The beneficiary sometimes pays renewal premiums out of the beneficiary's own funds. Where this is the case, the policyowner will still be able to change a revocable beneficiary designation, but the beneficiary is sometimes entitled to recover the premiums she or he paid. A collateral assignee usually has no duty to pay the premium, but if the assignee does pay, he or she can recover the premium paid.

The insurer's home office or authorized agents can receive the premium. If an unauthorized agent collects the premium and fails to remit it, the insurer will be bound if the agent had apparent authority.

The insurer has no duty to send notices of premium due unless there is a statute or policy provision to the contrary. However, where an insurer has sent premium notices, it cannot stop the practice without warning and lapse the policy of a policyowner who was relying on receiving the notice.

There is almost no excuse for nonpayment of the premium which is not based on some act or omission of the insurer. However, often the insurer has made an agreement or done something which will excuse nonpayment. The insurer's waiver of payment or of timely payment, refusal of tender, wrongful cancellation of the policy, or failure to collect the premium ordinarily excuses nonpayment. Where the insurer has sanctioned use of the mail for remitting premiums, and the policyowner mails the premium in what would ordinarily be sufficient time to reach the insurer, the insurer cannot lapse the policy because the premium was delayed or lost.

The policyowner ordinarily will not have a right to return of premiums once the risk has been assumed. There are exceptions, however, as where a minor-policyowner disaffirms a policy, or premiums were paid under a mistake of fact or in advance, or the policy provides for a return of premiums.

Policyowner dividends, paid to the owners of participating insurance policies, are a refund of excess premium. The policyowner owns the dividends and has a right to elect the way in which dividends will be paid. The usual options are cash payment, premium reduction, purchase of paid-up additions, or accumulation with interest. Purchase of one-year term insurance is sometimes permitted.

ILLUSTRATIVE CASE

In this case, the court held that payment of a premium by check was conditioned on the check's being honored when the insurer properly presented it for payment.

TRUDY C. NOBLE, Administratrix
v.
JOHN HANCOCK MUTUAL LIFE INSURANCE COMPANY [51]
Appeals Court of Massachusetts, Middlesex

Before HALE, C.J., and GRANT and ARMSTRONG, JJ.

HALE, Chief Justice.

This is an appeal by the plaintiff from a judgment of the Superior Court which dismissed her claim for the proceeds of a life insurance policy. The judge made findings of fact which we summarize below.

The plaintiff was the named beneficiary of a life insurance policy issued by the defendant to Nelson Noble, the plaintiff's husband. The policy provided for payment of $26,000 to the beneficiary if the insured should die while the policy was in full force. Quarterly premiums of $209.66 were due on (or within a thirty-one day grace period following) the twenty-third of March, June, September and December of each year, and had been paid through December 23, 1969. A notice of the premium due on March 23, 1970, was mailed to Nelson Noble at his home address. The defendant did not receive a payment of that premium by March 23 or within the grace period. On May 15, at which time Noble was confined to a hospital, Richard Klein, the defendant's district manager, had a telephone conversation with the plaintiff in which he explained to her that the premium on her husband's life insurance policy was overdue. He advised her to send him a check to cover the premium and she did so on May 17.

On or about May 28, while Nelson Noble was still hospitalized, the plaintiff received a notice from the defendant indicating that the next quarterly payment of $209.66 was due on June 23. The plaintiff became confused, thinking that the premium referred to in this notice was the one she had paid. She called the defendant's office and tried to contact Klein. She was informed that Klein was not in the office. She then talked with "one of the girls in the office" (whose identity and position are not apparent in the record) and explained the problem. The woman advised the plaintiff to stop payment on the original check and to send a new check and the premium notice that she had received. On May 28 the plaintiff stopped payment on the original check. Neither the plaintiff nor Nelson Noble (who had been released from the hospital around June 20) made a subsequent payment on the policy. Nelson Noble died on July 22, 1970.

1. The plaintiff argues that the defendant's receipt of the check mailed in accordance with Klein's instructions constituted an unconditional acceptance of the check as payment of the premium. We disagree. Absent an agreement to the contrary, a waiver or an estoppel, the receipt of a check constitutes only an acceptance conditional upon the check's being honored when properly presented. Merely giving the insurer possession of the check is not a payment of the premium. The payment would have become absolute if the check had been honored by the drawee on presentation, but the plaintiff prevented this occurrence by her stop payment order. Therefore, at the time of Nelson Noble's death, the March 23 premium payment was unpaid, the policy, by its terms, had lapsed, and the plaintiff was not entitled to any proceeds.

---

[51] 7 Mass. App. Ct. 97, 386 N.E.2d 735 (1979).

2. The plaintiff contends that she should nonetheless prevail because the defendant is estopped from asserting the lapse of the policy prior to the death of Nelson Noble because her failure to pay the premium due on March 23 resulted from her reliance on the suggestion of the defendant's agent that she stop payment on her original check.

"The basis of an estoppel is a representation . . . intended to induce a course of action on the part of the person to whom the representation is made, and where, as a consequence, there is detriment to the person relying on the representation and taking the action." *Capozzi's Case,* 4 Mass. App. 342, 347, 347 N.E.2d 685, 689 (1976), quoting *De Sisto's Case,* 351 Mass. 348, 351–352, 220 N.E.2d 923 (1966). The plaintiff's claim of an estoppel fails because the actions she took did not amount to reasonable reliance on the instructions of the defendant's agent. The woman in the defendant's office recommended a stop of the first check only in conjunction with the tender of another check. The record shows that plaintiff stopped payment on her original check as suggested but disregarded the essential second step of the instruction by failing to send another check. This selective compliance with the advice of the defendant cannot be said to be sufficient reliance to form the basis of an estoppel.

Judgment affirmed.

QUESTIONS FOR REVIEW

1. Contrast the legal significance of the initial premium with that of the renewal premiums for a life insurance policy.
2. With regard to the initial premium:
   a. What is meant by "presumption of payment?"
   b. Distinguish between conclusive and rebuttable presumptions.
3. What alternatives does an insurer have when it learns that a premium check has been dishonored? What are the possible legal effects if the insurer attempts to collect on the dishonored check?
4. Suppose an insurer has unconditionally accepted a promissory note in payment of a premium, and the policyowner fails to pay the note when due. What remedy does the insurer have? Do insurers usually accept promissory notes unconditionally? Why or why not?
5. Briefly summarize the preauthorized check plan for paying life insurance premiums. What are the principal arguments for and against the plan?
6. What are the principal advantages of the automatic premium loan? What are the disadvantages?
7. Under what circumstances is a life insurance company required to send premium notices?
8. Discuss briefly the insurer's duty with respect to the application of dividend accumulations when a premium remains unpaid at the end of the grace period.
9. Describe three situations in which the policyowner will be excused for nonpayment of a premium.

CHAPTER 13

Nonforfeiture Provisions and Policy Loans

CASH VALUES
NONFORFEITURE PROVISIONS
    The First Nonforfeiture Laws
    The Guertin Legislation
    The Cash Surrender Option
    The Extended Term Insurance Option
    The Reduced Paid-Up Insurance Option
    The Automatic Nonforfeiture Benefit
    Incomplete Nonforfeiture Option Transactions
    Additional Benefits
    The Beneficiary's Rights
POLICY LOANS
    Policy Loans Contrasted with True Loans
    Premium Loans and Cash Loans
    Amount of the Policy Loan
    Interest on Policy Loans
    Endorsement
    Deferment
    Extended Term and Reduced Paid-Up Policies
    The Beneficiary's Rights
    Repayment of Policy Loans
SUMMARY

The level premium, legal reserve system of life insurance results in cash values which can be used for nonforfeiture benefits or policy loans. The legal aspects of nonforfeiture options and policy loans are described in this chapter.

CASH VALUES

Nonforfeiture benefits or policy loans are possible where the life insurance policy has a cash value. Term policies often have no cash values. Under many term policies, the policyowner merely pays for pure insurance for a limited period.

The earliest policies were term policies. Life insurance for extended periods or for the whole of life did not become practical until development of the level premium, legal reserve system. Under this system, the same amount of annual premium is charged every year during an extended period—often, the insured's lifetime. Because the same amount is charged each year when the insured is young as when he or she is older, the insurer is given a larger premium in the early years than is needed for the policy's share of current-year claims. These excess funds become a part of the insurer's invested assets. The insurer establishes equivalent reserve liabilities to provide for the time in later years when the level premium will not be sufficient for the policy's share of the current-year claims.

This system results in a policy cash value which can be transferred to the policyowner or used to purchase extended term or paid-up insurance if the policyowner forfeits the policy. The cash value can also be advanced to the policyowner as a policy loan, or used to pay the premium while the policy remains in force.

NONFORFEITURE PROVISIONS

Because of the level premium system, the owner of a whole life or endowment policy, or a level term policy for the longer terms, contributes more in the early years than is required to meet her or his share of the current claims cost to the insurer. If the policy is kept in force, this apparent inequity will be remedied in later years when the policyowner will be paying less each year than her or his share. However, if the policy lapses, the policyowner will have contributed more than the cost of the protection provided up to that time. In the absence of nonforfeiture benefits, that difference is forfeited. In the early days of life insurance, this is exactly what happened to the policyowner whose policy lapsed for nonpayment of premiums. Most people then did not view this as unfair.

The First Nonforfeiture Laws

Some people, however, did view such forfeitures as unfair. Among them was Elizur Wright, the first insurance commissioner of Massachusetts. Largely because of his efforts, in 1861 Massachusetts enacted the first nonforfeiture law. This law required that whenever any policy lapsed, four fifths of its "net value" must be used to purchase extended term insurance. Similar laws were passed in other states in the next few decades, but this type of legislation received its first real impetus in connection with the standard policy provisions laws which resulted from the 1905 Armstrong Investigation in New York.

The standard policy provisions laws required that in the case of lapse of a whole life insurance contract that had been in effect for a minimum stated period (usually three years), the insurer must provide a cash surrender value. Alternatively, either paid-up whole life insurance for a reduced amount or extended term insurance for the net face amount, or both, must be offered in whatever amounts could be purchased by the net cash surrender value of the policy. One of these nonforfeiture benefits must be automatic—that is, it must become operative immediately upon the lapse of the policy if the policyowner did not make an election.

As a general rule, these early nonforfeiture benefits were computed on the American Experience Table of Mortality at a rate of interest not to exceed that stated in the law. This mortality table became outdated in the 1930s. In 1937, a committee under the chairmanship of Alfred N. Guertin was appointed to study the nonforfeiture situation. This committee's recommendations led to the adoption of two model statutes by the National Association of Insurance Commissioners (NAIC)—namely, the Standard Valuation Law and the Standard Nonforfeiture Law for Life Insurance. Together, these model statutes are often referred to as the Guertin legislation.

The Guertin Legislation

By January 1, 1948, the Guertin legislation had been made effective in every state by statute or by regulation. The model nonforfeiture legislation recommended by the Guertin Committee required that insurers use up-to-date mortality tables (including the 1941 Commissioners Standard Ordinary Mortality Table) and otherwise modernized the nonforfeiture requirements. One of the most important innovations was the separation of nonforfeiture benefits from policy reserves. Prior to this time, nonforfeiture values had been computed by subtracting from the policy reserve a declining and ultimately vanishing surrender charge. Under the Guertin legislation, the nonforfeiture benefits were to be calculated as specified in the law, without reference to the amount of the policy reserve.

The Guertin legislation requires that a paid-up nonforfeiture benefit is to be provided for every whole life or endowment insurance policy, and for every term policy running for more than 15 years, in case of lapse for nonpayment of premiums, if and when the specified formula produces a positive value. A cash surrender value must be provided if the policy has been in force for three years or more. The insurer must include tables of benefits in the policy and a statement of the methods used in calculating the benefits.

The 1941 Commissioners Standard Ordinary Mortality Tables, like their predecessors, became outdated, and new mortality tables were developed. These tables are referred to as the 1958 Commissioners Standard Ordinary Mortality Tables. These tables became the legally-required standard for minimum nonforfeiture values in every state by January 1, 1966.

In 1980, the NAIC adopted amendments to the standard valuation and nonforfeiture model statutes. These amendments included new mortality tables for ordinary life insurance, changes in the excess initial expense allowance used to determine minimum nonforfeiture values, and a system for automatic annual updating of the statutory valuation and nonforfeiture-interest-rates standards applicable to new business. All the states and the District of Columbia have enacted these amendments.

As a result of changing requirements, some policies now outstanding have nonforfeiture benefits based on laws which were effective prior to 1948, others have benefits based on laws effective between 1948 and 1966, and still others have benefits based on the 1958 tables or on the 1980 tables. Each policy is lawful as written, although each is different from those policies with nonforfeiture benefits based on a different set of laws. The reason for this is that new laws ordinarily cannot require changes in contracts already in effect.

The Cash Surrender Option

One of the nonforfeiture options provided by life policies with cash values is the cash surrender option. Under this option, a policyowner surrenders the policy to the insurer in return for the policy's cash surrender value. The cash surrender value is the amount of cash available to the policyowner on surrender of the policy before the policy matures. This value is determined by statute and by the terms of the policy. The illustrative policy in Appendix B defines the cash surrender values as follows:

> The term "cash surrender value" as used in the Policy means the cash value shown in the Table of Guaranteed Values . . . , less any existing indebtedness. . . . The table assumes that premiums have been paid to the end of the policy year indicated. . . . We will determine the cash value at any time within the policy year, with allowance for the time elapsed in such year and for the period premiums have been paid.

The table of guaranteed values has been calculated for $50,000 of whole life insurance on a 36-year-old male insured, rated standard. The cash values for the first five years are as follows:

End of Policy Year	Cash or Loan Value
1	$ 320.00
2	1,007.50
3	1,713.50
4	2,437.50
5	3,178.50

The policy states that these values have been calculated on the basis of the 1958 Commissioners Standard Ordinary Mortality Table. The policy further states that the cash values equal or exceed those required by the laws of the state governing the policy and that a detailed statement of method of computation has been filed with the state insurance department.

The policy requires that the policyowner surrender the policy to the insurer in exchange for the cash surrender value. According to most courts, the policyowner must comply with this policy requirement in order to be paid the cash surrender value by the insurer.[1]

The insurer ordinarily has the right to defer payment of the cash surrender value for up to six months from the date surrender is requested. This policy provision is required by state laws.[2] It is intended to protect the insurer from a drain on its cash and other current assets should severe adverse economic conditions cause large numbers of policyowners to surrender their policies.

The Extended Term Insurance Option

Extended term insurance is insurance for the face amount of the policy (less any unpaid policy loan and interest) extended for such period as the cash value will provide.

The illustrative policy in Appendix B provides the following:

> Extended Term Insurance. If the Premium Class shown [in the policy] is "Standard," you may continue the Policy as paid-up term insurance. The amount of such term insurance will be the Sum Insured less any indebtedness. The term period will begin on the due date of the first unpaid premium and will be such as the cash surrender value will provide as a net single premium at the Insured's then attained age. At the end of the term period all insurance under this Policy will terminate.

Most policies include a chart showing the period for which the insurance will be extended for each of the first 20 years. Such a chart appears in the illustrative policy in Appendix B. (These periods would change if there is an outstanding policy loan, however.) On request, the period will be computed for other years.

A legal question which sometimes arises with extended term insurance concerns the date on which the extended term insurance begins. The courts ordinarily hold that this date is the due date of the premium in default, not some later date such as the end of the grace period.[3] This is sometimes expressed in the policy. The illustrative policy states that "The term period will begin on the due date of the first unpaid premium . . ." The policy could, of course, specify a later date.

---

[1]Interstate Life & Acci. Co. v. Jackson, 71 Ga. App. 85, 30 S.E.2d 208 (1944); Board of Trustees of Unitarian Church v. Nationwide Life Ins. Co., 88 N.J. Super. 136, 211 A.2d 204 (1965).

[2]*See, e.g.,* ILL. REV. STAT. ch. 73, ¶ 841.2(1)(vi) (1985) (Ill. Ins. Code § 229.2) (1)(iv).

[3]Coons v. Home Life Ins. Co., 368 Ill. 231, 13 N.E.2d 482 (1938); Life & Cas. Ins. Co. v. Wheeler, 265 Ky. 269, 96 S.W.2d 753 (1936); Dressel v. Mutual Ben. Life Ins. Co., 154 S.W.2d 360 (Mo. Ct. App. 1941); Hutchinson v. National Life Ins. Co., 196 Mo. App. 510, 195 S.W. 66 (1917).

Another legal question that occasionally arises with extended term insurance concerns the deduction of any outstanding policy loan from both the cash value and the face amount of the policy in order to determine the amount of extended term insurance. This is the practice of insurers, but it is sometimes misunderstood by persons unfamiliar with insurance, who feel that it unfairly penalizes the policyowner. Actually, the procedure is fair, and the courts generally support it for two reasons.[4] First, the policy loan amount must be deducted from the cash value, as the loan amount has already been advanced to the policyowner. Second, deduction of the loan amount from the face value of the policy in order to determine the amount of extended term insurance is balanced by the longer term for which the lower amount of insurance is provided. Moreover, deduction of the loan amount from the face value is justified, because, otherwise, the policyowner who lapsed his or her policy with an outstanding loan against it would have a larger amount of insurance than would be the case if he or she had continued to pay the premiums.

For example, suppose a policyowner with a $50,000 policy takes out a $5,000 policy loan. Only $45,000 would be payable at the insured's death, as long as the loan remained unpaid, and the policy remained on a premium-paying basis (ignoring loan interest for purposes of this example). If the policy is switched to extended term insurance on October 11, the $5,000 loan will be deducted from the $50,000 face amount of the policy to determine the amount of extended term insurance which would be payable. If this were not done, the beneficiary would be entitled to $50,000 after the policy had lapsed on October 11, whereas she or he would have been entitled to only $45,000 before October 11 while the policy was still on a premium-paying basis. The cash value will purchase $45,000 of extended term insurance for a longer term than $50,000 of extended term insurance, however.

The Reduced Paid-Up Insurance Option

Reduced paid-up insurance is ordinarily available as one of the nonforfeiture options. The reduced paid-up nonforfeiture option provides paid-up insurance of the kind and for the duration provided by the policy immediately prior to lapse, in whatever amount the cash surrender value will purchase. That is, if the original policy was a whole life policy, the reduced paid-up policy will be a whole life policy. If the original policy was an endowment at age 65, the reduced paid-up policy will be an endowment at age 65. If the original policy was a 20-year term policy with 10 years yet to run, the reduced paid-up policy will be a term policy with 10 years yet to run.

---

[4]*See, e.g.*, Williams v. Union Central Life Ins. Co., 291 U.S. 170 (1934); Mayers v. Massachusetts Mut. Life Ins. Co., 11 F. Supp. 80 (E.D.N.Y. 1935); Miner v. Standard Life and Acci. Ins. Co., 451 F.2d 1273 (10th Cir. 1971).

The illustrative policy in Appendix B is a whole life policy. It provides the following reduced paid-up insurance nonforfeiture option:

> Paid-Up Insurance. You may apply the cash surrender value to purchase a fully paid whole life policy for a reduced amount of insurance. The amount of such insurance will be that amount which the cash surrender value will buy when applied as a net single premium at the Insured's then attained age as of the due date of the first unpaid premium. Reduced Paid-Up Insurance has cash and loan values.

The Automatic Nonforfeiture Benefit

If the policyowner fails to elect a nonforfeiture option, the policy must by law provide an automatic nonforfeiture benefit.[5] The illustrative policy provides the following:

> You may elect a Nonforfeiture Benefit Option within 60 days of the due date of the first unpaid premium. Your written election should be sent to us at our Home Office. If no election is made during this period, we will
>
> 1. If the Premium Class . . . is "Standard" automatically continue this Policy as Extended Term Insurance.
> 2. If the Premium Class . . . is "Rated" automatically continue this Policy as Paid-Up Insurance.

This is a typical automatic nonforfeiture benefit provision. Note that a standard policy provides extended term insurance. A rated, or substandard, policy provides reduced paid-up insurance.

Incomplete Nonforfeiture Option Transactions

If the insured dies before a nonforfeiture option transaction is complete, the question might be raised as to whether the nonforfeiture option benefit or the death benefit is payable.[6] There can be a significant difference between these two sums, and they might be payable to different persons. Therefore, a court action sometimes ensues where there is doubt concerning the completion of the nonforfeiture option process. Most of the cases in this area involve the cash surrender option, although, in some cases, the policyowner was attempting to exercise the extended term insurance option or the reduced paid-up insurance option.

---

[5]*See, e.g.,* ILL. REV. STAT. ch. 73, ¶ 841.2(1)(iii) (1985) (Ill. Ins. Code § 229.2(1)(iii)); TEX. INS. CODE ANN. art. 3.44a § 2(3) (Vernon 1981).

[6]Annot., 15 A.L.R. 3d 1317 (1967).

The general rule in these cases is that the right to exercise a nonforfeiture option is a continuing, irrevocable offer from the insurer to the policyowner.[7] When the policyowner accepts the insurer's offer according to its terms (exercises the option), the acceptance is binding on both parties, even if the insured dies before the insurer has completed its part of the transaction.[8] Thus, if a policyowner notified the insurer of his or her decision to take the cash surrender value and surrendered the policy, and the insured died before the insurer paid the cash surrender value, the majority of courts would hold that the insurer did not owe the death benefit to the beneficiary. Rather, the insurer would have to pay the cash surrender value to the policyowner, or to the policyowner's estate in the case of a policyowner-insured.

In one case, the court described a nonforfeiture option as an offer bought and paid for by the policyowner (the insured in this instance) as follows:

> The privilege to exercise the option of surrendering the policies for their cash value was one bought and paid for by the insured; such option is an offer contained in the policy contract and is from the company to the insured and it is his right to accept the offer, within a specified time, and his acceptance completes the contract; the company has no right to accept or reject; its obligation to pay is absolute.[9]

As with any other offer, however, an option must be accepted according to its terms. Thus, the policyowner must comply with the requirements for acceptance of a nonforfeiture option as set forth in the policy.

Where the insurer's offer is not accepted by the policyowner according to its terms, the policyowner has made a counteroffer. This counteroffer by the policyowner must be accepted by the insurer in order to be binding. In such a case, if the insurer has not accepted the policyowner's counteroffer at the time of the insured's death, the death benefit will be payable to the beneficiary. (At this point, a review of the section explaining offers and counteroffers in Chapter 2, "Contracts" might be helpful to the reader.)

For example, in one case,[10] a policyowner had a right to apply for the cash surrender value within one month of default in payment of the premium. Surrender of the policy was required. The premium due date was July 31. The premium was not paid. On August 4 and again on September 1, the policyowner requested the cash value. He did not surrender the policy, however, so the cash surrender option was not accepted according to its terms. The policyowner had, therefore, made a counteroffer to the insurer. The insured died on September 2 before the insurer accepted the counteroffer. The insurer was, therefore, liable for the face amount of the policy under the automatic

---

[7]Pacific States Life Ins. Co. v. Bryce, 67 F.2d 710 (10th Cir. 1933); Green v. American Nat'l Ins. Co., 452 S.W.2d 1 (Tex. Civ. App. 1970).

[8]Lipman v. Equitable Life Assur. Soc'y, 58 F.2d 15 (4th Cir. 1932).

[9]Pack v. Progressive Life Ins. Co., 239 Mo. App. 1, 187 S.W.2d 501 (1945).

[10]Conservative Life Ins. Co. v. Bollinger, 51 Ohio App. 191, 200 N.E. 149 (1935).

nonforfeiture benefit which provided for extended term insurance, rather than for the cash surrender value.

Additional Benefits

Life insurance policies frequently provide additional benefits, such as an accidental death benefit, disability benefits, or guaranteed insurability benefits. These benefits are not necessarily available after a nonforfeiture provision becomes effective. A clause in the policy excluding such additional benefits after the nonforfeiture provision takes effect is valid.

The illustrative policy contains three such clauses—one in the accidental death benefit rider, one in the disability benefit rider, and one in the guaranteed insurability benefit rider. The accidental death benefit rider states that "This Rider shall terminate upon . . . [t]he date the Policy is continued under a nonforfeiture benefit option."

If there is no provision expressly excluding additional benefits after continuation under a nonforfeiture provision, the courts look to the language of the contract to determine the intent of the parties. In some cases, additional benefits have been held payable and in others not payable.

The Beneficiary's Rights

Ordinarily, the policyowner has the right to exercise the nonforfeiture options. The policyowner can exercise the nonforfeiture options, including a surrender of the policy for its cash value, without the consent of a revocable beneficiary.

An irrevocable beneficiary's consent will be necessary if the policyowner wishes to surrender the policy for its cash value unless the policy specifically states otherwise.[11] An irrevocable beneficiary's consent to the exercise of the extended term or reduced paid-up insurance options is not ordinarily required. However, an irrevocable beneficiary has the right to remain beneficiary of extended term or reduced paid-up insurance provided under a nonforfeiture provision.[12]

POLICY LOANS

The owner of a life insurance policy with cash values can obtain money using the policy as security. This can be done in two ways. First, the policyowner can pledge the policy to a bank or other lending institution as security for a loan. Alternatively, the policyowner can receive an advance of cash from the insurer under the loan provision of the policy.

---

[11]Morse v. Commissioner, 100 F.2d 593 (7th Cir. 1938).
[12]O'Brien v. New England Mut. Life Ins. Co., 128 N.J. Eq. 590, 17 A.2d 555 (1941).

Policy loans were first made available by insurers on a voluntary basis. There were then no laws requiring policy loans. The automatic premium loan, or a practice similar to it, was in use as early as 1845[13] and was well established by the 1890s. Thus, the earliest policy loans were established to keep policies in force. This, of course, benefited both policyowners and insurers. Later, the policy loan privilege was expanded to permit policyowners to receive cash from the insurer.

Policy Loans Contrasted with True Loans

The term *policy loan* is a misnomer. A policy loan is not truly a loan. A loan is defined as the transfer of money by one person, the creditor, to another person, the debtor, upon agreement that the debtor will return to the creditor an equivalent sum at a later date (usually plus interest). A policy loan differs from a true loan in that the policyowner does not agree to repay the money transferred to her or him by the insurer. Rather, a policy loan is an advance of money which the insurer must eventually pay out under the policy. Thus, a policy loan does not create a creditor-debtor relationship between the insurer and the policyowner.

In one of the leading court decisions involving policy loans, Justice Oliver Wendell Holmes said:

> The so-called liability of the policyholder never exists as a personal liability, it is never a debt, but is merely a deduction in account from the sum the plaintiffs [the insurer] ultimately must pay.[14]

The illustrative policy in Appendix B provides that "This Policy is the sole security for any loan." The insurer must pay the cash surrender value of the policy to the policyowner on demand. As the insurer has the right to deduct the policy loan, plus interest, from the cash surrender value, the insurer is 100 percent secured against loss if the loan is not repaid and the policy is allowed to lapse. Moreover, as the loan value, plus interest, can be deducted from the proceeds after the insured's death, the insurer is also 100 percent secured if the loan has not been repaid when the insured dies. It is for these reasons that repayment of the loan and interest is not required. The foregoing is consistent with the view that a policy loan is not truly a loan, but rather an advance of money the insurer ultimately must pay.

Although the term *policy loan* is a misnomer, it is a term which has long been used throughout the life insurance industry. The term is, therefore, used in this book.

---

[13]Reidy, *The Policy Loan Provision*, in THE LIFE INSURANCE POLICY CONTRACT 189 (H. Krueger & L. Waggoner eds. 1953).

[14]Board of Assessors v. New York Life Ins. Co., 216 U.S. 517 (1910).

Premium Loans and Cash Loans

There are two types of policy loans—premium loans and cash loans. Premium loans are advances to the policyowner of policy cash values for the purpose of paying the premium. Automatic premium loans are advances made under a policy clause providing that, if the policyowner fails to pay a premium by the end of the grace period, the amount of the premium will automatically be advanced if there is a sufficient cash value. The illustrative policy in Appendix B provides the following:

AUTOMATIC PREMIUM LOAN

This provision will be in effect only if you have requested it in the application or in a written request at a time when no premium is unpaid beyond its grace period. You may cancel the effect of this provision in the same manner.

If this provision is in effect, any premium which remains unpaid at the end of a grace period will be paid by automatic loan. We may change the frequency of premium payment so that the interval between premium due dates is three, six, or twelve months after the first premium has been paid by automatic loan. If the loan value of this Policy is not sufficient to pay the premium due, the Nonforfeiture Benefit Options will apply.

Any automatic loan will be subject to the Policy Loan provisions.

Automatic premium loan provisions are not usually required by law. However, most insurers include such a provision in their policies, as it helps to prevent policy lapse.

Cash loans, or request loans as they are sometimes called, are advances of cash made to the policyowner by the insurer to be used for whatever purpose the policyowner wishes. Usually, when people speak of a "policy loan" they mean a cash loan. Nevertheless, premium loans are also policy loans. Premium loans and cash loans are advanced from the same cash values, have the same interest rates, and are both made on the sole security of the policy. Note that the illustrative policy quoted above states that an automatic premium loan "will be subject to the Policy Loan provisions." A policy provision permitting a policy loan under cash value policies is required in the states where most of the major life insurers are domiciled. Therefore, a policy loan provision will be found in most cash value policies.

Amount of the Policy Loan

The illustrative policy in Appendix B provides the following:

You may obtain a loan from us whenever this Policy has a loan value. The loan value is the amount which, with interest at the loan interest rate stated [in the policy] computed to the next premium due date, or to the next Policy anniversary if no further premiums are payable, will equal the cash surrender value on such date or anniversary. Any premium due and unpaid at the time the loan is made will be deducted from the loan proceeds.

Thus, the amount which can be obtained from the insurer as a policy loan changes over time. For example, at the end of policy year three, the illustrative policy has a cash surrender or loan value of $1,713.50. At the end of year five, this value is $3,178.50. In addition, the later the policy loan is taken out during the policy year, the higher will be the amount of money available to be advanced, as less interest must be charged by the insurer.

Interest on Policy Loans

The policyowner who takes out a policy loan does not promise to repay either the principal or the interest on the loan. The illustrative policy provides the following:

> We will charge daily interest on policy loans at the rate stated [in the policy]. Interest is payable on each policy anniversary. Any interest not paid when due is added to the loan.

However, if the interest accumulates so that the total of principal and interest is greater than the cash surrender value, the policy will expire. The illustrative policy contains the following clause:

> Whenever the indebtedness on this Policy is more than the Policy's guaranteed cash surrender value, this Policy terminates. We will mail a notice to your last known address, and to that of any assignee whose interest we have recorded, at least 31 days before such termination.

In other words, interest is payable, but it does not have to be paid. If the total of loan and accrued interest exceeds the maximum loan value at any time, the policy simply terminates.

The insurer must charge interest on a policy loan. The most important reason for this is that the insurer bases policy values on the assumption that the portion of the premiums unused in the early policy years will be invested at a projected rate of interest. If the cash value were advanced to the policyowner interest free, the intricate structure of the level premium would be adversely affected.

Nevertheless, the interest rate for a policy loan is not ordinarily the same as the rate assumed in calculating the policy values. Usually, the policy loan interest rate is higher, because the insurer wishes to discourage policy loans and because processing policy loans, many of which are for small amounts, is expensive.

All states have laws specifically regulating life insurance policy loan interest rates. Until a few years ago, the maximum interest rate most commonly allowed was eight percent. Then, in the early 1980s, the great majority of states enacted a variable policy loan interest rate statute based on the NAIC Model Policy Loan Interest Rate Bill.

This rush to allow variable policy loan interest rates resulted from the high interest rates policyowners could obtain on other investments in the early 1980s. Many policyowners took out policy loans at the rate established in their policies (as low as four percent in older policies) and invested the money in money market funds, certificates of deposit, and other investments yielding up to several times as much as the interest on the policy loans. This created a serious cash outflow problem for insurers and drained insurance policy values.

Variable policy loan interest rate laws will help to prevent similar problems in the future, although they do not affect the policy loan interest rates provided by policies already in force. Policies issued after the effective dates of these laws can include a provision that the policy loan interest rate will fluctuate with an indicator of other interest rates. Moody's Monthly Corporate Bond Yield Average is the indicator required by the NAIC Model Policy Loan Interest Rate Bill.[15] The model bill further provides that "The maximum rate for each policy must be determined at regular intervals at least once every 12 months, but no more frequently than once in any three month period."[16]

A variable policy loan interest rate benefits policyowners, beneficiaries, and insurers. Policyowners benefit because the policy loan interest rate can be set close to the rate that the insurer can earn on its new investments. The policy loan interest rate does not have to be set higher to protect the insurer from interest rate fluctuations. Beneficiaries benefit from variable policy loan interest rates because variable rates discourage policyowners from draining their policies of value, which frequently results in policy lapse or a lower death benefit. Insurers benefit, because they are protected from sudden large cash outflows resulting from demands for policy loans in times when interest rates on new investments are higher than policy loan interest rates.

Endorsement

The life policy is the sole security for a policy loan. At one time, many insurers required that the policy be delivered to the insurer for endorsement of the loan agreement upon it. Such endorsement is for the benefit of the insurer and can, therefore, be waived by the insurer. Today, most insurers do waive the requirement of endorsement, because endorsing the policy each time a loan is granted is expensive and inconvenient. Some insurers reserve the right to require endorsement at the insurer's option, however.

---

[15]§ 2(a).
[16]§ 3(d).

Deferment

The illustrative policy in Appendix B provides that the insurer can postpone, or defer, a policy loan for up to six months. This provision reads as follows:

> We have the right to postpone your loan for up to six months unless the loan is to be used to pay premiums on any policies you have with us.

As with the cash surrender deferment provision, the policy loan deferment provision is intended to protect life insurers in case unusual economic conditions cause large numbers of policyowners to seek policy loans. Such a situation could jeopardize the insurers' financial stability.

Ordinarily, the policy loan deferment provision is not utilized by the insurer. Policy loans are usually processed immediately. Even in times when policyowners are seeking policy loans in large numbers, such as in the early 1980s, insurers have resisted deferring loans.

Note that the deferment provision does not apply to premium loans. Even premium loans for payment of premiums on other policies issued by the insurer will not be deferred. The reason for this is that a premium loan does not require a cash payout by the insurer.

Extended Term and Reduced Paid-Up Policies

The policy loan provision does not apply to extended term insurance. The illustrative policy prohibits such loans as follows: "You cannot obtain a loan if this Policy is in force as Extended Term Insurance." The reason for this is that extended term insurance does not have policy loan values. Some policies, such as the illustrative policy, also have no cash surrender values for extended term insurance. Where extended term policies do have a cash surrender value, the value steadily decreases, and eventually there would be no security for a loan.

Where the policy is in force under the reduced paid-up insurance option, the policyowner can obtain a loan of the policy's cash value. However, if the accumulating interest causes the amount of the loan plus the interest to exceed the policy's cash value, and such interest is not repaid, the insurer can cancel the policy, just as if it were on a premium-paying basis, according to the majority of courts.[17]

If a policy loan is outstanding at the time one of the nonforfeiture options is exercised, the loan can be deducted in computing the amount available for the cash surrender value payout, or for the reduced paid-up whole life or extended term insurance premiums. The illustrative policy provides the following:

---

[17]*See, e.g.,* Jones v. Mutual Life Ins. Co., 216 Ala. 437, 113 So. 314 (1927).

> The term "cash surrender value" as used in this Policy means the cash value shown in the table of guaranteed values . . . , less any indebtedness. . . .
>
> You may apply the cash surrender value to purchase a fully paid whole life policy for a reduced amount of insurance. . . .
>
> The amount of . . . [extended] term insurance will be the Sum Insured less any indebtedness. . . . The term period will begin on the due date of the first unpaid premium and will be such as the cash surrender value will provide as a single net premium at the insured's then attained age.

Note that the amount of the policy loan, plus interest, is deducted twice in the case of extended term insurance. First, it is deducted from the table of guaranteed values to arrive at the cash surrender value. Next, it is deducted from the face amount of the policy to arrive at the amount of extended term insurance available. This procedure is fair, because the cash surrender value will purchase term insurance for a longer period if the face amount is reduced.

The Beneficiary's Rights

A revocable beneficiary ordinarily has a mere expectancy, rather than rights, under a life insurance policy. The revocable beneficiary's consent to a policy loan is, therefore, not required. Nor is the consent of an irrevocable beneficiary needed if the policy makes it clear that the policyowner has a right to obtain a policy loan without such consent.

A beneficiary has no right to recover from a policyowner-insured's estate the amount of a policy loan which the insurer deducts from the proceeds, according to the majority of courts.[18] The beneficiary is entitled only to the net proceeds, as such is the intention of the parties to the contract. The illustrative policy states that "[a]ny indebtedness will be deducted from any proceeds paid under this Policy."

Repayment of Policy Loans

A policy loan ordinarily can be repaid before the insured's death if the policyowner so desires. The illustrative policy in Appendix B states the following:

> If this Policy is in force and not on Extended Term Insurance, your loan can be repaid in full or in part at anytime before the Insured's death. However, any loan repayment must be at least $20 unless the balance due is less than $20, in which case the loan repayment must be for the full amount of the loan.

---

[18]Annot., 31 A.L.R. 2d 979 (1953).

Note that the policy says the loan can be repaid, not that it must be repaid. Moreover, there are two situations in which it ordinarily cannot be repaid—where the insured has died or where the policy is on extended term insurance. Some insurers do permit repayment after the insured's death, however, in order that the total proceeds can be distributed under a settlement agreement according to the policyowner's plan.

If the policyowner does not repay the loan, the insurer will obtain payment from one of two sources of money—the policy's cash surrender value or the death benefit proceeds.

SUMMARY

Under the level premium, legal reserve system, a cash value builds up in whole life policies, endowment policies, or term policies for the longer terms. This cash value can be given to the policyowner on lapse or used to purchase a nonforfeiture benefit. Alternatively, the policy can be kept in force, and the cash value can be advanced to the policyowner or used to pay the premium.

Nonforfeiture policy provisions are required by state nonforfeiture laws. Ordinarily, a policy has three nonforfeiture benefit options—cash surrender, extended term insurance, and reduced paid-up insurance. Under the cash surrender option, the policyowner surrenders the policy in return for its cash value. The insurer has the right to defer payment of the cash value for up to six months, but this rarely occurs.

Under the extended term insurance option, insurance for the face amount of the policy, minus any unpaid policy loan and interest, is extended for the period that the net cash value will provide. This period ordinarily begins on the due date of the premium in default, not at the end of the grace period. Any unpaid policy loan and interest are deducted from both the cash value and the face amount in computing the amount and duration of the extended term insurance. The reduced paid-up insurance option provides paid-up insurance of the kind and for the duration provided by the policy immediately prior to lapse, in whatever amount the cash surrender value will purchase.

If the policyowner fails to elect a nonforfeiture benefit, the automatic nonforfeiture benefit specified in the policy will apply. The automatic nonforfeiture benefit provision is required by law. For standard policies, the typical automatic nonforfeiture option is extended term insurance.

Occasionally, an insured person dies after the policyowner has attempted to exercise a nonforfeiture option, but before the transaction is complete. In these cases, the majority of courts have held that the option is a continuing, irrevocable offer from the insurer to the policyowner which, if accepted according to its terms, results in a contract binding on both parties. If the policyowner's acceptance differs from the terms of the option, the policyowner has made a counteroffer which must be accepted by the insurer in order to be binding.

If the policyowner wishes to receive the cash value but wishes to keep the policy in force, the insurer will advance the cash value to the policyowner. Such an advance is called a cash loan or request loan. The policyowner can also have the insurer apply the cash value to reduce or pay the premium. This is called a premium loan. Cash loans and premium loans are the two types of policy loans.

The term *policy loan* is a misnomer. A policy loan is actually an advance of money which the insurer must eventually pay out under the policy. A policy loan does not create a debtor-creditor relationship between the policyowner and insurer, because the loan and interest do not have to be repaid. The policyowner can repay them, however, before the insured's death if he or she desires (unless the policy is on extended term insurance).

The insurer must charge interest on a loan because it bases policy values on the assumption that the portion of the premiums unused in the early policy years will be invested. Variable policy loan interest rates are now allowed by most states to protect policyowners, beneficiaries, and insurers from the results of fluctuating interest rates. As with the cash surrender value, the insurer can defer making an advance to a policyowner for up to six months. If the loan plus interest accumulates so that the principal and the interest are greater than the cash surrender value, the policy will expire.

ILLUSTRATIVE CASE

In the following case, the insured owned two policies on his life with policy loans on both. The policy beneficiaries sued the insured's estate for reimbursement of the amounts of the loans, which amounts had been deducted from the policy proceeds. The trial court ruled in favor of the beneficiaries. The supreme court reversed.

In re SCHWARTZ' ESTATE[19]
Pennsylvania Supreme Court, Eastern District

ALLEN M. STEARNE, Justice.

The question involved is whether a "policy loan" upon a life insurance policy is a debt of such a nature as enables the designated beneficiary, upon the insured's death, to require the loan to be repaid from the insured's general estate, thus enabling the beneficiary to receive the full insurance proceeds. The court below ruled that it was such a debt and directed its repayment. This appeal followed.

George J. Schwartz, the decedent, was insured by two policies of life insurance, each in the amount of $5,000. In one policy decedent named two of his daugh-

---

[19]369 Pa. 574, 87 A.2d 270 (1952).

ters beneficiaries, and in the other he designated his first wife. Neither policy reserved the right to change beneficiaries. But each policy *obligated* the company to make "loans" to the insured to the limit of its cash surrender value. "Loans" were granted in the aggregate amount of $3,466.80.

By his will the testator-insured directed his executors "to pay my funeral expenses and all my just debts as soon after my decease as may conveniently be done." It was upon the theory that the "policy loans" created a debtor-creditor relationship between the insured and insurer, that the learned court below decreed that the beneficiaries were entitled to reimbursement from the general estate in order that they should receive the full face amounts of the policies.

In support of its ruling the court below relied upon our decision in Wilson's Estate, 363 Pa. 546, 70 A. 2d 354, wherein we decided that in an assessment of transfer inheritance tax, credit must be allowed for an indebtedness of the decedent-insured where a loan was made to him *by a bank,* and his life insurance policy, payable to designated beneficiaries, was pledged as collateral security. We said, at page 551 of 363 Pa., at page 356 of 70 A. 2d: "Decedent (settlor) merely assigned the insurance policies *as collateral* for his loan. As with any other collateral, when a loan is repaid the collateral is returned to the owner. Had the creditor bank used decedent-settlor's insurance collateral to liquidate its loan, the designated insurance beneficiaries could have enforced their claim against the estate of the decedent under their right of *subrogation,*[20] to the same extent as if they had been the original creditor."

In the case now before us, contradistinguished from the facts in Wilson's Estate, supra, the "debt" was owed to the *insurance company* and not to a third person with the insurance policy assigned as collateral. This raises the narrow but important question whether any sound difference exists between the fundamental natures of these transactions. More accurately: does such an insurance "loan" from the insuring company *upon the policy itself* create a debtor-creditor relationship?

The learned court below, and counsel at argument stated that they have been unable to find any reported case in this jurisdiction which has decided this question. Our own research has disclosed none. But courts in at least six other jurisdictions have considered the problem. They unanimously agree that a "loan" granted pursuant to a policy right does not create a debtor-creditor relationship. The nature of such a "policy loan" has recently been discussed in Fidelity Union Trust Co. v. Phillips, 5 N.J. Super. 529, 68 A. 2d 574. It is said, at page 575 of 68 A. 2d: "A clear distinction is drawn between a loan made by an insurance company to an insured against a life policy, and a collateral loan made by a third party secured by an assignment or pledge of the policy on the life of the borrower. The former 'is not a loan in the strict technical sense, for there is no obligation of repayment on the insured, but rather an advancement on the cash value of the policy, the repayment of which will reinstate the depleted insurance without the issuance of a new policy and the submission of evidence of insurability. A "loan" by the insurer in such circumstances does not give rise to the relationship of debtor and creditor." David

---

[20]Subrogation is the right given to a creditor to be substituted for another and to succeed to the other's rights. In this situation, the court says, the beneficiaries had the right to be substituted for the original creditor—that is, the creditor bank—and thus be repaid out of the estate of the decedent.

v. Metropolitan Life Insurance Co., 135 N.J.L. 106, 50 A. 2d 651, 653 (Sup. Ct. 1947), affirmed 136 N.J.L. 195, 54 A. 2d 731 (E. & A., 1947). Mr. Justice Holmes declared in Board of Assessors v. New York Life Insurance Co., 216 U.S. 517, 30 S. Ct. 385, 386, 54 L. Ed. 597, 1910, 'This is called a loan. It is represented by what is called a note, which contains a promise to pay the money. But as the plaintiff (insurance company) never advances more than it already is absolutely bound for under the policy, it has no interest in creating a personal liability, and therefore the contract on the face of the note goes on to provide that if the note is not paid when due, it shall be extinguished automatically by the counter credit for what we have called the reserve value of the policy. In short, the claim of the policy holder on the one side and of the company on the other are brought into an account current by the very act that creates the latter. The so-called liability of the policyholder never exists as a personal liability, it never is a debt, but is merely a deduction in account from the sum that the plaintiffs ultimately must pay.' Therefore, when an insurance company advances to an insured a sum of money against his policy, and upon the death of the insured retains the amount required to satisfy the 'loan' or advance, the beneficiary named in the policy is not entitled to recover from the estate of the insured the amount by which the insurance had been depleted by borrowings by the insured upon the policy.

* * * * *

Substantially the same rule was adopted by this Court in Black's Estate, 341 Pa. 264, 19 A. 2d 130. The insurance policy there included a provision almost identical with that now under consideration, except that payment by insurer was more accurately termed an "advance" rather than a "loan." Decedent had bequeathed his business to his son subject to payment of all his personal and business debts. A dispute arose between the son and the widow, as residuary legatee, as to whether certain items were debts or obligations payable out of the business. Concerning a cash advance to decedent from his insurance company, we said in 341 Pa. at page 270, 19 A. 2d at page 133: "The auditor and court below held that the advance was not such a debt as was required to be paid out of the business of decedent. With that conclusion we are in accord, for the association could not make any claim against the estate of decedent. It could not have proceeded against the decedent at the date of his death. Consequently there was no indebtedness, as clearly appears from a perusal of the agreement. The policy holder had the right to repay the advance made but he could not be compelled to do so."

While counsel for appellees point to factual distinctions between that case and the present one, such distinctions have no bearing on the legal principle here involved.

Legal digests and text writers appear to be equally unanimous. "Although a policy loan is termed a 'loan,' it differs from an ordinary commercial loan, and, in fact, is not a 'loan' in the ordinary sense of the word. It is merely a deduction from the sum insurer ultimately must pay, and is more accurately described as an advance": 44 C.J.S. Insurance, § 337, p. 1291. Accord: 29 Am. Jur. Insurance, § 463; Goldin on Insurance in Pennsylvania (2d ed.) page 631; 2 Couch on Insurance, § 335; Cooley's Briefs on Insurance (2d ed.) page 157.

Appellees argue that the insured's will and his testamentary scheme, considered in the light of his family circumstances, reveal that he intended his insurance beneficiaries to receive the full face amount of the policies. But the insured's *testamentary intent* is not the controlling consideration. We are obliged first to determine his *contractual* intent at the time he entered into the contracts of insurance wherein the rights of the insurance beneficiaries were created. We cannot interpret the meaning of contracts entered into on June 11, 1913, by speculating on testamentary intent adopted by insured in his testamentary scheme of April 2, 1949, nearly thirty-six years thereafter. The terms of the insurance contracts are clear and unambiguous; they give the insured an absolute right to demand at any time an advancement of any sum of money up to the reserve value of the policies. Under no discernible doctrine could it be held that the insured was incurring a *personal liability* by exercising this contract right. The insured could, of course, have directed by his will that the "policy loans" be paid out of his general assets so that the beneficiaries would receive the face amounts of the policies.[21] As he chose not to do this we have no power to do it for him. We cannot construe a direction to pay "debts" as applicable to an advancement of money which did not create a personal liability. As an insurance policy loan does not create a debtor-creditor relationship, the beneficiaries of these policies so encumbered are entitled only to the *net* proceeds.

Decree reversed at appellees' cost.

QUESTIONS FOR REVIEW

1. Summarize present statutory requirements concerning policy provisions for nonforfeiture benefits.
2. Outline briefly the limitations of the nonforfeiture benefits as compared to the benefits provided by a policy in force on a premium-paying basis.
3. Under the extended term insurance option:
   a. How is the amount of term insurance determined?
   b. How is the length of the term insurance period determined?
4. Under the reduced paid-up option:
   a. What kind of insurance is provided?
   b. How is the amount of insurance determined?
5. Suppose the policyowner surrendered the policy and requested the cash surrender value, and the insured died before the requested amount could be paid.
   a. On what grounds could both the policyowner and the beneficiary make claim for payment?
   b. What would you expect the court decision to be in this case? Why?
6. Explain what is meant by the statement, "The term *policy loan* is a misnomer."
7. Describe the two different types of policy loans which usually are available.
8. Most of the states now have variable policy loan interest rate laws. Describe the typical provisions of these laws.
9. What are the two situations under which the repayment of a policy loan is ordinarily prohibited?
10. Why is interest charged on policy loans?
11. What is the purpose of the provision reserving to the insurer the right to defer granting a request policy loan?

---

[21]It should be remembered, however, that the insurer is under no contractual obligation to accept repayment of the loan after the insured's death.

CHAPTER 14

Assignments and Other Transfers

ABSOLUTE ASSIGNMENTS
  Gifts
  Sales
  The Beneficiary's Rights on Absolute Assignment
COLLATERAL ASSIGNMENTS
  Collateral Assignment Forms
  The Beneficiary's Rights on Collateral Assignment
  Absolute Assignments Intended to Secure Loans
THE INSURER'S ROLE
  Absolute Assignment Clauses
  Collateral Assignment Clauses
  Clauses Prohibiting Assignment
  Consent of the Insurer
  Notice to the Insurer
  Validity of the Assignment
  Reassignment After Repayment of Debt
  Notice from the Insurer to the Assignee
REQUIREMENTS FOR ASSIGNMENT
  Compliance with the Policy Terms
  Legal Capacity of the Assignor
  Written Assignment
  Delivery
  Insurable Interest of the Assignee
SUCCESSIVE ASSIGNEES
ASSIGNMENTS BY THE BENEFICIARY
OTHER TRANSFERS
  Intestate Succession
  Wills
  Property Settlement Agreements and Divorce Decrees
  Sales of Assets
  Equitable Assignments
SUMMARY

One of the most important aspects of property ownership is the owner's legal power to transfer his or her rights in the property to another person. The owner ordinarily can transfer some or all of his or her rights, conditionally or unconditionally.

An assignment is a transfer of some or all of the ownership rights in property by one person, the assignor, to another person, the assignee. The word *assignment* is ordinarily used in reference to the transfer of choses in action although *assignment* can be used to denote the transfer of other ownership rights. *Assignment* also means a written document used to effect a transfer of rights in certain kinds of property, usually choses in action.

As a general rule, rights in an insurance policy are assigned for one of three purposes—to make a gift of the policy, to sell the policy, or to pledge the policy as security for a loan. When the policyowner wishes to give the policy away or to sell it, ordinarily an absolute assignment is made. If the policyowner wishes to pledge the policy for a loan, a collateral assignment usually will be made.

Ownership rights in life insurance policies can also be transferred in ways not ordinarily termed *assignments,* such as by intestate succession, by will, by property settlement or divorce decree, by a sale of assets, or by equitable assignment.

It is the purpose of this chapter to describe the various types of assignments, the requirements for assignment, and the rights and duties of the assignor, assignee, beneficiary, and insurer. The chapter will also briefly touch on the other ways in which rights in life policies are transferred.

ABSOLUTE ASSIGNMENTS

An absolute assignment of a life insurance policy is the irrevocable transfer by the policyowner of all of the policyowner's rights in the policy. Ordinarily, an absolute assignment is made in order to give the policy away or to sell it.

Gifts

If the policy is absolutely assigned to a person who exchanges nothing in return for it, the assignment is a gift. A gift is a voluntary transfer of property to another person, made without receiving consideration in return.

A gift requires contractual capacity on the part of the donor (the assignor in the case of a gift by assignment), voluntary intent to make a gift, delivery of the property to the donee (the assignee), and acceptance by the donee.[1] A valid gift must be a present transfer. A mere promise to make a gift in the future is unenforceable.

---

[1]Annot., 33 A.L.R. 2d 273 (1954).

Absolute assignments without consideration—that is, gifts—are usually made among family members. For example, a grandmother might purchase a life insurance policy on a grandchild's life and absolutely assign the policy to the grandchild when the grandchild reaches majority. Or, a person might wish to absolutely assign a policy on her or his own life to another family member in order to avoid estate taxes.

Sales

An absolute assignment made in return for consideration is a sale. Life insurance policies purchased for business purposes are sometimes absolutely assigned in return for consideration. For example, if a corporation owns a life insurance policy on the life of a key employee, the corporation might sell the policy to the key employee if the employee terminates employment. This would be done by means of an absolute assignment of the policy by the corporation to the employee, in return for consideration from the employee to the corporation.

The Beneficiary's Rights on Absolute Assignment

As a general rule, an irrevocable beneficiary's rights under an insurance policy cannot be destroyed by an absolute assignment without the beneficiary's consent. In the case of a revocable beneficiary, the courts have taken two views. According to one view, the absolute assignment, by itself, does not result in a change of beneficiary.[2] The assignee, as the new owner, can change the beneficiary if he or she desires, however. This appears to be the better view. The other view is that an absolute assignment destroys the interest of a revocable beneficiary.[3]

COLLATERAL ASSIGNMENTS

At one time, it was customary to secure a loan by designating the lender as irrevocable beneficiary of a life insurance policy owned by the borrower. This type of protection for lenders is rarely used today. Modern life insurance policies often include a significant cash value which can protect the lender during the insured's lifetime. A collateral assignment can give the assignee a right to the cash value on default of the loan, as well as a right to repayment from the death benefit. Thus, lenders prefer the protection of a collateral assignment to the protection afforded by being named irrevocable beneficiary.

---

[2]Continental Assur. Co. v. Conroy, 209 F.2d 539 (3d Cir. 1954); Rountree v. Frazee, 282 Ala. 142, 209 So.2d 424 (1968).
[3]Penn Mut. Life Ins. Co. v. Forbes, 200 Ill. App. 441 (1916).

A collateral assignment is a temporary transfer of some policy rights by the policyowner to a bank or other lender to provide security for a loan. The rights in the policy that are transferred are intended to revert to the policyowner when the loan has been repaid.

The policyowner has the primary obligation to repay the loan. The policy used as collateral is merely a secondary source of repayment if the policyowner defaults on the loan, or dies while the loan is outstanding. That is, the policyowner and the lender contemplate that the policyowner will repay a loan made to her or him and that the policy values will not be used for this purpose.

Collateral Assignment Forms

For many years the Assignment of Life Insurance as Collateral form approved by the Bank Management Commission of the American Bankers Association was the form widely used for collateral assignments. This form was jointly developed by the American Bankers Association and the Association of Life Insurance Counsel.

This collateral assignment form is no longer approved by the American Bankers Association because variations in state laws make it unsuitable for use in some states. The American Bankers Association now recommends that lenders obtain the proper form from the insurance department of the state where the assignment will be made.

Nevertheless, collateral assignment forms today incorporate many of the features of the original American Bankers Association form, and the original form is still in use in some states. A copy of the original form appears in Appendix E.

Under the American Bankers Association collateral assignment form, five rights are transferred to the lender. First, the sole right to collect the net proceeds of the policy at the death of the insured is transferred to the lender. The lender promises, however, that the excess of the proceeds over the amount of remaining debt will be paid to the beneficiary named by the policyowner. Second, the sole right to surrender the policy and receive the cash surrender value is transferred to the lender. Third, the sole right to obtain policy loans is transferred. The lender agrees that the right to surrender the policy or to make a policy loan will not be exercised unless there has been a default or failure to pay a premium by the policyowner, and notice of default has been mailed to the policyowner by the lender. Fourth, the policyowner transfers to the lender the sole right to receive dividends. Finally, the policyowner transfers to the lender the sole right to exercise the nonforfeiture options.

Other rights are reserved to the policyowner and are not transferred by the collateral assignment. These are the rights to collect disability benefits, to designate and change the beneficiary, and to elect an optional mode of settlement. The lender agrees, upon request, to forward the policy to the insurer for endorsement of beneficiary changes or settlement agreements made by the policyowner.

The lender under the American Bankers Association collateral assignment form is under no obligation to pay premiums. If the lender does pay premiums, however, the amount of premiums paid will be added to the debt owed by the policyowner.

The American Bankers Association collateral assignment form has a blank for the signature of the beneficiary. The beneficiary's consent to the terms of the assignment prevents conflicts between the beneficiary and the lender over the death benefit. It also eliminates the need for the beneficiary's consent when the lender wishes to exercise prematurity rights.

The Beneficiary's Rights on Collateral Assignment

If the beneficiary consents to the collateral assignment, the beneficiary cannot later object to repayment of the loan from the policy proceeds if there are no assets in the policyowner-insured's estate to repay the loan. For this reason, modern collateral assignment forms require the beneficiary's signature.

Where an irrevocable beneficiary does not consent to the assignment, the irrevocable beneficiary's rights are superior to the collateral assignee's. In other words, an irrevocable beneficiary has a vested interest in the policy which cannot be taken away without the beneficiary's consent.

As to a revocable beneficiary who does not consent to a collateral assignment, the majority rule is that the assignee's rights to the policy proceeds are superior to the beneficiary's rights.[4] The reasons for this rule were stated in one case as follows:

> From an every day, practical standpoint it is desirable to hold that an assignee of a policy containing a clause permitting a change of beneficiary and an assignment of the policy secures a right in the proceeds of the policy superior to the rights of the named beneficiary. If an assignee, in the absence of the consent of the beneficiary, does not obtain such right it will be practically impossible for an insured to borrow on a policy in time of need of financial aid in those cases where compliance with the form prescribed in the policy cannot be followed. No bank or individual would be likely to lend on the security of a policy where the right to enforce the reduction of the security to cash would only mature in case the insured outlived the beneficiary, and where the continued life of the policy depends upon the payment of the annual premium. As stated in the case of *Matter of Whiting, D.C.*, 3 F.2d 440, 441: "To hold that the beneficiary of such policy has a vested interest would be tantamount to destroying the 'changed beneficiary' provisions of the policy itself."[5]

---

[4]McAllen State Bank v. Texas Bank & Trust Co., 433 S.W.2d 167 (Tex. 1968).
[5]Davis v. Modern Industrial Bank, 279 N.Y. 405, 18 N.E.2d 639 (1939).

In a few states, however, the courts take the view that a revocable beneficiary has a right that is vested, subject to being divested. That is, the revocable beneficiary has a right to the policy proceeds that can be terminated only by changing the beneficiary, or by the beneficiary's consent to the assignment. Therefore, in these states, if a revocable beneficiary does not consent to a collateral assignment of the policy, a change of beneficiary before the assignment might be necessary.

Absolute Assignments Intended to Secure Loans

Although absolute assignments are used primarily for the gift or sale of a policy, they are sometimes used to secure a loan. In such instances, if the purpose of the assignment can be proved—that it was intended to serve as security for a loan and was not intended as a permanent transfer of all rights to the assignee—the general rule is that it will be treated as if it were a collateral assignment.

Illustrative of this rule is the case of *Albrent v. Spencer,*[6] decided by the Wisconsin Supreme Court in 1957. There, the policyowner made an absolute assignment of policies on his life as collateral security for the payment of a note on which approximately $140,000 was due. After the insured's death, the assignee collected the entire proceeds of the policies, satisfied the indebtedness, and retained the difference, allegedly amounting to approximately $90,000. The court summarized the question in the case as follows:

> We consider that the case presents the issue of whether it is against public policy for a creditor of the insured to avail himself of an absolute assignment of a previously pledged life insurance policy issued upon the life of the debtor, which assignment is intended to end the creditor-debtor relationship . . .
>
> It offends one's sense of justice that a creditor should realize more out of the proceeds of the policy than the principal and interest due on the loan for which the policy was pledged plus any expenditure of the creditor for premiums necessary to protect his security. To uphold the result reached below in the instant case would be to encourage creditors to bring pressure upon necessitous debtors to convert the rights of the creditor from that of the pledgee to that of owner in order that he might gamble upon the life of the insured in the hope of realizing the difference between the amount due on the loan and the face of the policy. In the instant case it is alleged that such difference amounted to the huge sum of approximately $90,000 . . .
>
> [A]ny purported absolute assignment by a debtor to a creditor of a policy, which had previously been pledged as security to the creditor is only valid between the immediate parties to the extent of enabling the creditor to realize the cash surrender value of the policy. If the creditor after receiving such absolute assignment and the creditor-debtor relationship

---

[6]275 Wis. 127, 81 N.W.2d 555 (1957).

is terminated, continues to hold the policy for the purpose of gambling upon the life of the insured, he becomes a constructive trustee[7] for the benefit of the estate of the deceased of any proceeds received upon the death of the insured, to the extent that such proceeds exceed the amount that would have been due such assignee if the creditor-debtor relationship had not been extinguished.

THE INSURER'S ROLE

The insurer has a crucial role in the assignment process. Many policies are drafted with assignment clauses which govern the method by which the assignment must be made in order to bind the insurer, or which prohibit assignment altogether. Even if no clause appears in the policy, the insurer must be notified of the assignment, or it will not be bound. Moreover, the insurer is not responsible for inquiring into the validity of the assignment unless it has knowledge of circumstances which make that validity questionable.

On the other hand, the insurer has certain duties toward the assignee. First, the insurer must not disregard an assignment which appears valid, unless the policy prohibits assignment. Second, the insurer is bound by law in some states to give the assignee notice of a premium due.

Absolute Assignment Clauses

Some insurers use an *ownership clause* to accomplish absolute assignments. The illustrative policy in Appendix B has such a clause. It reads in part as follows:

> You may name a new owner or contingent owner at any time while the Insured is living by filing a written request with us. Your written request will not be effective until it is recorded in our Home Office. Once recorded, the change will be effective as of the date you signed the request whether or not you or the Insured is alive when we record the change. However, the change will be subject to any payments made or other action taken by us before your request was recorded in our Home Office.

Other insurers require the use of an absolute assignment form which the policyowner must complete and return to the insurer. Still others require endorsement on the policy itself to effect an absolute assignment of the policy.

Collateral Assignment Clauses

Many life insurance policies contain a collateral assignment clause. The following clause from the illustrative policy in Appendix B is an example:

---

[7]A constructive trustee is the trustee of a trust created by construction of a court because the trustee, by wrongful means, holds a legal right to property the trustee should not, in equity and good conscience, hold.

You may assign this Policy as collateral for a loan without the consent of any revocable beneficiary. We are not bound by any assignment unless it is in writing and recorded at our Home Office. We are not responsible for the validity of any assignment. The rights of an assignee will at all times be subject to any indebtedness to us at the time the assignment is recorded by us, and, if applicable, to loans granted at anytime by us under the automatic premium loan provision of the Policy.

Note that this clause makes five important points. First, the consent of a revocable beneficiary is not necessary for a collateral assignment. This portion of the clause protects the assignee in those few states where the revocable beneficiary is considered to have a vested interest in the policy.

Second, the insurer requires notice of the assignment and states its intention not to be bound by the assignment in the absence of such notice.

Third, the insurer states its intention not to be responsible for the validity of a collateral assignment. This part of the absolute assignment clause is discussed in a subsection below.

Fourth, the insurer makes clear that an assignee's rights are subject to policy loans already advanced by the insurer. In other words, the insurer can deduct the amount of such loans from the cash surrender value or death benefit.

Finally, the insurer establishes its right to make automatic premium loans at any time, as it has a contractual duty to do this if the automatic premium loan provision is in effect.

Clauses Prohibiting Assignment

Life insurance policies providing a small amount of insurance, such as home service policies, sometimes contain clauses which prohibit assignment of the policy. If there is no statute which prevents the insurer from prohibiting such assignments, the clause is enforceable. The result in such a case will be that the insurer will have no duty to pay the assignee if an assignment is made.

Consent of the Insurer

If the life insurance policy requires the consent of the insurer to an assignment, the insurer must give its consent, or the assignee will have no rights against the insurer.[8] If the policy does not expressly require the insurer's consent, such consent is not necessary. The illustrative policy in Appendix B does not require the insurer's consent to an assignment, but many life insurance policies do require such consent.

---

[8]Thomas v. Metropolitan Life Ins. Co., 144 Ga. 367, 87 S.E. 303 (1915); Resnek v. Mutual Life Ins. Co., 286 Mass. 305, 190 N.E. 603 (1934); Hutsell v. Citizens' Nat'l Bank, 166 Tenn. 598, 64 S.W. 2d 188 (1933).

Notice to the Insurer

Policies often require that notice of an assignment be given to the insurer. The illustrative policy in Appendix B requires that the policyowner send the insurer a written request which will effect an absolute assignment on recording by the insurer. The policy further provides that the insurer will not be bound by a collateral assignment unless the assignment is in writing and recorded at the insurer's home office.

Such a notice requirement is for the protection of the insurer. The insurer can, therefore, waive the notice requirement, as a general rule. The insurer could, for example, waive a requirement of written notice and accept oral notice instead.

Where the insurer has notice of an assignment, the insurer should not pay out policy proceeds without regard to the rights of the assignee.[9] If the insurer does so, it might be compelled to pay again to the assignee.

If there is no policy provision requiring notice to the insurer of an assignment, the policy can be assigned without such notice. That is, in such a case the validity of an assignment does not depend upon notice to the insurer. However, the assignee would be wise to inform the insurer of the assignee's rights in the policy. An insurer is not liable to an assignee where the insurer pays the death benefit to the named beneficiary in ignorance of the assignee's rights.[10]

Validity of the Assignment

The assignment provision in most life insurance policies expressly states that the insurer assumes no responsibility for the validity of the assignment of the insurance contract. The validity of an assignment is governed by factors over which the insurer has no control and of which it often has no knowledge. Some of these factors are the mental competence of the assignor, the law of the state where the assignment is made, and whether there has been compliance with the formal requirements for assignment, such as delivery.

The court which decided *New York Life Insurance Co. v. Federal National Bank of Shawnee, Oklahoma*[11] stated the law regarding the insurer's responsibility for the validity of assignments. In that case, the policyowner-insured and the beneficiary joined in an assignment of the life insurance policy. The insurer advanced the full policy loan value to the assignee and, after the insured's death, paid the assignee the death benefits. The bank, acting as the beneficiary's guardian, sued the insurer to recover the face amount of the

---

[9]Morticians' Acceptance Co. v. Metropolitan Life Ins. Co., 321 Ill. App. 277, 53 N.E.2d 30 (1944), *aff'd,* 389 Ill. 81, 58 N.E.2d 854 (1945).

[10]Kot v. Chrysler Corp., 293 Mich. 688, 292 N.W. 531 (1940).

[11]151 F.2d 537 (10th Cir. 1945), *cert. denied,* 327 U.S. 778 (1946).

policy for the beneficiary. The bank alleged that the policyowner was mentally incompetent at the time the assignment was made. The court held that the insurer had no duty to inquire into the mental competency of the policyowner. When an insurer in good faith makes payment to an assignee of record, it cannot be required to pay a second time. Pertinent excerpts from this decision are as follows:

> No case has been cited, and our search has failed to reveal one, which has compelled an insurance company to pay a policy a second time when in good faith it has paid the amount of the policy to a new beneficiary or to an assignee, on the ground that the assignment or the change in beneficiary was void because of lack of mental capacity of the insured at the time the change was made, and that is so even though the original beneficiary did not join in the application for change of beneficiary or in the application for the assignment of the policy. The cases upon which the appellee relies to sustain its contention in this respect are not in point.
>
> There is yet another reason why the Bank may not prevail. That part of the policy which gave the insured the right to assign contains this provision: "The company assumes no responsibility for the validity of any assignment." This provision was a part of the contract made at a time when the parties were competent to contract, and must be given effect. There is no ambiguity or uncertainty as to the meaning of this provision. It can only mean that the Company shall not become liable by virtue of the assignment which for any reason was invalid. There was a good reason for the inclusion of such a provision. The Company had a large number of policy-holders. Many requests for the assignment of policies would be received. The Company no doubt realized that fraud, duress or undue influence might be practiced in many instances which would go to the validity of the assignment, or that assignments might be invalid for many other reasons, including impaired mental capacity or even lack of mental capacity to make the assignment. If the Company was to be charged with liability if an assignment was invalid for any of these reasons, it would of necessity be compelled to deny the right to assign, or in each instance would be compelled to carefully investigate the application before it was granted. This would place an impossible burden upon the Company. It was for these reasons that the Company in substance said to the insured: "We will give you the right to assign, but we shall not be liable if for any reason the assignment is invalid."

Clearly, the court in this case upheld the right of the insurer to pay an assignee in good faith. The court added an important comment, however, as follows:

> This provision would not, of course, protect the Company in case of an irregular assignment because that would put it upon notice, or in cases in which it had knowledge of the mental condition of the insured, or in cases in which it had knowledge of facts which should put it upon inquiry. But this is not such a case.

Thus, if the insurer knows the assignor is mentally incompetent, it cannot disregard that knowledge. Nor can it disregard irregularities on the face of a written assignment. Any facts known to the insurer that would arouse suspicion in the mind of a reasonable person must be investigated.

Reassignment After Repayment of Debt

Once the debt secured by a policy assigned as collateral has been repaid, the policyowner becomes entitled to the return of the rights assigned. The assignee will ordinarily reassign those rights to the policyowner.

Just as insurers do not assume responsibility for the validity of an assignment, neither do they assume responsibility for the validity of a reassignment. The insurer must have evidence of such a reassignment, however, before the owner of a policy which was collaterally assigned will be permitted to exercise the rights which the policyowner had transferred and which were reassigned to the policyowner. Such a reassignment might be a formal statement of the rights reassigned—signed and witnessed—or a simple statement on the letterhead of the assignee that the debt has been paid and all rights to the policy reassigned to the policyowner. If the insurer has doubts about the adequacy of the reassignment, it should seek advice of counsel.

Notice from the Insurer to the Assignee

Under the laws of a minority of states, the insurer is under a duty to notify an assignee of a premium due. For example, the California Insurance Code contains the following:

> When a policy of life insurance is, after the effective date of this section, assigned in writing as security for an indebtedness, the insurer shall, in any case in which it has received written notice of the name and address of the assignee, mail to such assignee a written notice, postage prepaid and addressed to the assignee's address filed with the insurer, not less than 10 days prior to the final lapse of the policy, each time the insured has failed or refused to transmit a premium payment to the insurer before the commencement of the policy's grace period or before such notice is mailed. The insurer shall give such notice to the assignee in the proper case while such assignment remains in effect, unless the assignee has notified the insurer in writing that such notice is waived.[12]

REQUIREMENTS FOR ASSIGNMENT

There are a number of formal requirements for a valid assignment which will bind the assignor, the beneficiary, and the insurer. The most important

---

[12]CAL. INS. CODE § 10173.2 (West Supp. 1988). *See also* ILL. REV. STAT. ch. 73, ¶ 846 (1985) (Ill. Ins. Code § 234); N.Y. INS. LAW § 3211(e) (McKinney 1985).

of these are compliance with the policy terms, legal capacity of the assignor (and of the beneficiary if his or her consent is necessary), and notice to the insurer. A written assignment and delivery of the assignment, or of the policy, are sometimes required also. Insurable interest of an absolute assignee is required in a very few states.

Compliance with the Policy Terms

The conditions for assignment stated in the policy ordinarily must be complied with, or the assignment cannot be enforced against the insurer. Thus, as noted above, the requirements that the insurer give consent to the assignment, or that written notice of the assignment be given to the insurer, must be observed or the assignment will not bind the insurer.

Legal Capacity of the Assignor

The assignor must have the required legal capacity to make an assignment. If the assignor is a minor, the assignment will be voidable by the minor unless a statute says otherwise. If the assignor lacks the mental capacity to make an assignment, the assignment will not be valid. In the absence of circumstances leading the insurer to believe the assignor does not have the requisite capacity, the insurer has no duty to ascertain the capacity of the assignor.

Written Assignment

An assignment does not have to be in writing, unless a statute or policy provision requires a written assignment. It is, nevertheless, customary and desirable to have a written assignment.

The written assignment does not have to be in any particular form to be legally effective. However, it must identify the policy and indicate the assignor's intention to transfer it to the assignee. A collateral assignment should precisely spell out the rights assigned and the duties of the parties. The assignor must, of course, sign the assignment. An irrevocable beneficiary also must sign the assignment; and, in some states, a revocable beneficiary must sign a collateral assignment.

Delivery

If there is no written assignment, delivery of the policy will usually be necessary. Where there is a written assignment, delivery of the assignment alone will be adequate.

Constructive, rather than actual, delivery will suffice. Constructive delivery is made when the assignor releases the policy or assignment with intent to be bound by it, as, for example, when the assignor puts it in the mail to be delivered to the assignee. Delivery to the assignee's agent, rather than to the assignee personally, will also constitute constructive delivery. Note that constructive delivery by an assignor to an assignee is much the same as constructive delivery of a policy by an insurer to an applicant.

Insurable Interest of the Assignee

The question of when the assignee must have an insurable interest in the life insured occurs only where there is an absolute assignment. A collateral assignment will not be held invalid for lack of insurable interest on the part of the assignee.

Assignments Made in Good Faith.   Absolute assignments, made in good faith and without intent to evade the law against wagering in human life, are valid in a majority of jurisdictions, even though the assignee has no insurable interest in the insured's life.[13] That is, if the policy is taken out by the insured, or by someone with an insurable interest in the insured's life, not for the purpose of later assigning the policy to a person who could not have taken it out originally, the owner can absolutely assign it to whomever she or he wishes. It does not matter that the absolute assignee has no insurable interest. This majority view is well stated by the Missouri Supreme Court in *Butterworth v. Mississippi Valley Trust Co.*[14] There the court said:

> There is some difference of opinion. But the prevailing view, and the greater weight of authority and the better and more soundly reasoned conclusions of the courts was tersely expressed by Mr. Justice Holmes in *Grigsby v. Russell,* 222 U.S. 149, 32 S.Ct. 58, 59, 56 L.Ed. 133, wherein, in ruling this precise question, he said, in part: "And cases in which a person having an interest lends himself to one without any, as a cloak to what is, in its inception, a wager, have no similarity to those where an honest contract is sold in good faith." The principle of the good faith of the assignment transaction runs like a scarlet thread through the better reasoned cases. The decided trend of adjudications unquestionably is to establish the rule that an insurable interest in the insured by the assignee of a policy of life insurance is not essential to the validity of the assignment if the party to whom it was issued in good faith had an insurable interest, and if the assignment was in good faith and not made to cover up a gambling transaction. We unequivocally approve that rule.
>
> Without the power of assignment life insurance contracts would lose much of their value. In a commercial age and with a commercial people,

---

[13] Annot., 30 A.L.R. 2d 1310 (1953).
[14] 362 Mo. 133, 240 S.W.2d 676 (1951).

and in recognition of commercial practices, the courts are not unaware of the frequent necessity for the transfer by assignment of such contracts in the usual course of every day business. To limit the assignment of such contracts otherwise valid to those having an insurable interest, and to thus ignore the bona fides of assignments of convenience or necessity, would not only impair the value of such contracts as a plan of estate building and economic protection but would work unconscionable injury to policyholders who are no longer financially able to or who no longer desire to continue such contracts.

The courts in a very few states have taken the view that an absolute assignee must have an insurable interest in the insured's life even if the assignment was made in good faith. They have based their decisions mainly on the rationale that an absolute assignment to an assignee without insurable interest would tend to encourage the murder of the insured as much as would the issuance of a policy to an applicant without an insurable interest.

Assignments Made in Bad Faith.   If the policy is taken out with the intent to assign it to a person with no insurable interest, the assignment will ordinarily be void, although the contract of insurance itself will be valid. The law strictly prohibits trafficking in human lives.

SUCCESSIVE ASSIGNEES

Occasionally, a policyowner assigns the same rights in the same policy to two different assignees. In such a situation, the insurer might be faced with conflicting assignees. Ordinarily, the insurer will pay the proceeds into court and let the court decide which assignee is entitled to the proceeds (interplead).

For example, suppose Timothy Davis assigns his $20,000 life insurance policy, in which he is the insured, to Martin Hemphill as security for a $20,000 loan. Mr. Davis delivers a written assignment to Mr. Hemphill but keeps the policy. Shortly after this, Mr. Davis delivers a written assignment of the same policy to James Chung as security for another $20,000 loan. Two weeks later and before payments have been made on either loan, Mr. Davis is killed in an airplane accident. Which assignee will be entitled to be paid the proceeds by the insurer, Mr. Hemphill or Mr. Chung?

First, suppose Mr. Chung had notified the insurer of the assignment immediately, and Mr. Hemphill failed to notify it at all. Suppose Mr. Hemphill was in Europe at the time of Mr. Davis' death and did not hear of it until his return. Meanwhile, the insurer, in good faith, paid the death benefit to Mr. Chung. The insurer would not have to pay Mr. Hemphill, because it paid Mr. Chung in good faith and in ignorance of the assignment to Mr. Hemphill.

Now, suppose that Mr. Chung notified the insurer of his assignment immediately and Mr. Hemphill notified the insurer of his assignment a week later. If Mr. Davis was accidentally killed a few days after the insurer received notice of Mr. Hemphill's assignment, who would receive the death benefit, Mr. Hemphill or Mr. Chung?

In the majority of states, in the absence of a statute to the contrary, Mr. Hemphill would be entitled to the money, under what is called the American rule. This rule states that the right of the first assignee is superior to that of a subsequent assignee. Here, Mr. Hemphill was the first assignee.

A minority of states follow the English rule. Under the English rule, the first assignee to give notice of his assignment to the insurer would be entitled to the death benefit, regardless of the order in which the assignments were made. Since Mr. Chung gave notice of his assignment one week before Mr. Hemphill gave notice of his, Mr. Chung would be entitled to the death benefit in those states which follow the English rule.

As one final example, suppose the policy had a face value of $50,000, and successive assignments had been made to Mr. Hemphill and Mr. Chung to secure a $20,000 loan made by each of them. Here, the insurer can pay Mr. Hemphill $20,000, pay Mr. Chung $20,000, and pay the remaining $10,000 to the named beneficiary.

ASSIGNMENTS BY THE BENEFICIARY

The beneficiary, like the policyowner, usually can transfer his or her rights in the life insurance policy. Before the insured's death, the beneficiary can transfer whatever rights he or she possesses.[15] An irrevocable beneficiary can transfer his or her rights. Ordinarily, such rights are vested, but subject to divestment if the policy expires or the beneficiary predeceases the insured. Even a revocable beneficiary can transfer his or her expectancy.

After the insured's death, the rights of the beneficiary to the policy proceeds become vested. The beneficiary's rights are then no different from rights to any other sum of money. Rights of this kind are usually assignable.

A policy provision prohibiting assignment is usually held ineffective to prevent an assignment by the beneficiary after the insured's death. This rule was expressed in one case as follows:

> The general rule, supported by a great wealth of authority, is that general stipulations in policies, prohibiting assignment thereof except with the insurers' consent, or upon giving some notice, or like conditions, have universally been held to apply only to assignments before loss, and, accordingly, not to prevent an assignment after loss.[16]

Spendthrift clauses in settlement agreements can, however, impose restrictions on the assignability of the proceeds by the beneficiary.[17]

---

[15]Sloan v. Breeden, 233 Mass. 418, 124 N.E. 31 (1919).

[16]Lain v. Metropolitan Life Ins. Co., 388 Ill. 576, 58 N.E. 2d 587 (1944).

[17]Chelsea-Wheeler Coal Co. v. Marvin, 134 N.J. Eq. 432, 35 A.2d 874 (1944); Michaelson v. Sokolove, 169 Md. 529, 182 A. 458 (1936).

OTHER TRANSFERS

Transfer of the policyowner's rights in a life insurance policy is some-times made in some way other than by a specific assignment of the policy. Such transfers can be made by intestate succession, by will, by property settlement agreement or divorce decree, or by sale of the assets of a business. In addition, actions which would not amount to a legal assignment of the policy sometimes result in an equitable assignment—that is, an assignment which would be enforced in an equitable action. These transfers will be discussed in this section.

Intestate Succession

A person who dies without a valid will dies intestate. The property of the person, who is called an "intestate," will pass to other persons according to the intestate statute of the relevant jurisdiction. If the intestate owned a life insurance policy insuring the life of another, a person or persons described in the intestate statute will succeed to the intestate's interests in the policy.

For example, suppose Georgia Appleton dies intestate, without debts, and that she owned a life insurance policy insuring her husband's life. Suppose that Mrs. Appleton had no children. If the intestate statute of her state of residence provides that an intestate's spouse will succeed to all of the intestate's property where the intestate has no children, her husband will become the policyowner.

Wills

A person who owns a life insurance policy on the life of another person has valuable property which can be transferred under the terms of her or his will. The policy need not be specifically mentioned in the will. If, for example, a testator who owned such a policy left all her or his property to a designated person, that person would become the policy's new owner.

Property Settlement Agreements and Divorce Decrees

A property settlement agreement or divorce decree can operate to modify the policyowner's rights in the policy. For example, a policyowner might be required to keep a life insurance policy in force for the benefit of a spouse or the children. Or, the policyowner might agree in a property settlement to transfer a policy to a spouse, or be ordered by the court to do so.

Sale of Assets

A sale of all the assets of a business will result in the transfer of a life insurance policy owned by the business. For example, in *Brand v. Erisman*,[18]

---

[18]172 F.2d 28 (D.C. Cir. 1948).

a partnership had purchased policies on the lives of the partners. When the partners later sold all the assets of the partnership, including all "contracts . . . rights or choses in action," the insurance policies were transferred to the purchaser along with the other assets of the business.

Equitable Assignments

An assignment which would not be enforceable in a legal action because it does not meet the requirements of a legal assignment will be enforced in an equitable action if fairness so requires. For example, in *Sundstrom v. Sundstrom*,[19] the Supreme Court of Washington held that the policyowner-insured had equitably assigned his life insurance policy to his wife, even though the legal requirements for an assignment had not been fulfilled. There were two claimants to the proceeds—the wife and the insured's mother. The insurer paid the benefits into the court and was dismissed from the lawsuit. The mother was the original beneficiary. The wife was named beneficiary of the policy several years after she and the insured had been married. The wife had worked and supported the insured, who had arthritis and was able to work only sporadically. Together, they had paid back to his parents the money the parents had charged him for furnishing care prior to his marriage. When that indebtedness had been reduced to a relatively small sum, the insured changed the beneficiary to his wife and gave her the policy, telling her that it was to be hers. Seven years later, the wife was seriously injured in an automobile accident. After a few weeks, her husband closed out their joint bank account and went back to his parents, taking with him the life insurance policy. The wife sued for divorce, but before the decree became final the insured died, after having changed the beneficiary back to his mother. On this set of facts, the court held that there was an equitable assignment in favor of the wife, reasoning as follows:

> We are convinced that this evidence, if believed by the trial court, fully warranted it in finding that the insured had made an equitable assignment of the policy to respondent [the wife] in 1932. It is apparent that he was at the time a hopeless cripple. For four years, his wife had faithfully worked to help support him, and had given him every attention possible. More than that, her earnings had been the principal means by which his personal, premarital debt to his parents had been reduced from five hundred eighty dollars to seventy dollars. Presumably he not only felt a deep affection for her, but also was sincerely grateful for all that she had done. In addition, he had agreed to transfer the policy to her as soon as *they* got "the folks" paid up. The language employed by him when he delivered the policy to her indicated that it was his intention then and there to invest her with full ownership of the proceeds thereof.
>
> It is true that no formal written assignment of the policy was executed, as required by the provision of the policy hereinabove quoted. But that

---

[19]15 Wash. 2d 103, 129 P.2d 783 (1942).

provision, as we have seen, is designed solely for the protection of the insurance company, and its rights are in no way involved here. Although the transaction between the insured and the respondent with reference to the transfer of the policy was simple and informal, it was only natural for a husband and wife to deal with each other in that way at a time when the relationship between them was one of affection and when there was no occasion for either of them to suspect the other of possible future double-dealing. Nor would it be expected that a wife, even if she were aware of the express requirements of the policy and were familiar with legal phraseology, would insist, under the circumstances then existing, that the terms of the transaction be reduced to writing. The evidence amply justifies the conclusion that it was the insured's intention on October 28, 1932, to transfer to respondent a present interest in the ultimate proceeds of the policy, that he delivered the policy to respondent for that purpose, and that by the form of expression which he then used he made an absolute appropriation of such proceeds to her, relinquishing further control or power of revocation with reference thereto. That being the case, the trial court had sufficient grounds for holding that the insured effected an equitable assignment of the insurance policy to the respondent.

SUMMARY

Transfer of a chose in action is ordinarily called an assignment. A gift or sale of the policy is done by absolute assignment, while a pledge of the policy is usually by collateral assignment.

An absolute assignment is the irrevocable transfer of all the policyowner's rights. An irrevocable beneficiary's rights cannot be destroyed by absolute assignment without the beneficiary's consent. An absolute assignment, by itself, does not affect the rights of a revocable beneficiary, according to one view. According to the other view, the rights of a revocable beneficiary are destroyed by an absolute assignment.

A collateral assignment is the temporary transfer of some of the policyowner's rights, made as security for a loan. When the loan is repaid, the rights transferred are ordinarily reassigned to the policyowner. Modern collateral assignment forms usually contain a line for the beneficiary's signature. If an irrevocable beneficiary does not consent to a collateral assignment, the beneficiary's rights are superior to the assignee's. According to the majority rule, a collateral assignee's rights are superior to the rights of a revocable beneficiary. An absolute assignment intended to secure a loan will be treated as a collateral assignment, as a general rule.

The insurer has a crucial role in the assignment process. Many policies are drafted with assignment clauses governing the method of assignment or requiring the insurer's consent. These clauses must be complied with, or the insurer will not be bound. Moreover, the insurer must be notified of the assignment. The insurer will not be liable to the assignee if it pays proceeds to other persons in ignorance of the assignee's rights. However, where the insurer has notice of a valid assignment, it cannot pay proceeds without regard to the assignee's rights.

The insurer does not take responsibility for the validity of an assignment. It has no control and, ordinarily, no knowledge of the factors which govern such validity. However, if it does know that the assignment might not be valid, it cannot disregard that knowledge.

The formal requirements for a valid assignment, binding on all parties, are compliance with the policy terms, legal capacity of the assignor, and notice to the insurer. A written assignment and delivery of the assignment, or of the policy, are sometimes required. The assignee of a collateral assignment need not have an insurable interest. An absolute assignee does not need an insurable interest if the assignment was made in good faith and not with intent to evade the law against wagering in human life, according to the majority rule.

The rights of successive assignees depend upon the order of the assignments in jurisdictions following the American rule. The first assignee's rights are superior to the rights of a later assignee. Under the English rule, the rights of the first assignee to give notice to the insurer are superior, regardless of the order of the assignments.

The beneficiary, like the policyowner, can transfer his or her rights in the policy before the insured's death. After the insured's death, ordinarily, even a policy provision prohibiting assignment will not prevent the beneficiary from transferring his or her right to the proceeds.

Rights in a life insurance policy can be transferred in ways other than by a specific assignment of the policy. Intestate succession, wills, property settlement agreements, divorce decrees, sales of assets, or equitable assignments often effect such transfers.

ILLUSTRATIVE CASE

This case involves a collateral assignment of a life insurance policy to a bank. The court discusses the rights of the assignee, assignor, and insurer.

JEFFERSON TRUST & SAVINGS BANK OF PEORIA,
Plaintiff-Appellee
v.
THE LINCOLN NATIONAL LIFE INSURANCE CO.,
Defendant-Appellant[20]
Appellate Court of Ilinois, Third District

STENGEL, Justice.

The assignee of a life insurance policy, Jefferson Trust & Savings Bank of Peoria (plaintiff), brought suit against defendant [Lincoln] National Life Insurance Company to recover the cash surrender value of the policy. Both parties filed mo-

---

[20]27 Ill. App. 3d 435, 325 N.E.2d 384 (1975).

tions for summary judgment. The circuit court entered summary judgment in favor of plaintiff and defendant appeals.

The policy contained an "automatic Premium Loan Privilege" which provided that any premium not paid before the expiration of the grace period was to be treated as paid and charged automatically as a loan against the policy with interest from the due date of the premium. Insured assigned the policy to plaintiff bank as collateral security for a loan, and the assignment was filed with the defendant as required by the policy. Both before and after the assignment, defendant made numerous loans under the automatic premium loan privilege. When plaintiff later surrendered the policy to obtain the cash surrender value, defendant set off all outstanding loans plus interest, and tendered $3,009.46. Plaintiff refused the tender, filed this action, and was awarded judgment for $7,768.50, from which judgment defendant appeals.

The amount in dispute represents loans against the policy made by defendant after the assignment. Plaintiff contends that the automatic loan privilege was revoked by the terms of the assignment and that notice of the assignment was sufficient to accomplish revocation. Defendant denies that notice of the assignment was written notice of revocation as required under the terms of the policy.

Paragraph 13 of the policy provides:

The Automatic Premium Loan Privilege will be granted either at the request of the Insured in the application for this policy or upon subsequent written request received by the Company at its Home Office prior to the expiration of the grace period allowed for payment of any premium. *This Privilege may be revoked at any time upon written notice to the Company at its Home Office* (emphasis added).

If the request has been made for the Automatic Premium Loan Privilege and such request remains unrevoked, any premium not paid before the expiration of the grace period shall be treated as paid and charged automatically as a loan against this policy with interest from the due date of the premium.

The assignment did not contain specific words of revocation of the loan privilege. Plaintiff contends, however, that specific words of revocation are unnecessary, and that the assignment given to defendant contained provisions so inconsistent with the automatic loan privilege that the privilege was revoked. Under the terms of the assignment, plaintiff acquired the sole right to obtain loans on the policy and had no obligation to pay premiums or interest on policy loans. Plaintiff argues that these two provisions of the assignment were patently inconsistent with the continuation of the automatic premium loan privilege which would permit the previous policyholder to impair the cash value of the policy by refusing to make payment of premiums.

Is such an inconsistency sufficient to revoke the automatic loan privilege? We think not.

In *Hoffman ex rel. Keithley v. New York Life Ins. Co.*, 230 Ill. App. 533 (2d dist., 1923), the insured executed two notes in lieu of premium payments which were liens against the policy, and then assigned the policy as security for a debt. The insured subsequently executed renewal notes against the policy. The assignee paid two annual premiums, and then applied for the cash surrender value of the policy. The assignee denied the right of the insurance company to deduct the outstanding loans from the cash value because he had no notice of the loans. The court held that the assignee stood in the shoes of his assignor, that it was his duty to ascertain the rights of the insured under the policy, and that the loans should be deducted from the cash surrender value.

Courts in other jurisdictions have similarly held that the cash surrender value due the assignee was subject to a setoff for premium loans made subsequent to the assignment, and have held that where the assignee has the policy with full opportunity to examine its provisions, the assignee is subject to the rights and conditions of that policy. In both of these cases the insurance companies had notice of the assignment.

The parties here agree that the original insurance policy was a valid binding contract and that as assignee of the policy, plaintiff took the policy subject to the same terms and conditions as the insured. The rule in Illinois is well established that an insurance policy is not a negotiable instrument and that an assignee takes subject to the conditions expressed in the policy and is in no better position than his assignor. We believe it is clear that, in the absence of a revocation, assignment of the policy in the case before us would not preclude defendant from setting off subsequent premium loans in computing the cash surrender value due plaintiff.

In support of its contention that the loan provision was revoked, plaintiff urges application of the rule that permits revocation of an offer by an act which is inconsistent with the continuation of the offer and which is brought to the attention of the non-revoking party. This rule can have no application in the case before us where a contract is already in existence and binding upon the parties in all of its provisions. Plaintiff also points to a comparable rule applicable to termination of a principal-agent relationship, citing *Van Houton v. Trust Co. of Chicago,* 413 Ill. 310, 109 N.E. 2d 187 (1952), where the court held that express notice by the agent to the principal that the agency is terminated is not essential. The court there stated the rule to be ". . . that *unless the parties have manifested otherwise* to each other, a principal or agent has notice that authority to do an act has terminated, or is suspended, if he knows, or has reason to know, should know, or has been given notification of the occurrence of an event from which the inference reasonably would be drawn." [Emphasis added.] This rule cannot support plaintiff's theory because here the contractual requirement of written notice is such a manifestation as would remove this case from the rule by the terms of the rule itself.

We must reject plaintiff's contention that the rules of law set forth in the cases involving revocation of offers and termination of agencies have any bearing on the case before us. Here the assignee stands in the position of its assignor and is subject to the automatic premium loan provision until it acts to revoke in writing, and such revocation is not effected by implication or mere constructive notice from the assignor by reason of the instrument of assignment.

If the premium loan provision had been revoked, either expressly or constructively, the insured's failure to pay premiums could have resulted in a forfeiture of the policy with an even greater impairment of the cash surrender value than would result from loans made under the automatic premium loan privilege. We conclude that the terms of the assignment permitted insured to impair the cash surrender value in any event and that plaintiff may actually be in a better position now than if revocation had occurred.

We hold that plaintiff, as assignee of a life insurance contract, took subject to the terms and conditions of the contract, including the provision that the automatic premium loan privilege could be revoked only upon written notice of revocation to defendant. The notice of assignment of the policy by the insured was not sufficient written notice to revoke the privilege. All outstanding premium loans plus interest must be set off against the cash surrender value of the policy.

The order of the circuit court granting summary judgment to plaintiff on the issue of liability is reversed, and defendant's motion for summary judgment is granted, and the cause is remanded for determination of damages consistent with this opinion.

Judgment reversed and remanded.

STOUDER, P.J., and BARRY, J., concur.

QUESTIONS FOR REVIEW

1. What is an assignment?
2. How does an absolute assignment differ from a collateral assignment?
3. What are the requisites for a valid assignment?
4. Is notice to the insurer essential for the validity of an assignment? Is such notice essential for any other purpose?
5. Under what circumstances does an absolute assignment constitute the making of a gift? A sale?
6. Why do most policies state that the insurer assumes no responsibility for the validity or effect of an assignment?
7. Contrast the rights of the beneficiary with those of a collateral assignee:
   a. When the beneficiary is revocable. When the beneficiary is irrevocable.
   b. When the beneficiary has joined in making the assignment. When the beneficiary has not joined in making the assignment.
8. What policyowner rights are transferred to the assignee under the American Bankers Association collateral assignment form? What policyowner rights are reserved to the assignor under the American Bankers Association collateral assignment form?
9. How have the courts generally interpreted the rights of the assignee and beneficiary when a policy is assigned absolutely for collateral purposes?
10. Describe the American and English rules regarding the rights of successive assignees.
11. What is meant by an equitable assignment?

CHAPTER 15

Lapse and Reinstatement

LAPSE AND EXPIRATION
REINSTATEMENT LAWS
REINSTATEMENT PROVISIONS
    Insurability
    Payment of Unpaid Premiums, with Interest
DEATH DURING THE REINSTATEMENT
APPLICATION REVIEW
CONTINUATION OF THE ORIGINAL CONTRACT
CONTESTABILITY OF THE REINSTATED POLICY
REINSTATEMENT AND THE SUICIDE CLAUSE
ADDITION OF NEW CONTRACT TERMS
LAW GOVERNING THE REINSTATED POLICY
SUMMARY

If a life insurance premium is not paid by the end of the grace period, the policy lapses. Thereafter, the policy is effective only as provided by its non-forfeiture section, if any. However, most life insurance contracts contain a reinstatement provision which enables the policyowner to return a lapsed policy to a premium-paying status and restores the benefits and privileges previously enjoyed.

The reinstatement provision gives the policyowner a right which can be valuable. If the policy has been in effect for several years, it might include privileges which are not available in policies currently offered. For example, the policy might contain settlement options which are no longer offered or which provide for more favorable interest or mortality assumptions than those in the insurer's new policies. Policy loan interest rates in a reinstated policy might be lower than rates in new policies. Prematurity rights attain significant value sooner in a reinstated policy than in one newly issued. Premium payments might be lower for the old policy than for the new policy. Ordinarily, the procedure for reinstatement is simpler than that involved in applying for a new policy.

Nevertheless, it is sometimes advisable for the owner of a lapsed policy to apply for a new one, rather than reinstate the original policy. The policyowner might prefer to have a universal or variable life insurance policy, rather than reinstate a regular whole life insurance policy. In order to reinstate a policy, the policyowner must pay all the back premiums with interest. Thus, if several years have passed since the policy lapsed, it could require a large cash outlay to reinstate it. Moreover, as the insured must be currently insurable if the policy is to be reinstated, insurability will not be a factor in deciding whether to reinstate the original policy or obtain a new one. If the insured is currently insurable, either can be done.

The purpose of this chapter is to describe lapse and reinstatement, and the major legal problems related to reinstatement.

LAPSE AND EXPIRATION

The word *lapse* has been defined as a "default in premiums before a policy has a nonforfeiture value."[1] After the policy has developed a nonforfeiture value, it is said to lapse "except as to the nonforfeiture benefits." The policy will expire on the termination of the applicable nonforfeiture benefit. For example, a policy might lapse for nonpayment of the premium due at the end of the grace period on October 2, 1988, but expire 10 years and 112 days later, on January 22, 1999, when the extended term insurance runs out.

As another example, the policyowner might decide to receive the cash surrender value after the policy has lapsed. Once the policy has been surrendered for its cash value, it expires.

REINSTATEMENT LAWS

Most states have laws requiring that life insurance policies issued or delivered in the state include a reinstatement provision. For example, the New York statute requires that life insurance policies contain the following:

> [A provision] that the policy shall be reinstated at any time within three years from the date of default, unless the cash surrender value has been exhausted or the period of extended insurance has expired, if the policyholder makes application, provides evidence of insurability, including good health, satisfactory to the insurer, pays all overdue premiums with interest at a rate not exceeding six per centum per annum compounded annually, and pays or reinstates any other policy indebtedness with interest at a rate not exceeding the applicable policy loan rate or rates determined in accordance with the policy's provisions. This provision shall be required only if the policy provides for termination or lapse in the event of a default in making a regularly scheduled premium payment.[2]

---

[1] L. DAVIDS, DICTIONARY OF INSURANCE 173 (6th ed. 1983).
[2] N.Y. INS. LAW § 3203(10) (McKinney 1985).

This may be contrasted with the Illinois statute, which requires:

A provision that in event of default in premium payments the value of the policy is applied to the purchase of other insurance as provided in this Section, and if such insurance is in force and the original policy is not surrendered to the company and cancelled, the policy may be reinstated within 3 years from such default, upon evidence of insurability satisfactory to the company and payment of arrears of premiums and the payment or reinstatement of any other indebtedness to the company upon the policy, with interest on the premiums at the rate of not exceeding 6% per annum payable annually and with interest on the indebtedness at the rate of not exceeding the rate prescribed by Section 229.5.[3]

A literal reading of the Illinois statute suggests that reinstatement does not have to be granted for term policies without a cash value, or for policies which have not been in force long enough to acquire a cash value. Nor is the granting of reinstatement required after any extended term insurance has expired, or after the cash value has been paid.

As a general rule, however, insurers are more liberal than the reinstatement statutes require. Reinstatement is usually to the insurer's advantage. Thus, insurers customarily include reinstatement provisions in their term policies, whether or not the statute requires it. They generally do not take advantage of their right to deny reinstatement after extended term insurance has expired.

Nevertheless, life policies usually forbid reinstatement if the policy has been surrendered for cash. The surrender of a policy is a deliberate act by the policyowner. It is not unreasonable to consider that cash surrender terminates the contractual relationship. Insurers discourage cash surrender by prohibiting reinstatement after cash surrender.

REINSTATEMENT PROVISIONS

Even where no statute or policy provision gives the policyowner the right to reinstate, the insurer and policyowner could agree to reinstate the policy. A policy provision is desirable, however, as it guarantees the right to reinstate, clarifies the terms of reinstatement, and helps to assure that all policyowners will be treated uniformly.

The reinstatement provision of a life insurance policy usually provides that, if the policy lapses for nonpayment of premium, it can be reinstated at any time within three years from the date of lapse. In some policies the period is five years. The policyowner must furnish evidence of the insured's insurability, including good health, which is satisfactory to the insurer. All unpaid back premiums must be paid with interest. If a policy loan was in

---

[3]ILL. REV. STAT. ch. 73, ¶ 836(1)(i) (1985) (Ill. Ins. Code § 224(1)(i)).

effect at the date of lapse, the loan must be repaid with interest, or the loan and interest must be restored as a lien against the policy proceeds.

The reinstatement provision in the illustrative policy in Appendix B reads as follows:

> If this Policy lapses due to an unpaid premium, it may be reinstated subject to the following conditions:
>
> 1. The Insured must be alive and still insurable by our standards; and
>
> 2. Any indebtedness which existed at the time of termination must either be paid or reinstated with interest compounded annually at the loan interest rate shown on page three; and
>
> 3. Each unpaid premium must be paid, with interest of 6% per annum compounded annually, from its due date to the reinstatement date; and
>
> 4. The request for reinstatement must be made by you in writing and submitted to our Home Office within 5 years after the date the Policy lapses; and
>
> 5. If you are not the Insured, the request for reinstatement must also be signed by the Insured if age 15 or older, last birthday, on the reinstatement date.
>
> A Policy which has been surrendered for its cash value may not be reinstated.

This provision is typical in most respects. It prohibits reinstatement if the policy has been surrendered for its cash value. However, expiration of the policy after it has been in effect as extended term insurance will not prevent the policyowner from reinstating the policy. This is more liberal than the provision required by the usual reinstatement statute.

Insurability

The illustrative policy states that "[t]he insured must be alive and still insurable by our standards" if the policy is to be reinstated. This requirement that the insured be insurable at the time of reinstatement prevents adverse selection.[4] Adverse selection means the tendency of persons who are poorer risks to seek insurance to a greater extent than do persons who are better risks.

It might be argued that to reinstate a lapsed policy after the insured has become uninsurable would place the insurer in no worse position than if the insured had become uninsurable while the policy continued on a premium-paying basis. This would be true if all lapsed policies were reinstated. As a matter of fact, they are not, and it is those insureds who have become unin-

---

[4] Adverse selection is also called "antiselection" or "selection against the insurer."

surable who are most interested in reinstatement. Life insurance involves the application of the law of large numbers to a group of insureds whose risks of death are reasonably comparable. Those who are still insurable are less apt to apply for reinstatement. Therefore, the mortality experience of the insurer would be adversely affected if reinstatement were permitted without the insurability requirement.

As a general rule, *insurability* has the same meaning, as used in connection with reinstatement, that it has in connection with an original application, except as to the insured's age. The insurer is free to consider such factors as habits, occupation, and finances, as well as the good health of the applicant for reinstatement, just as if it were considering an application for a new policy of life insurance.

Thus, the great majority of courts have held that *insurability* is a broader term than *good health* and includes the other factors just mentioned. This point of view is expressed in *Kallman v. Equitable Life Assurance Society*.[5] In that case, the policyowner-insured met the requirements of insurability as to his health, but reinstatement was refused because of his financial situation and the large amount of life insurance he was already carrying on his life. The insurer's refusal to reinstate was challenged in a court action filed shortly after the insured had committed suicide. The court upheld the insurer's decision saying:

> The distinction between "good health" and "insurability" might be illustrated in the case of a criminal condemned to death. On the eve of his execution he might be found to be in perfect physical condition, but it could not be reasonably contended that his situation did not affect his insurability. There are numerous circumstances which affect insurability. In Ginsberg v. Eastern Life Insurance Co. of New York . . . the court said that it is common knowledge that an insurance company will not reinstate a policy where it is known that the insured is financially insolvent and the circumstances show probability of suicide. . . .
>
> We are of the opinion that the language of the statute and of the policy "evidence of insurability satisfactory to the company" does not limit the inquiry upon an application for reinstatement to the good health or good physical condition of the insured. . . . Here, the insured's pecuniary circumstances coupled with his heavy over insurance, entirely out of line with his incoming financial condition, had a definite bearing upon his longevity and created a moral hazard which directly affected his insurability.

There are a few cases which support the position that the term *insurability* means the same as *good health* in connection with reinstatement.[6] This is decidedly a minority view, however.

---

[5]248 A.D. 146, 288 N.Y. S. 1032 (1936).
[6]*See, e.g.,* Missouri State Life Ins. Co. v. Hearne, 226 S.W. 789 (Tex. Civ. App. 1920); Smith v. Bankers Nat'l Life Ins. Co., 130 Neb. 552, 265 N.W. 546 (1936).

The illustrative policy reinstatement provision requires that the insured be "still insurable by [the insurer's] standards." Reinstatement provisions often require that evidence of insurability "satisfactory to the insurer" be furnished. There have been several interpretations of the meaning of the phrase "satisfactory to the insurer." On the one hand, it has been held that the judgment and conscience of the insurer's officers are controlling,[7] and, on the other hand, it has been held that if there is reasonable compliance with the insurer's insurability requirements, reinstatement should be compelled.[8]

The majority rule is that the courts will consider the practices of other insurers and judge whether the insurer's decision is reasonable on that basis. This position was summarized by the California Supreme Court in *Kennedy v. Occidental Life Insurance Co.*[9] as follows:

> The overwhelming weight of authority is to the effect that an agreement to reinstate an insurance policy upon "satisfactory evidence" of insurability does not give the insurer the power to act arbitrarily or capriciously, but that evidence which would be satisfactory to a reasonable insurer is all that is required.

Payment of Unpaid Premiums, With Interest

When the policyowner reinstates the policy, the insurer has the right under statute and case law to require the payment of all unpaid premiums, with interest. This puts the insurer in the position in which it would have been had the policy never lapsed and the insurer had had the premiums to invest. The illustrative policy requires that "[e]ach unpaid premium must be paid, with interest of 6 percent per annum compounded annually, from its due date to the reinstatement date."

The amount of interest which can be charged by the insurer in order to reinstate is spelled out in the statutes of many states. The most common rate is six percent, although a few states allow eight percent.

DEATH DURING THE REINSTATEMENT APPLICATION REVIEW

The conditions in the reinstatement provision of an insurance policy are conditions precedent. They must be met before the reinstatement can become effective. Therefore, if the insured dies after the reinstatement application has been submitted but before the conditions have been met, the beneficiary can receive only the nonforfeiture benefits under the lapsed policy, if any. In other words, merely completing an application for reinstatement is not enough to effect reinstatement if all the conditions are not met.

---

[7]Conway v. Minnesota Mut. Life Ins. Co., 62 Wash. 59, 112 P. 1106 (1911).
[8]Lane v. New York Life Ins. Co., 147 S.C. 333, 145 S.E. 196 (1928).
[9]18 Cal. 2d 627, 117 P.2d 3 (1941).

For example, suppose Therese Bixby is the owner of a life insurance policy insuring her life. The policy has a reinstatement provision identical to that in the illustrative policy in Appendix B. Ms. Bixby's policy lapses, and the extended term insurance becomes effective. Three years later, after the extended term insurance has expired, Ms. Bixby applies to have the policy reinstated and submits evidence of insurability. Two days after submitting the reinstatement application, Ms. Bixby dies in a fire without having submitted the unpaid premiums. The beneficiary will not be entitled to the benefits because Ms. Bixby failed to meet all the conditions for reinstatement.

Now suppose Ms. Bixby submitted the unpaid premiums with the reinstatement application. She dies before the insurer has had an opportunity to review the application and evidence of insurability. If the evidence of insurability clearly indicates that Ms. Bixby was insurable at the time of application, what is the insurer's liability?

The majority view is as follows: Where the policyowner has a contractual right to reinstate the policy and has performed the conditions precedent before the insured's death, the reinstatement will be effective, even though the insurer has not yet approved the reinstatement at the time of death.[10] Illustrative of this view is *Bowie v. Bankers Life Co.*,[11] a federal case construing Colorado law in which the policyowner-insured had applied for reinstatement, furnishing evidence of insurability satisfactory to a reasonable insurer and otherwise meeting all requirements specified in the policy. Before the insurer had approved the reinstatement application, the insured was drowned when his automobile plunged over a bridge and into a canal. The court held the reinstatement effective, saying:

> Where a policy contains a provision of this kind, where proof of insurability which is not open to valid objection as to form or substance is submitted within the authorized time, where payment of all premiums presently in arrears plus interest thereon is tendered, where the insured thus fully complies with the conditions of his contract, and where his death is wholly accidental and in no way involved in his proof of insurability, the policy is reinstated and the restoration relates back to the time of the submission of the application and the tender of the premiums.

On the other hand, a minority of courts take the position that the insurer must be permitted a reasonable time in which to approve or disapprove the application for reinstatement. If the insured should die during that time, the policy is not reinstated.[12]

---

[10]Annot., 164 A.L.R. 1057 (1946) *supp.* 105 A.L.R. 478 (1936).

[11]105 F.2d 806 (10th Cir. 1939), *aff'd on rehearing,* 121 F.2d 779 (1941).

[12]Exchange Trust Co. v. Capitol Life Ins. Co., 49 F.2d 133 (10th Cir. 1931); Rocky Mt. Sav. & Trust Co. v. Aetna Life Ins. Co., 199 N.C. 465, 154 S.E. 743 (1930); Gressler v. New York Life Ins. Co., 108 Utah 182, 163 P.2d 324 (1945).

The insurer must act promptly on an application for reinstatement, however, just as it must act promptly on an original application. As a general rule, the courts hold that an unreasonable delay in acting on the reinstatement application constitutes a waiver of the insurer's right to decline. Illustrative of this point of view is *Waldner v. Metropolitan Life Insurance Co.*[13] where the Kansas Supreme Court said:

> The defendant [the insurer] could not indefinitely hold the application for reinstatement without disapproving it, retain the money of the insured until long after her death, and thereafter escape liability on the ground the insured had not provided satisfactory proof of insurability.

CONTINUATION OF THE ORIGINAL CONTRACT

By the great weight of authority, a life insurance contract which is reinstated under the terms of a reinstatement provision is a continuation of the original contract and not the creation of a new contract.[14] Thus, reinstatement is ordinarily considered the exercise of a contractual right—cancelling the forfeiture—under the original policy, rather than the effecting of a new contract.

A few courts have held that the reinstated contract is a new contract, rather than a continuation of the original contract.[15] This is particularly apt to be true where the policyowner does not have a contractual right to reinstate[16] or where the policy terms are changed.[17]

Whether the reinstated contract is continuing or new can be an important question. First, the application of the incontestability and suicide provisions might differ if the contract was new, rather than continuing. Second, the insurer might have a right to add new conditions to a new contract, but not to one that is continuing. Finally, a continuing contract might be governed by laws different from those governing a new contract.

CONTESTABILITY OF THE REINSTATED POLICY

There are three points of view which have been taken by the courts regarding the contestability of a reinstated policy. The viewpoint in the great majority of jurisdictions is that the contestable period runs anew for the same period after reinstatement, but that the new contestable period applies only

---

[13]149 Kan. 287, 87 P.2d 515 (1939).

[14]*See, e.g.,* Trapp v. Metropolitan Life Ins. Co., 70 F.2d 976 (8th Cir. 1934); Prudential Ins. Co. v. Mason, 301 Mass. 82, 16 N.E.2d 69 (1938).

[15]*See, e.g.,* MacDonald v. Metropolitan Life Ins. Co., 304 Pa. 213, 155 A. 491 (1931).

[16]*See, e.g.,* Johnson v. Life Ins. Co. of Virginia, 169 So. 159 (La. Ct. App. 1936).

[17]Franklin Life Ins. Co. v. Parish, 109 F.2d 276 (5th Cir. 1940).

to statements made in the application for reinstatement.[18] The majority rule was explained in the case of *Sellwood v. Equitable Life Insurance Co. of Iowa*[19] as follows:

> The authorities reason that, since it is fundamental that fraud vitiates everything into which it enters . . . it cannot be supposed that the parties intended that an insured should have what Judge Learned Hand . . . characterized as "a license forever to cheat the insurer"; and that the reasons for the public policy that, absent fraud, statements by an insured in an application for insurance should be deemed to be representations and not warranties and that a limit should be set on the time within which the insurer should have the right to contest the policy for false statements of the insured in an application, apply to an application for reinstatement the same as to one for the original issuance of the policy itself. This view has been adopted by many authorities, regardless of whether the reinstatement be regarded as the continuation of the original contract of insurance or the making of a new one. . . . We adopt the rule that, upon reinstatement of a lapsed life insurance policy, the incontestable clause runs anew as to misrepresentations in the application for reinstatement. This rule is not only supported by the weight of authority, but also is a just and fair one.

States which have resolved the question of contestability by statutory enactment have adopted this majority rule. For instance, the West Virginia Insurance Code contains the following:

> The reinstatement of any policy of life insurance or annuity contract hereafter delivered or issued for delivery in this State may be contested on account of fraud or misrepresentation of facts material to the reinstatement only for the same period following reinstatement and with the same conditions and exceptions as the policy provides with respect to contestability after original issuance.[20]

A second and minor group of cases holds that the reinstatement itself is a separate agreement which, since it has no incontestable provision, can be contested for fraud at any time.

A very few courts have held that once the original contestable period has expired, the insurer is powerless to contest the policy. Thus, even if reinstatement has been procured by fraud, if the original contestable period has expired, the policy remains incontestable after reinstatement. The Arkansas and Utah courts adopted this position, but these states later adopted the majority position by statute. In 1986, the Supreme Court of North Carolina

---

[18] Annot., 23 A.L.R. 3d 743 (1969).
[19] 230 Minn. 529, 42 N.W.2d 346 (1950).
[20] W. VA. CODE § 33–13–26 (1982).

held that a policy could not be contested for misrepresentations in the reinstatement application made after the original contestable period had expired.[21]

An excellent summary of the three different views on this question is found in *Johnson v. Great Northern Life Insurance Co.,*[22] a North Dakota Supreme Court case decided in January 1945. In this case, the court said:

> . . . Neither the statutes nor the policy under consideration contain any provision to the effect that the incontestable clause in any way limits the right to contest a reinstatement. In such circumstances there seem to be three rules which find support in the authorities. One of these is that an incontestable clause in a policy has no application whatever to a reinstatement and the reinstatement may be contested at any time. Another is that an incontestable clause will prevent a contest of a reinstatement if the time in which the original policy was contestable has expired. The third rule is that the incontestability provision applies to the reinstatement in the same manner as it did to the original issuance of the policy; that is to say, the time within which the reinstatement may be contested is the same period thereafter as that within which the original policy might have been contested, and the grounds for such contest are limited to those which arise out of the negotiations leading to the reinstatement.
>
> The rule last stated appears to be the majority rule. . . . It is also the rule which seems to us to be best founded upon reason. We would reject the rule, first above stated, because, while not contrary to the contract or to express statute, it is contrary to legislative policy fairly to be inferred. This rule rests also upon the conception that the reinstatement is a new contract which is contrary to our holding in *Rott v. Provident Life Insurance Co., supra.* The second rule completely eliminates any requirements of good faith in the negotiations for reinstatement and is contrary to our holding in *New York Life Insurance Co. v. Hansen, supra.*
>
> We therefore adopt the rule last stated and hold that defendant may contest its reinstatement of the instant policy only during the same period of time thereafter as was fixed for contesting the original policy, or upon grounds expressly excluded from the operation of the incontestability provision.

One further point must be mentioned in connection with the contestability of a reinstated policy. This has to do with attachment of a copy of the reinstatement application to the policy. As a general rule, when a request for reinstatement reaches the insurer, the policy is in the hands of the policyowner. For that reason, the courts generally have held that it is not necessary that a copy of the reinstatement application be attached to the policy in order for the insurer to avail itself of a defense based upon misrepresentation in the application. However, some of the states have enacted statutes requir-

---

[21]Chavis v. Southern Ins. Co., 318 N.C. 259, 347 S.E.2d 425 (1986).
[22]73 N.D. 572, 17 N.W.2d 337 (1945).

ing the insurer to furnish a copy of the application to the policyowner or beneficiary on request.

REINSTATEMENT AND THE SUICIDE CLAUSE

Where the policy contains a suicide clause, usually the suicide period will not run anew from the date of reinstatement.[23] Most courts reach this conclusion on the theory that reinstatement does not create a new contract, but rather revives the original contract and continues it in force as from its original date.

Even in a jurisdiction where the reinstatement is considered to give rise to a new contract, the language of the policy might be such that the suicide clause will not run anew upon reinstatement. This was the holding in *Tatum v. Guardian Life Insurance Co.,*[24] an opinion written by a renowned judge, Learned Hand. This case contains an excellent discussion of the suicide and incontestable clauses, as they relate to reinstatement, as follows:

> Were we free to decide the point as res nova,[25] we should say that the reinstatement of a lapsed policy is not a new contract at all, when the insured can revive it merely by satisfying the company of his insurability and by paying the arrears. Those are the conditions upon what by the lapse has become a conditional obligation; but which is still an obligation from which the insurer cannot withdraw at will, being bound to approve if he is in fact satisfied . . . But although we are . . . to consider the policy as though it has been issued anew on February 14, 1933, it by no means follows that in construing it we must read it as though it spoke throughout from that date. By its very terms the policy is "reinstated"; the parties have thus chosen a word which presupposes, not a new contract, but the revival of an old one. The insured must pay not a single premium, but all arrears; and thereafter only at the old rate, however many years have passed. All benefits—*e.g.,* the surrender and loan value, term and paid-up insurance—go again into force as of the original date; they do not begin anew. Moreover, in the case at bar the defence of suicide was limited to one year from "the date hereof"; that is, the date upon the policy . . . Perhaps too the contrast between that phrase in the policy at bar and "the date of issue" in the incontestability clause, may be taken as some indication of a change of intent. Judged textually therefore, there is very good reason for holding that the clause speaks from the original date. It is of course true that our interpretation exposes the insurer to a risk which it would otherwise escape. An insured who had let a policy lapse might at any time within three years conceive the notion of getting it reinstated and then killing himself. Nevertheless we are disposed to hold that even on the theory of a new contract, which we

---

[23] Annot., 37 A.L.R. 3d 933, § 8 (1971).
[24] 75 F.2d 476 (2d Cir. 1935).
[25] *Res nova* means "a new matter."

should not ourselves have adopted, the reinstated policy is to be referred pro tanto[26] to the date of the original; at least that insurer who prepared the instrument must bear the doubts, so far as there are any. In the only decisions in which the point has arisen this has been the result . . . Though the new contract be a reissue of the policy as of the date of the renewal, it would force beyond all reason the meaning of the incontesta-bility clause to say that it barred a fraud which did not even exist when the policy became incontestable. The clause is one of limitation, not a license forever to cheat the insurer; unless construed in that preposterous way it must be an exception to the general principle that the policy as reinstated speaks from its old date. It may be the only exception; at least the suicide clause is not one.

Thus, Judge Hand ruled in this case that the suicide clause ran from the original policy date and not from the date of reinstatement, even though the law of the jurisdiction was that a reinstated policy was a new contract.

ADDITION OF NEW CONTRACT TERMS

The courts have held that an insurer cannot impose new contract terms at the time of reinstatement if the policyowner has a contractual right to rein-state the policy.[27] Some insurers have, for example, attempted to add a war hazard exclusion clause at the time of reinstatement. Assume that, at a time when an insurer was issuing policies without war hazard exclusion clauses, it issued to Oliver Ewing, age 23, a whole life policy with a reinstatement clause. Three years later, the policy lapsed for nonpayment of the premium. Two years after lapse, Mr. Ewing applies for reinstatement, submitting satis-factory evidence of insurability and the unpaid premiums plus interest. At this time, the insurer is issuing all of its new policies with a war hazard exclusion clause if the applicant is between the ages of 18 and 45. Can the insurer include a war hazard exclusion clause in Mr. Ewing's policy, as it is currently doing in all new policies issued to applicants in Mr. Ewing's age group? The cases indicate that it cannot.

In *Schiel v. New York Life Insurance Co.,*[28] a federal court, construing Arizona law, held that an insurer could not add an aviation hazard exclusion clause on reinstatement of a policy insuring the life of a prospective military pilot. There, the court said:

The Company made no claim that Schiel had become uninsurable for or-dinary life purposes in the amount originally written; in fact it conceded by its conduct that he was insurable for those purposes and in that amount. It declined, however, to reinstate the ordinary life policy except

---

[26]*Pro tanto* means "to a certain extent."
[27]Hogan v. John Hancock Mut. Life Ins. Co., 195 F.2d 834 (3d Cir. 1952).
[28]178 F.2d 729 (9th Cir. 1949), *cert. denied,* 339 U.S. 931 (1950).

upon a condition importing a concept of insurability at variance with the policy as written. This we think it might not do.

An understanding of the view taken may require some further analysis of the terms of the original policy. The clause relating to occupation has been quoted earlier. It provides that the policy is free of conditions as to residence, travel, occupation, and military and naval service . . . [T]he insurer had contracted that the policy was free of conditions pertaining to any legitimate occupation, whether in connection with the armed services or otherwise. The condition imposed on reinstatement of the ordinary life coverage for all practical purposes nullified the occupation clause. Under guise of reinstatement the insurer undertook to rewrite the contract in such fashion as to repudiate a risk assumed at the outset. If it could do that it could with equal facility have excluded altogether the risks of military service or travel, whereas the insured's liberty of action in all those matters was a measure of his insurability fixed and determined by the original contract. Without further laboring the point, we add only that the word "reinstate," as used in the policy, is entitled to be given its ordinary meaning, which is to restore to a former state or position.

This case states the general rule, that the provisions of a reinstated policy cannot be modified by new conditions imposed by the insurer. The rule is summarized in *Occidental Life Insurance Co. v. Fried,*[29] a federal court case construing Connecticut law, as follows:

An application for reinstatement, however, if accepted by the insurer, does not alter the terms and conditions of the basic contract of insurance; they customarily are already embodied in the policy itself, including any endorsements or documents attached. Upon reinstatement, the terms and conditions of the original policy do not change; premium rates, cash surrender value, loan value, beneficiary designation, an insured's indebtedness under the policy—in short, all basic obligations and rights—remain the same. The reinstatement provision is merely another contingent contractual feature of the policy pursuant to which the insured, having permitted his policy to lapse, is entitled, upon compliance with the conditions prescribed therein, including production of satisfactory evidence of insurability, to reinstatement of the original contract.

LAW GOVERNING THE REINSTATED POLICY

The law which governs the reinstated contract might depend on whether the contract is considered continuing or new. For example, laws mandating contract terms which were enacted between the original effective date and the reinstatement date will ordinarily be applicable if the contract is new, but not if it is continuing. In *Johnson v. Life Insurance Co. of Virginia,*[30] a statute

---

[29]245 F. Supp. 211 (D. Conn. 1965).
[30]169 So. 159 (La. Ct. App. 1936).

requiring that, after lapse, an amount equal to the reserve be applied to purchase extended term insurance was enacted after the original policy date, but before reinstatement. The reinstated policy lapsed. The court held that the reinstated contract was new, because the policyowner had no contractual right of reinstatement. Because the reinstated contract was new, it was subject to the statute. The beneficiary was, therefore, entitled to the face amount as extended term insurance.

In addition, a question has sometimes arisen as to which state's laws govern the reinstated policy. If, for example, the policyowner were living in State A when the policy was issued, but living in State B when it was reinstated, the laws of State A might govern if the policy were continuing, whereas State B's laws might govern if it were new.

SUMMARY

If a life insurance premium is not paid by the end of the grace period, the policy lapses except as to any nonforfeiture benefits. However, most life policies contain a reinstatement provision which is required by state statute. As reinstatement is usually to the insurer's advantage, these provisions tend to be more liberal than the reinstatement statutes require.

Reinstatement provisions ordinarily give the policyowner the right to reinstate a lapsed policy at any time within three (or five) years from the date of lapse if the policyowner complies with certain conditions precedent. The conditions precedent generally are as follows: The policyowner must submit to the insurer a reinstatement application; evidence of the insured's insurability, and all unpaid premiums, with interest as stated in the policy, and any policy loans, must be repaid with interest or restored as a lien against the policy proceeds.

Insurability in connection with reinstatement usually has the same meaning as it has in connection with the original application, except for age. Generally, the courts have held that *insurability* is a broader term than merely *good health* and includes such factors as habits, occupation, and finances. Insurability "satisfactory to the insurer," according to the majority view, means insurability satisfactory to a reasonable insurer.

If the insured dies after all the conditions precedent in the reinstatement provision have been complied with, but before the insurer has reviewed and approved the reinstatement application, the reinstatement will, nevertheless, be effective, according to the majority view. The minority view is that the insurer must be permitted a reasonable time in which to accept or reject the reinstatement application. The insurer must act promptly, however, or it might be held to have waived its right to reject the reinstatement application.

A reinstated policy is generally contestable for misstatements in the reinstatement application only, for the same length of time after reinstatement as the length of the original contestable period. However, the suicide period does not ordinarily run anew after reinstatement.

A reinstated policy, by the great weight of authority, is a continuing, rather than a new, contract. Therefore, the insurer is ordinarily prohibited from adding new contract terms to the reinstated policy.

ILLUSTRATIVE CASE

In this case, a beneficiary sued a life insurer for an amount allegedly due under a life policy which allowed reinstatement upon payment of all overdue premiums. A number of legal points in connection with reinstatement were discussed by the court.

DOROTHY M. FEDER, Plaintiff
v.
BANKERS NATIONAL LIFE INSURANCE COMPANY, Defendant [31]
Superior Court of New Jersey, Law Division

STAMLER, J. S. C.

Plaintiff Dorothy M. Feder sues for the proceeds of a life insurance policy issued by defendant Bankers National Life Insurance Co. upon the life of her deceased husband David Feder. The policy issued and was dated June 4, 1962 for the face amount of $50,000. The annual premiums were $854.40 and the insured elected to pay the premiums on a monthly basis of $77 each. The initial June and July 4 premiums were paid by the insured but the premium due August 4 was not paid. Under the standard nonforfeiture provisions of the policy the insured was entitled to a grace period for payment of the overdue premium of 31 days, during which time the policy would remain in force. Paragraph 2 of the policy relating to the grace period provides:

> In the payment of any annual premium or installment thereof under this policy, except the first, a grace of 31 days will be allowed, during which time the policy will remain in force.

On September 5 the grace period expired. On September 11, 1962 the insured executed a written application for reinstatement of the policy which was submitted to the company, together with two monthly premium payments on September 24, representing the monthly payments due in August and September. Following investigation the company approved of reinstatement of the policy on September 24, 1962. The subsequent premium for October was not paid, and again pursuant to the grace period provisions of the contract, the insured was permitted 31 days to make payment of that premium. The insured died on November 10, 1962.

The foregoing represents agreed facts. Only two factual determinations were required to be submitted to the jury.

Plaintiff contended that on November 7, 1962 (three days before death) the insured paid in cash $77 (the monthly premium charge) to defendant through its agent, and that acceptance of the premium constituted a waiver by defendant.

---

[31] 96 N.J. Super. 483, 233 A.2d 395 (1967), *aff'd,* 100 N.J. Super. 458, 242 A.2d 632 (1968), *cert. denied,* 52 N.J. 164, 244 A.2d 296 (1968).

Defendant denied that any such payment was made, and the jury agreed. There is therefore no substance to this contention of plaintiff.

Plaintiff then takes the position that the premium payment made on September 24 created a new premium period and that subsequent premiums were not due on the fourth of each month. She argues that the payment made on that date was for the period September 24 to October 24 and therefore the grace period would have terminated on November 24. Accordingly, it is urged that the assured's death on November 10 occurred within the grace period. Relying for the most part on cases treating with accident and health policies, plaintiff states that the company cannot claim a premium for any period of time in which no coverage is afforded. These contentions implicitly contain the acknowledged rule that no contractual obligation is supportable without underlying consideration.

The question then is: Does the acceptance on September 24 of the reinstatement application and premium create a new and different contract or is it the revival of the old?

Plaintiff contends that it is a new contract, with September 24 as its premium date. Defendant asserts that it is a reinstatement of the old contract, the premium date of which is fixed at September 4.

The authorities support defendant's view. The following relevant language is found in 3A Appleman, Insurance Law and Practice, § 1971, p. 700 (1967):

> It has been held that a reinstatement can only be brought about by a valid contract between the parties. To this end, there must be a meeting of minds of the parties, application and acceptance, valid consideration, and full knowledge of the circumstances under which the application is made and the money paid. Under this rule, the parties have the right to fix the terms of such reinstatement.
>
> The foregoing rule concerns the contract governing the reinstatement, which contract has its inception when the insured applies for reinstatement and its termination upon the acceptance by the insurer of that application. The question logically arises, then, as to whether the new policy is itself a different contract, a continuation of the intermediate contract, or a revival of the old.
>
> On this point, no case seems to hold that the intermediate contract, that is, the contract inducing the reinstatement, continues. There is a division of authority, however, upon the question as to whether the old contract is thereby automatically revived. A few courts have held that a new contract of insurance is thereby created, containing new warranties, new conditions, and the like, just as if no prior policy had ever existed. This is definitely a minority holding. The overwhelming majority of courts hold that the old contract is thereby reinstated and revived, and the new policy is merely a continuation of the old coverage.

As noted, most of the cases cited by plaintiff deal with reinstatement of accident or health policies. It is clear that life insurance policies must fall into a different category. A reinstated life policy continues at the same premium rate, instead of increasing to the age at which insurance is reinstated; the incontestability clauses and suicide provisions run from the earlier date; the cash surrender and loan value are reached at an earlier date; paid-up extended term options are sooner reached. There can be no doubt about the essential and important equities and reservations of right in a life policy over and beyond those of a reinstated accident and health policy. *Cf. Kampf v. Franklin Life Ins. Co.,* 33 N.J. 36, 161 A.2d 717 (1960), where the court stressed the importance of the "birth" date of a life policy and the advantages of an earlier "birth" date.

In *Acacia Mutual Life Ass'n v. Kaul,* 114 N.J.Eq. 491, 169 A. 36 (Ch.1933), the court said:

> The reinstatement of the policy was not the issuance of a new policy nor the reissuance of the original policy. It was the waiver of the lapse of the original policy, and the reinstatement of that policy in full force and effect according to its terms, all its terms. One of those terms is the incontestability clause. No contest can be made therefore on the original policy itself . . . (at p. 492, 169 A. at p. 36)

This language was directed to the insurer's claim, in its action for rescission of the policy, of fraudulent misrepresentations inducing the original insurance [sic] of the policy. (Rescission was granted in the case of the reinstatement contract and judgment rendered for the insurer). The above quotation is set forth for its reference to "all the terms" of an insurance contract being given full effect upon reinstatement.

The case of *New York Life Ins. Co. v. Weiss,* 133 N.J.Eq. 375, 32 A.2d 341 (E. & A. 1943), cited in the briefs of both parties, was a suit by the insurer to cancel and rescind a life insurance policy for fraudulent representations. Insofar as it is relevant at all, it stands only for the proposition that reinstatement is a contract separate and distinct from the original contract of insurance.

A foreign decision very similar to, if not indistinguishable from, the present case is *Travelers Protective Ass'n of America v. Ziegler,* 250 S.W. 1115 (Tex. Civ. App.1923). The insured in that case paid his last premium on January 15, 1921, covering the six months ending on June 30, 1921. The "dues" for the next six-month period should have been paid on or before June 30 to avoid the lapse which occurred by virtue of the Association's by-laws. The insured died on July 2, 1921.

> It [was] the contention of appellee that, as deceased was reinstated on *January 15, 1921,* and on that date paid the semi annual dues of $5.50, he had fully paid up to *July 15,* and consequently was not in arrears for the dues when he was killed on July 2. (at p. 1116)

In answer the court said:

> Under that contention deceased suffered no penalty whatever for becoming delinquent, but could by becoming delinquent at the end of each successive 6 months gain nearly a month free from dues and return to the fold. (at p. 1117)

It must therefore be concluded that notwithstanding the reinstatement, the original premium dates and policy dates remained and that the grace period had expired five days before death.

* * * * *

The ineluctable conclusion is that on all contentions plaintiff has failed to demonstrate her right to recover on the lapsed policy.

A judgment of no cause for action will be entered against plaintiff.

QUESTIONS FOR REVIEW

1. Distinguish between lapse and expiration.
2. List the requirements for reinstatement found in the usual reinstatement provision of a life insurance policy.
3. Distinguish between insurability and good health.
4. What is meant by adverse selection? How is the insurability requirement for reinstatement related to adverse selection?
5. What is the majority decision concerning the meaning of the phrase *satisfactory to the insurer* in connection with the evidence of insurability required for reinstatement?
6. Generally, reinstatement is considered to result in a continuation of the original contract. Under what conditions has reinstatement been held to create a new contract?
7. Describe the three judicial theories relating to the application of the incontestable clause in a reinstated policy.
8. What is the general rule as to the application of the original suicide clause to a reinstated policy?
9. On what grounds have the courts generally held that the insurer must not put new contract terms into a reinstated policy?

CHAPTER 16

Remedies

EQUITABLE PRINCIPLES
    No Adequate Remedy at Law
    Clean Hands
    Laches
    Equity and the Jury
INTERPLEADER
    Statutory Interpleader
    No Adequate Remedy at Law
    Interpleader Instituted by Plaintiff or Defendant
    Disinterested Stakeholder
    Claimants Claiming the Same Property
    Claimants in Different States
RESCISSION
    Grounds for Rescission
    Materiality
    Facts
    Innocent Versus Intentional Misrepresentation
    Fraud
    Adequate Remedy at Law
REFORMATION
    Grounds for Reformation
    Burden of Proof
DECLARATORY JUDGMENT
    Contract Interpretation
    Claims Questions
    Insurance Regulations
SUMMARY

The parties to a life insurance contract ordinarily have available to them the same remedies as are available to any contracting parties. Certain remedies are especially important to insurers because of the types of disputes which develop over life insurance contracts. The remedy of *interpleader*, for example, is often vital in dealing with disputes between two or more claimants to the policy benefits. Insurers sometimes seek the remedy of *rescission* where there has been a misrepresentation in an application for insurance. The remedy of *reformation* could be necessary where there has been a mistake in drafting the policy. Finally, a *declaratory judgment* might be sought to determine the rights of the parties where there is a dispute between the insurer and a claimant.

These remedies originated in the English courts of equity and are generally subject to equitable principles. Equitable principles will, therefore, be examined in this chapter, so that the reader can gain a better understanding of the remedies. The remedies themselves will also be examined in detail.

EQUITABLE PRINCIPLES

The courts of equity developed in England because of the rigidity of the common-law courts. Equity courts have, therefore, always been more flexible in their approach to dispensing justice than have law courts. Nevertheless, equity courts developed their own rules which had to be followed by a person requesting equitable relief. Although today courts of law and courts of equity have merged in most jurisdictions in the United States, and legal and equitable relief are often sought from the same judge in the same court action, many equitable principles still prevail. The most important of these equitable principles are discussed below.

No Adequate Remedy at Law

The function of equity is to supplement—not to replace—the law. Therefore, the plaintiff must not have an adequate remedy in an action at law if he or she wants to be heard by a court of equity. In most situations, the legal remedy, which is usually money damages, is sufficient to do justice to the plaintiff. But in some situations, money damages will not suffice.

For example, suppose Bruce McDonald's neighbor has built a fence that juts onto Mr. McDonald's property. Mr. McDonald does not want money damages. He wants the fence removed.

Or, suppose Mr. McDonald's neighbor holds excessively loud parties night after night which are interfering with Mr. McDonald's sleep and damaging his health. Again, money damages will not suffice. Mr. McDonald wants the noise to stop.

Finally, suppose Mr. McDonald's neighbor has contracted with Mr. McDonald to sell him a piece of land she owns which adjoins Mr. McDonald's land. Mr. McDonald wants this land so that he can enlarge his back yard and have room for swings for his children. The neighbor now says she has changed her mind and does not wish to transfer the land to Mr. McDonald. Money damages will not suffice here, either. Mr. McDonald wants that particular land.

In each of these situations, Mr. McDonald could seek an equitable remedy, because the legal remedy of money damages will not bring him relief. In the first case, the court could command the neighbor to remove the fence. This command is called a "mandatory injunction"—a command that the person do something. In the second case, the court could command the neighbor to stop holding the loud parties. This command is called a "prohibitory injunction"—a command that the person stop doing something. In the last case, the court could command the neighbor to convey the land to Mr. McDonald. This command is called a decree for "specific performance" of the contract between Mr. McDonald and his neighbor, which is a type of mandatory injunction.

In each case, the court would enforce its command. If the neighbor did not obey, he or she could be jailed or fined for contempt of court. In the case of the contract for the sale of land, the court itself could convey the land to Mr. McDonald.

Clean Hands

One important maxim of equity is that "a person who comes into equity must come with clean hands." This means that the plaintiff in a suit in equity will be denied relief if she or he has acted unfairly or dishonestly as to the matter at issue. The equity court was originally called "the court of the King's conscience." Equity courts still consider themselves courts of conscience. A court of conscience will not spend its time and the public's money in helping a person who has acted inequitably.

For example, suppose Anna Olsen, an elderly widow, hired a broker to sell a piece of farmland she owned. The broker, knowing the land to be worth much more than Mrs. Olsen thought because of a new highway which was going to be built near it, offered to buy the land himself. Mrs. Olsen contracted to sell the land to the broker for much less than its true value. Later, Mrs. Olsen found out about the new highway and the land's true value. Mrs. Olsen refused to transfer title to the land to the broker.

If the broker tries to force Mrs. Olsen to transfer the land to him through a suit in equity for specific performance of the contract, the equity court will deny the broker's request. He does not have clean hands because of his unfair conduct.

Laches

Another maxim of equity is that "equity aids the vigilant." This means that the plaintiff in equity must not unreasonably delay in enforcing his or her rights, if such delay harms the defendant. Where the plaintiff has unreasonably delayed, and the defendant has been harmed by the delay, the plaintiff will be guilty of *laches*. Equitable relief will be denied to a plaintiff who is guilty of laches.

For example, suppose Roscoe Foster watched his neighbor, Maria Alvarez, construct a building, the north wall of which encroached on Mr. Foster's land. Suppose Mr. Foster knew of the encroachment from the beginning but said nothing to Ms. Alvarez during the many months the building was under construction. When the building was nearly complete, suppose Mr. Foster asked the equity court to issue a mandatory injunction forcing Ms. Alvarez to remove the encroachment from his land. The court will not act, because Mr. Foster is guilty of laches—an unreasonable delay in enforcing his rights, a delay which harmed Ms. Alvarez.

Equity and the Jury

Ordinarily, in a court of law, questions of fact are decided by a jury and questions of law by the judge. If a case involves a dispute as to what actually happened or what was, in fact, said or done by either of the parties, the jury will hear the evidence and decide what happened. This is called a finding of fact. The judge, however, makes the ruling on the legal effect of the facts so decided.

In a court of equity, there ordinarily is no jury. There, the judge has the power to decide every question, whether of law or fact, which comes before the court. The constitutionally-guaranteed right to a jury trial does not apply in courts of equity.[1] If it seems advisable, the judge in an equity court sometimes submits a question of fact to a jury for decision, but as a general rule, the finding of the jury will be advisory only.

This aspect of equity is illustrated in a 1949 case brought in the United States District Court for the District of Maryland.[2] In that case, an insurance company brought an action to cancel (rescind) two policies of life insurance on the ground that the insured had misrepresented material facts in the applications. The defendants requested a jury trial, but the court held that the issues were equitable, rather than legal, and that there was no right to a jury trial. The opinion reads in part as follows:

> It is very well known that the Federal rules of civil procedure while generally merging law and equity cases for procedural matters, were not intended to destroy the distinction between law and equity with respect to the matter of jury trials. In a typical case for equitable relief, such as the instant case, there was no right to a jury trial. On the contrary it is well established both by federal and Maryland law and judicial decisions that in equity cases, where there is no adequate remedy at law, there is no right to a jury trial at common law or by statute.

---

[1] In some states, there are statutes providing for trial of fact issues by a jury in certain equitable actions.

[2] Connecticut Gen. Life Ins. Co. v. Candimat Co., 83 F. Supp. 1 (D. Md. 1949).

INTERPLEADER

When two or more persons claim money or other property which is being held by a third person who does not claim to be the owner, the third person can give the property to the court and ask the court to decide who is entitled to it. This is the equitable remedy of *interpleader*. Interpleader is important to insurers, because they frequently find themselves faced with conflicting claimants to insurance proceeds. When a life insurance policy has been in force for many years—with beneficiary changes, assignments made and released, policy lapses and reinstatements, and other policy transactions occurring—there can be conflicting claims among successive beneficiaries, beneficiaries and assignees, beneficiaries and persons claiming community property rights, and so forth.

When an insurer is faced with conflicting claims for policy proceeds, its position would be difficult indeed without the interpleader remedy. Ordinarily, only a court can, with safety to the insurer, decide who among the claimants is entitled to the proceeds. Payment by the insurer to one claimant, if that claimant is not the one entitled to the proceeds, usually means that the insurer will have to pay the same claim twice.

Without interpleader, the insurer would also be exposed to the danger that each claimant would sue it in a separate legal action. This is called a "multiplicity of lawsuits." Each claimant conceivably could win her or his lawsuit and, thus, subject the insurer to multiple liability. Interpleader prevents this, because once the conflicting claimants are joined in an interpleader suit, they will be prevented by the court from beginning or continuing another legal action to recover the proceeds. The court commands the claimants not to begin, or to desist from, such actions. In other words, it tells them not to do, or to stop doing, something. This is a prohibitory injunction.

One court gave the following concise description of the reasons the interpleader remedy was developed:

> The fundamental basis for interpleader is to permit the holder of a fund who admits he is not the owner of it to put the fund in the hands of the court, so that claimants with substantial contentions may fight out their claims to it and so that the holder will be shielded from the danger of deciding at its peril who is rightfully entitled to the fund, as well as from the burden of defending and danger of losing separate lawsuits brought by each claimant.[3]

A further reason for development of the interpleader remedy is that it conserves judicial resources. Adjudication of the rights of all claimants in one suit, rather than in two or more suits, prevents duplication of effort by the courts.

---

[3]United Benefit Life Ins. Co. v. Katz, 155 F. Supp. 391 (E.D. Pa. 1957).

Unfortunately, there is some expense involved in connection with interpleader, and at least part of this expense, as a general rule, is payable out of the policy proceeds. Thus, the funds which ultimately reach the payee are ordinarily diminished by the interpleader action. For this reason and also because court action means delay in performing a service which is usually performed promptly, an insurer often encourages conflicting claimants to settle the matter among themselves. If they are unwilling to do this, however, the insurer usually must seek interpleader to protect itself.

Statutory Interpleader

Many of the equitable rules of interpleader have been liberalized by federal and state interpleader statutes and court rules. Interpleader in the federal courts is governed by the federal Interpleader Act[4] and federal Rule of Civil Procedure 22. Under the Interpleader Act, diversity of citizenship between the insurer and one of the claimants is necessary. Also, there must be $500 or more in controversy.

No Adequate Remedy at Law

As with other types of equity suits, there must be no adequate remedy at law, or interpleader will not be allowed. In almost all cases in which a life insurer seeks interpleader, there is no adequate remedy at law. Certainly this is the case where there is a reasonable doubt as to which of two or more conflicting claimants is entitled to insurance proceeds.

Where there is not a reasonable doubt as to which of the claimants is entitled to the proceeds, some courts deny interpleader because the insurer has an adequate remedy at law.[5] According to these courts, an insurer should pay the claimant entitled to the proceeds and defend itself if the claimant who is not entitled files an action at law. Usually, however, there will be a reasonable doubt as to who is entitled to the funds, and hence, no adequate remedy at law.

Moreover, other courts have held that a stakeholder need not make a judgment as to whether or not there is a reasonable doubt as to which claimant is entitled. One court said:

> The jurisdiction of a federal court to entertain a bill of interpleader is not dependent upon the merits of the claims of the defendants. . . . It is our opinion that a stakeholder, acting in good faith, may maintain a suit in interpleader for the purpose of ridding himself of the vexation and ex-

---

[4]28 U.S.C.A. §§ 2361, 1335 & 1397 (West 1976 & 1978).

[5]Great Am. Reserve Ins. Co. v. Sanders, 525 S.W.2d 956 (Tex. Sup. Ct. 1975); Kurz v. New York Life Ins. Co., 168 So.2d 564 (Fla. Dist. Ct. App. 1964), *motion denied* 174 So.2d 537 (Fla. Sup. Ct. 1965); Rio Grande Nat'l Life Ins. Co. v. Schmidt, 292 S.W.2d 864 (Tex. Civ. App. 1956).

pense of resisting adverse claims, even though he believes that only one of them is meritorious. As the Supreme Court said in *Myers v. Bethlehem Corporation,* 303 U.S. 41, 51 ". . . Lawsuits also often prove to have been groundless; but no way has been discovered of relieving a defendant from the necessity of a trial to establish the fact."[6]

Interpleader Instituted by Plaintiff or Defendant

An insurer can interplead in one of two ways. First, it can file a bill of interpleader as a plaintiff. The bill of interpleader permits the insurer to pay the proceeds into the court and requires the conflicting claimants to bring their claims before the court—that is, to interplead their claims. The court will often dismiss the insurer from the suit at this point. The insurer is then discharged of all liability. The court will go on to decide which claimant is entitled to the funds.

Second, if one claimant sues the insurer before the insurer has filed a bill of interpleader, the insurer can usually defend itself by filing a cross bill of interpleader. The other claimant, or claimants, will then be brought into the suit, and the insurer dismissed from it.

Disinterested Stakeholder

Ordinarily, in order to institute an interpleader suit or defend with a cross bill of interpleader, the person holding the money or other property, called the stakeholder, must claim no interest in the property held. He or she must be a disinterested stakeholder. An insurer holding life insurance policy proceeds is usually a disinterested stakeholder. The insurer itself makes no claim to the proceeds.

Sometimes the insurer does have an interest in the proceeds. In such a case the insurer can file a bill in the nature of interpleader. The insurer is not then required, as in strict interpleader, to be a disinterested stakeholder.

For example, sometimes an insurer disputes the amount claimed. In one case, the insured changed the beneficiary from his first to his second wife, then took out a policy loan. After his death, the first wife claimed that the insurer had no right to change the beneficiary or grant the loan. When the insurer tendered the policy proceeds minus the loan, there was a controversy as to the amount of the insurer's liability. The court held that the insurer was not a disinterested stakeholder. The insurer was, therefore, denied interpleader.[7] In such a case, a bill in the nature of interpleader would be appropriate.

---

[6]Hunter v. Federal Life Ins. Co., 111 F.2d 551 (8th Cir. 1940).

[7]Williams v. Penn Mut. Life Ins. Co., 160 Miss. 408, 133 So. 649 (1931), *aff'd* 163 Miss. 324, 140 So. 875 (1932).

Claimants Claiming the Same Property

In an interpleader suit, the claimants must be claiming the same property. Again, this is usually the case where an insurer is the stakeholder. The conflicting claimants will be claiming the same policy proceeds.

Claimants in Different States

A problem arises when the claimants reside in different states. Suppose, for example, an insurer is domiciled in Illinois but is licensed to do business in Texas and Florida. The insurer can be sued in both Texas and Florida, because it does business in those states. Now suppose there are two conflicting claimants to the same life insurance proceeds—one living in Texas and the other in Florida. The insurer is in danger of being sued in each of those states. The insurer needs a court where both claimants can be served in an interpleader suit. Neither the Texas state courts nor the Florida state courts will do. The Texas state courts have no jurisdiction over the Florida resident, and the Florida state courts have no jurisdiction over the Texas resident.

A federal interpleader action is the answer to this problem. The federal interpleader statute confers the power of nationwide service of process upon a federal district court in any district where a claimant lives "or may be found."[8] The insurer could, therefore, institute an interpleader suit in a federal district court in either Texas or Florida. The district court can enter an order restraining the claimants from beginning or continuing a court action elsewhere. The insurer can pay the policy proceeds into the district court and be dismissed from the suit, leaving the conflicting claimants to litigate their rights there.

RESCISSION

The equitable remedy of rescission is also important to insurers. The contract is void from the beginning if it is rescinded.

Rescission can be accomplished in three ways. First, by an agreement of the parties; second, by one of the parties declaring rescission of the contract if a legally sufficient ground exists, accompanied by tender of the consideration (this method is ineffective for life insurers because of the incontestable clause, as explained below); or third, by a decree of rescission issued by a court of equity.

If there has been a material misrepresentation in the application for insurance, and the insurer discovers the misrepresentation while the insured is alive[9] and within the contestable period, the insurer will generally pursue a

---

[8]28 U.S.C.A. § 2361 (West 1978).

[9]A suit for rescission after the insured's death can be maintained where the words "during the lifetime of the insured" are omitted from the incontestable clause. This will be discussed in Chapter 17, "Policy Contests."

rescission of the contract. The insurer will usually first attempt to effect a rescission by agreement with the policyowner. The insurer will tender the premiums back to the policyowner and tell the policyowner it wishes to rescind. If the policyowner agrees and accepts the premiums, the rescission will be effective.

If the policyowner will not agree to rescind, the insurer will usually sue in equity for rescission. Merely declaring a rescission of the contract will not suffice in the case of a life insurance contract because of the incontestable clause. If the insured lived beyond the contestable period, the insurer would lose its material misrepresentation defense. The incontestable clause ordinarily states that the insurer will not contest the validity of the policy, except for nonpayment of premiums, after it has been in force during the insured's lifetime for two years from the policy date. If the insured died more than two years after the policy date, the insurer could not contest the validity of the policy. Unless it had another defense, it would have to pay the proceeds. Therefore, the insurer will ordinarily sue for rescission in equity. If the equity court grants the rescission, all that will be payable by the insurer will be the amount of the premiums paid.

Grounds for Rescission

There are a number of circumstances in which one party will have a right to rescind the contract. All of these grounds for rescission must have occurred either before, or at the time that, the contract was entered into. They cannot have occurred after the contract is in force.

One ground for rescission of a contract is a mistake by both parties as to a material fact. For example, suppose Anthony Levato contracts to sell Eric Bergstrom a house for $75,000. Unknown to either Mr. Levato or Mr. Bergstrom, the house had been destroyed by fire two days before. Mr. Bergstrom is entitled to rescission of the contract due to a mutual mistake of fact. If Mr. Bergstrom has paid any money to Mr. Levato, the court will direct Mr. Levato to return it.

A second ground for rescission, in a minority of jurisdictions, is a mutual mistake of law. For example, suppose Thomas Wells contracts to buy a push-cart from Joan Wolska for $700. The contract is entered into on the assumption that Mr. Wells could sell his handmade belt buckles from the push-cart on the streets of the town in which he lives. Unknown to Mr. Wells and Ms. Wolska, several days earlier a municipal ordinance was enacted forbidding sales of merchandise from push-carts. Mr. Wells would be entitled to rescission of the contract due to a mutual mistake of law in those jurisdictions that recognize this ground.

The third ground for rescission, and the ground of importance to insurers, is misrepresentation of a material fact. In order for the insurance principle to function properly, it is necessary that the insurer select the lives to be insured so that the mortality actually experienced will approximate that which the insurer assumed under the mortality tables used. Misrepresentation of material facts in the insurance application interferes with the proper functioning of this principle.

In order to determine whether it wishes to enter into an insurance contract, the insurer requests detailed information concerning the proposed insured's health, family history, occupation, activities, and so forth. In some instances, the insurer has the proposed insured examined by a physician. The insurer might also obtain an inspection report giving general information on the health, habits, finances, and reputation of the proposed insured. Even where there is a physical examination and inspection report, information contained in the application can be material.

In other instances, the insurer does not have the insured examined or obtain an inspection report but relies entirely on the information in the application in making its risk selection decision. In such instances, misrepresentation of a material fact in the application will usually give the insurer a right to rescind.

For example, suppose Raymond Hansen submits an application for life insurance on his own life. On the application, there is the following question: "Have you ever had, or been told by a physician that you had, a heart disorder or disease?" Mr. Hansen answers no, although he was hospitalized because of a heart attack six months earlier. Four months after the effective date of the policy, the insurer becomes aware of Mr. Hansen's heart attack. The insurer has a ground for rescission of the insurance contract because of Mr. Hansen's misrepresentation of a material fact.

Materiality

Contracts can be rescinded when there is a mutual mistake, or a misrepresentation by one party, only as to a fact which is material. The test of the materiality of a fact is whether, if a party had known the fact, she or he would have entered into the contract. If the party would not have entered into the contract knowing the fact, the fact is material.

In the case of the applicant who indicated that he had had no heart trouble when in fact he had had a heart attack, the insurer would not have issued the policy if it had known of the heart attack. It would have issued a substandard policy or none at all. This was, therefore, a misrepresentation of a material fact.

Misrepresentation of a fact which is not material will not be a ground for rescission. Suppose, for example, that an applicant states her date of birth as September 17, 1955, when it was actually September 19, 1955. This would be a misrepresentation of fact, but it would not be material. The insurer's decision to accept or reject the application would not have been different if it had known the truth.

Often, the answers to questions in the application concerning ill health or treatment by a physician are equally immaterial. For example, suppose an applicant discloses a visit to his physician and states as the reason for the visit "ankle sprain." Even if the condition was not technically a sprain, the misrepresentation would not ordinarily be material, because the insurer's decision would not be affected by it. The test of materiality has been codified in the New York Insurance Code as follows:

> No misrepresentation shall be deemed material unless knowledge by the insurer of the facts misrepresented would have led to a refusal by the insurer to make such contract.[10]

Facts

A misrepresentation of fact is a misrepresentation of a circumstance existing in the past or the present. With respect to the future, the only misrepresentation possible is a misrepresentation of intention, as when a promise is made with the intention of not keeping it. Otherwise, a prediction or opinion about the future is ordinarily not a misrepresentation of fact, as no one can know the future. Misrepresentations of opinion are misrepresentations of fact if made by an expert who has information not available to the other party.

Innocent Versus Intentional Misrepresentation

In general contract law, material misrepresentation innocently made by one party to a contract will give the other party the right to rescind the contract, just as will an intentional misrepresentation. This is not always the rule, however, where misrepresentations by applicants for life insurance contracts are concerned. In some states, the material misrepresentation by an applicant must be intentional if the insurer is to be granted rescission.

If, for example, Raymond Hansen, in the example above, had thought his chest pains resulted from indigestion, and his doctors had not told him he had had a heart attack, his misrepresentation would have been innocent. In a minority of states, the insurer would not be able to rescind on the ground of material misrepresentation in such an instance. However, in the majority of states, such innocent material misrepresentation is a ground for rescission.

Fraud

Fraud involves an intentional misrepresentation communicated to another person who is injured as a result of relying on the misrepresentation. An intentional material misrepresentation of fact made by an insurance applicant to an insurer, which induces the insurer to issue an insurance policy it would not otherwise issue, is fraud. The insurer is injured because it has insured a risk it would not have insured if it had known the truth.

---

[10]N.Y. Ins. Law § 3105(b) (McKinney 1985).

Adequate Remedy at Law

If evidence of material misrepresentation is discovered after the death of the insured, but prior to the expiration of the contestable period, the evidence can ordinarily be used by the insurer in defense of a lawsuit by the beneficiary if the incontestable clause includes the phrase *during the lifetime of the insured,* or words to that effect.[11] This phrase stops the running of the incontestable clause at the insured's death. In such circumstances, the insurer has an adequate remedy at law. The equitable remedy of rescission is, therefore, not available.

Assume, for example, that Chester Horner, insured, dies of leukemia three months after issuance of a life insurance policy. The death certificate states that the illness was of two years duration, and an investigation supports this statement. The illness was diagnosed two years prior to death, and Mr. Horner was informed of the diagnosis. Nevertheless, his answers to the application questions gave no hint of ill health of any kind, even though two of the questions, if honestly answered, would have elicited information about the leukemia. This, of course, is misrepresentation of a material fact. The insurer will deny the claim for the death benefit in accordance with its usual procedures. If the beneficiary sues, the insurer will show the court that information material to the appraisal of the risk was misrepresented at the time of application. This will ordinarily constitute an effective defense for the insurer. Consequently, the insurer has an adequate remedy at law, and equitable rescission is not available to it.

In most jurisdictions the situation described above would be changed, however, if the wording of the incontestable clause did not include the phrase *during the lifetime of the insured.* Without the phrase, the incontestable clause continues to run, and the beneficiary could wait until after two years from the policy date to sue. At that time, the policy would be incontestable for misrepresentations in the application. Therefore, if the phrase *during the lifetime of the insured* is not included, the insurer has no adequate remedy at law and can sue for rescission of the contract after the insured's death. The suit for rescission would, of course, have to be brought during the contestable period.

REFORMATION

Reformation is the equitable remedy by which a written contract is revised or intepreted to express the original intent of the parties when the contract, as written, fails to do so. The purpose of reformation is not to make a

---

[11]The illustrative policy in Appendix B contains the following language: "We will not contest the validity of this Policy, except for nonpayment of premiums, after it has been in force during the Insured's lifetime for two years from the Policy Date."

new contract but to reform the existing contract to reflect the original agreement of the parties.

Life insurance policies are prepared with the utmost care, and machine procedures are utilized to assure a high degree of accuracy. Mistakes are sometimes made, however, and a mistake in a life insurance policy is often serious. Perhaps 20-year endowment values were inadvertently included in a 20-pay life policy. Possibly a typist moved a decimal point one place to the right. Perhaps figures have been reversed. In any case, the insurer must inform the policyowner of the error as soon as it is discovered. The insurer must explain the nature of the error and request permission to correct it.

Assume, however, that the policyowner does not grant permission to correct the error. The policy states the face value as $100,000 instead of $10,000, and the policyowner states a firm intention to enforce it according to its written terms. At this point, the insurer's lawyer considers the equitable remedy of reformation.

Grounds for Reformation

The general rules which apply to the reformation of other written contracts usually apply also to insurance contracts.[12] The three grounds for reformation of contracts are mutual mistake, unilateral mistake, and misrepresentation.

Mutual mistake occurs where the writing does not conform to the original agreement, and the parties are not aware of the discrepancy. For example, suppose an applicant applies for an annuity of $5,000 per year. By mistake the policy reads $5,000 per month. A year later the insurer discovers the error and seeks to correct it. The annuitant refuses, and demands $5,000 per month. The equity court will reform the contract to reflect the parties' original intent if the insurer can provide clear and convincing proof of the terms of the original agreement.[13]

Where one party knows of the mistake, and the other does not—that is, unilateral mistake—the contract can be reformed according to the modern trend. A denial of relief would enable the party who knows of the mistake to benefit at the expense of the mistaken party. Reformation acts to conform the writing to the original agreement. There is no hardship on either.party, as each is getting what he or she originally bargained for.

A case where the court discussed reformation for mistake is *Flax v. Prudential Life Insurance Co.*[14] There, the policyowner had converted his policy to paid-up whole life insurance in the amount of $2,755. Due to what the law

---

[12]Annot., 32 A.L.R. 3d 661 (1970).
[13]Travelers Ins. Co. v. Bailey, 124 Vt. 114, 197 A.2d 813 (1964).
[14]148 F. Supp. 720 (S.D. Cal. 1957).

has continued to call a "scrivener's error"—that is, an error of the person who wrote the contract—the cash value amount reflected in the written contract was $5,495.26. The policyowner attempted to recover this cash value from the insurer, but the insurer counterclaimed for reformation of the contract. Reformation was granted by the court, which said:

> The defendant [the insurer] had no knowledge of the existence of the mistake until during the month of June 1954, at which time, in the course of processing an application by the plaintiff for a loan on the policy, it discovered it. The defendant immediately notified the plaintiff of the mistake and requested him to join in the reformation of the policy to rectify it, which he has refused to do.
>
> [W]hen, either through mutual mistake or unilateral mistake by one party which is known to the other, the policy does not express the intention of the parties, reformation may be had either when an action is instituted by the insured to enforce its provisions or in a direct action brought by the insurer to make the policy speak verity.
>
> From time immemorial, it has been the function of equity as administered in the federal courts to remedy what is known as "scrivener's mistakes"—mistakes performed by the person who drafted the instrument in such a manner that it did not express what was *actually* agreed. In an early case, the Supreme Court of the United States stated the principle and the reasons for it in this manner:

> > There are certain principles of equity, applicable to this question, which, as general principles, we hold to be incontrovertible. The first is, that where an instrument is drawn and executed, which professes or is intended to carry into execution an agreement, whether in writing or by parol, previously entered into, but which, *by mistake of the draftsman, either as to fact or law, does not fulfil, or which violates, the manifest intention of the parties to the agreement, equity will correct the mistake, so as to produce conformity of the instrument to the agreement.* The reason is obvious: the execution of agreements, fairly and legally entered into, is one of the peculiar branches of equity jurisdiction; and if the instrument which is intended to execute the agreement be, from any cause, insufficient for that purpose, *the agreement remains as much unexecuted, as if one of the parties had refused, altogether, to comply with his engagement;* and a court of equity will, in the exercise of its acknowledged jurisdiction, afford relief in the one case, as well as in the other, *by compelling the delinquent party fully to perform his agreement, according to the terms of it, and to the manifest intention of the parties.* So, if the mistake exists, not in the instrument, which is intended to give effect to the agreement, but in the agreement itself, and is clearly proved to have been the result of ignorance of some material fact, a court of equity will, in general, grant relief, according to the nature of the particular case in which it is sought. [Emphasis added.]

. . . To summarize: The plaintiff either did or did not know of the mistake. *If he did*, it appearing that the mistake *was not known* to the insurer, we have the type of unilateral mistake for which relief by way of reformation is granted. *If he did not* know the mistake, we have a case of mutual mistake for which reformation also lies. Indeed, relief may be granted by disregarding the printed words which the scrivener erroneously failed to delete.

. . . So, if plaintiff's present demands were allowed, he would receive something which he did not bargain or pay for,—something for nothing. The language of the Persian poet applies:

"Sue for a Debt he never did contract,

And cannot answer—

Oh, the sorry trade."[15]

It would be neither good morals nor good law to sanction the application of such a policy to business relations.

On the other hand, a ruling for the defendant avoids a palpable injustice and still allows the plaintiff the full benefit of the contract *he and the company intended* to make.

Judgment will, therefore, be for the defendant.

The court, thus, held that the insurer could pay the amount that should have been stated in the policy.

Misrepresentation, either innocent or intentional, can also be a ground for reformation. In this case, the contract will be reformed to reflect the expressed intent of the parties, even though the misrepresenting party might have actually intended the contract to differ from that expressed intent. In misrepresentation cases, the party seeking reformation knows what he or she has agreed to but is deluded as to the content of the contract he or she signed.

For example, suppose Robert Feldman agrees to buy 100 acres of farmland. However, the contract Mr. Feldman signs, which was prepared by the other party, obligates him to buy 200 acres. Mr. Feldman can sue for reformation of the written contract to make it reflect his agreement. Note that Mr. Feldman does not wish to rescind the contract. He wants to purchase the 100 acres. He merely wants the contract to reflect his agreement.

Where an insurer, through misrepresentation of the contents of a policy, leads the applicant to believe the policy provides coverage not actually stated in the policy, the courts have reformed the policy to conform to the applicant's and the insurer's original agreement.

Burden of Proof

There is a strong presumption by the courts that a written contract correctly expresses the intention of the parties. For this reason, reformation will

---

[15]Khayyám, *Rubáiyát of Omar Khayyám of Naishápúr* (E. FitzGerald, trans.) in IMMORTAL POEMS OF THE ENGLISH LANGUAGE 360 (O. Williams ed. 1961).

be granted only if the plaintiff can produce clear and convincing proof of the terms of the original agreement. Clear and convincing proof is stronger proof than that usually required in civil (noncriminal) court actions. The usual level of proof required to sustain the burden of proof in civil actions is a preponderance of the evidence or, simply, more convincing proof than the other side presents. Clear and convincing proof, on the other hand, is proof which will produce a firm belief in the judge's mind of the truth of the allegations sought to be established. Thus, the burden of proof on the plaintiff in a reformation suit is more difficult to sustain than that in most civil actions.

DECLARATORY JUDGMENT

Declaratory judgment suits have their roots in equity, although, today, the right to a declaratory judgment is granted by federal or state statute. The federal Declaratory Judgment Act[16] was enacted in 1934. Most states have declaratory judgment acts patterned on the Uniform Declaratory Judgments Act.[17]

A declaratory judgment, as the name implies, is a judgment that declares the rights of the parties involved in the suit. It differs markedly from other suits in equity or actions at law in that it does not require either of the parties to take any action or to pay money to the other.

Applied to life insurance contracts, the declaratory judgment has many possibilities. Questions involving contract interpretation, claims, and the legality of insurance regulations are among those which can be resolved.

Contract Interpretation

Questions involving the interpretation of the insurance contract can be resolved by a declaratory judgment. This is illustrated in *Liner v. Penn Mutual Life Insurance Co.*[18] In the *Liner* case, the court interpreted two life insurance polices—one naming the insured's son and the other his daughter as beneficiary. These policies had been intended by the policyowner-insured to provide for the educational expenses of the beneficiaries. Both policies provided that, on the death of the insured, the proceeds were to be held under the interest option with interest payable to the insured's widow, as trustee, during the minority of each beneficiary. The widow was given the right to withdraw $500 per year in a lump sum under each policy until the insurer received an affidavit from a college stating that the beneficiary of the policy was enrolled there. After receipt of the affidavit, $1,250 per year could be withdrawn.

---

[16]28 U.S.C.A. § 2201 (West 1982 & Supp. 1987).

[17]The Uniform Declaratory Judgments Act was approved by the National Conference of Commissioners on Uniform State Laws and the American Bar Association in 1922.

[18]286 A.D. 517, 145 N.Y.S.2d 560 (1955).

Both policies contained accidental death coverage, and the insured died under such circumstances that this additional benefit was payable. The question was whether the specific amounts that could be withdrawn would be doubled, since the amount payable was doubled. The beneficiaries asked for declaratory judgments to that effect, while the insurer contended that the accidental death benefit merely doubled the sum payable and had no effect on the withdrawal privileges, which remained unchanged. The trial court held in favor of the contention of the insurer, and the beneficiaries appealed.

The appellate court reversed and discussed the question in this way:

> The purpose of the insured throughout these transactions was to protect his children during approximately the first twenty years of their lives and to insure that they would receive a college education. The period during which he desired to assist them was substantially certain and known to him; it would not vary according as he might or might not die an accidental death. Regardless of the manner in which he might die, he wished to assist his children through college so that they could take care of themselves. That would require twenty years, not forty. Yet the insurance company interprets the withdrawal privileges so that the duration of the protection period varies according to the way in which the insured met his death. We think the desired protection period would be the same in either case.

> * * * * *

> We conclude that the withdrawal privileges under Option D should be doubled. Nothing else would satisfy the purpose of the insured to provide for his children during a fixed period of their lives which would not vary according to the manner of his death, and nothing else would satisfy his direction set forth in the supplemental contract that the extra $5,000 be distributed "in addition to and together with" the basic death benefit.

> The judgments should be reversed and judgments granted to the plaintiffs declaring that $1,000 may be withdrawn each year until receipt of the affidavit mentioned in the change of beneficiary and $2,500 per year thereafter.

Claims Questions

Life insurers have found the declaratory judgment helpful in a number of claims situations. Most life insurers do not deny a claim unless they believe such an action is justified. However, sometimes evidence is in the hands of the beneficiary, her or his attorney, or others, which has not been made available to the insurer. The declaratory judgment provides the insurer a method for bringing the matter into court for resolution.

For example, if a claim is presented for disability benefits, and the insurer denies liability on the ground that the insured is not disabled according to the policy terms, an action for a declaratory judgment is one of the most effective ways of clarifying the rights of the parties.

Another claims situation in which a suit for declaratory judgment can sometimes assist the insurer is denial of the accidental death benefit. It is often said that, where the accidental death benefit is denied, payment of the face amount "finances a lawsuit." If there is a good possibility that a lawsuit against the insurer will be filed, an immediate action by the insurer for a declaratory judgment offers one way to have the facts ascertained while evidence is fresh and while witnesses are still available.

This same advantage is occasionally present where a claim for the face amount itself is denied. Even though the insurer is convinced of the soundness of its decision, it, nevertheless, remains vulnerable to a suit by the beneficiary until the expiration of the statute of limitations or the period of time for suit specified in the policy. During that time, witnesses might die or become widely scattered, and the ascertainment of the facts becomes progressively more difficult.

In addition, some states have statutory penalties imposed for wrongful and vexatious delay in settling life insurance claims. A court decision unfavorable to the insurer, made after the expiration of the period specified in these statutes, means the insurer will have to pay a statutory penalty, as well as the policy proceeds. In certain instances, a declaratory judgment action filed shortly after the loss has occurred might enable the insurer to avoid the penalty.

Insurance Regulations

Where an insurer questions the legality of an insurance regulation, the insurer might join the insurance commissioner in a suit for declaratory judgment. Without a declaratory judgment the insurer is left with the choice of either complying with a regulation it believes is illegal or refusing to comply. Refusing to comply could result in fines or other penalties if the insurer was wrong about the regulation's legality.

SUMMARY

Four remedies which developed in equity are of special importance to insurers. These are interpleader, rescission, reformation, and the declaratory judgment.

In most instances, these remedies are governed by the general principles of equity. One of these principles requires that the plaintiff in equity have no adequate remedy at law. The usual remedy at law is money damages. Those seeking relief in equity ordinarily want some other type of relief, such as a mandatory or prohibitory injunction, which is not available at law. Another principle of equity is that a person seeking an equitable remedy must come into equity with clean hands—that is, the person must have acted fairly and honestly. A third principle is that the plaintiff must not delay seeking relief in equity, if such delay would harm the defendant. If the plaintiff so delays, he or she will be guilty of laches and will be denied relief by the equity court.

Interpleader is an equitable remedy which allows an insurer, faced with conflicting claimants to policy proceeds, to pay the proceeds to the court and be dismissed from the case. The court will enjoin the claimants to litigate the matter among themselves. Without interpleader, the insurer would be in danger of paying more than once and of having to defend a multiplicity of lawsuits.

The equitable remedy of rescission allows an insurer to have the life insurance contract cancelled within the contestable period if there has been misrepresentation in the application. The misrepresentation must be of a fact which is material to the risk. A material fact is a fact which, if known to the insurer, would have kept it from entering into the contract. In some states, the misrepresentation must be intentional (fraudulent), rather than innocent, or the insurer cannot rescind.

Reformation is the equitable remedy whereby a written contract is revised or interpreted to conform to the original agreement of the parties. The grounds for reformation are mutual mistake, unilateral mistake, and misrepresentation. Reformation will be granted only when the plaintiff can produce clear and convincing proof of the terms of the original agreement.

Declaratory judgment suits have origins in equity, although, today, the right to institute a declaratory judgment suit is granted by federal or state statute. A declaratory judgment is a judgment that declares the rights of the parties, without requiring either party to take any action or pay any money to the other.

ILLUSTRATIVE CASE

The usefulness of the remedy of interpleader is demonstrated again and again in cases involving the life insurance contract. The following case is included as an illustration of its use.

*GREAT AMERICAN RESERVE INSUR-
ANCE COMPANY,* Petitioner
v.
VIOLET SANDERS, Respondent[19]
Supreme Court of Texas

POPE, Justice.

Great American Reserve Insurance Company filed an interpleader suit in district court naming as defendants the insured's ex-wife, Violet Sanders, and surviving widow, Jessie Sanders. The petition also named Hill Metropolitan Funeral Directors, Inc. because of an assignment to it by Violet Sanders for part of the insurance proceeds to cover the insured's funeral expenses. The trial court

---

[19]525 S.W.2d 956 (1975).

awarded the $5000 insurance proceeds to Violet Sanders, less $1208.60 awarded to the funeral home by virtue of its assigned interest, and less $500 attorney fees to the insurer-stakeholder, Great American Reserve Insurance Company. The court of civil appeals reversed and remanded. We reverse the judgment of the court of civil appeals and affirm that of the trial court.

This case presents us with two separate questions. First, whether there was a bona fide claim made by each of the rival claimants such as will allow the insurer-stakeholder to resort to the equitable remedy of interpleader. Second, whether Article 3.62, Vernon's Tex.Ins.Code Ann., imposes an absolute duty upon an insurer to either pay a claimant or interplead rival claimants within 30 days of the time demand is made for the proceeds.

The case was submitted to the trial court upon an agreed statement of facts. Nathaniel and Violet Sanders were married in 1960. They obtained a divorce on July 30, 1969, and Violet was awarded custody of their five minor children. The court ordered Nathaniel Sanders to pay $35.00 per week for child support.

Nathaniel Sanders married Jessie Mae Sanders in February, 1971. They separated in early summer of 1971, though no divorce action was brought by either party. Subsequent to this separation, in September, 1971, Violet Sanders threatened to bring contempt proceedings against Nathaniel because of his failure to make child support payments. Nathaniel proposed instead that he take out a $5000 life insurance policy, with Violet as beneficiary, and also that he begin making regular support payments. Nathaniel secured a certificate of insurance from Great American Reserve Insurance Company through a group plan available to employees of the City of Dallas. Violet was named as beneficiary and was given possession of the certificate.

Nathaniel's failure to make regular support payments continued and on February 14, 1973, a Dallas County Domestic Relations Court entered a commitment for contempt against him because of his delinquent child support payments amounting to $2478.00. The commitment was suspended, however, as long as Nathaniel made the $35.00 per week payments.

Nathaniel Sanders died on April 3, 1973. Violet Sanders assigned $1213.60 to Hill Metropolitan Funeral Directors, Inc. from the insurance proceeds. On May 9, 1973, both Violet and Jessie Mae filed proof of death with the insurer, and claimed the proceeds of the policy. Great American Reserve filed its petition in interpleader on June 15, 1973, wherein it admitted liability under the policy, and deposited the $5000.00 proceeds in the registry of the court. Great American alleged that it had honest doubts as to who was entitled to the proceeds, and asked $500 for attorney fees.

The trial court granted an agreed partial summary judgment in favor of the funeral home for $1208.60, by virtue of its assigned interest in that amount by Violet Sanders. Great American was awarded $500 out of the fund for attorney fees, and the trial court determined that Violet Sanders was entitled to the balance.

Violet appealed the trial court's award of $500 to the insurer for attorney fees, and also appealed the trial court's refusal to award her attorney fees and a 12% penalty provided for in Article 3.62, Tex.Ins.Code Ann. The court of civil appeals held that Great American had a duty to make an investigation within thirty days after the claim for proceeds was made, in order to determine who was entitled to the proceeds. According to that court, this investigation would have revealed the indisputable merit of Violet's claim and shown that Jessie's claim was entirely spurious. The court also held that Article 3.62 required the insurer to either pay a claimant within 30 days of demand for the proceeds, or to file its petition in intervention within this same period. We think that the court of civil appeals has placed a burden on the insurer not contemplated by Article 3.62.

Great American was entitled to maintain an interpleader suit if there existed a reasonable doubt, either of fact or law, as to which of the rival claimants was entitled to the proceeds of the policy. If the insurer's doubt is a reasonable one, and for that reason it in good faith declines to pay the named beneficiary, but admits liability and deposits the funds into court, it is liable only for the face amount of the policy.

We must examine the nature of the conflicting claims in order to determine whether or not Great American was faced with a reasonable doubt as to which claim was superior. Violet Sanders was the named beneficiary, and had possession of the certificate of insurance. According to Article 3.48, Tex.Ins.Code Ann., an insurer may pay the named beneficiary of a policy without concern for further liability unless it receives notice of an adverse, and bona fide, claim to the proceeds.

Great American in this case was faced with an adverse claim, filed on the same day as Violet's claim, by Jessie Mae Sanders. An investigation of this claim would reveal that Jessie Mae was Nathaniel's wife at the time he took out the certificate of insurance, at all times when premiums were paid, and at the time of his death.

These facts raise the possibility that Jessie Mae was entitled to the proceeds, or some part thereof, on the ground that Nathaniel's act of naming his ex-wife beneficiary of a policy purchased with funds of the community of Nathaniel and Jessie Mae, was constructive fraud upon Jessie Mae. It was held in *Givens v. Girard Life Ins. Co.,* 480 S.W.2d 421, 426 (Tex.Civ. App.–1972, writ ref'd n. r. e.) that the widow "establishes constructive fraud prima facie by proof that life insurance was purchased with community funds for the benefit of an unrelated person, and the beneficiary then has the burden to justify such use of community funds."

The beneficiary may rebut the prima facie case by showing special circumstances which justify the purchase of the life insurance. Obviously, the fact that the unrelated person is named as beneficiary and has possession of the policy does not rebut the prima facie case. The fact that the policy was to secure delinquent support payments for the benefit of the insured's minor children may be sufficient justification for the purchase of the policy, but this is not a determination which the insurance company should have to make.

The question of whether use of community funds is constructive fraud upon the wife is a difficult one. It is stated in Johanson, *Revocable Trusts and Community Property: The Substantive Problems,* 47 Tex.L.Rev. 537, 568 (1969):

> As a group the cases do not give clear guidelines. At best, they point up the factors that bear on the decision whether a transfer is likely to be held in constructive fraud of the wife's rights. Among the factors that have been emphasized are the relationship of the transferee to the transferor or his wife; whether there are special circumstances that tend to justify the transfer; the value of the assets transferred in relation to the total value of the community estate; and whether the wife has adequately been provided for out of the remaining community property and the separate property of the husband.

To require the insurance company in this case to discover every fact that may be a circumstance justifying use of the community funds, decide which facts are true and which are false, and apply the law of constructive fraud to those facts would defeat the very purpose of interpleader. An insurance company should not be compelled to act as judge and jury. Since we hold that interpleader was properly available to Great American, we also uphold the trial court's award to it of $500 attorney fees.

The court of civil appeals held that Great American was not in good faith in failing to interplead within 30 days under Article 3.62. That statute assesses a 12% penalty and reasonable attorney fees against the insurance company in favor of the rightful claimant where the company has failed to pay the claimant within 30 days. Several cases have held that where circumstances exist which make interpleader a proper remedy, as in this case, failure to pay the money into the court within 30 days after demand does not make the insurer liable for the penalty and attorney fees. In this case, the interpleader suit was filed thirty-seven days after the demands for the proceeds were received. We are not deciding whether in another case a period of delay before interpleading the competing claimants might be so unreasonable as to justify imposition of the statutory penalty.

We reverse the judgment of the court of civil appeals and affirm that of the trial court.

QUESTIONS FOR REVIEW

1. What conditions are prerequisite to the plaintiff who seeks relief in equity?
2. Distinguish between the two types of injunctions.
3. Describe the equitable remedy of specific performance.
4. Discuss equity and the jury.
5. Give an illustrative situation which might lead an insurer to seek each of the following remedies in equity: interpleader, rescission, reformation, and declaratory judgment.
6. What is a "disinterested stakeholder?"
7. What are some of the grounds upon which rescission can be sought?
8. What is the significance of the legal concept of materiality in relation to rescission?
9. Describe the nature of the judgment in a suit for declaratory judgment.

CHAPTER 17

Policy Contests

VALID, VOID, AND VOIDABLE CONTRACTS

MATERIAL MISREPRESENTATION

MISREPRESENTATION STATUTES
Fraudulent or Material Misrepresentation
Misrepresentation Related to the Cause of Loss

BREACH OF CONDITIONS

CONTEST OF THE POLICY

DEVELOPMENT OF THE INCONTESTABLE CLAUSE
Warranties
Representations

CONFLICT WITH OTHER PROVISIONS
The Majority View
The Minority View
The Model Statute
Misstatement of Age Clause

CONTESTS NOT BARRED BY THE
INCONTESTABLE CLAUSE
Fraudulent Impersonation
Lack of an Insurable Interest
Policy Procured With Intent to Murder

CONTESTABILITY OF DISABILITY AND
ACCIDENTAL DEATH INSURANCE

THE PHRASE *DURING THE LIFETIME
OF THE INSURED*
The Statutory Remedy
Omission of the Phrase

DATE FROM WHICH THE CONTESTABLE
PERIOD RUNS

SUMMARY

A contest of a life insurance policy is a court action to determine the validity of the policy. If there has been material misrepresentation in the application, the insurer might institute a suit to rescind the policy, or defend, on the ground that the policy is invalid, a lawsuit instituted by the beneficiary. These are policy contests.

Contracts are invalid if there are certain defects in their formation. In general contract law, a contract can be rescinded at any time, on the ground that the contract is invalid, by a party who discovers that there was material misrepresentation by the other party at the time of the contract's formation. This is a basic rule of general contract law.

However, life insurance policies have a unique clause—the incontestable clause—which abrogates this basic rule after a specified period of time, usually two years. In other words, because of the incontestable clause, ordinarily a life insurer can rescind the policy or defend against payment of the proceeds, on the ground that the policy is invalid, only during the first two years following the policy issue date. The purpose of this chapter is to discuss policy contests, particularly as they are affected by the incontestable clause.

VALID, VOID, AND VOIDABLE CONTRACTS

Contracts are said to be valid, void, or voidable. A valid contract is enforceable in either a court of law or of equity, depending upon the remedy sought. Certain requirements relating to offer, acceptance, consideration, competency of the parties, and legality of purpose must be met if an agreement is to be a valid informal contract. These were discussed in Chapter 2, "Contracts."

To say a contract is "void" is actually a contradiction in terms, since the word *contract* means an agreement enforceable by court action. Where the agreement is not enforceable by court action, it is not a contract. The terms *void contract,* or *contract void ab initio* (from the beginning), are commonly used, however, and are used in this book.

For example, a life insurance contract will be void *ab initio* where the required insurable interest is not present. Insurable interest is of such fundamental importance that its absence will make an attempted life insurance contract void—that is, no contract at all.

A voidable contract is enforceable until a party who has the right to do so takes some action to disaffirm—that is, to avoid—the contract. An informal contract is ordinarily voidable if there are certain defects in its formation. A party's lack of contractual capacity, mutual mistake of the parties, or material misrepresentation by a party are some of the formation defects which will make the contract voidable by one or more of the parties.

MATERIAL MISREPRESENTATION

This chapter deals primarily with life insurance policy contests due to material misrepresentation. If one party has misrepresented a material fact which induces the other party to enter into a contract he or she would not have entered into knowing the truth, the other party can sue for rescission, or defend an action for performance of the contract.

Material misrepresentation in the application for a life insurance contract is most commonly discovered when the insurer is investigating an early death claim. An early death claim is a claim for life insurance benefits where the insured died soon after the policy became effective. Material misrepresentation is not significant with respect to claims under older policies because of the incontestable clause, as will be discussed below. When material misrepresentation is discovered while investigating an early death claim, the claim can be denied on that basis. As the insurer would not have entered the contract as applied for if it had known the truth, the insurer is entitled to deny the claim and refund the premiums paid.

Sometimes, however, material misrepresentation is discovered while the insured is still living. Perhaps the insurer is investigating a disability claim by the insured, or reviewing a second application for insurance on the insured's life. When the insurer receives an application, it is routine practice for it to search its records for policies already in force or applications submitted on the same life. The insurer must do this to control the aggregate amount of insurance it issues on one life. During such claim or application reviews, information is sometimes discovered which leads to an investigation revealing health history that has been misrepresented by a living insured. Whenever information of this kind is revealed during the contestable period, the insurer usually takes prompt action to rescind the policy. Ordinarily, this means that the insurer, after verifying its information completely enough to support a court action, notifies the policyowner that it elects to rescind the policy and is returning the premiums paid. If the policyowner refuses the refund of premiums, the insurer initiates a suit to have the court rescind the policy.

One reason that most life insurers take prompt action to rescind where material misrepresentation is discovered while the insured is still living is that the insurer might lose the right to rescind if it knew the facts and, nevertheless, treated the contract as continuing in force, or failed to object within a reasonable length of time. A second reason is that the incontestable clause is required by law to establish a deadline—in most states, two years from the policy issue date—beyond which the insurer cannot contest the policy's validity on the ground of material misrepresentation or breach of a condition precedent.

MISREPRESENTATION STATUTES

Most of the states have enacted statutes defining the type of misrepresentation that must have occurred if the insurer is to contest the policy.

Fraudulent or Material Misrepresentation

Many misrepresentation statutes state that the misrepresentation must either have been made with intent to deceive—that is, fraudulently—or be material to the risk. The Illinois statute falls into this group and reads as follows:

> No such misrepresentation or false warranty shall defeat or avoid the policy unless it shall have been made with actual intent to deceive or materially affects either the acceptance of the risk or the hazard assumed by the company.[1]

In some states, misrepresentation statutes prohibit an insurer from using a misrepresentation in the application to contest the policy unless the misrepresentation was fraudulent. A misrepresentation that is material, but not fraudulent, will not suffice. Ohio, for example, requires the following:

> No answer to any interrogatory made by an applicant in his application for a policy shall bar the right to recover upon any policy issued thereon, or be used in evidence at any trial to recover upon such policy, unless it is clearly proved that such answer is willfully false, that it was fraudulently made, that it is material, and that it induced the company to issue the policy, that but for such answer the policy would not have been issued, and that the agent or company had no knowledge of the falsity or fraud of such answer.[2]

Where the insurer claims the misrepresentation was made fraudulently, the insurer must prove there was intent to deceive on the part of the person who made the misrepresentation. However, the courts will infer intent to defraud if the facts clearly indicate that there could be no other explanation.

For example, in one Pennsylvania case, the applicant had had at least 13 consultations with four different physicians in a city 100 miles from her home within two years of the date of application. Yet, she stated in her application that there had been no consultations with any physician within the past seven years. The court said:

> The consultations were clearly of such important character and of such recent occurrence as could not be forgotten, and the insured must have been fully cognizant that she hid them from the insurer by her false answer. In this connection, we said in *Evans v. Penn Mutual Life Ins. Co.,* 322 Pa. 547, 553, 186 A. 133, 138: "The circumstances preceding and attending the making of the statements may be such that the insured must be said to have been aware of their falsity at the time or that an inference of fraud is otherwise irresistible, as for instance where an unreported illness or disability of insured was so serious and so recent that he could not have forgotten it."[3]

---

[1]ILL. REV. STAT. ch. 73, ¶ 766 (1985) (Ill. Ins. Code § 154).
[2]OHIO REV. CODE ANN. § 3911.06 (Page 1971).
[3]Bailey v. Pacific Mut. Life Ins. Co., 336 Pa. 62, 6 A.2d 770 (1939).

Misrepresentation Related to the Cause of Loss

A few states take the position that material misrepresentation cannot be used as a basis for a contest of the policy unless the misrepresentation related to the actual cause of loss. For example, in Missouri, the misrepresentation statute reads as follows:

> No misrepresentation made in obtaining or securing a policy of insurance on the life or lives of any person or persons, citizens of this state, shall be deemed material, or render the policy void, unless the matter misrepresented shall have actually contributed to the contingency or event on which the policy is to become due and payable, and whether it so contributed in any case shall be a question for the jury.[4]

Under a statute of this kind, the insurer would not be permitted to defend a claim denial on the basis of material misrepresentation in the application if the misrepresented facts related to a malignancy, and the insured died of a heart attack. Only if the insured died of the malignancy could the insurer defend the claim denial.

BREACH OF CONDITIONS

When a life insurance contract is voidable by the insurer, the reason is usually that there was a material misrepresentation in the application. However, the breach of a condition precedent to effectiveness of the contract can also cause the contract to be voidable by the insurer. Such conditions precedent are incontestable after the contestable period has expired, according to the majority view.

For example, most life policies state that a proposed insured must be in good health when the policy is delivered. This is a condition precedent to the effectiveness of the policy. Suppose, for example, that Jerome Wiseman, a proposed insured, was in good health at the time he filled out and signed the application for life insurance. Mr. Wiseman answered all questions on the application truthfully. The application indicated Mr. Wiseman had had no significant health problems. However, two weeks after submitting the application, and before the policy had been issued, Mr. Wiseman unexpectedly suffered a massive heart attack. Shortly thereafter, the soliciting agent went to Mr. Wiseman's office to deliver the policy and left it with his secretary who did not mention the reason for Mr. Wiseman's absence. The policy had a two-year incontestable clause. Two years and three months after the policy was delivered, Mr. Wiseman had another heart attack from which he died.

While processing the claim for the death benefit, the insurer learned of the first heart attack. The insurer cannot contest the validity of the policy on the ground that a condition precedent to the policy's effectiveness was not

---

[4]Mo. Ann. Stat. § 376.580 (Vernon 1968).

met. The incontestable clause prevents such a contest after the contestable period has expired.

Note that here there was no misrepresentation by Mr. Wiseman. He answered all questions truthfully. This, then, is an example of a breached condition precedent which cannot be used to contest the validity of the policy after the contestable period. If, however, during the contestable period the insurer had learned of Mr. Wiseman's heart condition, the insurer could have contested the policy.

Such conditions precedent differ from exceptions to coverage and limitations of the risk. While the conditions relate to the effectiveness of the policy, exceptions and limitations spell out the risk the insurer is assuming under the policy. Examples of exceptions and limitations of the risk are the suicide clause, the war hazard exclusion clause, the aviation hazard exclusion clause, and the misstatement of age clause.

Unfortunately, some of the courts have not distinguished between conditions precedent to effectiveness of the policy on the one hand, and exceptions and limitations of the risk under the policy on the other. As will be explained in the section in this chapter entitled "Conflict with Other Provisions," this lack of understanding has resulted in a conflicting body of law.

CONTEST OF THE POLICY

The word *contest,* as applied to the incontestable clause, means a court action challenging the validity of the policy.[5] This is the majority rule. A contest can occur by the insurer's defense of an action at law brought by the policyowner or beneficiary. A contest can also be initiated by the insurer as a suit in equity against the policyowner to rescind the policy.

If the insurer files an answer in defense or brings suit within the contestable period, it will not matter that the court's judgment is not rendered until after the contestable period has expired. The insurer will have contested within the contestable period.

Generally speaking, action taken by the insurer outside of court is not a contest. Denial of liability, repudiation of the policy, or tender of premiums do not constitute a contest. Nevertheless, if an insurer tenders premiums to the policyowner, and the policyowner agrees to rescind, accepts the premiums, gives a release, and surrenders the policy, this will protect the insurer from liability.[6]

A suit to have the contract reformed so that it will conform to the original agreement of the parties is not a contest of the policy. Thus, the incon-

---

[5]*See, e.g.,* American Life Ins. Co. v. Stewart, 300 U.S. 203 (1937); Densby v. Acacia Mut. Life Ass'n, 64 App. D.C. 319, 78 F.2d 203 (1935); Fields v. Universal Life & Acci. Ins. Co., 424 S.W.2d 704 (Tex. Civ. App. 1968).

[6]Eichwedel v. Metropolitan Life Ins. Co., 216 Mo. App. 452, 270 S.W. 415 (1925); Telford v. Metropolitan Life Ins. Co., 228 N.Y.S. 54 (1928).

testable clause does not prevent the insurer from seeking reformation after the contestable period has expired.[7]

DEVELOPMENT OF THE INCONTESTABLE CLAUSE

An incontestable clause ordinarily provides that, after the policy has been in force for two years from the issue date and during the lifetime of the insured, the validity of the policy will be incontestable. For example, the clause in the illustrative policy reads as follows:

> We will not contest the validity of this Policy, except for nonpayment of premiums, after it has been in force during the Insured's lifetime for two years from the Policy Date. This provision does not apply to any rider providing accidental death or disability benefits.

Incontestability means that the insurer cannot challenge the validity of the policy—that is, defend a lawsuit for policy benefits or initiate a suit in equity to rescind the policy—on the basis of material misrepresentation in the application or failure of conditions precedent to effectiveness.[8]

This clause is unique to life insurance. In fact, it is directly opposed to a basic rule of contract law—that fraud vitiates a contract. Generally speaking, in life insurance, this rule must be revised to read, "Fraud vitiates a contract unless it is a life insurance contract with an incontestable clause, and the contestable period has expired."

What, then, is so unusual about the life insurance contract that insurers should be required by law to include in it a provision contrary to a basic rule of contract law? To answer this question, it is necessary to know something about the history of insurance generally, and, particularly, the history of warranties and representations.

Warranties

In the early days of insurance, statements made by an insurance applicant were considered to be warranties. A warranty is a statement guaranteed to be true in all respects. If the statement is untrue in any respect, even though the applicant does not know it is untrue, and even though the statement is not material, the contract can be rescinded. A warranty is part of the contract.

The warranty doctrine was first applied in marine insurance where it did not result in hardship to the insured because, ordinarily, no extensive period of time elapsed between the making of the contract and any dispute that

---

[7]Annot., 7 A.L.R. 2d 504 (1949). Schaefer v. California-Western States Life Ins. Co., 262 Cal. App. 2d 840, 69 Cal. Rptr. 183 (1968); Johnson v. Consolidated Am. Life Ins. Co., 244 So. 2d 400 (Miss. 1971).

[8]See the discussion of breaches of conditions precedent above.

might arise about its validity. When the doctrine of warranties was applied to life insurance, however, it did create hardships.

Often life insurance premiums had been paid over a long period of time and the misstatements concerned were trivial, yet the insurer would disaffirm the contract at the death of the insured. The beneficiary was left without policy benefits unless he or she sued the insurer and won. The beneficiary's lawsuit was made difficult because he or she had to defend against an alleged misstatement in the application made many years earlier and about which the beneficiary might know little or nothing. Ordinarily, the person who had made the statement—the insured—was dead. Thus, the beneficiary was seriously handicapped in a dispute about the exact truth of statements in the application.

During the latter half of the 18th and early part of the 19th centuries, warranties in insurance contracts were enforced with technical exactness by the courts of England and the United States. If warranted facts were not true exactly as stated, the insurer could avoid the contract at any time. Insurers found that by the latter half of the 19th century, their readiness to litigate with respect to every deviation from the absolute truth in the application was creating distrust in the public. Insurers had gained a reputation, as one commentator put it, of being "the great repudiators."

The London Indisputable Life, an English insurer, was the first to attempt to counteract the distrust thus created. In 1848, it included a provision in its charter relinquishing the right to contest a policy for any reason whatsoever. In 1864, in the United States, the Manhattan Life Insurance Company introduced the first policy clause providing for incontestability.

By the time of the Armstrong Investigation in 1905, a majority of life insurers in the United States were voluntarily including an incontestable clause in their policies. The Standard Policy Provisions Law, enacted in New York following the Armstrong Investigation, included a mandate that life policies include an incontestable clause. Later, the Committee of Fifteen, appointed in the wake of the Armstrong Investigation, recommended model state legislation which also included an incontestable clause. This was subsequently enacted into law by a majority of the states.

Representations

A representation, as contrasted with a warranty, is not a part of the contract itself, but is a statement by an applicant of facts upon which the insurer bases its decision whether or not to issue the applied-for policy. Moreover, unlike a warranty, a representation need not be true in all respects, but need only be true as to facts material to the risk. Where the statements are representations, the insurer cannot rescind the contract or defend a suit for benefits on the ground of misrepresentation of a fact unless the fact is material. If the statements are warranties, the insurer could so defend or rescind, whether or not the misrepresented fact is material to the risk.

Modern state insurance codes commonly require that life insurance policies contain a provision declaring that, in the absence of fraud, all statements in the application shall be deemed representations and not warranties. Thus, the doctrine of warranties, as applied to life insurance, has become mainly of historical interest.

CONFLICT WITH OTHER PROVISIONS

The rule in the majority of states is that the incontestable clause relates only to contests of the validity of the policy. Moreover, it is generally agreed by lawyers and students of the life insurance contract that life insurers originally included the incontestable clause as a waiver of their right to contest the policy for misstatements by the applicant. Nevertheless, the way in which insurers have typically worded the clause has cast doubt on this. Incontestable clauses usually read something as follows: "This policy shall be incontestable after it has been in force during the lifetime of the insured, for a period of two years from the issue date, *except for nonpayment of premiums."* [Emphasis added.]

A logical question concerning such a clause is this: "Why does the incontestable clause say it is not applicable to the nonpayment of premiums if the purpose of the clause is to prevent a contest in the event of a misstatement in the application?" Sometimes, an incontestable clause states that it does not apply to the war hazard exclusion clause or some similar clause, and the same question can be asked in that instance.

If these exceptions or limitations had never been included in the incontestable clause, there would probably have been little question as to its legal effect. The word *contest* would have been accepted as meaning a court challenge to the validity of the contract, based on rules applicable to contracts generally. The incontestable clause would have been accepted for what it was undoubtedly intended to be—a pledge of good faith in the form of a waiver, after a specified period of time, of any legal right the insurer might otherwise have had to challenge the validity of the contract.

When a life insurer denies a claim on the basis that premiums were not paid by the end of the grace period or that the insured was killed as the result of military service, it is denying the claim on a different basis than when it asserts it has no liability because the contract is invalid by reason of material misrepresentation. When the insurer contends it has no liability because renewal premiums were not paid, or because the insured died as a result of military service, it is assuming the validity of the contract and alleging a failure to fulfill its conditions, or a violation of its terms. It is not contending that the policy is not valid. A policy provision stating that the contract will be incontestable except for nonpayment of premiums, or death as a result of military activities, creates doubt as to the meaning the insurer intended to give to the word *contest*.

Moreover, if an insurer states that the incontestable clause does not apply to the nonpayment of premiums but does not mention the war hazard exclusion clause, does this mean the insurer cannot defend a claim based on the death of a soldier in war under the war hazard exclusion clause if the contestable period has expired? A maxim of contract interpretation—*expressio unius est exclusio alterius*—has led some courts to rule that it does.

Expressio unius est exclusio alterius means that the expression of one thing implies the exclusion of another. In other words, in a contract the expression of one or more things of a class implies the exclusion of all in the class which are not expressed. Nonpayment of premiums, the war hazard exclusion clause, the suicide clause, and similar clauses comprise the class in this instance. According to the courts in some jurisdictions, therefore, if the policy were to state that the incontestable clause was not applicable to nonpayment of premiums and to the suicide clause, but did not mention the war hazard exclusion clause or aviation hazard exclusion clause, the latter two clauses would not be effective after the contestable period because these clauses had not been specifically excluded from the operation of the incontestable clause.[9]

The Majority View

Probably the best statement of the majority view concerning the impact of the incontestable clause on other policy provisions is found in *Metropolitan Life Insurance Co. v. Conway*.[10] This opinion was written in 1930 by Judge Benjamin Cardozo who later became a Justice of the United States Supreme Court. The suit was between an insurer and the Superintendent of Insurance of New York. The Superintendent had refused to approve an aviation hazard rider which limited recovery to the payment of the reserve if the insured's death occurred due to certain aviation activities. The Superintendent took the position that the provisions of the rider were inconsistent with the incontestable clause required by New York law. It was as if the Superintendent were saying to the insurer: "After two years from the date of issue, the incontestable clause prohibits you from contesting the policy. Yet, you are now requesting permission to include in your policies a provision expressly declaring that if the insured should, at any time, meet death by reason of aviation activities, you will not be liable for more than the reserve."

---

[9]*See, e.g.*, Mutual Reserve Fund Life Ass'n v. Austin, 142 F. 398 (C.C.A. Mass. 1905); Fore v. New York Life Ins. Co., 180 Ark. 536, 22 S.W.2d 401 (1929); Goodwin v. Provident Saving Life Assur. Soc'y, 97 Iowa 226, 66 N.W. 157 (1896); Bernier v. Pacific Mut. Life Ins. Co., 173 La. 1078, 139 So. 629 (1932).

[10]252 N.Y. 449, 169 N.E. 642 (1930).

The insurer's position was that it was free to specify risks that it was unwilling to assume throughout the life of the contract, even though the policy became incontestable after two years. Thus, the insurer argued that under a policy with an aviation hazard exclusion, the insurer, in paying only the reserve if death occurred due to aviation activities, was carrying out the terms of the policy and not contesting it. The lower appellate court decided for the insurer. The Court of Appeals of New York upheld that decision as follows:

> We agree with the Appellate Division in its holding that rider and statute in this instance are consistent and harmonious. The provision that a policy shall be incontestable after it has been in force during the lifetime of the insured for a period of two years is not a mandate as to coverage, a definition of the hazards to be borne by the insurer. It means only this, that within the limits of the coverage the policy shall stand, unaffected by any defense that it was invalid in its inception, or thereafter became invalid by reason of a condition broken. Like questions have arisen in other jurisdictions and in other courts of this state. There has been general concurrence with reference to the answer.

The Minority View

Although *Conway* represents the majority view, there is, as previously stated, a minority view also. The same question concerning aviation riders was presented to the Louisiana Supreme Court in *Bernier v. Pacific Mutual Life Insurance Co.*[11] two years after *Conway* was decided. The Louisiana court in *Bernier* took the minority view, stating:

> The provision in a life insurance policy, making the contract incontestable after a stated period, means something more than that the insurer cannot then contest the validity of the policy on the ground of breach of a condition; it means that the company cannot then contest its obligation to pay, on due proof of the death of the insured, the amount stated on the face of the policy, except for a cause of defense that is plainly excepted from the provision making the policy incontestable.

Thus, the court in *Bernier* in effect held that the incontestable clause was a mandate to coverage and that an insurer could not "contest its obligation to pay" except for a reason plainly reserved in the wording of the incontestable clause itself. A few other courts have taken a similar view, although not always for the same reasons.

The Model Statute

Because of this divergence of opinion in the courts, the Life Insurance Association of America and the American Life Convention appointed a

---

[11]173 La. 1078, 139 So. 629 (1932).

committee in 1947 to draft a recommended statutory provision. This committee drafted a statutory provision adopting the majority position of *Conway*. It reads as follows:

> A clause in any policy of life insurance providing that such policy shall be incontestable after a specified period shall preclude only a contest of the validity of the policy, and shall not preclude the assertion at any time of defenses based upon provisions in the policy which exclude or restrict coverage, whether or not such restrictions or exclusions are excepted in such clause.

This model statute has been enacted by a few states.

Misstatement of Age Clause

The relationship of the misstatement of age clause and the incontestable clause should be mentioned. A misstatement of age clause allows the insurer to pay benefits according to the amount of insurance the premiums would have purchased at the insured's correct age where the age was misstated in the application.

Because the age of the insured has such a vital relationship to the risk of death, a misstatement of age clause was commonly used by life insurers before the introduction of the incontestable clause. With the growing use of the incontestable clause, however, the question arose as to whether an adjustment for misstatement of age could be made after the expiration of the contestable period. In other words, was this also a contest of the policy which would be barred by the incontestable clause after the expiration of the contestable period?

In some of the earlier policies, misstatement of age was listed in the incontestable clause as one of the exceptions. Thus, the incontestable clause was held not to prevent an adjustment for misstatement of age in such instances, since it was specified as an exception in the clause.

Where a misstatement of age clause is not excepted in the incontestable clause, the majority of courts have reached the conclusion that there is no conflict between the two clauses. For instance, in one 1939 case,[12] the court said:

> The suit is based on a life insurance policy issued to Oliver P. Langan, a citizen of Missouri, with his wife (plaintiff) as beneficiary. The policy is for the face amount of $10,000, annual premium $434, age of insured stated as 53 and contract commencing January 13, 1927. The policy provides that after one year from its date it shall be incontestable except for nonpayment of premiums, and also contains the following: "If the age of

---

[12]Langan v. United States Life Ins. Co., 344 Mo. 989, 130 S.W.2d 479 (1939).

the Insured has been understated, the amount payable hereunder shall be such as the premium paid would have purchased at the correct age; if the age of the Insured has been overstated the company will return the excess premium, or premiums, paid."

In his application, the insured stated that he was born on July 14, 1873, and that his age at nearest birthday was 53 years.

. . . The beneficiary (plaintiff) furnished sworn proof of death to the defendant, in which she stated that insured was born on July 14, 1871, and that she derived this information from the family Bible. A statement furnished by the undertaker also stated that insured was born on July 14, 1871.

. . . [Plaintiff] contended that the defendant could not legally avoid paying the face amount of the policy for two reasons: (1) Because of the provision in the policy for incontestability; (2) because the age adjustment clause in the policy comes within the prohibition of our statute dealing with misrepresentations, which reads as follows: "No misrepresentation made in obtaining or securing a policy of insurance on the life or lives of any person or persons, citizens of this state, shall be deemed material, or render the policy void, unless the matter misrepresented shall have actually contributed to the contingency or event on which the policy is to become due and payable, and whether it so contributed in any case shall be a question for the jury."

. . . [The insurer] contends: (1) The incontestability provision is not applicable because defendant is not contesting the provisions of the policy, but is only seeking to confine its liability within the express terms of the policy; (2) that the misrepresentation statute does not apply because it refers only to misrepresentations made to obtain a policy and not to terms agreed upon and expressly written in the policy itself.

. . . [W]e conclude that the weight of authority is that an incontestable clause does not prevent the enforcement of an age adjustment clause contained in the same policy.

CONTESTS NOT BARRED BY THE INCONTESTABLE CLAUSE

The general rule is that after the expiration of the contestable period, all contests relating to the validity of the policy are barred. Like most rules, this has its exceptions. These exceptions—fraudulent impersonation, lack of an insurable interest, and procurement of the policy with an intent to murder—are discussed in this section.

Fraudulent Impersonation

Where application is made to insure the life of one person, but another person, fraudulently impersonating the proposed insured, signs the application or takes the medical examination, the incontestable clause will not bar the insurer from contesting the policy at any time. This is the majority rule.

For example, in *Obartuch v. Security Mutual Life Insurance Co.,*[13] a suit was filed for death benefits on the life of Frank Obartuch. The insurer admitted that the contestable period had elapsed but denied liability on the ground that the application was either not signed, or not knowingly signed, by Frank Obartuch. Moreover, the insurer alleged that a person unknown to it was fraudulently substituted for Frank Obartuch at the medical examination. The court's conclusions of law were as follows:

> 1. That it is contrary to public policy for any person to obtain life insurance by substituting an individual other than the named insured for medical examination, and a policy secured by such substitution is void;
>
> 2. That the incontestable clause in the policies in suit does not preclude the defense that the person examined by the defendant's medical examiner was not Frank Obartuch, but someone else who impersonated said Frank Obartuch.
>
> 3. That said policies did not constitute a valid contract with Frank Obartuch and, if valid at all, were contracts upon the life of the person examined by the defendant's medical examiner.
>
> 4. That there was never any valid contract of life insurance upon the life of Frank Obartuch because he never knowingly signed any application therefor or authorized any other person to sign an application for him.

Quoting another case, *Maslin v. Columbian National Life Insurance Co.,*[14] the court pointed out:

> There cannot be the slightest doubt that the person whom an insurance company intends to make a contract with and intends to insure is the person who presents himself for physical examination.
>
> * * * * *
>
> The defendant's only contract was with the man who made the application and took the examination.

In the *Ludwinska* case,[15] a similar situation is considered. The person named as the insured was an imbecile and the application for insurance was made by her sister who also impersonated the named insured at the medical examination. The court held that if anyone was insured it was the sister and not the one named in the policy.

---

[13]114 F.2d 873 (7th Cir. 1940), *cert. denied,* 312 U.S. 696 (1941).

[14]3 F. Supp. 368 (S.D.N.Y. 1932).

[15]Ludwinska v. John Hancock Mut. Life Ins. Co., 317 Pa. 577, 178 A. 28 (1935).

Lack of an Insurable Interest

The incontestable clause does not bar a policy contest based on lack of an insurable interest, according to the majority view.[16] It is well established that a person cannot enter into a valid and enforceable contract insuring the life of another person if the beneficiary has no insurable interest in the life of the insured. Such a contract is void from the beginning, as against public policy. If a contract containing an incontestable clause is void from the beginning, the incontestable clause which is part of the contract necessarily fails also. In other words, if no contract came into existence in the first place, the incontestable clause never existed either.

Policy Procured with Intent to Murder

If the policy was procured with the intent to murder the insured, the incontestable clause will not bar a contest of the policy.[17] Again, the policy is void from the beginning, and the incontestable clause is not operative.

For example, in *Henderson v. Life Insurance Co. of Virginia*,[18] the insured, a 15-year-old boy, was apparently induced by his foster father, James R. Thomas, the applicant and beneficiary, to sign an application indicating consent to the insurance on his life (if the application was in fact signed by the insured and not by someone else). James R. Thomas falsely represented that he was the insured's natural father. Thus, Thomas took out eight policies on the insured's life with six different insurers. Thomas then murdered the insured, was caught, convicted, and sentenced to life imprisonment.

The insured's administratrix sued for the benefits on behalf of the insured's estate because Thomas, the named beneficiary, was disqualified from receiving the benefits. The question before the court was whether the insurer was prevented from contesting the validity of the contracts because the contestable period had elapsed. The court said:

> [T]he incontestable clause does not constitute a bar to the defense that the insurance was procured with the express purpose of murdering the insured and thus derive the benefits thereunder, or the defense that a contract was wagering. Both of these circumstances make the contract

---

[16]*See, e.g.*, Aetna Life Ins. Co. v. Hooker, 62 F.2d 805 (6th Cir. 1933), *cert. denied,* 289 U.S. 748 (1933); Carter v. Continental Life Ins. Co., 73 App. D.C. 60, 115 F.2d 947 (1940); Home Life Ins. Co. v. Masterson, 180 Ark. 170, 21 S.W.2d 414 (1929); Charbonnier v. Chicago Nat'l Life Ins. Co., 266 Ill. App. 412 (1932); Wharton v. Home Sec. Life Ins. Co., 206 N.C. 254, 173 S.E. 338 (1934); Clement v. New York Life Ins. Co., 101 Tenn. 22, 46 S.W. 561 (1898).

[17]Goldstein v. New York Life Ins. Co., 133 N.Y. Misc. 106, 231 N.Y.S. 161 (1928); Columbian Mut. Life Ins. Co. v. Martin, 175 Tenn. 517, 136 S.W.2d 52 (1940).

[18]176 S.C. 100, 179 S.E. 680 (1935).

void as against public policy, and no rights in favor of any one can accrue thereunder. As one court pointedly said, the incontestable clause is no more a part of the contract than any of its other provisions, and, when the contract falls, it brings with it all of its constituent parts.

Thus the court held that no benefits were payable to anyone.

CONTESTABILITY OF DISABILITY AND ACCIDENTAL DEATH INSURANCE

When the incontestable clause was introduced, life insurance itself was the only coverage offered in a life insurance contract. Therefore, the early legislation requiring incontestable clauses related only to life insurance.

In the years that followed, life insurers began offering disability coverages, either as clauses in the life insurance policy or as riders to it. Since that time, many cases have been decided concerning the contestability of disability provisions and of accidental death provisions as well.

Many courts have recognized that life insurance and disability insurance are essentially different and that those differences provide sound reasons for holding that the statutory incontestable requirements for life insurance do not apply to disability provisions.

Disability insurance claims, unlike life insurance claims, are often made before the contract has been in force for a long period of time. Witnesses, including the insured, are usually readily available. Moreover, when disability provisions are held to be contestable, the person penalized is generally the contracting party, and not a beneficiary as with life insurance. Granting the contracting party immunity from the consequences of her or his own misrepresentation or fraud is often difficult to justify.

In 1922, the National Convention of Insurance Commissioners recommended that statutes requiring incontestable clauses be amended to permit life insurers to except disability and accidental death provisions from the operation of the incontestable clause. An amendment of this kind has since been incorporated into the statutes of about one half of the states.

The insurer's right to exclude disability and accidental death provisions from the operation of the incontestable clause was upheld in the case of *Equitable Life Assurance Society v. Deem*[19] where the court said:

> The policy as a whole includes three separate kinds of insurance, which constitute in reality three major promises of insurance protection, life, accident and disability. It seems entirely clear that the insurer intended to avail itself of the statutory authority to make the incontestable clause inapplicable to the latter two of these risks, and thus excepted from the clause those provisions of the policy relating to them.

* * * * *

[19] 91 F.2d 569 (4th Cir. 1937), *cert. denied,* 302 U.S. 744 (1937).

While ambiguities which fairly exist in insurance policies must be re-solved in favor of the insured, it is not permissible for courts by a strained and over-refined construction of ordinary words to create an ambiguity which would not otherwise exist. . . . And while the incontest-able clause is a valuable feature of life insurance and is to be liberally construed to effectuate its beneficent purpose, there is no reason to deny to the insurer the option given by statute to except from its operation the additional features of disability and double indemnity benefits, where its purpose to do so has been definitely expressed. "To make a contract in-contestable after the lapse of a brief time is to confer upon its holder extraordinary privileges. We must be on our guard against turning them into weapons of oppression."

Thus, where the incontestable clause contains an appropriate exception, the majority of the courts have upheld the insurer's right to contest the valid-ity of the disability provisions, even after the expiration of the contestable period. However, some courts have denied insurers this right. Numerous cases have arisen on this question, and the decisions are highly conflicting.

By the weight of authority, if no specific exception is made in the incon-testable clause, disability provisions and accidental death provisions are held subject to the incontestable clause, as is life insurance. After the expiration of the contestable period, the validity of such a policy cannot be contested with respect to any of its provisions.

THE PHRASE *DURING THE LIFETIME OF THE INSURED*

Most life insurance policies today include the phrase *during the lifetime of the insured,* or similar wording, in the incontestable clause. The illustrative policy in Appendix B states the following: "We will not contest the validity of this Policy, except for non-payment of premiums, after it has been in force *during the Insured's lifetime* for two years from the Policy Date." [Emphasis added.]

The phrase *during the lifetime of the insured* has not always been in-cluded in the incontestable clause. The original incontestable clauses con-tained no such wording. It was assumed that the death of the insured stopped the running of the contestable period. In other words, it was assumed that if the insured died during the contestable period, the policy would never be-come incontestable.

However, in 1918, in *Monahan v. Metropolitan Life Insurance Co.,*[20] the plaintiff challenged this assumption. The facts of *Monahan* were these: The insured died during the contestable period. The claim made for the death benefit was denied on the basis of breach of the warranties in the application.

---

[20]283 Ill. 136, 119 N.E. 68 (1918).

Thereupon, the beneficiary waited until the expiration of the contestable period before bringing suit.

The policy clause read as follows:

> After two years this policy shall be noncontestable, except for nonpayment of premiums.

The Illinois Supreme Court interpreted this clause literally. As the contestable period had expired at the time suit was filed, the court said the insurer was precluded from defending on the basis of breach of warranties in the application. In short, the court held that the insured's death did not stop the running of the contestable period.

The Statutory Remedy

Following the *Monahan* decision, an insurer's only remedy in similar situations would have been to bring suit for rescission during the contestable period. In many instances, this would have been inconvenient. In other instances, it would have been impossible—as where the insured died near the end of the contestable period.

For these reasons, shortly after the *Monahan* decision Illinois and New York amended their statutes to permit the inclusion of the phrase *during the lifetime of the insured* in incontestable clauses. Soon thereafter, the National Convention of Insurance Commissioners recommended legislation permitting the inclusion of the phrase *during the lifetime of the insured* in the incontestable clause.

Today, when a life insurance policy includes an incontestable clause with this phrase, the courts generally agree that if the insured dies before the expiration of the contestable period the policy never becomes incontestable. In other words, when the insured's death occurs before the end of the contestable period, the policy has not been in force for "two years during the lifetime of the insured." No matter how long the beneficiary waits to sue, the insurer can contest the validity of the policy.

Omission of the Phrase

Where the incontestable clause contains the phrase *during the lifetime of the insured* and the insured dies during the contestable period, the insurer can at any time defend a lawsuit brought by the beneficiary on the ground of material misrepresentation or breach of a condition precedent. The insurer, therefore, has an adequate remedy at law. Because it has an adequate remedy at law, it cannot bring suit in equity for rescission of the contract.

However, some insurers feel that it would be to their advantage to have the facts decided in the equity court where there is ordinarily a judge deciding them, rather than in a court of law where a jury will probably decide. For this reason, these insurers often omit the words *during the lifetime of the insured* from the incontestable clause. If these words are not included in the incontestable clause, and the insured dies during the contestable period, the insurer will ordinarily lose the right to contest the validity of the policy after the contestable period expires. The insurer, thus, does not have an adequate remedy at law and is entitled to bring an action in equity to have the policy rescinded. These insurers feel that the added burden of instituting a suit in equity is offset by the advantage of having the facts decided by a judge, rather than a jury.

Massachusetts Mutual Life Insurance Co. v. Goodelman,[21] decided by the United States District Court for the Eastern District of New York in 1958, illustrates the availability of the equitable remedy of rescission where the phrase *during the lifetime of the insured* is omitted from the incontestable clause.

This case concerned a policy issued on February 27, 1956, insuring the life of Leon Goodelman in the amount of $100,000. The insured died on December 22, 1957, only slightly more than two months before the expiration of the contestable period. Within the contestable period, the insurer elected to rescind the policy and tendered the premiums paid on it. The insurer based this decision on material misrepresentation, as the insured did not disclose that he was suffering from diabetes and arteriosclerosis when the application was completed. The beneficiary would not agree to rescind.

On February 20, 1958, seven days before the expiration of the contestable period, the insurer instituted a suit in equity for rescission of the contract. It took this action because the incontestable clause did not contain the phrase *during the lifetime of the insured.* After the expiration of the contestable period, the beneficiary sued the insurer for the proceeds of the policy (the "second action" mentioned in the quotation below) and filed a motion that the insurer's suit in equity for rescission be dismissed on the ground that the insurer had an adequate remedy at law. The court denied this motion to dismiss as follows:

> The grounds urged by defendant for dismissal of the instant action for rescission is that the sole issue between the parties is basically legal in nature; that the plaintiff has a complete and adequate remedy at law in that it can assert its claims of fraud and misrepresentation in the aforesaid second action and thus assure the present defendant of her right to a trial by jury of that action.
>
> The principal issue on this motion is whether the Mutual Company had the right to resort to a court of equity with its claims for rescission or should have delayed action until the beneficiary sued on the policy and then interposed its defenses in such action. Mutual contends that if it had delayed bringing its action beyond the two year period from date of issue of the policy, it would have lost its right to defend by the operation of the incontestability clause in the contract. It reads as follows:

---

[21]160 F. Supp. 510 (E.D.N.Y. 1958).

Incontestability. This policy . . . shall be incontestable after it has been in force for a period of two years from its date of issue.

It is crystal clear from a mere reading of the provision that if Mutual had any remedy pertaining to the policy, such remedy must be asserted within the two year period, in this case prior to February 27, 1958. It could not be availed of beyond that time.

. . . Mutual was not precipitate in instituting its action for rescission. It delayed doing so until its claim was about to be outlawed by the incontestability clause. In fact, barely one week remained for it to take action or forfeit its right to do so. In a similar rescission case, American Life Insurance Co. v. Stewart, 300 U.S. 203, 57 S.Ct. 377, 379, 81 L.Ed. 605, the plaintiff's right to resort to equity by way of claim for rescission was upheld. Mr. Justice Cardozo writing for the Court, said:

If the policy is to become incontestable soon after the death of the insured, the insurer becomes helpless if he must wait for a move by some one else, who may prefer to remain motionless till the time for contest has gone by. . . . Accordingly an insurer, who might otherwise be condemned to loss through the mere inaction of an adversary, may assume the offensive by going into equity and there praying cancellation.

The court, thus, held that the insurer did not have a remedy at law and could bring its action in equity. If the incontestable clause had included the words *during the lifetime of the insured,* the insurer would have had a remedy at law and could not have instituted action in the equity court.

DATE FROM WHICH THE CONTESTABLE PERIOD RUNS

Many policy provisions include the usual statutory language and make the policy incontestable after it has been in effect for two years from "date of issue." As the policy date and the date when the policy was issued are often different, there can be a question as to which of these dates is the one from which the contestable period shall be computed.

The majority of courts hold that if the insurance does not become effective until after the date of issue, the contestable period begins to run from the date of issue. However, where the policy bears a date of issue later than that on which the insurance becomes effective, as in the case of a backdated policy, the period will be held to begin on the earlier date. In this, as in other instances, the terms of the policy will be construed most favorably toward the insured and beneficiary to give incontestability at the earliest possible time.

SUMMARY

If there has been a material misrepresentation in an application for life insurance, the insurer will often wish to contest the validity of the policy. A policy contest is a court action in which the insurer sues in equity court to rescind the contract, or defends a denial of benefits in a lawsuit brought by the beneficiary. The insurer can contest the policy's validity if there has been either material misrepresentation in the application or breach of a condition precedent to effectiveness of the policy. Some states have statutes prohibiting policy contests unless the misrepresentation is fraudulent or material. Others have statutes prohibiting policy contests unless the misrepresentation is related to the cause of loss.

The incontestable clause of a life insurance policy states that the validity of the policy cannot be contested once the contestable period has passed. The incontestable clause relates to contests of the validity of the policy and not to denial of benefits under policy exceptions and limitations, according to the majority view. The exceptions and limitations are ordinarily effective after the contestable period has passed.

Certain policy contests are not barred by the incontestable clause. Even after the contestable period has expired, fraudulent impersonation, lack of an insurable interest, and procurement of the policy with intent to murder the insured are grounds for a contest of the policy.

Disability and accidental death coverages in a life insurance policy are often specifically excluded from the operation of the incontestable clause. Statutes in many states permit such an exclusion. If no exclusion is included in the incontestable clause, the majority view is that the policy will become incontestable as to the disability and accidental death coverages, just as to the life coverage, when the contestable period has expired.

Most incontestable clauses today include the phrase *during the lifetime of the insured*. This phrase stops the running of the contestable period if the insured dies before the policy has become incontestable. In other words, the policy will never become incontestable if the insured dies during the contestable period and the incontestable clause contains this phrase. The insurer will be able to defend a lawsuit on the ground that the policy is invalid whenever the suit is brought. The insurer, therefore, has an adequate remedy at law and cannot sue in equity for rescission. Some insurers feel that the right to sue in equity where there is ordinarily a judge deciding the facts, rather than a jury, is to the insurer's advantage. Some of those insurers do not include the phrase *during the lifetime of the insured* in the incontestable clause so as to preserve their right to sue for rescission in equity if the insured dies within the contestable period.

ILLUSTRATIVE CASE

In this case the court discussed the meaning of the term *contest* and held that, in order to contest a life insurance policy, the insurer would either have to file suit within the contestable period, or defend a lawsuit brought within the contestable period.

*PROVIDENT NATIONAL BANK, Testa-
mentary Trustee under the Last Will
and Testament of James A. Lefton,
Plaintiff,*

v.

*CONTINENTAL ASSURANCE COM-
PANY, Defendant*[22]
United States District Court,
E. D. Pennsylvania

MEMORANDUM OPINION
VanARTSDALEN, District Judge.

Plaintiff, as testamentary trustee, under the Last Will and Testament of James A. Lefton, has filed a motion for a judgment on the pleadings pursuant to Rule 12(c) of the Federal Rules of Civil Procedure. This court has diversity jurisdiction and Pennsylvania law is applicable. All of the facts necessary for determination are contained in the pleadings. The only issue remaining is a question of law, and a judgment on the pleadings is appropriate. The undisputed facts are as follows and will be considered as findings of fact to the extent that such may be necessary under Rule 12(c), Federal Rules of Civil Procedure.

On November 1, 1969, defendant, for a valuable consideration, executed and delivered to James A. Lefton, a member of the American Marketing Association, a life insurance policy under Certificate of Insurance issued under the terms of Group Life Insurance Policy No. L29775, insuring members of the American Marketing Association. The face amount of the policy was $40,000.00.

The insurance policy in question under Paragraph 17, General Provisions, contains the following language:

"This Policy shall be incontestable after two (2) years from its date of issue, except for nonpayment of premium. No statement made by any Insured relating to his insurability shall be used in contesting the validity of the insurance under the Policy with respect to which such statement was made after such insurance has been in force prior to the contest for a period of two (2) years during such Insured's lifetime nor unless it is contained in a written instrument signed by such Insured."

James A. Lefton died on February 26, 1971. Defendant, by letter dated July 26, 1971, advised plaintiff that they were denying the claim under this policy. By stipulation of counsel for the purposes of the motion for judgment on the pleadings, the parties agree that "the Continental Assurance Company has begun no lawsuit or litigation seeking to contest the insurance policy herein involved up to the time of the filing of the Complaint in the above captioned matter."

Defendants deny coverage due to an alleged misrepresentation as to the health of Lefton. The effective date of the insurance policy was November 1, 1969. This suit was instituted on November 2, 1971, one day after the two year incontestability clause of Paragraph 17 of the policy became effective. The only issue involved

---

[22]343 F.Supp. 29 (1972).

is a question of law as to the meaning of the first sentence of the incontestability clause.

Plaintiff contends that the policy becomes incontestable two years after its effective date unless the insurance company contests the policy by a law suit or affirmative defense in a law suit during a two year period from date of issuance of the policy. Defendants contend that its notice to plaintiff denying liability on the policy within the two-year period is sufficient and that it need not contest the policy by law suit or affirmative defense to a law suit within two years from date of issuance of the policy.

There are three Pennsylvania Superior Court cases that have considered the present issue and all have construed the exact language of this policy to mean that the insurance company must either file suit or affirmatively defend a law suit brought during the two-year contestability period in order to effectively "contest" the policy.

In *Prudential Insurance Co.* v. *Ptohides,* 122 Pa.Super. 469, 186 A. 386 (1936), the "incontestability clause" was quoted as follows: "This policy shall be incontestable after one year from the date of issue, except for nonpayment of premium, ..." *Id.* at 470–471, 186 A. at 386. The court posed the following question at page 472, 186 A. at page 387: "Second. What kind of action must be taken by the company in order to institute a valid contest of its liability?" In amplification of that question, the court said at page 474, 186 A. at Page 388, "In other words, is the contest contemplated by the clause a contest in court, either by the institution, within the time limited, of appropriate proceedings for the surrender and cancellation of the policy, or by making a defense to a suit brought within the period upon the policy?" The court answered this question by saying that appropriate proceedings in a court are essential to a valid contest by the insurer. In the case of *Kessler* v. *National Life & Accident Insurance Company,* 124 Pa.Super. 319, 188 A. 377 (1936), the court citing the *Ptohides* case stated:

> "In Prudential Insurance Company v. Ptohides, 122 Pa.Super. 469, 186 A. 386, decided July 10, 1936, it was held that the only legally effective way in which an insurer may 'contest' its liability under a policy, upon the ground of fraud in its procurement, is by offensive or defensive proceedings in a court. That is, either by the institution, within the time limited, of appropriate proceedings for cancellation, or by making a defense to a suit brought within the period upon the policy. It was repeated in that case, citing Feierman v. Eureka Life Ins. Co., 279 Pa. 507, 124 A. 171, and Cohen, et al. v. Metropolitan Life Ins. Co., 112 Pa.Super. 314, 171 A. 106, that the death of the insured during the period of contestability does not affect either the running of that period or the obligation of the insurance company to act within the time specified if it desires to contest its liability."

The case of New York Life Insurance Company v. Del Bianco, 161 Pa.Super. 566, 56 A.2d 319 (1948), affirms the position previously taken by the court in *Ptohides & Kessler, supra.*

In the case of Franklin Life Insurance Company v. Bieniek, 312 F.2d 365 (3rd Cir. 1962), the Third Circuit Court of Appeals considered the aforementioned Pennsylvania Superior Court cases and held them to express the applicable Pennsylvania law with respect to the meaning of the incontestability clause here in question and held that a letter of notice is insufficient. It is abundantly clear that Pennsylvania law requires that the insurer "contest" the policy by either bringing an action or defending an action within the contestability period or be forever barred by the terms of the incontestability clause.

Defendant cites two cases which he contends support his position. There is dicta in the case of Feierman v. Eureka Life Ins. Co., 279 Pa. 507, 124 A. 171 (1924), which can be construed as saying that the incontestability clause such as in this case does not require a "contest" by the legal action, as follows:

> "The great weight of authority supports the position that the insurer must at least disavow liability within the contestable period to be relieved,—not necessarily by legal action, but some definite step, specifying the ground of complaint, in such form as to effect a cancellation of the contract. The clause means precisely what its language states: the policy will not be challenged, opposed, or litigated, and is indisputable after two years. During this period, the company may contest it for any sufficient reason. The incontestable clause is for the benefit of the insurer, in that it induces people to insure in the company, and requires no act of the insured to put it in motion or aid in the discovery of facts on which it may fasten to the insurer's benefit. Therefore insured's death within the time does not stop investigation or relieve of the duty to investigate false representations or other fraudulent circumstances on which the policy is based. The knowledge that false representations have been made must be ascertained within the two years, and, in the same time, the company, by some act, must rescind, cancel or notify the insured or the beneficiary that it will no longer be bound by the policy."

The Pennsylvania Superior Court in Prudential Ins. Co. v. Ptohides, *supra,* clearly distinguished the holding from the dicta in *Feierman, supra,* 122 Pa.Super. at 474, 186 A. at 388, by stating: "In view of the question actually involved in that case [Ptohides], this language cannot properly be interpreted as a decision by our Supreme Court that mere notice to an insured, or, in case of his death, to his beneficiary, that the company intends to contest its liability, upon a specified ground, is sufficient." The Superior Court further stated that had the matter come squarely before the State Supreme Court, it would have held that mere notice, in the absence of legal proceedings would be insufficient. In Prudential Ins. Co. v. Himelfarb, 362 Pa. 123, 66 A.2d 257 (1949), the Court held that the filing of a bill in equity to rescind within the period of incontestability, but served thereafter, was sufficient. No State Supreme or Superior Court case has ever held that mere notice, absent a legal proceeding, would avoid the incontestability clause.

Defendant's reliance on the case of Carpentieri v. Metropolitan Life Insurance Company, 138 Pa.Super. 1, 10 A.2d 37 (1939), is factually inapplicable. The incontestability clause in the *Carpentieri* case is materially different from the language here involved. The relevant part of the clause in *Carpentieri* is as follows: "This Policy shall be incontestable after it has been in force, during the lifetime of the Insured, for a period of one year from its date of Issue, ..." *Id.* at 5, 10 A.2d at 38. Naturally, the phrase, "during the lifetime of the insured," modifies the effect of the contestability period; for if an insured dies within one year of the date of the issuance of the policy, the incontestability clause by its terms does not become effective. In *Carpentieri,* the court clearly distinguished the clause and its effect from those in *Feierman, Kessler* and *Ptohides*.

For the above reasons, plaintiff's motion for a judgment on the pleadings must be granted.

QUESTIONS FOR REVIEW

1. Discuss valid, void, and voidable contracts.
2. Define the term *policy contest*.
3. How does the breach of a condition precedent to effectiveness of the policy relate to policy contests?
4. Discuss the history of the incontestable clause.
5. Define the term *warranty*.
6. Define the term *representation*.
7. Explain the effect the incontestable clause would have if:
   a. Death was the result of suicide within two years.
   b. There had been a misstatement of age.
8. Under what circumstances are policy contests not barred by the incontestable clause?
9. Does the incontestable clause apply to disability and accidental death coverages? Explain.

CHAPTER 18

Contract Performance

ESTABLISHING THE PROPER PAYEE
    No Named Beneficiary
    Executor or Administrator Beneficiaries
    Trustee Beneficiaries
    Assignee Beneficiaries
    Incompetent Beneficiaries
    Homicide Beneficiaries
    Common Disasters
    Conflicting Claimants
    Unclaimed Benefits
SUICIDE
    The Suicide Exclusion
    Policies Without a Suicide Exclusion
    Suicide and the Accidental Death Benefit
DISAPPEARANCE OF THE INSURED
    Mysterious Disappearance
    Explainable Disappearance
    Keeping the Policy in Force
    Reappearance
WAR OR AVIATION HAZARD EXCLUSIONS
COMPUTATION OF THE BENEFIT AMOUNT
RELEASES
COMPROMISE SETTLEMENTS
UNFAIR CLAIM SETTLEMENT PRACTICES ACT
THE REASONABLE EXPECTATIONS DOCTRINE
CLAIMS LITIGATION
    Compensatory Damages
    Punitive Damages
SUMMARY

A contract is performed when the acts required by the contract are done. A life insurance contract is performed when all the promises it contains have been carried out. Ordinarily, this happens when the insured has died, and the benefits are paid to the beneficiary.

A life insurance contract requires that proof of loss be submitted after the insured's death. The illustrative policy in Appendix B provides the following:

> If the Insured dies while this policy is in force, we will pay the sum insured to the Beneficiary, when we receive at our Home Office due proof of the Insured's death, subject to the provisions of this Policy.

Thus, the insurer's claims adjuster will check to make certain the policy was in force at the insured's death. Due proof of the insured's death is usually made by means of a certified death certificate submitted by the beneficiary. Life insurers consider it an essential part of their responsibilities to pay death benefits as promptly as possible, as the benefits are often necessary for the support of the insured's survivors. In the great majority of cases no problems are encountered, and the death benefit is paid promptly.

In some instances, however, the insurer encounters legal problems in performing the contract. The purpose of this chapter is to explore significant legal problems related to life insurance contract performance.

ESTABLISHING THE PROPER PAYEE

Ordinarily, the beneficiary designation has been properly drafted, and there is no question as to whom the benefit is payable. In a small minority of cases, however, there is a problem in establishing the proper payee. The problems involved in these cases will be discussed in this section.

No Named Beneficiary

Under most ordinary life insurance contracts, if there is no surviving beneficiary at the death of the insured, the policy provides that the benefits will be paid to the policyowner or to the policyowner's estate. Some policies, notably group life policies covering federal government employees or persons in the armed services, provide a listing of contingent beneficiaries, in order of preference, if there is no named beneficiary. Under this government insurance, these are the insured's widow or widower, children and descendants of deceased children, per stirpes, parents or parent, estate, or next of kin. The term *per stirpes* is discussed in Chapter 10, "Beneficiary Designations and Changes."

Executor or Administrator Beneficiaries

A policyowner-insured sometimes names the executor or administrator of his or her estate as primary beneficiary. At other times, the executor or administrator will be the proper payee under the policy terms because all named beneficiaries have predeceased the insured.

When an executor or administrator is the claimant, the insurer will require evidence of her or his appointment by the court. Ordinarily, a certified copy of the letters of administration appointing an administrator, or letters testamentary appointing an executor, are requested by the insurer.

Trustee Beneficiaries

When a trustee is named beneficiary, the insurer will need evidence of the trustee's appointment and power to act before paying the trustee. The insurer will require a certified copy of the trust agreement in some situations. Sometimes, the original trustee named in the trust has died or resigned or has been removed. In that case, the insurer must be certain that the person claiming to be the successor trustee has been appointed. If the trustee of a testamentary trust is the policy beneficiary, the will creating the trust must be probated to be certain the will is valid. In addition, the testamentary trustee must qualify before the trustee can be paid the benefits.

Assignee Beneficiaries

Collateral transfers, or assignments, of life insurance policies are often made by policyowners when they borrow money. Assignment of the policy to the lender secures the loan made to the policyowner. Usually, today, these assignments are made pursuant to the terms of an assignment form which gives the assignee—usually a bank or other lending institution—the right to receive from the insurer as much of the net proceeds of the policy as the assignee, by affidavit filed with the insurer, claims to be due under the assignment. The form provides that the remainder of the proceeds, if any, is to be paid in accordance with the latest beneficiary designation, mode of settlement or other assignment then of record.

In the absence of a statute to the contrary, a beneficiary with vested rights in a life insurance policy can assign his or her right to the proceeds to another person. The proceeds are then payable to the person receiving the right—the assignee.

Incompetent Beneficiaries

Generally speaking, a minor or mentally incompetent person cannot give the insurer a binding release for payment of the proceeds. For this reason, payment of proceeds where the beneficiary is incompetent requires careful handling. Often the involvement of the insurer's lawyers is required.

A release can be disaffirmed by a minor during her or his minority or within a reasonable time after she or he reaches majority. For this reason, whenever a minor is the beneficiary, the insurer must carefully examine the relevant state laws to determine what benefits, if any, can be paid directly to the minor and what benefits must be paid to a guardian of the minor's estate, or held at interest for the minor until her or his majority.

In some states, a minor over a certain age, usually 15 or 16, can make specified contracts for life, accident, or health insurance and can give a binding release for benefits payable to the minor under such a contract. The Alabama statute provides the following:

(a) Any person of competent legal capacity may contract for insurance.

(b) Any minor of the age of 15 years or more, as determined by the nearest birthday, may, notwithstanding his minority, contract for annuities or for insurance upon his own life, body, health, property, liabilities or other interests or on the person of another in whom the minor has an insurable interest. Such a minor shall, notwithstanding such minority, be deemed competent to exercise all rights and powers with respect to, or under:

(1) Any contract for annuity or for insurance upon his own life, body or health; or

(2) Any contract such minor effected upon his own property, liabilities or other interests or on the person of another, as might be exercised by a person of full legal age, and may at any time surrender his interest in any such contracts and give valid discharge for any benefit accruing or money payable thereunder.

Such a minor shall not, by reason of his minority, be entitled to rescind, avoid or repudiate the contract nor to rescind, avoid or repudiate any exercise of a right or privilege thereunder; except, that such a minor, not otherwise emancipated, shall not be bound by any unperformed agreement to pay by promissory note or otherwise, any premium on any such annuity or insurance contract.

(c) Any annuity contract or policy of life or disability insurance procured by or for a minor under subsection (b) of this section, shall be made payable either to the minor or his estate or to a person having an insurable interest in the life of the minor.[1]

Thus, for example, if a 15-year-old minor in Alabama contracted for life insurance on the life of his or her child and named himself or herself beneficiary, the minor could give a binding release for the benefits.

In many instances, the minor is not the policyowner, and a statute such as the one quoted above does not apply. For example, a parent might name a minor child the beneficiary of the parent's insurance policy. In such an instance, some states have a statute allowing an insurer to make limited payments to a parent or to another person caring for the minor. A few states

---

[1] ALA. CODE § 27–14–5 (1986).

have a statute allowing an insurer to pay out limited amounts directly to a minor who has reached a specified age. The Montana statute reads as follows:

> Any minor domiciled in this state who has attained the age of 16 years shall be deemed competent to receive and to give full acquittance and discharge for a payment or payments in aggregate amount not exceeding $3,000 in any one year made by a life insurer under the maturity, death, or settlement agreement provisions in effect or elected by such minor under a life insurance policy or annuity contract, provided such policy, contract, or agreement shall provide for the payment or payments to such minor and if prior to such payment the insurer has not received written notice of the appointment of a duly qualified guardian of the property of the minor.[2]

In the absence of a statute permitting payment without a guardian, only a court-appointed guardian of the minor's estate has competence to give a binding release where a minor is the beneficiary. However, appointment of a guardian of the minor's estate requires a court hearing with attendant delays and expenses. When a claim is filed by the guardian of a minor's estate, the insurer will require a certified copy of the court order of appointment.

Ordinarily, a parent must be appointed guardian of her or his child's estate by the court, as would any other person, or the parent will not be able to give a binding release. The parent's status as guardian of the minor's person usually does not make the parent legally competent to give a binding release without such court appointment. Nor does the appointment as guardian of the minor's person of someone who is not the minor's parent make that person competent to give a binding release for the proceeds, unless that person has been appointed as guardian of the minor's estate also.

If no guardian of the minor's estate is appointed and no statute permits payment by the insurer without such a guardian, the insurer ordinarily must hold the proceeds at interest until the minor beneficiary reaches the age of majority. The beneficiary can then give a binding release.

As with minors, beneficiaries who are mentally incompetent cannot give the insurer a binding release. If the court has appointed a guardian of the incompetent beneficiary's estate, the payment can be made to such a guardian. If the beneficiary is institutionalized, small amounts of insurance proceeds are sometimes paid to a trust account maintained for the beneficiary by the institution.

Homicide Beneficiaries

For reasons of public policy, a beneficiary who intentionally and wrongfully kills the insured is usually disqualified from receiving the life insurance

---

[2]Mont. Code Ann. § 33–15–502(1) (1987).

proceeds. The law protects human life and prohibits that which encourages murder. The law does not allow people to profit from their own wrongdoing.

Justifiable Homicides.   Unless there is a state statute to the contrary, the killing must be wrongful to disqualify the beneficiary. For example, a killing in lawful self-defense is not wrongful. If the beneficiary kills in lawful self-defense, he or she will not be disqualified from receiving the proceeds.[3] Such a killing is justifiable homicide. Nor will an accidental killing of the insured by the beneficiary disqualify the beneficiary.[4] Finally, if the beneficiary was insane at the time he or she killed the insured, the beneficiary will not be disqualified unless the policy specifically provides otherwise.[5]

Lesser Degrees of Wrongful Killing.   There are a number of gradations of wrongful killing. Not all wrongful killing is murder. A wrongful killing can be classified as first-degree murder, second-degree murder, voluntary manslaughter, involuntary manslaughter, reckless homicide, and so forth. Each state has its own classifications of wrongful killing. The classification of the homicide, as well as the law of the state in regard to homicide beneficiaries, must be carefully examined by the insurer to determine if the beneficiary is disqualified.

In one case, a state statute provided that a beneficiary would be disqualified only if the beneficiary was convicted of the insured's murder. A beneficiary in that state was convicted of voluntary manslaughter of the insured, not of murder. The court held that the beneficiary was entitled to the proceeds.[6] But, in another state, the beneficiary was disqualified from receiving the proceeds when her culpable negligence resulted in the insured's death.[7] Culpable negligence is a lesser degree of wrongful killing than voluntary manslaughter. Thus, where homicides of a lesser degree are involved, the laws of the relevant state must be carefully examined. The insurer often must file a bill of interpleader and pay the proceeds to the court in order to protect itself.

Acquitted Beneficiary.   Sometimes, the beneficiary is acquitted of the murder of the insured after being tried in a criminal proceeding. Such acquittal does not necessarily mean that the beneficiary is entitled to receive the proceeds. A suit to enforce payment of life insurance proceeds is a civil action, and the rules of evidence in civil actions are different from those in criminal proceedings. It is possible for a person to be acquitted of a charge of murdering the insured, yet be judged disqualified to receive the proceeds

[3]Provident Life & Acci. Ins. Co. v. Carter, 345 So. 2d 1245 (La. Ct. App. 1977).
[4]Franklin Life Ins. Co. v. Strickland, 376 F. Supp. 280 (N.D. Miss. 1974).
[5]Holdom v. Ancient Order of United Workmen, 159 Ill. 619, 43 N.E. 772 (1895); Simon v. Dibble, 380 S.W.2d 898 (Tex. Civ. App. 1964).
[6]Rose v. Rose, 79 N.M. 435, 444 P.2d 762 (1968).
[7]Quick v. United Benefit Life Ins. Co., 287 N.C. 47, 213 S.E.2d 563 (1975).

in a civil action. Thus, suppose Jeffrey Brown, the insured, is killed by Barbara Brown, his wife and primary beneficiary. If she is acquitted of the charge of murder in a criminal proceeding by reason of temporary insanity, she still could be judged disqualified to receive the life insurance benefits in a civil action.[8]

Policies Procured in Good Faith.   In instances where the insured has procured the policy, or where the beneficiary has procured the policy in good faith and without intent to murder the insured, the benefits will be payable to someone, even though the beneficiary is disqualified because she or he killed the insured. The question then arises as to whom the benefits should be paid. The state law must be consulted on this point also. Some states have statutes which provide that the contingent beneficiary will receive the proceeds.[9] Other states have statutes providing that the proceeds shall be paid as if the homicide-beneficiary had predeceased the insured.[10] Still others provide that the benefits are payable to the insured's estate[11] or to the insured's nearest relative.[12] Where there is no statute, the majority of courts have held that the contingent beneficiary is entitled to the proceeds. A minority of courts have held that the executor or administrator of the insured's estate is the proper payee.

Policies Procured with Intent to Murder.   In the rare instance where it is proved that the beneficiary purchased an insurance policy with the intent to murder the insured, the insurer does not have to pay the proceeds to anyone, according to the majority view. In such an instance, the policy is void. For example, in *Ellis v. John Hancock Mutual Life Insurance Co.*,[13] the United States District Court for the Eastern District of Arkansas held that a person who purchased (or instigated the purchase of) a policy on the life of another, with intent to murder the insured, could not recover the proceeds and that the policies were void from their inception. The court stated the following:

> Less than one month before William Scroggins' death, William and Sharon Scroggins, his bigamous wife, procured from Farmers an insurance policy on the life of William Scroggins. Said policy named Sharon Scroggins as primary beneficiary and her two daughters by a previous marriage were named as second beneficiaries . . .

---

[8]*See* United States v. Kwasniewski, 91 F. Supp. 847 (E.D. Mich. 1950). There, a contingent payee was disqualified from receiving the remaining proceeds, although he was acquitted of the murder of the primary payee by reason of insanity. *See also* California-Western States Life Ins. Co. v. Sanford, 515 F. Supp. 524 (E.D. La. 1981).

[9]*E.g.*, Or. Rev. Stat. § 112.515 (1984).

[10]*E.g.*, R. I. Gen. Laws § 33–1.1–11 (1970).

[11]*E.g.*, Okla. Stat. Ann. tit. 84 § 231 (West Supp. 1988).

[12]Tex. Ins. Code Ann. § 21.23 (Vernon 1981).

[13]586 F. Supp. 649 (1984).

The plaintiff, administrator of the estate, contends that although Sharon Scroggins is the named beneficiary . . . she conspired and in fact contracted with Ruby Lee Henry and Randall James to have William Scroggins murdered. Ruby Henry and Randall James are now serving 30– and 40–year terms, respectively, for the death of William Scroggins. Plaintiff contends that since Sharon Scroggins conspired and contracted to have William Scroggins killed, under Arkansas law, the proceeds of the policies go to the estate. Farmers contends that not only did Sharon Scroggins conspire to have William Scroggins killed, but that she procured the policy with Farmers with the purpose and intent of having William Scroggins killed. Therefore, Farmers contends that the Farmers policy is void *ab initio*.

. . . What is the legal effect, regarding the validity of the Farmers' policy and the distribution of the proceeds, if Sharon Scroggins conspired to have William Scroggins killed?

. . . Since the Court has concluded that for purposes of this suit, the evidence indicates that Sharon Scroggins conspired and contracted to have her husband killed, it must also conclude that Sharon Scroggins cannot recover the proceeds as a beneficiary under the policies. It is well settled in Arkansas that when the beneficiary in a life insurance policy wrongfully kills the insured, public policy prohibits a recovery by the beneficiary.

The next question is whether the Farmers policy is void *ab initio*, thereby precluding any liability on the part of Farmers. The general rule of law is that a life insurance policy is void from its inception and the insurer is relieved of all liability upon the subsequent homicide of the insured where it is proved that a beneficiary procured the policy possessing a then present intention to murder the insured.

It was Sharon Scroggins who expressed the interest in the life insurance policy and who made the original inquiry. It was Sharon Scroggins who became agitated and cursed when she was told her husband's signature was required. Although William Scroggins did, in fact, go to the insurance agent, sign the application, and submit himself to a 15 minute standard physical conducted by a paramedic, the Court is of the opinion that William Scroggins did not participate in the procuring of the insurance in such a manner as to become, in effect, the party who contracted with the insurance company. In fact, William Scroggins was nothing but a mere innocent instrumentality in Sharon's scheme, and Sharon procured the policy with the present intention to murder the insured.

The court, therefore, held that no benefits were payable to anyone, because the policy was void.

Common Disasters

If the insured and the primary beneficiary are killed in a common disaster, the insurer must determine whether they died simultaneously. If both were killed at the same instant, or if they died in such a way that it cannot be determined who died first, the state's simultaneous death act will apply.

A simultaneous death act provides that, unless there is a clause in the policy to the contrary, where an insured and beneficiary die simultaneously, or where it is impossible to tell who died first, it will be deemed that the beneficiary died first. State simultaneous death acts are patterned on the Uniform Simultaneous Death Act drafted by the National Conference of Commissioners on Uniform State Laws.

Although the simultaneous death acts of the states vary somewhat, that of Illinois is typical. It reads as follows:

> No sufficient evidence of survivorship. If the title to property or its devolution depends upon priority of death and there is no sufficient evidence that the persons have died otherwise than simultaneously and there is no other provision in the will, trust agreement, deed, contract of insurance or other governing instrument for distribution of the property different from the provisions of this Section:
>
> (a) The property of each person shall be disposed of as if he had survived.
>
> * * * * *
>
> (d) If the insured and the beneficiary of a policy of life or accident insurance have so died, the proceeds of the policy shall be distributed as if the insured had survived the beneficiary.[14]

If the beneficiary survives the insured for even a short time, the state's simultaneous death act will not apply. If the policy or beneficiary designation has a time clause, that clause might determine who is to receive the proceeds. A time clause provides that the beneficiary must survive the insured by a specified number of days, or the benefits will be paid as if the beneficiary had died before the insured. The time clause in the illustrative policy in Appendix B reads as follows:

> If any beneficiary dies simultaneously with the Insured or during the 14 days immediately following the date of death of the Insured, the proceeds of the Policy shall, unless otherwise provided in the application or in a written request, be paid to the same payee or payees and in the same manner as if the deceased beneficiary had died before the Insured. Any reference in this Policy to a beneficiary living or surviving shall mean living on the 15th day immediately following the date of death of the Insured.

If the policyowner has entered into a settlement agreement naming a contingent payee, the contingent payee will receive the remaining proceeds when the primary payee dies. This will be true whether the primary payee and insured die simultaneously, or whether the primary payee survives the insured. A settlement agreement is often a good way to solve the problems connected with short-term survivorship. See the discussion on this subject in Chapter 11, "Settlement Agreements, Trusts, and Wills."

---

[14]ILL. REV. STAT. ch. 110 ½, ¶ 3–1 (1985).

Conflicting Claimants

Sometimes, the insurer is faced with two or more claimants for the proceeds. This can happen for a variety of reasons. For example, a policyowner-insured might have entered into a property settlement agreement in which he or she agreed to maintain the spouse or minor children as beneficiaries. If the policyowner-insured then names a second spouse or someone else as beneficiary, there might be two or more conflicting claimants for the proceeds. Or, as another example, a policyowner-insured might have partially completed a beneficiary change at the time of his or her death. If the intended beneficiary claims the insured substantially complied with the policy provisions regarding beneficiary change, but the original beneficiary denies this, the insurer will again be faced with conflicting claimants.

When there are conflicting claimants, the insurer ordinarily will encourage them to settle their differences. If the conflicting claimants agree on a division of the benefits, and each gives the insurer a release from all claims to the benefits, the insurer can pay the claimants according to their agreement. If the claimants will not agree, and if there is any question as to which person is entitled to the proceeds, the insurer usually will pay the proceeds to the court in an interpleader action. Interpleader is discussed in Chapter 16, "Remedies."

Unclaimed Benefits

Sometimes, the insurer cannot find the proper payee of a life insurance benefit. When this happens, the insurer does not become the owner of such unclaimed benefits. Rather, the benefits become subject to the unclaimed property statute of one of the states. Usually, this will be the unclaimed property statute of the state of the beneficiary's last known address. If no address is known, the statute of the insurer's state of domicile will govern.[15]

Nearly all the states have unclaimed property statutes. Most of these statutes are based upon the Uniform Disposition of Unclaimed Property Act, drafted by the National Conference of Commissioners on Uniform State Laws. An unclaimed property statute also applies to other types of unclaimed property and not just to unclaimed insurance benefits. Unclaimed deposits held by banks is one example. These statutes are sometimes called escheat statutes, but this is a loose use of the term *escheat*. *Escheat* means reversion of ownership of property to the state in the absence of persons legally entitled to take claim to the property. Under most unclaimed property statutes, the state merely holds and uses the property.

Ordinarily, the state law provides that the insurer will hold the unclaimed benefits for seven years, after which time they will be considered abandoned.

---

[15]Texas v. New Jersey, 379 U.S. 674 (1965), *supp. by* Texas v. New Jersey, 380 U.S. 518 (1965).

The benefits must then be reported to the state. State officials will advertise their existence in a newspaper and send a notice to the beneficiary's last known address. If no one claims the benefits, the insurer must pay them to the state.

The state has full use of the funds, but under most unclaimed property statutes the beneficiary can claim them from the state at any time. In some states, however, the state becomes the owner of the property after holding it for a specified number of years. In that case, the property is said to escheat to the state.

SUICIDE

Suicide is the intentional killing of oneself. The suicide of an insured person can substantially affect the performance of the life insurance contract. The effect of an insured's suicide is discussed in this section.

The Suicide Exclusion

Most modern life insurance policies contain a provision which states that death benefits will not be payable if the insured dies by suicide within a certain period, usually two years, after the policy becomes effective. The insurer will return only the amount of the premiums paid, less any indebtedness. The illustrative policy in Appendix B has the following provision:

> If the Insured dies by suicide, while sane or insane, within two years from the Policy Date, our liability will be limited to the amount of the premiums paid, less any indebtedness.

The suicide clause represents a compromise between two competing interests. On the one hand, the best interests of the policyowners as a group must be considered. If the insurer made no effort to prevent a person who was contemplating suicide from securing life insurance benefits for her or his dependents, the other policyowners would have to share the resulting higher costs of life insurance.

On the other hand, the economic loss to the insured's dependents is just as great when the insured commits suicide as when she or he dies in some other manner. The purpose of life insurance is to protect against the economic loss resulting from the insured's death.

A policy provision such as the one quoted above is generally believed to furnish sufficient protection against those who might be tempted to have their beneficiaries profit from their contemplated suicides. Few people will apply for life insurance with the intention of waiting two years before committing suicide. At the same time, the provision also protects the beneficiary of an insured who commits suicide two or more years after the policy becomes effective.

Suicide Statutes.   Some states have statutes defining the period during which the risk of suicide can be excluded from a life insurance contract. The Tennessee statute quoted below is typical:

[T]he following causes of death may be excepted by a provision in the policy:
  (a) Suicide committed, while sane or insane, within two (2) years from the date of issue of the policy.[16]

A few states specify a one-year period. One state, Missouri, provides that suicide shall not be a defense to the payment of the death benefit unless suicide was contemplated by the insured at the time of application.[17] As it would be impossible in most suicide situations to prove an intent of this kind, the effect of the Missouri statute is to nullify the suicide provision of life insurance policies issued in Missouri.

While Sane or Insane.   Policy exclusions excepting risk of death by suicide, without the added words *while sane or insane,* are usually interpreted to refer only to the insured's suicide while he or she is sane. If the suicide clause excludes risk of death by suicide while sane or insane, self destruction by an insane insured ordinarily will not be covered during the exclusion period. However, courts in a minority of jurisdictions hold that an insane insured must have had an intention to kill himself or herself and a consciousness of the physical nature and consequences of his or her act. In other words, if the insured was unable to resist his or her insane impulses, or was so insane as to not understand what he or she was doing, the suicide exclusion will not apply.

Burden of Proof.   The majority of modern suicide cases concern the factual question of whether the insured's death was, or was not, suicide. When an insurer denies a claim on the ground of suicide, the burden is on the insurer to prove suicide by evidence sufficient to convince the jury.

For example, in *Still v. Metropolitan Life Ins. Co.,*[18] the insured died as a result of three bullet wounds in the chest. There were powder burns on his shirt and skin, indicating that the gun was fired at close range. The insured was found sitting in his automobile in a parking lot. The court said:

There was evidence that the decedent was having financial difficulty; that he had recently been involved in an automobile accident in which a person had been killed and a claim was pending against him on account of

---

[16]TENN. CODE ANN. § 56–7–302(5) (1980).
[17]MO. ANN. STAT. § 376.620 (Vernon 1968).
[18]118 Ga. App. 832, 165 S.E.2d 896 (1968).

it; and that he was depressed. It was also shown that the decedent purchased a gun two days before his death; and that this was the gun found just below his hands in his automobile. One of the bullets passed through the body into the seat. There were no signs of violence. A physician, who was also the coroner that investigated the death, testified that the decedent could have fired into his body three times before losing consciousness.

On the other hand, there was evidence that the decedent was not depressed; that just before his death he appeared as normal as always; that he had a cast on his right arm as a result of the automobile accident; and that although it would not be impossible, it would be difficult to fire a pistol with that hand. There was some testimony that the decedent sometimes carried money in a long type billfold chained to his belt or in his coat pocket, and that this was not found among his personal effects; that decedent could have been shot and robbed.

In a case such as this, until the evidence preponderates against death by homicide, the jury is obliged to presume that homicide was the case, i.e., there is a presumption against suicide which remains until so dispelled. . . .

The jury decided the presumption had been overcome and that the decedent had committed suicide. There is ample evidence to support their conclusion and it will not be disturbed.

The suicide period of the policy had yet to expire. Therefore, the court ruled that the death benefit was not payable because the death was caused by suicide. The insurer was liable only for the amount of the premiums paid.

In another case, *Angelus v. Government Personnel Life Ins. Co.*,[19] the court held that the insurer had not sustained its burden of proving that the insured committed suicide. There, the insured, a young marine, died of a gunshot wound in the head from a gun he was holding. The question before the court was whether the insured's death was by suicide. The court said:

[The insured] was assigned to a guard company for temporary duty, which was to terminate the day of his death.

His guard duties required that he be familiar with a .45 calibre automatic pistol. On numerous occasions, while acting as corporal of the guard, he had given instructions on the use of the automatic pistol and on safety precautions to be observed while handling it.

Throughout decedent's [the insured's] tour of duty with the guard, all pistols assigned to personnel on post or on duty were kept with a loaded clip inserted, but no round of ammunition was in the chamber. It was common knowledge among members of the guard that all pistols in actual physical custody of guard personnel were loaded.

Decedent is described as a happy-go-lucky individual with no known disturbing problems. He was a good worker, cheerful, and competent in his temporary additional duty assignment. One of his associates states:

[19]51 Wash. 2d 691, 321 P.2d 545 (1958).

"He was an exceptionally good natured marine and I never knew him to worry or sweat anything. I had known him a good while and was a very close friend of his. It always appeared to me life was just a big joke to him and I told him several times he ought to take things more seriously."

About eleven a.m. the day of his death, decedent talked with Corporal Last, who reported that he

"* * * seemed to be in a very good mood. He was especially happy because he was off guard and had liberty that night."

About five p.m. of the same day, Sergeant Nelson asked decedent "when he was coming back to work with me in fire control. He told me that he would be down in the morning and ready to go to work."

About five-thirty p.m. decedent and Corporal Tishler, with whom he was going on liberty, entered hut No. 5. Decedent talked with Corporal Ball, who stated:

". . . He was laughing and seemed to be in very good spirits as he was going on liberty and he was kidding me because I had the duty. He walked into the head [lavatory] to comb his hair and I heard him laugh and then the report of the .45."

While Corporal Tishler was combing his hair, decedent grabbed a pistol belt hanging on a peg, pulled the pistol out of the holster, "jacked a round into the chamber," put the pistol to his head, and said, "here's to it," and fired the pistol. He died several hours later.

On previous occasions, decedent had been observed playing a modified version of "Russian Roulette" with a .45 calibre automatic pistol, the same type which caused his death. He would squeeze the release on the clip, allow it to slide down, then pull the slide to the rear, and release it. If the clip dropped about half an inch, the slide would not pick up a round from the clip and place it in the chamber. The clip was then locked in place, the pistol placed at his temple, and the trigger pulled. In truth, this is not "Russian Roulette," which is played with a revolver and not an automatic pistol. His safety depended upon sleight-of-hand and not chance.

"He would never do it unless he was just trying to 'shake someone up.' He always laughed afterwards."

One witness stated that *the clip was not in the weapon* when it was recovered from the floor after the shooting. Another witness stated, when describing the weapon after the shooting,

"The pistol was fully cocked with one (1) round in the chamber and three (3) rounds in the magazine *when recovered*."

This suggests the hypothesis that the decedent believed he had released the clip and caused it to drop, so that the slide had not "jacked a round into the chamber" of the pistol. If this be true, he was mistaken.

* * * * *

We agree with the trial court; appellant did not establish suicide by a preponderance of the evidence.

The judgment is affirmed.

Policies Without a Suicide Exclusion

Some policies contain no clause excluding from coverage deaths caused by suicide. In the absence of a suicide clause, the benefit will ordinarily be payable if the insured dies as a result of suicide. There are two exceptions to this general rule.

First, if the insured purchased the policy in contemplation of suicide, the death benefit will not be payable. This is because such a purchase is a fraud on the insurer. Second, if the insured was sane at the time of the suicide, and the insured's estate is the beneficiary, the death benefit will not be payable, as a general rule.

Suicide and the Accidental Death Benefit

The accidental death benefit will not be payable if the insurer can establish that the insured committed suicide. A suicide is not an accidental death. The insured who commits suicide can forsee the death and could have prevented it.

DISAPPEARANCE OF THE INSURED

Insured persons sometimes disappear. The beneficiary who believes the absent insured is dead is then faced with the problem of proving the death. The legal problems created by the disappearance of the insured are discussed in this section.

Mysterious Disappearance

Sometimes, the disappearance of an insured person is without explanation. This is called mysterious disappearance. Most state laws provide that a person who has mysteriously disappeared will be presumed to be dead if certain criteria have been met. Ordinarily, there are four criteria. First, the person must have been continuously absent from her or his home for a specified period of time, usually seven years. Second, the absence must have been without explanation. Third, persons most likely to have heard from the missing person must have heard nothing. Fourth, the beneficiary must have been unable to locate the missing person by diligent search and inquiry.

The presumption of death is rebuttable. This means that a person who wishes to refute the presumption of death is permitted to present evidence that the missing person is alive. If evidence is presented to show that the missing person is alive, the question of survival will be decided by the jury. If such evidence is not offered, the presumption of death will stand and the court will declare the missing person dead.

The Uniform Absence as Evidence of Death and Absentee's Property Act, which is in effect in two states, abolishes the presumption of death. This model act provides that the issues of whether and when death occurred are to be submitted to the jury for decision in each case.

Explainable Disappearance

Some disappearances are explainable. There are two types of explanation for the disappearance of an insured. First, there might be reason to believe the insured purposely disappeared. Second, the missing insured might have been exposed to a specific peril, such as an airplane crash.

There are a number of reasons to believe that an insured person purposely disappeared. The insured might have been in financial or marital difficulty, or a fugitive from the law. Sometimes, the insured has told others that he or she planned to disappear. The insurer can use such circumstances in an attempt to rebut the presumption that the insured is dead.

Where the missing insured was exposed to a specific peril, such as an airplane crash, a boating accident, or a fire, the beneficiary will often be able to prove the death by circumstantial evidence without waiting for the presumption of death to arise. For example, suppose a small boat containing the insured and several other persons capsized in a violent storm at sea, and the bodies of all on board were recovered except that of the insured. The beneficiary would probably be able to establish the insured's death by circumstantial evidence without waiting for the presumption of death to arise.

Keeping the Policy in Force

Many life insurance policies on the lives of persons missing for extended periods expire for nonpayment of premiums before the presumption of death arises. The beneficiary is then faced with the problem of proving that the insured actually met death sometime prior to the date the policy expired. If the beneficiary fails to prove this, no benefits are payable.

When an insured has disappeared, the beneficiary should keep the policy in force until the insured's death has been established judicially. If it can then be proved that the insured died on a date prior to the end of the period during which premiums were paid, the overpayment of premiums can be recovered from the insurer.

Reappearance

Sometimes, an insured reappears after having been declared dead by a court and after the full benefits have been paid to the beneficiary. Generally speaking, the insurer then has the right to recover the money because it was paid under a mistake of fact.

However, if less than the full amount of the benefits was paid in a compromise settlement of a doubtful claim (also called an accord and satisfaction), the benefits cannot be recovered by the insurer. The courts will not disturb a compromise settlement.

WAR OR AVIATION HAZARD EXCLUSIONS

These exclusions have been discussed in detail in Chapter 8, "Added Benefits and Limitations." War hazard exclusion clauses are either status clauses or result clauses. Where there is a status clause, the insurer must determine whether the insured was in the military service in time of war when he or she died. If a result clause is involved, the insurer ordinarily must determine if the insured died as a result of military activities.

The aviation hazard exclusion usually limits the benefit payable if death occurs as a result of certain specified aviation activities. The increasing safety of aviation has resulted in a liberalization of aviation restrictions. Today, the restrictions ordinarily do not apply if the insured is a fare-paying passenger on a regularly-scheduled flight.

COMPUTATION OF THE BENEFIT AMOUNT

In the majority of life insurance claims, the benefit amount is computed by first adding the following items:

1. The death benefit, which is ordinarily the face amount of the policy, but may be a reduced amount if the policy is under the reduced, paid-up non-forfeiture option. Also included under this item are any adjustments required as the result of a misstatement of age.
2. Any paid-up additions.
3. Any accidental death benefit payable.
4. Any premiums paid in advance, including, under some policies, refund of any premium paid beyond the month in which death occurred.
5. Any *post mortem* dividends or dividend accumulations.
6. Any interest required by state law because of delay in payment.

From the total will be deducted:

1. Any unpaid policy loans plus accrued interest.
2. Any premium payable but unpaid at the date of death.

The remainder is the amount payable.

If death was the result of suicide during the suicide exclusion period, the liability of the insurer under most policies is limited to the amount of premiums paid, without interest. If death was the result of war or aviation activities, and death from these causes was a risk not assumed under the contract, the liability is ordinarily the amount of premiums paid or the amount of the reserve, whichever is larger.

RELEASES

A release is the giving up of a right or claim by the person who has it. Thus, if a creditor has a right to receive a sum of money from a debtor, the creditor can release that right. The written release must be delivered to the debtor to be effective.

In some states, if the release is sealed by the giver, the person who receives the release need not give consideration in exchange for it. A seal is an impression or writing made on a document, or a substance such as wax affixed to the document, evidencing an intention that the document be sealed.

In many states, however, consideration must be given by the recipient of the release to the giver of the release, or the release will not be valid. Consideration for the release of one debt is not provided by the payment of a different debt. This becomes important to life insurers when the insurer denies a claim for the accidental death benefit. If the beneficiary gives the insurer a release of the beneficiary's claim to the accidental death benefit, the insurer's payment to the beneficiary of the death benefit (one debt) is not consideration for the beneficiary's release of the accidental death benefit (another debt). The attempted release of the claim to the accidental death benefit would be invalid for lack of consideration. However, if the insurer paid a sum in addition to the death benefit, not necessarily amounting to the entire accidental death benefit, there would be consideration for the release.

COMPROMISE SETTLEMENTS

A compromise settlement is an agreement between two or more persons to settle a matter in dispute between them and the performance of the promises made in the agreement. *Compromise settlement* is the term most frequently used in insurance contract performance contexts. *Accord and satisfaction* is a more accurate term, however, as *accord and satisfaction* applies to contract disputes, whereas *compromise settlement* applies to contract disputes and other disputes as well.

Where the existence or amount of a debt is in dispute, the debt can be discharged by a compromise settlement. For example, suppose a beneficiary claimed that the insured had died in an accident, whereas the insurer claimed that disease was the cause of death. There would be a dispute as to the existence of the debt for the accidental death benefit. Suppose also that under the policy, the amount of the accidental death benefit was $100,000. If the beneficiary agreed with the insurer to accept $50,000 in discharge of the disputed debt, and the insurer paid the beneficiary this amount, they would have agreed to a compromise which was then settled by the insurer's payment of the $50,000.

UNFAIR CLAIM SETTLEMENT PRACTICES ACT

The Unfair Trade Practices Model Act, drafted by the National Association of Insurance Commissioners (NAIC), contains a section which deals with unfair claim settlement practices.[20] This section was added to the Unfair

---

[20]UNFAIR TRADE PRACTICES MODEL ACT § 4(9).

Trade Practices Model Act in 1972. Many states have incorporated statutes based on this section into their laws.

The Unfair Claim Settlement Practices section mandates that the insurer promptly and thoroughly investigate claims and settle any claim on which liability has become reasonably clear. Among other prohibitions, it forbids misrepresentations as to coverage, delay in communications regarding claims, and attempts to settle for less than the policy provides.

The NAIC has also drafted an Unfair Claims Settlement Practices Model Regulation to implement the act. The model regulation "defines certain standards which, if violated with such frequency as to indicate a general business practice, will be deemed to constitute unfair claims settlement practices."[21]

The Unfair Trade Practices Act provides that the insurance commissioner can punish an insurer for unfair claims settlement practices. Punishment can be in the form of a fine or suspension or revocation of the offending insurer's license.

THE REASONABLE EXPECTATIONS DOCTRINE

A doctrine which permits the courts to honor the reasonable expectations of policyowners and beneficiaries has been emerging since the 1960s. The reasonable expectations doctrine can be stated as follows: The reasonable expectations of policyowners and beneficiaries will be honored, even though the strict terms of the policy do not support those expectations.

The implementation of the reasonable expectations doctrine has resulted in what one author termed "judge-made insurance."[22] The claimant's actual expectation of coverage, the insurer's part in creating that expectation, and the unfairness of a policy provision are factors which can influence the court to grant coverage where the policy does not provide it.

For example, in one case,[23] an airplane passenger purchased a round-trip ticket from Los Angeles to Dayton, Ohio. Before leaving Los Angeles, he purchased an accidental death policy covering the round-trip from a vending machine and mailed the policy to his wife, the named beneficiary. The policy stated that it covered "travel on . . . scheduled air carriers."

As part of his return trip, the insured planned a flight from Terre Haute, Indiana, to Chicago, Illinois. The flight from Terre Haute to Chicago was cancelled, and the insured was forced to take an unscheduled air carrier, rather than the scheduled carrier he had planned to take. He was killed when the unscheduled carrier crashed.

---

[21]UNFAIR CLAIMS SETTLEMENT PRACTICES MODEL REGULATION § 2.

[22]Abraham, *Judge-Made Law and Judge-Made Insurance: Honoring the Reasonable Expectations of the Insured*, 67 VA. L. REV. 1151 (1981) [hereinafter Abraham].

[23]Steven v. Fidelity and Cas. Co., 58 Cal. 2d 862, 377 P.2d 284, 27 Cal. Rptr. 172 (1962).

The court held that the $62,500 in benefits was payable, because "[i]n this type of standardized contract, sold by a vending machine, the insured may *reasonably expect* coverage for the whole trip which he inserted in the policy, including reasonable substituted transportation necessitated by emergency." [Emphasis added.]

Note that the terms of the contract were not ambiguous. As was stated in Chapter 2, "Contracts," under traditional contract rules the courts do not impose their interpretation where the terms of the contract are clear and unambiguous. Thus, the reasonable expectations doctrine is a departure from these traditional contract rules.

This departure has been criticized by a number of legal scholars. They argue that it results in two conflicting bodies of contract law, one with a rationale that courts should not interpret clear and unambiguous contract language, and the other with a rationale that the reasonable expectations of the policyowner should be honored, despite clear and unambiguous language to the contrary of those expectations. Second, they argue that the court considers the reasonable expectations of one party only, the policyowner, and not the reasonable expectations of the insurer. This creates uncertainty for the insurer which will result in higher premium charges. Finally, some informed policyowners will have coverage provided them that they did not reasonably expect merely because an average policyowner would have expected it.[24]

Examples of reasonable expectations cases include those involving temporary insurance under a conditional premium receipt where the courts have held that the policyowner could reasonably expect immediate coverage on payment of premium,[25] cases where the policy contained coverage restrictions which made the policy of little value to the policyowner,[26] and cases where there were inconspicuous exclusions.[27]

It is likely that the reasonable expectations doctrine will continue to expand. It is hoped that a discrete set of legal principles for granting insurance coverage based on reasonable expectations will be developed to guide insurers.

CLAIMS LITIGATION

Denials of life or health insurance claims can result in lawsuits between a policyowner or beneficiary and the insurer. Such lawsuits can be a costly

---

[24]Abraham, *supra* note 23; Note, *The Reconstruction of Insurance Contracts Under the Doctrine of Reasonable Expectations,* 18 J. MARSHALL L. REV. 155 (1984) (authored by Scott B. Krider).

[25]Damm v. National Ins. Co. of Am., 200 N.W. 2d 616 (N.D. 1972).

[26]Kievet v. Loyal Protective Life Ins. Co., 34 N.J. 475, 170 A. 2d 22 (1961).

[27]Karol v. New Hampshire Ins. Co., 120 N.H. 287, 414 A. 2d 939 (1980).

additional expense for an insurer. This is particularly true today, because an insurer's improper denial of a claim can result in the imposition of money damages beyond the policy benefits. These additional money awards are called extra-contract damages.

If, however, an insurer's claims adjusters thoroughly investigate a claim, act with reasonable dispatch, give equal consideration to the claimant's rights and the rights of the insurer, reach a proper claims decision, and communicate that decision with a clear explanation to the claimant, many claims lawsuits can be avoided.

When an insurer is sued on a claim it has denied, there are several types of expenses which it can incur. First, there is the expense resulting from the time the insurer's employees (including attorneys employed by the insurer) and agents spend assisting in the defense of the suit. While outside attorneys are usually hired to present the defense of the suit in court, employees and agents of the insurer are frequently called on to help the outside attorneys. Outside attorneys are attorneys who work in law firms and are not employed full-time by the insurer.

Second, the costs of litigation can be substantial. These costs include not only outside attorney's fees but costs for investigation, transcripts, expert witness fees, travel, and a number of other expenses necessary for the proper defense of the lawsuit. A trial will ordinarily cost several thousand dollars. Lengthy, complex trials can cost much more.

Third, if the insurer loses the lawsuit, it will likely have to pay compensatory damages to the plaintiff. Compensatory damages are the money which the court awards to the plaintiff to compensate for a wrong done to him or her. In addition, the court could order the insurer to pay punitive damages to the plaintiff. Punitive damages are awarded to a plaintiff to punish a defendant who has acted in a malicious, fraudulent, or oppressive manner toward the plaintiff. Punitive damages—also called exemplary damages—are awarded to make an example of the defendant and, thus, dissuade others from similar behavior.

Compensatory Damages

Compensatory damages fall into several categories. First, if an insurer loses a lawsuit, it will have to pay contract damages. Contract damages are the money which a court finds that the insurer owes under the terms of the insurance contract.

Second, an insurer who loses a lawsuit might have to pay extra-contract compensatory damages. Extra-contract damages are awards of money in addition to that payable under the contract.[28] For example, an insurer might have to pay the plaintiff's attorney's fees as extra-contract compensatory

---

[28]Extra-contract damages include punitive damages, as well as extra-contract compensatory damages.

damages. These, like the insurer's own attorney's fees, can be substantial. Also, court costs might be assessed against an insurer which loses a lawsuit.

A prevailing plaintiff might also recover other extra-contract compensatory damages from the insurer. For example, there might be an award of damages for the plaintiff's emotional distress and anxiety caused by the insurer's wrongful denial of a claim. The insurer, in such cases, can also be compelled to pay other losses of a prevailing plaintiff, provided the losses are legally the result of the insurer's wrongful conduct.

Punitive Damages

Punitive damages historically have been awarded in tort lawsuits, but have not been awarded in contract lawsuits. A tort is a wrongful act causing harm. Where the wrongful act was intentional and outrageous, most courts have allowed the jury to award punitive damages. For example, assault is a tort for which punitive damages have been awarded.[29]

Punitive damages historically have not been recoverable in contract lawsuits unless the conduct constituting the breach of contract was also a tort.[30] The primary purpose of contract remedies has been to compensate the plaintiff, rather than to punish or make an example of the defendant.

In 1957, the California appellate courts began developing the tort of breach of the covenant of good faith and fair dealing, which covenant they said was implied in insurance contracts.[31] Breach of the implied covenant of good faith and fair dealing is both a breach of contract and a tort. Where such a breach occurs, punitive damages can be awarded if the insurer's conduct is found to be malicious, fraudulent, or oppressive.

A breach of the implied covenant of good faith and fair dealing is sometimes called bad faith. To characterize a breach of the implied covenant of good faith and fair dealing as bad faith is misleading. Bad faith in this context does not mean "positive misconduct of a malicious or immoral nature."[32] Rather, it means that the insurer denied a claim without a reasonable basis. In California, where most of the law of extra-contract damages against insurers has arisen, an insurer violates the covenant of good faith and fair dealing when it "unreasonably denies or delays payment . . . without giving the insured's interest at least as much consideration as its own."[33] If the insurer in California is guilty of bad faith, the court can award extra-contract compensatory damages to the plaintiff.

---

[29]Maxa v. Neidlein, 163 Md. 366, 163 A. 202 (1932).

[30]Boise Dodge, Inc. v. Clark, 92 Idaho 902, 453 P.2d 551 (1969).

[31]Gruenberg v. Aetna Ins. Co., 9 Cal. 3d 566, 510 P.2d 1032, 108 Cal. Rptr. 480 (1973); Silberg v. California Life Ins. Co., 11 Cal. 3d 452, 521 P.2d 1103, 113 Cal. Rptr. 711 (1974).

[32]Neal v. Farmers Ins. Exchange, 21 Cal. 3d 910, 582 P.2d 980, 148 Cal. Rptr. 389 (1978).

[33]Austero v. National Cas. Co., 84 Cal. App. 3d 1, 148 Cal. Rptr. 653 (1978).

Where an insurer has denied a claim without a reasonable basis, and it is also determined that the insurer acted with malice, oppression, or fraud, punitive damages could be assessed against the insurer. *Malice* means conduct which is intended to cause injury, or despicable conduct which is carried on with a willful and conscious disregard of the rights of others. *Oppression* means despicable conduct that subjects a person to cruel and unjust hardship in conscious disregard of that person's rights. *Fraud* means intentional misrepresentation, deceit, or concealment of a material fact known to a person with the intention of thereby causing injury to another.[34]

For example, in the landmark California case of *Fletcher v. Western National Life Insurance Co.,*[35] the plaintiff was an impoverished laborer with eight children and a fourth grade education who had purchased a disability income policy from the defendant in 1963. He sustained back and leg injuries in 1965 while lifting a 361-pound bale of rubber. Numerous doctors examined him and agreed that this accident had disabled him. The insurer paid the plaintiff the $150 per month for over a year but then seized upon a statement in one of the medical reports to demand that this money be returned. This statement was that the "plaintiff's disability was contributed to by a preexistent congenital defect in the lumbosacral spine and a preexisting osteoarthritis condition." The insurer did not investigate to determine if the plaintiff knew of a preexisting defect, but accused him of misrepresentation in his application for the policy.

The plaintiff filed suit, after which disability income payments were made only at long intervals and only after repeated demands by the plaintiff's attorney. The lack of regular payments caused great hardship for the plaintiff and his family.

The plaintiff asked the court for a declaration that he was entitled to the policy benefits, so long as he was disabled; for compensatory and punitive damages for intentional infliction of emotional distress; and for compensatory and punitive damages for fraud in inducing him to buy the policy.

The court held that the insurer had acted in an outrageous manner, and that its actions caused the plaintiff to be frightened, worried, and upset. The plaintiff, therefore, was entitled to damages for emotional distress.

The court also held that the plaintiff could recover in tort for breach of the implied covenant of good faith and fair dealing. The court said:

> An insurer owes to its insured an implied-in-law duty of good faith and fair dealing that it will do nothing to deprive the insured of the benefits of the policy. . . . The violation of that duty sounds in tort notwithstanding that it may also constitute a breach of contract . . . [P]unitive damages may be recovered upon a proper showing of malice, fraud or oppression even though the conduct constituting the tort also involves a breach of contract.

---

[34]CAL. CIV. CODE § 3294 (West Supp. 1988).
[35]10 Cal. App. 3d 376, 89 Cal. Rptr. 78 (1970).

The court, therefore, affirmed the trial court's awards of $60,000 in compensatory damages and $180,000 in punitive damages against the insurer, as well as $10,000 in punitive damages against the insurer's claims manager.

Although California is the forerunner in this area, it is by no means the only state in which punitive damages are a concern to insurers. To date, courts in about one third of the states have adopted the concept of the implied covenant of good faith and fair dealing or some similar theory of liability, and have allowed punitive damages against life and health insurers. For example, the Idaho Supreme Court held that an award of punitive damages against an insurer requires an "act which is an extreme deviation from reasonable standards of conduct, and that the act was performed by the defendant with an understanding of or a disregard for its likely consequences."[36] Moreover, punitive damages are awarded pursuant to statute in some states. Rhode Island has enacted a statute allowing punitive damages.[37] Other states have statutes which subject the insurer to extra-contract damages for bad faith failure or delay in paying a claim.

A few courts have expressly rejected or limited the California approach.[38] Courts of some states have not yet taken a position. Insurers must be wary of those states which have not taken a position, as such a state could unexpectedly adopt a position similar to California's. For example, Alabama courts had held that, in the absence of fraud, an insurer would be liable only for breach of contract if it improperly denied a claim. Then, in 1981, the Alabama Supreme Court authorized recovery for a separate tort arising out of a claim denial. The new tort of bad faith now exists in Alabama.[39]

Damage Amounts.   Because the primary purpose of punitive damages is to punish and make an example of the defendant, the amount of the award is tailored to the defendant's wealth. One court said, "It follows that the wealthier the wrongdoing defendant, the larger the award of exemplary damages need be in order to accomplish this objective.[40] Punitive damages awards against insurers are, therefore, sometimes calculated as a percentage of the insurer's net worth. The size of the compensatory damages and the type of offense committed by the insurer are sometimes taken into account in determining the size of the punitive damages award. Such punitive damages awards have been in the millions of dollars.[41]

---

[36]Linscott v. Ranier Nat'l Life Ins. Co., 100 Idaho 854, 606 P.2d 958 (1980).

[37]R.I. GEN LAWS § 9–1–33 (Supp. 1982).

[38]*See e.g.,* Kewin v. Massachusetts Mut. Life Ins. Co., 409 Mich. 401, 295 N.W.2d 50 (1980); Spencer v. Aetna Life & Cas. Co., 227 Kan. 914, 611 P.2d 149 (1980).

[39]Gulf Atlantic Life Ins. Co. v. Barnes, 405 So. 2d 916 (Ala. 1981); Chavers v. National Security Fire & Cas. Co., 405 So. 2d 1 (Ala. 1981).

[40]Neal v. Farmers Ins. Exchange, 21 Cal. 3d 910, 582 P.2d 980, 148 Cal. Rptr. 389 (1978).

[41]Sparks v. Republic Nat'l Life Ins. Co., 132 Ariz. 529, 647 P.2d 1127 (1982), *cert. denied,* 459 U.S. 1070 (1982). In the *Sparks* case, the Arizona Supreme Court awarded the plaintiffs $1,551,000 in compensatory damages, $80,000 in attorney's fees, and $3,000,000 in punitive damages.

Countervailing Forces.   In the mid-1980s, countervailing forces to the increase in the number of punitive damages awards against insurers began to appear. First, the difficulty of obtaining property and casualty insurance made tort reform, including the limitation of punitive damages, an issue of growing national interest.

Second, there have been recent cases in which the courts have imposed a higher standard of proof upon plaintiffs. For example, in 1986 the Arizona Supreme Court, in *Linthicum v. Nationwide Life Insurance Co.*,[42] held that punitive damages should be awarded only where there is clear and convincing evidence of "reprehensible conduct combined with an evil mind over and above that required for the commission of a tort . . . " This case significantly reduces the circumstances where punitive damages are appropriate in Arizona, a state where bad faith actions have been a serious threat to insurers. Third, in 1986 the United States Supreme Court in *Aetna Life Insurance Co. v. Lavoie*[43] reversed a punitive damages award of $3.5 million where the deciding vote in the lower court had been cast by a judge who had a substantial interest as a plaintiff in other bad faith litigation.

The insurer had argued that the award of punitive damages violated its constitutional rights under the Contracts Clause, under the excessive fines clause of the Eighth Amendment, and under the Due Process Clause of the Fourteenth Amendment of the United States Constitution. Justice Burger, in writing the United States Supreme Court opinion, noted that "[t]hese arguments raise important issues which, in an appropriate setting must be resolved . . ." Moreover, in *Bankers Life & Casualty Co. v. Crenshaw,*[44] decided by the Court in 1988, although the Court declined to rule on the constitutionality of punitive damages because the insurer's constitutional challenges had not been timely raised, Justice O'Connor, in a concurring opinion in which Justice Scalia joined, indicated an interest in addressing the constitutionality of punitive damages. Insurers have thus been encouraged to raise constitutional arguments in cases where the plaintiff claims punitive damages.

Third, a coalition of insurers and insurance trade associations drafted a model bill which imposes a higher standard of proof on plaintiffs in punitive damage actions; sets a cap on the amount of damages which may be awarded; defines the base on which such damages may be awarded; and limits the introduction of evidence concerning the insurer's financial worth. In 1985, Montana enacted a law requiring that punitive damages claims be proven by clear and convincing evidence; that a cap be placed on the amount of punitive damages that may be recovered; and that evidence of the insurer's financial worth be limited.[45] The insurance industry is pressing for more such legislative relief.

---

[42]150 Ariz. 326, 723 P. 2d 675 (1986).
[43]475 U.S. 813 (1986).
[44]108 S. Ct. 745 (1988).
[45]MONT. CODE ANN. § 27–1–221 (1988).

Finally, the United States Supreme Court decided, in *Pilot Life Insurance Co. v. Dedeaux,*[46] that state common-law tort actions against employers' group health insurers were preempted by the Employee Retirement Income Security Act (ERISA).[47] That is, the insured must pursue her or his remedies under ERISA, which does not provide for punitive damages, jury trials, or damages for emotional distress. The impact of this ruling is enormous, as vast numbers of people are covered under group life and health policies, and most group policies are governed by ERISA.

SUMMARY

A life insurance contract is performed when all the promises it contains are carried out. Ordinarily, this is a routine matter that involves obtaining from the beneficiary a completed claim form and proof of the insured's death, computing the amount of benefits due, and paying out the benefits. Occasionally, however, problems arise in adjusting the claim.

The insurer sometimes must investigate to determine the proper payee. If no beneficiary has been named, the policy will usually provide that the proceeds are payable to the policyowner or the policyowner's estate (where the policyowner is the insured). If the executor or administrator of the insured's estate is the beneficiary, the insurer will require evidence of his or her appointment by the court. Likewise, when a trustee is named beneficiary, the insurer will require evidence of the trustee's appointment in the deed of trust. If the policy was collaterally assigned, the insurer will require an affidavit from the assignee stating the amount of proceeds due the assignee.

Incompetent beneficiaries cannot give the insurer a binding release for payment of the proceeds. In the case of minor incompetents, a court-appointed guardian of the minor's estate can receive the proceeds and give a binding release, or the proceeds can be held at interest until the minor reaches majority. In some states, statutes allow small amounts to be paid directly to a minor. The guardian of the estate of a mentally incompetent person can receive benefits on behalf of the incompetent and give a binding release.

A beneficiary who wrongfully kills the insured will usually be disqualified to receive the life insurance benefits. Each state has its own law governing such disqualification. Acquittal of the beneficiary in a criminal trial does not necessarily mean that the beneficiary will qualify to receive the benefits, as the rules of evidence in criminal and civil trials differ. If the policy was procured in good faith and without intent to murder the insured, the benefits will be payable to someone—usually the contingent beneficiary or the insured's estate. If the policy was procured with intent to murder the insured, no proceeds are payable to anyone, according to the majority view.

---

[46]107 S. Ct. 1549 (1987).

[47]Pub. L. No. 93–406, 88 Stat. 829 (codified as amended in scattered sections of 5, 18, 26, 29, 31 and 42 U.S.C.).

If the insured and beneficiary die simultaneously in a common disaster, the state simultaneous death act provides that it will be presumed that the beneficiary died first. If the beneficiary survives the insured for a short time (several hours, for example) the act will not apply. However, if there is a time clause in the policy or beneficiary designation, the beneficiary must survive the insured for the period of time specified in the clause if the beneficiary is to receive the benefits.

Where there are conflicting claimants who cannot resolve their differences, the insurer will ordinarily file a bill of interpleader and deposit the benefits with the court. Unclaimed benefits will be turned over to the state after a certain period of time has elapsed—usually seven years.

No death benefits will be payable if the policy contains a suicide exclusion, and the insured commits suicide during the suicide period (usually within two years after the policy is effective). If the suicide exclusion clause includes the words *while sane or insane,* self-destruction by an insane insured ordinarily will not be covered. The burden of proving suicide falls on the insurer. If the insurer can establish that the insured died by suicide, no accidental death benefits will be payable, as a suicide is not an accidental death.

Where an insured mysteriously disappears, a presumption of death will arise after seven years in most states if the insured was continuously absent without explanation, if the persons most likely to hear from the insured have heard nothing, and if the insured cannot be located by diligent search and inquiry. If the missing insured was exposed to a specific peril, the beneficiary will often be able to prove the death by circumstantial evidence without waiting for the presumption of death to arise.

Claims adjusters must take the requirements of the Unfair Claim Settlement Practices Act into account when adjusting claims. An increasing number of courts also require that the reasonable expectations of the policyowner or beneficiary be honored.

Where a claim has been denied, the claimant sometimes sues the insurer. Claims litigation can be expensive for insurers, as legal fees, court costs, damages to compensate the plaintiff for emotional distress, and punitive damages sometimes are assessed against insurers, in addition to contract damages. Proper claims handling is, therefore, important, as it helps to protect the insurer from liability as well as assuring that claimants receive fair treatment.

ILLUSTRATIVE CASE

In the following case, the beneficiaries were unable to establish that the insured had perished as a result of a specific peril, in this instance a fire. The insurers introduced competent evidence supplying an explanation for the insured's disappearance.

Geneva ROBERTS, Plaintiff-Appellant,
v.
WABASH LIFE INSURANCE CO.,
Defendant-Appellee
Geneva ROBERTS, Plaintiff-Appellant,
v.
MODERN WOODMEN OF AMERICA,
Defendant-Appellee
Forrest ROBERTS et al.,
Plaintiffs-Appellants,
v.
OCCIDENTAL LIFE INSURANCE CO.,
Defendant-Appellee[48]
Court of Appeals of Indiana, First District

RATLIFF, Judge.

STATEMENT OF THE CASE

Geneva Roberts filed actions against Wabash Life Insurance Co. and Modern Woodmen of America, and her four sons filed an action against Occidental Life Insurance Co. in an effort to collect the proceeds of policies which had been issued insuring the life of their husband and father, Clarence Roberts. The Brown Circuit Court entered judgment in favor of the insurance companies after trial of the consolidated actions. We affirm.

FACTS

Clarence Roberts and his wife, Geneva, lived approximately three miles north of Nashville, Indiana, at the intersection of Road 135 and Grandma Barnes Road. Located west of their house was a barn which they utilized as a garage and storage area. On November 18, 1970, Ella Cummings, a neighbor of Clarence Roberts, observed leaves burning at the base of a tree located near the barn on the Roberts' property. In retrospect Mrs. Cummings surmised that she could have extinguished the small fire herself if she had stopped at that time. Instead, she went to her home and called the fire department at 6:15. When the fire engine arrived at 6:30, the barn was already destroyed; witnesses recalled that the fire spread rapidly through the structure. Several vehicles were parked in the east portion of the barn. Neighbors and passers-by managed to save only one of the vehicles, Clarence Roberts' pick-up truck.

Because of the limited water supply, the firemen directed their efforts primarily toward protecting nearby buildings. Eventually they moved across the debris spraying water to cool the ashes. Their path led them to a shotgun lying across the charred remains of a body.

The Brown County coroner took the body to Indianapolis for an autopsy. Funeral services were conducted for Clarence Roberts, and the body was buried at a

---

[48]410 N.E. 2d 1337 (1980).

local cemetery. Because the investigation of the fire produced a long list of perplexing questions for which the investigators could not find plausible answers, the body was exhumed on December 21, 1970.

After the wife and sons of Clarence Roberts were unsuccessful in their attempts to collect approximately $640,000 in life insurance proceeds, they filed actions against the insurance companies. The evidence at trial reflected contrasting images of Clarence Roberts.

Clarence Roberts' attorney and physician described Roberts as a very civic-minded person who enjoyed an excellent reputation in the community. During the late 1960s, Clarence Roberts experienced financial problems due to losses suffered by several grain elevators which he owned. Lawsuits were filed against him during the summer of 1969. Roberts reportedly became increasingly despondent.

In June 1970 Clarence Roberts hinted of suicide during a conversation with his attorney. After discussing but rejecting the possibility of filing a petition in bankruptcy, Roberts told another attorney on November 3, 1970, ". . . my widow will be the richest one in Brown County."

Some persons surmised that Clarence Roberts accidentally set the barn afire while shooting himself. Roberts kept gasoline for his lawn mower in the barn, and the fact was offered as an explanation for the rapid burning of the structure. The autopsy revealed no gunshot wound. Although the shotgun had been fired, the position of the gun over the body was not compatible with the substantial recoil which would have followed its firing.

Clarence Roberts obtained a loan from Wabash Life Insurance Co. in 1967 or 1968 for the purpose of financing construction of an apartment complex. The relationship turned into a fiasco. Wabash eventually alleged that Roberts had submitted altered bills and fictitious bills for which Wabash had paid Roberts. At the time of trial Wabash estimated that the fraudulent bills totalled a minimum of $131,000 and perhaps more than $200,000.

Alvin Haggard, who owned Al's Friendly Tavern, had known Clarence Roberts for forty years. Roberts confided in Haggard concerning his financial problems. According to Haggard, Roberts "wanted to get out of the mess he was in." Haggard never heard Roberts mention suicide. In mid-September 1970 Roberts showed Haggard a card for a Swiss bank account. Clarence Roberts told Haggard that Roberts had more than $100,000 on deposit in his own Swiss bank account.

Several people who were acquainted with Clarence Roberts saw Roberts in Morgantown on the morning of November 17, 1970. Roberts was accompanied by a man who was not known by Roberts' friends in Morgantown. The man, who was approximately the same size as Roberts but older than Roberts, was wearing a dirty brown plaid shirt. The stranger suffered from some sort of seizure while in Morgantown. Clarence Roberts put the man into Roberts' car and drove toward Nashville.

Early in the afternoon of November 18, 1970, a bank officer went to the home of Clarence Roberts. He wanted to discuss with Roberts a note on which the bank suspected Roberts had forged the signature of his brother, Carson Roberts. Clarence Roberts, who was aware of the bank's suspicions, did not respond to the knock on the door.

Charles Roberts saw his cousin, Clarence Roberts, mulching leaves at Clarence Roberts' home late in the afternoon of November 18, 1970. Charles talked with Clarence briefly. Clarence, who was wearing a solid-color blue shirt, commented that his wife, Geneva, and his son, Loren, had gone to Columbus for supper. Clarence invited Charles to join him for a sandwich, but Charles declined the invitation. Charles departed. Fifteen minutes later, Charles Roberts received word of a fire at Clarence Roberts' property. Charles returned to Clarence's property approximately twenty-five minutes after Charles' departure; the roof of the barn had already collapsed due to the fire.

The Brown County coroner was concerned with establishing identity as well as cause of death for the body found amidst the debris of Clarence Roberts' barn. The body was severely burned, and the only distinctive piece of clothing to survive the fire was a portion of a brown plaid shirt. Dr. Benz, who performed the autopsy, deemed definite identification of the body impossible. Dr. Benz noted an absence of carbonous material in the respiratory tract and an absence of internal burning of the respiratory tract, but tests showed the presence of 80–86% carbon monoxide in the blood. Dr. Benz opined that the person had died from the carbon monoxide intoxication prior to the fire.

In December the bank repossessed Clarence Roberts' pick-up truck. The bank's representative soon became aware of a massive leakage of fumes into the cab of the truck. Inspection revealed thirty or more holes in the exhaust system. The holes looked as if they had been made with a hammer and punch.

On the morning after the fire, the coroner located Clarence Roberts' Masonic ring beneath several inches of ashes. The ring showed little fire damage. An expert witness testified that the solder in the ring should have melted at a much lower temperature than the temperature required to disintegrate the fingers, hands, and arms. The witness, John Kennedy, studied photographs which had been taken during and after the fire and also examined some of the bones from the body. Kennedy believed that the area where the body was found had been saturated with flammable liquid which caused an accelerated rate of burning. Kennedy expressed the opinion that the body had been soaked with a flammable liquid and burned after the limbs had been removed.

A blood sample taken from the body was reported as type AB. Clarence Roberts' military records indicated that his blood type was B. The Roberts challenged the reliability of the blood-typing efforts and also suggested that military records frequently are inaccurate.

X-rays from Clarence Roberts' medical records were compared with x-rays taken of the body. The expert witnesses had differing opinions concerning the validity of the comparison as well as the similarities and dissimilarities detectable by the comparison.

A tooth discovered near the body was identified as a lower right second molar. Clarence Roberts' lower right second molar had been removed several years prior to the fire. The Roberts' witnesses insisted that the tooth could be a first molar rather than a second molar. Other witnesses pondered the question of why other teeth had not been found.

Donald Barrett testified that Clarence Roberts had been in Barrett's tavern in Mentone, Indiana, at least twenty times prior to November 18, 1970. He was usually with a woman who was not Geneva Roberts. Barrett testified that Roberts and that woman were in his tavern in April 1972. Other acquaintances of Clarence Roberts testified that they saw Roberts in 1974 and in 1975.

Radiologists, anthropologists, pathologists, dentists, law enforcement officers, investigators, relatives, and friends offered differing opinions as to whether the body found on November 18, 1970, was that of Clarence Roberts. The trial court ultimately entered judgment in favor of the insurance companies in the actions filed by the wife and sons of Clarence Roberts.

ISSUES

1. Did the Roberts prove by a preponderance of the evidence that the body which was found amidst the debris on Clarence Roberts' property on November 18, 1970, is the body of Clarence Roberts?
2. Does the evidence lead solely to a conclusion that the Roberts are entitled to the relief which they seek?
3. Did the trial court erroneously disregard certain . . . common law presumptions of death?

* * * * *

DISCUSSION AND DECISION

Issues One and Two

The Roberts' lawsuits are based upon two theories. First, the Roberts contend that the burned body is that of Clarence Roberts. The Roberts had the burden of proving that contention. In order for the Roberts to be entitled to relief from the negative judgment, the evidence must lead solely to a conclusion opposite that reached by the trial court.

The Roberts assert that the evidence leads solely to a conclusion that they should have been granted the relief which they seek. They have painstakingly set forth the evidence most favorable to their position, and they have attempted to show lack of credibility in that evidence which is unfavorable to them.

An appellate court will not weigh the evidence or assess the credibility of witnesses. The two adjectives which best describe the evidence in this case are "voluminous" and "conflicting." The evidence does not lead solely to a conclusion opposite that reached by the trial court.

Issue Three

As their second theory the Roberts argue that, regardless of whether the body was proven to be that of Clarence Roberts, the wife and sons are entitled to a presumption of death under the . . . common law because more than seven years had passed between the date of Clarence Roberts' disappearance and the date of the trial. The insurance companies respond that, even if the wife and sons are entitled to a presumption of death due to the passing of time, the Roberts failed to prove that death occurred prior to the lapse of the life insurance contracts.[1]

When a person is inexplicably absent from home for a continuous period of seven years, fails to communicate with those persons who would be most likely to hear from him, and cannot be found despite diligent inquiry and search, that person is presumed to be dead. The Roberts introduced evidence from which the trier of fact could conclude that Clarence Roberts had been absent from home without

---

[1]All of the life insurance contracts had expired by August 12, 1972, due to non payment of premiums.

explanation for a continuous period exceeding seven years, that he had not communicated with his family and friends during that period, and that diligent search for him had proven futile. The Roberts insist that the burden of proof shifted to the insurance companies after the Roberts introduced evidence giving them the benefit of the presumption of death.

In *Fuller v. Supreme Council of Royal Arcanum*, (1917) 64 Ind.App. 49, 60, 115 N.E. 372, Judge Hottel explained that

> "[c]ertain evidence may give rise to a presumption in favor of the party having the burden of proof, which will impose upon the adverse party the necessity or duty of going forward with the evidence, but the burden of proof is not thereby shifted. The burden of the issue continues where the law places it though some presumptions in favor of the party who bears it may require the adverse party to go forward with the proof.

We quote also from *Equitable Life Assurance Society v. James, supra,* at page 188 of 73 Ind.App., at page 12 of 127 N.E.:

> "The presumption of death which arises after a continuous absence for a period of seven years, of one who left his home for a temporary purpose, and from whom no tidings have been received, is not a conclusive presumption, but may be rebutted by proof of facts and circumstances inconsistent with, and sufficient to overcome, such presumption. When, in an action of this kind, there is any evidence tending to rebut the presumption of death, arising from such absence, it is for the jury to say whether such evidence is sufficient to rebut the presumption. . . ."

Although the burden of proof did not shift to the insurance companies, the insurance companies did have an obligation to go forward with evidence to rebut the presumption of death.

Clarence Roberts was having severe financial difficulties at the time of his disappearance. His dealings with Wabash Life Insurance Co. were, at best, questionable and perhaps fraudulent. Clarence Roberts allegedly had forged a signature in order to obtain a loan, and he knew that he was about to be called to answer for doing so. Roberts expressed dissatisfaction concerning his relationship with his wife and children, and he was seen on numerous occasions in the company of a woman who was not his wife. Roberts confided in a friend that he "wanted to get out of the mess he was in" and that he had a Swiss bank account with a balance exceeding $100,000. This evidence could reasonably lead a trier of fact to a conclusion that Clarence Roberts had the motives and the financial ability to absent himself from his home indefinitely without communicating with his family and friends.

Additionally, the life of Clarence Roberts was insured for approximately $640,000. Roberts disappeared on the same day that a body was found in the debris left after his barn was destroyed by fire. Investigation of the fire revealed evidence of possible murder and arson.[2] The disappearance of Clarence Roberts could reasonably be viewed as a part of a scheme to defraud the life insurance companies.

---

[2]Clarence Roberts was indicted for murder and kidnapping in 1975.

The trial court, as trier of fact, wrote in finding number eleven: "The evidence introduced at the trial of the cause further indicates that the disappearance of the insured, Clarence Roberts, on November 18, 1970, is explainable by a reasonable hypothesis other than his death on that date."

* * * * *

Having carefully considered each of the issues presented for review, we hold that the Roberts have failed to demonstrate reversible error.

Judgment affirmed.

ROBERTSON, P.J., and NEAL, J., concur.

QUESTIONS FOR REVIEW

1. Describe the problem insurers face at the death of the insured when a minor is named as beneficiary. Describe the way in which some states have alleviated this problem.
2. If no beneficiary survives the insured, what usually happens to the policy benefits?
3. What problems do insurers face when the beneficiary kills the insured? How are these problems usually handled?
4. What is the problem which the state simultaneous death acts are designed to solve?
5. Explain how the suicide of the insured affects the performance of the life insurance contract (a) if there is a suicide clause in the policy, and (b) if there is no suicide clause.
6. What conditions must be met for an insured to be presumed to be legally dead? After the insured has been presumed to be legally dead, and the insurer has paid a death benefit, suppose the insured reappears.
   a. What are the insurer's rights if the full death benefit has been paid?
   b. What are the insurer's rights if, as a compromise, less than the full death benefit has been paid?
7. Indicate the different items which the insurer might have to take into account in calculating the total death benefit to be paid to a beneficiary.
8. Describe the doctrine of reasonable expectations, and the process by which it has become law.
9. What are contract damages? What are punitive damages? What is the purpose of punitive damages?

CHAPTER 19

Group Insurance

HISTORY OF GROUP LIFE INSURANCE

GROUP LIFE INSURANCE DEFINITIONS
    Employer-Employee Groups
    Creditor Groups
    Labor Union Groups
    Trusteed Groups
    Association Groups
    Credit Union Groups
    Discretionary Groups

GROUP LIFE INSURANCE STANDARD PROVISIONS
    Grace Period Provision
    Incontestable Clause
    Application Provision
    Evidence of Insurability Provision
    Misstatement of Age Provision
    Settlement Provision
    Certificate Provision
    Conversion Privileges
    Continuation of Coverage During Disability
    Creditor Group Life Insurance Certificates
    Nonforfeiture Provisions

DEPENDENT GROUP LIFE INSURANCE

GROUP MASTER POLICIES AND CERTIFICATES

THE ACTIVELY-AT-WORK REQUIREMENT
    Actively at Work Full-Time
    Increase in the Amount of Life Insurance

TERMINATION OF GROUP INSURANCE
    Definition of *Termination*
    Date of Termination

GROUP POLICY PREMIUMS AND DIVIDENDS
    Dividends
    Creditor Group Life Insurance Rates

THE POLICYHOLDER AS AGENT

CONFLICT OF LAWS

FEDERAL TAXATION OF GROUP LIFE INSURANCE

ERISA AND GROUP INSURANCE

SECTION 89 DISCRIMINATION TESTING
  Qualification Tests
  Discrimination Tests
  Employees Excluded
  Highly Compensated Employees
  Plans
  Other Section 89 Rules

FEGLI AND SGLI

GROUP HEALTH INSURANCE

WHOLESALE AND FRANCHISE INSURANCE

SUMMARY

A book about life insurance law would not be complete without a chapter about group insurance. Group insurance is an almost universal employee benefit in the United States. Group life insurance in force in the United States at the end of 1986 amounted to $2,801 billion, or 41.7 percent of the total life insurance in force. Group life insurance in force has grown spectacularly since its beginnings in 1911 and continues to grow, having more than quadrupled since 1972.[1] Group health insurance now provides the great majority of health benefits paid by life and health insurers in the United States.[2]

Many of the rules of law which apply to individual life or health insurance also apply to group insurance. There are also many rules of law unique to group insurance. The most important of these latter rules will be sketched in this chapter. This chapter does not purport to be a comprehensive explanation of group insurance law. Such an explanation would require a space many times that allotted here.

HISTORY OF GROUP LIFE INSURANCE

The earliest group life insurance policies were written to cover loss of life among a group of persons during a voyage. In the early 1800s, slave traders insured the lives of shiploads of slaves being transported to America from Africa. The slave traders were the beneficiaries of these contracts. In 1854, the Manhattan Life Insurance Company insured the lives of 180 Chinese laborers who were being transported from China to Panama to work on the Panama Canal.

---

[1] AMERICAN COUNCIL OF LIFE INSURANCE, LIFE INSURANCE FACT BOOK UPDATE 10 (1987).
[2] HEALTH INSURANCE ASSOCIATION OF AMERICA, SOURCE BOOK OF HEALTH INSURANCE DATA: 1988 UPDATE 4–7.

The first group life insurance plans, in the form we know group life insurance today, were established in 1911 and 1912. All the employees of the companies involved were insured under group master policies issued to their employers. The relationships of the people and companies—insurer, employer, employees, and beneficiaries—were essentially the same as those under the more than 600,000 group master policies now in force in the United States.

Modern group insurance began with the efforts of those in charge of Montgomery Ward and Company to replace the failing Montgomery Ward employees' mutual benefit association with an insured plan covering all employees. Such associations of employees provided a small death benefit and temporary disability benefits through dues and assessments of their members.

The officers of Montgomery Ward developed a plan and began negotiations with several insurers in 1910. In 1912, the Equitable Life Assurance Society of the United States (Equitable) issued a group insurance policy which covered all Montgomery Ward employees. Although Equitable had issued a number of earlier group policies—the first in 1911 to the Pantasote Leather Company of Passaic, New Jersey—these earlier group policies actually stemmed from the negotiations between Equitable and Montgomery Ward.

The Montgomery Ward policy established a pattern for employer-employee group life insurance policies. It insured the lives of the 2,912 employees of Montgomery Ward for the benefit of beneficiaries selected by the employees at a premium to be paid by the employer. The lives of all employees were insured, regardless of insurability. The employer was not a beneficiary. Although there have been variations from this scheme, as with contributory policies where the employee pays part of the premium, it is essentially the scheme followed today.

By 1915, several other major life insurers had begun to issue group life insurance policies. There was widespread criticism of such insurance, however. Many insurance executives felt it was unsound to issue life insurance without individual underwriting. Some felt that charging lower premiums for group life insurance was unfairly discriminatory.

Such criticisms were quieted somewhat in 1917 when the National Association of Insurance Commissioners (NAIC) developed a standard definition of group life insurance and standard policy provisions for group life insurance policies. In the years that followed, the group life insurance concept was broadened and refined in a series of model bills developed by the NAIC. This process continues with the most recent of these amendments to the current model being adopted by the NAIC in 1986. Most of the states have enacted group life insurance statutes based on one of these versions of the group life insurance model bill developed by the NAIC.

The states with group life insurance statutes based on the NAIC models have statutes defining group life insurance and statutes mandating standard provisions which must be included in group life insurance policies. The next two sections deal with these definitions and with mandated standard group life insurance policy provisions.

GROUP LIFE INSURANCE DEFINITIONS

The 1917 model bill defined group life insurance as "that form of life insurance covering not less than 50 employees, with or without medical examination," under a policy issued to the employer. The premiums were to be *noncontributory*—that is, paid by the employer—or *contributory*—that is, paid jointly by the employer and employees. Under policies where the employer paid the premium, all the eligible employees had to be insured or "all of any class or classes thereof determined by conditions pertaining to the employment." If the premium were paid by employer and employees jointly, at least 75 percent of those eligible had to be insured. The amounts of life insurance were to be based on a plan prohibiting individual selection. That is, the employee's position within the group could be used as a basis for the amount, but two similarly situated employees could not be insured for different amounts. Finally, the employer could not be a beneficiary.

This definition has been expanded and revised over the years. In 1946, for example, the definition was revised to reduce the number of required lives from 50 to 25. In the 1954 model bill, the number was reduced to 10. The current model bill, now called a model act,[3] states no minimum number of required lives for employer-employee groups.

The 1946 revision of the model bill recognized a number of types of groups in addition to employer-employee groups. It also recognized the right of an insurer to require evidence of individual insurability.

Revisions to the model bill have been made many times. As a result of these revisions, the provisions of a state's group life insurance law depend upon which version of the model bill the state followed, at least in those states which have patterned their laws on the model bill. Some states have not based their group life insurance laws on the model bill, and several have no statutory definition of group life insurance, although all have some statutory requirements relating to group life insurance. Thus, group life insurance statutes vary considerably among the states.

The current group life insurance model act recognizes the following as eligible groups: (1) employees of an employer; (2) debtors of a creditor or creditors; (3) members of a labor union or similar employee organization; (4) employees of two or more employers, or members of one or more labor unions or similar employee organizations, or employees of one or more em-

---

[3]In the 1980 model, the word *bill* was changed to *act*. The meaning of *model bill* and *model act* is, for practical purposes, the same. A bill introduced into a legislature becomes an act if passed.

ployers and members of one or more labor unions (trusteed groups); (5) members of an association or associations; (6) members of a credit union or credit unions; and (7) groups which are deemed to be valid at the discretion of the commissioner of insurance (discretionary groups).

Employer-Employee Groups

Employer-employee groups were the first type of group insured and the only type allowed under the 1917 model bill. It is by far the most important type of group. Nearly 90 percent of the group master policies issued in the United States are issued to employer-employee groups.[4]

Under the current model act the policy can be issued either to the employer or to the trustees of a fund established by the employer. The model act permits the policy to define the term *employees* as including employees of subsidiary corporations. *Employees* can also be defined as the employees, individual proprietors, and partners of affiliated businesses if the employer and affiliated business are under common control. Retired and former employees can be included in the group, as can directors of a corporate employer.

Earlier model bills required that a minimum number of employees be insured when the policy is issued. The current model act contains no such requirement. The current model act also contains no requirement that the policyholder pay part of the premium, and no requirement that at least 75 percent of eligible employees be covered under contributory policies. These requirements were found in earlier model bills and appear in the group life insurance laws of some states. The current model act has, however, retained the requirement, contained in earlier model bills, that 100 percent of eligible employees be covered under noncontributory policies, except employees who reject such coverage in writing. Finally, an insurer can exclude or limit coverage on any person as to whom evidence of insurability is not satisfactory.

Creditor Groups

Under the current model act, a policy covering debtors of a creditor or creditors can be issued to the creditor, its parent holding company, or to a trustee or an agent designated by two or more creditors. The premium can be paid by the creditor, the debtors, or both. The amount of insurance on the life of a debtor cannot exceed the amount of the debt. The insurer can exclude debtors on whom evidence of insurability is not satisfactory.

Benefits under a creditor group life insurance policy are paid to the creditor. This is the only type of group life insurance in which the policyholder is also the beneficiary. The benefit payment reduces or extinguishes the debtor's obligation, however.

---

[4]AMERICAN COUNCIL OF LIFE INSURANCE, LIFE INSURANCE FACT BOOK 30 (1986).

Certain requirements which appeared in earlier model bills have been eliminated in the current model act, but still appear in the creditor group life insurance laws of some states. Notably, these requirements were (1) that a debt payable in a lump sum be payable within 18 months; (2) that there be a ceiling on the amount of life insurance; (3) that the group have 100 new entrants during the first policy year; and (4) that a contributory group cover at least 75 percent of eligible debtors.

Labor Union Groups

In labor union groups, the labor union or other employee organization is the policyholder. Union members, or classes of union members, are insured for the benefit of persons other than the union, its officials, its representatives, or its agents. Under the current model act, the premium can be paid from union funds or from members' contributions, or both. Under noncontributory policies, all eligible members must be covered.

Earlier model bills required that the labor union group have 25 members when the policy is issued and that at least 75 percent of eligible members be covered in contributory plans. These requirements appear in the labor union group life insurance laws of some states.

Trusteed Groups

A group life insurance policy can be issued to a trust established by two or more employers, by one or more labor unions, or by one or more employers and one or more labor unions. The employees or union members are insured for the benefit of persons other than an employer or union.

In contributory groups, the policy must cover all eligible members who do not reject such coverage in writing. Insureds can contribute funds to pay part or all of the premium under the current model act. This was not true under earlier model bills. In addition, requirements as to minimum group size found in earlier model bills are not found in the current model act.

Association Groups

The current model act has added, as an eligible group, the members of an association, or of one or more associations under a trust. The association must have been organized and maintained for at least two years for purposes other than that of obtaining insurance. It must have at least 100 members when the insurance goes into force.

Credit Union Groups

The current model act has also added, as an eligible group, the members of a credit union, or of one or more credit unions under a trust. The credit union groups insure their members for the benefit of persons other than the credit union. In other words, this type of group insurance is not creditor insurance. Its purpose is to protect the credit union member, not the credit union. The credit union member designates the beneficiary.

Discretionary Groups

The current model act allows for groups which do not fall into any of the categories described above, as long as the group meets the requirements specified in the act. These requirements are that the policy be in the best interests of the public, result in economies of acquisition or administration, and provide benefits reasonable in relation to the premiums charged.

The model act attempts to deal with the problems that group insurers experience when they issue a group master policy in one state, and a second state attempts to regulate the policy as to persons living in the second state. Some states will not allow group insurers to cover their residents under a group master policy issued in another state unless the group is a type recognized by the first state. The model act provides that if the commissioner of insurance of any state where the model act has been adopted finds that the group qualifies as a discretionary group, coverage under the group policy can be offered in all other states which have adopted the model act. This reciprocal provision reads in part as follows:

> No [discretionary] group life insurance policy may be offered in this state by an insurer under a policy issued in another state unless this state or another state having requirements substantially similar to [the discretionary group requirements of the model act] has made a determination that such requirements have been met.

GROUP LIFE INSURANCE STANDARD PROVISIONS

The standard provisions sections of the model act specify certain provisions which must be included, in substance, in a group life insurance policy. These provisions can be made more favorable to the insureds or more favorable to the policyholder and equally favorable to the insureds. There are 12 standard provisions and a supplementary bill relating to conversion privileges. Unlike the group life insurance definitions sections, the group life standard provisions sections of the current model act are substantially similar to those in earlier model bills. Where there are differences, they will be pointed out in the following subsections.

Grace Period Provision

A group life insurance policy must contain a provision granting a grace period of 31 days for the payment of any premium due except the first. The grace period provision requirement is the same as that for individual life insurance policies, with a notable exception. This exception is explained in the following paragraphs.

The group life policy will be in force during the grace period unless the policyholder gives the insurer written notice of discontinuance in advance of the date of discontinuance and in accordance with the terms of the policy. Thus, if a policyholder does not give written notice of discontinuance and does not pay the premium, the policy will still be in force during the whole grace period, after which time it will lapse. Or the policy might be in force for none or part of the grace period if the policyholder gives the discontinuance notice.

If the policy is in force for part or all of the grace period, the model act states that "The policy may provide that the policyholder shall be liable to the insurer for the payment of a pro rata premium for the time the policy was in force during such a grace period." The reason the policyholder will owe a premium for the portion of the grace period when the policy was in force is that the insurer must pay claims for deaths of insured persons occurring during this period. If the policyholder does not pay the insurer the pro rata premium for the grace period, the insurer can sue to recover it. Such an unpaid premium can amount to many thousands of dollars in the case of a large group. Ordinarily, under an individual life insurance policy, the insurer cannot sue to recover a premium not paid during the grace period, although the insurer can recover the unpaid premium out of the death benefits if the insured dies during the grace period.

Incontestable Clause

There are actually two kinds of contestable periods provided by a group master policy. First, the model act provides that the validity of the group master policy itself will be incontestable except for nonpayment of premiums after it has been in force for two years. Contests of the validity of a group master policy are relatively rare, however. Such contests usually involve misrepresentation of the employer-employee relationship. The cases are in conflict as to whether the incontestable clause precludes a group insurer from defending a lawsuit for death benefits on the ground that the policyholder and the insured did not have an employer-employee relationship. For example, in *John Hancock Mutual Life Insurance Co. v. Dorman*[5] the court held that the incontestable clause in a group life policy prevented the insurer from defending a suit for death benefits on the ground that a director of the policyholder-corporation was not covered because the director was not an employee. The insurer argued that the policy was invalid as to the director, but the court ruled that after the contestable period had expired, the insurer could not show that the director lacked the attribute of being an employee.

In another case with similar facts, *Simpson v. Phoenix Mutual Life Insurance Co.*,[6] the court held that employment was a condition precedent to cov-

---

[5]108 F.2d 220 (9th Cir. 1939).
[6]24 N.Y.2d 262, 247 N.E.2d 655 (1969).

erage, not a limitation of the risk, and hence was not contestable after the contestable period. The court said, "The hallmark of the distinction between conditions and limitations is discoverability." The court decided that the question of whether Simpson was or was not a full-time employee could have been investigated and the answer discovered when the certificate was issued to him. After the contestable period, therefore, the insurer was barred from using Simpson's employment status to defend against paying the claim for death benefits.

In *Fisher v. Prudential Insurance Co.,*[7] on the other hand, the court held that the insurer could defend a claim for benefits on the ground that the insured had never been an employee of the policyholder, even though the contestable period had expired. The plaintiff argued that the insurer could no longer contest the validity of the policy, but the court said the incontestable clause was never intended to enlarge the coverage of the policy or to force an insurer to insure lives it never intended to cover.

This last case seems to the authors to represent the better view. Moreover, the current model act provides that no incontestable provision "shall preclude the assertion at any time of defenses based upon provisions in the policy which relate to eligibility for coverage."

The second type of contestable period relates to evidence of insurability submitted by insureds. Ordinarily, insureds do not submit evidence of insurability in order to be covered by a group life insurance policy. However, if an employee under a contributory plan applies for coverage after the deadline, evidence of insurability usually will have to be submitted. Evidence of insurability will have to be submitted if the employee is a member of a class eligible for amounts of life insurance in excess of the insurer's guaranteed issue limit.

The evidence of insurability, often called a *health certificate,* is an application form with questions pertaining to the proposed insured's health. As with individual insurance, this evidence of insurability will be approved or rejected at the insurer's home office. Also, as with individual insurance, there is a specified contestable period after which the validity of the insured's coverage will be incontestable as to misstatements in the evidence of insurability.

The model act requires group life policies to contain a clause such as the following:

> [N]o statement made by any person insured under the policy relating to his insurability shall be used in contesting the validity of the insurance with respect to which such statement was made after such insurance has been in force prior to the contest for a period of two years during such person's lifetime, nor unless it is contained in a written instrument signed by him.

---

[7]107 N.H. 101, 218 A.2d 62 (1966).

Application Provision

The application provision is closely related to the incontestable clause. The application provision required by the model act has three parts.

First, the group life policy must provide that a copy of the application of the policyholder, if any, be attached to the master policy when it is issued. This corresponds to some degree to the entire contract provision included in individual life insurance policies.

Second, the group life policy must provide that all statements made by the policyholder, or by the persons insured, shall be deemed representations and not warranties. The legal effect of making all statements representations and not warranties is the same in group insurance as in individual insurance. That is, misstatements must be material to the risk if the insurer is to contest the validity of the policy based on the misstatements.

Third, the group life policy must provide that no statement made by an insured shall be used in a contest of the policy unless a copy of the instrument containing the statement is, or has been, furnished to the insured or, in the event of the insured's death or disability, to his beneficiary or administrator.

Because group policies often insure large numbers of persons, it would be virtually impossible, in many cases, to require that the instrument containing the statement be attached to and made part of the policy, as with individual life insurance. Thus, the model act requires only that a copy of the instrument (usually an evidence of insurability) be furnished to the insured, or after the insured's death, to her or his beneficiary or administrator.

Evidence of Insurability Provision

Under the model act, group life policies are required to have "a provision setting forth the conditions, if any, under which the insurer reserves the right to require a person eligible for insurance to furnish evidence of individual insurability satisfactory to the insurer as a condition to part or all of his coverage."

When a person eligible to be insured under a contributory plan chooses not to be insured, then later changes his or her mind and applies for the insurance, there is a possibility that a change in health induced the change of mind. Insurers, therefore, require evidence of insurability in such a situation and in some other situations also. The situations in which the insurer will require evidence of insurability must be spelled out in the group policy, according to the model act.

Misstatement of Age Provision

The model act requires that group life policies contain the following: A "provision specifying an equitable adjustment of premiums or of benefits or of both to be made in the event the age of a person insured has been misstated, such provision to contain a clear statement of the method of adjustment to be made."

Settlement Provision

The model act requires that a group life insurance policy include a provision that death benefits shall be payable to the person the insured has designated as beneficiary, "except that where the policy contains conditions pertaining to family status the beneficiary may be the family member specified by the policy terms."

The insured under a group life policy ordinarily has the right to name the beneficiary. Except for creditor plans, the policyholder cannot be named the beneficiary, but, otherwise, the insured is unrestricted in her or his choice of beneficiary. In other respects, the general rules applicable to individual life insurance beneficiary designations also apply to beneficiary designations under group life insurance. Usually, the designation is revocable, and the insured can change the beneficiary whenever she or he wishes by complying with the policy procedures for beneficiary change.

In the event there is no designated beneficiary, the group policy itself can provide for one, as with individual insurance. In some group policies, this will be the insured's estate. Or, the group policy can provide for a succession beneficiary designation, making proceeds payable to the first relative living as described in a list of the insured's relatives, as spouse, children, parents, and brothers and sisters. The objective of a succession beneficiary provision is to avoid the necessity of having a personal representative appointed to make claim for life insurance benefits payable to the insured's estate.

Under the model act, the policy can also reserve to the insurer the right to pay up to $2,000 "to any person appearing to be equitably entitled thereto by reason of having incurred funeral or other expenses incident to the last illness or death of the person insured." This is a facility-of-payment clause. If it is included in the policy, the insurer can, at its option, pay small amounts to anyone who has assumed the expenses of the insured's last illness or burial.

Settlement options are not required in group policies by the model act. Nevertheless, one or two settlement options are usually provided under group life insurance contracts, although it is not customary to permit elaborate settlement arrangements. Usually, either the fixed period installment option or the fixed amount installment option is available—sometimes both. A life income option is sometimes provided and may be available by special agreement with the insurer, even when it is not expressly provided for in the policy itself.

The settlement provision required by the model act does not pertain to creditor insurance, nor do the certificate provision, the conversion provisions, or the provision for continuation of coverage during disability, all of which are discussed below. These provisions are not appropriate to creditor insurance.

Certificate Provision

Under the model act, the group life master policy must also provide that the insurer will issue certificates to the policyholder for delivery to each of the insured persons. The certificate must specify the insurance protection provided for the insured, to whom the benefits will be paid, and the rights of the insured to convert to individual insurance if his or her group insurance terminates. The model act also requires a provision regarding continuation of insurance in the event of the insured's total disability. This provision must be described in the certificate.

Ordinarily, today, certificates are combined with booklets describing the group insurance policy. These booklet-certificates generally provide information in addition to that required by the model act.

Conversion Privileges

The model act requires that employees be allowed to convert their group coverage, without providing evidence of insurability, to an individual policy on termination of employment or termination of the group master policy. Conversion is an important aspect of group insurance and will be described in some detail in this section.

Conversion at Termination of Employment. The requirement of a conversion privilege at termination of the insured's employment is one of two required provisions granting an insured the right to convert her or his group life insurance coverage to an individual life insurance policy. This standard provision gives the insured a right to convert when her or his coverage under the group policy, but not the group policy itself, terminates because of termination of employment or termination of membership in an eligible class.

Employment can terminate in a number of ways—because the insured resigned, was discharged, or was laid off. The employee might also be transferred from a class of employees eligible for group life insurance to a class that is ineligible. If an employee terminates employment for any reason, he or she must have the right to obtain an individual life insurance policy from the group insurer without providing evidence of insurability. However, the insurer is not required to issue an individual policy unless the person whose group insurance terminated applies for the individual policy and pays the first premium within the conversion period. The conversion period begins on termination of employment and lasts 31 days. Earlier model bills required that the person converting have the right to choose any form of individual life insurance policy, except term insurance, that is being issued by the insurer to applicants of the person's age and for the applied-for amount. The current model act allows the insurer to offer term insurance also as a conversion option if it wishes to do so.

The model act provides that the conversion amount shall be no more than the amount the person was entitled to under the group policy. Under the model act, "the amount of any life insurance for which such person becomes eligible under the same or any other group policy within 31 days after such termination" is subtracted. The individual policy does not have to include disability benefits or other supplementary coverages. The premium for the individual policy must be at the customary rate for the kind of policy, for the amount of coverage, for the class of risk in which the insured is placed at the time of conversion, and for her or his attained age on the date the individual policy becomes effective.

To illustrate, suppose Donna McCracken is insured for $35,000 under her employer's group life insurance policy. She quits her job and goes to work for another company within 31 days after her resignation, where she becomes eligible for $20,000 of group life insurance. In addition to her new group life coverage of $20,000, Ms. McCracken will have the right to purchase up to $15,000 of individual life insurance from her former employer's insurer without providing evidence of insurability.

Conversion at Policy Termination. In the event the group policy terminates, or is amended to terminate the insurance of a class of employees, an employee whose coverage ceases can convert to an individual life insurance policy. However, such an employee must have been insured under the group policy for at least five years.

The individual policy can provide the lesser of $10,000 and the amount of insurance the employee had under the group policy, minus the amount of group insurance for which he or she becomes eligible within 31 days of termination.

Other features of this conversion privilege are the same as those on conversion at termination of employment. However, some employees will be ineligible for conversion at group policy termination because of the five-year rule. Also, conversion at termination of the group policy is apt to provide less insurance than conversion at termination of employment.

To illustrate, suppose Peter Van Eck is insured for $35,000 under his employer's group life insurance policy when it terminates. Mr. Van Eck has been insured for more than five years. Another group policy is issued to the same policyholder before 31 days have elapsed. Under this policy, Mr. Van Eck has $20,000 of life insurance. Mr. Van Eck has a right to receive an individual life insurance policy in the smaller of two amounts—$10,000 or the former coverage minus the present coverage. The former coverage, $35,000, minus the present coverage, $20,000, is $15,000. Thus, Mr. Van Eck can purchase up to $10,000 of individual life insurance without providing evidence of insurability. Contrast Mr. Van Eck's conversion rights with those of Ms. McCracken in the example above.

Extension of Death Benefit Provision. The model act requires a provision for a death benefit in the highest amount for which an individual life insurance policy would have been issued if an employee dies during the conversion period and before an individual policy becomes effective. It does not matter that the employee did not apply for an individual policy. The provision will be effective whether or not the employee applied. Ordinarily, the practical effect of this clause is to extend the group policy coverage during the 31-day conversion period.

Supplementary Bill Relating to Conversion.   A supplementary bill prepared by the NAIC relates to the conversion privilege. It does not require a policy provision and, thus, is not a part of the group life standard provisions section of the model act, but is in a separate section of its own. The supplementary bill extends to a maximum of 60 days the period during which the employee can apply for an individual policy, unless the employee has been notified of the conversion rights at least 15 days before the end of the conversion period. It does not require that the extension of coverage, described in the subsection above, be provided beyond the end of the conversion period, however. The supplementary bill has been enacted by many states.

Continuation of Coverage During Disability

The model act includes a new requirement for continuation of coverage under the group policy during total disability. This requirement does not appear in earlier model bills.

The provision for continuation of insurance during total disability applies to employer-employee groups only. The insured employee can continue coverage during her or his total disability by paying to the policyholder the portion of the premium she or he would have paid if there had been no disability. The continuation is to be for six months unless the insurer approves continuation under another policy provision, or the policy terminates earlier.

Creditor Group Life Insurance Certificates

Insurers issuing creditor group life insurance are required by the model act to issue certificates of insurance to the creditor-policyholder. The creditor must deliver a certificate of insurance to each debtor. The certificate of insurance must describe the insurance coverage and specify that the death benefit shall first be applied to reduce or extinguish the indebtedness.

Nonforfeiture Provisions

While most group life insurance is yearly renewable term insurance without cash values, some group life insurance does build cash values. Where the group life insurance is on a plan other than term, the policy must contain nonforfeiture provisions equitable to the insureds and to the policyholder.

However, these need not be the same as nonforfeiture provisions required for individual life insurance policies.

DEPENDENT GROUP LIFE INSURANCE

The earlier model bills did not provide for life insurance covering the lives of the insured's dependents. The current model act contains a section entitled "Dependent Group Life Insurance." This section provides that a group life policy (except for a creditor policy) can insure the employees or members against loss due to the death of a spouse or dependent child. The premium for this dependent life insurance can be paid by the policyholder, the employee or member, or both. In noncontributory plans with dependent coverage, spouses and all dependent children must be covered. However, the insurer can exclude or limit the coverage of a spouse or dependent child whose evidence of insurability is unsatisfactory.

The amounts of life insurance for a covered spouse or dependent child cannot exceed 50 percent of the amount of the employee's or member's life insurance. The certificate must contain a statement describing the dependent insurance.

An employee can convert his or her group dependent life insurance along with the insurance on the employee's own life. Conversion of dependent insurance can be made at the time of termination of the employee's employment or at termination of the group policy.

The model act further requires that a conversion privilege shall be available to dependents themselves under two circumstances. First, at the death of the insured employee or member, a surviving dependent can convert to an individual policy. Second, if the dependent's group life coverage terminates because the dependent ceases to be a qualified family member, the dependent can convert. Divorce of a dependent spouse or maturity of a dependent child would be the usual reasons a dependent ceased to be a qualified family member.

In many respects, the model act reflects the current practice of insurers regarding dependent life insurance, although the model act tends to be more liberal as to benefits and conversion by dependents. Group life insurance covering the lives of spouses and dependent children is authorized by statute in many states and is issued in others by permission of the commissioner of insurance.

GROUP MASTER POLICIES AND CERTIFICATES

When an insurer contracts to provide group insurance, it issues a master policy to the policyholder, which is an employer, a union, an association, a trust, or other entity. The master policy, along with the application from the policyholder and applications from insured persons, if any, constitute the contract of insurance, according to the general rule.

The insurer ordinarily issues certificates or booklet-certificates to the policyholder for distribution to the insured persons. The certificate explains the insurance to the insured person. It usually does not contain all of the provisions found in the master policy. The certificate is not the contract of insurance, according to the general rule. However, the master policy and certificate will be construed together by a court to determine the provisions of the contract. Ambiguities or conflicts between the master policy and the certificate will be construed to give the insured the broadest coverage. In other words, if the certificate contains terms more favorable to the insured than those contained in the master contract, the terms in the certificate will prevail.

THE ACTIVELY-AT-WORK REQUIREMENT

Group policies covering employees commonly contain an actively-at-work requirement. An eligible employee must be actively at work on the date her or his insurance is to become effective, or the employee will not be covered. Generally, absent employees become insured on the first day they return to work after becoming eligible.

The actively-at-work requirement prevents persons who are too ill to work from being insured under the group policy. Ordinarily, those who are actively at work are reasonably able-bodied. Thus, the actively-at-work requirement is an important underwriting tool.

Actively-at-work requirements are stated in many different ways in group policies. The courts have generally upheld them as valid and unambiguous.

McLean v. Metropolitan Life Insurance Co.,[8] illustrates the operation of the actively-at-work clause. There, the employee, a factory worker, began work on June 18, 1951, and worked until September 1, 1951, when he went on leave due to disability. He never returned to work. On September 16, 1951, he would have become eligible for group insurance coverage if he had been actively at work. He died on February 5, 1952. The court held that he was not covered under the policy, saying:

> The Court finds nothing ambiguous about the term "actively at work," and, from the facts stipulated, John H. McLean was not "actively at work" at any time after September 1, 1951. In fact he was totally disabled, unable to work, and did not appear at his place of employment after September 1, 1951.
>
> Furthermore, the fact that he was totally disabled by reason of an accidental injury incurred in the course of his employment and could not be actively at work in no way met the requirements of the group policy.
>
> The Court finds that the terms of the group policy are clear and that the insurance never became effective in the case of John H. McLean. Judgment is therefore rendered for the defendant with costs.

---

[8] 78 Ohio L. Abs. 464, 153 N.E.2d 349 (Ct. Com. Pleas 1957).

. . . John H. McLean became eligible for insurance ninety days after June 18, 1951, or September 16, 1951. His insurance became effective on that date provided he was "actively at work" on that date. If he was not "actively at work" on that date, then his insurance became effective on the next following day on which he was "actively at work."

Actively at Work Full-Time

In some group policies, the actively-at-work clause is phrased to require that the employee be actively at work full-time. Some courts have held that the term *full-time* is ambiguous. Where the term is defined in hours, as "full-time means 30 or more work hours per week," the courts are less likely to hold it ambiguous.

Increase in the Amount of Life Insurance

Where there is an increase in the amount of group life insurance covering an employee, it is customary to require that the increase will not become effective unless the employee is actively at work. The increase will become effective if and when an absent employee returns to active work.

For example, in *Smillie v. Travelers Insurance Co.,*[9] the group life insurance policy provided for an increase in the amount of life insurance for insured employees who were actively at work on June 1, 1977. One insured employee, Charles M. Smillie II, was confined to the hospital from May 20, 1977, until his death on June 4, 1977. The court held that the increased coverage was not effective for Mr. Smillie. The beneficiary received the amount of insurance in effect before the increase.

TERMINATION OF GROUP INSURANCE

Group life insurance policies cover the members of employee groups, union groups, association groups, or other groups. A person can be insured under the group policy only if he or she is a member of the group. As a general rule, a person's group insurance terminates when he or she ceases to be a member of the group.

Although there can be various provisions in employer-employee group policies for extending coverage under some circumstances, such policies typically provide that an employee's group coverage ceases when her or his employment ceases. A termination provision might read as follows:

The insurance of an insured employee shall automatically terminate on the earliest of the following dates:

(a) The date of termination of such employee's active status in any of the eligible classes of employment;

---

[9]102 Mich. App. 780, 302 N.W.2d 258 (1980).

(b) The date of termination of this policy; and,

(c) If this is a contributory plan, the date of expiration of the last period for which the participant has made a contribution.

For purposes of this discussion, the relevant subsection of this provision is subsection (a). Thus, if the death of an insured employee occurs prior to the date his or her employment terminates, the employee will have been insured, and the death benefit will be payable. If the death occurs after that date, the person will not have been insured on the date of death (except for coverage provided during the conversion period or during disability).

Definition of *Termination*

Questions sometimes arise as to what constitutes termination of employment. If an employee resigns,[10] retires,[11] or is discharged by the employer,[12] ordinarily, the employee is held to have terminated employment. If the employee does not express an intention to resign, this can sometimes be inferred from other circumstances. Thus, where an employee did not formally resign but told his wife he was quitting and applied for unemployment compensation, the court held he had terminated employment.[13]

A mere absence from work,[14] or a leave of absence,[15] is not held to be termination of employment, as a general rule. The courts are divided as to whether layoffs or strikes constitute a termination of employment. As to strikes, the majority view is that the striking employee has, in effect, quit her or his employment upon joining the strike and that, therefore, the employment terminated.

When a division of a policyholder-company is sold, there can be a question as to whether the employees working in the division terminated employment. In *Pan American Life Insurance Co. v. Garrett*,[16] an electric company sold its transportation division to another company. The employees continued working in their jobs, but for the buyer-company. The court held that the

---

[10]Wyatt v. Security Benefit Life Ins. Co., 178 Kan. 91, 283 P.2d 243 (1955); Murphy v. Chrysler Corp., 306 Mich. 610, 11 N.W.2d 261 (1943); Metropolitan Life Ins. Co. v. Cole, 163 Va. 906, 178 S.E. 43 (1935). See Annot., 68 A.L.R. 2d 8 (1959).

[11]Young v. Minton, 49 Ga. App. 545, 176 S.E. 662 (1934); Lynch v. Central States Life Ins. Co., 281 Ill. App. 511 (1935).

[12]Kowalski v. Aetna Life Ins. Co., 266 Mass. 255, 165 N.E. 476 (1929); Szymanski v. John Hancock Mut. Life Ins. Co., 304 Mich. 483, 8 N.W.2d 146 (1943); Lineberger v. Security Life & Trust Co., 245 N.C. 166, 95 S.E.2d 501 (1956).

[13]Gilby v. Travelers Ins. Co., 248 F.2d 794 (8th Cir. 1957).

[14]Shea v. Aetna Life Ins. Co., 292 Mass. 575, 198 N.E. 909 (1935); Smith v. Aetna Life Ins. Co., 198 N.C. 578, 152 S.E. 688 (1930); Thompson v. Pacific Mills, 141 S.C. 303, 139 S.E. 619 (1927).

[15]Peyton v. Metropolitan Life Ins. Co., 148 So. 721 (La. Ct. App. 1933); MacDonald v. Pennsylvania Mut. Life Ins. Co., 122 Pa. Super. 288, 186 A. 234 (1936).

[16]199 S.W.2d 819 (Tex. Civ. App. 1946).

employees had terminated employment with the seller-company and were no longer insured under the group insurance policy covering its employees.

Date of Termination

The date of an employee's termination from employment is sometimes difficult to determine. A leave of absence or layoff intended to be temporary can become permanent due to illness or other circumstances. Because of this, many group policies contain a provision stating that when such temporary leaves or layoffs continue for a period of two (sometimes three) months, the employee's employment will be considered terminated unless the employer elects to consider it continued.

GROUP POLICY PREMIUMS AND DIVIDENDS

Group policy premiums are typically remitted to the insurer by the policyholder. As with individual insurance, the premium is payable prior to the period of coverage. Group premiums might be paid from the funds of the policyholder, from the funds of the insured persons, if the state law permits, or from the funds of both. Where the entire premium is paid from the policyholders' funds, the plan is called "noncontributory." Where the insured persons contribute at least part of the premium, the plan is called "contributory." Under noncontributory plans, an enrollment card ordinarily will be completed by each eligible employee, even though all eligible employees will be covered. The enrollment card serves as a record of coverage and as a beneficiary designation form. Usually, under group insurance contributory plans, the employee must sign an application and authorize deduction of the premium contribution from his or her salary.

Legal problems relating to premium payment more often occur where the plan is contributory. For example, where an insured employee makes the required contribution, but the policyholder fails to remit it to the insurer, the courts are divided as to whether the employee's coverage terminates.[17]

Dividends

As with individual insurance policies, group policies can provide for a return of part of the premium. Such a return of premium is usually called a dividend when the insurer is a mutual company, and a premium refund or retroactive rate credit when the insurer is a stock company.

---

[17]Holding that the employee's coverage terminates, Magee v. Sun Life Assur. Co., 182 Miss. 287, 180 So. 797 (1938); Longley v. Prudential Ins. Co., 161 S.W.2d 27 (Mo. Ct. App. 1942); Woehr v. Travelers Ins. Co. 134 N.J. Eq. 38, 34 A.2d 136 (1943); Rivers v. State Capital Life Ins. Co., 245 N.C. 461, 96 S.E.2d 431 (1957): cf., All States Life Ins. Co. v. Tillman, 226 Ala. 245, 146 So. 393 (1933); Greer v. Equitable Life Assur. Soc'y, 180 S.C. 162, 185 S.E. 68 (1936).

The insured persons are not usually entitled to receive any dividends or premium refunds that become payable under a group insurance policy. The policyholder is entitled to receive the dividend or premium refund. Under some state laws, however, if the dividend or premium refund exceeds the premiums that the policyholder has paid, the excess must be used for the benefit of the insureds.

Creditor Group Life Insurance Rates

Unlike property and liability insurers, life insurers have generally been exempt from rate regulation. The exception is creditor group life insurance.

The competitive situation that pertains to creditor group life insurance is exactly the opposite of that which pertains to other types of group life insurance. The creditor is both the policyholder and the beneficiary in creditor insurance. In employee group life insurance, the employer is usually the policyholder, but it is forbidden for the employer to be the beneficiary. In some instances, the creditor is also the agent and, thus, receives a commission on the sale of the policy, and, as policyholder, sometimes receives dividends or premium refunds. The creditor is not required to pay any of the premium. Finally, the creditor, as policyholder, makes the decision as to which policy it will purchase.

Under these circumstances, the insurer that offers the policy at a higher premium rate will be at a competitive advantage. The creditor who purchases the policy gets more commission if the rate is higher. The debtors, who have no choice as to which policy is purchased, ordinarily must pay the higher premiums.

Because of this reverse competition in the group creditor insurance field, group creditor statutes and regulations are designed to establish maximum rates. Most states have enacted laws patterned on the NAIC Model Credit Insurance Bill which requires that benefits equal a reasonable percentage of premium. Other states have established a scale of premium rates which the insurer cannot exceed without permission of the insurance commissioner. Still other states merely require the insurer to file its creditor group insurance rates with the insurance commissioner.

THE POLICYHOLDER AS AGENT

In employer-employee groups, the policyholder often assumes many administrative duties, including enrolling eligible employees, collecting employee contributions, distributing certificates, providing forms for beneficiary changes, and transmitting claim forms to the insurer. It is not surprising, therefore, that it is sometimes contended that the employer is the agent of the insurer in carrying out these administrative duties.

The majority rule is that the policyholder is not the agent of the insurer but rather is the agent of the insured employees. A growing minority view holds that the policyholder is the agent of the insurer. This is a complex area of the law. The policyholder might be the insurer's agent for some purposes in a particular state, but not for other purposes. The question of the policyholder's agency is often crucial in determining the rights of the insureds.

For example, in *Kaiser v. Prudential Insurance Co.*,[18] the insured had named his first wife as beneficiary of his group life insurance, changing the designation to his daughter when his first wife died. Later, he remarried. After his death his second wife, Elizabeth Kaiser, brought suit for the proceeds, claiming that the insured had submitted a change of beneficiary form to the employer naming her, Elizabeth, as the new beneficiary and that the employer had acknowledged the change. The insurer never received this form.

The group policy provided that an insured could make a beneficiary change at any time "by written notice through the employer to the Company at its Home Office, on a form furnished by it." The question in the case was this: Was the employer the insurer's agent for receipt of the change of beneficiary form? If so, receipt by the employer of the change of beneficiary form would be receipt by the insurer. The court said:

> An employer is not precluded as a matter of law from acting as agent of the insurer with respect to receipt of notice from the employee as to change of beneficiary, or in the matter of acknowledging that a change has been effected. . . . [W]e are constrained to determine that the language of the policy and of the certificate in question relating to change of beneficiary must be construed to mean that the employer is the agent of the insurer in receiving notice of change of beneficiary and in acknowledging that such change has been effectuated.

Thus, as the employer was acting for the insurer, receipt by the employer of the insured's change of beneficiary form was receipt by the insurer. The change of beneficiary was, therefore, effective. The court in this case followed the minority rule.

CONFLICT OF LAWS

A group insurance policy often is issued by an insurer domiciled in one state to an employer domiciled in another state, with insureds and beneficiaries residing in yet other states. Therefore, questions can arise as to which state's law must be applied. Conflict of laws rules are used to determine the answers.

Generally, the validity and effect of a contract are to be determined by the law of the place of contracting. The place of contracting is the place where the last act necessary to put the contract into force was performed. The last act is ordinarily delivery of the policy. Thus, the law of the employer's state of domicile will usually govern. A few courts have, however, fol-

---

[18]272 Wis. 527, 76 N.W.2d 311 (1956).

lowed the center of gravity or grouping of contacts rule by which the law of the place that has the greatest interest in the outcome of the case will be applied.

Thus, the performance of the contract will sometimes be governed according to the law of the state where the group policy was delivered, and sometimes according to the law of the state where the certificate was delivered. Which law applies will depend on the conflict of laws rules of the state where the case is tried. Sometimes, this is a critical difference. The outcome of the case can depend on which state's law governs.

In *Poffenbarger v. New York Life Insurance Co.,*[19] the court was faced with the question of whether to apply the law of the District of Columbia where the group policy was delivered or the law of West Virginia where the certificate was delivered. The court said:

> Defendant contends [that] . . . this case should be governed by District of Columbia law inasmuch as it was there that the group policy was delivered to the Trustees. It is well established in West Virginia that the *lex loci contractus* [the law of the place where the contract is made] governs the nature, construction and validity of contracts. However, beyond that general principle, neither statute nor decisional law is available to indicate West Virginia's choice of the law to be applied in this troublesome area of group insurance contracts and the delivery of certificates thereunder. In the absence of state decisional law, it is the responsibility of the federal court to determine what the highest state court would find the law to be on this point if the same case were before it. . . . [I]t is not unreasonable to assume that our West Virginia court in a case such as this might choose to apply the relatively new "grouping of contacts" theory of the conflict of laws. This theory would permit the forum [court] to apply the law of the jurisdiction most intimately concerned with the outcome of the particular litigation. In the present case the State of West Virginia would appear to have a legitimate concern in the outcome of the litigation. This manifest interest of a state in the area of insurance on its residents was recognized in another context by the Supreme Court in *McGee v. International Life Ins. Co.,* 355 U.S. 220, 78 S.Ct. 199, 2 L.Ed.2d 223 (1957). It occurs to me that a West Virginia Court would and should recognize as significant the fact that the certificate was delivered in this state to the insured who was a resident of the state at the time, and that the plaintiff-beneficiary, as a West Virginia resident, is properly and logically entitled to litigate her claim in this forum. Additionally, it is noted that West Virginia legislation relative to group life insurance demonstrates a valid concern in regard to the issuance and delivery of such certificates in this state.
>
> The totality of these contacts and circumstances alone might well persuade the West Virginia Court to apply West Virginia law . . . Certainly such a conclusion would not offend the basic principles of justice.

---

[19]277 F. Supp. 726 (S.D. W. Va. 1967).

FEDERAL TAXATION OF GROUP LIFE INSURANCE

This book does not purport to explain the taxation of life insurance. Nevertheless, the federal tax law has had such an impact on the development of group life insurance that some mention of this must be made.

The Internal Revenue Code provides that the cost of group term life insurance paid by the employer is tax-exempt to the insured employee up to $50,000 of coverage.[20] Moreover, the amount of premium paid by the employer is tax-deductible to the employer as a business expense. This provision of the Internal Revenue Code has been in effect for two decades. It has had the effect of encouraging employers to purchase group term life insurance and has resulted in a valuable benefit for employees.

The amount of premium paid by an employer for group permanent life insurance, however, is not tax-exempt to an employee. It is subject to taxation as additional compensation to the employee. The great majority of group life insurance has, therefore, been issued as term insurance.

ERISA AND GROUP INSURANCE

The Employee Retirement Income Security Act of 1974 (ERISA)[21] has a substantial impact on group insurance plans. ERISA is applicable to group life and health insurance plans covering employees, except governmental and church plans, plans maintained for the purpose of complying with workers' compensation laws, and certain plans covering nonresident aliens. Group life and health insurance plans covering employees (as well as many other types of nonpension plans providing benefits for employees) are called employee welfare benefit plans under ERISA. An employer is not required to establish an employee welfare benefit plan. If an employer has an employee welfare benefit plan, however, the plan is subject to the numerous requirements stated in ERISA. These requirements are complex and apply differently to different types of plans. This section will briefly describe the most important of these requirements.

An employee welfare benefit plan must be established pursuant to a written instrument. This instrument must describe how the plan is to be financed and how benefits are to be received. The plan instrument usually names one or more fiduciaries who will administer the plan. Ordinarily, the employer, someone working for the employer, or a trustee will be named plan administrator. A plan administrator must act solely for the benefit of the plan participants and beneficiaries.

Employee welfare benefit plans are divided into two classes—major plans and minor plans. More requirements are imposed on major plans than on

---

[20]26 U.S.C.A. § 79 (West Supp. 1987).

[21]Public Law No. 93–406, 88 Stat. 829 (codified as amended in scattered sections of 5, 18, 26, 29, 31, and 42 U.S.C.).

minor plans. A plan is a minor plan if it has fewer than 100 participants and the benefits are provided from the employer's general assets, insurance contracts, or both. All other plans are major plans.

Reporting and disclosure are important responsibilities of plan administrators. A summary plan description must be provided to all participants and must be filed with the federal Department of Labor when the plan is initiated. This summary plan description must describe the plan in a manner that can be understood by the average plan participant. An annual report must be filed with the Internal Revenue Service. The annual reports of minor plans are simplified to reduce the costs of compliance for these plans.

ERISA requires that a reasonable claims procedure be set forth in the summary plan description. In the case of an insured employee welfare benefit plan, the insurer's claims procedures will suffice. A fiduciary who will review claim denials must be indicated in the plan. This can be the plan administrator, an insurer, or other person or organization.

SECTION 89 DISCRIMINATION TESTING

Section 89 of the Internal Revenue Code,[22] added to the code by the Tax Reform Act of 1986, greatly impacts employer-sponsored group term life insurance plans and health plans (whether insured or employer-funded). To protect the benefits from taxation, each of an employer's life and health plans must satisfy a set of qualifications and discrimination tests. Personal income taxes will be levied on highly compensated employees if benefit plans offer or provide them with more coverage than permitted, as compared with other employees.

Qualifications Tests

Section 89 applies qualifications tests to welfare benefit plans. First, the employer must provide employees with reasonable notice of the benefits available. Second, the plan must be in writing, legally enforceable by employees, maintained for the exclusive benefit of employees, and established with the intent of being maintained indefinitely. The penalty for failure to meet this qualifications test is inclusion in the income of all participants (not just the highly compensated) of the value of the coverage provided.

Another qualifications test must also be met if tax penalties are to be avoided. In order to pass this test, the plan must not be discriminatory with regard to its terms.

Discrimination Tests

Discrimination tests include coverage, eligibility, and benefit tests. Once the qualifications tests have been met, a coverage test is applied. This cover-

---

[22]26 U.S.C.A. § 89 (1988).

age test will be met if 80 percent of the nonhighly compensated employees are covered. If this coverage test is met, the discrimination test is passed. This is not as simple as it sounds, however, as employers are not permitted to disregard employees who have other core health coverage[23] in their calculations. Where the plan is contributory, it is quite likely that the 80 percent coverage level will not be met.

If the plan does not pass the 80 percent coverage test, eligibility and benefit tests must be passed. The employer will first test to see if at least 50 percent of eligible employees are nonhighly compensated. If not, the employer will test to see if the percentage of nonhighly compensated employees is at least as great as the percentage of highly compensated employees who are eligible. If the plan fails this test also, there will be tax penalties. If the plan passes this test, another eligibility test must be applied. The employer must now test to see whether 90 percent of the nonhighly compensated employees are eligible for a benefit worth at least 50 percent of the most valuable benefit available to a highly compensated employee. Again, if the plan fails this test, there will be tax penalties.

If the plan passes the 90 percent/50 percent eligibility test, the employer will apply a benefit test. The employer will test to see whether the average benefit for nonhighly compensated employees is at least 75 percent of the average benefit for highly compensated employees Once more, there will be tax penalties if the plan fails this test. If it passes this benefit test, the discrimination test is passed.

Employees Excluded

Some employees can be excluded from the employer's calculations. Newly hired employees with less than one year of service (six months for core health plans), part-time employees normally working fewer than 17½ hours a week, seasonal employees working fewer than six months per year, employees under age 21, union employees, and nonresident aliens can be excluded.

Highly Compensated Employees

A highly compensated employee is any employee who, during the preceding year, was a 5 percent owner of the employer; received compensation above $75,000; was in the top 20 percent of employees (as to amount of compensation) and received more than $50,000 in compensation; or was an officer and received over 150 percent of certain limits set by the Internal Revenue Code ($30,000 in 1988).

---

[23]Noncore coverage is dental, vision, psychological, orthodontic, and elective cosmetic surgery coverage. Other health coverage is core coverage.

Plans

For purposes of Section 89, each option or different benefit offered is considered to be a different plan and may need to be tested separately. For example, if an employer provides life insurance equal to one times pay to hourly employees and two times pay to salaried employees, the employer has two life insurance plans. Employee and dependent coverages will be considered separate plans.

Other Section 89 Rules

Section 89 has many other rules which affect discrimination testing. For example, all employees of a controlled group of businesses are treated as employed by a single employer. Eligibility and benefit tests may be applied separately with respect to employees in each of the employer's separate lines of business or operating units. Section 89 imposes new reporting requirements.

A complete description of the manifold complexities of Section 89 is far beyond the scope of this book. Undoubtedly, Section 89 will help shape the employer-employee group life and health insurance plans of the future.

FEGLI AND SGLI

The Federal Employees' Group Life Insurance Act of 1954[24] established a plan of group life insurance for nearly all the civilian employees of the federal government. The Federal Employees' Group Life Insurance Plan (FEGLI) is the largest group life insurance plan in the world.

The Federal Employees' Group Life Insurance Act authorized the Civil Service Commission to purchase "from one or more life insurance companies a policy or policies" of group insurance to provide the benefits outlined by the act. The insurer or insurers from whom the insurance was to be purchased were required to: (1) be licensed in 48 states and the District of Columbia; and (2) have group life insurance in force in an amount equal to at least one percent of the total amount of employee group life insurance in the United States in all life insurers.

When the act became effective in 1954, eight insurers met these requirements. For ease of administration, however, the Civil Service Commission elected to purchase only one policy. This policy was purchased from the Metropolitan Life Insurance Company. The policy became effective on August 29, 1954. The other qualifying insurers participated as reinsurers. Provision is made in the law for reinsurance by smaller life insurers also. At the present time, more than 360 life insurance companies are reinsuring a part of this business.

---

[24]5 U.S.C.A. §§ 8701–8716 (West 1967 & Supp. 1987).

By reason of the reinsuring arrangements, the conversion privilege available to the insured employees differs somewhat from that provided under the usual employee's group life insurance policy. For example, if the employees of the A.B.C. Manufacturing Company are insured under a group life insurance policy issued by the Argus Life Insurance Company, a terminating employee is entitled to have an individual life insurance policy issued to her or him by the Argus Life Insurance Company without evidence of insurability. Under FEGLI, however, the converting insured can purchase an individual policy from any participating insurer that has applied for authority to issue individual life insurance contracts and that has met the requirements set out by the Civil Service Commission.

The Civil Service Commission, not the insurer, is responsible for furnishing to each insured employee a certificate that states the benefits to which that employee is entitled, the beneficiary of those benefits, and the persons to whom claims are to be submitted. The certificate must include a summary of all the provisions of the policy that affect the insured.

The law creating the Servicemen's Group Life Plan (SGLI) was enacted in 1965.[25] SGLI is supervised by the Veterans' Administration. SGLI is structured in a manner similar to FEGLI. That is, a primary insurer issues the group policy and other insurers provide reinsurance for the primary insurer. SGLI is available to all members of the uniformed services on active duty and to certain members of the Ready Reserve and Retired Reserve.

The interpretation of the Federal Employees' Group Life Insurance Act is generally a matter for the federal courts. One court explained this as follows:

> The construction of the federal statute is, in the first instance, a federal question. There is no well developed body of state law on the issue here presented, nor is there any overwhelming state interest that would suggest here that Congress intended that the courts look to the various states for the procedural rules to be applied in naming beneficiaries in federal insurance policies. In the interest of uniformity it is much better that the federal courts here develop a separate body of law rather than look to state law—and fifty different interpretations.[26]

Questions involving the determination of family relationships, however, are sometimes answered in accordance with state law. This rule is summarized in the case of *Metropolitan Life Insurance Co. v. Thompson.*[27] The court discussed the application of state law, rather than federal law, to questions of family relationships as follows:

> [T]here being no federal law of domestic relations, whether a particular claimant falls within the federally-defined classification [of beneficiaries] must often be resolved with reference to state law.

---

[25]38 U.S.C.A. §§ 765–779 (West 1979 & Supp. 1987).
[26]Sears v. Austin, 292 F. 2d 690 (9th Cir. 1961), *cert. denied* 368 U.S. 929 (1961).
[27]368 F.2d 791 (3rd Cir. 1966).

GROUP HEALTH INSURANCE

Until 1983, the NAIC had not developed a model act for group health insurance contracts. As a result, such contracts are not subject, in most states, to the detailed regulation applying to group life insurance contracts. However, many states have a statutory definition of eligible groups for group health insurance plans, and required policy provisions are specified in some states.

Group health insurance is patterned in many respects on group life insurance. For example, both group life and group health insurance are issued as master policies with group certificates distributed to the insured persons. The actively-at-work and termination provisions in a group health insurance contract operate similarly to those in a group life insurance contract. Conflict of laws rules apply to group health insurance just as they apply to group life insurance. Group health premium and dividend payments are similar to those for group life. Similar questions occur regarding the agency of the policyholder.

In other respects, group health insurance resembles individual health insurance. This will be explained in Chapter 20, "Health Insurance." Some unique aspects of group health insurance will also be discussed in that chapter.

WHOLESALE AND FRANCHISE INSURANCE

Wholesale life insurance and franchise health insurance are hybrids between individual and group insurance. Wholesale or franchise insurance covers a group of people, with an individual insurance policy issued to each insured in the group. There is usually an agreement with an employer or association that the insurer may sell the wholesale or franchise policies to employees or members. The premiums will ordinarily be deducted from employees' wages by an employer and remitted to the insurer. An association will usually collect the premiums from the members and remit them to the insurer.

The NAIC has drafted a model act defining franchise insurance which has been adopted by about one half the states. Several other states have statutes or regulations governing franchise insurance which are not based on the model act.

Franchise insurance is defined in the model act to be individual accident and health insurance issued to five or more employees of one employer or ten or more members of a trade or professional association or union. Members of other associations, formed for purposes other than obtaining insurance, and with a two-year active existence and a constitution or by-laws, can also be issued franchise insurance. Most states have laws defining franchise insurance, the majority of these laws patterned on the model act.

SUMMARY

Group life insurance has grown spectacularly since its beginnings in 1911, and now amounts to over 40 percent of all life insurance in force in the United States. Group health insurance provides the great majority of health benefits paid by health insurers.

Group life insurance covers employer-employee groups, creditor groups, labor union groups, trusteed groups, association groups, credit union groups, and other groups at the discretion of the insurance commissioner. Not all these are permissible groups in all states, but the types of groups permitted by state statutes has continued to expand.

Most states have statutes which specify certain provisions which must be included in group life policies. These are the grace period provision, incontestable clause, application provision, evidence of insurability provision, certificate provision, and conversion provisions, among others. Some of these provisions are similar in purpose to those found in individual life policies, but others, such as the certificate and conversion provisions, are unique to group life insurance.

The group master policy issued to the employer, union, or other policyholder, along with the application from the policyholder and any applications from insured persons, constitute the insurance contract. Nevertheless, the certificate and master policy will be construed together by a court to give the insured person the broadest coverage. Conflicts between master policy and certificate will be resolved in the insured person's favor.

The most important type of group contract is the employer-employee contract. These contracts have an actively-at-work provision which requires that an eligible employee be actively at work on the date his or her insurance is to become effective. If the employee is not actively at work on that date, the employee will be covered on the first day he or she returns to work. The actively-at-work requirement is an important underwriting tool which assures that those in the group are reasonably able-bodied. The courts generally uphold actively-at-work clauses.

Group insurance usually terminates when the insured ceases to be a member of the group, although there are often provisions extending the insurance for a period of time after termination of group membership. Employees cease to be a member of the employee group on termination of employment. If an employee resigns, retires, or is discharged, employment has terminated. Absence from work is not termination, as a general rule. The courts are divided as to whether a striking employee has terminated employment.

The policyholder often assumes many duties necessary to administer a group insurance plan. The majority rule is that the policyholder is the agent of the employees for carrying out these duties. A growing minority view is that the policyholder is the agent of the insurer. The policyholder can be the agent of the employees for some purposes and the agent of the insurer for other purposes.

The growth of group term life insurance has been spurred by tax laws which exempt the cost of this coverage, up to $50,000 face amount, from income taxation to an employee where the premium is paid by the employer. Group permanent life insurance is not similarly tax-exempt, and, for this reason, most group life insurance is term insurance. The employer can deduct the premium it paid as a business expense.

ILLUSTRATIVE CASE

This case concerns the actively-at-work clause in a group life insurance policy.

SMITH

v.

FOUNDERS LIFE ASSURANCE
COMPANY OF FLORIDA[28]
Court of Appeals of Georgia

BANKE, Chief Judge.

Daisy Smith sued Founders Life Assurance Company to recover $22,000 in death benefits allegedly owed her pursuant to a group insurance policy covering the employees of the Macon-Bibb County Water and Sewerage Authority, which had employed her deceased husband, George Edward Smith, prior to his death. She also sought a bad-faith penalty, punitive damages, and attorney fees pursuant to OCGA § 33-4-6. Concluding as a matter of law that Mr. Smith was not covered under the terms of the policy, the trial court granted the insurance company's motion for summary judgment and denied Mrs. Smith's motion for summary judgment. Mrs. Smith appeals.

After working for the Macon-Bibb County Water and Sewerage Authority for many years, Mr. Smith was forced to cease working on March 24, 1983, due to the illness which ultimately resulted in his death. At the time of his death, which occurred on June 6, 1983, he was considered by the Authority to be a full-time employee on sick leave.

Prior to June 1, 1983, the Authority's employees, including Mr. Smith, had been covered by a policy of group insurance issued by Prudential Insurance Company. The Prudential policy expired on that date and was replaced by a policy issued by the appellee, Founders Life Assurance Company. Founders Life denied Mrs. Smith's claim for death benefits on the ground that Mr. Smith had not been "actively employed" or "actively working" between the effective date of the policy and the date of his death. Thereafter, Mrs. Smith submitted a claim for death benefits to Prudential Insurance Company, which paid her the full amount of such benefits due under the terms of its policy.

---

[28] 175 Ga. App. 262, 333 S.E.2d 5 (1985).

The Founders policy specifies that "each employee actively employed 30 or more hours per week . . . on the date of issue hereof is eligible for insurance from the date of issue . . ." However, the policy further provides as follows: "EFFECTIVE DATES OF INSURANCE. Each eligible employee shall become insured automatically on the date he becomes eligible for insurance *except that an employee who is not actively at work . . . on such date shall not become insured until the next following day on which he is actively at work . . .*" (Emphasis supplied.) The term "actively at work" is defined elsewhere in the policy to mean "the actual expenditure of time and energy in the service of the employer . . ."

Although Mr. Smith was undoubtedly "actively employed" by the Authority at the time of his death and was thus an "eligible" employee under the terms of the policy, it is undisputed that he had not been "actively at work" at any time between the date of his death and the policy's issue date. Therefore, under the unambiguous provisions of the policy governing the "effective dates of insurance," the coverage never took effect as to him. It necessarily follows that the trial court was correct in granting Founders Life's motion for summary judgment and in denying the appellant's motion for summary judgment. We reject the appellant's contention that a fact issue exists as to whether the coverage became effective by estoppel, there being no suggestion in the record that Founders Life ever collected any premium payments from Mr. Smith, through the agency of his employer or otherwise. This fact distinguishes the present case from such cases as *Cason v. Aetna Life Ins. Co.,* 91 Ga.App. 323, 332, 85 S.E.2d 568 (1954), and *American Home Mut. Life Ins. Co. v. Harvey,* 99 Ga.App. 582(1)(b), 109 S.E.2d 322 (1959).

Judgment affirmed.

McMURRAY, P.J., and BENHAM, J., concur.

QUESTIONS FOR REVIEW

1. On what grounds were the early group life insurance plans criticized?
2. Briefly summarize the 1917 standard group life insurance definition.
3. List four groups that are recognized as eligible groups for group life insurance under the current NAIC model act.
4. Briefly discuss each of the following required provisions for group life insurance policies under the model act:
   a. The grace period provision.
   b. The misstatement of age provision.
   c. The incontestable provision.
5. Briefly summarize the conversion rights that must be granted under a group life insurance policy:
   a. If an employee's group coverage terminates because employment terminates.
   b. If an employee's group coverage terminates because of termination of the group policy.
6. Contrast the position of the group policyholder in an employee group plan with that of a creditor group policyholder.
7. Describe the purpose of the actively-at-work provision.

8. Under which of the following situations could there be a question as to the termination of an employee's insurance under her or his employer's group life insurance plan?

   a. The employee resigns.

   b. The employee is discharged.

   c. The employee goes on strike.

9. What has been considered the majority rule with respect to the policyholder as an agent of the insurer or of the insured? The minority rule?

10. What is the purpose of the Federal Employees' Group Life Insurance Act of 1954?

11. How has the federal income tax law spurred the growth of group life insurance?

CHAPTER 20

Health Insurance

THE UNIFORM INDIVIDUAL ACCIDENT AND
SICKNESS POLICY PROVISIONS LAW
 Restatement of the Uniform Law in Simplified Language
 Persons Covered
 Required Provisions
 Optional Provisions
DEFINITIONS OF TERMS
 Injury and Sickness
 Hospital
 Physician
PREEXISTING CONDITIONS
BENEFIT PROVISIONS
MANDATED BENEFITS
EXCLUSIONS AND LIMITATIONS
CANCELLATION AND RENEWAL PROVISIONS
MEDICARE AND MEDICARE
SUPPLEMENT POLICIES
LONG-TERM CARE POLICIES
GROUP HEALTH INSURANCE
 The Group Health Insurance Model Acts
 Coordination of Benefits Provisions
CONTINUATION OF GROUP HEALTH COVERAGE
SUMMARY

There are several kinds of health insurance. One kind provides for reimbursement of medical, hospital, or surgical expenses when an insured person is ill or has suffered an accident. Another kind provides for replacement of lost income when an insured person is unable to work due to disability. Still others provide for vision or dental care expenses or accidental death and dismemberment benefits. A new type of health insurance provides for expenses of long-term care in a nursing home.

Health insurance is written under both individual and group contracts. Group health insurance covers many more people in the United States than does individual health insurance. Nevertheless, individual health insurance has been more heavily regulated than group health insurance, due in part to the absence, until 1983, of a model group health insurance law drafted by the National Association of Insurance Commissioners (NAIC). Individual health insurance will, therefore, receive more attention in this chapter.

The law of health insurance has much in common with the law of life insurance. For example, most of the principles of contract and agency law that apply to life insurance apply also to health insurance. Many of the rules of law relating to accidental injury under the accidental death benefit provisions of life insurance policies apply also to accidental injury under health insurance policies. Disability benefits in life and in health policies are often governed by the same laws. Nevertheless, health insurance is also governed by unique statutory and case law. The purpose of this chapter is to briefly describe the laws unique to health insurance.

THE UNIFORM INDIVIDUAL ACCIDENT AND SICKNESS POLICY PROVISIONS LAW

From 1912 until 1950, individual health insurance policies were subject to a Uniform Standard Policy Provisions Law which required such policies to contain certain standard policy provisions in the exact words and in the order set out in the law. This resulted in inflexibility and cumbersome policy language. Therefore, in 1950, the NAIC recommended a Uniform Individual Accident and Sickness Policy Provisions Law which has since been adopted with few variations by all the states.[1]

The term *accident and sickness insurance* is an older term for what now is called "health insurance." The term *health insurance* will be used in this book except when referring to the uniform law.

Accident and sickness insurance is defined in the uniform law as "insurance against loss resulting from sickness or from bodily injury or death by accident, or both." The uniform law applies to health policies insuring one person or insuring a person and certain of his or her family members and dependents. It does not apply to workers' compensation insurance, liability insurance, reinsurance, blanket insurance, or group insurance. Moreover, the uniform law does not apply to life, endowment, or annuity contracts or to any accidental death, dismemberment, or disability coverages in such policies.

---

[1]Wisconsin adopted the Uniform Accident and Sickness Policy Provisions Law but repealed it in 1975 and replaced it with other legislation which contains some of the provisions of the uniform law.

Restatement of the Uniform Law in Simplified Language

In 1979, the NAIC adopted the Restatement of the NAIC Uniform Individual Accident and Sickness Policy Provisions Law in Simplified Language. The restatement is intended as a guideline for those drafting individual health policies which must be written in simplified—that is, readable—language. Because many states now have laws requiring simplified language in individual health policies, this was a needed modernization of the uniform law. The simplified restatement was not intended to change the meaning of the uniform law but merely to restate its required provisions and some of its optional provisions in readable language. Where the uniform law is quoted in the following sections, the simplified language will be used.

Persons Covered

The individual health policy must insure only one person, or more than one person if the policy is applied for by an adult member of a family and the additional persons are certain family members or dependents. The additional persons who can be insured under the policy are the applicant's spouse, dependent children or any of the applicant's children under a specified age not exceeding nineteen years, and any other dependents of the applicant.

Generally, individual health insurance policies provide that children of the insured are eligible for coverage until they are 19, or until 23 if they are full-time students. A number of states have enacted laws requiring that a mentally or physically handicapped child who is incapable of self-support be permitted to remain insured past the limiting age.

All states have legislation requiring the inclusion of newborn children under their parents' health insurance policies. The NAIC has endorsed a Model Newborn Children Bill requiring that both individual and group health policies cover newborn children from the moment of birth. This bill has been enacted into law by well over four-fifths of the states; other states have independent legislation regarding newborns. If payment of an additional premium is required to provide coverage for the newborn child, these laws typically permit the insurer to require that notice of the birth of the child be given the insurer and that the additional premium be submitted within 31 days of the birth. If this is not done, the insurance coverage will not continue beyond the 31-day period.

Required Provisions

The Uniform Individual Accident and Sickness Policy Provision Law sets out provisions which are required to be included in all individual health insurance policies. These include an entire contract provision, a provision for a time limit on certain defenses (similar in some respects to an incontestable clause), a grace period provision, a reinstatement provision, several claims provisions, a provision limiting the time in which legal actions can be brought, and a change of beneficiary provision.

Entire Contract Provision. Each individual health insurance policy must provide that the "policy [with the application and attached papers] is the entire contract between the Insured and the Company." An individual health policy also must state that no change in the policy is valid unless approval of the change is made by an executive officer of the insurer and is endorsed on the policy. Finally, there must be a statement that no agent has the authority to change the policy or waive any of its conditions. The entire contract provision in an individual health insurance policy is thus similar to that in an individual life insurance policy.

Time Limit on Certain Defenses Provision. The first section of the time limit on certain defenses provision has the same general purpose as an incontestable clause in a life insurance policy. There are, however, differences between the two.

As with the incontestable clause, the basic purpose of the first section of the time limit on certain defenses provision is to limit the period of time in which an insurer will be permitted to rescind the policy, or to defend a claim denial, due to a material misrepresentation in the application. The first part of a time limit on certain defenses provision might read as follows:

> After three years from the issue date only fraudulent misstatements in the application shall be used to void the policy or deny any claim for loss incurred or disability that starts after the three year period.

Thus, after the individual health policy has been in effect for the required period of time, which cannot exceed three years,[2] it will be incontestable, except for fraudulent misstatements in the application. Note that there are several important differences between the time limit on certain defenses provision found in health insurance policies and the incontestable clause found in life insurance policies. First, the contestable period in the health policy is usually three years, instead of two years as in the life policy. Second, fraud is specifically excluded from the operation of the health policy time limit on certain defenses provision. Fraud is not ordinarily excluded in a life policy incontestable clause. The life policy will be incontestable even if the misrepresentation was fraudulent. These differences reflect the wider variety of claims problems encountered in health insurance.

The time limit on certain defenses clause can have optional wording in those individual health policies which provide the insured the right to con-

---

[2]One third of the states have reduced the three-year period to a two-year period. The insurer can always use a shorter period if it wishes, as that would be more favorable to the insured.

tinue the policy in force until age 50 or after or, in the case of a policy issued after age 44, for at least five years from its issue date. Such long-term individual health policies can contain a provision stating that "[a]fter this policy has been in force for three years during the Insured's lifetime (excluding any period during which the Insured is disabled), the Company cannot contest the statements in the application." Note that this provision does not except fraud and that it contains the phrase *during the lifetime of the insured*. It is, therefore, much the same as the life policy incontestable clause.

The time limitation on certain defenses provision contains a second section dealing with preexisting diseases or conditions. It reads as follows: "No claim for loss incurred or disability that starts after 3 years from the issue date will be reduced or denied, because a sickness or physical condition not excluded by name or specific description before the date of loss had existed before the effective date of coverage."

The important topic of preexisting conditions will be discussed in a later section.

Grace Period Provision.   A grace period provision is required to be included in an individual health insurance policy. Unlike the grace period for life insurance policies, which is usually 31 days, the grace period for individual health policies can be as short as seven days for weekly premium policies or 10 days for monthly premium policies. However, the grace period must be 31 days if premiums are payable on any basis but weekly or monthly. As with life insurance, the coverage remains in force during the grace period of a health insurance policy.

Where an individual health insurance policy is renewable at the insurer's option (optionally renewable policies), the grace period provisions must include a statement that, if the insurer gives timely notice of its intention not to renew the policy beyond the period for which a premium has been paid, there will be no grace period. Thus, if the insurer has notified the insured of its intention not to renew the policy beyond a specified date, there will be no grace period for the premium that would otherwise have become due on that date. Such a provision would read essentially as follows:

> Grace Period: This policy has a 31-day grace period. This means that if a renewal premium is not paid on or before the date it is due, it may be paid during the following 31 days. The grace period will not apply if, at least 30 days before the premium due date, the Company has delivered or mailed to the Insured's last address shown in the Company's records written notice of the Company's intent not to renew this policy. During the grace period, the policy will stay in force.

If a claim arises during the grace period, the insurer can reserve the right to deduct any unpaid premium from the settlement. This right is not a required part of the grace period provision but is a separate optional provision.

Reinstatement Provision. The reinstatement provision required to be included in individual health insurance policies differs considerably from that in life policies. If a reinstatement application is not required, the individual health policy must provide that the insurer's acceptance of a premium after lapse will automatically reinstate the policy. If the insurer requires an application for reinstatement and issues a conditional premium receipt to the applicant, the reinstatement will be effective as of the date the reinstatement is approved by the insurer. If the insurer fails to act on the reinstatement application within 45 days of the date of the conditional receipt, the policy will be reinstated automatically.

A reinstated individual health policy covers only losses resulting from accidents that occur after the effective date of reinstatement, or from sicknesses which begin more than 10 days after the reinstatement. Thus, there is a 10-day waiting period for sickness coverage after reinstatement.

Except for this 10-day waiting period, the rights and duties of the insured and insurer are the same under a reinstated policy as they were prior to the reinstatement, but subject to any provisions added in connection with the reinstatement. Thus, an individual health policy can be reinstated subject to restrictive conditions which were not part of the policy prior to lapse. In other words, the reinstatement of a lapsed health policy does not necessarily mean the policy is fully restored to its former status. In this way, it differs from a reinstated life insurance policy, to which the insurer usually cannot add new conditions.

Claims Provisions. Individual health insurance policies are required to include several provisions relating to health insurance claims. First, there is a notice of claim provision. The insurer must be given notice of a claim within 20 days after the occurrence or commencement of any loss covered by the policy, or as soon thereafter as is reasonably possible. Some claims, such as an accidental death claim, for example, will be based on the occurrence of a loss. Others, such as a disability income claim or a claim for hospital benefits, will be based on a loss that commences on a certain date and might continue for some time. Notice, therefore, must be given to the insurer within 20 days after the occurrence of a loss in the one instance, or the commencement of a loss in the other.

Where it is not reasonably possible for an insured to give such notice to the insurer within 20 days, later notice will suffice. For example, suppose the insured were struck by a fast-moving truck and were in a coma for an extended period of time. It might not be reasonably possible for the insured to provide notice within the 20-day period. Notice to the insurer can be given by another person on the insured's behalf, however.

If the policy provides disability income coverage for a period of at least two years, the insurer can include a provision requiring notice of continuance of disability.

Second, an individual health insurance policy must provide that the insurer will furnish claim forms within 15 days of the date it receives notice of claim. If claim forms are not furnished within 15 days, the policy must provide that the claimant will be considered to have fulfilled the proof of loss requirements if she or he merely files written proof of the occurrence on which the claim is based and of the character and extent of the loss.

Third, the policy must provide that written proof of loss must be furnished to the insurer within 90 days of the date of loss except in the case of claims for disability income payments. In the case of disability income claims, proof of loss must be furnished within 90 days after the end of the period for which payment is due. The policy must also provide that if it is impossible for the insured to comply with these requirements, it will be sufficient if he or she furnishes such proof as soon as possible, but no later than one year from the date proof of loss would otherwise have been required.

Note the difference between the requirements for notice of claim and those for proof of loss. Notice of claim must be given within 20 days, but 90 days are allowed to present proof of loss, because proof of loss might require a doctor's statement, or a death certificate in the case of an accidental death benefit.

Fourth, an individual health policy must specify that a claim will be paid immediately upon receipt of proof of loss unless periodic payments are involved. Periodic payments, such as disability income payments, must be made at least monthly.

Fifth, the policy must provide that all benefits are payable to the insured if the insured is alive. Accidental death benefits must be payable to a named beneficiary or to the insured's estate if no beneficiary is named. Other accrued benefits which are unpaid at the insured's death are payable either to the insured's estate or to a named beneficiary, at the insured's option.

Finally, the policy must include a provision that the insurer at its own expense shall have the right to have the insured physically examined during the time a claim is pending. The insurer also has the right to make an autopsy in case of the insured's death, unless forbidden by law.

Legal Actions Provision.   The individual health policy must provide that no action at law or in equity can be brought against the insurer until 60 days after written proof of loss has been furnished to the insurer in accordance with the policy terms. Nor shall such an action be brought after three years from the time written proof of loss has been furnished. In other words, if the insured or beneficiary decides to sue the insurer, the suit cannot be brought earlier than 60 days, or later than three years, after claim proofs have been submitted.

Beneficiary Change Provision.   If an individual health insurance policy provides a death benefit, a change of beneficiary provision is also required.

This provision must state that unless the policyowner has designated an irrevocable beneficiary, the right to change the beneficiary is reserved. It must also state that the consent of a revocable beneficiary shall not be required for the policyowner to surrender, assign, or otherwise deal with the policy.

Optional Provisions

If the insurer includes certain optional provisions in an individual health insurance policy, the uniform law requires that those provisions must be as favorable to the insured as the optional provisions in the uniform law. The optional provisions include payment of claims provisions, a misstatement of age provision (essentially the same as that in a life policy), overinsurance provisions, an illegal occupation provision, and a provision excluding from coverage any loss resulting from the use of intoxicants and narcotics.

Payment of Claims Provisions.   In addition to the required payment of claims provisions, the insurer can, at its option, include certain other provisions relating to claims payment. One of these optional provisions concerns benefits payable to the insured's estate or to a minor or other incompetent person. Such a provision can read as follows:

> If benefits are payable to the Insured's estate or a beneficiary who cannot execute a valid release, the Company can pay benefits up to $1,000 to someone related to the Insured or beneficiary by blood or marriage whom the Company considers to be entitled to the benefits. The Company will be discharged to the extent of any such payment made in good faith.

If the health policy provides payment for hospital, medical, surgical, or nursing services, there can be a provision that the insurer can, at its option, pay the benefits directly to the hospital, physician, or other provider of care. However, if the insured directs otherwise in writing by the time proofs of loss are filed, the insurer must follow the insured's direction.

Change of Occupation Provision.   An insurer can include in an individual health insurance policy a provision relating to a change by the insured to an occupation either more or less hazardous than the insured's occupation at the time of application. If, on the one hand, the insured becomes ill or has an accident at a time when she or he is engaged in a more hazardous occupation, the benefit will be adjusted to the amount the premium paid would have purchased at the more hazardous occupation. That is, the benefit will be adjusted downward, but there will be no adjustment of premium.

If, on the other hand, the insured changes to a less hazardous occupation, the insurer must reduce the premium rate accordingly. The insurer must also return the excess unearned premium.

Overinsurance Provisions.   Insurers wish to discourage overinsurance. Overinsurance occurs when there is an amount of insurance which is excessive in relation to the loss insured against. For example, if a person is covered for disability income insurance in excess of his or her disposable income, the person is overinsured. It would be profitable for the person to be disabled. There would be temptation to submit claims where there is a borderline, or even a nonexistent, disability. Even if the disability income insurance equaled or was slightly less than the insured's disposable income, he or she might prefer to receive the disability income rather than work. This would also be overinsurance. Just as with loss of income due to disability, a person can be overinsured for medical or hospital expenses, or other types of losses.

Overinsurance is a serious problem which the health insurance industry and the insurance regulators have not yet solved. Compensation for actual losses—not windfall profits—is an objective much to be desired. Overinsurance of some people creates higher premiums for all. As premiums get higher, poorer people can afford less insurance.

The optional overinsurance provisions in the uniform law are inadequate to solve the problem of overinsurance. Nevertheless, they do help to mitigate it.

These optional overinsurance provisions deal with situations where there is more than one health policy covering the same loss issued by the same insurer, or where there is coverage of the same loss by two or more insurers. There is also an overinsurance provision in the uniform law dealing with disability income benefits which are too high in relation to earnings.

Generally speaking, overinsurance provisions allow the insurer to make a proportional reduction in its benefit payment if the insured has other health insurance coverage for the same loss, and the insurer had not been notified of the other coverage before the loss. The insurer must return the premiums for the excess insurance.

For example, suppose an insured had two or more health insurance policies with one insurer covering the same loss. Usually, this will be possible only with policies which are not underwritten individually, such as policies sold by machine. The uniform law provides that an individual health policy can include a provision that insurance covering a particular loss issued by the insurer in excess of a stated amount shall be void. Alternatively, there can be a provision that the insured can elect among the policies she or he has with the insurer. Such a provision might read: "Other Insurance in This Insurer: If the Insured has more than one policy of hospital expense insurance, only one policy chosen by the Insured will be effective. The Company will refund all premiums paid for all the other policies."

There are also two optional provisions concerning insurance with other insurers. One provision is to be included in policies covering losses on an expense-incurred basis. The other is to be included in policies covering losses on a nonexpense-incurred basis. An example of a policy which pays benefits on an expense-incurred basis would be a policy which pays 80 percent of incurred expenses for a semi-private hospital room. An example of a policy which pays on a nonexpense-incurred basis would be a policy which pays $150 per day while the insured is hospitalized, regardless of the expenses incurred.

These optional overinsurance provisions limit the insurer's liability to a specified portion of the total loss suffered by the insured where the insured has "other valid coverage." The overinsurance provision can be drafted to include in the definition of "other valid coverage" that provided by group insurance, Blue Cross-Blue Shield plans, and so forth.

The last optional overinsurance provision deals with the relation of the insured's earnings to his or her disability income benefits. If this provision is included and the total amount of benefits payable under all valid disability income coverages on the insured exceeds a specified percentage of the insured's earnings, the disability income benefit payable will be adjusted downward. That is, the amount payable by an insurer with a relation-of-earnings-to-insurance provision in its policy is limited to a proportionate part of the benefits that would otherwise be payable. However, the benefits payable under all disability income coverages cannot be reduced below $300 a month unless the total coverage is less.

Illegal Occupation Provision.   Another optional provision which the insurer can include in an individual health policy is the illegal occupation provision. This provision can read as follows: "The Company will not be liable for any loss which results from the Insured committing or attempting to commit a felony or from the Insured engaging in an illegal occupation."

Thus, for example, if a person insured under an individual health policy providing hospital benefits is injured as a result of a gunshot wound received during his or her commission of a burglary, any resulting hospital expenses would not be payable under the policy.

Intoxicants and Narcotics Provision.   The purpose of this provision is similar to that of the illegal occupation provision. This provision can read as follows: "The Company will not be liable for any loss resulting from the Insured being drunk or under the influence of any narcotic unless taken on the advice of a physician."

DEFINITIONS OF TERMS

A number of terms are usually defined in a health insurance policy. Among these are the terms *injury, sickness, hospital,* and *physician.*

Injury and Sickness

Health policies generally insure against loss resulting from injury or sickness. Therefore, these terms are often defined in the policy.

The NAIC Model Regulation to Implement the Individual Accident and Sickness Minimum Standards Act (NAIC Accident and Sickness Minimum Standards Regulation) has been adopted in about one third of the states. This regulation requires a definition of accident no more restrictive than the following:

> Injury or injuries, for which benefits are provided, means accidental bodily injury sustained by the insured person which are the direct cause, independent of disease or bodily infirmity or any other cause and occurs while the insurance is in force. Injuries shall not include injuries for which benefits are provided under workmen's compensation, employer's liability or similar law, motor vehicle no-fault plan, unless prohibited by law, or injuries occurring while the insured person is engaged in any activity pertaining to any trade, business, employment, or occupation for wage or profit.

Under the model regulation, the definition of sickness cannot be more restrictive than the following:

> Sickness means sickness or disease of an insured person which first manifests itself after the effective date of insurance and while the insurance is in force. There will be a probationary period which will not exceed thirty (30) days from the effective date of the coverage of the insured person. Sickness shall not include sickness or disease for which benefits are provided under any workman's compensation, occupational disease, employer's liability or similar law.

Note that the injury must be sustained, or the sickness or disease must first manifest itself while the policy is in force.

Hospital

The insurer's intent under hospital policies is to provide benefits if the insured is confined in a hospital but not if she or he needs only custodial care. For this reason, many policies define the term *hospital*. Such definitions must be carefully drafted, or they will fail of their purpose.

For example, in *Travelers Insurance Co. v. Page*[3] the health policy included a definition of *hospital* which read as follows:

> The term *hospital* as used herein means an institution which meets all of the following tests: (a) It is engaged primarily in providing medical care and treatment of sick and injured persons on an in-patient basis at the patient's expense and maintains diagnostic and therapeutic facilities for surgical and medical diagnosis and treatment of such persons by or under the supervision of a staff of duly qualified physicians; (b) It continuously provides twenty-four hour a day nursing service by or under the supervision of registered graduate nurses and is operated continuously with organized facilities for operative surgery; and (c) It is not, other than incidentally, a place of rest, a place for the aged, a place for drug addicts, a place for alcoholics or a nursing home.

---

[3]120 Ga. 72, 169 S.E.2d 682 (1969).

The insured was confined in a psychiatric nursing home where there were facilities for suturing and other minor surgery. There were no facilities for major surgery—indeed, the plaintiff admitted that if any of the patients had required even a tonsillectomy, the patient would have been transferred to a general hospital. The insurer, therefore, contended that the institution was not a hospital, as the term was used in the policy. The court, however, contended that the policy definition of *hospital* did not mention major surgery and that to impose a requirement that the facility must be equipped to do major surgery would be going beyond the terms of the policy. The court said:

> We must, therefore, in construing the term most favorably to the insured, construe it to mean that the facilities for any "operative" surgery continuously maintained as provided in the policy is a sufficient compliance therewith. To say that operative surgery means that an institution to be a hospital under the policy must have facilities for both minor and major surgery would be equivalent to saying that it must have facilities for all surgery. The policy does not require this. If the policy had even gone so far as to specify major surgery, we could not require that the hospital have facilities for all major surgery; neither can we require that it have facilities for all types of operative surgery. The policy did not require it and neither can we.

The NAIC Accident and Sickness Minimum Standards Model Regulation requires that the term *hospital* be defined no more restrictively than the following:

> A Hospital is an institution operated pursuant to law and is primarily and continuously engaged in providing or operating, either on its premises or in facilities available to the hospital on a prearranged basis and under the supervision of a staff of duly licensed physicians, medical, diagnostic and major surgical facilities for the medical care and treatment of sick or injured persons on an in-patient basis for which a charge is made and provides 24 hour nursing service by or under the supervision of registered graduate professional nurses.

The definition can exclude convalescent homes, rest homes, and nursing facilities; facilities primarily affording custodial, educational or rehabilitative care; facilities for the aged, drug addicts or alcoholics; and military hospitals.

Physician

Health insurance policies frequently define the term *physician* in order to limit payments under the policy to expenses for treatment given by a qualified practitioner. Some states regulate this definition by statute, however, to prevent insurers from defining *physician* narrowly. Illinois, for example, requires that benefits payable for the expenses of any medical treatment must be payable on an equal basis for the services of any person licensed to give the treatment.[4] The following illustrative definition should meet the requirements of such statutes:

> *Physician* means a licensed practitioner of the healing arts performing services within the scope of his license as provided by the laws of the jurisdiction in which such practitioner resides.

PREEXISTING CONDITIONS

A preexisting condition is a physical or mental condition of the insured that existed prior to the effective date of the insured's health insurance policy. Individual health insurance policies typically provide that the insurer will pay benefits for losses resulting from an accident that occurs, or a sickness that first manifests itself, after the effective date of the policy. Thus, for example, if the insured receives medical treatment after the effective date of the policy for injuries suffered in an accident that occurred before the effective date, the claim will be properly denied. However, if an illness existed without symptoms at the time the policy became effective, it would be covered because it had not manifested itself prior to the effective date. The word *manifest* means "to show plainly."

Older policies did not use the term *first manifest,* but rather covered losses for sickness commencing after the effective date of the policy. Sicknesses sometimes have their origins in conditions which existed prior to the policy effective date, but of which there were no symptoms. This language in the older policies, applied to such conditions, caused misunderstandings and disputes between insureds and insurers. Many states, therefore, require that health policies use the words *first manifest* in defining the term *sickness.* If the *first manifest* language is used, only preexisting conditions which exhibited symptoms prior to the policy effective date will be excluded.

The NAIC Accident and Sickness Insurance Minimum Standards Model Regulation contains the following definition of the term *preexisting condition:*

> "Pre-existing condition" shall not be defined to be more restrictive than the following: Pre-existing condition means the existence of symptoms which would cause an ordinarily prudent person to seek diagnosis, care or treatment within a five (5) year period preceding the effective date of the coverage of the insured person or a condition for which medical advice or treatment was recommended by a physician or received from a physician within a five (5) year period preceding the effective date of the coverage of the insured person.

This further limits the definition of *preexisting condition* to a condition first manifesting itself within a five-year period before the policy effective date.

---

[4]ILL. REV. STAT. ch.73 ¶ 982(b) (1985) (Ill. Ins. Code § 370(b)).

As previously noted, the Uniform Individual Accident and Sickness Policy Provisions Law requires a provision which precludes denial or reduction of a claim arising three years after the policy issue date, if the denial is based on a condition which has not been specifically excluded by name. Thus, if an applicant has had treatment for a back injury and states this on the application, the underwriter could decide to accept the application but issue the policy with an amendment rider excluding benefits for medical treatment or hospitalization resulting from disease or injury to the lower back. Under a policy with such an exclusion amendment, the claims examiner can properly deny a claim for benefits for such treatment throughout the period in which the policy remains in force.

BENEFIT PROVISIONS

Health insurance policies provide a wide array of coverages. Hospital, medical, and surgical expense coverages and disability income coverages are the most important. Major medical policies provide a relatively new but important type of coverage. These policies are intended to cover the major expenses that result from long periods of hospital confinement or expensive surgical procedures.

Medicare supplement policies provide health insurance coverage for those expenses Medicare does not cover. There has been much recent regulation of Medicare supplement policies. This will be discussed in a later section.

Health policies can also provide accidental death and dismemberment benefits. Some limited policies provide benefits only if the insured is injured as the result of an accident or only if she or he contracts a specified disease, such as cancer. Some policies limit coverage to travel accidents. Vision and dental care expense policies are becoming more common—usually as group insurance. Long-term care insurance provides benefits when the insured is confined to a nursing home.

MANDATED BENEFITS

Many of the health insurance statutes enacted over the past several years have mandated various types of benefits. Among such laws have been those mandating coverage for newborn and handicapped children of the insured, alcoholism and drug addiction treatment, maternity expenses, outpatient treatment, home health care, and treatment of mental illness. Moreover, laws have been enacted requiring that treatment by chiropractors, podiatrists, optometrists, psychologists, and other health professionals be covered in health policies.

These statutes usually apply to both individual and group health insurance policies. They have been voluminous, diverse, and sometimes conflicting, creating serious compliance problems for insurers, especially in regard to group health insurance.[5]

In addition to these specific mandated benefits, many states have adopted minimum standards for individual hospital, medical, surgical, major medical, and disability income policies. In 1976, the NAIC adopted a Model Individual Accident and Sickness Insurance Minimum Standards Act and model regulations to implement it. The NAIC Model Minimum Standards Regulation requires, for example, that basic hospital incurred-expense policies provide at least 80 percent of a semi-private room rate or, alternatively, at least $30 per day for 31 days. Eighty percent of miscellaneous hospital expenses up to $1,000 (or, alternatively 10 times the room and board charge) with a $100 deductible must be provided.

By 1988 one half of the states had enacted laws or adopted regulations requiring minimum standards in individual health policies. In some states, these statutes and regulations do not follow the NAIC models. This lack of uniformity has been a source of concern to the health insurance industry because of the expense of conforming to different standards in different states.

EXCLUSIONS AND LIMITATIONS

Most individual health insurance policies list some conditions for which benefits will not be paid. Generally, these conditions are listed in a section of the policy entitled "Exclusions and Limitations." These exclusions and limitations differ from one type of health insurance policy to another. Disability income policies, for instance, typically include few exclusions or limitations. Usually, benefits under such policies are not payable in the event the disability results from war, attempt to commit suicide, or self-inflicted injury. Injuries or illnesses for which benefits are payable under workers' compensation laws ordinarily will not be covered.

Hospital expense policies often contain more exclusions. Thus, a hospital-surgical policy might exclude losses incurred as a result of:

1. Injury or sickness for which the insured is entitled to benefits under Medicare or any Workers' Compensation, Occupational Diseases Law, or any similar law.
2. Care or treatment received while confined in facilities provided by the Veterans Administration unless there is a legal obligation for the insured to pay for the treatment or services provided.
3. Sickness contracted or injury sustained as a result of war, declared or undeclared, or any act or hazard of war.

---

[5] R. Younger, Mandated Insurance Coverage—The Achilles Heel of State Regulation? (1982).

4. Injury or sickness of the insured while in the military, naval, air force, or other armed services of any country. (The pro rata unearned premium for any period of such service will be returned to the insured upon request.)

5. Pregnancy, childbirth, abortion, miscarriage, or any complications thereof.

6. Any attempt at suicide, whether sane or insane, or any intentionally self-inflicted injury.

7. Dental treatment of the teeth or gums unless required by injury to natural teeth.

State legislatures and insurance departments have reduced the number of allowable exclusions in the past several years. For instance, the insurer cannot exclude treatment for tuberculosis in some states. In some states, treatment for alcoholism cannot be excluded. Treatment for mental illness is also frequently required to be covered, although benefits may be limited for such treatment.

CANCELLATION AND RENEWAL PROVISIONS

Individual health insurance policies often include restrictions on renewability. Some health insurance policies include optional cancellation provisions which allow the insurer to cancel them at any time. All that is necessary is to give the policyowner the required notice and refund the premium paid for coverage beyond the cancellation date. The number of these freely cancellable policies is diminishing, however. Their issuance is being discouraged by legislatures and insurance departments.

A second type of individual health insurance policy is optionally renewable. That is, it cannot be cancelled by the insurer at any time, but the insurer can refuse to renew it. The insurer must give the policyowner notice of its intention not to renew. Many states limit the insurer's right to refuse renewal. Some do not permit the insurer to refuse renewal except on a policy anniversary. Thus, if the health policy were issued on March 1, 1989, the insurer could not refuse to renew it until March 1, 1990, even though the premiums were payable monthly or quarterly. This guarantees at least one year's coverage. Other states forbid the insurer to refuse renewal except under certain specified conditions.

Next, there are individual health policies which can be continued at the option of the policyowner. In this category are noncancellable, or noncancellable and guaranteed renewable, policies. The NAIC reccommends that the states require these terms to be used as follows:

> The terms "non-cancellable" or "non-cancellable and guaranteed renewable" may be used only in a policy which the insured has the right to continue in force by the timely payment of premiums set forth in the policy (1) until at least age 50, or (2) in the case of a policy issued after

age 44, for at least five years from its date of issue, during which period the insurer has no right to make unilaterally any change in any provision of the policy while the policy is in force.

About one fourth of the states requires this terminology.

Finally, there are guaranteed renewable policies. Guaranteed renewable policies—in those states which require the terminology recommended by the NAIC—are the same as noncancellable, or noncancellable and guaranteed renewable policies except that under a guaranteed renewable policy, the insurer may make changes in premium rates by classes.

A number of states require that renewability provisions appear on the face page of the policy. Renewability provisions are important. The policyowner should not have to search the policy to ascertain them.

The importance of complying with a state statute requiring renewability provisions to appear on the policy's face page is illustrated by *Caswell v. Reserve National Insurance Co.*[6] *Caswell* involved a policy that was nonrenewable at the insurer's option. The insured had been paid benefits for expenses resulting from a heart attack, after which the insurer offered to renew the policy only on the condition that a rider be attached to the policy excluding payment of future benefits for heart and circulatory system diseases. The insurer maintained that, as it had the right to refuse renewal outright, it had the right to insert a new exclusion in the policy and refuse renewal unless the exclusion was accepted. The policyowner tendered the renewal premium and insisted on renewal of the policy as it was originally written. The insurer refused, and the policyowner sued, claiming the benefits would have been payable under the terms of the policy as originally written.

The policyowner contended that the policy was in violation of a Louisiana statute requiring renewability provisions to appear on the face page of the policy as follows:

> In any case where the policy is subject to cancellation or renewal at the option of the insurer, there shall be prominently printed on the first page of such policy a statement so informing the policyholder.

The insurer contended that the renewability provision appeared on the first page of the policy proper and that the outside, or cover page, should not be considered as being part of the policy. The court, however, noted that the cover page included a few items of policy information and held, therefore, that the renewability provision did not appear upon the face page of the policy as required, saying:

> Therefore, we hold that as a matter of law the requirements of the statute were not complied with in that the page on which the caveat was inserted was not the first page of the policy as was required.

---

[6]272 So. 2d 37 (La. Ct. App. 1973).

The court, therefore, held that the policyowner could not be required to accept a new exclusion as a condition of renewal and that benefits were payable as contended.

MEDICARE AND MEDICARE SUPPLEMENT POLICIES

Medicare is a government program which provides hospital, medical, and surgical benefits for most persons aged 65 and over and for certain disabled persons who are younger. The Medicare program is made up of two parts: a basic plan covering hospital room and board and related expenses (Part A Medicare) and a supplementary medical plan which provides for the cost of physicians' services (Part B Medicare).

Medicare covers, with various limitations, the costs of the following: inpatient hospital care, post-hospital extended care in a skilled nursing facility, home health services, hospice care, physicians' services, prescription drugs, x-rays and other diagnostic tests, ambulance services, splints, casts, rental of hospital beds, prosthetic devices, braces, artificial body parts, and physical therapy, among other benefits. Medicare benefits were greatly expanded by Congress's enactment of the Medicare Catastrophic Coverage Act of 1988.[7] As of January 1, 1989, Medicare will cover inpatient hospital expenses after payment of an annual deductible (approximately $564 in 1989). As of January 1, 1990, Medicare beneficiaries will have to pay no more than a "catastrophic limit" per calendar year (approximately $1,370 in 1990) for covered charges by physicians. As of January 1, 1991, Medicare will pay for the prescription drugs of a Medicare beneficiary who is not hospitalized, subject to a 50 percent coinsurance payment by the Medicare beneficiary in 1991, 40 percent in 1992, and 20 percent thereafter. (Prescription drugs of those hospitalized were already paid for under the prior law.) As of January 1, 1989, Medicare pays for 150 days of skilled nursing facility care, subject to a coinsurance payment by the Medicare beneficiary (approximately $164 in 1989).

Although Medicare provides substantial benefits, there are significant gaps that can be bridged by additional health insurance purchased from private insurers, called Medicare Supplement or Medigap health insurance policies. The deductibles and coinsurance payments required by Medicare can be difficult for an aged person to pay. Moreover, private duty nurses, routine physical check-ups, vision and dental care, hearing examinations and hearing aids, and immunizations are among those services not covered by Medicare.

Supplementary private health insurance is an important protection for the elderly. Such Medicare supplement insurance is regulated by both federal and state law. A federal law, known as the Baucus Amendment,[8] encourages the adoption by all states of the Medicare supplement insurance standards

---

[7]Pub. L. 100–360.
[8]42 U.S.C.A. §1395ss (West 1983).

contained in the NAIC Medicare Supplement Insurance Minimum Standards Model Act and Regulation.

The NAIC Medicare Supplement Insurance Minimum Standards Model Act and Regulation were developed for use by states which have not enacted the NAIC Individual Accident and Sickness Insurance Minimum Standards Act, but which desire to establish minimum standards for Medicare supplement insurance policies. After the enactment of the Medicare Catastrophic Coverage Act of 1988, the NAIC drafted changes to the model act and regulation to reflect changes in the Medicare law.

The model act and regulation require certain definitions of terms found in Medicare supplement policies, such as the terms *accidental means, convalescent nursing home, hospital, mental and nervous disorders, nurses, physician,* and *sickness.* The model act and regulation prohibit certain policy provisions and outline minimum benefit standards for Medicare supplement policies. The model act and regulation also establish loss ratio standards and required provisions disclosing the terms of the policy. An outline of policy coverage must be given to applicants for Medicare supplement policies. Finally, the replacement of Medicare supplement policies is governed by these model laws.

LONG-TERM CARE POLICIES

Medicare does not pay for long-term nursing home care. In recent years, the public has become increasingly aware of this gap in coverage and concerned about the exhaustion of savings and other resources that can result from long-term nursing home care. Because the elderly population is growing at a rate three times faster than that of the general population, the market for long-term care policies is substantial.

In 1987, the National Association of Insurance Commissioners adopted a Long-Term Care Model Act. One half of the states have some type of long-term care insurance legislation, including one third which have legislation patterned on the model act. Other states have pending legislation based on the model act.

The purpose of the Long-Term Care Insurance Model Act is to promote the availability of long-term care insurance products, to protect applicants for long-term care insurance from deceptive sales or enrollment practices, to establish standards for long-term care insurance, to facilitate public understanding of the product, and to facilitate flexibility and innovation in the development of long-term care insurance.

The model act applies to insurance policies providing at least 12 months of coverage in a setting other than an acute care unit of a hospital, including both group and individual policies. Excluded from the definition are Medicare supplement policies, hospital expense and indemnity policies, medical-surgical expense coverage, disability income coverage, accident only policies, specified disease only policies, and limited health benefit policies.

Under the model act, group long-term care policies can be issued to employers, labor organizations, or a combination of these under a trust; to professional, trade, or occupational associations; to other associations; and to other groups in the discretion of the insurance commissioner.

Long-term care insurance policies cannot "be cancelled, nonrenewed, or otherwise terminated on grounds of the age or the deterioration of the mental or physical health of the insured" under the model act. Such policies cannot "provide coverage for skilled nursing care only or provide significantly more for skilled care in a facility than coverage for lower levels of care." This latter provision is required because the majority of persons needing long-term care require primarily intermediate or custodial care, not skilled care. This is the essence of long-term care insurance.

According to the model act, long-term care policies, other than group policies, cannot use a definition of the term *preexisting condition* that is more restrictive than the following:

> Preexisting condition means a condition for which medical advice or treatment was recommended by, or received from a provider of health care services, within six months preceding the effective date of coverage of an insured person.

Long-term care policies, again excepting group policies, cannot exclude "coverage for a loss or confinement which is the result of a preexisting condition unless such loss or confinement begins within six months following the effective date of coverage of an insured person." The six-month limitation periods in both the above provisions can be extended by the insurance commissioner.

Most long-term policies currently in force are individual policies. Insurance experts believe that group policies will probably account for most long-term care insurance in the future. Laws patterned on the Long-Term Care Insurance Model Act will likely spur the growth of group long-term care insurance.

GROUP HEALTH INSURANCE

Group health insurance contracts are, in many respects, governed by the same rules of law as are individual health insurance contracts. Group health insurance contracts cover the same losses as do individual health insurance contracts—that is, medical, hospital and surgical expenses, loss of income due to disability, loss due to accidental death or dismemberment, dental and vision care expenses, long-term care expenses, and so forth. As with individual health insurance, dependents of the insured can also be covered under a group health insurance policy. Moreover, health coverages mandated by state laws usually apply to both individual and group health insurance policies.

The Group Health Insurance Model Acts

In 1983, the NAIC adopted a Group Health Insurance Definition and Group Health Insurance Standard Provisions Model Act. The permissable groups under this model act parallel those in the current Group Life Insurance Model Act. That is, under the Group Health Insurance Model Act, group health insurance can be issued to an employer, a creditor, a labor union, a trust established by employers and unions, an association, a credit union, or other group which in the insurance commissioner's opinion is in the public interest. The Group Health Insurance Model Act provides for dependent group health insurance.

A number of the required group health policy provisions are similar to the required provisions for group life insurance policies. There are, however, a number of provisions in each model act which are not found in the other, because the provision is appropriate to one type of insurance but not to the other. For example, the Group Health Insurance Model Act requires "[a] provision that the insurer shall have the right and opportunity to examine the person of the individual for whom claim is made when and so often as it may reasonably require during the pendency of claim under the policy. . . ." The Group Health Insurance Model Act also requires provisions relating to disability claims and to preexisting conditions. About one fourth of the states have group health insurance laws patterned on this model act.

The Group Health Insurance Mandatory Conversion Privilege Model Act was adopted by the NAIC in 1976. About one third of the states have laws based on this model act. Another third have laws governing conversions by group health insureds to individual health policies which are not based on the model act.

Coordination of Benefits Provisions

As with individual health insurance, overinsurance under group health insurance policies is a serious problem. Insurers attempt to control overinsurance in group health insurance by including a coordination of benefits provision in their group health policies. A coordination of benefits provision specifies that benefits will not be paid for amounts reimbursed by other group insurers. It limits total benefits if the insured has multiple group health insurance to 100 percent of expenses covered, and designates the order in which the group insurers are to pay benefits.

Overinsurance is an especially difficult problem in group health insurance. The same accident can entitle the insured person to benefits from his or her employer's group health insurer, a workers' compensation insurer, an automobile liability insurance carrier, an individual health insurer, or a spouse's employer's group insurer. Moreover, overinsurance is even more difficult to ascertain and control where group health insurance benefits are involved than it is in the case of individual health policies. Overinsurance under individual health policies can be controlled by appropriate policy provisions and to a certain extent through underwriting requirements. If issuance of an individual health policy would result in the applicant's being overinsured, the insurer can disapprove the application entirely, or offer the applicant a reduced amount of insurance.

In group insurance, however, it is not practical to underwrite each insured person. Moreover, coverage under a group plan often results automatically from a person's employment. Thus, coordination of benefits provisions are an important tool used by insurers in their efforts to reduce overinsurance.

In 1985 the NAIC adopted completely revised Group Coordination of Benefits Regulations and Guidelines, taking into account such modern realities as two-worker families, dependent children of divorced insureds, and covered retirees who found full-time employment elsewhere and thus had double group health coverage. An efficient, fair coordination of benefits system requires that all group policies reflect the same rules. Most of the states have adopted the Group Coordination of Benefits Regulation.

CONTINUATION OF GROUP HEALTH COVERAGE

In 1986, Congress enacted the Consolidated Omnibus Budget Reconciliation Act (COBRA)[9] which requires that employers sponsoring group health plans offer continuation of coverage under the plan to employees and their spouses and dependent children who have lost coverage because of the occurrence of certain qualifying events. COBRA applies to both self-funded and insured health plans and to most employers. Employers with fewer than 20 employees, the federal government, and churches do not have to comply.

Employees and their spouses and dependent children have a right to continue group health coverage for 18 months if they lose coverage due to a reduction in the employee's work hours or to termination of employment for reasons other than the employee's gross misconduct. Spouses and dependent children have a right to continue coverage for three years if they lose coverage due to the death of the employee, the divorce or legal separation of the employee and spouse, the employee's entitlement to Medicare, or a child's ceasing to qualify as a dependent. Bankruptcy of the employer that results in loss of coverage can also trigger the right to continuation coverage.

When an employer's group health plan becomes subject to COBRA, the employer must notify covered employees and their dependents of their rights under COBRA. The employee or a family member must notify the plan administrator of a divorce, legal separation, or a child ceasing to qualify as a

---

[9]Pub. L. No. 99–272, tit. X, 100 Stat. 82, 222 (1986).

dependent. The employer must notify the plan administrator of the employee's death, reduction in hours or termination of employment, or Medicare entitlement. The plan administrator must then notify the person losing coverage of her or his right to continue coverage.

If an eligible person chooses to continue coverage, she or he must pay for the coverage, unless the employer elects to pay for part or all of it. The coverage must be identical to coverage provided under the plan to similarly situated employees or family members. The person cannot be required to provide evidence of insurability in order to continue group health coverage.

Continuation coverage terminates if the employer no longer provides health coverage for any of its employees, if the premium is not paid on time, or if the covered person either becomes covered under another group health plan or becomes entitled to Medicare. If continuation of coverage rights terminate solely because of expiration of the time period, the covered person can convert to a conversion health plan maintained by the employer.

COBRA continuation coverage has been criticized for a number of reasons. First, it conflicts with the numerous state laws already enacted on the subject. Second, critics say penalties for infractions of COBRA are unduly harsh. Third, administration of COBRA continuation coverage is difficult and uncertain.

SUMMARY

Health insurance covers losses suffered by the insured as a result of illness or accident. Some health insurance policies cover hospital, medical, and surgical expenses. Some replace lost income when the insured is disabled and unable to work. Others provide accidental death or dismemberment benefits, travel accident insurance, vision or dental care benefits, or long-term care benefits. Group health policies cover more people than individual health policies, but individual health policies are more heavily regulated.

Individual health policies must conform to the provisions of state law. Nearly all states have laws patterned on the NAIC Uniform Individual Accident and Sickness Policy Provisions Law. The uniform law provides that an individual health insurance policy is a policy covering one person, or covering an applicant and certain of his or her family members and dependents.

The individual health policy provisions required by the uniform law include an entire contract provision, a provision for a time limit on certain defenses, a grace period provision, a reinstatement provision, several claims provisions, a provision limiting the time in which legal actions can be brought, and a change of beneficiary provision. Most of these provisions differ somewhat from life policy provisions.

The time limit on certain defenses provision found in health policies is similar to the incontestable clause in a life policy, but the contestable period in a health policy usually runs for three years, rather than two as in a life policy, and does not except fraud. In addition, the health policy clause deals with preexisting conditions. Under a health policy, a preexisting condition cannot be the basis for reduction or denial of a claim after the policy has been in force for three years unless the condition is excluded by name.

The grace period provision allows for shorter grace periods for weekly or monthly premium health policies than the grace period in life policies. The reinstatement provision of a health policy differs from that in a life policy in that the insurer can add new restrictive conditions.

A health insurer can include certain optional provisions in an individual health insurance policy. Some of these optional provisions are the change of occupation provision, the misstatement of age provision, the overinsurance provisions, the illegal occupation provision, and the intoxicants and narcotics provision.

Probably the most important of these optional provisions are the overinsurance provisions. Overinsurance occurs when an insured has more than one source of coverage and stands to make a profit if she or he becomes ill or has an accident. Overinsurance is a serious problem which the insurance industry has not yet solved.

The definitions of terms in health policies are of crucial importance. *Injury, sickness, hospital,* and *physician* are terms which are often defined in the policy. Some states have regulations governing the way in which these terms shall be defined. The terms *injury* or *sickness* are usually defined to include only injuries that occurred or sicknesses that first manifested themselves after the effective date of the policy.

Many state laws mandate certain benefits which must be included in both individual and group health insurance policies. These include coverage of newborn and handicapped children of the insured, alcoholism and drug addiction treatment, maternity expenses, outpatient treatment, home health care, and treatment of mental illness. In addition, many states have laws mandating that claims for covered treatment provided by chiropractors, podiatrists, optometrists, psychologists, and other health professionals be honored.

Individual health insurance policies have four basic types of provisions governing the right to continue the policy. Some policies contain clauses making the policy freely cancellable at any time by the insurer. These clauses are being discouraged by legislatures and insurance departments. Other individual health policies have clauses which allow the insurer to refuse to renew the policy. Still others are noncancellable or guaranteed renewable. The premium rate of a policy which is guaranteed renewable can be changed by the insurer. This is not true of noncancellable policies. Some states have laws mandating that cancellation and renewal provisions appear on the face page of the policy.

Medicare supplement policies provide coverage for hospital and medical expenses not covered by Medicare. Such policies must conform to the standards contained in the NAIC Medicare Supplement Insurance Minimum Standards Model Act and Regulation in those states which have laws patterned on these models. Medicare does not cover long-term care in a nursing home. Long-term care insurance policies can fill this gap in coverage. Many states have enacted long-term care insurance laws, most patterned on the NAIC Long-Term Care Insurance Model Act.

Group health insurance policies cover the same losses that individual health policies cover, and many rules of individual health insurance apply to group policies as well. Overinsurance is a problem for group health insurers, just as it is for individual health insurers. Coordination of benefits clauses in group policies help to reduce overinsurance.

COBRA requires continuation of health benefits under most employers' group health plans if employees, their spouses, or dependent children lose coverage because of the occurrence of certain qualifying events. The person continuing coverage must pay for the coverage which will last 18 months or three years, depending on the reason for loss of coverage.

ILLUSTRATIVE CASE

This case deals with the definition of *sickness* in a health policy.

KATHRYN L. MCDANIEL, Appellant

v.

STATE FARM MUTUAL INSURANCE COMPANY,
A Corporation, Appellee[10]

Court of Appeals of Kansas

Before FOTH, C. J., and ABBOTT and MEYER, JJ.

FOTH, Chief Judge.

This is an action to recover benefits under a health insurance policy. Plaintiff appeals from the trial court's holding that her condition was not covered by the policy's insuring clause definition:

> Sickness means any sickness or disease of a Covered Person *first manifesting itself* while this policy is in force with respect to such person and shall include all complications arising therefrom. [Emphasis added.]

The case was submitted to the trial court on deposition testimony, exhibits and stipulations. The court entered the following findings of fact and conclusions of law:

> 1. The plaintiff made written application for a· health insurance policy with the defendant's agent, Quincy Seymour, on January 27, 1976. Mr. Seymour was the scrivener of the application in that he wrote out plaintiff's answers to questions asked of her from the application form. Plaintiff's application was accepted by defendant and a policy issued effective as of the day of application.

> 2. On February 26, 1976, plaintiff consulted Dr. Ducey and gave a history of severe headaches, blurred vision, fatigue, and an episode of syncope or unconsciousness. She told Dr. Ducey she had experienced these symptoms for the past two or three months.

---

[10]3 Kan. App. 2d 174, 591 P.2d 1094 (1979).

3. On March 2, 1976, plaintiff was admitted by Dr. Ducey to the Wesley Medical Center for a complete examination. Upon admission to the hospital, she gave essentially the same history concerning her complaints and the length of their duration that she had earlier given Dr. Ducey, all as more fully set out in the record. However, plaintiff did not relate these symptoms to any particular illness or disease.

4. After running tests, it was the opinion of Dr. Ducey and his consultants that plaintiff was suffering from an arterio venous malformation right frontal lobe. One symptom consistent with this diagnosis was the plaintiff's lack of concern for the symptoms that she had complained of to Dr. Ducey and upon admission to the Wesley Medical Center.

5. Although plaintiff was not aware of the condition of an arterio venous malformation prior to or at the time of the effective date of the policy, that fact does not determine whether or not there is coverage under the defendant's policy for her condition.

6. The words 'manifesting itself' as used in the policy's definition of *sickness* means that point in time when the sickness or disease becomes symptomatic and not necessarily when the exact nature of the sickness or disease is diagnosed by a physician after extensive testing.

7. Dr. Ducey testified, and the Court so finds, that the history of complaints presented to him by the plaintiff were symptoms of an arterio venous malformation right frontal lobe. These symptoms were being experienced prior to the effective date of the policy based upon the history given Dr. Ducey and the Wesley Medical Center by plaintiff. Therefore, plaintiff's arterio venous malformation was symptomatic and manifesting itself prior to the effective date of the policy. Accordingly, the defendant's policy does not cover the plaintiff's medical and hospital expenses incurred because of the arterio venous malformation right frontal lobe.

8. Based upon the above findings and the Kansas case law, the Court hereby enters judgment in favor of the defendant. Costs taxed to plaintiff.

We affirm on the basis of the trial court's findings, with the following additional observations:

First, appellant does not attack the finding (No. 2) that all the symptoms of February 26, 1976, had existed for at least two months—*i.e.,* since at least one month prior to the effective date of the policy. Appellant's sole contention on appeal, although expressed in different ways, is that before an illness "manifests itself" under the policy it must be clear to the policyholder, regardless of whether it is diagnosable by the physician.

Second, despite appellant's efforts to distinguish them we believe this case is controlled by *Southards v. Central Plains Ins. Co.,* 201 Kan. 499, 441 P.2d 808 (1968), and *Bishop v. Capitol Life Ins. Co.,* 218 Kan. 590, 545 P.2d 1125 (1976). In *Southards* the plaintiff had purchased credit insurance (health and accident) in conjunction with the purchase of a car on a conditional sales contract. The effective date of the insurance policy was September 27, 1965. Later that same fall, plaintiff was treated for anemia and was given a blood transfusion. After a second transfusion in January, plaintiff was told by his doctor that he had Bright's disease. The insurance company denied coverage because the policy excluded coverage " 'where the sickness or disease was *contracted* prior to the effective date of the Policy.' " (201 Kan. p. 500, 441 P.2d p. 810. Emphasis added.) The trial court held there was no coverage.

On appeal, plaintiff asserted that, since the sickness did not occur until after the policy was issued, it did not originate, or was not "contracted," until after the effective date of the policy. The insurer argued that, although *disabiity* did not ensue until after the policy date, the *disease* was present at the date of issuance in such a stage as to be manifest to one versed in medical science.

The Supreme Court first delineated the applicable rules in *Southards*, 201 Kan. at 499, Syl. ¶¶ 3 and 4, 441 P.2d at 809–10:

> It is the general rule that the origin or inception of a sickness or disease, within the meaning of a health and accident policy requiring that sickness and disease be contracted after the effective date of the policy, is that point in time when the disease becomes manifest or active or when there is a distinct symptom or condition from which one learned in medicine can diagnose the disease.
>
> Knowledge of his condition on the part of one afflicted with a disease is not essential to establish the existence or date of origin of the disease.

Applying those rules to the facts of the case, the court decided "[t]hat on September 27, 1965, the date on which the policy was issued, [plaintiff] was afflicted with glomerulonephritis to the extent that it was active and manifest to those who specialized in medicine." 201 Kan. at 505, 441 P.2d at 813. The Court concluded its opinion by citing language from *Minear v. Benefit Association of Railway Employees*, 169 Kan. 199, 205, 218 P.2d 244 (1950):

> . . . The policy provided indemnity only for disability resulting from illness contracted and beginning during the life of the policy. Obviously, the company would not be insuring an applicant against an illness or disease from which he was already suffering. . . . 201 Kan. at 506, 441 P.2d at 814.

The result was to affirm the denial of coverage.

In *Bishop* the plaintiff had purchased a "debtor-creditor" insurance policy providing that the insurer would make the debtor's monthly payments should he become totally disabled by reason of sickness. The policy excluded coverage for disability resulting from " 'a sickness or disease *existing* prior to the effective date' " of the policy. 218 Kan. at 591, 545 P.2d at 1126. Emphasis added.

Almost seven months after issuance of the policy, plaintiff entered the hospital complaining of chest pains and shortness of breath. He was given a complete medical examination, and it was diagnosed that he was suffering from hardening of the arteries. His doctor concluded that he had suffered "an old heart attack," evidenced by the presence of an old scar on the wall of his heart. Plaintiff was then treated for arteriosclerotic heart disease and released. When the insurer denied coverage, plaintiff brought suit.

On appeal, the Supreme Court upheld the trial court's judgment in favor of the insurer. The Court, citing *Southards*, stated the rule and issue in this manner:

> A similar controversey was before this court in *Southards*, wherein we stated the test of the origin or inception of a sickness or disease, within

the meaning of a health and accident policy requiring that sickness and disease be contracted after the effective date of the policy, to be that point in time *when the disease becomes manifest or active or when there is a distinct symptom or condition from which one learned in medicine can diagnose the disease.* This is the rule followed by the majority of courts which have considered the question and it is controlling in the instant case. Thus, we focus our attention on the issue of whether the disease causing *plaintiff's disability was manifest or active prior to the date of the policy, or whether there was a distinct symptom from which one learned in medicine could diagnose the disease prior to the date of the policy.* 218 Kan. at 592, 545 P.2d at 1127. [Emphasis added.]

After reviewing the evidence, the Court concluded that plaintiff's disability was "manifest" prior to the date of the policy because the symptoms exhibited by plaintiff three months after the policy was issued were the same symptoms shown when he was examined six months prior to the issuance of the policy. In light of this fact, the court could not say that the symptoms of heart disease "were not active or manifest to one learned in medicine prior to the effective date of the policy." 218 Kan. at 596, 545 P.2d at 1129.

In those cases, it will be seen, the policy language attempted to exclude preexisting conditions even though not ascertained or *ascertainable.* The court limited the policy language by holding that the disease must have "manifested" itself by symptoms before it could be said to be preexisting. If it did so "manifest" itself as to be diagnosable before the policy's effective date it was not covered. That, it was said, was the rule followed by the majority of the courts.

In this case the policy language is that previously employed by the court, *i.e.,* that the illness must have "manifested" itself. We think the language was designed to fit the judicial pronouncements, and that it is the equivalent of saying that there must be symptoms which would lead a physician to diagnose the illness, and not that the insured be aware of the existence of the disease.

Here, the symptoms exhibited by plaintiff after the effective date of the policy were found to be the same as those which she suffered one or two months prior to the issuance of the policy. On the basis of these symptoms plaintiff's doctor ordered the examinations and conducted the consultations with specialists which resulted in the diagnosis of her condition. Had she come to him with the same symptoms when she suffered from them before the policy was issued, he would have followed the same course and reached the same diagnosis. Under the rule stated in *Southards* and *Bishop,* plaintiff's disease first "manifested itself" prior to the effective date of the policy. The trial court therefore correctly found no coverage, and its judgment is affirmed.

QUESTIONS FOR REVIEW

1. List five provisions required by the NAIC Uniform Individual Accident and Sickness Policy Provisions Law to be included in an individual health insurance policy.
2. Briefly summarize the entire contract policy provision in an individual health policy.

3. List two ways in which the grace period provision in individual health insurance policies can differ from the grace period provision in individual life insurance policies.

4. If an individual health insurance policy is reinstated effective as of September 5, and the insured becomes ill on September 10, will benefits be payable for loss incurred as the result of such illness? Why or why not?

5. What is the purpose of the time limit on certain defenses provision?

6. List four optional provisions that can be, but are not required to be, included in an individual health insurance contract.

7. For what reasons do insurers endeavor to discourage overinsurance?

8. List and briefly summarize two policy provisions that can be included in an individual health insurance policy for the purpose of reducing the benefits payable if the insured has two or more policies providing the same type of benefits.

9. Define and differentiate between a cancellable health insurance policy and one that is optionally renewable. What is the difference between a noncancellable health insurance policy and a policy that is guaranteed renewable?

10. What is a preexisting condition? When does the NAIC Uniform Individual Accident and Sickness Policy Provisions Law require that preexisting conditions be covered?

11. When will an employee, the employee's spouse, or dependent children have a right to continuation of a group health coverage under COBRA? Who pays for such continuation coverage?

CHAPTER 21

Life and Health Insurance Advertising

PROMOTIONAL LITERATURE PRESENTED
BY AGENTS

WAIVER, ESTOPPEL, AND GROUP
INSURANCE ADVERTISING

DIRECT RESPONSE INSURANCE ADVERTISING
  Direct Response Advertisements Binding the Insurer
  Interstate Direct Response Advertising

REGULATION BY FEDERAL AGENCIES

STATE LAWS GOVERNING INSURANCE
ADVERTISING
  State Laws Governing all Advertising
  State Laws Governing
    Insurance Advertising
  Model Unfair Trade Practices Act
  Model Rules Governing Advertisements of Accident
    and Sickness Insurance
  Model Rules Governing the Advertising of Life
    Insurance

SUMMARY

The creation of life and health insurance advertisements which are not only effective marketing tools but also in compliance with the law is no easy task.[1] Nevertheless, careful compliance with advertising laws is vital, because advertising is highly visible and sanctions for noncompliance can be severe. An understanding of life and health insurance advertising law is, therefore, necessary for those engaged in the creation of insurance advertisements, in the

---

[1]See R. Ismond, Insurance Advertising: Ethics and Law (1968); Wolkoff, *Making Sure Your Marketing is Legal*, National Underwriter, Life & Health Edition (Aug. 30, 1980).

sale of insurance products, or in regulatory compliance. Such understanding can also help claims adjusters, as advertising material must sometimes be taken into account in adjusting claims.

An insurance advertisement is, for purposes of this discussion, any written or spoken material designed to promote public interest in life or health insurance or to induce the purchase of life or health insurance policies. Life and health insurance advertising is done through prepared sales presentations, promotional literature, direct mail, newspapers, magazines, radio, and television.

The law governing life and health insurance advertisements includes law governing advertisements generally, as well as law governing insurance advertisements specifically. Each state has its own advertising laws. However, insurance advertising is often done across state lines. Interstate advertising can create an especially complex situation, as the laws of two or more states are involved. Federal laws can also apply in some insurance advertising situations. This chapter contains a description of the case law, statutes, and regulations governing life and health insurance advertising.

PROMOTIONAL LITERATURE PRESENTED BY AGENTS

Agents use various types of promotional literature during the solicitation of insurance sales. Often, these are intended as estimates or illustrations and are not intended to be part of the insurance contract. The parol evidence rule (discussed in Chapter 2, "Contracts") ordinarily precludes the admission into court proceedings of evidence outside a written contract to vary the terms of the contract. Therefore, the majority rule is that written statements regarding surplus earnings, dividends, accumulations, and so forth which are not attached to the policy, or referred to in the policy, are not part of the contract.[2] If the insurer has clearly indicated that such a statement is intended only for purposes of illustration, the court is even more likely to hold that it is not part of the contract.

If the written estimate or illustration is attached to the policy or if the policy refers to it, however, the courts sometimes hold that it is part of the contract. For example, in one case a sheet of paper with illustrations showing the amount of surplus earnings which would be apportioned to a life insurance policy at the end of 20 years was pasted to the policy. It followed a statement on the first page of the policy that "the Benefits, Statements and Values on the succeeding pages of this Policy are made a part hereof." The court held that the amount of surplus earnings specified in the illustration sheet was a guaranteed amount, rather than an estimate. That amount was, therefore, declared to be payable to the policyowner.[3]

---

[2]Annot., 17 A.L.R. 3d 777 (1968).
[3]Legare v. West Coast Life Ins. Co., 118 Cal. App. 663, 5 P.2d 682 (1931).

Although an estimate or illustrative statement is not ordinarily part of the contract, such a statement must be made in good faith. A person who has been induced to enter into an insurance contract by intentionally false statements is not without remedy. She or he will have grounds to sue the insurer for fraud, or for rescission or reformation of the contract.[4]

WAIVER, ESTOPPEL, AND GROUP INSURANCE ADVERTISING

Although waiver and estoppel are not ordinarily available to broaden coverage under an individual life or health insurance policy,[5] group insurance has been treated differently by the courts, because the insured person usually has no opportunity to read the group master policy.[6] Group insureds depend on promotional and explanatory literature and their group certificates for an understanding of their insurance coverage. When these contain terms more favorable to the insured than the terms of the master policy, the insurer is often held to have waived the terms in the master policy, or is estopped to deny the more favorable statements in the literature or certificates. For example, in one case, a group life insurance master policy required yearly proof of disability in order for an insured to qualify for waiver of premium. The insurer's promotional literature stated that the insured merely needed to submit proof of disability "from time to time." The insured submitted no proof of disability before his death, but the plaintiff beneficiary was able to prove that the insured had been disabled from the termination of his employment until his death. The court held that the insurer had waived the more rigorous requirement of the master policy and allowed the plaintiff-beneficiary to recover the death benefits.[7]

DIRECT RESPONSE INSURANCE ADVERTISING

Many insurers solicit an inquiry about, or the sale of, an insurance policy without the use of a soliciting agent. This type of solicitation is called direct response insurance solicitation. Other terms for this type of solicitation are *mail order, direct mail,* or *mass merchandising,* but *direct response* is the most accurate term.

Direct response insurance solicitation is done by direct mail or media advertisements. Media used include newspapers, magazines, radio, and television. The direct response method is primarily used to sell life and health

---

[4]Rohrschneider v. Knickerbocker Life Ins. Co., 76 N.Y. 216 (1879); Standard Acci. Ins. Co. v. Harrison-Wright Co., 207 N.C. 661, 178 S.E. 235 (1935).

[5]Annot., 1 A.L.R. 3d 1139 (1965).

[6]Annot., 36 A.L.R. 3d 541 (1971).

[7]Lewis v. Continental Life & Acci. Co., 93 Idaho 348, 461 P.2d 243 (1969).

policies which are supplemental to the basic policies sold through the regular agency marketing method.

Many legal questions result from direct response solicitation. This section will deal with the most important of these questions.

Direct Response Advertisements Binding the Insurer

Often, with direct response solicitation, the applicant simply clips the application form from a newspaper, magazine, or direct mail brochure and applies directly to the insurer. The applicant has no opportunity to discuss the terms of the contract with an agent of the insurer but must rely on the advertisement for an understanding of the contract. Courts in some jurisdictions have held that the advertisement is, therefore, binding on the insurer.

In one case, an insurer had inserted an advertising brochure with an application form into local newspapers.[8] The brochure advertised a family hospital benefit policy. The plaintiff had sent in the application and received a policy. His wife became hospitalized, but the insurer denied hospital benefits because the wife's illness began before the effective date of the policy. The plaintiff filed a declaratory judgment action asking the court to determine whether hospitalization of his wife, due to the preexisting illness, was covered.

The policy did contain an exclusion for preexisting illness. This exclusion was mentioned in the brochure, but in such a way that the court felt the average reader would not have understood it. The court looked to the dominant theme of the advertisement which was immediate, unqualified coverage. The court made this statement:

> [W]here the dominant theme of such advertising, constantly and prominently repeated, is that the insured is immediately covered upon payment of his initial premium "without any qualification whatsoever" and is intended to be so understood by the person who reads it, the fact that one or more caveats may be found inserted within the copy which would or could be read by a sophisticated or suspicious reader to limit or qualify the extent or immediacy of coverage does not necessarily alter or erase the dominant theme of the solicitation, or the overall meaning, intent, and effect of the language therein to the average reader.

The court, therefore, held that the hospital benefits were payable. The opinion contains the following statement about direct response advertising:

> It seems clear to this court that where a health and accident insurer engages in a plan of solicitation by means of advertising in public newspapers of general circulation, without the intervention of agents, and without physical examinations or medical statements as a condition of the issuance of insurance or of coverage, but where the policy is put in-

---

[8]Craver v. Union Fidelity Ins. Co., 37 Ohio App. 2d 100, 307 N.E.2d 265 (1973).

to effect by application of the insured on a form attached to the advertising solicitation and the payment of a premium, and where it is obvious the solicitation is intended to and does in fact induce the reader to apply for and secure the policy of insurance, the insurance company is bound by any representations, promises, warranties or undertakings contained in such solicitation.

In another case, a direct response advertisement for travel accident insurance was placed in an automobile club publication.[9] The question before the court in that case was whether the direct response advertisement with its application form constituted a complete offer by the insurer. If so, the mailing of the application with a premium check was an acceptance which completed the contract of insurance.

The advertisement read: "ENROLL NOW . . . and take along this '365' Travel Accident Insurance wherever you may go . . . Your club membership automatically qualifies you to enroll." In much smaller type on the application form was printed: "I . . . understand that protection becomes effective the date my certificate of insurance is issued."

The plaintiff's wife applied for travel accident insurance on June 2, 1976, by mailing in a premium check and the completed application. The wife died as the result of an automobile accident on June 3. On June 4, the insurer received the application and premium check and mailed a certificate of insurance to the applicant. When the death benefits were claimed, the insurer denied liability on ground that the insurance was not in effect at the time of death.

The court held that the death benefits were payable, because the advertisement was a complete offer, and the mailing of the application and the premium check was an acceptance of that offer. The contract of insurance was created at the time of acceptance, which was one day before the applicant's death. The court stated that the reasonable expectations of the applicant governed, and that the applicant could reasonably expect that she was covered because of statements in the advertisement. Quoting from a similar case from another jurisdiction, the court pointed out that:

[W]hen the potential insurance purchaser cannot consult with an agent to ascertain the parameters of the proposed policy, the concept of an informed meeting of the minds is a myth unless the insurance company clearly and explicitly explains the policy in its literature. To effectuate this goal, the reasonable expectations which such literature raises or does not rebut must govern the interpretations of such policies.[10]

The NAIC Model Unfair Claims Settlement Practices Act, adopted by the National Association of Insurance Commissioners in 1972 as a part of the Model Unfair Trade Practices Act, contains a section aimed at direct response insurance. This section prohibits attempting "with such frequency as

---

[9]Riordan v. Automobile Club, 100 Misc. 2d 638, 422 N.Y.S.2d 811 (1979).
[10]Fritz v. Old Am. Ins. Co., 354 F. Supp. 514 (S.D. Tex. 1973).

to indicate a general business practice . . . to settle a claim for less than the amount to which a reasonable man would have believed he was entitled by reference to written or printed advertising material accompanying or made part of an application." Many states have adopted the Model Unfair Claims Settlement Practices Act.

Interstate Direct Response Advertising

Direct response advertising is often done on an interstate basis. Earlier in this century, an insurer licensed to do business in one state might send direct response advertising material into other states in which it was not licensed and sell policies there. During the 1960s, states began passing unauthorized insurers acts which made it unlawful to transact direct response insurance business in a state having such an act unless the insurer was licensed there.[11] Because of these laws, the problem of unlicensed insurers selling insurance by direct response advertising almost disappeared by the 1970s.[12]

Today, the insurer must be licensed, and the policy approved in every state in which the advertisement appears (unless the advertisement says that the policy will not be sold in the state). The advertisement itself must comply with the laws of those states where the policy will be sold. The insurer must comply with countersignature laws in some states.[13] Thus, interstate marketing of direct response insurance involves a number of legal hurdles for insurers.

The lack of uniformity among the policy provisions laws and advertising laws of the states makes necessary a careful review of policy forms and advertising by an insurer's compliance personnel. An insurer must take care that direct mail advertising is not sent into a state where the insurer is not licensed to do business. Dissemination of media advertisements into states where the insurer is not licensed can be difficult to control, as newspapers and magazines are often circulated in many states. Radio and television broadcasts also cross state lines. An insurer usually puts disclaimers in its media advertising if that advertising will be distributed or broadcast in states where the insurer is not licensed. These disclaimers say that the policy will not be sold in those states. This will ordinarily protect the insurer from insurance department action against it.[14]

---

[11]Many of these laws are based on model acts drafted by the National Association of Insurance Commissioners. These model acts are the Unauthorized Insurers Model Statute, the Unauthorized Insurers Process Act, and the Unauthorized Insurers False Advertising Process Act.

[12]Beavan & Braybrooks, *The Sale of Insurance Through the Mail,* CLU JOURNAL 18, April 1982.

[13]Countersignature laws are discussed in Chapter 4, "Agency in Life and Health Insurance."

[14]See Symon, *Mass Merchandising of Life Insurance,* A.L.I.A. LEGAL SECTION PROCEEDINGS 259 (1975).

REGULATION BY FEDERAL AGENCIES

The McCarran-Ferguson Act provides that the Federal Trade Commission Act is to be applicable to the business of insurance only "to the extent that such business is not regulated by State Law." Since 1945, when the McCarran-Ferguson Act was adopted, there have been efforts by the Federal Trade Commission (FTC) to assert jurisdiction over insurance advertising—particularly interstate direct response advertising. In response to these efforts, the states have passed laws regulating advertising. Thus, within the boundaries of states which have their own laws governing advertising, the FTC is barred from enforcing the Federal Trade Commission Act proscription of false, deceptive, or misleading advertising.

The United States Postal Service (USPS) has the power to deny use of the mail to carry material which is contrary to the public interest. Thus, the USPS has occasionally been involved in regulation of direct response advertising where fraudulent or misleading advertisements have been sent through the mail. In addition, the mail fraud statute[15] provides that the use of the mail to perpetrate frauds and swindles can result in fines and imprisonment for the guilty persons.

The Federal Communications Commission (FCC) indirectly controls advertising on radio or television. The FCC has the power to revoke or refuse to renew a broadcaster's license if the broadcaster has disseminated false or misleading advertising. Broadcasters, therefore, review advertisements carefully before broadcasting them. If a broadcaster feels an advertisement could cause criticism by the FCC, it might refuse to broadcast the advertisement.

The Internal Revenue Service (IRS) has concerned itself with advertising of deferred annuities. A deferred annuity is a contract which provides that the purchaser pay premiums to the insurer but defer receiving annuity payments from the insurer until a later date. This is in contrast to an immediate annuity contract which provides for payments from the insurer commencing one month to one year after purchase of the annuity, depending on the frequency of the periodic payments.

The IRS opposes advertisements which state that deferred annuities are tax shelters. A tax shelter typically allows some part of the taxpayer's income to escape taxation entirely, but the purchase of a deferred annuity does not ultimately avoid tax. Such annuities are tax deferral devices, but the IRS has also opposed overemphasis on the tax deferral aspect of deferred annuities. In addition, the IRS has been concerned with advertisements for deferred annuities which disparage the taxing authorities. Statements such as "Don't let Uncle Sam take away one half your interest" are unacceptable to the IRS.

Finally, the IRS frowns upon undue emphasis on the savings aspect of deferred annuities in advertisements. There has been pressure to end the tax deferred status of deferred annuities, because they were being advertised as savings accounts. The Tax Equity and Fiscal Responsibility Act of 1982

---

[15]18 U.S.C.A. § 1341–45 (West 1984 & Supp. 1987).

(TEFRA)[16] significantly altered the tax deferred status of annuity contracts. The retirement income and lifetime payout guarantees of deferred annuities are the proper features to emphasize in advertisements.

The Securities and Exchange Commission (SEC) has also been concerned with annuity advertising. In April 1979, the SEC stated in a release that it "remained very concerned with the proliferation of contracts which, while styled annuities, are clearly different in their essential terms from traditional annuities and are marketed in a manner involving the offer and sale of securities." The release further stated that in order to avoid compliance with the federal securities laws, sellers of such contracts must bear significant mortality and investment risks. The contracts must also be advertised in such a way that they do not relegate the annuity features to fine print while emphasizing features calculated to appeal to investors who desire to "maximize tax-deferred capital accumulation rather than to acquire conventional annuity plans."

STATE LAWS GOVERNING INSURANCE ADVERTISING

Insurance advertising is governed by state advertising laws which govern all types of advertising. It is also governed by laws which specifically apply to insurance advertising.

State Laws Governing All Advertising

Most states have laws that declare the dissemination of deceptive advertising of any sort a misdemeanor. This, of course, includes insurance advertising. Most of these laws are based on the Printer's Ink Model Statute. This model statute was first developed in 1911.

State court cases and statutes also prohibit the use of a person's name or likeness for advertising purposes without that person's permission. Such a use is one form of the tort of invasion of privacy. The person whose name or likeness is so used can sue the advertiser for money damages. Invasion of privacy is discussed in Chapter 22, "Privacy and Insurance."

State Laws Governing Insurance Advertising

All the states have passed laws specifically governing insurance advertising. Most are patterned on model laws drafted by the NAIC. These NAIC model laws include the model Unfair Trade Practices Act,[17] the model Rules

---

[16]Pub. Law. No. 97–248, 96 Stat. 324 (codified in scattered sections of 26, 28, 29, 31, 42, 45, 47, 49 and 50 App. U.S.C.).

[17]The official title of this model act is "An Act Relating to Unfair Methods of Competition and Unfair and Deceptive Acts and Practices in the Business of Insurance." We will refer to the model act by its popular name, the "Unfair Trade Practices Act."

Governing Advertisements of Accident and Sickness Insurance,[18] and the model Rules Governing the Advertising of Life Insurance. These model laws and the state statutes and regulations based on them will be discussed in this section.

Model Unfair Trade Practices Act

The McCarran-Ferguson Act provides that the Federal Trade Commission Act will apply to the interstate business of insurance to the extent it is not regulated by state law. This spurred the passage of uniform state laws governing insurance advertising. Prior to the passage of the McCarran-Ferguson Act in 1945, there had been only unrelated, sporadic attempts by the states to regulate insurance advertising. Soon after the McCarran-Ferguson Act was passed, the NAIC, in cooperation with the insurance industry, drafted the model Unfair Trade Practices Act. Almost all the states have laws based on this model act. The rest have other laws governing unfair trade practices.

The model Unfair Trade Practices Act declares that its purpose is to ". . . regulate trade practices in the business of insurance in accordance with the intent of Congress as expressed in the [McCarran-Ferguson Act]." It aims to fulfill this purpose by defining and prohibiting unfair trade practices. Among the unfair trade practices prohibited are defamation, unfair discrimination, rebating, unfair claims settlement practices, and false advertising.

The model Unfair Trade Practices Act contains a general prohibition against any form of insurance advertising which is "untrue, deceptive or misleading." In addition, the model act spells out specific types of false advertising which are unfair trade practices. Among these are: (1) a misrepresentation of the "benefits, advantages, conditions or terms of any insurance policy"; (2) a misrepresentation as to "the dividends or share of the surplus to be received on any insurance policy" or "previously paid on any policy"; (3) a misrepresentation either of an insurer's financial condition or "as to the legal reserve system upon which any insurer operates"; (4) the use of a name or title of an insurance policy which misrepresents the policy's true nature; and (5) a misrepresentation of an insurance policy "as being shares of stock."

The model Unfair Trade Practices Act provides that the insurance commissioner shall have power to investigate an insurer's affairs to determine if it ". . . has been or is engaged in . . . any unfair or deceptive act or practice." The commissioner can summon the insurer to a hearing if the commissioner has reason to believe there has been such an act or practice. If, after the hearing, the commissioner determines that the insurer has committed an unfair trade practice, the commissioner must issue an order to the insurer to

---

[18]The term *health insurance* is preferred modern usage. *Accident and sickness insurance* is an older term which is falling into disuse.

cease and desist the practice. The commissioner can at his or her discretion fine the insurer up to $50,000 in any six-month period, depending on the number of violations committed and on whether the insurer knew, or reasonably should have known, it was violating the act. The commissioner can also suspend or revoke the insurer's license to do business in that state if the insurer knew, or reasonably should have known, it was violating the act. Thus, the penalties for false advertising can be severe.

Model Rules Governing Advertisements of Accident and Sickness Insurance

In 1955 and 1956, the NAIC, in cooperation with the insurance industry and the FTC, developed a comprehensive code of rules designed to govern accident and health insurance advertising. The rules were intended to supplement a state's Unfair Trade Practices Act. The NAIC recommended that each state insurance department adopt the model Rules Governing Advertisements of Accident and Sickness Insurance. Only three states—Alaska, Hawaii, and Montana—have not yet adopted rules governing accident and health insurance advertising.

Interpretive guidelines were added to the model rules to aid insurance commissioners in administering the rules and to help insurers to develop advertising in compliance with the rules. The interpretive guidelines were not intended by their drafters to be a part of the rules. Nevertheless, some states have adopted the interpretive guidelines along with the rules. In those states, the interpretive guidelines are a part of the state regulation of advertising and have the force of law.

Most states that have adopted the model rules have adopted them with variations.[19] Because most states have their own versions of the model rules, an insurance advertisement must be checked against the regulations of any state in which it will be disseminated.

Preamble.   The model rules begin with a preamble which reads in part as follows:

> Although modern insurance advertising patterns much of its design after advertising for other goods and services, the uniqueness of insurance as a product must always be kept in mind in developing advertising of accident and sickness insurance. By the time an insured discovers that a particular insurance product is unsuitable for his needs, it may be too late for him to return to the marketplace to find a more satisfactory product. Hence, the insurance-buying public should be afforded a means by which it can determine, in advance of purchase, the desirability of the competing insurance products proposed to be sold. This can be accomplished by

---

[19]These variations have been noted in a compilation by the Life and Health Compliance Association, entitled, "A & H Advertising Requirements by State" (May 1987).

advertising which accurately describes the advantages and disadvantages of the insurance product without either exaggerating the benefits or minimizing the limitations. Properly designed advertising can provide such description and disclosure without sacrificing the sales appeal which is essential to its usefulness to the insurance-buying public and the insurance business. The purpose of the rules and interpretive guidelines is to establish minimum criteria to assure such a proper and accurate description and disclosure.

Purpose.   The purpose of the model rules is "to assure truthful and adequate disclosure of all relevant information in the advertising of accident and sickness insurance. This purpose is intended to be accomplished by the establishment of, and adherence to, certain minimum standards and guidelines of conduct in the advertising of accident and sickness insurance . . ." Interpretive Guideline 1, notes that "Disclosure is one of the principal objectives of these rules . . ."

Applicability.   The model rules are applicable to any "accident or sickness or medical, surgical or hospital expense" insurance advertisement when the advertisement is intended for "presentation, distribution or dissemination" in the state. Insurance advertisement is broadly defined as follows:

> An advertisement for the purpose of these rules shall include: (1) printed and published material, audio visual material, and descriptive literature of an insurer used in direct mail, newspapers, magazines, radio scripts, TV scripts, billboards, and similar displays; and (2) descriptive literature and sales aids of all kinds issued by an insurer, agent, or broker for presentation to members of the insurance buying public, including but not limited to circulars, leaflets, booklets, depictions, illustrations, and form letters; and (3) prepared sales talks, presentations, and material for use by agents, brokers, and solicitors.

The model rules also mandate that:

> Every insurer shall establish and at all times maintain a system of control over the content, form, and method of dissemination of all advertisements of its policies. All such advertisements, regardless of by whom written, created, designed or presented, shall be the responsibility of the insurer whose policies are so advertised.

This puts the burden of compliance with advertising law squarely upon the insurer.

Definitions.   The model rules contain various relevant definitions such as the definition of *advertisement* noted above. *Policy* for the purpose of the model rules is defined as any accident or sickness "policy, plan, certificate, contract, agreement, statement of coverage, rider or endorsement." The model rules will not apply, however, to advertisements of disability, waiver of premium, or double indemnity benefits included in life insurance, endowment, or annuity contracts.

Exceptions, reductions and *limitations* are distinguished in the definitions section. For the purpose of the model rules, an exception is any provision in a policy whereby coverage for a specified hazard is entirely eliminated; it is a statement of risk not assumed under the policy. A reduction, on the other hand, is any provision which reduces the amount of the benefit. Where there is a reduction a risk of loss is assumed, but payment upon the occurrence of such loss is limited to some amount or period less than would be otherwise payable had such reduction not been used. A limitation is any provision which restricts coverage but which is not an exception or reduction. A definition of *hospital* in a policy is an example of a limitation.

An important revision to the model rules, made in 1974, was the inclusion of definitions of three types of advertisements, *institutional advertisements, invitations to inquire,* and *invitations to contract.* The insurance industry advisory committee had strongly recommended that clear distinctions be made among these types of advertisements. The NAIC responded by including definitions of *institutional advertisement, invitation to inquire,* and *invitation to contract* in the model rules. According to the model rules, an institutional advertisement has as its sole purpose the promotion of the reader's or viewer's interest in the concept of accident or sickness insurance, or the promotion of the insurer. Some requirements which apply to invitations to inquire or invitations to contract do not apply to institutional advertisements. Institutional advertisements are the least stringently regulated of the three types of advertisements.

An invitation to inquire has as its objective the creation of a desire to inquire further about the product. It is limited to a brief description of the loss for which the benefit is payable. It "may contain . . . [t]he dollar amount of benefit payable, and/or . . . [t]he period of time during which the benefit is payable; provided the advertisement does not refer to cost." If the advertisement specifies either the dollar amount of benefit payable or the period of time during which the benefit is payable it must contain, in effect, the following provision:

> For costs and further details of the coverage, including exclusions, any reductions or limitations and the terms under which the policy may be continued in force, see your agent or write to the company.

An invitation to inquire is more strictly regulated than an institutional advertisement but not as strictly regulated as an invitation to contract.

An invitation to contract includes terms and cost of the insurance advertised. Terms and cost are the elements necessary to a prospective purchaser to enable her or him to decide whether to purchase the insurance. Because a decision to purchase the insurance may be made on the basis of the advertisement alone, invitations to contract are more strictly regulated than invitations to inquire or institutional advertisements.

Method of Disclosure of Required Information. Either of two methods is permitted for the disclosure of information required to be included in insurance advertisements. Required information, such as exceptions, reductions, or limitations can be set out conspicuously and in close conjunction with the statements to which such information relates. Alternatively, such information may be put under appropriate and prominent captions, such as "Exceptions," "Exclusions," or "Conditions Not Covered." The interpretive guidelines prohibit the use of captions such as "Extent of Coverage" or "Only These Exclusions." The interpretive guidelines state that these do not provide adequate notice of the significance of the material.

Form and Content of Advertisements. The model rules provide that the form and content of an advertisement of an accident or sickness insurance policy shall be sufficiently complete and clear to avoid deception, or the capacity or tendency to mislead or deceive. The state commissioner of insurance has the authority to determine whether the advertisement is misleading. In making such a determination, the commissioner must examine the overall impression that the advertisement may be reasonably expected to create upon a person of average education or intelligence, within the segment of the public to which it is directed. Different standards for advertisements will be required for publications of general circulation than for scholarly, technical, or business publications, presumably because the readers of the latter will have a higher level of education.

The model rules state the following:

> Advertisements shall be truthful and not misleading in fact or in implication. Words or phrases, the meaning of which is clear only by implication or by familiarity with insurance terminology, shall not be used.

If such insurance terminology is used, the terms used must be defined in the advertisement.

Advertisements of Benefits Payable, Losses Covered, or Premiums Payable. The model rules provide that advertisements cannot omit information or use words or illustrations which might mislead readers regarding benefits, losses, coverage, or premiums. There is an interpretive guideline containing no less than 40 illustrations of what must, or must not, appear in insurance advertisements. The following are examples:

1. An advertisement which describes any benefits that vary by age must disclose that fact.
2. An advertisement which states or implies immediate coverage or guaranteed issuance of a policy is unacceptable unless suitable administrative procedures exist so that the policy is issued within a reasonable period of time after the application is received by the insurer.

3. An advertisement which uses the word *plan* without identifying it as an *insurance plan* is not permissible.
4. An advertisement which fails to disclose that the definition of *hospital* does not include a nursing home, convalescent home or extended care facility, as the case may be, is unacceptable.

It can be seen from these examples that a careful study of the model rules and interpretive guidelines is necessary for persons who develop accident and health insurance advertising.

The model rules prohibit the use of certain words or phrases "in a manner which exaggerates any benefits beyond the terms of the policy." Note that these words or phrases are not forbidden, as long as they do not exaggerate the benefits. The interpretive guidelines list terms which must be used with caution to avoid exaggerating benefits. Some of these terms are *all, full, complete, comprehensive, up to,* and *as high as.*

Descriptions of policy exceptions, reductions, or limitations which are worded so as to imply that these are benefits are prohibited. The negative features of exceptions, reductions, or limitations must be fairly described. For example, a waiting period must not be described as a "benefit builder."

The model rules prohibit the use of words or phrases such as *tax free, extra cash,* or *extra income* in advertisements for hospital benefit policies. Such words or phrases are forbidden because they have the "effect of misleading the public into believing the policy advertised will, in some way, enable them to make a profit from being hospitalized." The interpretive guidelines give additional examples of prohibited words and phrases. The interpretive guidelines note that "[i]llustrations which depict paper currency or checks showing an amount payable are deceptive and misleading and are not permissible."

Advertisements of hospital benefits are prohibited if they state that the amount of the benefit is payable on a monthly or weekly basis when, in fact, the amount of the benefit payable is based upon a daily pro-rata basis relating to the number of days of confinement. The model rules also mandate that "[w]hen the [hospital] policy contains a limit on the number of days of coverage provided, such limit must appear in the advertisement."

The model rules regulate advertisements of health policies covering specified diseases or limited accidents, such as travel accidents. They prohibit advertisements which imply coverage beyond the terms of a specified disease. For example, an advertisement for a cancer-only policy cannot be written to imply that there is coverage for other diseases. Different terms which refer to the same disease cannot be used to imply broader coverage than is provided. Moreover, advertisements for specified disease policies or for limited accident policies must be conspicuously labeled as such in prominent type. Such a label might read "THIS IS A CANCER ONLY POLICY" or "THIS IS AN AUTOMOBILE ACCIDENT ONLY POLICY."

Direct response advertisements must not imply that the product advertised is "low cost," because no agent commissions are payable. The reason stated for this prohibition is that ". . . the cost of advertising and servicing such policies is a substantial cost in the marketing of a direct response insurance product."

The model rules require that invitations to contract disclose exceptions, reductions, and limitations affecting the basic provisions of the policy. They also require that a waiting, elimination, probationary, or similar time period between the effective date of the policy and the effective date of coverage be disclosed. Finally, they forbid the use of words such as *just, only,* or *merely* to describe exceptions, reductions, or limitations, so as to make them seem unimportant.

A preexisting condition provision must be disclosed in advertisements which are invitations to contract. It must be disclosed "in negative terms." In other words, the advertisement must not make the preexisting condition provision appear to be a benefit, rather than an exclusion. Moreover, the term *preexisting condition* cannot be used without a definition. The advertisement cannot imply that the applicant's physical condition or medical history will not affect the issuance of the policy or the payment of a claim. Finally, advertisements with application forms must contain a question worded substantially as follows:

> Do you understand that this policy will not pay benefits during the first ____
> year(s) after the issue date for a disease or physical condition which you
> now have or have had in the past _____ YES

Disclosure of Renewability, Cancellability, and Termination Provisions. The model rules require that invitations to contract disclose provisions relating to renewability, cancellability, termination, or modification of benefits. Such disclosure must be made "in a way which will not minimize or render obscure the qualifying conditions." The interpretive guidelines provide the following examples: "This policy can be cancelled by the company at any time," or "Renewable at the option of the insurer."

Testimonials and Endorsements. The model rules mandate that testimonials or endorsements by third parties be genuine and represent the current opinion of the author. If the person making the testimonial has an interest in the insurer, this must be disclosed in the advertisement. Stockholders, directors, officers, or employees of the insurer fall under this rule. In addition, if the testimonial has been paid for, this must be disclosed in the advertisement. When a testimonial refers to benefits paid, the specific claim data must be retained by the insurer for four years or until the report has been filed at the next examination of the insurer by the state insurance department. The interpretive guidelines explain that this gives the insurance department the means to verify the authenticity of testimonials used in advertising efforts.

Use of Statistics. The model rules require that statistics used in advertisements be relevant and accurate. An advertisement cannot imply that statistics used are derived from the policy advertised unless this is true. The source of any statistics used must be cited in the advertisement.

The model rules prohibit the use of words such as *liberal* or *generous* relating to claim settlements. Moreover, the model rules state that "[a]n unusual amount paid for a unique claim for the policy advertised is misleading and shall not be used."

Disparaging Statements. The model rules forbid statements in an insurance advertisement which disparage other insurers. Unfair or incomplete comparisons of policies or benefits of other insurers are also forbidden.

Jurisdictional Licensing and Status. The model rules prohibit an insurer from implying that it is licensed in jurisdictions where it is not licensed, when the advertisement appears in those jurisdictions. Also forbidden is any implication that an insurer or its policies are endorsed by state or federal governments. For this reason, words such as *official,* when used to describe applications or policies, are not permissible, as they have a tendency to mislead.

Identity of the Insurer and Policy. The insurer's identity must be clearly disclosed in the advertisement. An advertisement which is an invitation to contract must identify the form number of the policy advertised.

Special Offers. Advertising that implies that purchasers will receive a lower group insurance rate, when such a rate is not applied, is prohibited. Nor can insurers advertise limited offers which imply that the purchaser will receive a special rate if he or she purchases during the period of the offer when, actually, the rate would remain the same if the purchaser applied later. The model rules also prohibit overemphasis on any reduced initial premium rate. Finally, the model rules prohibit the use of "safe driver's awards" or similar special awards in advertisements for accident or sickness insurance.

Statements About an Insurer. Misleading statements about an insurer's assets, corporate structure, financial standing, age, or relative position in the insurance business are prohibited. For example, an insurer which has been organized only a relatively short time may not advertise that it is old. The model rules also prohibit inclusion of a recommendation by a commercial rating system in an advertisement unless the advertisement clearly indicates the purpose and scope of the recommendation. For example, an advertisement may state that "The Careful Insurance Company is rated A + (excellent) by A. M. Best Company, independent insurance analysts, on the basis of operating performance and financial strength."

Enforcement Procedures. The model rules mandate that each insurer maintain a file of all its advertisements. A note must be attached to each advertisement in the file indicating the manner and extent of the advertisement's distribution, and the form number of any policies advertised. The advertisements must be kept on file for four years or until the next examination report on the insurer is filed, whichever is the longer time.

Those insurers which must file an annual statement with the state must also file a certificate of compliance with the state's advertising laws. The certificate of compliance must be executed by an officer of the insurer. In the certificate the officer must state that, to the best of her or his knowledge, information, and belief, the insurer's advertisements, disseminated during the past year, complied with the advertising laws of the state.

Model Rules Governing the Advertising of Life Insurance

The model Rules Governing the Advertising of Life Insurance were adopted by the NAIC in 1975. They govern the advertising of life insurance policies and annuity contracts. Sixteen states have adopted rules which closely follow the NAIC model. Nine states have other regulations governing advertisements of life insurance. The rest have not adopted life insurance advertisement regulations. Thus, the regulation of life insurance advertisements is less uniform than that of health insurance.

Life insurance advertising has presented fewer problems than have been presented by health insurance advertising. Therefore, regulation of life insurance advertising is less complex. Unlike the model Rules Governing Advertisements of Accident and Sickness Insurance, the model Rules Governing the Advertising of Life Insurance include no interpretive guidelines.

The model life insurance advertisement rules are, however, patterned on the model accident and sickness insurance advertisement rules. Many sections are substantially the same. For this reason, only the sections which are unique to the model life insurance advertisement rules will be discussed here.

Definitions. In the model life insurance advertisement rules, the terms *policy, insurer,* and *advertisement* are defined substantially the same way that they are in the model accident and sickness insurance advertisement rules. The terms *exception, reduction,* and *limitation* are not defined in the model life insurance advertisement rules. Neither are the terms *institutional advertisement, invitation to inquire,* and *invitation to contract.* These types of advertisements are not distinguished in the model life insurance advertisement rules. This is a major departure from the model accident and sickness insurance advertisement rules.

Form and Content of Advertisements. Unique to the model life insurance advertisement rules is a section which deals with the use of terms such as *investment, profit,* and *savings,* in connection with life insurance policies or annuity contracts. It is forbidden to use such terms in a misleading way.

Disclosure Requirements. If a life insurance advertisement uses a term such as *no medical examination required,* when policy issuance is not guaranteed upon application, the term must be accompanied by an equally prominent statement that policy issuance could depend upon answers to health questions. Advertisements of life insurance policies must clearly indicate that the policy advertised is a life insurance policy if the name of the policy does not include the words *life insurance.*

Advertisements of life insurance policies with level premiums, but with benefits which increase or decrease with the age of the insured, must disclose the changing benefit feature. An advertisement for a policy with nonlevel premiums must prominently describe the premium changes.

Life insurance policy advertisements must not imply that dividends are guaranteed. Dividend illustrations must be based on the insurer's current dividend scale. Such illustrations must contain a statement that they are not guarantees or estimates of future dividends. Advertisements must not state that the policyowner will share in the general account assets of the insurer.

In 1976, a subsection regulating advertisements of deferred annuities and deposit funds was added to the model life insurance advertisement rules. This subsection deals primarily with disclosure of interest rates. It also requires that when a deferred annuity or deposit fund does not provide a cash surrender value prior to commencement of benefit payments, the advertisement must disclose that fact.

SUMMARY

Life and health insurance advertisements are not ordinarily considered part of the contract, especially if they are not referred to in the policy or attached to it. In group insurance, however, if there is advertising at variance with the contract, the insurer can be estopped to deny terms more favorable to the insured which appear in the advertising, or the insurer can be held to have waived the less favorable contract terms. Direct response advertisements also have been held binding on the insurer because the applicant has no opportunity to confer with an agent to gain an understanding of the insurance.

Direct response insurance is frequently sold on a multistate basis. A direct response insurer must be licensed, and the policy approved in every state in which the advertisement appears, unless the advertisement says that the policy will not be sold in that state. The advertisement itself must comply with the laws of those states where the policy will be sold. The lack of uniformity among state laws governing policy provisions and advertising can make this a difficult task.

The laws governing life and health insurance advertisements include laws governing advertisements generally, as well as specific life and health insurance advertising laws. Insurance advertising regulation is primarily done by the states, although the federal government is sometimes involved through the Federal Trade Commission, the United States Postal Service, the Federal

Communications Commission, the Internal Revenue Service, and the Securities and Exchange Commission.

Most states have passed statutes based on the NAIC Model Unfair Trade Practices Act. This act includes a section prohibiting false insurance advertising. Supplementing these statutes are regulations, adopted by the state insurance departments, which govern the advertising of life and health insurance. Many of these regulations are based on the NAIC model Rules Governing Advertisements of Accident and Sickness Insurance and the NAIC model Rules Governing the Advertising of Life Insurance. These model rules spell out in detail how life and health insurance advertisements must be structured. Their aim is to ensure that advertisements do not mislead prospective purchasers of insurance.

ILLUSTRATIVE CASE

This case concerns an accident policy covering students. The pamphlet advertising the policy did not contain an exclusion found in the policy. The court, therefore, held that there was coverage despite the exclusion.

EUGENE E. LAWRENCE et al., Appellants

v.

PROVIDENTIAL LIFE INSURANCE COMPANY, Appellee[20]
Supreme Court of Arkansas

ROBINSON, Justice.

The question on appeal is whether, under the terms of a policy of accident insurance, the assured is entitled to recovery for medical expenses he sustained by reason of an injury to his son, who was insured under the policy. The specific issue is whether the nature of the injury and resulting expenses were excluded under the provisions of the policy.

The appellee, Providential Life Insurance Company writes a type of accident insurance called "The Providential School Plan". Among other things, this insurance provides indemnity to the extent of $5,000 for medical expenses for "teachers, students, and non-teaching personnel". Parents of students were solicited to purchase the policy to protect themselves against medical expenses they might incur by reason of injury to their children. The solicitation of parents was made by the insurance company distributing to the school children, to take home, a pamphlet advertising the policy. The pamphlet explained the benefits provided by the policy, those things not covered by the policy and the amount of premium. The pamphlet also contained a pocket on one side where currency or a check could be inserted by the parents in payment of the premium in the event they decided to take the insurance. The pamphlet could then be sent to the insurance company and it became the application of the sender asking that the applicant's child or children be included in a master policy to be issued to the school attended by the children. In

---

[20]238 Ark. 981, 385 S.W.2d 936 (1965).

this instance the policy was issued to the Brookland Public School District, Brookland, Arkansas.

The printed matter in the application appears to be complete in giving full information about what is not covered by the policy. At least the application shows on its face what the applicant understood was not covered by the policy. The application states:

> THIS INSURANCE DOES NOT COVER . . . Dental expenses of any kind except those resulting from accidental injury to whole, sound natural teeth, eyeglasses, contact lenses or prescriptions therefor; intentionally self-inflicted injuries, injury for which benefits are payable under any Workmen's Compensation Act or Law; an act of war whether such war be declared or undeclared; any form of sickness, disease or infection except pyogenic infections incurred through an accidental cut or wound; services rendered by members of the insured's immediate family or as a part of the school duties by a physician retained by the school system. Expense for physiotherapy, diathermy, heat treatment in any form, antibiotic therapy, manipulation or massage will be payable only when such treatment is performed in hospital to a resident bed patient.

The policy as issued, in addition to the foregoing exclusions named in the application, excluded from coverage, among other things, fighting and "any aggravation of a pre-existing condition". Neither of these exclusions were mentioned in the application made on a printed form prepared by the insurance company. Thus, it will be seen that the exclusion provision of the policy is broader than the exclusion provision of the application.

The policy, when issued, was sent to the Brookland School. A copy was not sent to the applicant, the parent. It is not shown that the insurance company had any reason to believe that the parents of the children named in the policy would ever see the policy.

Appellant, Eugene E. Lawrence, father of David Lawrence, sent in an application in the aforesaid manner naming his children, including David, to be insured. David is afflicted with hemophilia. Some time after the delivery of the policy, David received a cut to the inside of a lip while fighting with another boy. Due to the fact that he was afflicted with hemophilia, the cut did not stop bleeding for a long time. It was necessary to send him to a hospital in Memphis. The hospital and doctor bills finally amounted to $2,454.15. A claim was made against the insurance company; payment was refused on the ground that the policy did not cover an injury due to fighting and that it did not cover an aggravation of a pre-existing condition of hemophilia.

The cause was submitted to the court sitting as a jury on a stipulation of facts. The court rendered a judgment in favor of the insurance company. The assured has appealed.

If the exclusions named in the policy are controlling, the assured cannot recover. On the other hand, if the statement in the application setting out the things not covered by the policy is to prevail, injuries due to fighting or an aggravation of a pre-existing condition are not excluded. One of the contentions of the insurance company is that the exclusions listed in the pamphlet should not prevail because there is a notation thereon that the pamphlet is not a policy. Of course the pamphlet is not a policy, but it did become an application.

At this point it might be well to mention that the policy provides that any form of disease or sickness is not covered by the policy. Although hemophilia may be designated as a disease, the assured is not precluded from recovering on that ground because this court has held many times that the aggravation of a pre-existing dormant condition is not a valid defense in a suit on an accident policy.

We now reach the question of which should prevail—those things listed in the application as not being covered by the insurance or those things listed in the policy as not covered. In the case of *Woodmen of the World Life Ins. Society v. Counts,* 221 Ark. 143, 252 S.W.2d 390, Counts applied for a policy providing double indemnity for accidental death. The policy, as issued, did not contain the double indemnity feature. The insured was accidentally killed. This court held that the insurance company was liable for double indemnity; that it was the duty of the insurance company to write the type of insurance named in the application, or to issue no policy. There, the court quoted with approval from *Robinson v. United States Ben. Soc.,* 132 Mich. 695, 94 N.W. 211; "The duty of the defendant was to issue the policy in compliance with the terms of the application. If it chose to insert inconsistent provisions, it was its duty to call the attention of the insured to them, so that he might accept or refuse the policy. The insured has the right to assume that his policy will be in accordance with the terms of his application, and he cannot be bound by a different policy until he has had the opportunity to ratify or waive the inconsistent provisions."

In the case at bar, the application, the form of which was prepared by the insurance company, clearly states those things not covered by the policy. The insurance company had no right to add other exclusions to the policy without the approval of the applicant.

Appellee suggests that although the stipulation shows that the insured was injured in a fight, there is no showing that he received an accidental injury within the meaning of the policy. The complaint alleges that the insured was accidentally injured. It is stipulated that he was injured in a fight with a fellow student. The inference is that the injury was accidental. There is no showing that the insured was the aggressor or that he was not acting in self defense. In *Maloney v. Maryland Casualty Co.,* 113 Ark. 174, 167 S.W. 845, the court said: If an injury occurs without the agency of the insured, it may be logically termed 'accidental,' even though it may be brought about designedly by another person."

There is no dispute about the amount involved, which is $2,454.15. Since it has been decided that the appellant is entitled to recover, it necessarily follows that he is entitled to 12 per cent penalty on the amount sued for and a reasonable attorney's fee. In the circumstances, we believe a $1,000.00 fee would be appropriate.

Reversed.

QUESTIONS FOR REVIEW

1. Why has promotional material for group life insurance been treated differently in the courts than similar material for individual life insurance?
2. What is meant by *direct response insurance advertising*? Indicate some of the legal hurdles which face an insurer which uses direct response insurance advertising on an interstate basis.

3. Describe the nature of the authority over insurance advertising which is possessed by each of the following:
   a. Federal Trade Commission.
   b. United States Postal Service.
   c. Federal Communications Commission.
   d. Internal Revenue Service.
   e. Securities and Exchange Commission.

4. In a state with an unfair trade practices act based on the NAIC model, what legal sanctions can the insurance commissioner impose on an insurer which violates the unfair trade practices act by its advertising practices?

5. How are the terms *exceptions, reductions,* and *limitations* defined in the model Rules Governing Advertisements of Accident and Sickness Insurance?

6. Define the following:
   a. Institutional advertisements
   b. Invitations to inquire
   c. Invitations to contract
   Which is the most strictly regulated? Why?

7. What must be disclosed in an advertisement which contains a testimonial or endorsement?

8. In a life insurance advertisement which uses a term such as "no medical examination required" when policy issuance is not guaranteed upon application, what additional statement must appear?

CHAPTER 22

Privacy and Insurance

HISTORY OF PRIVACY LAW
  The Tort of Invasion of Privacy
  Constitutional Protection of Privacy
FEDERAL PRIVACY LEGISLATION
  The Fair Credit Reporting Act
  The Privacy Act of 1974
STATE PRIVACY LAWS
THE NAIC MODEL PRIVACY ACT
  Pretext Interviews
  Notice of Insurance Information Practices
  Disclosure Authorization Forms
  Investigative Consumer Reports
  Access to Recorded Personal Information
  Correction, Amendment, or Deletion of Information
  Adverse Underwriting Decisions
  Disclosure Limitations and Conditions
  Enforcement
AIDS AND PRIVACY
SUMMARY

Privacy is a word with no single commonly accepted definition. Privacy can mean quite different things to different people. The members of the Privacy Protection Study Commission, which was created by Congress in 1974 to recommend privacy legislation, could not agree on a definition after two years of studying privacy. The tort of invasion of privacy has not one definition, but four.

A definition often repeated by the courts is that the right to privacy is "the right to be let alone." This definition does not fit well when we are discussing the right to privacy in insurance transactions, however. A more workable definition in that context is "the right to fair personal information practices."

HISTORY OF PRIVACY LAW

The legal right to privacy is of relatively recent origin. It did not exist at English common law. Before 1890, no American court had granted relief for an invasion of the right to privacy. There then appeared a famous and influential article by Samuel D. Warren and Louis D. Brandeis entitled *The Right to Privacy*.[1] In this article, the authors argued that the growing excesses of the press made necessary a distinct remedy for invasion of privacy. Thereafter, the right to privacy began to receive protection in statutes and court cases. A body of tort law providing damages for invasion of privacy developed.

The Tort of Invasion of Privacy

The tort of invasion of privacy has taken four distinct forms. The first form is appropriation of a person's name or likeness by another person for the other person's benefit. For example, there will ordinarily be an invasion of a person's privacy if that person's name or photograph are used for advertising purposes without his or her consent.

The second form of invasion of privacy is unreasonable intrusion upon a person's seclusion or solitude or into the person's private affairs. Invasion of a person's home or eavesdropping on her or his private conversations by means of a telephone wiretap are examples of this form of invasion of privacy.

The third form is the public disclosure of private facts about a person. Thus, publication in a newspaper that a person does not pay his or her debts is an invasion of privacy.

The fourth form of invasion of privacy consists of placing a person in a false light in the public eye. Publishing a photograph of an honest waiter to illustrate an article about dishonest waiters was held to be an invasion of privacy in one case.[2]

There are several defenses to invasion of privacy lawsuits. First, if the plaintiff consented to the invasion of his or her privacy, the consent will bar recovery, as is true for other torts. Second, there is a privilege to report on and discuss public figures or newsworthy persons. An ordinary person could be newsworthy if he or she receives an honor or experiences a calamity. This privilege can bar recovery for public disclosure of private facts. Third, there is a qualified privilege of the defendant to further his or her own legitimate interests. For example, reasonable investigations of insurance applicants or insurance claims are privileged and, therefore, cannot serve as grounds for a lawsuit based on invasion of privacy.

Unlike defamation, truth is not a defense to a lawsuit for invasion of privacy. In other words, a public disclosure of private facts, even though the facts are true, will be actionable at law.

---

[1]S. Warren & L. Brandeis, *The Right to Privacy*, 4 HARV. L. REV. (1890).
[2]Valerni v. Hearst Magazines, 99 N.Y.S.2d 866 (Sup. Ct. 1949).

Constitutional Protection of Privacy

In addition to the tort actions just described, certain protections against government intrusion into individual privacy have been found in the federal Constitution by the United States Supreme Court. Although the right to privacy is not explicitly mentioned in the Constitution, the Court has held that it is implied. In *Katz v. United States*,[3] the Court held that while a person's general right to privacy is largely left to state law, various provisions of the federal Constitution protect personal privacy from government invasion. Moreover, the Congress of the United States has stated in the Privacy Act of 1974[4] that "the right to privacy is a personal and fundamental right protected by the Constitution of the United States." Constitutional protection from government intrusion extends to privacy against arbitrary intrusion by the police; privacy in marriage, procreation, contraception and child rearing; political privacy; and privacy in communications and records, among others.

FEDERAL PRIVACY LEGISLATION

In recent times, public concern over invasions of privacy has increased along with the increase in government regulation and record keeping, and with the growing impact of the computer. The federal government, credit bureaus, insurers, and many other organizations gather and store ever vaster quantities of personal information. The concern that some of these data may be inaccurate or misused, with harm to the persons involved, has spurred the enactment by Congress of laws regulating personal information collection, retention, and use. The Fair Credit Reporting Act[5] and the Privacy Act of 1974 are the federal privacy laws of greatest importance to insurers.

The Fair Credit Reporting Act

In 1970, Congress enacted the Fair Credit Reporting Act (FCRA). The FCRA was intended to insure that credit reporting agencies act "with fairness, impartiality and a respect for the consumer's right to privacy." Insurers and others who use consumer reports have duties under the FCRA also.

A consumer report is "any written, oral or other communication of any information by a consumer reporting agency bearing on a consumer's credit worthiness, credit standing, credit capacity, character, general reputation, personal characteristics or mode of living" for use in determining whether the consumer can obtain employment, credit, or insurance to be used primarily for personal or family purposes. A consumer is a natural person under the FCRA. The FCRA does not protect businesses.

---

[3] 389 U.S. 347 (1967).
[4] 5 U.S.C.A. § 552a (West 1977 & Supp. 1987).
[5] 15 U.S.C.A. §§ 1681a–1681t (West 1982 & West Supp. 1987).

An investigative consumer report, as opposed to a consumer report, means a report "obtained through personal interviews with neighbors, friends or associates of the consumer reported on or with others with whom he is acquainted or who may have knowledge" about the consumer. Specific factual credit information obtained directly from a credit reporting agency is not considered an investigative consumer report. The FCRA imposes additional requirements where an investigative consumer report is involved. It requires that the consumer be given advance notification that such a report might be made and a statement informing the consumer that she or he can request a disclosure of the nature and scope of the investigation.

A consumer reporting agency is any entity which for money, or on a cooperative nonprofit basis, regularly prepares consumer reports and furnishes them to others. Consumer reporting agencies must comply with the extensive requirements of the FCRA. Information can be released by a consumer reporting agency only on court order, on request of the consumer, or to a person the agency believes has a legitimate business need for the information. Certain obsolete information cannot be reported. Reasonable procedures to guard against improper reporting must be maintained. The consumer reporting agency must disclose to the consumer the nature and substance of all information, except medical information, in its files at the time of the request, certain sources of the information, and the recipients of the information. If a person disputes the information in his or her file, the information must be verified or deleted.

Insurers are also required by the FCRA to make certain reports to consumers. An insurer which makes an adverse decision based on a consumer report must inform the person involved of the adverse decision and, at the same time, supply the name and address of the consumer reporting agency which made the report on which the decision was based. An adverse decision would include either denial of insurance or an increase in the charge for the insurance.

It is unlawful under the FCRA for an insurer to obtain information on a consumer from a consumer reporting agency under false pretenses. A person who knowingly and willfully obtains such information without a legitimate business need for the information, in connection with a business transaction involving the consumer, could be fined up to $5,000, imprisoned up to one year, or both.

Insurers are ordinarily concerned with the FCRA in three ways. First, at the time a risk is assessed, the insurer may obtain consumer reports or investigative consumer reports. Second, claims investigations may necessitate obtaining such reports. Third, insurers are employers and may obtain such reports in order to make an employment decision.

The Privacy Act of 1974

Congress had two purposes in enacting the Privacy Act of 1974 (the Privacy Act). First, the Privacy Act governs the collection, retention, use, and disclosure of government records on individuals. Second, the Privacy Act established the Privacy Protection Study Commission. The purpose of the Commission was to study the uses of personal information in the United States and to recommend privacy legislation. The Commission issued a final report in 1977.

This report, entitled *Personal Privacy in an Information Society,* covers personal information handling by both government and private industry. Sixty-seven pages of the report are devoted to "The Insurance Relationship." The Commission determined that the insurance industry is among society's largest gatherers and users of information about individuals. The report examines "the way records about an individual affect his place in the insurance relationship today, and . . . the problems industry record-keeping practices pose from a privacy protection viewpoint." The report recommends three public-policy objectives concerning the collection, retention, and use of personal information: "(1) to minimize intrusiveness; (2) to maximize fairness; and, (3) to create a legitimate enforceable expectation of confidentiality."

The Commission recommended that the Fair Credit Reporting Act be amended, and other federal laws enacted to govern personal information gathering and use by insurers and to "give the individual actionable rights against insurance institutions and support organizations" if they did not comply with the law. Although such federal laws were not enacted, the report provided the impetus for the development of the NAIC Insurance Information and Privacy Protection Model Act (the NAIC Model Privacy Act).

STATE PRIVACY LAWS

As was pointed out at the beginning of this chapter, tort law protecting people from invasion of privacy has been developing in the various states for nearly a century. In addition, the states have enacted statutes making confidential much data held by state agencies. For example, in some states a coroner's report is available only to a person to whom the cause of death is a "material issue." Medical records are usually recognized as personal and private and are protected from public disclosure. Adoption records, social service records, educational records, personnel files, and tax returns are often protected from disclosure by state laws.

State privacy legislation affecting insurance record keeping was minimal prior to the development of the NAIC Model Privacy Act. Some states have made use of their Unfair Trade Practices Act to regulate record-keeping practices to a limited extent. A few states have passed laws regulating forms that a person must sign to authorize disclosure of medical information about herself or himself. Some of these laws have precise requirements as to the form and content of such authorization forms. Insurers have had to develop forms which will comply with the various state laws.

Beyond the regulation mentioned above, however, there was little state insurance recordkeeping privacy regulation before the adoption of the NAIC Model Privacy Act. Nevertheless, most insurers have voluntarily instituted measures to safeguard the confidentiality of records, to conduct periodic evaluations of recordkeeping practices, to allow customers to have access to information collected during a background check, and to review the operating practices of the investigative firms they employ.

THE NAIC MODEL PRIVACY ACT

The Insurance Information and Privacy Protection Model Act (Model Privacy Act) was adopted by the NAIC in 1979, with a revised version adopted in 1980. Virginia was the first state to enact a law based on the Model Privacy Act, followed shortly by Arizona, California, Connecticut, Georgia, Illinois, Kansas, Montana, and North Carolina. New Jersey and Oregon later enacted laws patterned on the model act. Other states are considering enactment of such laws.

The Model Privacy Act establishes "standards for the collection, use and disclosure of information gathered in connection with insurance institutions, agents or insurance-support organizations." Insurance-support organizations presumably include the Medical Information Bureau (MIB) (a trade association, composed of a large number of insurers, which provides for the exchange of medical information among its members), investigative agencies, claims adjustment agencies and credit bureaus. The NAIC stressed the importance of balancing the insurer's need for information and the public's need for fairness in insurance information practices. The law protects only natural persons who are residents of the state where the law is enacted. Those obtaining insurance for business purposes are not protected.

The Model Privacy Act has five stated purposes: (1) to minimize intrusiveness; (2) to establish a regulatory mechanism to enable natural persons to ascertain what information is being or has been collected about them in connection with insurance transactions; (3) to enable such persons to have access to such information for the purpose of verifying or disputing its accuracy; (4) to limit the disclosure of information collected in connection with insurance transactions; and, (5) to enable insurance applicants and policyowners to obtain the reasons for adverse underwriting decisions. The remainder of this section contains a discussion of the requirements of the Model Privacy Act.

Pretext Interviews

A pretext interview occurs when an interviewer, in an attempt to obtain information about someone, makes a misrepresentation or refuses to identify himself or herself. The interviewer might pretend to be someone else, pretend to represent someone he or she does not represent, or misrepresent the purpose of the interview. It is ordinarily unlawful under the Model Privacy Act for an insurer, an agent, or an insurance-support organization, such as an investigative or claims adjustment agency, to conduct a pretext interview in connection with an insurance transaction.

There is one exception to this rule. Pretext interviews can be conducted in claims investigations if there is a reasonable basis for suspecting fraud, material misrepresentation, or material nondisclosure. Such pretext interviews can be conducted with anyone except a person who has a privileged relationship with the person being investigated. Privileged relationships would probably include those between husband and wife, doctor and patient, or attorney and client, although the term is not defined in the model act.

Notice of Insurance Information Practices

Under the Model Privacy Act, an insurer or agent must provide notice of insurance information practices to applicants for insurance. With certain exceptions, policyowners[6] must also be provided with such notice when there is a policy renewal or reinstatement or a request for a change in benefits. The exceptions are where information is collected only from the policyowner or, in the case of renewal, where there has been a similar notice given within the past 24 months.

The notice must be given promptly. Applicants must be given the notice when the collection of information from a third person is begun. Where information is collected only from the applicant, the notice must be given when the policy is delivered.

If notice must be given when a policy is renewed, it must be given by the renewal date. In the case of policy reinstatement or change in insurance benefits, if notice is required, it must be given at the time the request for reinstatement or change in benefits is received by the insurer.

The notice of insurance information practices must be in writing. It must state whether personal information may be collected from persons other than the proposed insured. The types of personal information that may be collected and the types of sources and investigative techniques that may be used must be disclosed. The notice must disclose that certain types of persons may receive personal information without prior authorization by the person to whom the information relates. These include persons who need the information to provide services to the insurer; other insurers or agents who need the information to prevent or detect fraud, misrepresentation, or nondisclosure, or to perform functions in connection with insurance transactions; medical professionals where a medical problem is involved; persons conducting certain research or audits; and persons who will use the information in marketing.

The notice must also state the types of personal information that may be disclosed without prior authorization. The notice must state that the person involved has a right of access to the information and the right to correct or amend it. A statement that insurance-support organizations may retain infor-

---

[6]Group certificateholders are included where the insurance is individually underwritten.

mation and disclose it to other persons must be contained in the notice. Finally, the notice must state that, upon request, a person proposed for coverage can receive a description of procedures which allow access to or correction of personal information, and a description of the circumstances under which personal information may be disclosed without prior authorization.

Disclosure Authorization Forms

Disclosure authorization forms are signed by an applicant or insured to indicate consent to disclosure of personal information about her or him. The required content of disclosure authorization forms is spelled out in the model act. The form must be dated and written in plain language. The form must specify the types of persons authorized to disclose such information, the nature of the information which can be disclosed, and the types of persons to whom the information can be disclosed. The form must also specify the purpose for which the information is collected.

Disclosure authorizations are not valid after certain time periods spelled out in the model act. The applicant or insured can authorize a shorter period of time if he or she wishes. The form must provide for this. Finally, the applicant or policyowner must be notified that he or she is entitled to receive a copy of the authorization form.

Investigative Consumer Reports

An investigative consumer report under the Model Privacy Act is a report about a person's character, general reputation, personal characteristics, or mode of living obtained from neighbors, friends, associates, acquaintances, or others. When an investigative consumer report is to be prepared, the insurer or agent must inform the person investigated that she or he can request to be interviewed also. Notice must be given that a person can receive a copy of the investigative report upon request if she or he is not interviewed.

Access to Recorded Personal Information

Upon request and after proper identification, a person has a right of access to information about him or her in the possession of an insurer, agent, or insurance-support organization. The person must be informed of the nature and substance of the information and allowed to have a copy on request. The person must be informed of the identity of the persons or organizations to whom the information has been disclosed, if this has been recorded, or else of the persons to whom such disclosure is normally made. The person must also be given a summary of procedures for requesting correction, amendment, or deletion of information. Institutional sources of the information must be disclosed. A reasonable fee can be charged for providing this information.

Medical-record information can be disclosed to the person involved or to a medical professional designated by the person. A medical professional is defined as "any person licensed or certified to provide health care services." Physicians, dentists, nurses, optometrists, and other categories are listed in the model act.

There is one important exception to the access requirement. The model act provides the following:

> The rights granted to all natural persons by this subsection shall not extend to information about them that relates to and is collected in connection with or in reasonable anticipation of a claim or civil or criminal proceeding involving them.

This limitation applies to the correction, amendment, or deletion of information as well.

Correction, Amendment, or Deletion of Information

A person who wishes to correct, amend, or delete personal information about herself or himself must send a written request to the insurer, agent, or insurance-support organization holding the information. The holder of the information must either comply with the request or notify the person of its refusal, the reasons for the refusal, and that the person has a right to file a supplementary statement.

If the holder of the information complies with the request for correction, amendment, or deletion, the person involved must be notified of the compliance. The correction, amendment, or deletion must be furnished to certain others designated by the person and to certain insurance-support organizations.

In the case of a refusal to correct, amend, or delete information, the person involved has a right to file a statement of what the person believes is the correct information with the holder. This statement must be made available to anyone reviewing the disputed information.

Adverse Underwriting Decisions

Adverse underwriting decisions include declinations and terminations of coverage or offers to insure at higher than standard rates. An insurer responsible for an adverse underwriting decision must provide the applicant, policyowner, or proposed insured with the reason for the decision or with notice that the reason will be given upon request. The person involved also has a right to the specific items of personal and privileged information that support the reason for the adverse decision, unless the insurer reasonably suspects criminal activity, fraud, material misrepresentation, or material nondisclosure. Medical-record information can be disclosed either to the person involved or to a medical professional designated by the person.

Inquiries by insurers, agents, or insurance-support organizations regarding previous adverse underwriting decisions must include a request for the reasons for the decision. The same applies to inquiries as to previous coverage through a residual market mechanism. A residual market mechanism is an arrangement by which persons obtain insurance when they cannot do so through ordinary channels.

An insurer cannot base an adverse underwriting decision solely on a previous adverse underwriting decision or previous coverage through a residual market mechanism. An adverse underwriting decision can be based, however, on further information obtained from another insurer responsible for a previous adverse underwriting decision.

An adverse underwriting decision cannot be based solely on personal information received from an insurance-support organization whose primary source of information is insurers. However, an insurer can base an adverse underwriting decision on further personal information, such as a statement by another insurer that its file contains the source of the information supplied by the insurance-support organization, that the information is medical-record information or was furnished by the person reported on, and that the information is accurate.

Disclosure Limitations and Conditions

Disclosure of personal information to third parties by an insurer, agent, or insurance-support organization can be made with written authorization of the person reported on, or under certain conditions without such authorization. As noted above, the required contents of authorization forms have been spelled out in the NAIC Model Privacy Act. The conditions under which the insurer, agent, or insurance-support organization can disclose personal information without written authorization are also spelled out. They include disclosure to persons who need the information to perform a service for the disclosing insurer, agent, or insurance-support organization; disclosure to other insurers, agents, or insurance-support organizations to detect or prevent fraud; disclosures to other insurers, agents, or insurance-support organizations connected with an insurance transaction involving the person reported on; disclosure of a person's medical problem to the person's physician or other medical professional; disclosure to insurance regulatory authorities; disclosure to other government authorities by the insurer to protect itself from illegal activities; disclosure pursuant to a subpoena or search warrant; and certain disclosures in connection with scientific research, audits, and marketing.

Enforcement

The NAIC Model Privacy Act provides that the state commissioner of insurance shall have the power to investigate to determine whether an insurer or agent doing business in the state is complying with the act. The commissioner can also investigate an insurance-support organization acting on behalf of an insurer or agent doing business in the state, or where a state resident is affected.

If the commissioner's investigation leads to a reasonable belief that there has been a violation of the act, the commissioner can conduct a hearing at which the person complaining and the insurer, agent, or insurance-support organization can testify and present other evidence. If a violation is found, the commissioner can issue an order requiring the insurer, agent or insurance-support organization to cease and desist from such conduct. An insurer, agent, or insurance-support organization subject to an order of the commissioner can obtain a review by a court. Violation of a valid cease and desist order can result in a fine of up to $10,000 for each violation or up to $50,000 for violations constituting a "general business practice."

In addition to this procedure for enforcement, the NAIC Model Privacy Act has a section providing for equitable actions (injunctions) to enforce a person's right of access to, or correction of, information, or his or her right to be given reasons for adverse underwriting decisions. Finally, a person who knowingly and willfully obtains personal information from an insurer, agent, or insurance-support organization under false pretenses can be fined as much as $10,000, imprisoned up to one year, or both.

AIDS AND PRIVACY

Concerns about the confidentiality of Acquired Immune Deficiency Syndrome (AIDS) test results have been voiced by some people. One survey showed that only 52 percent of people in the United States believe that life insurance companies will keep AIDS testing results confidential.[7] The insurance industry, however, has long been committed to keeping medical information confidential, so that only those with a business need to know will have access to it. The American Council of Life Insurance (ACLI) and the Health Insurance Association of America (HIAA), in their *Position Paper on AIDS and Insurance,* stated that

> insurers will continue to maintain their excellent record of confidentiality regarding sensitive medical information. After all, this is only sound business practice, since the price of carelessness has always been the loss of consumer confidence. With AIDS, companies have more reason for care.

The absence of reported court cases in which an insurance applicant or an insured has prevailed in an invasion of privacy action against an insurer seems

---

[7]*American Council of Life Ins. & Health Ins. Ass'n of Am., Public Attitudes About AIDS and Underwriting Practices Survey Highlights* (1988).

to bear out the claim of the ACLI and HIAA that insurers do protect the confidentiality of medical information.

As one example of insurance industry concern for the privacy of applicants and insureds, the Medical Information Bureau, which had been placing AIDS antibody test results in codes that specifically designated the AIDS antibody test, has now modified this procedure and places the test results in a code that designates only general blood abnormalities. Thus, the MIB no longer maintains a specific record of AIDS antibody test results.

The National Association of Insurance Commissioners has attempted to allay privacy concerns of the public regarding underwriting for AIDS. In 1987 the NAIC adopted a bulletin proposed for issuance by insurance departments entitled "Medical/Lifestyle Questions on Applications and Underwriting Guidelines Affecting AIDS and ARC." The statement in the proposed bulletin that "insurance support organizations shall be directed by insurers not to investigate, directly or indirectly, the sexual orientation of an applicant or beneficiary," is apparently directed at concerns about privacy, as well as concerns about underwriting discrimination against homosexuals, the group hardest hit by the AIDS epidemic. The proposed bulletin also requires that whenever an applicant is requested to take an AIDS-related test in connection with an application for insurance, the use of such a test must be revealed to the applicant and his or her written consent obtained. This is clearly aimed at maintaining fair personal information practices for insurance applicants.

SUMMARY

Privacy has no single commonly accepted definition. One definition is "the right to be let alone." As to privacy in insurance transactions, a more workable definition is "the right to fair personal information practices."

The tort of invasion of privacy takes four distinct forms. First, appropriation of a person's name or likeness by another person for the other person's benefit can be an invasion of privacy. Second, an unreasonable intrusion upon a person's seclusion or solitude or into the person's private affairs can be an invasion of privacy. Third, invasion of privacy can take the form of public disclosure of private facts about a person. Finally, placing a person in a false light in the public eye can constitute an invasion of privacy.

The federal Constitution provides protection against government intrusions into individual privacy in the areas of intrusion by the police; privacy in marriage, procreation and child rearing; and political privacy, among others.

Congress has enacted laws regulating personal information collection, retention, and use. The Fair Credit Reporting Act and the Privacy Act of 1974 are the federal privacy laws of greatest importance to insurers. The purpose of the Fair Credit Reporting Act is to ensure that credit reporting agencies act fairly, impartially, and with a respect for the consumer's right to privacy.

The Privacy Act of 1974 was enacted to govern the retention, use, and disclosure of government records on individuals and to establish the Privacy Protection Study Commission. The purpose of the Commission was to study the uses of personal information in the United States and to recommend privacy legislation. The report of the Commission provided the impetus for the development of the NAIC Insurance Information and Privacy Protection Model Act.

State privacy legislation affecting insurance recordkeeping was minimal prior to the development of the NAIC Model Privacy Act. Laws based on the model act have been adopted in over one fourth of the states.

The model act establishes standards for the collection, use, and disclosure of information about applicants and insureds. The model act governs pretext interviews and investigative consumer reports, provides for notice of insurance information practices, and regulates the form and content of disclosure authorization forms. The model act also provides for access to recorded personal information and for correction, amendment, or deletion of that information. It mandates that an insurer responsible for an adverse underwriting decision provide a reason for the decision. Finally, the model act governs the disclosure of personal information by an insurer to third parties.

The AIDS epidemic has raised new public concerns about the confidentiality of medical information collected by insurers. Insurers and regulators are attempting to address those concerns through fair personal information practices.

ILLUSTRATIVE CASE

In this case, the court discusses the right to privacy. The court pointed out that only unwarranted invasions of privacy are actionable. The right of privacy does not prohibit the communication of matters of a private nature if there is a duty to communicate.

GALEN D. SENOGLES, Appellant,

v.

SECURITY BENEFIT LIFE INSURANCE
COMPANY, Appellee[8]
Supreme Court of Kansas

KAUL, Justice:

This is an appeal from a summary judgment rendered for the defendant-appellee (Security Benefit Life Insurance Company), in an action for damages for invasion of privacy. At the time judgment was rendered the trial court had before it the pleadings, a deposition of Galen D. Senogles, plaintiff-appellant, taken by defendant, supporting affidavits filed with defendant's motion, the briefs of the parties, and the proceedings of a pretrial conference.

---

[8]217 Kan. 438, 536 P.2d 1358 (1975).

The question presented is whether communication to a third party of medical information received by defendant from plaintiff's physicians, under authorization given by plaintiff in connection with an application for life insurance, was made under such circumstances that the transmission thereof was qualifiedly or conditionally privileged.

The facts are not in dispute and are substantially set forth in the trial court's memorandum decision which we quote in pertinent part:

"This is an action to recover $50,000 in damages from the defendant life insurance company, based upon an alleged invasion of the right of privacy of the plaintiff and an alleged breach of the confidential relationship between the plaintiff and defendant, all based upon the transmittal by the defendant of certain medical information applicable to the plaintiff to Medical Information Bureau, an association which provides under certain terms and conditions medical information to member life insurance companies for certain purposes in connection with underwriting risks.

"The facts applicable to defendant's motion for summary judgment are undisputed. On or about February 22, 1972, plaintiff applied to the defendant for a policy of health insurance, application No. 0040037. The application for insurance signed by plaintiff included the following authorization:

"'I hereby authorize any licensed physician, medical practitioner, hospital, clinic or other medical or medically related facility, insurance company or other organization, institution, or person, that has any records or knowledge of me or my health, to give to the Security Benefit Life Insurance Company any such information.'

"As a result of the authorization, the defendant did receive medical information applicable to plaintiff. The information received was to the effect as follows:

"(a) Chest pain, significant but ill defined, no cause indicated, not listed elsewhere—information obtained from attending physician, surgeon, hospital, sanatorium or clinic—within first year, but not known to be present at time of inquiry or application;

"(b) Cardiac arrhythmia, premature contractions or not listed elsewhere (this includes any arrhythmia, not listed elsewhere, except sinus arrhythmia)—information obtained from attending physician, surgeon, hospital, sanatorium or clinic—within first year, but not known to be present at time of inquiry or application.

"(c) Asthma, primary or allergic—information obtained from attending physician, surgeon, hospital, sanatorium or clinic—under treatment, not surgical—within second year.

"Pursuant to its contract with M.I.B., the aforementioned medical information was forwarded to M.I.B. on or about April 10, 1972, in a coded form.

"M.I.B is a nonprofit, unincorporated trade association formed to conduct a confidential exchange of information between offices of about 700 member life insurance companies. All members of the association are required to comply with rules and regulations which include a requirement that all information received through the M.I.B will be held confidential and will be kept in such a manner that its confidential character will be maintained. The rules further provide that a member insurance company can obtain information from M.I.B only after first obtaining medical authorization from their applicant. Pursuant to this rule, Union Central Insurance Company requested medical information applicable to the plaintiff and received the medical information summarized above in a coded form. By reason of the medical information received by the defendant, and pursuant to the terms of the conditional receipt issued by the defendant, the defendant declined to accept plaintiff's application for insurance and returned to plaintiff, the premium paid by the plaintiff at the time of his application. Plaintiff gave no instructions to any representative of the defendant concerning their authority to secure medical information and what defendant could do with such medical information, other than the written instructions set forth in the insurance application. The only information received by the defendant based upon plaintiff's written authorization set forth in the insurance application were the medical reports from Dr. R. M. Brooker dated March 17, 1972, Dr. James K. L. Choy, dated March 2, 1972, and Dr. Horace T. Green, dated March 27, 1972, copies of which are attached as exhibits herein." (Emphasis supplied.)

The trial court then proceeded to discuss some of our recent decisions in actions for invasion of right of privacy; namely, *Johnson v. Boeing Airplane Co.,* 175 Kan. 275, 262 P.2d 808; and *Munsell v. Ideal Food Stores,* 208 Kan. 909, 494 P.2d 1063. The trial court relied primarily upon our opinion in *Munsell* in reaching its decision.

At oral argument, defendant's counsel, with consent of plaintiff's counsel, agreed to and has supplied us with a copy of the constitution and rules of the Medical Information Bureau, hereafter referred to as M.I.B.

Before dealing with the precise question presented, we should observe that the trial court rendered its judgment solely on the basis of the existence of a qualified privilege. It did not consider whether plaintiff actually had a case for invasion of right of privacy and, if so, whether plaintiff had shown any damages suffered as a result thereof. In this connection defendant says plaintiff was unable to set forth any damages. Plaintiff takes the position that malice is not in the case; that it was neither necessary to plead it nor prove it. In his deposition plaintiff admitted that he had given no written or oral instructions to defendant, or its agents, other than what appears in the authorization included in the application. In this connection we note that in the authorization, heretofore set out verbatim in the trial court's memorandum decision, the plaintiff authorizes *inter alia* an insurance company or other organization to give to defendant any records or knowledge of defendant's health. Neither party attempts to explain the effect, if any, of including "insurance company or other organization" in this context within the authorization. We shall give it no significance in our consideration. Neither shall we give consideration to the fact that no express limitation on the use or further communication of medical information was imposed upon defendant by the terms of the authorization.

In view of the posture of the case as presented on appeal we shall confine our decision to the sole question whether, under the particular facts and circumstances shown, the transmission of the medical information to M.I.B. was made in a manner which rendered it qualifiedly privileged. We are not concerned with any question relating to the unauthorized disclosure by a physician concerning a patient which might constitute an actionable invasion of the patient's right to privacy.

Although litigation was scarce until recent times, a citizen's right to privacy has long been recognized in this jurisdiction. Right of privacy was defined in *Johnson v. Boeing Airplane Co.,* supra, wherein we held:

> "The doctrine of the 'right of privacy' is defined as 'the right to be let alone,' the right to be free from unwarranted publicity, the right to live without unwarranted interference by the public in matters with which the public is not necessarily or legitimately concerned, and the right to be free from unwarranted appropriation or exploitation of one's personality, private affairs and private activities."

The definition in *Johnson* was quoted with approval in *Munsell* wherein we pointed out the distinction between the torts of defamation and invasion of privacy and set out and adopted what was said to be the general rule concerning invasions of the right to privacy in these words:

> ". . . It is clear from the decisions that only unwarranted invasions of the right of privacy are actionable. The corollary to this rule is that a 'warranted' invasion of the right of privacy is not actionable. Appellant urges that we recognize and apply here the rule that the right of privacy does not prohibit the communication of any matter though of a private nature, *when the publication is made under circumstances which would render it a privileged communication according to the law of libel and slander.* This rule is recognized in 41 Am.Jur., Privacy, § 20, p. 940; *Brents v. Morgan,* 221 Ky. 765, 299 S.W. 967, 55 A.L.R. 964; and in the first comprehensive article on the subject of the 'Right to Privacy' in 4 Harvard Law Review 193, at page 216 published by Samuel D. Warren and Louis D. Brandeis in 1890. We hold that the rule is sound and should be applied in the case at bar." (208 Kan. p. 923, 494 P.2d p. 1075.) (Emphasis supplied.)

Based upon the *Munsell* case the trial court reasoned that under the circumstances attendant herein the communication by defendant to M.I.B. was qualifiedly privileged and, in the absence of an affirmative allegation of malice, entered judgment for the defendant. We believe the reasoning of the trial court was sound and that it made a proper disposition of the case.

Plaintiff argues that *Munsell* is distinguishable on the facts and that the holding therein does not support the trial court's decision. We agree the facts surrounding the publication in *Munsell* are not "four square" to the facts shown in the instant case, but the general principles of law upon which the decision in *Munsell* was predicated are applicable here.

Our decision in *Munsell* was followed by our opinions in *Dotson v. McLaughlin,* 216 Kan. 201, 531 P.2d 1; and *Froelich v. Adair,* 213 Kan. 357, 516 P.2d 993, in which the thrust of *Munsell* was elaborated upon. In *Froelich* and *Dotson* we further defined the boundaries for the protection of privacy and gave recognition to the analysis of the right of privacy and the four tort classifications made by Professor Prosser (Prosser Law of Torts, [4th Ed.], Right of Privacy, § 117, p. 802) and incorporated in Restatement of the Law (Second), Torts, Tentative Draft No. 13, § 652. The classifications are set out in our holding in syllabus ¶ 1 in *Dotson* and need not be repeated here. The *Froelich* case dealt with what has been labeled "Intrusion Upon Seclusion", while in *Dotson* we held that plaintiff had failed to make out a case under any of the concepts defined in Restatement, *supra*.

In the *Dotson* opinion we spoke of our holding in *Munsell* in this fashion:

> ". . . There we held that only *unwarranted* invasions of the right of privacy are actionable and that the right of privacy does not prohibit the communication of any matter though of a private nature, when the publication is made under circumstances which would render it a privileged communication according to the law of libel and slander." (216 Kan. p. 206, 531 P.2d p.5.)

In the *Froelich* opinion we reaffirmed what was said in *Munsell* to the effect that the right of privacy does not prohibit communication of a matter of a private nature when the publication is made under circumstances which would render it a privileged communication according to the law of libel and slander.

The principal thrust of plaintiff's argument on appeal is that the *Munsell* case is not on "all fours" with the case at bar and that, therefore, the trial judge erred in basing his decision on *Munsell*. From what has been said it is readily apparent that even though *Munsell* may not be on "all fours" factually, the principles of law enunciated therein are applicable and control the disposition of the instant case. Concerning an action for invasion of privacy, based upon the communication of matters of a private nature, *Munsell* settled these principles—(1) a warranted invasion of privacy is not actionable; (2) communication or publication of a matter even of a private nature made, under circumstances which would render it a privileged communication according to the law of libel and slander, will not support an action; and (3) generally, the issue whether a publication is qualifiedly privileged is a question of law to be determined by the court.

We turn then to the precise question whether the circumstances under which the instant communication was made were such as to render it qualifiedly privileged.

The subject of qualified privilege is not new to this court. In the early case of *Kirkpatrick v. Eagle Lodge*, 26 Kan. 384, the distinction between absolute and qualified privilege was pointed out and it was held that the publication in question, which consisted of allegedly false and libelous statements made about the plaintiff in connection with his expulsion from a fraternal organization, was made on an occasion and in such a manner as to prevent an inference of malice, which the law draws from unauthorized communications, and affords a qualified defense, depending upon the absence of malice. Following *Kirkpatrick* numerous cases appear in our reports wherein qualified privilege has been found to exist in various factual situations and liability was denied in the absence of proof of malice. In such cases the burden of proof is on the plaintiff to establish malice.

In the case of *Faber v. Byrle*, 171 Kan. 38, 229 P.2d 718, 25 A.L.R.2d 1379, this court elaborated on the distinction between absolute and qualified privilege and considered the latter in depth. The definition of qualifiedly privileged appearing in 33 Am.Jur., Libel and Slander, § 126, pp. 124–126, was quoted and adopted by this court. It reads:

" '. . . A communication made in good faith on any subject matter in which the person communicating has an interest, or in reference to which he has a duty, is privileged if made to a person having a corresponding interest or duty, even though it contains matter which, without this privilege, would be actionable, and although the duty is not a legal one, but only a moral or social duty of imperfect obligation. The essential elements of a conditionally privileged communication may accordingly be enumerated as good faith, an interest to be upheld, a statement limited in its scope to this purpose, a proper occasion, and publication in a proper manner and to proper parties only. The privilege arises from the necessity of full and unrestricted communication concerning a matter in which the parties have an interest or duty, and is not restricted within any narrow limits.' " (p. 42, 229 P.2d p. 721.)

The essence of the above quoted definition is restated in 50 Am.Jur.2d, Libel and Slander, § 195, pp. 698–699.

We believe the communication and the surrounding circumstances under which it was made in the instant case falls within the boundaries of the definition. Defendant had an interest in the medical information which it forwarded to the M.I.B. by reason of which, through its membership, it would receive information pertaining to other applicants for insurance. Defendant had a duty under its contract of membership with M.I.B. M.I.B. had a duty to furnish the information to other members when the requirements of M.I.B. rules were met.

Defendant's counsel vigorously argues that the duty to transmit information was not only required by the contractual relationship between M.I.B. and its members, but was a duty involving the public interest; that it was a legitimate business procedure and vital to the life insurance industry. Defendant's argument is supported by the record.

In the instant case there is no evidence of bad faith on the part of defendant. It is undisputed that the medical information in question was not divulged to the public or to anyone who did not have a legitimate interest in the health of the plaintiff. Our examination of the rules of M.I.B. and affidavits of Joseph C. Wilberding, Executive Director of Medical Information Bureau, indicates the M.I.B. rules are geared to protect against misuse of the information and that it is to be revealed only to home office employees of member companies who directly pass upon the transaction. Medical information is released to a member company only when it has a signed medical authorization from the involved applicant in its home office files.

In this connection Mr. Wilberding stated in his affidavit:

"In order to maintain the strictest security and confidentiality in the exchange of information, M.I.B. had promulgated a number of rules and regulations which must be adhered to by its members. M.I.B. information is not to be made known to insurance agents or anyone else except the member insurance company home office underwriting or claims personnel. General Rules of M.I.B. provide that before a member insurance company can ask for details of medical codes, said member must have in its home office files signed medical authorization from the involved applicant authorizing the member company to obtain information from other insurance companies. . . ."

In addition to the security measures outlined by Mr. Wilberding in his affidavit, rules of M.I.B., which we have examined, provide for strict limitation of the use and possession of code books; that correspondence regarding the meaning of code symbols must be between officers of member companies and the executive director of M.I.B.; and that correspondence regarding medical impairments of applicants may be conducted only by medical directors of other companies.

In a recently published article appearing in Vol. 4 (1974) Rutgers Journal of Computers And The Law, the author makes a comprehensive analysis of the purposes and activities of M.I.B. He concludes:

> "The MIB serves an invaluable function in the life insurance industry by meeting underwriters' informational needs. The proved ability to set premiums which result from use of the MIB benefits the policyholders. It is they who bear the burden of increased costs if an applicant is assessed for premiums inadequate to cover the risk of loss he represents."

We are satisfied there is a valid business interest in the communication in question; it was made in good faith; and M.I.B. and member companies had a corresponding interest; and that the information was limited in scope to a proper purpose, published in a proper manner and to proper parties only. In other words, the communication here falls within the definition of qualified privilege adopted by this court in *Faber v. Byrle,* supra and followed in other cases cited.

There is no evidence that the privilege accorded to defendant had been lost by abuse thereof. The record reveals that Union Central Life Insurance Company, a member company, had received in its home office information concerning plaintiff and had contacted plaintiff's physicians. The record further shows, however, that Union Central had previously received an application from plaintiff with the signed medical authorization attached.

We have found no reported decisions involving the activities of M.I.B. However, our attention is directed to *Johns v. Associated Aviation Underwriters,* 203 F.2d 208 (5th Cir. 1953), where, in applying Texas law, the Fifth Circuit Court of Appeals found the existence of a qualified privilege in a libel action based upon a report of an underwriters association concerning a pilot's qualifications. The association performed a service for insurance companies similar to that rendered by M.I.B. to its members. The relationship of the parties and the circumstances surrounding the publication of the report were similar to those shown to exist in the case at bar. The court stated the applicable rule in these words:

> "A communication made in good faith on any subject, in which the person reporting has an interest and in reference to which he has a duty, is conditionally or qualifiedly privileged if made to a person having a corresponding interest or duty. . ."

Apparently, California has encoded the rule concerning qualified privilege in such cases. *Mayer v. Northern Life Ins. Co.,* D.C., 119 F.Supp. 536 (1953), was labeled a defamation action. The complaint alleged that defendant (Northern Life) had caused false medical information to be recorded in the records of an agency subscribed to by life insurance companies. The agency is not identified in the opinion, but apparently rendered a service similar to that performed by M.I.B. In applying California law the court said:

". . . However, the allegations of the complaint disclose that this is a case of qualified privilege within the provisions of Section 47(3) of the Civil Code of the State of California. . . . (p. 536.)

The section of the California Code (West's Annotated, California Codes [Civil] § 47), referred to reads:

"A privileged publication or broadcast is one made—

    .   .   .   .   .

"3. In a communication, without malice, to a person interested therein, (1) by one who is also interested, or (2) by one who stands in such relation to the person interested as to afford a reasonable ground for supposing the motive for the communication innocent, or (3) who is requested by the person interested to give the information."

Since plaintiff had failed to allege malice the court determined that his complaint failed to state a claim upon which relief could be granted and dismissed the action.

We agree with defendant that cases involving agency credit reporting wherein a communication to those with a legitimate business report is generally deemed qualifiedly privileged are analogous in many respects to the case at bar. In the recent case of *Kansas Electric Supply Co. v. Dun and Bradstreet, Inc.,* 448 F.2d 647 (10th Cir. 1971). The Tenth Circuit Court of Appeals, in applying Kansas law, approved a jury instruction to the effect that credit reports of Dun and Bradstreet were conditionally privileged.

The judgment is affirmed.

SCHROEDER, J., dissenting.

FROMME, J., not participating.

QUESTIONS FOR REVIEW

1. Tell what is meant by *privacy,* as it relates to insurance operations.
2. Describe the different forms of the tort of invasion of privacy.
3. What are the defenses to lawsuits based upon invasion of privacy?
4. How does the Fair Credit Reporting Act relate to the operations of insurers?
5. Suppose an insurer makes an adverse decision based on a consumer report. What rights does the person involved have?
6. Review the purposes of the NAIC Model Privacy Act.
7. What are pretext interviews?
8. Discuss the "notice of insurance information practices" that must be provided by insurers. Summarize the types of information contained in such notices.
9. How is the subject of adverse underwriting decisions handled in existing state privacy laws?
10. Suppose a person learns that some of an insurer's information about her or him is false. What can the person do in a state with privacy laws based on the NAIC Model Privacy Act?

CHAPTER 23

Insurers and Agents as Employers

STATUTORY PROTECTION OF EMPLOYEES
  Federal Employment Statutes
  State Employment Statutes and Municipal Ordinances
DISPARATE TREATMENT AND DISPARATE
IMPACT DISCRIMINATION
  Disparate Treatment Discrimination
  Disparate Impact Discrimination
EMPLOYMENT PRACTICES AND DECISIONS
  Bona Fide Occupational Qualifications
  Advertising
  Applications and Interviews
  The Immigration Reform and Control Act of 1986
  Job Performance Evaluations
  Uniform Standards for Job Performance
  Preferences of Coworkers or Customers
SEXUAL HARASSMENT, PREGNANCY DISCRIMINATION,
AND REVERSE DISCRIMINATION
  Sexual Harassment
  Pregnancy Discrimination
  Reverse Discrimination
AFFIRMATIVE ACTION
RETALIATION BY THE EMPLOYER
PENALTIES FOR EMPLOYMENT DISCRIMINATION
WRONGFUL DISCHARGE
SUMMARY

The insurance industry employed nearly two million people in the United States in 1985. Moreover, employment in the insurance industry continues to rise, having increased from approximately one million people employed in 1960.[1] Because the insurance industry employs so many people, those who

---

[1] AMERICAN COUNCIL OF LIFE INSURANCE, LIFE INSURANCE FACT BOOK 95 (1986).

manage insurance companies, insurance agencies, and insurance brokerage businesses have a special need to know the basic rules of employment law. The purpose of this chapter is to enable the reader to recognize existing and potential employment problems. Early recognition of employment problems by managers greatly assists the persons in the company who are responsible for handling such problems—often those in the personnel, human resources, or law departments. If managers understand the bases on which employment decisions can lawfully be made and the bases on which it is unlawful to make employment decisions, many potential problems can be averted.

STATUTORY PROTECTION OF EMPLOYEES

The United States Congress and the great majority of state legislatures have enacted statutes which protect employees from discrimination in employment. The most important of these statutes are outlined in this section.

Federal Employment Statutes

One of the most important employment statutes is the federal Civil Rights Act of 1964. Title VII of this act prohibits discrimination in employment based on race, color, religion, sex, or national origin.[2] These are called protected classes.

Other federal statutes also protect employees from discrimination. The Age Discrimination in Employment Act of 1967[3] and its amendments protect job applicants and employees over the age of 40 from discrimination based on age. The Equal Pay Act of 1963 prohibits an employer from paying employees of one sex more than employees of the other sex for the same work unless the pay difference is based on a seniority system, a merit system or another factor other than sex.[4]

In addition, private employers which have contracts with the federal government for procurement of property or nonpersonal services involving amounts exceeding $2,500 are essentially prohibited from making employment decisions based on a person's mental or physical handicap if that handicap is unrelated to the person's ability to fulfill the job requirements.[5] Other federal statutes have been held to prohibit employment discrimination, but the statutes mentioned above are the principal sources of federal antidiscrimination law.

---

[2] 42 U.S.C.A. § 2000(e) et seq. (West 1981).
[3] 29 U.S.C.A. §§ 621–634 (West 1985 & Supp. 1987).
[4] 29 U.S.C.A. § 206(d) (West 1978).
[5] 29 U.S.C.A. § 793 (West Supp. 1987).

State Employment Statutes and Municipal Ordinances

Most states have their own laws which prohibit employment discrimination. The Illinois Human Rights Act[6] is fairly typical of these statutes. It prohibits employment discrimination based on race, color, religion, national origin, ancestry, age, sex, marital status, handicap, or unfavorable discharge from military service. The classes of protected persons differ among the states. Some state statutes include classes not listed in the Illinois statute. Some do not protect classes of persons protected under Illinois law.

There are also many cities and towns which have municipal ordinances prohibiting employment discrimination and agencies to enforce those ordinances. The state and municipal laws which apply to an employer depend upon the location of the employer's business. An insurer's branch or field offices might have different employment laws applying to them than the laws applying to the home office.

Which states, cities, and towns have enacted statutes or passed ordinances forbidding employment discrimination, and the protections afforded by those statutes and ordinances, is well beyond this overview of employment law. However, employers and managers must become familiar with the state and municipal antidiscrimination laws which apply to them, as well as with the federal laws which apply everywhere in the United States.

DISPARATE TREATMENT AND DISPARATE IMPACT DISCRIMINATION

There are two major types of employment discrimination which the courts have identified in enforcing antidiscrimination laws. These are *disparate treatment* and *disparate impact* employment discrimination.

Disparate Treatment Discrimination

Disparate treatment occurs when an employer bases an employment decision on a person's race, religion, national origin, sex, age, and so forth. For example, disparate treatment occurs when an employer refuses to hire a qualified job applicant because the applicant is a woman, is black, or follows a particular religion. This type of discrimination is clearly unlawful. It is easier to identify than disparate impact discrimination.

Disparate Impact Discrimination

Disparate impact discrimination occurs when an apparently nondiscriminatory job requirement has a disproportionately large adverse effect on the opportunities of people in one of the protected classes. The courts have held

---

[6]ILL. REV. STAT. ch. 68 ¶¶ 1–101 to 9–102 (1985 & Supp. 1986).

disparate impact discrimination to exist when a job requirement is not closely related to the person's ability to perform the job. Disparate impact discrimination is just as unlawful as disparate treatment discrimination. It is also as damaging to the people it affects.

An understanding of disparate impact discrimination can be gained by a review of *Griggs v. Duke Power Co.,*[7] a landmark United States Supreme Court case. In that case, Willie S. Griggs and twelve other black employees at the Duke Power Company's Dan River Station in Draper, North Carolina, filed a class action against their employer, Duke Power Company, alleging unlawful discrimination on the part of the employer. A class action is a lawsuit brought by a representative member, or members, of a large group of persons on behalf of all the members of the group.

Before July 2, 1965, the effective date of the Civil Rights Act of 1964, Duke Power Company employed blacks in only one of its five operating departments at the Dan River Station—the labor department. The wage for the highest-paying job in the labor department was less than the lowest wage paid in the four other operating departments. In 1955, the company began requiring a high school education or its equivalent before it would assign a newly-hired person to any operating department other than the labor department, or before transferring current employees to the more desirable departments.

In 1965, when blacks were no longer restricted to the labor department, the company instituted a policy of requiring potential transferees from the labor department and from other less desirable jobs to pass two standardized aptitude tests before any transfer would be granted to an employee who did not have a high school education. The two tests were the Wonderlic Personnel Test which purports to measure general intelligence, and the Bennett Mechanical Comprehension Test. The company also required all newly-hired employees to have a high school education or its equivalent and to pass the two tests. The two tests were not designed or intended to measure the ability of an employee to perform a particular job at the Dan River Station. Moreover, the score required, for an applicant to be hired or for an employee to be transferred, was close to the national median for high school graduates. Approximately one half of the nation's high school graduates would, therefore, be unable to achieve a satisfactory score on these tests.

Duke Power Company applied the testing and education requirements fairly to blacks and whites alike. The trial court found that the tests were "not administered, scored, designed, intended or used to discriminate because of race or color." However, because blacks in North Carolina had been discriminated against in the schools, they had received an education inferior to that received by most whites. The 1960 census statistics show that 12 percent of black males in North Carolina had completed high school, while 34 percent of white males had done so. Because of their inferior educational

---

[7]401 U.S. 424 (1971).

opportunities, blacks did worse than whites on the tests, and a greater percentage of blacks than whites was, therefore, barred from employment opportunities at the Dan River Station.

Finally, the evidence introduced at the trial showed that employees who had not completed high school or taken the aptitude tests continued to perform satisfactorily and to make progress in departments at the Dan River Station for which the high school and test criteria were now prerequisites. In other words, the job requirements were not closely related to a person's ability to perform the job.

In *Griggs,* the United States Supreme Court held that Title VII of the Civil Rights Act of 1964 prohibits employment practices which are fair in form but discriminatory in operation if the employment practice is not closely related to job performance. This criterion has been applied to prevent the use of such factors as height and weight requirements, arrest records, and other standards that, even when applied fairly to all, have had the effect of disqualifying more blacks than whites, more women than men, and so forth.

For example, if a job in a factory requires that an object weighing 30 pounds be lifted several times each hour, a height or weight requirement for that job will not ensure that a job applicant will be able to lift the object. The proper method of selecting someone with the necessary strength is to test the applicant's strength directly by having him or her lift the object.

EMPLOYMENT PRACTICES AND DECISIONS

Employment practices and decisions begin with the employer's advertisements for the job—its want ads—and continue throughout employment until the employee's termination by resignation, discharge, or retirement. With few exceptions, employment practices or decisions cannot lawfully be based on age, religion, national origin, or sex. They can never be based on race or color.

An applicant for any job should be tested to see how well she or he can perform the actual job. Any test or job requirement should be directly related to determining whether the applicant can perform the duties of the job for which she or he has applied. Screening devices, such as height and weight requirements, education requirements, or required tests which are not directly related to the applicant's abilities to perform the duties of the job might have a disparate impact on minorities, women, and members of other protected classes. If the screening devices have such a disparate impact, they are unlawful.

Bona Fide Occupational Qualifications

In a very few circumstances, age, sex, religion, or national origin can be used to screen applicants. In such a case, it is necessary to establish that the use of such a characteristic is a *bona fide occupational qualification.* A bona fide occupational qualification is a characteristic upon which it is usually unlawful to base an employment decision, but upon which such a decision can lawfully be based as to the job in question. For example, it is usually unlawful to base an employment decision on a person's sex. If the job in question is that of locker-room attendant in a women's locker room, however, sex is a bona fide occupational qualification. The employer can lawfully require that the applicant be female.

As another example, a parochial school which is seeking a teacher of religious instruction might require applicants to be members of the religious group operating the school. This would be a bona fide occupational qualification.

Advertising

When an insurer, insurance agency, or insurance brokerage business is seeking job applicants, it might advertise in newspapers and trade journals. Any language in the advertisement which expresses or implies a preference for applicants of a particular race or color or which indicates that applicants of a particular race or color will receive less consideration is always prohibited. The regulations issued by the federal agencies which interpret the Age Discrimination in Employment Act prohibit employers from using help wanted notices or advertisements which "contain such terms and phrases as 'age 25 to 35,' 'young,' 'boy,' 'girl,' 'college student,' 'recent college graduate' or others of a similar nature, [because] such a term or phrase deters the employment of older persons and is a violation of the act."[8] It is, however, permissible to specify a minimum age less than 40, such as "not under 18" or "not under 21."

Help wanted notices or advertisements can specify an age, sex, religion, or national origin requirement only when the requirement meets the strict standards of a bona fide occupational qualification, as described above.

Applications and Interviews

The application and employment interview are essential tools for gathering information about a job applicant in order to evaluate the applicant's ability to do the job. The application and interview should be designed to elicit only information relating to the applicant's abilities to do the job. Information which is not related to the applicant's abilities to do the job or which is not required for other legitimate reasons[9] should not be elicited. State employment laws vary as to what information can be requested on an application or during an interview. It is the responsibility of the employer's

---

[8]29 C.F.R. § 1625.4 (1987).

[9]An employer can ask for the person's social security number for F.I.C.A. withholding purposes, for example.

attorney to review hiring procedures and ensure compliance with all applicable laws.

Supervisors, managers, and others who conduct job interviews should
take care to avoid actions which could create liability for the employer. First,
questions of a job applicant eliciting information which might be used as the
basis for a discriminatory hiring decision should be avoided. For example, it
would be unnecessary and unwise to ask an applicant for a typist's job which
church he or she attended. This has nothing to do with the applicant's typing
abilities. Even though the question is a friendly attempt to get acquainted
with the applicant, it could be viewed by an unsuccessful applicant as the
basis of a decision not to hire. Other examples of questions which should be
avoided are the following:

1. What social organizations do you belong to?
2. Are you married?
3. Have you ever been arrested?
4. How old are you?

Question one, "What social organizations do you belong to?" might elicit
the name of a social organization which reveals the applicant's religion or
national origin. Except in the rare instances in which they are a bona fide
occupational qualification, religion or national origin are not related to an
applicant's ability to perform a job satisfactorily.

Question two, "Are you married?" elicits information which cannot be
used to make an employment decision, according to the law of most states. It
is information which has no relationship to the applicant's abilities to perform
the job. After the hiring decision is made, an employee can be asked her or
his marital status for insurance or other legitimate purposes.

Question three, "Have you ever been arrested?" also elicits information
which cannot be used to make an employment decision. The members of
several minority groups are arrested at a greater rate than members of non-
minority groups. If an employer bases a hiring decision on the number of
times an applicant has been arrested, this would affect minorities disproportionately and would, therefore, be unlawful. However, the employer can inquire about convictions. Convictions for offenses which adversely reflect on
an applicant's ability to perform a job satisfactorily can be considered in
making the hiring decision.

Question four, "How old are you?" should be avoided. Under federal law,
age cannot be considered as a factor in employment decisions if the person is
over 40. The only legitimate concerns an employer has with respect to an
applicant's age before the hiring decision is whether the applicant has reached
the age of majority (18 to 21 depending on the state).

While the inquiries noted above are not unlawful in themselves, an unsuccessful applicant might convince a court that the information elicited was
the basis for an unlawful employment decision. This could happen even

though the decision actually was based on job-related criteria. If the employer does not have non-job-related information, such a claim by an unsuccessful applicant will be unlikely. In short, the safest procedure is to ask only for information related to the applicant's abilities to perform the job. If other information is to be elicited, the employer's attorney should assess the situation.

Immigration Reform and Control Act of 1986

There are some questions that an employer must ask of job applicants in order to avoid hiring illegal aliens. These duties are imposed by the federal Immigration Reform and Control Act of 1986. An employer cannot lawfully hire an employee without checking the applicant's identity and authorization for employment. An employee must sign a form devised by the Immigration and Naturalization Service (INS) verifying employment eligibility. The employee also must present documentation such as a driver's license, birth certificate, passport, voter's registration card, social security card, or INS employment authorization.

The act also prohibits discrimination against employees and job applicants because of their national origin or citizenship status, as long as they are not illegal aliens. The antidiscrimination provisions were included in the act to prevent employers from rejecting job applicants with foreign accents or appearances in order to protect themselves from penalties if the applicant turns out to be an illegal alien. Congress intended that an employer's good faith compliance with the identity and authorization verification procedures described above would protect the employer.

Job Performance Evaluations

As with other employment practices, job performance evaluations must not be based on the employee's race, color, sex, age, and so forth. Job performance evaluations should be based only on the employee's job performance.

Job performance evaluations should be made periodically. Many employers evaluate their employees' job performances annually. The time interval can be longer or shorter according to the employer's preference.

Although such periodic job performance evaluations are not required by law, they help to avoid discrimination suits because they offer a regularly scheduled opportunity to discuss the employee's job performance. An employee ordinarily files a discrimination charge because the employee believes that her or his failure to get a raise or promotion, or some other adverse employment decision, was based on a prohibited criterion, such as the employee's race, sex, national origin, or age. In other words, the employee believes it was something other than her or his job performance which led the employer to make the adverse employment decision.

Periodic job performance evaluations can reduce discrimination suits by providing an opportunity for the employer to explain to the employee the bases on which his or her work is being evaluated and the reasons for any adverse employment decision. The employee is more likely to understand what is expected by the employer if there are periodic job performance evaluations. Often, the employee's misunderstandings or misconceptions about the job can be eliminated.

Another benefit of periodic job performance evaluations is their role in an employer's defense of a discrimination charge. Periodic written job performance evaluations should greatly aid an employer in demonstrating that an adverse employment decision was not based on race, sex, national origin, or age, but on poor performance. Even if an employee's job performance evaluations reflect good work, but an expected promotion went to another employee, the employer should be able to show why the employee who received the promotion deserved it.

An effective job performance evaluation can be conducted in the following way. First, the employee receives a detailed written roster of her or his job duties, called a job description or duty list. In the job description, the job is broken down into its various duties. Next to each duty, there is a space where the supervisor writes her or his evaluation of the employee's performance. The employee is given an opportunity to review the supervisor's written job performance evaluation, and the supervisor and employee discuss the evaluation. The employee can then be told the basis for a raise, promotion, demotion, probation, and so forth.

Second, all employees receive job performance evaluations and reviews of those evaluations on a regular basis. If an employer evaluates only the poor performers, and there are poor performers in one or more protected classes, discrimination suits are likely. If the employer evaluates only the good performers, the poor performers might believe discrimination is involved. Thus, the best practice is to evaluate the job performance of all employees.

Third, the employer strives to make all job performance evaluations accurate and honest. An inaccurate or dishonest job performance evaluation does the employer a disservice. For example, if the employee is given a better rating than he or she deserves and is later demoted or fired, it will be more difficult and perhaps impossible for the employer to demonstrate the basis for the demotion or firing. The documentation of the employee's poor performance won't exist because the employee's supervisor gave the employee a "break," rather than an accurate and honest evaluation.

Fourth, the employer strives to make the job performance evaluation detailed, rather than general. A detailed job performance evaluation assists the employee in understanding exactly what the employer wants and how to improve her or his performance.

Fifth, the employer gives employees written job performance evaluations and reviews those evaluations at the proper time. A written job performance evaluation which is drafted after a discrimination suit is filed, to justify the employment action complained of, will be given no weight by a court or administrative agency. At the time an adverse employment decision is made, a written job performance evaluation should be given to the employee and a review of the evaluation made.

Sixth, the employer fully documents the employee's job performance. Time sheets and written reports on the employee's job performance are maintained. Without documentation, it is difficult for an employer to rebut a charge of discrimination. The documentation must be maintained in an even-handed manner, however, because a discrimination charge is essentially an allegation that one person was treated differently from others who were similarly situated. For example, if time sheets are kept, they should be kept for all employees similarly situated and not just for some.

Even-handed treatment and documentation are the keys to the defense of discrimination complaints. Even if adverse actions taken by the employer against an employee were, in fact, nondiscriminatory and completely justified, the employer must have evidence to support its position. The evidence is, in large part, documentation of the reasons the employer took the action.

Finally, the employer tailors the time interval for job performance evaluations to the circumstances. For a new employee who has just started a job, job performance usually should be evaluated frequently until the employee knows what is expected. The same is true for an employee on probation who needs to be more closely supervised than others.

Uniform Standards for Job Performance

Job performance evaluations will be effective only if the employer establishes uniform standards for job performance. For example, if a manager decides that five instances of unexcused tardiness are necessary to put an employee on probation, that standard must be applied to all employees in a similar position. The manager who applies different standards to employees in similar positions is more likely to be charged with discriminatory conduct than the manager who applies uniform standards. Such a discrimination charge can result in great expense for the employer.

For example, suppose Josephine Manning has 10 clerk-typists working for her. Several clerk-typists frequently arrive at work late without satisfactory explanations. Ms. Manning informs the employees that from that day forward, any employee who arrives at work late more than twice without satisfactory explanation will be put on probation. After two weeks, A and B, two of the clerk-typists, have each arrived late twice. Ms. Manning likes A but has never had a friendly relationship with B, although B's work is usually better than A's. Ms. Manning talks to A about A's tardiness. A and B are each late one more time. Ms. Manning puts B on probation but gives A one more chance before putting A on probation.

Here A and B were not treated uniformly, even though each had violated the same rule. If B were in a protected class—if B were, for example, a black, a woman, or over 40—and A were not in a protected class, B might be able to convince a court that Ms. Manning had unlawfully discriminated, even though that was not Ms. Manning's intention. Ms. Manning might have treated B differently for reasons unrelated to B's race, sex, or age, but if Ms. Manning cannot show a business reason for treating B differently from A, Ms. Manning's company might be found liable for discrimination. If a manager treats whites, males, or blacks preferentially, the manager's motive for doing so is irrelevant.

Managers must treat all employees objectively and according to uniform standards. Managers should avoid making exceptions in applying company rules.

Preferences of Co-Workers or Customers

Employment decisions can almost never lawfully be based on the preferences of co-workers or customers for an employee of a certain race, sex, age, or similar non-job-related criterion. For example, if a woman is being considered for a job which has previously been held only by men, and the co-workers are all men who would prefer not to have a woman in their group, the employer cannot lawfully consider the co-workers' preferences in making the hiring decision. If the woman is the best-qualified person for the job, it is irrelevant that her co-workers would be men who do not wish to work with her. If the employer denies her the job for this reason, this would be unlawful discrimination.

Similarly, the preferences of customers must not be a factor in an employment decision. Simply because the employer believes that customers would prefer a white, a male, or a gentile in the job, the employer cannot lawfully base employment decisions on the customers' preferences. Limited exceptions can be made to this rule where personal privacy of customers is a consideration, as where the employer is hiring a locker-room attendant.

SEXUAL HARASSMENT, PREGNANCY DISCRIMINATION, AND REVERSE DISCRIMINATION

The kinds of discrimination which have been discussed so far are discrimination based on a person's race, color, national origin, sex, age, religion, handicap, veteran status, ancestry, marital status, or unfavorable discharge from military service. There are, however, three special kinds of discrimination for which an employer can be liable. These are sexual harassment, discrimination because of pregnancy, and reverse discrimination. These special kinds of discrimination are discussed in this section.

Sexual Harassment

The Equal Employment Opportunity Commission (EEOC) includes sexual harassment as a type of sex discrimination which is barred by Title VII of the Civil Rights Act of 1964. The EEOC's guidelines on sexual harassment provide that "unwelcome sexual advances, requests for sexual favors, and other verbal or physical conduct of a sexual nature" constitute unlawful sexual harassment under certain conditions.[10] First, it will be sexual harassment if submission to the sexual conduct is an express or implied condition of the employee's employment. Second, it will be sexual harassment if the employee's submission to or rejection of the sexual conduct is the basis for an employment decision, such as a decision to promote or fire the employee. Finally, it will be sexual harassment if the sexual conduct substantially interferes with the employee's work performance or creates an intimidating, hostile, or offensive working environment.

Sexual harassment encompasses many types of behavior that can occur in the work place. For example, a male supervisor who promises to promote a female employee if she has a sexual relationship with him clearly commits sexual harassment. The female employee's opportunity for advancement depends on her submission to her supervisor's request. This is sexual harassment because the person making the employment decision is the same one making the unlawful demand.

In a situation such as this, the EEOC guidelines hold the company liable for violation of Title VII, even if the supervisor's superiors had no knowledge of the supervisor's unlawful demand. The courts are divided as to whether liability should be imposed on the employer which had no knowledge of the sexual harassment. Most courts impose liability on an employer which knows or should have known of sexual harassment committed by a supervisor but fails to investigate or stop the harassment.

Although the clearest cases of sexual harassment involve unwelcome sexual advances of supervisors toward employees who report to them, sexual harassment can also occur between employees of equal rank. Once the employer knows of such behavior by an employee toward another employee, it has a duty to investigate and stop the unlawful behavior. If the employer chooses not to investigate and fails to take corrective action, it could be liable for sexual harassment.

Sexual harassment can occur between persons of the same sex, as well as between persons of opposite sexes. Men as well as women can be victims of sexual harassment.

It requires judgment to determine whether the behavior of one employee toward another constitutes sexual harassment. An innocent flirtation or a request for a date probably will not constitute sexual harassment. Repeated

---

[10]29 C.F.R. § 1604.11 (1987).

unwelcome sexual advances and demands for dates are more likely to constitute sexual harassment. When the sexual advances or demands are directed toward an employee by his or her supervisor, sexual harassment is even more likely to be found by the court.

Pregnancy Discrimination

Women who are disabled by pregnancy or by medical conditions related to pregnancy must be treated the same as disabled men or disabled nonpregnant women.[11] EEOC guidelines require employers to treat disabilities due to pregnancy the same as other disabilities with respect to all terms and conditions of employment.[12]

A pregnant woman must be allowed to work until she is determined to be physically unable to work by appropriate medical personnel. The determination of her disability must be based on her actual physical condition. A pregnant woman must not be forced to stop working merely because it is her sixth month of pregnancy or because of some other predetermined factor which is unrelated to her actual physical condition.

A pregnant woman sometimes becomes disabled for an extended period of time after her child is born if there is a complication of childbirth. Alternatively, a woman might be able to resume her job a few days after giving birth. Once her physician finds that she is able to resume her job, she is not entitled to remain at home and return to work whenever she chooses unless the same would be true for a disabled male or nonpregnant female (except for those states which require an employer to allow an employee maternity leave). If, however, a disabled male or nonpregnant female can take off an additional period of time after the disability has ended, then the woman who has had a disability resulting from pregnancy is entitled to do the same. An employer lawfully can and often does require all employees to return to work as soon as their disabilities have ended. As long as disabilities resulting from pregnancy and pregnancy-related conditions are treated the same as other disabilities with respect to the terms and conditions of employment, ordinarily there is no unlawful discrimination. Some states—California, for example—require special treatment for pregnant employees, such as a right to reinstatement in their jobs.

As an example, suppose a male employee has a back injury which prevents him from performing his job for three months. Upon his return to work, his employer gives him the seniority that he would have had had he worked those three months. The employer permits him to resume the same position he had before his injury. The employer also pays his medical and hospital bills and gives him disability income payments while he is absent from work.

---

[11] 42 U.S.C.A. § 2000e(k) (West 1981).
[12] 29 C.F.R. § 1604.10(b) (1987).

A woman who works for the same employer becomes pregnant and her physician states that she is unable to perform her job. The employer must treat her disability from pregnancy the same as the employer treated the male employee's disability from back injury. In other words, the woman would be entitled to payment of medical and hospital bills by her employer and to disability income payments while she is disabled. When the woman's physician says she is no longer disabled, and she returns to work, she is entitled to the same treatment received by the male employee with the back injury. Seniority rights, retirement benefits, accrued vacation, and service credit of a woman on disability leave due to pregnancy must be determined as if the disability were unrelated to pregnancy.

If an employer does not require a statement from a physician that a male worker or nonpregnant female worker is disabled before that worker is entitled to receive disability benefits, then no such statement can be required from the pregnant worker. Similarly, if a male worker or nonpregnant female can return to work after a disability without a physician's statement that the disability is no longer present, then such statement cannot be required of an employee disabled by pregnancy.

Reverse Discrimination

In the United States, every person is protected from employment discrimination based on race, sex, religion, and so forth. If a white male Protestant is subjected to discrimination because he is white, he is a victim of race discrimination. If he is subjected to discrimination because he is male, he is a victim of sex discrimination. If he is subjected to discrimination because he is a Protestant, he is a victim of religious discrimination.

In other words, those who have not ordinarily been discriminated against are protected against discrimination, just as are those who have been discriminated against. Discrimination against persons who are not ordinarily discriminated against is called reverse discrimination. Reverse discrimination is unlawful.

AFFIRMATIVE ACTION

Under Executive Order 11246, the federal government requires all individuals and businesses which are awarded federal contracts to agree not to discriminate against any employee or job applicant on the basis of race, color, religion, sex, or national origin. Executive Order 11246 also requires a statement by such federal contractors in advertisements for employees that all applicants will be considered solely on the basis of their qualifications.

Nonconstruction contractors and subcontractors having 50 or more employees and a federal contract exceeding $50,000 in a 12-month period are, in addition, required to have written affirmative action plans. Affirmative action plans are used to remedy the effects of past discrimination by requiring the hiring of women and members of other protected classes that have been excluded from fair representation in many types of jobs. Affirmative action plans are a temporary measure to bring those who have been unfairly excluded from certain types of jobs into such jobs in numbers which are representative of their membership in the population generally. Many employers institute affirmative action plans as a good business practice, even if they are not legally required to do so.

RETALIATION BY THE EMPLOYER

An employer cannot discipline an employee who opposes the employer's unlawful employment practices. An employee who has "made a charge, testified, assisted or participated in any manner in an investigation, proceeding or hearing" concerning an employment practice unlawful under Title VII cannot be disciplined because of such participation.[13]

For example, suppose Larry Henderson reasonably believes that he didn't get the promotion he deserved because of his race. Mr. Henderson files a charge of discrimination with the EEOC. Vernon Cook, an associate of Mr. Henderson's, assists Mr. Henderson in presenting his case to the EEOC by testifying. Connie Walters, Mr. Henderson's and Mr. Cook's supervisor, is outraged when she learns of the discrimination charge. She believes that she did not discriminate and that Mr. Henderson's job performance did not justify a promotion.

Ms. Walters must be careful to treat Mr. Henderson and Mr. Cook the same as other employees. She must not permit their involvement in the discrimination charge to affect her treatment of these two employees. This does not mean that she cannot discipline either or both for violating a company rule, just as she would have done had there been no discrimination suit. But neither employee can be disciplined because of his involvement in the discrimination charge. Ms. Walters cannot retaliate against Mr. Henderson or Mr. Cook.

Even if the allegations in the discrimination charge are untrue, such retaliation itself will be a violation of the law. Suppose there was insufficient evidence to support Mr. Henderson's claim of discrimination, and Ms. Walters is found not to have denied Mr. Henderson the promotion because of his race. If Ms. Walters treated Mr. Henderson or Mr. Cook differently from other employees because of their participation in the discrimination charge, Ms. Walters violated Title VII. This Title VII violation is separate from the discrimination alleged in the charge.

Thus, managers employed by insurance companies, insurance agencies, or insurance brokerage businesses must take care not to respond emotionally if an employee files a charge of discrimination. Retaliation of any kind will

---

[13]42 U.S.C.A. § 2000e–3(a) (West 1981).

make a successful defense of the charge more difficult while subjecting the employer to additional liability.

PENALTIES FOR EMPLOYMENT DISCRIMINATION

Employment discrimination can be costly to an employer. For example, an employer could be sued by a group of rejected applicants who were denied employment because of the employer's use of a test or job requirement which was not directly related to an applicant's ability to do the job. Suppose the job requirements were height and weight requirements which disqualified more women than men and which were unrelated to the job. The employer could be sued by the rejected women applicants. If the women were successful in their suit, each woman who could demonstrate an economic loss might be eligible for back pay. Back pay consists of all the payments, including wages and fringe benefits, which the women would have received if the employer had not discriminated against them. In some instances, back pay can be given for a period beginning two years before the complaint was filed. The women might also be entitled to have their attorneys' fees and court costs paid by the employer. The judge could order the employer to discontinue the height and weight requirements in its selection process and order that the women be hired.

This is only one example of the many risks faced by employers who discriminate. The judge has much discretion and will fashion the remedy to fit the circumstances of each case. It is, therefore, wise for each insurer, insurance agency, or insurance brokerage business to review its employment practices in order to make certain that its job requirements are sufficiently related to the job and that they do not result from conscious or unconscious bias.

WRONGFUL DISCHARGE

The most significant development in employment law in the 1970s and 1980s has been the erosion of the employment-at-will rule. The employment-at-will rule can be defined as follows: An employer can dismiss an employee who was hired for an indefinite period of time without cause and without notice. While for many years union and government employees have had protection against wrongful discharge, before 1970 a non-union, private sector employee, hired for an indefinite period of time, ordinarily could be discharged at the will of the employer. Both contract and tort theories of wrongful discharge of these employees have now developed. The leading case was *Peterman v. Teamsters*,[14] decided in California in 1959. In that case, the employee refused to commit perjury on behalf of the employer. The court held

---

[14]174 Cal. App. 2d 184, 344 P.2d 25 (1959).

that the employer's discharge of the employee breached a covenant of good faith and fair dealing implied in the at-will employment contract. The term *at-will employment contract* does not necessarily mean a written contract, but rather the agreement between the employer and employee as to the terms of the employment. Following California's lead, courts in other states began to apply the implied covenant of good faith and fair dealing to at-will employment contracts.[15]

Other contract theories also developed. In one case, the court held that employee expectations of employment tenure based on the employer's handbooks and policy statements were enforceable in breach of contract actions.[16] Courts in other states have made similar holdings.[17]

The leading wrongful discharge case using a tort theory is *Nees v. Hocks*,[18] decided in Oregon in 1975. In that case, the employee was discharged for requesting jury duty over his employer's objections. The court held that the employer was liable for tort damages because the employer's actions undermined the public policy in favor of jury service. The public policy tort theory has been adopted by courts in other states. For example, in Connecticut, a quality control supervisor protested deviations from food labeling requirements. The court held that he could recover tort damages if he could prove that his dismissal was caused by his protests.[19] Damages for wrongful discharge have also been granted in cases where the employee was discharged because the employer was trying to avoid providing the employee with certain employee benefits.

The great majority of the states have now allowed recovery of damages for wrongful discharge, either in tort or for breach of contract. The employer will, however, escape liability unless the employee can show breach of an implied covenant of good faith and fair dealing, breach of an employment contract, or that the employer's actions were against public policy.

Regular job performance evaluations can assist the employer in establishing the reasons for the discharge. Review and revision of employee handbooks and similar materials can be an important preventive measure. Disciplinary and discharge procedures can be scrutinized and changed if necessary. Insurers, insurance agencies, and brokerage businesses can protect themselves from liability for wrongful discharge by attention to such preventive measures.

---

[15]K Mart v. Ponsock, 732 P.2d 1364 (1987); Fortune v. National Cash Register Co., 373 Mass. 96, 364 N.E. 2d 1251 (1977); Monge v. Beebe Rubber Co., 114 N.H. 130, 316 A.2d 549 (1974).

[16]Toussaint v. Blue Cross & Blue Shield, 408 Mich. 579, 292 N.W. 2d 880 (1980).

[17]Duldulao v. St. Mary of Nazareth Hosp. Center, 115 Ill. 2d 482, 505 N.E. 2d 314 (1987); Aiello v. United Airlines, Inc., 818 F.2d 1196 (5th Cir. 1987); Thompson v. Kings Entertainment Co., 653 F. Supp. 871 (E.D. Va. 1987).

[18]272 Or. 210, 536 P.2d 512 (1975).

[19]Sheets v. Teddy's Frosted Foods, Inc., 179 Conn. 471, 427 A.2d 385 (1980).

SUMMARY

The insurance industry is a major employer in the United States. Managers who work for insurers, insurance agencies, and insurance brokerage businesses need to know how to recognize existing and potential employment problems.

Federal, state, and municipal governments have enacted statutes prohibiting employment discrimination. These statutes protect job applicants and employees from discrimination in employment based on race, color, religion, sex, national origin, age, and, in some instances, based on handicap, veteran status, ancestry, marital status, or unfavorable discharge from military service.

Federal law prohibits disparate treatment discrimination and disparate impact discrimination. Disparate treatment discrimination occurs when an employer bases an employment decision on a person's race, religion, national origin, sex, age, or another prohibited criterion. Disparate impact discrimination occurs when a job requirement which is not closely related to a person's ability to perform the job results in a disproportionately large adverse effect on the job opportunities of people in one of the protected classes.

With few exceptions, employment practices or decisions cannot be based on age, religion, national origin, or sex. They can never be based on race or color. Employment practices and decisions begin with advertisements for the job, and involve job applications, interviews, promotions, demotions, raises in pay, probation, job performance evaluations, disciplinary actions, and termination.

Job performance evaluations are an important tool for reducing the likelihood of discrimination complaints. Job performance evaluations give the employer an opportunity to discuss the employee's job performance and thereby eliminate misunderstandings between employer and employee.

Uniform job standards also help to prevent discrimination charges. Uniform job standards assure that employees in the same position will be treated alike.

Employers must avoid discrimination charges arising from sexual harassment of employees, pregnancy discrimination, and reverse discrimination. Some employers with federal contracts must have written affirmative action plans to remedy the effects of past discrimination. Employers cannot lawfully retaliate against an employee who has made a charge of discrimination or testified in a discrimination proceeding.

Employment discrimination can be costly to an employer. Managers can help prevent discrimination charges by avoiding job practices and decisions which are likely to lead to such charges.

Before 1970 a nonunion, private sector employee, hired for an indefinite period, ordinarily could be discharged at the will of the employer, without notice and without cause. Both contract and tort theories of wrongful discharge of these employees have now developed.

ILLUSTRATIVE CASE

In this case an employee brought a successful wrongful discharge action against her employer, based on breach of contract.

NORA E. DULDULAO, Appellee,

v.

SAINT MARY OF NAZARETH
HOSPITAL CENTER,
Appellant[20]

Supreme Court of Illinois

Justice THOMAS J. MORAN delivered the opinion of the court:

Plaintiff, Nora E. Duldulao, brought this action in the circuit court of Cook County, alleging that defendant, St. Mary of Nazareth Hospital Center, discharged her from its employ in violation of the terms of an employee handbook. Plaintiff claimed that the handbook, distributed by defendant, created enforceable contractual rights. Both parties moved for summary judgment. The trial court denied plaintiff's motion but granted defendant's motion, entering judgment in favor of defendant. The appellate court reversed both rulings. This court allowed defendant's petition for leave to appeal.

Defendant raises [these] issues for review: (1) Did the employee handbook in this case create contractual terms binding defendant to a particular procedure for terminating plaintiff's employment? (2) Did defendant in fact terminate plaintiff's employment in accordance with the provisions of the employee handbook?

Defendant initially hired plaintiff in 1968, and rehired her in 1970 when she returned from a brief stay in the Philippines. In 1971 she was promoted to head nurse, and in 1972 she was named staff development coordinator of the department of nursing. She served in this position until September 14, 1981, when defendant reorganized several of its departments. Plaintiff became human resources development coordinator, a position which she claims was identical to her previous position. Defendant, however, submitted the affidavits of supervisors who claim that plaintiff's new position included new duties and responsibilities. On December 11, 1981, plaintiff was given a sheet entitled "Probationary Evaluation" and also a "Final Notice" informing her that she was terminated as of the end of the day. Both sheets listed essentially the same alleged infractions:

> "Unsatisfactory performance was demonstrated by the failure to properly monitor the Legal Implications of Documentation seminar and the Patient Education seminar. Further unsatisfactory performance was demonstrated by failure to follow instructions regarding CPR recertification and monitoring of the Patient Education Seminar."

Plaintiff claims that her termination violated procedural rights she had by virtue of an implied contract with defendant. The terms of this contract, plaintiff claims, are to be found in an employee handbook distributed by defendant. Defend-

---

[20]115 Ill. 2d 482, 106 Ill. Dec. 8, 505 N.E.2d 314 (1987).

ant first published an employee handbook before plaintiff was rehired in 1970. The record before us does not reveal the contents of this initial employee handbook other than the fact that it required two weeks' notice for the dismissal of probationary employees. Plaintiff's deposition reveals that she did not discuss the contents of this handbook during her rehiring interview in 1970, although she became aware of it some time after returning to work, and subsequently used it in training sessions for new employees.

In 1975 defendant published a revised employee handbook. At the beginning of this handbook is the following note, signed by Sister Stella Louise, president of the hospital:

"N.B. The Personnel Policies of Saint Mary of Nazareth Hospital Center are presented in this booklet in a summarized form. Further details regarding any policy may be obtained by consulting the master file in the Personnel Department.

It is then necessary that every employee of Saint Mary of Nazareth Hospital Center be well informed on hospital policy and other pertinent information that will assist him in directing his total efforts toward the best patient care possible. A booklet containing hospital and personnel policy is given to each employee. As a new policy change is finalized, a copy will be given to every employee to be read and placed in his booklet. If a policy needs clarification, your Supervisor or Department Head will be happy to assist you in its interpretation.

Please take the time to become familiar with these policies. They are designed to clarify your rights and duties as employees. Your observance of these policies will produce a safe and pleasant environment in which to work and assure you a respected place in Saint Mary's family of employees."

Among other things the 1975 handbook modified the previous policy which had required two weeks' notice for dismissal of a probationary employee. The 1975 handbook, as amended by a policy statement finalized on June 18, 1981, provided that "[a]n employee may be terminated without notice but for just cause during the initial probationary period." The probationary period was to last 90 days, unless "extended up to 180 days by the department head for just cause." Once an employee successfully completed the probationary period he or she was to become a "permanent employee." Permanent employees could be terminated only with "proper notice and investigation." The amendments to the handbook provided that "[p]ermanent employees are never dismissed without prior written admonitions and/or investigation that has been properly documented." Except in the case of extremely serious offenses the handbook required three warning notices before a permanent employee could be dismissed.

The contractual status of employee handbooks has been the subject of a great deal of litigation in recent years. Several courts have rejected the notion that an employee handbook or manual can ever create binding contractual obligations. However, the overwhelming majority of courts considering the issue have held that an employee handbook may, under proper circumstances, be contractually binding.

This court has never specifically addressed the issue of employee handbooks. Our appellate court, however, has addressed the issue several times, with conflicting results. In *Carter v. Kaskaskia Community Action Agency* (1974), 24 Ill. App.3d

1056, 322 N.E.2d 574, the court held that an employee manual, which was introduced after the employee began working and was written with input from the employees, created enforceable contractual rights. However, in *Sargent v. Illinois Institute of Technology* (1979), 78 Ill. App.3d 117, 33 Ill. Dec. 937, 397 N.E.2d 443, the court distinguished *Carter* and held that the handbook in question was not binding because it was given to the employee when he first began work and was not specifically "bargained for." Still another appellate decision, *Kaiser v. Dixon* (1984), 127 Ill. App.3d 251, 82 Ill. Dec. 275, 468 N.E.2d 822, rejected *Sargent* and held that an employee manual may be binding notwithstanding that it was not "bargained for."

Federal courts applying Illinois law have reflected the split in our appellate court. Two Federal cases have followed *Sargent*. However, since *Kaiser*, several Federal courts applying Illinois law have followed *Kaiser* as the better reasoned approach.

Nearly all courts agree on the general rule, that an employment relationship without a fixed duration is terminable at will by either party. Those courts which hold that an employee handbook can never create enforceable job security rights appear to apply this general rule as a limit on the parties' freedom to contract. The majority of courts, however, interpret the general "employment-at-will rule" as a rule of construction, mandating only a presumption that a hiring without a fixed term is at will, a presumption which can be overcome by demonstrating that the parties contracted otherwise. We agree with the latter interpretation.

We find particularly persuasive the opinion of the Supreme Court of Minnesota in *Pine River State Bank v. Mettille* (Minn. 1983), 333 N.W.2d 622, which analyzed an employee handbook in terms of the traditional requirements for contract formation: offer, acceptance, and consideration. In *Pine River* an employee handbook was distributed to the plaintiff several months after he began working for defendant. The handbook contained a section entitled "Job Security" which described the generally secure nature of employment in the banking industry. The court held that this section of the handbook did not constitute an offer because it contained no definite promises. The handbook, however, also contained a section entitled "Disciplinary Policy," which stated that "[i]f an employee has violated a company policy, the following procedure will apply * * *", followed by a step-by-step process of progressive discipline ending with "[d]ischarge from employment for an employee whose conduct does not improve as a result of the previous action taken." The court held this to be a specific offer for a unilateral contract—the bank's promise in exchange for the employee's performance, *i.e.*, the employee's labor. By performing, the employee both accepted the contract and provided the necessary consideration, and thus the bank's dismissal of the plaintiff without the benefit of the progressive disciplinary procedures constituted a breach of the employment contract.

Following the reasoning in *Pine River*, we hold that an employee handbook or other policy statement creates enforceable contractual rights if the traditional requirements for contract formation are present. First, the language of the policy statement must contain a promise clear enough that an employee would reasonably believe that an offer has been made. Second, the statement must be disseminated to the employee in such a manner that the employee is aware of its contents and reasonably believes it to be an offer. Third, the employee must accept the offer by commencing or continuing to work after learning of the policy statement. When these conditions are present, then the employee's continued work constitutes consideration for the promises contained in the statement, and under traditional principles a valid contract is formed.

Applying the above principles to the case at bar it is apparent that the document entitled "Employee Handbook" created an enforceable right to the particular disciplinary procedures described therein. The amended handbook states that "[a]t the end of 90 calendar days since employment the employee becomes a permanent employee and termination contemplated by the hospital *cannot occur* without proper notice and investigation." (Emphasis added.) It states that permanent employees *"are never* dismissed without prior written admonitions and/or an investigation that has been properly documented" (emphasis added), and that "three warning notices within a twelve-month period *are required* before an employee is dismissed, except in the case of immediate dismissal." (Emphasis added.) The reservation as to "immediate dismissal" does not detract from the definiteness of the offer, because that term is well defined. An "immediate dismissal" justifies dismissal "without notice for a grave and valid reason," and the list of examples of grave offenses includes such offenses as "Mistreatment of a patient," "Fighting on hospital premises," "Unauthorized Possession of Weapons," and "Reporting to work under the influence of intoxicants." The handbook also lists offenses which are specifically *not* subject to immediate dismissal, such as "Deliberate Violation of Instructions," "Unwillingness to Render Satisfactory Service," and "Unauthorized Absence." An employee reading the handbook would thus reasonably believe that, except in the case of a very serious offense, he or she would not be terminated without prior written warnings. Furthermore, the handbook creates rights even for probationary employees who may be terminated "without notice but for just cause."

Moreover, the handbook contains no disclaimers to negate the promises made. In fact, the introduction to the handbook states just the opposite, that the policies in the handbook "are designed to clarify your *rights* and duties as employees." (Emphasis added.) Thus, the handbook language is such that an employee would reasonably believe that after the expiration of the initial probationary period the progressive disciplinary procedure would be part of the employer's offer.

Finally, it is undisputed that defendant gave the handbook to plaintiff and intended that plaintiff become familiar with its contents. In fact, a significant part of plaintiff's duties as an employee consisted of instructing new employees on the contents of the handbook. There is no question but that plaintiff continued to work with knowledge of the handbook provisions. Under these circumstances the handbook's provisions became binding on the employer.

A more difficult question is whether or not defendant complied with the provisions of the handbook. It is undisputed that plaintiff had been working for more than 90 days and was receiving benefits only available to "permanent" employees. Defendant, however, claims that plaintiff had been transferred to a new position, and therefore reverted to probationary status. In support of this argument defendant cites an amendment to the handbook, finalized on September 3, 1981, which states that "[a]ll promotions and transferred employees must successfully pass a designated probationary period." This provision means, defendant argues, that once plaintiff had been transferred she could be terminated without the benefit of the progressive disciplinary procedures required for permanent employees.

We disagree. The handbook states that an employee may be terminated without notice during the *"initial* probationary period" (emphasis added), a period which ends "[a]t the end of 90 calendar days since employment." There is nothing in the policy statement on transfers to indicate that an employee serving a *"designated* probationary period" loses the right to progressive disciplinary procedures which vested when the employee successfully passed the *"initial* probationary period." (Emphasis added.) In addition, in distinguishing between "permanent" and "probationary" employees for disciplinary purposes the handbook notes that only "permanent" employees are eligible for employee benefits. It is undisputed that plaintiff continued to receive vacation pay and other benefits after the September 14, 1981, reorganization, as she had following her prior promotions. In fact, plaintiff's supervisors at the hospital claimed in their depositions that plaintiff, upon transfer, had occupied a hybrid "permanent probationary" status.

Moreover, the policy statement on transfers and promotions specifically states that its purpose is to "provide employees with approved promotional or transfer opportunities." The statement provides a procedure which begins with the posting of vacant positions and the employee's filing of a "Request for Transfer Form." The policy statement thus appears to apply only to *voluntary* transfers, and it is undisputed that plaintiff's transfer was not voluntary.

Ambiguous contractual language is generally construed against the drafter of the language, and in the absence of evidence to the contrary we must conclude that the "designated probationary period" does not divest an employee of rights vested at the end of the "initial probationary period." We must also conclude that the designated probationary period applies only to employees who *request* transfer or promotion. It is clear that plaintiff's alleged infractions did not fit into the category of extremely serious offenses warranting "immediate dismissal," and it is undisputed the plaintiff did not receive the progressive disciplinary procedures normally required for permanent employees in a nonimmediate-dismissal situation. Since defendant can point to no reason why plaintiff would not be entitled to the progressive disciplinary procedures, other than the reasons we have rejected above, we must agree with the appellate court that the failure to provide plaintiff with the required process violated her contractual rights.

* * * * *

For the reasons stated above, the judgment of the appellate court is affirmed insofar as it reversed the orders of the circuit court. The cause is remanded to the circuit court of Cook County with directions to enter summary judgment for the plaintiff and for such further proceedings as are consistent with this opinion.

Affirmed in part and remanded, with directions.

QUESTIONS FOR REVIEW

1. List three federal statutes which protect employees against discrimination. Discuss the type, or types, of employment discrimination each statute prohibits.
2. Contrast disparate treatment discrimination and disparate impact discrimination.
3. Define the term *bona fide occupational qualification*.
4. Is it permissible for an advertisement for job applicants:
   a. To imply a preference for applicants of a particular race or color?
   b. To specify a minimum age, such as "not under 18"?
5. Why is it inadvisable to elicit information about a job applicant that is not related to the applicant's ability to perform the duties of the job?

6. Describe how the following can help prevent employment discrimination complaints:

    a. Job performance evaluations.

    b. Uniform standards for job performance.

7. The EEOC's guidelines on sexual harassment provide that "unwelcome sexual advances, requests for sexual favors and other verbal or physical conduct of a sexual nature" constitute sexual harassment under three conditions. What are these conditions?

8. Is it unlawful employment discrimination to force a pregnant female employee to stop working because it is her sixth month of pregnancy?

9. Define the terms *reverse discrimination* and *affirmative action.*

10. Can an employer lawfully discipline an employee:

    a. For filing a job discrimination charge against the employer?

    b. For testifying against the employer at a job discrimination hearing?

11. Define the employment-at-will rule. How has this rule been modified in recent years?

Appendixes

Appendix A. Insurance Application Form

WASHINGTON National INSURANCE COMPANY

APPLICATION FOR LIFE/HEALTH/ANNUITY - PART I

MEDICAL
NON-MEDICAL

- PLEASE PRINT -

1. Proposed Insured/Annuitant | Birthplace (State) | Birthdate M D Y | Age | Sex | Height | Weight

John (First)   A. (Middle)   Doe (Last)   Illinois   SS#   05 05 53   34   M   5'11"   180

Single χ Married Widowed Divorced Separated

2. Address   Number and Street | City | State | Zip Code

1234 Center Street   Evanston   Ill.   60200

Previous Address (within 2 years)

3. Name of Employer | **a.** Address - No. and St. | City | State | Zip Code

XYC Company, Inc.   16 Oak St.   Evanston   Ill.   60200

b. Occupation   **c.** Duties | **d.** How Long Employed? **e.** Former Occupation

Salesman   Sales   15 Yrs.   Mos.   Student

f. Avg. Mo. Earned Income   **g.** Avg. Mo. Unearned Income | **4.** Address premium notices and correspondence to:

$ 2,500 $ None   χ Insured/Annuitant   Owner   Employer   Payor

5. LIFE INSURANCE | **6. ANNUITY**   Annuity Contract   Annuity Rider

Basic Plan of Insurance   Amount

a. Deferred
  Single Purchase   -   Amount $
  Periodic Purchase   -   Amount $
  Maturing at Age
  Waiver of Payment

a.   Whole Life   b. $ 50,000
c. χ WP   e.   Payor Benefits
d. χ ADB f. χ Guaranteed Insurability   g. $

Additional Rider Benefits   Amount/Units

b.   Single Purchase Immediate - Amount $

h.   i.   Plan

j.   k.   Amount Paid $

7. Is this Policy/Contract being applied for under a Tax Qualified Retirement Plan?   Yes   No

l.   m.

If yes, indicate type   TDA   401 Corp.   403a
HR-10 Keogh   IRA   Deferred   Other
Comp.

n. Shall Automatic Premium Loan provision be operative if available in basic plan of insurance? χ Yes   No

Purchase Payment Allocation:

Amount Paid $ COD

Employer   %   Employee   %

8. HEALTH INSURANCE

Occupational Class

Disability Income Form   Monthly Benefit   Max. Ben. Period   Elim. Period

Rider   Benefit   Rider   Benefit   Rider   Benefit

Business Expense Form   Monthly Benefit   Elimination Period
(Submit Business Expense Questionnaire)

Major Med. Policy Form   Deductible   Maximum Benefit
In-Full Hospital Rider ($100 Deductible only)   ☐ Rider

Hospital Indemnity Form   Daily Hosp. Ind. $ Elimination Period

Other (Specify Form and Benefits)   Amount Paid $

9. Present Coverage on Proposed Insured - List all Life/Health/Annuity coverage in force.   ✓ if none

Company or Service Plan	Year of Issue	Amt. of Life Ins.	Amt. of Annuity	Amt. of ADB	Benefits: Indicate Mo./Wkly Dis. Inc. Bus. Exp. Ben. Per.	Hospitalization Rm. Ben. Surgery	Major Medical Deductible Max. Ben.
ABC Ins.	1972	$10,000	-	$10,000			

Is this coverage to replace any Insurance or Annuity?   Yes χ No   If replacing Life Insurance or Annuity, complete Replacement Proposal. If replacing Health Insurance, termination date of such insurance is

10. MODE: χ ANN   SA   QR   PAC   MDO
   MDH   GA   SD - No. of Payments

11. Total Amount Paid in Exchange for Receipt $

02336

(1-83)

605

PART I - CONTINUED

12. Beneficiaries   Primary   Relationship   Contingent   Relationship

Jane Margaret Doe   Wife   James Mark Doe   Son

COMPLETE FOR FAMILY COVERAGE AND CHECK TYPE OF COVERAGE DESIRED   Life Ins.   Health Ins.

13. **Full names** of dependents proposed for coverage

	Relationship	Birthplace (State)	Birthdates M D Y	Age	Height/ Weight	Present Life Ins.
	Spouse					
Children			XXX		XXX	
			XXX		XXX	
			XXX		XXX	
			XXX		XXX	

14. **a.** Spouse's occupation, duties   **b.** Spouse's other health coverage   **c.** Avg. Mo. Inc. **d.** SS#
$

COMPLETE QUESTIONS 15 AND 19—27 FOR PAYOR BENEFITS

15. **a.** Full name of proposed payor. Please print.

Birthplace (State)	Birthdate M D Y	Age	Sex	Height	Weight	Relationship to Insured

b. Payor's occupation   **c.** Mailing Add. No., Street, City, State, Zip Code   **d.** SS#

COMPLETE IF APPLICANT/OWNER IS NOT PROPOSED INSURED/ANNUITANT

16. Proposed ownership designation applies to ☐ Life ☐ Annuity - Please print full names   Relationship to Insured/Annuitant

Owner   SS#

Contingent   SS#

Proposed Insured/Annuitant, if a minor, is to become Owner: ☐ At Owner's death ☐ At age 21 or upon prior death of the Owner
Owner's mailing address: Number and Street   City   State   Zip Code

17. **SPECIAL REQUESTS:** Identify Life/Health/Annuity   18. **HOME OFFICE ENDORSEMENTS:**

Questions 19—24 must be answered if applying for Life or Health Coverage or WP on an Annuity Contract.

Has **any person** proposed for insurance, so far as you know or believe: **Yes No**

Identify question and individual to whom details apply.

19. Any income payable during disability other than policies listed under question no. 9?   X

20. Been refused new insurance or reinstatement or had insurance postponed, limited, offered, or quoted on a substandard or rated basis?   X

22a - Sports pilot; 600 hours per year.

21. Any other application for personal Life or Health Insurance pending with this or any other company?   X

22. In the past two years, participated in: (If yes, attach questionnaire):
    a) Aviation activities as pilot or crew member? X
    b) Hazardous activities, sports, avocations, hobbies? .   X

23. Smoked cigarettes within the past year? If so, indicate quantity per day   X

24. Used narcotics, barbiturates, amphetamines, psychedelic drugs, frequently or been treated for drug usage or alcoholism?   X

Questions 25—27 should be answered if applying for Life or Health Coverage or WP on an Annuity Contract.

ANSWER THE FOLLOWING QUESTIONS AND GIVE FULL DETAILS — NAMES; AILMENTS; TREATMENT; DATES; PHYSICIANS' NAMES AND ADDRESSES; RECOVERY DATES; ETC.

Has **any person** proposed for insurance, so far as you know or believe: **Yes No**

Identify question and individual to whom details apply.

25. Ever had symptoms or been diagnosed as having disorder, disease, or persistent discomfort of —
    a) Respiratory System (lungs, bronchi, trachea, etc) such as TB, asthma, emphysema, bronchitis?   X

PART I - CONTINUED

Yes No

b) Circulatory System (heart, blood, arteries, veins, etc) such as high blood pressure, heart attack, murmur, rheumatic fever?   X

              27a - Dr. Jones - checkups each year

c) Digestive System (esophagus, stomach, intestine, liver, gall bladder, etc) such as ulcer, cirrhosis, hemorrhoids, bleeding?   X   15 Main   Evanston, Ill.

d) Nervous System (brain, nerves, etc) such as paralysis, fainting, epilepsy, convulsions, mental or nervous disorders?   X

e) Muscular and Skeletal Systems (muscles, bones, joints, spine, etc) such as neck or back problems, fracture. arthritis?   X

f) Genito-urinary System (kidney, bladder, reproductive organs, etc) such as infection, bleeding, male or female disorders?   X

g) Glandular System (thyroid, pancreas, adrenal, lymph glands, etc) such as diabetes, or abnormal growth or function?   X

h) Breast disorder or menstrual irregularity?   X

26. Ever had impaired sight or hearing, cancer or growth, venereal disease. hernia, or skin disease?   X

27. Within the past five years:

a) Been treated by or consulted any physician, health practitioner or psychologist?............   X

b) Had surgery or operation?   Has either been advised. or is either contemplated?   X

c) Been on, or now on, prescribed diet or medication?   X

d) Received disability, Worker's Compensation or pension benefits?   X

Give name and address of personal or family physician(s).

     Dr. M. D. Jones, 15 Main St., Evanston, Ill.

The undersigned represent(s) and agree(s), to the best of his (her) knowledge or belief, that the foregoing statements and answers are complete, true and correctly recorded and agree(s) to be bound by all statements and answers made or to be made in this application consisting of Part I and Part II (if said Part II is required by the Company). The undersigned further expressly agree(s) as follows: 1. This application and any policy issued in consequence thereof shall constitute the entire Contract. No agent is authorized to make or modify contracts, to waive any of the Company's rights or requirements or to bind the Company by making or receiving any promise, representation or information, unless the same be in writing, submitted to the Company, and made a part of such contract. 2. Except as otherwise provided in the Conditional Receipt bearing the same date as this application, the insurance applied for shall not become effective until the policy is delivered to and accepted by the Owner and the entire first premium is actually paid while all of the answers in Part I and Part II of this application continue to be complete and true answers. 3. The Company is authorized to amend any portion of this application pertaining to Life Insurance/Annuity by making an appropriate notation of any corrections or changes in the space designated "Home Office Endorsements," and the acceptance of any policy issued on this application shall constitute a ratification of any such amendment; provided, in those States where it is required by Statute, regulation or Insurance Department Ruling, any amendment as to amount, classification, plan of insurance or benefits shall be made only with written consent of the undersigned. 4. Unless otherwise stated in Question 16, the Proposed Insured/Annuitant will be the Owner of any policy issued on this application.

Signed At   _Evanston, Ill._

           City   State

Date   _Jan 10_   19_88_

                              John N Doe

                              Proposed Insured/Annuitant

                              Spouse (If coverage applied for)

Witnessed By   _Sam Smith_

                Writing Agent

                           Applicant/Owner if other than Proposed Insured/Annuitant

INSURANCE COMPANY

SUPPLEMENTAL APPLICATION FOR LIFE/HEALTH INSURANCE — Part 1

Your application for Life or Health Insurance is hereby amended to include the following questions. This Supplemental Application will be attached to, and made a part of your policy, if issued.

In the past 5 years did you, any member of your family, or co-habitant:

a. Have a fever of more than three weeks duration, weight loss of more than 15 pounds in two months, diarrhea of more than one months duration, skin rash or oral lesions (infections or sores of the mouth)? **No**

If yes, please explain.

_____

_____

_____

_____

_____

b. Have Acquired Immune Deficiency Syndrome (AIDS), AIDS-Related Complex (ARC) or any other immunological deficiency? **No**

If yes, please explain.

_____

_____

_____

_____

_____

Signed At ___*Evanston, Ill*_____   ___*John A Doe*_____
                    City   State   Proposed Insured

Date ___*Jan 10*_____ 19 *88*___   _____
                                                          Spouse (If coverage applied for)

Witnessed By ___*Sam Smith*_____   _____
                        Writing Agent   Applicant/Owner if other than Proposed Insured

B422

Adult Application Part 2	**WASHINGTON NATIONAL INSURANCE COMPANY** **EVANSTON, ILLINOIS 60201** **Declarations to Medical Examiner**

Proposed Insured........ *John* .... *A.* .... *Doe*
First Name .... Middle initial .... Last name

Birth Date:
Month **5** Day **5** Year **53**   Insurance Applied For: ☒ Life   Amount $ **50,000**
☐ Health   Monthly Indemnity $ ....

1. a. Name and address of your personal physician? *Dr. H. David Jones, 15 Main St., Evanston, Ill.*
(If none, so state)
b. If consulted within the last five years give date, reason, and treatment prescribed.... *checkups each year*

2. Have you ever been treated for or ever had any known indication of:

	Yes	No
a. Disorder of eyes, ears, nose, or throat?	☐	☒
b. Dizziness, fainting, convulsions, headache; speech defect, paralysis or stroke; mental or nervous disorder?	☐	☒
c. Shortness of breath, persistent hoarseness or cough, blood spitting; bronchitis, pleurisy, asthma, emphysema, tuberculosis or chronic respiratory disorder?	☐	☒
d. Chest pain, palpitation, high blood pressure, rheumatic fever, heart murmur, heart attack or other disorder of the heart or blood vessels?	☐	☒
e. Jaundice, intestinal bleeding; ulcer, hernia, appendicitis, colitis, diverticulitis, hemorrhoids, recurrent indigestion, or other disorder of the stomach, intestines, liver or gallbladder?	☐	☒
f. Sugar, albumin, blood or pus in urine; venereal disease; stone or other disorder of kidney, bladder, prostate or reproductive organs?	☐	☒
g. Diabetes; thyroid or other endocrine disorders?	☐	☒
h. Neuritis, sciatica, rheumatism, arthritis, gout, or disorder of the muscles or bones, including the spine, back, or joints?	☐	☒
i. Deformity, lameness or amputation?	☐	☒
j. Disorder of skin, lymph glands, cyst, tumor, or cancer?	☐	☒
k. Allergies; anemia or other disorder of the blood?	☐	☒
l. Excessive use of alcohol, tobacco, or any habit-forming drugs?	☐	☒
3. Are you now under observation or taking treatment?	☐	☒
4. Have you had any change in weight in the past year?	☐	☒

5. Other than above, have you within the past 5 years:

	Yes	No
a. Had any mental or physical disorder not listed above?	☐	☒
b. Had a (checkup) consultation, illness, injury, surgery?	☒	☐
c. Been a patient in a hospital, clinic, sanatorium, or other medical facility?	☐	☒
d. Had electrocardiogram, (X-ray) other diagnostic test?	☒	☐
e. Been advised to have any diagnostic test, hospitalization, or surgery which was not completed?	☐	☒
6. Have you ever had military service deferment, rejection or discharge because of a physical or mental condition?	☐	☒
7. Have you ever requested or received a pension, benefits, or payment because of an injury, sickness or disability?	☐	☒
8. Family History: Tuberculosis, diabetes, cancer, high blood pressure, heart or kidney disease, mental illness or suicide?	☐	☒

DETAILS of "Yes" answers. (IDENTIFY QUESTION NUMBER, CIRCLE APPLICABLE ITEMS: Include diagnoses, dates, duration and names and addresses of all attending physicians and medical facilities.)

5(b) and (d) — Dr. Jones — checkups each year

	Age if Living?	Cause of Death?	Age at Death?
Father	60		
Mother	59		
Brothers and Sisters No. Living	2		
No. Dead			

9. Females only:

	Yes	No
a. Have you ever had any disorder of menstruation, pregnancy or of the female organs or breasts?	☐	☐
b. To the best of your knowledge and belief are you now pregnant?	☐	☐

The undersigned represents that the foregoing statements and answers are complete, true and correctly recorded, and shall form a part, designated as Part 2, of the application for insurance.

Signed at *Evanston, Ill.* on *Jan 10* 19 **88**   *John A Doe*
Signature of Proposed Insured

Witnessed by........ *Julice Hershel, M.D.*
Medical Examiner

O 1033-3   (6-74)

Appendix B. Whole Life Insurance Policy Form

Whole Life Insurance Policy

If the Insured dies while this Policy is in force, we will pay the Sum Insured to the Beneficiary, when we receive at our Home Office due proof of the Insured's death, subject to the provisions of this Policy.

Right to Examine and Return Policy Within 10 Days

You may, at any time within 10 days after receipt of this Policy, return it to us at our Home Office or to the Agent through whom it was purchased, and we will cancel it. The return of the Policy will void it from the beginning and any premium paid will be refunded to the owner.

Muriel L Crawford   *George P. Kendall.*
Secretary   President

Signed for the Company at Evanston, Illinois, on the Policy Date.

WHOLE LIFE INSURANCE POLICY

Premium Payable for A Stated Period
or Until Prior Death of Insured

Sum Insured Payable at Death

Non-Participating

Washington national®
INSURANCE COMPANY
EVANSTON, ILLINOIS 60201

OP 800   Page 1   (5-85)

Alphabetical Guide To Your Policy

Provision	Section
Automatic Premium Loan	16
Beneficiary	4
Cash Values*	Page 3A (B-C)
Change of Beneficiary	4
Collateral Assignment	5
Common Disaster	4
Computation of Guaranteed Values	20
Definitions	1
Entire Contract	2
Extended Term Insurance*	18
Grace Period	8
Incontestability	11
Incorrect Age or Sex	6
Indebtedness	13
Loans	15
Nonforfeiture Benefit Options*	18
Non-Participating	12
Ownership	3
Paid-Up Insurance	18
Policy Exchange Privilege	17
Premiums	7
Premium Refund at Death	9
Reinstatement	14
Right to Examine Contract	Page 1
Settlement Options	Page 8
Suicide	10
Table of Guaranteed Values	19

*Pages 3B and C are not included if your policy does not contain additional benefit rider(s) with cash value(s).

Additional Benefits

The additional benefits, if any, listed on page 3 are described in the additional benefit agreements that follow page 10.

Page 2

```
INSURED:                    JOHN A DOE

AGE AND SEX:                    34 MALE

POLICY NUMBER:                2 222 299

POLICY DATE:        FEBRUARY  01, 1988

SUM INSURED:                   $50,000

PREMIUM CLASS:                STANDARD
```

PAGE 3

POLICY SPECIFICATIONS

INSURED   JOHN A DOE   AGE 34   SEX MALE

POLICY DATE   FEBRUARY 01, 1988   2 222 299   POLICY NUMBER

SUM INSURED $50,000

PREMIUM CLASS   STANDARD

SCHEDULE OF BENEFITS AND PREMIUMS

BENEFIT DESCRIPTION	SUM INSURED	BENEFIT TERMINATES	ANNUAL PREMIUM	PREMIUM PERIOD
WHOLE LIFE	$50,000	LIFE	$783.25	LIFE
DISABILITY PREMIUM WAIVER		FEB 01, 2019	$25.00	31 YEARS
ACCIDENTAL DEATH BENEFIT	$50,000	FEB 01, 2024	$50.00	36 YEARS
GUARANTEED INSURABILITY	$10,000	FEB 01, 1997	$27.20	9 YEARS

TOTAL PREMIUM $885.45

PAGE 3 (CONT'D)

```
INSURED     JOHN A DOE                    2 222 299    POLICY NUMBER
                          SCHEDULE OF TOTAL PREMIUMS

      BEGINNING
MONTH  DAY  YEAR        ANNUAL      SEMIANNUAL        QUARTERLY         MONTHLY

  FEB   01  1988    $   885.45   $   452.65    $    231.35    $     77.30
  FEB   01  1997    $   858.25   $   438.75    $    224.25    $     75.00
  FEB   01  2019    $   833.25   $   425.75    $    217.75    $     72.50
  FEB   01  2024    $   783.25   $   400.25    $    204.75    $     68.00
```

PAGE 3 (CONT'D)

```
                                    2 222 299    POLICY NUMBER

INSURED    JOHN A DOE               AGE 34       SEX  MALE

                TABLE OF GUARANTEED VALUES
                       WHOLE LIFE
                SUM INSURED $   50,000
```

END OF POLICY YEAR	CASH OR LOAN VALUE	PAID-UP INS. VALUE	EXTENDED INSURANCE YEARS	DAYS
1	$ 305.00	$ 1,150	1	310
2	937.00	3,300	5	28
3	1,588.50	5,450	7	211
4	2,259.00	7,450	9	201
5	2,947.50	9,450	11	39
6	3,653.50	11,300	12	122
7	4,376.00	13,150	13	115
8	5,115.50	14,850	14	37
9	5,871.50	16,550	14	264
10	6,645.00	18,150	15	78
11	7,434.50	19,700	15	216
12	8,240.50	21,200	15	320
13	9,062.00	22,600	16	29
14	9,898.00	23,950	16	77
15	10,748.00	25,300	16	104
16	11,611.50	26,550	16	111
17	12,486.50	27,750	16	100
18	13,373.50	28,900	16	74
19	14,271.50	30,000	16	35
20	15,179.50	31,050	15	348
@60	20,627.00	36,250	14	213
@62	22,460.00	37,700	14	12
@65	25,184.50	39,650	13	60

```
    NON-FORFEITURE FACTOR       FIRST YEAR       1945.32050
                                2 TO 20 YEARS    734.99400.
                                THEREAFTER       712.07800
                        0
    POLICY LOAN INTEREST RATE IS 8% (PAID IN ARREARS) COMPOUNDED ANNUALLY

                        0
                        PAGE 3 A
```

1. Definitions

We, our, us – The Washington National Insurance Company.

You, your – the owner of this Policy.

Policy Date – the effective date of coverage under the Policy and the date from which policy anniversaries, policy years, policy months and premium due dates are determined. The Policy Date is also the Date of Issue of this Policy.

Policy Anniversary – the same day and month as the Policy Date for each succeeding year this policy remains in force.

Attained age – the Insured's age at issue plus the number of years and completed months from the Policy Date.

Written request – in a written form satisfactory to us, signed by you and filed in our Home Office at Evanston, Illinois.

Indebtedness – unpaid policy loans and unpaid loan interest.

In force – the Insured's life remains insured under the terms of this Policy.

Insured – the person whose life is insured under this Policy as shown on page three.

Beneficiary – the person or entity to receive the proceeds in the event of the Insured's death.

Proceeds – the amount we are obligated to pay under the terms of this Policy when it is surrendered, matures or when the Insured dies.

2. Entire Contract

We have issued this Policy in consideration of the application and payment of the premiums. A copy of the application is attached and is a part of this Policy. The Policy with the application makes the entire contract. All statements made by or for the Insured will be considered representations and not warranties. We will not use any statement in defense of a claim unless it is made in the application and a copy of the application is attached to this Policy when issued.

Only our President, one of our Vice Presidents, our Secretary or our Actuary has the authority to modify or waive any provision in this Policy, and then only in writing. No Agent or other person has the authority to change or waive any provision of this Policy.

3. Ownership

You, as the owner of this Policy, are named as owner in the application. You may exercise all the rights and options that this Policy provides, while the Insured is living, subject to the rights of any irrevocable beneficiary. If you are not the Insured and you die before the Insured,

your estate will become the owner unless you have made a written request naming a contingent owner.

You may name a new owner or contingent owner at any time while the Insured is living by filing a written request with us. Your written request will not be effective until it is recorded in our Home Office. Once recorded, the change will be effective as of the date you signed the request whether or not you or the Insured is alive when we record the change. However, the change will be subject to any payments made or other action taken by us before your request was recorded in our Home Office.

4. Beneficiary

The beneficiary named in the application will receive the death proceeds unless you name a new beneficiary. In that event, we will pay the death proceeds to the beneficiary named in your last change-of-beneficiary request as provided in this Policy.

You may name a new beneficiary by filing a written request with us. The written consent of any irrevocable beneficiary will be required. Your change-of-beneficiary request will not be effective until recorded by us at our Home Office. Once recorded, the change will be effective as of the date you signed the request whether or not you or the Insured is alive when we record the change. However, the change will be subject to any payments made or other action taken by us before your request was recorded in our Home Office.

Unless otherwise provided in the application or in a written request, if more than one primary beneficiary is named in the application, death proceeds will be paid in equal shares to the primary beneficiaries who survive the Insured. If none survive, death proceeds will be paid in equal shares to the contingent beneficiaries who survive the Insured. If no beneficiary survives the Insured, death proceeds will be paid to you, if you are living, otherwise to your estate.

If any beneficiary dies simultaneously with the Insured or during the 14 days immediately following the date of death of the Insured, the proceeds of this Policy shall, unless otherwise provided in the application or in a written request, be paid to the same payee or payees and in the same manner as if the deceased beneficiary had died before the Insured. Any reference in this Policy to a beneficiary living or surviving shall mean living on the 15th day immediately following the date of death of the Insured.

5. Collateral Assignment

You may assign this Policy as collateral for a loan without the consent of any revocable beneficiary. We are not bound by any assignment unless it is in writing and recorded at our Home Office. We are not responsible for the validity of any assignment. The rights of an assignee will at all times be subject to any indebtedness to us at the time the assignment is recorded by us, and, if applicable, to loans granted at anytime by us under the automatic premium loan provision of the Policy.

6. Incorrect Age or Sex

This Policy is issued at the age shown on page three, which should be the age attained by the Insured on the last birthday prior to the Policy Date. If the Policy Date falls on the Insured's birthday, the age should be the Insured's attained age on the Policy Date.

If the Insured's age or sex is incorrectly shown on page three, we will adjust the proceeds payable under this Policy to the proceeds the premium would have purchased at the correct age and sex based upon our rates in effect when this Policy was issued.

7. Premiums

The first premium is due on the Policy Date. Future premium due dates are determined by the frequency of payment you selected in the application. The amount of premiums, their due dates, and the period of years for which they are payable are shown on page three.

You may change the frequency of premium payment on any premium due date so that the interval between premium due dates is exactly twelve, six or three months. Other intervals may be permitted with our consent. The premium for any frequency will be based on our rates in effect on the Policy Date.

Each premium must be paid on or before its due date, or within the grace period. Premiums can either be mailed to us at our Home Office or paid to an authorized agent. Upon request, we will give you a receipt signed by our President or Secretary.

8. Grace Period

We will allow a period of 31 days after the premium due date for payment of each premium after the first. This is the grace period. If the Insured dies during the grace period before the premium is paid, we will deduct one month's premium from the death proceeds of this Policy.

If any premium is not paid on or before its due date, that premium is in default. If that premium is still unpaid at the expiration of the grace period, this Policy terminates except for any nonforfeiture benefits.

9. Premium Refund at Death

Any portion of a paid premium which applies to a period beyond the end of the policy month of the Insured's death will be added to the proceeds payable under this Policy.

Premiums waived under any disability rider attached to this Policy will not be refunded.

10. Suicide

If the Insured dies by suicide, while sane or insane, within two years from the Policy Date, our liability will be limited to the amount of the premiums paid, less any indebtedness.

11. Incontestability

We will not contest the validity of this Policy, except for nonpayment of premiums, after it has been in force during the Insured's lifetime for two years from the Policy Date. This provision does not apply to any rider providing accidental death or disability benefits.

12. Non-Participating

The premium rates for this Policy are guaranteed. Therefore, the Policy will not participate in any surplus earnings of the Company.

13. Indebtedness

Indebtedness will be deducted in any settlement under this Policy.

14. Reinstatement

If this Policy lapses due to an unpaid premium, it may be reinstated subject to the following conditions:

1) The Insured must be alive and still insurable by our standards; and

2) Any indebtedness which existed at the time of termination must either be paid or reinstated with interest compounded annually at the loan interest rate shown on page three; and

3) Each unpaid premium must be paid, with interest of 6% per annum compounded annually, from its due date to the reinstatement date; and

4) The request for reinstatement must be made by you in writing and submitted to our Home Office within 5 years after the date the Policy lapses; and

5) If you are not the Insured, the request for reinstatement must also be signed by the Insured if age 15 or older, last birthday, on the reinstatement date.

A Policy which has been surrendered for its cash value may not be reinstated.

15. Policy Loans

You may obtain a loan from us whenever this Policy has a loan value. The loan value is the amount which, with interest at the loan interest rate stated on page three computed to the next premium due date, or to the next Policy anniversary if no further premiums are payable, will equal the cash surrender value on such date or anniversary. Any premium due and unpaid at the time the loan is made will be deducted from the loan proceeds. You cannot obtain a loan if this Policy is in force as Extended Term Insurance. This Policy is the sole security for any loan.

We have the right to postpone your loan for up to six months unless the loan is to be used to pay premiums on any policies you have with us.

We will charge daily interest on policy loans at the rate stated on page three. Interest is payable on each policy anniversary. Any interest not paid when due is added to the loan.

If this Policy is in force and not on Extended Term Insurance, your loan can be repaid in full or in part at any time before the Insured's death. However, any loan repayment must be at least $20 unless the balance due is less than $20, in which case the loan repayment must be for the full amount of the loan.

Any indebtedness will be deducted from any proceeds paid under this Policy.

Whenever the indebtedness on this Policy is more than the Policy's guaranteed cash surrender value, this Policy terminates. We will mail a notice to your last known address, and to that of any assignee whose interest we have recorded, at least 31 days before such termination.

16. Automatic Premium Loan

This provision will be in effect only if you have requested it in the application or in a written request at a time when no premium is unpaid beyond its grace period. You may cancel the effect of this provision in the same manner.

If this provision is in effect, any premium which remains unpaid at the end of a grace period will be paid by automatic loan. We may change the frequency of premium payment so that the interval between premium due dates is three, six, or twelve months after the first premium has been paid by automatic loan. If the loan value of this Policy is not sufficient to pay the premium due, the Nonforfeiture Benefit Options will apply.

Any automatic loan will be subject to the Policy Loan provisions.

17. Policy Exchange Privilege

While this policy is in force with no premium in default, you may exchange the Policy for another form of Policy. Our approval is needed. An additional payment and evidence the Insured is then insurable under our underwriting rules then in effect may be required.

18. Nonforfeiture Benefit Options

If you discontinue premium payments after this Policy has a cash value, you may, subject to the following conditions and limitations, choose one of these Options:

(a) Cash Surrender. You may surrender the Policy to us for its cash surrender value. Once the Policy is surrendered, it is no longer eligible for reinstatement.

(b) Paid-Up Insurance. You may apply the cash surrender value to purchase a fully paid whole life policy for a reduced amount of insurance. The amount of such insurance will be that amount which the cash surrender value will buy when applied as a net single premium at the Insured's then attained age as of the due date of the first unpaid premium. Reduced Paid-Up Insurance has cash and loan values.

(c) Extended Term Insurance. If the Premium Class shown on page three is "Standard," you may continue the Policy as paid-up term insurance. The amount of such term insurance will be the Sum Insured less any indebtedness. The term period will begin on the due date of the first unpaid premium and will be such as the cash surrender value will provide as a net single premium at the Insured's then attained age. At the end of the term period all insurance under this Policy will terminate.

You may elect a Nonforfeiture Benefit Option within 60 days of the due date of the first unpaid premium. Your written election should be sent to us at our Home Office. If no election is made during this period, we will

1) If the Premium Class shown on page three is "Standard" automatically continue this Policy as Extended Term Insurance under Option (c); or

2) If the Premium Class shown on page three is "Rated" automatically continue this Policy as Paid-Up Insurance under Option (b).

Any insurance provided under Option (b) or (c) may be surrendered at any time for its then present value. If surrendered within 30 days of a policy anniversary, the present value will not be less than the value on that anniversary.

The term "cash surrender value" as used in this Policy means the cash value shown in the Table of Guaranteed Values on page three, less any existing indebtedness.

We may delay paying the cash surrender value for up to six months from the date surrender is requested.

19. Table of Guaranteed Values

This Policy's guaranteed values are shown in the table on page three. The table assumes that premiums have been paid to the end of the policy year indicated and that there is no indebtedness. We will determine the cash value at any time within a policy year, with allowance for the time elapsed in such year and for the period premiums have been paid. We will furnish values upon request for policy years not shown.

20. Computation of Guaranteed Values

Reserves, cash and present values, and net single premiums are calculated on the basis of the Commissioner's 1958 Standard Ordinary Mortality Table except that calculations for Extended Term Insurance are based on the Commissioner's 1958 Extended Term Insurance Table. Both tables assume continuous functions, age last birthday, with interest at the rate of 4% compounded annually. Computations are made on the assumption that death benefits are paid immediately upon death. In making these calculations the premium for, or the value of, any additional benefit provided by rider is excluded.

Cash values are calculated by the Standard Non-Forfeiture Value Method; using the non-forfeiture factor or factors shown in the Table of Guaranteed Values. The amount of Paid-Up Insurance or the term of Extended Insurance which could be purchased at any time is that which the cash surrender value would purchase when applied as a net single premium at the Insured's attained age.

The cash values and non-forfeiture benefits provided by this Policy equal or exceed those required by the laws of the state governing this Policy. A detailed statement of the method of computation of non-forfeiture values has been filed with the insurance supervisory official of such state.

Settlement Options

Election of Options

You may elect to have all or part of the proceeds of this Policy applied under one of the following settlement options. You may cancel or change a previous election, but only if you do so prior to the death of the Insured or the endowment maturity date of the policy, if applicable. If you do not elect a settlement option prior to the Insured's death, the beneficiary may do so provided the election is made within one year after the date of death of the Insured. Any settlement option election will be subject to the limitations and conditions set forth on page 8.

Any election or cancellation of a settlement option must be in writing in a form satisfactory to us. At the time an option is elected, we will prepare an agreement to be signed which will state the terms and conditions under which payments will be made. Any change of beneficiary will cancel any previous election of a settlement option.

OPTION 1 - Income for a Fixed Period

We will pay the proceeds in equal installments over a period of from one to thirty years. The amount of each installment will be based upon the period and the frequency of the installments selected from Table 1 on page 9.

OPTION 2 - Income for Life

We will pay a monthly income during a person's lifetime. The monthly income may be a life annuity only - Option 2(A), a life annuity with a minimum guaranteed period of 5, 10, or 20 years - Option 2(B), or an installment refund life annuity - Option 2(C), as shown in Table 2 on page 9. Payments will be at least equal to the amount shown in Table 2. Higher payments may be made at our discretion.

OPTION 3 - Income of a Fixed Amount

We will pay the proceeds in equal installments in the amount and at the intervals agreed upon until the proceeds applied under this option, with interest at 2 1/2% per annum, are exhausted. The final installment will be for the then remaining balance only.

OPTION 4 - Interest Income

We will hold the proceeds on deposit and pay or credit interest at the rate of 2 1/2% per annum. Payment of interest will be at such times and for such periods as are agreeable to you and us.

OPTION 5 - Joint and Survivor Income for Life

We will pay an income during the lifetime of two payees, and continuing until the death of the survivor. This option includes a minimum guaranteed period of 10 years. Payments will be at least equal to the amount shown in Table 3. Higher payments may be made at our discretion. On request, we will furnish minimum income information for age combinations not shown in the table.

OPTION 6 - Joint and Two-thirds Survivor Income for Life

We will pay an income (the "original amount") during the time two persons both remain alive, and two-thirds of the original amount during the remaining lifetime of the survivor. Payments during the time both payees are alive will be at least equal to the amount shown in Table 3. Higher payments may be made at our discretion. On request, we will furnish minimum income information for age combinations not shown in the table.

Limitations/Conditions

1. The amount applied under any Settlement Option must be at least $2,000 and must be sufficient to provide a periodic installment or interest payment of at least $20.

2. An Option will be available without our consent only if the proceeds are payable to a natural person receiving for his or her own benefit.

3. We may require proof of the age of any payee under Option 2, 5, or 6. We also may require evidence that the payee is living at the time any payment is due.

4. The first payment under an Option will be due on the date proceeds are applied, except under Option 4 it will be due at the end of the first payment interval.

Death of Payee

If the last surviving payee dies while receiving payments under an Option, we will pay as follows:

1. If Option 1 was elected, an amount equal to the commuted value of any unpaid installments.

2. If Option 2(B) or 5 was elected, an amount equal to the commuted value of any unpaid installments for the guaranteed period.

3. If Option 2(C) was elected, an amount equal to the commuted value of any unpaid installments required to equal the amount of proceeds applied under the Option.

4. If option 3 or 4 was elected, an amount equal to any proceeds still on deposit plus accrued interest.

5. If Option 2A or 6 was elected, an amount equal to any unpaid installment due prior to the death of the payee under Option 2A or the last survivor under Option 6.

Commuted values under Option 1 will be calculated by us using 2 1/2% interest per year, compounded annually. Commuted values under Options 2(B), 2(C), or 5 will be calculated by us using interest compounded annually at the rate of 2 1/2% per year, or the rate of interest used in the calculation of the amount of the monthly installments, whichever is higher. Unless we have agreed otherwise in writing, payment shall be made in one sum to the payee's estate.

Surrender of Benefits

Unless the right was reserved in the Settlement Option election, no payee is allowed to (a) assign or borrow against the proceeds of an Option, (b) receive any installment payments in advance, or (c) make any changes in the provisions elected. All benefits shall be exempt from the claims of creditors to the maximum extent permitted by law.

Excess Interest

We may pay or credit excess interest of such amount and in such manner as we determine.

Settlement Option Tables

Monthly installments are shown per $1,000 of proceeds and are calculated using an interest rate of 2 1/2% per year, compounded annually. Installment amounts under Options 2, 5, and 6 depend on the sex and age last birthday of the payee or payees on the date the first installment is due. Installments for any age or combination of ages not shown in Table 2 or 3 (Minimum age 50) will be furnished by us on request.

TABLE 1 -- Income for a Fixed Period

(Annual, semiannual, or quarterly installments shall be determined by multiplying the monthly installment by 11.865, 5.969, or 2.994 respectively.)

Years	Monthly Installment	Years	Monthly Installment	Years	Monthly Installment	Years	Monthly Installment	Years	Monthly Installment	Years	Monthly Installment
1	$84.28	6	$14.93	11	$8.64	16	$6.30	21	$5.08	26	$4.34
2	42.66	7	12.95	12	8.02	17	6.00	22	4.90	27	4.22
3	28.79	8	11.47	13	7.49	18	5.73	23	4.74	28	4.12
4	21.86	9	10.32	14	7.03	19	5.49	24	4.60	29	4.02
5	17.70	10	9.39	15	6.64	20	5.27	25	4.46	30	3.93

TABLE 2 -- Income for Life

Age of Payee		2A Life Annuity	2B Guaranteed Period			2C Installment Refund	Age of Payee		2A Life Annuity	2B Guaranteed Period			2C Installment Refund
Male	Female		5 Years	10 Years	20 Years		Male	Female		5 Years	10 Years	20 Years	
46	51	$4.08	$4.07	$4.03	$3.87	$3.83	66	71	$7.05	$6.88	$6.41	$5.04	$5.85
47	52	4.16	4.15	4.11	3.93	3.89	67	72	7.32	7.12	6.58	5.08	6.02
48	53	4.25	4.24	4.19	3.99	3.96	68	73	7.61	7.38	6.75	5.12	6.19
49	54	4.35	4.33	4.28	4.05	4.03	69	74	7.92	7.65	6.93	5.15	6.38
50	55	4.45	4.43	4.37	4.11	4.10	70	75	8.25	7.93	7.11	5.17	6.57
51	56	4.55	4.53	4.46	4.17	4.16	71	76	8.61	8.24	7.29	5.20	6.78
52	57	4.66	4.64	4.56	4.24	4.25	72	77	9.00	8.55	7.47	5.22	7.00
53	58	4.78	4.75	4.66	4.30	4.34	73	78	9.41	8.89	7.65	5.23	7.23
54	59	4.90	4.86	4.76	4.37	4.42	74	79	9.86	9.24	7.83	5.24	7.48
55	60	5.02	4.99	4.87	4.43	4.51	75	80	10.35	9.61	8.00	5.25	7.74
56	61	5.16	5.11	4.98	4.49	4.61	76	81	10.87	10.00	8.17	5.26	8.02
57	62	5.30	5.25	5.10	4.56	4.70	77	82	11.44	10.40	8.33	5.26	8.32
58	63	5.45	5.39	5.23	4.62	4.81	78	83	12.05	10.82	8.46	5.27	8.63
59	64	5.61	5.54	5.35	4.68	4.92	79	84	12.71	11.25	8.62	5.27	8.97
60	65	5.77	5.70	5.49	4.74	5.03	80	85	13.44	11.69	8.74	5.27	9.33
61	66	5.95	5.87	5.63	4.80	5.15	81	85 and over	14.22	12.14	8.85	5.27	9.71
62	67	6.15	6.05	5.77	4.85	5.27	82		15.07	12.60	8.96	5.27	10.12
63	68	6.35	6.24	5.92	4.91	5.41	83		15.99	13.06	9.05	5.27	10.56
64	69	6.57	6.44	6.08	4.96	5.55	84		17.00	13.52	9.13	5.27	11.02
65	70	6.80	6.66	6.24	5.00	5.69	85 and over		18.09	13.96	9.19	5.27	11.52

TABLE 3 -- Joint and Survivor Life Income

OPTION 5
Joint Life Income with Installments Guaranteed for 10 Years

Age of Payee M F	F50	M50 F55	M55 F60	M57 F62	M58 F63	M59 F64	M60 F65	M62 F67	M65 F70	M70 F75
50 55	$3.57	$3.75	$3.91	$3.97	$4.00	$4.02	$4.05	$4.10	$4.16	$4.25
55 60	3.67	3.91	4.14	4.23	4.27	4.31	4.35	4.43	4.53	4.68
56 61	3.69	3.94	4.18	4.28	4.32	4.37	4.41	4.49	4.61	4.77
57 62	3.71	3.97	4.23	4.33	4.38	4.42	4.47	4.56	4.69	4.86
58 63	3.73	4.00	4.27	4.38	4.43	4.48	4.53	4.63	4.77	4.96
59 64	3.74	4.02	4.31	4.42	4.48	4.53	4.59	4.70	4.84	5.05
60 65	3.76	4.05	4.35	4.47	4.53	4.59	4.65	4.76	4.92	5.15
61 66	3.77	4.07	4.39	4.52	4.58	4.64	4.70	4.83	5.00	5.25
62 67	3.79	4.10	4.43	4.56	4.63	4.70	4.76	4.89	5.08	5.36
63 68	3.80	4.12	4.46	4.60	4.68	4.75	4.82	4.96	5.16	5.46
64 69	3.82	4.14	4.50	4.65	4.72	4.80	4.87	5.02	5.24	5.57
65 70	3.83	4.16	4.53	4.69	4.77	4.84	4.92	5.08	5.31	5.67
66 71	3.84	4.18	4.56	4.73	4.81	4.89	4.97	5.14	5.39	5.77
67 72	3.85	4.20	4.60	4.76	4.85	4.93	5.02	5.20	5.46	5.88
68 73	3.87	4.22	4.62	4.80	4.89	4.98	5.07	5.25	5.54	5.98
69 74	3.88	4.24	4.65	4.83	4.92	5.02	5.11	5.31	5.60	6.08
70 75	3.89	4.25	4.68	4.86	4.96	5.05	5.15	5.36	5.67	6.18

OPTION 6
Joint Life Income with Two-thirds to Survivor

Age of Payee M F	F50	M50 F55	M55 F60	M57 F62	M58 F63	M59 F64	M60 F65	M62 F67	M65 F70	M70 F75
50 55	$3.97	$4.19	$4.42	$4.51	$4.56	$4.61	$4.66	$4.75	$4.91	$5.17
55 60	4.16	4.42	4.70	4.81	4.87	4.93	4.99	5.11	5.31	5.64
56 61	4.20	4.46	4.75	4.87	4.94	5.00	5.06	5.19	5.39	5.74
57 62	4.24	4.51	4.81	4.94	5.00	5.07	5.13	5.27	5.48	5.84
58 63	4.27	4.55	4.87	5.00	5.07	5.13	5.20	5.35	5.57	5.95
59 64	4.31	4.61	4.93	5.07	5.13	5.21	5.28	5.43	5.66	6.06
60 65	4.35	4.66	4.99	5.13	5.20	5.28	5.36	5.51	5.75	6.17
61 66	4.39	4.70	5.05	5.20	5.28	5.35	5.43	5.60	5.85	6.30
62 67	4.43	4.75	5.11	5.27	5.35	5.43	5.51	5.68	5.95	6.41
63 68	4.47	4.80	5.18	5.34	5.42	5.50	5.59	5.77	6.05	6.54
64 69	4.51	4.85	5.24	5.41	5.49	5.58	5.67	5.86	6.18	6.67
65 70	4.56	4.91	5.31	5.48	5.57	5.66	5.75	5.95	6.26	6.80
66 71	4.60	4.96	5.37	5.55	5.64	5.74	5.83	6.04	6.35	6.94
67 72	4.64	5.01	5.44	5.62	5.72	5.82	5.92	6.13	6.47	7.08
68 73	4.68	5.06	5.50	5.70	5.79	5.90	6.01	6.23	6.58	7.22
69 74	4.73	5.12	5.57	5.77	5.87	5.98	6.09	6.32	6.69	7.37
70 75	4.77	5.17	5.64	5.84	5.95	6.06	6.17	6.41	6.80	7.52

WASHINGTON NATIONAL INSURANCE COMPANY
Evanston, Illinois

Attached to and Forming a

Part of Policy No. `772222299`

Issued on the Life of. John A. Doe

Effective Date February 1, 1988

AVIATION EXCLUSION PROVISION

The liability under this Policy shall be limited to the amount specified below if the death of the Insured occurs as a result of travel or flight in any kind of aircraft while the Insured (1) is a pilot, officer or member of the crew of such aircraft, or (2) is participating in aeronautic or aviation training during such flight, or (3) is in a military, naval or air force aircraft while under flight orders or on flying status in the military, naval or air forces of any country. Descent from or with any kind of aircraft in flight shall be deemed to be part of such flight.

In event the Insured's death should occur under any of the conditions defined above, the Company's liability shall be limited to the payment of a single sum equal to the greater of (a) the premiums paid on this Policy, decreased by any indebtedness on or secured by this Policy, or (b) the reserve under this Policy, less any indebtedness on or secured by this Policy; provided, however, that in no event shall such liability be greater than the amount payable in the absence of this provision. If no basis for the computation of reserves is specified in this Policy, reserves shall be computed according to the Commissioners 1941 Standard Ordinary Mortality Table, with 3% interest and on the basis of the Commissioners Reserve Valuation Method.

The limitations of liability contained herein shall also apply to any reduced paid-up insurance or extended term insurance put in force in accordance with any non-forfeiture provisions contained in this Policy, and shall be included in any policy to which this Policy may be changed or converted.

If this Policy has attached thereto any supplementary contract for an additional benefit in the event of accidental death, the conditions and exceptions contained therein shall not be affected by this provision.

The provision of this Policy entitled "Incontestability" is hereby amended to read as follows:

This Policy shall be incontestable after 2 years from its date of issue except (a) for non-payment of premiums, (b) as to any provision for an additional benefit in the event of accidental death, (c) as to any provision for benefits in the event of total and permanent disability and (d) for the limitation of benefits contained in the provision entitled Aviation Exclusion Provision.

AMENDMENT OF APPLICATION

It is agreed and understood that my original application for insurance under the above designated Policy is hereby amended to permit the inclusion in such Policy of the foregoing Aviation Exclusion Provision and that such provision shall be attached to and made a part of such Policy.

Dated at _Evanston, Ill._ this _8_ day of _Feb._, 19_88_

John A Doe

The foregoing Aviation Exclusion Provision shall become operative as of the Effective Date shown above.

WASHINGTON NATIONAL INSURANCE COMPANY

Muriel L Crawford

SECRETARY

O 1109

(1-69)

WASHINGTON NATIONAL INSURANCE COMPANY
EVANSTON, ILLINOIS 60201

WAIVER OF PREMIUM DISABILITY BENEFIT RIDER

THIS RIDER IS A PART OF THE POLICY TO WHICH IT IS ATTACHED

Benefit

We will waive premiums for the Policy while the Insured is totally disabled. However, the Insured must be totally disabled for six consecutive months to qualify for this benefit. Waiver of any premium is subject to the terms of this Rider and the Policy.

Disability must commence:

1) on or after the effective date of this Rider; and

2) while this Rider is in force with no premium more than 31 days overdue; and

3) on or after the policy anniversary on which the Insured's age is 5; and

4) before the policy anniversary on which the Insured's age is 65.

Definition of Total Disability

Total disability is defined as follows. It is the Insured's inability to:

1) engage in an occupation for remuneration; or

2) engage in an occupation for profit.

The inability must result from:

  (a) an injury; or

  (b) a sickness.

Occupation is defined as follows:

1) It is any occupation for which the Insured is qualified by reason of:

  (a) an education; or

  (b) some training; or

  (c) some experience.

2) It is also any occupation for which the Insured could become qualified by reason of:

  (a) an education; or

  (b) some training; or

  (c) some experience.

Engaging in an occupation for remuneration; or engaging in one for profit, include:

1) being a homemaker; and

2) attending school as a full time student;

if that is the Insured's principal occupation at the time total disability begins.

Total disability shall also include the following. If the Insured has totally lost:

1) the sight of both eyes; or

2) the use of both hands; or

3) the use of both feet; or

4) the use of one hand and one foot;

then the Insured is totally disabled. We will waive premiums as long as:

1) such loss of sight continues; or

2) such loss of use continues.

Risks Not Covered

Certain risks are not covered. They are as follows. We will not waive premiums if total disability results from:

1) intentionally self-inflicted injury while sane; or

2) self-inflicted injury while insane; or

3) war, or any act of war; whether or not the Insured is in military service. The term "war" includes armed aggression resisted by:

  (a) the armed forces of any country; or

  (b) any international organization; or

  (c) any combination of countries.

Notice of Claim

Written notice of claim must be received:

1) at our Home Office; and

2) during the Insured's lifetime; and

3) during the continuance of total disability;

unless it can be shown that such notice was given as soon as reasonably possible.

Proof of Disability

We must receive due proof of total disability before we will waive any premium. Afterwards, we may ask for proof that total disability continues. This will be done at reasonable intervals. After two years, "reasonable intervals" shall mean annually; or less often at our option. As part of due proof, we may require the Insured to be examined by a medical examiner of our choice. We will pay for the examination. We will advise you of this requirement. We will do so in writing.

Commencement of Benefits

We will waive premiums beginning with the first premium due after the date total disability begins. If any such premium has been paid, we will refund it to you. However, no premium which became due more than one year prior to the time we receive written notice of disability will be waived or refunded. If disability begins during the Grace Period of a premium in default, we will not waive the payment of that premium. Premiums will be waived in accordance with the mode of payment in effect at the time disability begins. Any premium we waive will not be deducted in any settlement under the Policy.

Discontinuance of Benefits

You must again pay premiums beginning with the policy month following the earliest of:

1) termination of the Insured's total disability; or

2) failure of the Insured to have a medical exam when we request one; or

3) failure to furnish due proof that the Insured is still totally disabled when we request it.

We will advise you of the premium due date. We will do so in writing.

Termination of Rider

This Rider shall terminate upon the earliest of:

1) the anniversary of the Policy on which the Insured's age is 65; or

2) when any premium: (a) for the Policy; or (b) for this Rider is in default beyond the end of its grace period; or

3) the date the Policy matures; or

4) the date the Policy terminates; or

5) the date the Policy is surrendered; or

6) the date the Policy is continued under a non-forfeiture benefit option, if any.

Any termination of this Rider will be without prejudice to any existing claim.

Cancellation

You may cancel this Rider by written request. This can be done on the due date of any premium. The Policy must be sent to us.

Consideration

This Disability Benefit is granted in consideration of:

1) the application; and

2) the payment of the additional premium specified on page three of the Policy.

Payment of the additional premium is subject to the same conditions as the premium for the Policy. However, the additional premium shall cease to be payable whenever this Rider terminates or is cancelled.

Effective Date

Unless otherwise specified on page three of the Policy, the effective date of this Rider shall be the policy date of the Policy.

Nonforfeiture Benefit Limitations

If the Policy to which this Rider is attached contains nonforfeiture values, any insurance contained under the nonforfeiture value provisions in the basic Policy shall not include the benefits provided by this Rider.

WASHINGTON NATIONAL INSURANCE COMPANY

Muriel L. Crawford

SECRETARY

WASHINGTON NATIONAL INSURANCE COMPANY
EVANSTON, ILLINOIS 60201

ACCIDENTAL DEATH BENEFIT RIDER

THIS RIDER IS A PART OF THE POLICY TO WHICH IT IS ATTACHED

Benefit

We will pay the Accidental Death Benefit when we receive due proof of the accidental death of the Insured. The amount payable is shown on page three of the policy. We will pay the Beneficiary. Any payment is subject to the provisions of the Policy and this Rider.

Proof of the accidental death must show that death resulted solely and directly from: 1) an accidental bodily injury; or 2) an accidental drowning. Such death must occur on or after the effective date of this Rider:

1. while this Rider was in force with no premium more than 31 days overdue; and

2. within 90 days after the accidental injury; and

3. on or after the Policy anniversary on which the Insured's age is five; and

4. before the Policy anniversary on which the Insured's age is 70.

Definition of Accidental Death

Accidental death means death resulting directly and solely from:

(a) an accidental bodily injury visible on the surface of the body or disclosed by an autopsy;

(b) a disease or infection resulting from ptomaine poisoning or from an accidental bodily injury as described and beginning within 30 days after the date of the injury; or

(c) an accidental drowning.

Risks Not Covered

Certain risks are not covered. We will not pay the Accidental Death Benefit if the Insured's death results from any of the following causes:

1. Intentionally self-inflicted injury while sane; or

2. Self-inflicted injury while insane; or

3. Participation in an assault; or

4. Participation in a felony; or

5. Travel or flight in or descent from any kind of aircraft: (a) on which the Insured is a pilot, officer or member of the crew; or (b) on which the Insured has duties aboard; or (c) which is being operated for any training or instructional purpose; or (d) on which the Insured is being flown for the purpose of descent while in flight; or

6. Any bodily or mental infirmity existing before or beginning after the accident; or

7. Any infection or disease existing before or beginning after the accident, except a disease or infection as provided in the definition of "accidental death"; or

8. Any drug, medication or sedative voluntarily taken unless: (a) administered by a licensed physician; or (b) taken as prescribed by a licensed physician; or

9. Alcohol in combination with any drug, medication or sedative; or

10. Suicide, whether sane or insane; or

11. Any poison, gas or fumes voluntarily taken, absorbed or inhaled; or

12. War or any act of war, whether or not the Insured is in military service. The term "war" includes war declared or undeclared. It also includes armed aggression resisted by: (a) the armed forces of any country; and (b) any international organization or combination of countries.

Termination

This Rider shall terminate upon the earliest of:

1. The Policy anniversary on which the Insured's age is 70; or

2. When any premium for the Policy or this Rider is in default beyond the end of its grace period; or

3. The date the Policy terminates; or

O 2359-1   (3-83)

4. The date the Policy matures; or

5. The date the Policy is surrendered; or

6. The date the Policy is continued under a nonforfeiture benefit option.

Any termination shall not affect an existing claim.

Benefits Suspended

This Rider shall automatically be suspended during any period for which premiums are being waived under a Disability Benefit Rider attached to the Policy.

Cancellation

You may cancel this Rider on the due date of any premium. Your written request should be sent to our Home Office. The Policy should accompany your request.

Right of Autopsy

We shall have the right to examine the Insured's body. We shall have the right to perform an autopsy. However, our right expires 30 days after we receive due proof of the Insured's accidental death. Our right to an autopsy is subject to local law.

Consideration

This Benefit is granted in consideration of: 1) the application; and 2) the payment of the additional premium stated on page three of the Policy. Such payment is subject to the same conditions as the Policy's premiums. The additional premium shall cease to be payable when: 1) this Rider terminates; or 2) the Rider is cancelled.

Effective Date

The effective date of this Rider shall be the policy date of the Policy; unless otherwise specified on page three.

Nonforfeiture Benefit Limitations

Any nonforfeiture benefit option provisions in the Policy apply only to the Policy. Such provisions shall not include these Rider benefits.

WASHINGTON NATIONAL INSURANCE COMPANY

Muriel L. Crawford

SECRETARY

WASHINGTON NATIONAL INSURANCE COMPANY
EVANSTON, ILLINOIS 60201

INSURED SUBSTITUTION RIDER

THIS RIDER IS A PART OF THE POLICY TO WHICH IT IS ATTACHED

Benefit

You may exchange this Policy for a new policy on the life of a new Insured if:

1) this Policy is in force with no premium more than 31 days overdue; and

2) evidence of insurability of the new In--sured, satisfactory to us, is furnished; /and

3) the exchange is made prior to the policy anniversary on which the original Insured's age is 65.

An exchange is subject to the provisions of this Rider and the Policy. The exchange will be made upon: 1) your written request (and any assignee); and 2) surrender of this Policy.

Date of Exchange

The date of exchange shall be the same day of the month as the policy date of this Policy coincident with or next following: 1) the date we approve your exchange request: or 2) the date of payment for any cost of the exchange; whichever is later. We will advise you of this date. We will do so in writing.

New Policy Specifications

The policy date of the new policy shall be: 1) the policy date of this Policy; or 2) the first anniversary of this Policy following the birth date of the new Insured: whichever is later. The new policy shall be issued on the same plan of insurance as this Policy.

The sum insured of the new policy may be: 1) equal to the sum insured of this Policy (Option 1); or 2) such amount as the cash value of this Policy on the date of exchange will provide when transferred to the new policy (Option 2). You may elect either option. You must do so in writing. Option 2 is subject to our minimum amount rules.

Additional benefits may be included in the new policy only with our consent. We will require: 1) evidence of insurability of the new Insured; and 2) an additional payment for the benefit(s).

The suicide and incontestability provisions of the new policy will be operative from the date of exchange. The new policy will be subject to any existing collateral assignments of this Policy.

Cost of Exchange

The cost of the exchange is determined as follows:

1) Premiums on this Policy must be paid to the date of exchange. Premiums may be paid for a period beyond this date. If so, we will refund such premiums to you.

2) Premiums for the new policy will be based on: (a) our rates in effect on the date of exchange for the plan and sum insured of the new policy; (b) the new Insured's issue age on the policy date of the new policy; and (c) the class of risk of the new Insured on the date of exchange.

3) The amount of the first premium for new policy is as follows. It is the amount necessary to pay premiums from the date of exchange to the next regular premium due date. This date is determined by the frequency of payment you select in the application for exchange. We will: 1) calculate this amount; and 2) advise you accordingly. We will do so in writing. Payment is due on or before the date of exchange.

4) Any indebtedness on this Policy on the date of exchange will be transferred to the new policy. However, such indebtedness may exceed the loan value of the new policy. If so, the excess must be paid to us. Payment must be made on or before the date of exchange. We will: 1) calculate the excess amount; and 2) advise you of the amount due. We will do so in writing.

5) If Option 1 is elected, this Policy and the new policy may have different cash surrender values. If so, we will do as follows:

(a) If the cash surrender value of this Policy exceeds the cash surrender value of the new policy; we will pay the excess to you.

(b) If the cash surrender value of the new policy exceeds the cash surrender value of this Policy; we will

O 2367

(2-83)

require that you pay such excess to us. State premium tax; if applicable, will be added to the amount due.

Termination

This Rider shall terminate upon the earliest of:

1) the Policy anniversary on which the Insured's age is 65; or

2) when any premium for the Policy is in default beyond the end of its grace period; or

3) The date the Policy terminates; or

4) the date the Policy matures; or

5) the date the Policy is surrendered; or

6) the date the Policy is continued under a nonforfeiture benefit option.

General Provisions

This Rider is subject to all of the provisions contained: 1) in the Policy; and 2) in any Rider attached thereto insofar as such provisions are applicable to and not in conflict with this Rider. If the Policy to which this Rider is attached contains nonforfeiture benefit option provisions, any insurance contained under those provisions in the Policy shall not include the benefits provided by this Rider.

WASHINGTON NATIONAL INSURANCE COMPANY

Muriel L. Crawford

SECRETARY

WASHINGTON NATIONAL INSURANCE COMPANY
EVANSTON, ILLINOIS 60201

GUARANTEED INSURABILITY RIDER

THIS RIDER IS A PART OF THE POLICY TO WHICH IT IS ATTACHED

Option Dates

Each policy anniversary on which the Insured's age is 25, 28, 31, 34, 37, 40, or 43, and which occurs after the Effective Date of this Rider shall be an Option Date. However, any Option Date shall be canceled if the right to purchase additional insurance on that date is previously exercised under an "Advance Purchase Privilege."

Benefit

You may purchase a new policy on the life of the Insured on each Option Date if the Policy and this Rider are in force. However, your purchase will be subject to the provisions of the Policy and this Rider. Evidence of insurability will not be required.

Your written request for a new policy must be received by us on or within 60 days before the Option Date. Payment of the first premium must also be made on or before that date. The Option Date shall be the policy date of the new policy. The new policy will be effective on that date if the Insured is living and the first premium has been paid.

The new policy may be any form of Life or Endowment policy we then issue. The premium for the new policy will be based on the same risk classification as this Policy. It will be calculated using our rates then in use for the plan elected and for the then attained age of the Insured. If this Policy on the Option Date contains a disability benefit provision, a similar provision may be included in the new policy without evidence of insurability. However, the disability benefit will be included only if the Insured is not then totally disabled as defined in such provision. We will require evidence of insurability if any additional benefits are to be included in the new policy. We will also require an additional payment for such benefits.

The maximum amount of insurance you may purchase on any Option Date is the option amount shown on page three of this Policy. The minimum amount is the amount we will issue based on our rules in effect on the Option Date. However, the maximum amount may be increased as described in "Advance Purchase Privilege."

The incontestability and suicide provisions in the new policy shall be operative from the policy date of this Policy.

If you do not exercise your option to purchase a new policy on an Option Date, the option expires on that date.

Advance Purchase Privilege

Your right to purchase insurance on a future Option Date may be exercised immediately upon the happening of any of the following events:

1. the Insured's marriage; or

2. each birth of a living child to the Insured and his or her spouse; or

3. each legal adoption of a child by the Insured.

"Marriage" means a marriage ceremony legally performed by a third person.

The maximum amount of insurance you may purchase increases if there is a multiple birth or if more than one child is adopted on the same day. The maximum amount is the option amount shown on page three of the Policy multiplied by the number of children liveborn or adopted.

We must receive within 90 days of the event:

1. your written application for the new policy; and

2. proof satisfactory to us that the event happened.

The policy date of the new policy shall be the date of your application. The new policy shall be effective on the policy date or the date we receive the first premium, whichever is later, provided the Insured is then living.

The exercise of this Advance Purchase Privilege shall automatically cancel the next Option Date. If you do not exercise the privilege, it shall expire on the 90th day following the event.

Consideration

The consideration for this Rider is the application for the Policy and this Rider and the payment of the additional premium shown on page three of the Policy. Payment of the additional premium is subject to the same conditions as

O 2363

(10-82)

the premium for the Policy. However, the additional premium shall cease to be payable whenever this Rider terminates.

General Provisions

The payment of premiums for this Rider shall not increase the cash, loan or non-forfeiture values under the Policy.

This Rider is subject to all of the terms and conditions contained in the Policy insofar as such terms and conditions are applicable to and not in conflict with this Rider.

If the Policy to which this Rider is attached contains non-forfeiture values, any insurance contained under the non-forfeiture value provisions in the basic Policy shall not include the benefits provided by this Rider.

Effective Date

The effective date of this Rider shall be the policy date of the Policy.

Termination

This Rider shall terminate upon the earliest of:

1. the termination date shown on page three of the Policy; or

2. when any premium for the Policy or this Rider is in default beyond the end of its grace period; or

3. the date the Policy matures, terminates, is surrendered or continued under a non-forfeiture benefit option; or

4. upon cancellation or expiration of all Option Dates.

Cancellation

You may cancel this Rider on the due date of any premium by written request accompanied by the Policy for endorsement.

WASHINGTON NATIONAL INSURANCE COMPANY

Muriel L. Crawford

SECRETARY

WASHINGTON NATIONAL INSURANCE COMPANY   FOR MORE INFORMATION ABOUT THIS POLICY PLEASE CONTACT:
ORDINARY LIFE DEPARTMENT   02/02/88   HOME OFFICE
1630 CHICAGO AVENUE   POLICY NUMBER   HOME OFFICE
EVANSTON, ILLINOIS   60201   77-2222299-   WASHINGTON NATIONAL INS CO
                                                                         1630 CHICAGO AVENUE
                                                                         EVANSTON IL   60201

              STATEMENT OF POLICY COST AND BENEFIT INFORMATION
                      PREPARED FOR: DOE, JOHN A

              AGE BASIS: 34   ISSUE BASIS: STANDARD

BASIC POLICY   WHOLE LIFE

POL	----------	ANNUAL PREMIUMS	----------		GUAR AMT(2)	GUARANTEED CASH	
					PAYABLE	SURRENDER VALUE	
YR	COVERAGE	PRM WV	A D B	TOTAL	ON DEATH	TOTAL	INCR
		(1)					
01	783.25	25.00	50.00	858.25	50,000	305	305
02	783.25	25.00	50.00	858.25	50,000	937	632
03	783.25	25.00	50.00	858.25	50,000	1,589	652
04	783.25	25.00	50.00	858.25	50,000	2,259	670
05	783.25	25.00	50.00	858.25	50,000	2,948	689
10	783.25	25.00	50.00	858.25	50,000	6,645	3,697
20	783.25	25.00	50.00	858.25	50,000	15,180	8,535
31	783.25	25.00	50.00	858.25	50,000	25,185	10,005

(AGE 65)

EFFECTIVE POLICY LOAN INTEREST RATE IS 8.00% PAID IN ARREARS.

	SURRENDER	NET PAYMENT
	COST INDEX	COST INDEX
YEAR 10	5.601	15.665
YEAR 20	6.920	15.665

AN EXPLANATION OF THE INTENDED USE OF
EACH OF THESE INDEXES IS PROVIDED IN
THE LIFE INSURANCE BUYER'S GUIDE.

(1) PREMIUM PAYMENTS ARE WAIVED IN THE EVENT OF TOTAL DISABILITY.
(2) DEATH BENEFITS ARE DOUBLED IN THE EVENT OF DEATH DUE TO ACCIDENTAL DEATH.
(3) THE INFORMATION CONTAINED IN THIS POLICY SUMMARY IS GENERAL IN NATURE. A COMPLETE STATEMENT OF
    COVERAGE CAN ONLY BE FOUND IN THE POLICY.
(4) ALL FIGURES ASSUME RENEWAL OF THE RENEWABLE TERM COVERAGES, WHEN APPLICABLE.

THIS POLICY MAY AT ANY TIME WITHIN TWENTY (20) DAYS AFTER ITS RECEIPT BE RETURNED TO THE COMPANY.
UPON ITS RETURN THE POLICY WILL BE CONSIDERED VOID FROM ITS INCEPTION AND THE PREMIUM WILL BE
REFUNDED TO THE OWNER.

WASHINGTON NATIONAL INSURANCE COMPANY   FOR MORE INFORMATION ABOUT THIS POLICY PLEASE CONTACT:
ORDINARY LIFE DEPARTMENT   02/02/88   HOME OFFICE
1630 CHICAGO AVENUE   POLICY NUMBER   HOME OFFICE
EVANSTON, ILLINOIS 60201   77-222299-   WASHINGTON NATIONAL INS CO
                                                                      1630 CHICAGO AVENUE
                                                                      EVANSTON IL 60201

                         STATEMENT OF POLICY COST AND BENEFIT INFORMATION (CONTINUED)
                         PREPARED FOR: DOE,JOHN A

                         AGE BASIS: 34   ISSUE BASIS: STANDARD

BENEFIT   GUARANTEED INSURABILITY
POL   ANNUAL
YR   PREMIUM

01-05   27.20
09   27.20

(EXPIRY)

(1) THE INFORMATION CONTAINED IN THIS POLICY SUMMARY IS GENERAL IN NATURE. A COMPLETE STATEMENT OF
    COVERAGE CAN ONLY BE FOUND IN THE POLICY.
(2) ALL FIGURES ASSUME RENEWAL OF THE RENEWABLE TERM COVERAGES, WHEN APPLICABLE.

Appendix C. Dividend Provisions

DIVIDEND PROVISIONS

Annual Dividends. Dividends such as the company may apportion shall be payable at the end of each policy year after the first while this policy is in force other than as extended term insurance. The Owner may elect in writing to have each dividend applied under one of the following methods:

1. Premium Payment. Used toward the payment of premiums.

2. Paid-Up Additions. Used to buy a participating paid-up life insurance addition to this policy. The net value of each paid-up life insurance addition shall not be less than the dividend used to purchase that addition. Paid-up additions may be surrendered at any time.

3. Dividend Accumulation. Left on deposit with the company to earn interest at a rate not less than 3.5% per year. Any dividend accumulations not applied under the Credits to Avoid Lapse provision will be added to the sum payable at the death of the Insured or upon surrender for cash. Dividend accumulations may be withdrawn at any time.

4. Cash. Paid in cash.

The company will change the dividend method for any dividends payable after the company receives a written request for such change. If no election has been made, method 3 shall apply.

Dividend Credits. Dividend Credits are any dividend accumulations and any current dividend payable under dividend methods 1 or 3.

Dividend At Death. The company will pay a portion of the dividend which would have been paid if the Insured had lived to the end of the policy year in which the Insured died. If such a dividend is paid, the company will also pay a portion of the interest on any dividend accumulations which would have been payable if the Insured had lived to the end of such policy year. This dividend and interest on any dividend accumulations payable at the time the Insured dies will be based on the dividend scale in effect at the time the company receives notice of the Insured's death.

Election of Paid-Up Policy. The company will, upon receipt of a written election and the surrender of dividend credits, endorse this policy as a participating paid-up policy. The dividend credits surrendered must be equal to the net single premium increased by 3% for an amount of paid-up insurance equal to the difference between the Amount of Basic Plan insurance and the amount of reduced paid-up insurance then available under the Non-Forfeiture Provisions. Such paid-up insurance shall be payable under the same conditions as the insurance under the Basic Plan.

Election of Matured Endowment. The company will, upon receipt of a written election and the surrender of this policy and dividend credits, mature this policy as an endowment. This election may be made when the sum of the dividend credits and the cash surrender value are equal to the amount of insurance then in force under the Basic Plan.

633

Appendix D. War Hazard Rider

WASHINGTON NATIONAL INSURANCE COMPANY

Evanston, Illinois

Attached to and Forming a

Issued on the Life of...

Part of Policy No..

Effective Date...

AVIATION AND WAR RISK EXCLUSION PROVISION

The term "Home Area" as used in this provision means only the fifty states of the United States, the District of Columbia, Canada, Canal Zone, Puerto Rico and the Virgin Islands; "war service" means being in the military, naval or air forces or any civilian force auxiliary thereto of any country (a) at war, declared or undeclared, or (b) involved in any conflict between the armed forces of countries, international organizations, or combinations thereof.

The liability under this Policy shall be limited to the amount specified below if the death of the Insured:

1. occurs as a result of an act of war, declared or undeclared, if such act occurs outside the Home Area while the Insured is in war service and if death occurs while the Insured is in war service outside the Home Area or within 6 months after his return to the Home Area or within 6 months after his termination of service in such forces, whichever is the earlier date; or

2. occurs within 2 years after the date of issue of this Policy as a result of an act of war, declared or undeclared, if such act occurs outside the Home Area while the Insured is not in war service, and death occurs outside the Home Area or within 6 months after returning to the Home Area; or

3. occurs inside or outside the Home Area whether or not the Insured is in war service and as a result of operating or riding in or descending from any kind of aircraft if the Insured is a pilot, officer or member of the crew of such aircraft or is giving or receiving any kind of training or instruction or has any duties aboard such aircraft or requiring descent therefrom.

In event the Insured's death should occur under any of the conditions defined above, the Company's liability shall be limited to the payment of a single sum equal to the greater of (a) the premiums paid on this Policy, decreased by any indebtedness on or secured by this Policy, or (b) the reserve under this Policy, less any indebtedness on or secured by this Policy; provided, however, that in no event shall such liability be greater than the amount payable in the absence of this provision. If no basis for the computation of reserves is specified in this Policy, reserves shall be computed according to the Commissioners 1941 Standard Ordinary Mortality Table, with 3% interest and on the basis of the Commissioners Reserve Valuation Method.

The limitations of liability contained herein shall also apply to any reduced paid-up insurance or extended term insurance put in force in accordance with any non-forfeiture provisions contained in this Policy, and shall be included in any Policy to which this Policy may be changed or converted.

If this Policy has attached thereto any supplementary contract for an additional benefit in event of accidental death, the conditions and exceptions contained therein shall not be affected by this provision.

The provision of this Policy entitled "Incontestability" is hereby amended to read as follows:

This Policy shall be incontestable after 2 years from its date of issue except (a) for non-payment of premiums, (b) as to any provision for an additional benefit in the event of accidental death, (c) as to any provision for benefits in the event of total and permanent disability and (d) for the limitation of benefits contained in the provision entitled Aviation and War Risk Exclusion Provision.

AMENDMENT OF APPLICATION

It is agreed and understood that my original application for insurance under the above designated Policy is hereby amended to permit the inclusion in such Policy of the foregoing Aviation and War Risk Exclusion Provision and that such provision shall be attached to and made a part of such Policy.

Dated at...this.....................day of.., 19........

....

The foregoing Aviation and War Risk Exclusion Provision shall become operative as of the Effective Date shown above.

WASHINGTON NATIONAL INSURANCE COMPANY

Muriel L Crawford

SECRETARY

O 1105

Appendix E. American Bankers Association Assignment Form

FORM DESIGNED, PRINTED, AND DISTRIBUTED BY
AMERICAN BANKERS ASSOCIATION
BANK MANAGEMENT COMMISSION

Form No. 10—LIFE INSURANCE ASSIGNMENT (REVIEWED AND APPROVED 1950)

ASSIGNMENT OF LIFE INSURANCE POLICY AS COLLATERAL

A. *For Value Received* the undersigned hereby assign, transfer and set over to _____

_____ of _____

its successors and assigns, (herein called the "Assignee") Policy No. _____ issued by the

_____

(herein called the "Insurer") and any supplementary contracts issued in connection therewith (said policy and contracts being

herein called the "Policy"), upon the life of _____

of _____ and all claims, options, privileges, rights, title and interest therein
and thereunder (except as provided in Paragraph C hereof), subject to all the terms and conditions of the Policy and to all
superior liens, if any, which the Insurer may have against the Policy. The undersigned by this instrument jointly and severally
agree and the Assignee by the acceptance of this assignment agrees to the conditions and provisions herein set forth.

B. It is expressly agreed that, without detracting from the generality of the foregoing, the following specific rights are included
in this assignment and pass by virtue hereof:
1. The sole right to collect from the Insurer the net proceeds of the Policy when it becomes a claim by death or maturity;
2. The sole right to surrender the Policy and receive the surrender value thereof at any time provided by the terms of the
   Policy and at such other times as the Insurer may allow;
3. The sole right to obtain one or more loans or advances on the Policy, either from the Insurer or, at any time, from other
   persons, and to pledge or assign the Policy as security for such loans or advances;
4. The sole right to collect and receive all distributions or shares of surplus, dividend deposits or additions to the Policy now
   or hereafter made or apportioned thereto, and to exercise any and all options contained in the Policy with respect thereto;
   provided, that unless and until the Assignee shall notify the Insurer in writing to the contrary, the distributions or shares
   of surplus, dividend deposits and additions shall continue on the plan in force at the time of this assignment; and
5. The sole right to exercise all nonforfeiture rights permitted by the terms of the Policy or allowed by the Insurer and to
   receive all benefits and advantages derived therefrom.

C. It is expressly agreed that the following specific rights, so long as the Policy has not been surrendered, are reserved and
excluded from this assignment and do not pass by virtue hereof:
1. The right to collect from the Insurer any disability benefit payable in cash that does not reduce the amount of insurance;
2. The right to designate and change the beneficiary;
3. The right to elect any optional mode of settlement permitted by the Policy or allowed by the Insurer;
   but the reservation of these rights shall in no way impair the right of the Assignee to surrender the Policy completely with all
   its incidents or impair any other right of the Assignee hereunder, and any designation or change of beneficiary or election of a
   mode of settlement shall be made subject to this assignment and to the rights of the Assignee hereunder.

D. This assignment is made and the Policy is to be held as collateral security for any and all liabilities of the undersigned,
or any of them, to the Assignee, either now existing or that may hereafter arise in the ordinary course of business between
any of the undersigned and the Assignee (all of which liabilities secured or to become secured are herein called "Liabilities").

E. The Assignee covenants and agrees with the undersigned as follows:
1. That any balance of sums received hereunder from the Insurer remaining after payment of the then existing Liabilities,
   matured or unmatured, shall be paid by the Assignee to the persons entitled thereto under the terms of the Policy had this
   assignment not been executed;
2. That the Assignee will not exercise either the right to surrender the Policy or (except for the purpose of paying premiums)
   the right to obtain policy loans from the Insurer, until there has been default in any of the Liabilities or a failure to pay any
   premium when due, nor until twenty days after the Assignee shall have mailed, by first-class mail, to the undersigned at the
   addresses last supplied in writing to the Assignee specifically referring to this assignment, notice of intention to exercise
   such right; and
3. That the Assignee will upon request forward without unreasonable delay to the Insurer the Policy for endorsement of any
   designation or change of beneficiary or any election of an optional mode of settlement.

F. The Insurer is hereby authorized to recognize the Assignee's claims to rights hereunder without investigating the reason for
any action taken by the Assignee, or the validity or the amount of the Liabilities or the existence of any default therein, or
the giving of any notice under Paragraph E (2) above or otherwise, or the application to be made by the Assignee of any
amounts to be paid to the Assignee. The sole signature of the Assignee shall be sufficient for the exercise of any rights under
the Policy assigned hereby and the sole receipt of the Assignee for any sums received shall be a full discharge and release
therefor to the Insurer. Checks for all or any part of the sums payable under the Policy and assigned herein, shall be drawn
to the exclusive order of the Assignee if, when, and in such amounts as may be, requested by the Assignee.

G. The Assignee shall be under no obligation to pay any premium, or the principal of or interest on any loans or advances on
the Policy whether or not obtained by the Assignee, or any other charges on the Policy, but any such amounts so paid by the
Assignee from its own funds, shall become a part of the Liabilities hereby secured, shall be due immediately, and shall draw
interest at a rate fixed by the Assignee from time to time not exceeding 6% per annum.

H. The exercise of any right, option, privilege or power given herein to the Assignee shall be at the option of the Assignee,
but (except as restricted by Paragraph E (2) above) the Assignee may exercise any such right, option, privilege or power
without notice to, or assent by, or affecting the liability of, or releasing any interest hereby assigned by the undersigned, or
any of them.

I. The Assignee may take or release other security, may release any party primarily or secondarily liable for any of the Liabilities, may grant extensions, renewals or indulgences with respect to the Liabilities, or may apply to the Liabilities in such order as
the Assignee shall determine, the proceeds of the Policy hereby assigned or any amount received on account of the Policy by the
exercise of any right permitted under this assignment, without resorting or regard to other security.

J. In the event of any conflict between the provisions of this assignment and provisions of the note or other evidence of any
Liability, with respect to the Policy or rights of collateral security therein, the provisions of this assignment shall prevail.

K. Each of the undersigned declares that no proceedings in bankruptcy are pending against him and that his property is not
subject to any assignment for the benefit of creditors.

Signed and sealed this _____ day of _____, 19_____

_____   _____(L.S.)

Witness   Insured or Owner

_____   _____

                                                       Address

_____   _____(L.S.)

Witness   Beneficiary

                                                       Address

INDIVIDUAL ACKNOWLEDGMENT

STATE OF _____
COUNTY OF _____ }ss:

On the _____day of _____ 19 _____, before me personally came

_____, to me known to be the individual _____ described in and who

executed the assignment on the reverse side hereof and acknowledged to me that _____ he _____ executed the same.

_____
Notary Public

My commission expires_____

CORPORATE ACKNOWLEDGMENT

STATE OF _____
COUNTY OF _____ }ss:

On the _____ day of _____19_____, before me personally came _____

_____, who being by me duly sworn, did depose and say that he resides in _____

that he is the _____ of _____, the corporation described in and which executed the assignment on the

reverse side hereof; that he knows the seal of said corporation; that the seal affixed to said assignment is such corporate seal; that

it was so affixed by order of the Board of Directors of said corporation, and that he signed his name thereto by like order.

_____
Notary Public

My commission expires_____

* * * * *

Duplicate received and filed at the home office of the Insurer in _____, this _____ day of _____ 19_____

By_____
Authorized Officer

NOTE: When executed by a corporation, the corporate seal should be affixed and there should be attached to the assignment a certified copy of the resolution of the Board of Directors authorizing the signing officer to execute and deliver the assignment in the name and on behalf of the corporation.

BMC 136-6-1941

Appendix F. Late Remittance Offer

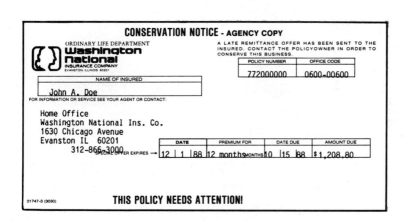

Appendix G. Reinstatement Application Form

<table>
<tr><td colspan="2">

Washington national
INSURANCE COMPANY
EVANSTON ILLINOIS 60201

</td><td colspan="2">

APPLICATION FOR REINSTATEMENT
LIFE AND/OR HEALTH INSURANCE

</td></tr>
</table>

Insured's Name (Please print full name)	Date of Birth
Mary Roe	January 1, 1958

Mailing Address	Policy Number
1234 Main Street	0000000

Occupation	Amount Paid with this Application $	Premium Due Date
Lawyer	30.00	March 12, 1988

The undersigned hereby declare(s) that the following statements and answers are complete and true and are made to induce the Company to reinstate the above numbered policy.

ALL QUESTIONS MUST BE ANSWERED

I. Since the date of the Application for the policy, have:

1. The INSURED
2. The Insured Spouse (if Family Plan or Family Term benefits are included in this Policy)
3. The Insured CHILD or CHILDREN (if Family Plan or Family Term benefits are included in this Policy)
4. The PURCHASER (if the Policy is a Juvenile Policy which includes Purchaser Waiver of Premium benefits)

Explain "Yes" answers. Include names, dates, disorders and physicians.

	Yes	No
a. Had any injury or change in health?	☐	☒
b. Been a patient in a hospital, clinic or sanitorium?	☐	☒
c. Had any treatment or examination or been a patient of any physician or practitioner?	☐	☒
d. Smoked cigarettes within the past year? If so, indicate quantity per day	☐	☒
e. Used narcotics, barbiturates, amphetamines, psychedelic drugs, marijuana or been treated for drug habit or alcoholism?	☐	☒
f. Participated in any hazardous sport or flown other than as a fare paying passenger?	☐	☒
g. Applied for any life or health insurance with this or any other company?	☐	☒
h. Been declined, postponed or rated for insurance or for reinstatement in this or any other company?	☐	☒

II. INSURED'S Height: 5 ft. 5 in. Weight 125

The undersigned expressly agree(s) as follows: (1) the policy shall not be reinstated until the Company has received payment of all arrears and has approved this application at its Home Office; (2) the terms and conditions of the incontestable provision in said policy shall apply to a reinstatement thereof made upon this application, but the period of time specified in said provision shall rum from the date of approval of this application by the Company; and (3) if said reinstatement application is approved the Company shall be under no liability nor shall any insurance be restored with respect to any person now deceased or with respect to any person who would not be covered under said policy on the date of this application had there been no default in premium payment.

AUTHORIZATION

To: Any licensed physician, medical practitioner, hospital, clinic or other medically related facility, the Veterans Administration, insurance or reinsurance company, consumer reporting agency, government agency, Medical Information Bureau, Inc., benefit plan administrator, employer, and the agent through whom application is being made.

(1) I authorize you to release the following to Washington National Insurance Company for purposes of determining eligibility for insurance benefits under an existing policy or claims for benefits:

Full information including copies of records concerning medical examinations, history and treatment, character and general reputation, habits, occupation, income, finances, aviation activities, and hazardous activities of the undersigned and all minor children proposed for coverage.

(2) I authorize Washington National Insurance Company or its reinsurers to release any information to the Medical Information Bureau, Inc., to a benefit plan administrator, to other insurance or reinsurance companies and to persons or organizations performing business or legal services in connection with my application, or as may be otherwise lawfully required.

(3) I know that I may receive a copy of this authorization upon request. I agree this authorization shall be valid for two and one-half years from its date and that a photographic copy of it shall be as valid as the original. I acknowledge receipt of the Notice of Information Practices, which includes the Fair Credit Reporting Act Notice and Medical Information Bureau Notice.

(4) ☐ I elect to be interviewed if an investigative consumer report is prepared in connection with this application.

Dated _May 1_, 19 _88_   _Mary Roe_
Signature of Insured

Sam Smith
Witness

Check if Applicable	☐ Signature of SPOUSE (Family—Term) ☐ Signature of PURCHASER (Juvenile) ☐ Signature of OWNER if other than Insured

Name of Owning Corporation, Partnership, ect., if applicable

Agency/District	Agent	Code/Agency	Mode of Payment

B 394

NOTICE OF INFORMATION PRACTICES

In addition to the information provided by you, we may also obtain information from physicians or other medical professionals; from hospitals or other medical-care institutions; from the Medical Information Bureau, the Veterans Administration, government agencies, public records, insurance or reinsurance companies, agents, consumer reporting agencies and financial institutions. We may also obtain information from your friends, neighbors, associates, and past and present employers, either directly or through an investigative consumer report.

FAIR CREDIT REPORTING ACT NOTICE

If an investigation is conducted in connection with your application, you are entitled, under the Federal Fair Credit Reporting Act, to disclosure of the nature and scope of that investigation. If a consumer investigative report is prepared, you may obtain a copy of such report as provided in the section entitled "Your Right To Information In Our Files". Further information regarding the investigation and any investigative consumer reports may be obtained by mailing your request to the office identified at the end of this notice. The type of information we may obtain includes any which relates to your mental and physical health, character and general reputation, habits, finances, occupation, income, insurance coverage, and participation in aviation and other hazardous activities. If insurance is sought for members of your family, similar information may be requested about them.

As permitted by law, Washington National Insurance Company or our agent may disclose personal information about you without your authorization when such disclosure is necessary to conduct our business.

MEDICAL INFORMATION BUREAU NOTICE

We may make a brief report regarding your insurability to the Medical Information Bureau, a non-profit membership organization of life insurance companies, which operates an information exchange on behalf of its members. If you apply for life or health insurance coverage, or submit a claim for benefits to a Bureau member company, the Bureau, upon request, will supply such company with the information it may have in its file.

Upon receipt of a request from you, the Bureau will arrange disclosure to you of any information it may have in your file. (Medical information will be disclosed only to your attending physician.) If you question the accuracy of the information contained in the Bureau's file, you may contact the Bureau and seek a correction in accordance with the procedures set forth in the Federal Fair Credit Reporting Act. The address of the Bureau's information office is Post Office Box 105, Essex Station, Boston, Massachusetts 02112; telephone number (617) 426-3660.

OTHER DISCLOSURES

There are other circumstances in which disclosure of personal information may be made:

• to persons or organizations which perform a business or professional function for us;

• to other insurers, agents or insurance-support organizations to enable them to perform their function in connection with an insurance transaction involving you, or to detect or prevent insurance fraud or other misrepresentation;

• to a medical professional for the purpose of informing you of a medical problem of which you may not be aware;

• to an insurance regulatory authority;

• to a law enforcement or other government authority to prevent or prosecute fraud or other unlawful activities;

• for the purpose of conducting scientific research, including actuarial or underwriting studies;

• to our affiliated companies in connection with the marketing of an insurance product or service; and

• to a group policyholder for the purpose of reporting claims experience or conducting an audit of the Company's or the agent's operations.

In each case, only that personal information which is reasonably necessary to accomplish the business purpose will be disclosed. Information obtained by an insurance-support organization may be retained by it and disclosed to other persons as permitted by the Federal Fair Credit Reporting Act and other applicable laws.

YOUR RIGHT TO INFORMATION IN OUR FILE

You have a right of access to recorded personal information about you which we have in our files and which is reasonably locatable and retrievable. Within 30 business days after we receive your request for access, we will inform you of the nature and substance of the recorded personal information and the name of any institutional source of such information. You may come to the Company and photocopy the information, or if you prefer, we will photocopy and mail it to you. We may ask you to pay a reasonable charge to cover the cost of providing the copies.

We will also provide the identity, if recorded, of those persons to whom we have disclosed the information in the two years preceding the date of your request. If the identity of those persons is not recorded, we will provide you with the names of those persons and organizations to whom such information is normally disclosed.

Your right of access includes any medical information we may have about you, but we will disclose medical information only to the medical professional you designate, providing he or she is licensed to provide medical care with respect to the condition to which the information relates. Your right of access does not include any information which relates to and is collected in connection with or in reasonable anticipation of a claim or civil or criminal proceeding.

DISPUTED INFORMATION

You may request, in writing, that recorded personal information be corrected, amended, or deleted from our files. We will notify you if we comply with your request. If we do not comply, we will notify you within 30 business days after we receive your written request and will provide the reasons for our refusal. You will then have the opportunity to file with us a concise statement of your position regarding the disputed personal information. We will include your statement in our files and will provide it with any subsequent disclosure of recorded personal information.

If we correct, amend, or delete disputed personal information from our records, or if we refuse and you file a concise statement with us, we will furnish the additional information or fact of deletion to any insurance support organization that furnished the disputed information to us and to any person you designate who may have received the disputed information within the preceding two years.

Please send any questions concerning our information practices or your access to information in our files to:

Director of Public Affairs
Washington National Insurance Company
1630 Chicago Avenue
Evanston, Illinois 60201

THIS NOTICE MUST BE GIVEN TO THE PROPOSED INSURED(S)/POLICYHOLDER

REINSTATEMENT CONDITIONAL RECEIPT

Ordinary Department

This form is to be used only as a conditional receipt for the deposit on an application for reinstatement of a lapsed Ordinary Policy.

Washington National INSURANCE COMPANY EVANSTON, ILLINOIS 60201

_____, 19____

RECEIVED from _____ , the sum of

_____ Dollars, as a deposit on account of

premium on Policy No. _____ issued or assumed by WASHINGTON NATIONAL INSURANCE COMPANY

upon the life of _____ , application for
reinstatement of which has this day been made.

The above amount is received by me merely for transmittal to and subject to acceptance and approval by the Company at its Home Office, and such tender of payment shall not revive or restore said policy or constitute payment of all or any protion of any premium thereunder unless so accepted and approved. This receipt is issued upon the express understanding that if the Company declines to approve such application it shall have the right to reject said payment, in which case the above amount will be refunded and this receipt shall become null and void.

_____ Agent

Appendix H. Life Insurance Buyer's Guide

Life Insurance Buyer's Guide

This guide can show you how to save money when you shop for life insurance. It helps you to:

- Decide how much life insurance you should buy

- Decide what kind of life insurance policy you need, and

- Compare the cost of similar life insurance policies.

Prepared by the
National Association of Insurance
Commissioners

Reprinted by

Washington National
INSURANCE COMPANY
Evanston, Illinois 60201 ● A Washington National Corporation Financial Service Company

The National Association of Insurance Commissioners is an association of state insurance regulatory officials. This association helps the various Insurance Departments to coordinate insurance laws for the benefit of all consumers. You are urged to use this Guide in making a life insurance purchase.

**This Guide Does Not Endorse
Any Company Or Policy**

Buying Life Insurance

When you buy life insurance, you want a policy which fits your needs without costing too much. Your first step is to decide how much you need, how much you can afford to pay and the kind of policy you want. Then, find out what various companies charge for that kind of policy. You can find important differences in the cost of life insurance by using the life insurance cost indexes which are described in this guide. A good life insurance agent or company will be able and willing to help you with each of these shopping steps.

If you are going to make a good choice when you buy life insurance, you need to understand which kinds are available. If one kind does not seem to fit your needs, ask about the other kinds which are described in this guide. If you feel that you need more information than is given here, you may want to check with a life insurance agent or company or books on life insurance in your public library.

3

Choosing the Amount

One way to decide how much life insurance you need is to figure how much cash and income your dependents would need if you were to die. You should think of life insurance as a source of cash needed for expenses of final illnesses, paying taxes, mortgages or other debts. It can also provide income for your family's living expenses, educational costs and other future expenses. Your new policy should come as close as you can afford to making up the difference between (1) what your dependents would have if you were to die now, and (2) what they would actually need.

Choosing the Right Kind

All life insurance policies agree to pay an amount of money if you die. But all policies are not the same. There are three basic kinds of life insurance.

1. Term insurance

2. Whole life insurance

3. Endowment insurance

Remember, no matter how fancy the policy title or sales presentation might appear, all life insurance policies contain one or more of the three basic kinds. If you are confused about a policy that sounds complicated, ask the agent or company if it combines more than one kind of life insurance. The following is a brief description of the three basic kinds:

4

Term Insurance

Term insurance is death protection for a "term" of one or more years. Death benefits will be paid only if you die within that term of years. Term insurance generally provides the largest immediate death protection for your premium dollar.

Some term insurance policies are "renewable" for one or more additional terms even if your health has changed. Each time you renew the policy for a new term, premiums will be higher. You should check the premiums at older ages and the length of time the policy can be continued.

Some term insurance policies are also "convertible." This means that before the end of the conversion period, you may trade the term policy for a whole life or endowment insurance policy even if you are not in good health. Premiums for the new policy will be higher than you have been paying for the term insurance.

Whole Life Insurance

Whole life insurance gives death protection for as long as you live. The most common type is called "straight life" or "ordinary life" insurance, for which you pay the same premiums for as long as you live. These premiums can be several times higher than you would pay initially for the same amount of term insurance. But they are smaller than the premiums you would eventually pay if you were to keep renewing a term insurance policy until your later years.

5

Some whole life policies let you pay premiums for a shorter period such as 20 years, or until age 65. Premiums for these policies are higher than for ordinary life insurance since the premium payments are squeezed into a shorter period.

Although you pay higher premiums, to begin with, for whole life insurance than for term insurance, whole life insurance policies develop "cash values" which you may have if you stop paying premiums. You can generally either take the cash, or use it to buy some continuing insurance protection. Technically speaking, these values are called "nonforfeiture benefits." This refers to benefits you do not lose (or "forfeit") when you stop paying premiums. The amount of these benefits depends on the kind of policy you have, its size, and how long you have owned it.

A policy with cash values may also be used as collateral for a loan. If you borrow from the life insurance company, the rate of interest is shown in your policy. Any money which you owe on a policy loan would be deducted from the benefits if you were to die, or from the cash value if you were to stop paying premiums.

Endowment Insurance

An endowment insurance policy pays a sum or income to you — the policyholder — if you live to a certain age. If you were to die before then, the death benefit would be paid to your beneficiary. Premiums and cash values for endowment insurance are higher than for the same amount of whole life insurance. Thus endowment insurance gives you the least amount of death protection for your premium dollar.

6

Finding a Low Cost Policy

After you have decided which kind of life insurance fits your needs, look for a good buy. Your chances of finding a good buy are better if you use two types of index numbers that have been developed to aid in shopping for life insurance. One is called the "Surrender Cost Index" and the other is the "Net Payment Cost Index." It will be worth your time to try to understand how these indexes are used, but in any event, use them only for comparing the relative costs of similar policies. LOOK FOR POLICIES WITH LOW COST INDEX NUMBERS.

What is Cost?

"Cost" is the difference between what you pay and what you get back. If you pay a premium for life insurance and get nothing back, your cost for the death protection is the premium. If you pay a premium and get something back later on, such as a cash value, your cost is smaller than the premium.

The cost of some policies can also be reduced by dividends; these are called "participating" policies. Companies may tell you what their current dividends are, but the size of future dividends is unknown today and cannot be guaranteed. Dividends actually paid are set each year by the company.

Some policies do not pay dividends. These are called "guaranteed cost" or "nonparticipating" policies. Every feature of a guaranteed cost policy is fixed so that you know in advance what your future cost will be.

7

The premiums and cash values of a participating policy are guaranteed, but the dividends are not. Premiums for participating policies are typically higher than for guaranteed cost policies, but the cost to you may be higher or lower, depending on the dividends actually paid.

What Are Cost Indexes?

In order to compare the cost of policies, you need to look at:

1. Premiums

2. Cash values

3. Dividends

Cost indexes use one or more of these factors to give you a convenient way to compare relative costs of similar policies. When you compare costs, an adjustment must be made to take into account that money is paid and received at different times. It is not enough to just add up the premiums you will pay and to subtract the cash values and dividends you expect to get back. These indexes take care of the arithmetic for you. Instead of having to add, subtract, multiply and divide many numbers yourself, you just compare the index numbers which you can get from life insurance agents and companies:

1. LIFE INSURANCE SURRENDER COST INDEX — This index is useful if you consider the level of the cash values to be of primary importance to you. It helps you compare costs if at some future point in time, such as 10 or 20 years, you were to surrender the policy and take its cash value.

2. LIFE INSURANCE NET PAYMENT COST INDEX — This index is useful if your main concern is the benefits that are to be paid at your death and if the level of cash values is of secondary importance to you. It helps you compare costs at some future point in time, such as 10 or 20 years, if you continue paying premiums on your policy and do not take its cash value.

There is another number called the Equivalent Level Annual Dividend. It shows the part dividends play in determining the cost index of a participating policy. Adding a policy's Equivalent Level Annual Dividend to its cost index allows you to compare total costs of similar policies before deducting dividends. However, if you make any cost comparisons of a participating policy with a nonparticipating policy, remember that the total cost of the participating policy will be reduced by dividends, but the cost of the nonparticipating policy will not change.

How Do I Use Cost Indexes?

The most important thing to remember when using cost indexes is that a policy with a small index number is generally a better buy than a comparable policy with a larger index number. The following rules are also important:

(1) Cost comparisons should only be made between similar plans of life insurance. Similar plans are those which provide essentially the same basic benefits and require premium payments for approximately the same period of time. The closer policies are to being identical, the more reliable the cost comparison will be.

8

9

(2) Compare index numbers only for the kind of policy, for your age and for the amount you intend to buy. Since no one company, offers the lowest cost for *all* types of insurance at *all* ages and for *all* amounts of insurance, it is important that you get the indexes for the actual policy, age and amount which you intend to buy. Just because a "shopper's guide" tells you that one company's policy is a good buy for a particular age and amount, you should not assume that all of that company's policies are equally good buys.

(3) Small differences in index numbers could be offset by other policy features, or differences in the quality of service you may expect from the company or its agent. Therefore, when you find small differences in cost indexes, your choice should be based on something other than cost.

(4) In any event, you will need other information on which to base your purchase decision. Be sure you can afford the premiums, and that you understand its cash values, dividends and death benefits. You should also make a judgment on how well the life insurance company or agent will provide service in the future, to you as a policyholder.

(5) These life insurance cost indexes apply to new policies and should not be used to determine whether you should drop a policy you have already owned for awhile, in favor of a new one. If such a replacement is suggested, you should ask for information from the company which issued the old policy before you take action.

10

Important Things to Remember-A Summary

The first decision you must make when buying a life insurance policy is choosing a policy whose benefits and premiums most closely meet your needs and ability to pay. Next, find a policy which is also a relatively good buy. If you compare Surrender Cost Indexes and Net Payment Cost Indexes of similar competing policies, your chances of finding a relatively good buy will be better than if you do not shop. **REMEMBER, LOOK FOR POLICIES WITH LOWER COST INDEX NUMBERS**. A good life insurance agent can help you to choose the amount of life insurance and kind of policy you want and will give you cost indexes so that you can make cost comparisons of similar policies.

Don't buy life insurance unless you intend to stick with it. A policy which is a good buy when held for 20 years can be very costly if you quit during the early years of the policy. If you surrender such a policy during the first few years, you may get little or nothing back and much of your premium may have been used for company expenses.

Read your new policy carefully, and ask the agent or company for an explanation of anything you do not understand. Whatever you decide now, it is important to review your life insurance program every few years to keep up with changes in your income and responsibilities.

11

Appendix I. Adjustable Life Insurance Application and Policy Forms

washington national INSURANCE COMPANY

APPLICATION FOR ADJUSTABLE LIFE INSURANCE - PART I

☑ NEW POLICY SL 9999999
☐ INCREASE/ADDITION TO EXISTING POLICY # _____

☐ MEDICAL
☐ NON—MEDICAL

Questions **1** through **7** relate to the Proposed Insured under the policy (PLEASE PRINT)

Questions **1A.** through **6A.** relate to the Proposed Other Insured under the policy (PLEASE PRINT)

1. Name

First	Middle	Last
JANE	S	DOE

☐ Single, ☒ Married, ☐ Widowed, ☐ Divorced ☐ Separated

Birthplace (State)	Birthdate M D Y	Age	Sex	Height	Weight
IL	05 16 52	35	F	5'8"	130

SS # 491-00-0000

2. Address Number and Street
123 SUNNY STREET

City	State	Zip Code
MAINTOWN	VT	00000

3. Occupation MANAGER   Duties SALES - MGR

Name of Employer JANES BOUTIQUES

Address of Employer No. and St	City	State	Zip Code
456 ELM	MAINTOWN	VT	00000

4. List all Life Insurance now in force.

Name of Company	Face Amount	Amount of ADB	Year of Issue
NONE			

5. Insurance Applied For Amount

a. Adjustable Life _ _ _ II _ _ _ _ _ b $ 50,000
c. ☒ Level Death Benefit (Option 1)
d. ☐ Increasing Death Benefit (Option 2)
e. ☒ Disability Waiver _ _ f ☐ A D B _ _ _ _ g $ _____
h. ☐ Guaranteed Insurability _ _ _ _ _ _ _ _ i $ _____
j. ☐ Children's Adjustable Life _ _ _ _ _ _ k $ _____
l. ☐ Cost of Living

6. Beneficiaries (Print full names and relationships. Give date of birth, if a minor)

Primary	Relationship
JOHN RAY DOE	HUSBAND

Contingent	Relationship
BARBARA JUNE DOE	DAUGHTER

7. Complete For Children's Rider

FULL NAMES OF CHILDREN	Birthdates M D Y	Age

1A. Name

First	Middle	Last

☐ Single, ☐ Married, ☐ Widowed, ☐ Divorced ☐ Separated

Birthplace (State)	Birthdate M D Y	Age	Sex	Height	Weigh

SS #

2A. Address ☐ Same as Question 2. Number and Street

City	State	Zip Code

3A. Occupation   Duties

4A. List all Life Insurance now in force.

Name of Company	Face Amount	Amount Of ADB	Year of Issue

5A. Insurance Applied For Amount

a. Adjustable Life _ _ _ _ _ _ _ _ _ _ _ b $ _____
c. ☐ Disability Waiver _ _ d ☐ A D B _ _ _ e $ _____
f. ☐ Guaranteed Insurability _ _ _ _ _ _ g $ _____
h. ☐ Cost of Living

6A. Beneficiaries (Print full names and relationships. Give date of birth if a minor)

Primary	Relationship

Contingent	Relationship

8. The Owner Of This Policy Shall Be
☒ A Insured
☐ B Other _____ (Print full name and relationship to Insureds)
Owner is ☐ Individual ☐ Trustee ☐ Corporation ☐ Partnership
Contingent _____ (Print full name and relationship to Insureds)
Address of Owner name in (B.) _____
Street City State Zip Code
Social Security or Tax ID No. of Owner name in (B.)

9. SPECIAL REQUESTS

10. HOME OFFICE ENDORSEMENTS

11. MODE OF PLANNED PREMIUM PAYMENT
☐ ANN ☐ SA ☒ QR ☐ PAC ☐ SD

13. Send premium notices and correpondence to:
☒ Insured Residence ☐ Insured Business ☐ Owner

02771

12. a. PLANNED PERIODIC PREMIUM $ 400.00
b. AMOUNT OF INITIAL PREMIUM $ 400.00

14. AMOUNT PAID IN EXCHANGE FOR RECEIPT $ 400.00

PART I · CONTINUED

Has any person proposed for insurance, so far as you know or believe:

	Yes	No
15. Been refused new insurance or reinstatement, or had insurance postponed, limited, offered, or quoted on a substandard or rated basis?...............	☐	☑
16. Any insurance or annuity which this coverage is to replace or change? (If yes, complete proposal for Policy Replacement)..........................	☐	☑
17. Any other application for Life Insurance pending with this or any other company?................	☐	☑
18. In the past two years participated in: (If yes, attach questionnaire)		
a) Aviation activities as pilot or crew member?..	☐	☑
b) Hazardous activities, sports, avocations, hobbies?....................................	☐	☑
19. Smoked cigarettes within the past year? If so, indicate quantity per day......................	☐	☑
20. In the past two years, used narcotics, barbiturates, amphetamines, psychedelic drugs or been treated for drug usage or alcoholism?..................	☐	☑

Identify question and individual to whom details apply.

ANSWER THE FOLLOWING QUESTIONS AND GIVE FULL DETAILS — NAMES; AILMENTS; TREATMENT; DATES; PHYSICIANS' NAMES AND ADDRESSES; RECOVERY DATES; ETC.

Has any person proposed for insurance, so far as you know or believe:

	Yes	No
21. Ever had symptoms or been diagnosed as having disorder, disease, or persistent discomfort of —		
a) Respiratory System (lungs, bronchi, trachea, etc) such as TB, asthma, emphysema, bronchitis?.	☐	☑
b) Circulatory System (heart, blood, arteries, veins, etc) such as high blood pressure, heart attack, murmur, rheumatic fever?..................	☐	☑
c) Digestive System (esophagus, stomach, intestine, liver, gall bladder, etc) such as ulcer, cirrhosis, hemorrhoids, bleeding?....................	☐	☑
d) Nervous System (brain, nerves, etc) such as paralysis, fainting, epilepsy, convulsions, mental or nervous disorders?......................	☐	☑
e) Muscular and Skeletal Systems (muscles, bones, joints, spine, etc) such as neck or back problems, fracture, arthritis?.................	☐	☑
f) Genito-urinary System (kidney, bladder, reproductive organs, etc) such as infection, bleeding, male or female disorders?...................	☐	☑
g) Glandular System (thyroid, pancreas, adrenal, lymph glands, etc) such as diabetes, or abnormal growth or function?..........................	☐	☑
22. Ever had impaired sight or hearing, cancer or growth, venereal disease, hernia, or skin disease?.......	☐	☑
23. Within the past five years:		
a) Been treated by or consulted any physician, health practitioner or psychologist?..........	☐	☑
b) Been a patient in a hospital or clinic?	☐	☑
c) Had surgery or operation? Has either been advised, or is either contemplated?..........	☐	☑
d) Been on, or now on, prescribed diet or medication?	☐	☑

Identify question and individual to whom details apply.

Give name and address of personal or family physician(s).

IN EXCELLENT HEALTH

PART I - CONTINUED   999999

The undersigned represent(s) and agree(s) as follows:

1. To the best of his (her) knowledge or belief, the above statements and answers are complete, true and correctly recorded.

2. To be bound by all statements and answers made or to be made in this application consisting of Part I and Part II (if said Part II is required by the Company).

3. This application and any policy issued shall constitute the entire Contract.

4. No agent is authorized to: (a) make or modify contracts; (b) waive any of the Company's rights or requirements.

5. Except as provided in the Receipt bearing the same date as this application, the insurance applied for shall not become effective until the policy is delivered to and accepted by the Owner and the entire first premium is paid while all of the answers in Part I and Part II of this application continue to be complete and true answers.

6. Acceptance of any policy issued on this application shall constitute approval of any change made by the Company in the space designated "Home Office Endorsements". However, any change in amount, classification, plan insurance, age at issue or benefits shall be made only with written consent of the undersigned.

Signed At _Maintown Vt_   _Jane S Doe_
           City   State   Insured Signature

Date _10 - 18 - 87_   19___
                          Other Insured Signature (If coverage applied for)

Witnessed By _John Smith_
           Licensed Resident Agent   Owner's Signature, if other than Insured

Adjustable Life Insurance Policy

We agree to pay the death benefit to the beneficiary after receipt of due proof of the death of the Insured while this policy is in force and before the maturity date, subject to the provisions of this policy.

We agree to pay the cash value to the Owner if the Insured is living on the maturity date.

Right to Examine and Return Policy Within 20 Days

You may, at any time within 20 days after receipt of this Policy, return it to us at our Home Office or to the Agent through whom it was purchased, and we will cancel it. The return of the Policy will void it from the beginning and any premium paid will be refunded to the owner.

Muriel L Crawford   *George P. Kendall*

Secretary   President

Signed for the Company at Evanston, Illinois, on the Policy Date.

Adjustable Life Insurance Policy — Endowment Maturing at Age 95

Death Benefit payable at death prior to Maturity Date

Any Cash Value payable on Maturity Date

Adjustable Death Benefit — Flexible Premiums payable during lifetime of Insured until the Maturity Date

Nonparticipating

Washington National®
INSURANCE COMPANY
EVANSTON, ILLINOIS 60201

Page 1

UL 115   (5-87)

Alphabetical Guide To Your Policy

Provision	Section
Accumulated Value	21
Annual Illustrative Report	10
Basis of Computations	30
Beneficiary	4
Cash Loans	16
Changes in Existing Insurance Coverage	20
Collateral Assignment	5
Continuation of Insurance	27
Cost of Insurance Rates	23
Death Benefit	18
Definitions	1
Effective Date of Coverage	11
Endowment at Age 95	28
Entire Contract	2
Grace Period	14
Incontestability	8
Incorrect Age or Sex	6
Interest and Repayment	17
Interest on Death Benefit	19
Interest Rates	24
Monthly Deduction	22
Non-Participating	9
Ownership	3
Partial Surrender	26
Premiums	13
Reinstatement	15
Settlement Options (Election)	31
Suicide	7
Surrender	25
Surrender Charge	Page 3
Table of Guaranteed Values	29
Termination of Coverage	12

Additional Benefits

The additional benefits, if any, listed on page 3 are described in the additional benefit agreements that follow page 10.

Page 2

INSURED: JANE S DOE

POLICY NUMBER: 9 999 999

POLICY DATE: FEBRUARY 22, 1988

```
                        POLICY SCHEDULE

INSURED          JANE S DOE                    AGE   35   SEX   FEMALE

POLICY DATE      FEBRUARY 22, 1988          9 999 999   POLICY NUMBER

INSURANCE CLASS  NONSMOKER

MATURITY DATE    FEBRUARY 22, 2048***      MONTHLY ANNIVERSARY DAY  22

INITIAL SPECIFIED AMOUNT      $50,000      DEATH BENEFIT OPTION      1

MINIMUM FIRST YEAR PREMIUM FOR POLICY

        ANNUAL       SEMI-ANNUAL        QUARTERLY          MONTHLY

        $491.64        $245.82          $122.91            $40.97

INITIAL PREMIUM AMOUNT              $122.91

PLANNED PERIODIC PREMIUM           $400.00      PAYABLE    QUARTERLY*

GUARANTEED FIRST YEAR INTEREST RATE          8.900 %

MINIMUM GUARANTEED INTEREST RATE             4.500 % **

MONTHLY POLICY FEE                           $4.00


MAXIMUM POLICY LOAN RATE                     7.40 % IN ADVANCE

       BENEFIT            INITIAL BENEFIT    BENEFIT        INITIAL
     DESCRIPTION              AMOUNT      TERMINATES***  MONTHLY PREMIUM

ADJUSTABLE LIFE INSURANCE        $50,000    FEB 22, 2048      $40.25
DISABILITY BENEFIT                          FEB 22, 2018      $.72




   * DUE ON QUARTERLY ANNIVERSARY DAY AND PAYABLE TO MATURITY DATE

  ** THE ACTUAL CURRENT INTEREST RATE(S) CREDITED MAY BE HIGHER.

 *** IT IS POSSIBLE THAT COVERAGE WILL EXPIRE PRIOR TO THE MATURITY
     DATE SHOWN EVEN IF SCHEDULED PREMIUMS ARE PAID IN A TIMELY MANNER.

                        PAGE THREE
```

INSURED   JANE S DOE   AGE   35   SEX   FEMALE

INSURANCE CLASS NONSMOKER   9 999 999   POLICY NUMBER

MAXIMUM COST OF INSURANCE RATES* PER $1000.00
(SEE SECTION 23 IN POLICY)

THE FOLLOWING TABLE SHOWS THE MONTHLY GUARANTEED MAXIMUM INSURANCE
RATES. ATTAINED AGE IN THE TABLE BELOW IS THE AGE LAST BIRTHDAY ON
THE POLICY ANNIVERSARY ON OR PRECEDING THE MONTHLY ANNIVERSARY DAY.

ATTAINED AGE	MONTHLY RATE
35	0.17853
36	0.18363
37	0.18873
38	0.19469
39	0.20319
40	0.21255
41	0.22922
42	0.24840
43	0.26674
44	0.28675
45	0.30676
46	0.32677
47	0.34929
48	0.37347
49	0.39933
50	0.42768
51	0.45854
52	0.49358
53	0.53195
54	0.57116
55	0.61492
56	0.67705
57	0.74684
58	0.82431
59	0.90946
60	1.00144
61	1.10109
62	1.21014
63	1.32772
64	1.45472

PAGE THREE (CONT)

INSURED   JANE S DOE   AGE   35   SEX   FEMALE

INSURANCE CLASS NONSMOKER   9 999 999   POLICY NUMBER

ATTAINED AGE	MONTHLY RATE
65	1.59283
66	1.74207
67	1.90415
68	2.08164
69	2.27627
70	2.49147
71	2.72728
72	2.98712
73	3.27192
74	3.58682
75	3.93361
76	4.31493
77	4.73170
78	5.18315
79	5.66853
80	6.18705
81	6.74486
82	7.34293
83	8.22544
84	9.21922
85	10.29576
86	11.44790
87	12.67361
88	13.97426
89	15.36072
90	16.85005
91	18.47514
92	20.29451
93	22.44349
94	25.22305

* THE ACTUAL CURRENT COST OF INSURANCE RATES CHARGED MAY BE LOWER.

PAGE THREE (CONT)

```
INSURED          JANE S DOE                AGE    35      SEX    FEMALE

INSURANCE CLASS  NONSMOKER                 9 999 999    POLICY NUMBER

EFFECTIVE DATE   FEBRUARY 22 1988          SPECIFIED AMOUNT    $50,000
```

THE FOLLOWING TABLE SHOWS THE SURRENDER CHARGES WHICH APPLY FROM
THE EFFECTIVE DATE FOR THE ABOVE SPECIFIED AMOUNT:

COVERAGE YEAR	SURRENDER CHARGE
1	$603.75
2	603.75
3	603.75
4	603.75
5	603.75
6	603.75
7	603.75
8	603.75
9	603.75
10	0.00

NOTE: THESE SURRENDER CHARGES ARE NOT AFFECTED BY SUBSEQUENT DECREASES
        IN THE SPECIFIED AMOUNT.

PAGE THREE (CONT)

```
INSURED         JANE S DOE                         AGE   35    SEX  FEMALE

INSURANCE CLASS  NONSMOKER                     9 999 999    POLICY NUMBER

                     TABLE OF GUARANTEED VALUES *
                       ADJUSTABLE LIFE INSURANCE
                  INITIAL SPECIFIED AMOUNT    $50,000.00

       END OF                    EXTENDED INSURANCE          REDUCED
     POLICY YEAR    CASH VALUE   YEARS        DAYS           PAID-UP

         1      $        867.60     7            60      $       6,063
         2             2,185.00    19           121             14,629
         3             3,789.69    25            29             24,312
         4             5,466.12    30            90             33,615
         5             7,217.58    35             1             42,567

         6             9,046.52    39           151             51,186
         7            10,953.19    44           151             59,483
         8            12,941.99   * * MATURES * *               67,484
         9            15,018.38   * * MATURES * *               75,213
        10            17,789.49   * * MATURES * *               85,593

        11            20,054.64   * * MATURES * *               92,722
        12            22,423.68   * * MATURES * *               99,644
        13            24,900.76   * * MATURES * *              106,373
        14            27,484.14   * * MATURES * *              112,890
        15            30,168.89   * * MATURES * *              119,179

        16            32,959.11  . * * MATURES * *             125,254
        17            35,860.21   * * MATURES * *              131,131
        18            38,879.05   * * MATURES * *              136,846
        19            42,020.74   * * MATURES * *              142,410
        20            45,294.03   * * MATURES * *              147,846

      @ 60            67,912.47   * * MATURES * *              177,295
      @ 65            91,325.03   * * MATURES * *              199,230


   BASED ON GUARANTEED VALUES, THE POLICY MATURES AT. AGE  95.

 * ASSUMING MINIMUM INTEREST RATES AND MAXIMUM COST OF INSURANCE RATES




                            PAGE THREE A
```

Part I -- General Provisions:

1. Definitions:

We, Our, Us -- the Washington National Insurance Company.

You, Your -- the owner of this Policy.

Accumulated Value -- see Part V, Non-Forfeiture Provisions, for definition.

Attained Age -- the Insured's age at issue plus the number of completed years from the Policy Date.

Beneficiary -- the person or entity to receive the death benefits in the event of the Insured's, or Other Insured's, death.

Cash Value -- the Accumulated Value less the applicable Surrender Charge(s) from the original Specified Amount and any approved increase, or, if greater, any excess payments (see Section 13) and interest credited thereon. However, this amount cannot be greater than the Accumulated Value.

Covered Insured -- the Insured, or Other Insured(s) covered under a rider in force on this Policy.

Death Benefit -- the amount of money we will pay if the Insured dies while this Policy is in force.

Debt -- unpaid policy loans and unpaid loan interest due to us and secured by this Policy.

Excess Interest Rate(s) -- the difference between the current interest rate(s) and the Minimum Guaranteed Interest Rate (see Section 24).

Increase -- an increase in the Specified Amount for the Insured. See Section 20, Changes In Existing Coverage.

Increase Year -- the twelve Monthly Anniversary Days beginning with the effective date of an approved increase.

In Force -- in effect and providing insurance protection on the Insured's life.

Insured -- the person on whose life this Policy is issued, as shown on the Schedule Page.

Monthly Anniversary Day -- the same date as the Policy Date, but in any subsequent month.

Monthly Deductions -- the amount to be deducted from the Surrender Value on any Monthly Anniversary Day necessary to pay the Cost Of Insurance, plus the cost of additional benefits provided by rider(s), plus the monthly policy fee, for the following month.

Other Insured -- person(s) insured under "Other Insured Rider(s)" if any, attached to this Policy.

Planned Periodic Premium -- the designated premium amount which we have been requested to bill (see the Schedule Page).

Policy Anniversary -- the same date and month as the Policy Date, on each succeeding year this Policy remains in force.

Policy Date -- the date of issue of this Policy, as shown in the Schedule Page.

Proceeds -- the amount we will pay under the terms of this Policy when it matures or is surrendered, or when an insured dies while this Policy is in force.

Proof Of Death -- proof of the interest of the claimant (ordinarily, a valid Death Certificate and properly completed Claimant's Statement).

Specified Amount -- the amount of coverage in force pursuant to the original application, as amended by increases or decreases, if any.

Surrender Value -- the cash value, less any debt.

Written Request -- in writing, in a form satisfactory to us, signed by you and received by us at our Home Office at Evanston, Illinois.

2. Entire Contract:

We have issued this Policy in consideration of the application and payment of one Planned Periodic Premium. The entire contract consists of: The application; the Policy and Riders, if any; any supplemental applications or Schedule Page Amendments; and, any application(s) for reinstatement on record in our Home Office. The application for the Policy and any supplemental application(s) for increases shall be made a part of the Policy. To be effective, any change in or waiver of the terms of the contract must be in writing and signed by an Elected Officer of the Company.

We rely on all statements made by or for the Insured or Other Insureds in the application(s). These statements are considered to be representations and not warranties. We may use any statements made in the application, a supplemental application or an application for reinstatement, in defense of a claim.

3. Ownership:

You, as the owner of this Policy, may exercise all the rights and options that this Policy provides, while the Insured is living, subject to the rights of any irrevocable beneficiary. If you are not the Insured and you die before the Insured, your estate will become the owner unless you have named a contingent owner.

You may name a new owner or contingent owner at any time while the Insured is living by filing a written request with us. Your written request will not be effective until it is recorded in our Home Office. Once recorded, the change will be effective as of the date you signed the request, whether or not either you or the Insured is alive when we record the change. However, our liability resulting from such change will be subject to any payments made or other action taken by us before your request was recorded in our Home Office.

4. Beneficiary:

The beneficiary on the policy date will be as designated in the application.

A new beneficiary may be named from time to time by a written request signed by the owner and any irrevocable beneficiary.

A change of beneficiary will not take effect until recorded by us. When a change of beneficiary has been so recorded, whether or not the person insured is then alive, it will take effect as of the date the written request was signed. Any payment made or any action taken or allowed by us before the change of beneficiary is recorded will be without prejudice to us.

If any beneficiary dies simultaneously with the Insured or during the 14 days immediately following the date of death of the Insured, the proceeds of this policy shall, unless otherwise provided in the application or in a written request, be paid to the same payee or payees and in the same manner as if the deceased beneficiary had died before the Insured. Any reference in this Policy to a beneficiary living or surviving shall mean living on the 15th day immediately following the date of death of the Insured.

5. Collateral Assignment:

You may assign this policy as collateral for a loan without the consent of any revocable beneficiary. We are not bound by any assignment unless it is in writing and recorded at our Home Office. We are not responsible for the validity of any assignment. The rights of an assignee will at all times be subject to any debt to us at the time the assignment is recorded by us, and, if applicable, to loans granted at any time by us.

6. Incorrect Age or Sex:

If we find that our records are incorrect as to the age or sex of the Insured or Other Insured, the proceeds or death benefit payable shall be adjusted. We will pay the amount which would be purchased by the most recent monthly deduction at the correct age or sex. (The monthly deduction is described in the Non-Forfeiture Provisions Section.)

7. Suicide:

If the Insured commits suicide, while sane or insane, within two years from the Policy Date, our liability will be limited to the amount of the premiums paid, less any debt and Partial Surrenders, and less the costs of any Riders.

If the Insured commits suicide, while sane or insane, within two years from the effective date(s) of any increase in insurance or any reinstatement, our total liability shall be the cost of the increase or reinstatement.

8. Incontestability:

We will not contest the validity of this Policy after it has been in force for two years during the lifetime of the Insured from its date of issue or its last date of reinstatement, except as to increases in the Specified Amount. We will not contest the validity of this Policy with respect to any increase in the Specified Amount after such increase has been in force for two years during the lifetime of the Insured. So long as the Policy is contestable as to any portion of its coverage, we reserve the right to require such forms as may be necessary to obtain medical or other records.

9. Non-Participating:

This Policy is Non-Participating and will not share in our profits or surplus earnings. We will pay no dividends on this Policy.

The Company reserves the option to credit interest rates higher than guaranteed or to charge cost of insurance rates lower than guaranteed (see Sections 23-24).

10. Annual Report:

We shall send a report to the owner, at least once each year, which shows: the current accumulated and cash values; the current specified amount; the death benefit; the amount of premiums paid (and any interest earned); and, any outstanding policy loans, loan interest charges, or partial surrender.

You may also request an Illustrative Report on your policy at any time. You may be required to pay a nominal charge for this service.

11. Effective Date of Coverage:

The effective date of coverage under this Policy shall be as follows:

1. For all coverage issued pursuant to the original application, the effective date shall be the Policy Date;

2. For any approved increase under this Policy, or other addition to coverage by Rider, the effective date shall be the Monthly Anniversary Day that falls on or which next follows the date we approve the supplemental application, if any. The effective date will be subject to the payment of any minimum premium requirements;

3. For any insurance that has been reinstated, the effective date shall be the the date we approve the application for reinstatement.

12. Termination of Coverage:

All coverage under this Policy shall terminate when any one of the following events occur:

1. The Insured dies;

2. The Policy matures;

3. The Policy lapses upon expiration of the Grace Period;

4. The Policy is surrendered.

Part II -- Premium Provisions:

13. Premiums:

One Planned Periodic Premium is due on the Policy Date and must be paid to place this Policy in force. Future premium due dates are determined by the frequency of payment you selected in the application. The amount of Planned Periodic Premium Payments, their due dates, and the period of years for which they are scheduled to be payable are shown on the Schedule Page.

The amount and frequency of actual premium payments will affect cash values and the duration of insurance. (See the Non-Forfeiture Provisions Section.) To preserve the status of the policy as life insurance for federal tax purposes, we reserve the right to limit premium payments.

The Minimum First Year Premiums are shown on the Schedule Page. On any Monthly Anniversary Day in policy year one, the sum of the premiums paid must at least equal an amount computed by multiplying the Minimum First Year Monthly Premium times the number of months that the Policy has been in force, including the month following that Monthly Anniversary Day.

When an increase in Specified Amount is approved, there will be an additional minimum first year premium requirement for the Increase Year.

You may change the frequency and amount of Planned Periodic Premium Payments. We reserve the right to limit the amount of increases in such payments to preserve the status of the Policy as Life Insurance for federal tax purposes. Planned Periodic Premium Payments will be subject to our rules regarding minimum amounts.

Excess payments made during the life of this Policy are total premiums, less any partial surrender(s), in excess of the greater of the:

(1) Minimum first year premium and the minimum first year premium for any approved increase multiplied by the number of years and fractional years each coverage was in force; or

(2) Minimum first year premium, and the minimum first year premium for any approved increase, plus the sum of all the monthly deductions which were made in the second and subsequent years for the number of years and fractional years each coverage was in force.

This definition of excess payments is not affected by any subsequent decreases in the Specified Amount.

Additional premium payments may be made at any time prior to the Maturity Date. The amount of such payments is subject to the same restrictions as for Planned Periodic Premiums.

14. Grace Period:

On any Monthly Anniversary Day in Policy year one, the sum of premiums paid, less any partial surrender, cannot be less than (1), plus (2), plus (3) where:

(1) is the Minimum First Year Monthly Premium shown on the Schedule Page, times the number of months that this Policy has been in force, including the month following that Anniversary Day; and

(2) is the Minimum First Year Monthly Premium for any approved increase, times the number of months that the increase has been in force, including the month following that Monthly

Anniversary Day; and

(3) is the cost of any Riders added after the Policy date.

If this first year sum has not been paid, a Grace Period of 61 days shall be allowed to make up any deficiency.

On any Monthly Anniversary Day after the first Policy year, a Grace Period of 61 days will be allowed to make up any premium deficiency: (A) if the surrender value on that Monthly Anniversary Day is not sufficient to cover the Monthly Deduction for the following month, and, (B) if the sum of the premiums paid, less any partial surrenders, is less than (1), plus (2), plus (3) where:

(1) is the Minimum First Year Monthly Premium for the Policy multiplied by the number of months it has been in force; and

(2) is the Minimum First Year Monthly Premiums for any approved increase multiplied by the number of months it has been in force; and

(3) is any increase in the Cost of Insurance for the Policy, including any Riders added on the Policy Date, plus the cost for any Riders added after the Policy Date.

If a claim arises during the Grace Period, any deficiency in premiums or unpaid monthly deductions will be deducted from the death benefit.

A written notice of any premium deficiency will be sent to your last known address (and to any assignee of record) at least thirty days prior to termination of your coverage. If the premium on the written notice is not received by the end of the grace period, the Policy terminates (See Section 12).

15. Reinstatement:

If this Policy lapses upon expiration of the Grace Period, it may be reinstated at any time within five years after the date of lapse and prior to the Maturity Date. We will reinstate the Policy when we receive:

1. Satisfactory evidence of insurability;

2. A minimum payment of the lesser of (a) or (b) where:

(a) is the Minimum First Year Monthly Premium shown on the Schedule Page times the number of months for which that premium was not paid, plus the Minimum First Year Monthly Premium for any approved increase times the number of months for which that

premium was not paid; and

(b) is an amount such that the Policy's surrender value will be equal to or greater than the Monthly Deduction for the next 3 months.

You may repay any Policy debt. If you do repay any Policy debt, we will reinstate the cash value as of the date of lapse, increased by your reinstatement payment. If you do not repay any debt, we will eliminate that debt, and reinstate the surrender value as of the date of lapse, increased by your reinstatement payment.

If you are not the Insured, the request for reinstatement must also be signed by the Insured if age 15 or older, last birthday, on the reinstatement date.

The effective date of a reinstatement shall be the date we approve the application for reinstatement.

Part III -- Loan Provisions:

16. Cash Loans:

We will make a loan to you, on the sole security of this Policy, upon your written request while this Policy is in force. The maximum amount of such loan will be the loan value as of the date of the loan. The loan value will be the cash value, less any debt, less the monthly deductions until the next Policy anniversary, less the loan interest to the next Policy anniversary. Cash loan requests may be deferred for a period of up to six months at our option (except a loan used to pay premiums on any Policy the Owner may have with the Company).

17. Interest and Repayment:

Interest on loans will be payable in advance at the rate shown in the schedule page. All interest not paid when due will be added to the loan and will accrue interest at the same rate. If the loan is repaid before the date to which interest is paid, any unearned interest will be refunded.

A loan may be repaid in whole or in part at any time while this Policy is in force during the lifetime of the Insured. Failure to repay a loan or to pay interest on it will not terminate this Policy unless the total debt against the Policy equals or exceeds the cash value.

Part IV –– Insurance Coverage:

18. Death Benefit:

We will pay the death benefit when we receive due proof in our Home Office that the Insured died while this Policy was in force. The amount of the death benefit will depend upon: (A) The Death Benefit Option in effect on the date of the death; (B) The Specified Amount on the date of death; (C) Any debt. Any debt will be deducted from the death benefit payable under this Policy.

Should death occur following a partial surrender of the Policy, but prior to the subsequent monthly anniversary day, the death benefit will be reduced by amount equal to the reduction in accumulated value (see Section 26).

This Policy offers two Death Benefit Options.

Option 1: The death benefit will be the greater of: (A) The Specified Amount on the date of death; or (B) the amount calculated from the following table.

Option 2: The death benefit will be the greater of: (A) The Specified Amount plus the Accumulated Value on the date of death; or (B) the amount calculated from the following table.

Death Benefit as a Percentage
of the Accumulated Value

Age	%	Age	%	Age	%	Age	%
Under 41	250	50	185	60	130	70	115
41	243	51	178	61	128	71	113
42	236	52	171	62	126	72	111
43	229	53	164	63	124	73	109
44	222	54	157	64	122	74	107
45	215	55	150	65	120	75-90	105
46	209	56	146	66	119	91	104
47	203	57	142	67	118	92	103
48	197	58	138	68	117	93	102
49	191	59	134	69	116	94	101
						95+	100

This is how you calculate the death benefit from the above table.

- Locate the attained age.
- Multiply the corresponding percentage by the Accumulated Value.

The Death Benefit Option in effect for this Policy is shown on the Schedule Page.

The death benefit payable upon the death of any person insured under any Rider shall be as provided by such Rider. Death benefits payable under a Rider are not subject to any debt to us, unless so provided in the Rider. Unless an Optional Method Of Settlement is elected, the death benefit shall be paid in one sum to the designated beneficiary. If no beneficiary survives, the death benefit shall be paid in one sum to you, if living, otherwise to your estate.

19. Interest on Death Benefit:

If the death benefit is not paid in one sum, or under an Optional Method Of Settlement, within 30 days following receipt of proof of death, or the time provided by statute, whichever is less, we will pay interest on the unpaid benefit. Interest will be at a rate declared by us or the rate provided by statute, whichever is greater. Such interest will accrue from the date we receive proof of death to the date of payment, but not for more than one year, or the period of time provided by statute, whichever is greater.

20. Changes in Existing Insurance Coverage:

A change in existing coverage (including any coverage provided by Riders) might disqualify the Policy as life insurance for federal tax purposes. If such a change is requested, it will be disallowed unless you elect a partial surrender in order to avoid such disqualification.

Otherwise, the owner can, by written request, make the following changes.

INCREASE
The following will apply to any increase in the Policy's Specified Amount on the Insured, other than as provided by a Cost of Living Rider.

(1) An increase can be requested after the first policy year. Any request for an increase will be subject to evidence of insurability satisfactory to us. However, no evidence of insurability will be required if the increase is provided by a Guaranteed Insurability Rider, or if the Death Benefit is under Option 1 and the request is for an increase not to exceed the amount of an excess payment made with your request for the increase.

(2) Any increase approved by us will be in force as of the effective date shown on the Schedule Page amendment, subject to minimum first year premium requirements for the Increase Year.

(3) Each increase will have its own schedule of surrender charges. Any subsequent reduction or termination of such an increase will not result in removal or reduction of that surrender charge schedule.

DECREASE
A decrease can be requested after the second policy year. However, no decrease will be permitted within twelve months of a prior increase. It will become effective on the Monthly Anniversary Day following our

receipt of the written request, or on the day we receive it if we receive it on a Monthly Anniversary Day.

Such decrease will reduce the Specified Amount in the following order:

(1) It will decrease the insurance provided by the most recently approved increase;

(2) It will decrease the approved increase(s) successively by the most recent effective dates; and

(3) It will decrease the Initial Specified Amount.

However, any surrender charges in the Policy will not be affected by the decrease.

No request for a decrease will be given effect which would reduce the Specified Amount to the lesser of $25,000 or the Policy's initial Specified Amount.

DEATH BENEFIT OPTION

A change in the death benefit option may be requested. If the request is to change from Option 2 to Option 1, the Specified Amount will be increased by the amount of the Accumulated Value so that the new Specified Amount for Option 1 will equal the Option 2 death benefit on the date of change. If the request is to change from Option 1 to Option 2, the Specified Amount will be decreased by the sum of the Option 1 Specified Amount and the amount of the Accumulated Value less the Option 1 Death Benefit so that the new death benefit for Option 2 will equal the Option 1 death benefit on the date of change. This means that the amount of the death benefit will not immediately change when the death benefit option is changed. The death benefit option change will go into effect on the Monthly Anniversary Day following the date we receive the request, or on the day we receive it if we receive it on a Monthly Anniversary Day.

Part V -- Non-Forfeiture Provisions:

21. Accumulated Value:

The Accumulated Value on the date of issue shall be 100 percent of the initial premium amount (as shown on the Schedule Page), less the monthly deduction for the month following the Policy Date.

The Accumulated Value on each Monthly Anniversary Day shall be calculated as (1), minus (2), plus (3), plus (4), minus (5), where:

(1) is the Accumulated Value on the preceding Monthly Anniversary Day;

(2) is any partial surrender made since the preceding Monthly Anniversary Day;

(3) is 100 percent of all premiums received on this Policy since the preceding Monthly Anniversary Day;

(4) is one month's prorated interest (see Interest Rate(s) Provision) on item (1), minus (2), plus (3); and

(5) is the monthly deduction for the month following that Monthly Anniversary Day provided the surrender value is sufficient to cover that deduction. If the surrender value is not sufficient, the monthly deduction is taken from the premium payment. If the premium payment was insufficient, then the Grace Period provision will apply.

The Accumulated Value on any day other than a Monthly Anniversary Day shall be the Accumulated Value as of the preceding Monthly Anniversary Day, less any partial surrender made since the preceding Monthly Anniversary Day, plus 100 percent of all premiums received on this Policy since the preceding Monthly Anniversary Day, plus pro-rated interest to that day.

If the Policy terminates on a Monthly Anniversary Day, item (5) will be added to the Accumulated Value.

22. Monthly Deduction:

The monthly deduction is the sum of:

A) the cost of insurance for the Insured as determined on a monthly basis, calculated by multiplying (1) by the result of (2) minus (3), where:

(1) is the Monthly Cost Of Insurance Rate (see the the Cost Of Insurance Rates Provision);

(2) is the death benefit on the Monthly Anniversary Day, divided by 1.0036748; and,

(3) is the Accumulated Value on the Monthly Anniversary Day before subtracting the Monthly Deduction for the next month (see Section 21); and

B) the cost of additional benefits provided by Riders, if any; and

C) the monthly policy fee shown on the Schedule Page.

The monthly deduction is subtracted from the surrender value each month.

23. Cost of Insurance Rates:

The maximum guaranteed Monthly Cost Of Insurance Rates are shown on the Schedule Page(s). Those rates may be reduced at our option but may may not be increased. The cost of additional benefits for any Rider attached to this Policy will not be affected by the Cost Of Insurance Rates shown on the Schedule Page unless the cost of such Rider is also based on those rates.

Any reduction or increase in the current Monthly Cost Of Insurance Rates charged will be on a non-discriminatory basis toward any one Insured and will apply equally to all Insureds of the same age, sex, and classification whose Policies have been in force the same length of time, but any increase will never exceed the maximum rates shown on the Schedule Page. The current Cost Of Insurance Rates we charge will be determined annually by us based upon our expectations as to future mortality experience.

24. Interest Rate:

The Minimum Guaranteed Interest Rate used in calculating Accumulated Values is .36748% per month, compounded monthly. This is equivalent to 4.5% per year, compounded yearly. Each year we will guarantee current interest rate(s), which may be higher but can never be lower than the Minimum Guaranteed Rate, to calculate Accumulated Values for the next year.

The Minimum Guaranteed Rate will be applied to that portion of the Accumulated Value equal to any debt. The current interest rate(s) will apply to the balance of the Accumulated Value.

25. Surrender:

Any time after the first policy year, and during the Insured's life and before the Maturity Date, the owner may return this Policy to us and request its surrender value. The surrender value is the cash value on the date of surrender, less any debt, plus the pro-rated monthly deduction for the portion of the month between the date of surrender and the following Monthly Anniversary Day. The Cash Value of any Paid-Up Insurance surrendered within 30 days of a Policy Anniversary shall not be less than the Cash Value on such Anniversary.

Unless an Optional Method of Settlement is elected (see Settlement Option Provision) we will pay the surrender value to the Owner in one sum. Such proceeds are subject to the interest of any assignee of record. We reserve the right to defer paying the surrender value for up to six months from the date a validly executed request and this Policy are received at our Home Office.

The coverage provided in this Policy ends on the date we receive the Policy and a properly completed surrender request in our Home Office.

26. Partial Surrender:

The Owner may elect to make a Partial Surrender of this Policy. It must be made during the lifetime of the Insured and prior to the Maturity Date. The request must be in writing. It will be subject to these conditions:

- Each partial surrender is subject to a charge equal to the greater of $25.00, or 12 months excess interest on the amount withdrawn. The excess interest would be at the then current rate guaranteed on new premium payments.

- The minimum amount that can be withdrawn is $500.

- Only one Partial Surrender may be made in each Policy Year.

- The amount withdrawn, including the charge described above, cannot exceed the surrender value, less six times the current monthly deduction.

Partial Surrender requests may be deferred for a period of up to six months at our option, unless the withdrawn amount is to be used to pay premiums on any Policies you have with us.

The Accumulated Value and the Cash Value immediately after a Partial Surrender will be the Accumulated Value and the Cash Value immediately prior to the surrender reduced by the Partial Surrender amount withdrawn, which includes the charge described above. Also, the Death Benefit will be reduced by an amount equal to the reduction in Accumulated Value. As a result, if the Death Benefit is Option 1, the Specified Amount will be reduced by an amount equal to the reduction in Accumulated Value. (See Section 18 – Death Benefit).

27. Continuation of Insurance:

Insurance coverage under this Policy and any benefits provided by Rider(s) will be continued so long as there is no premium deficiency (see Grace Period Provision) or so long as the surrender value is sufficient to cover the monthly deduction. This provision shall not continue the Policy beyond the Maturity Date nor continue any Rider beyond the date for its termination as provided in the Rider. The surrender value on the Maturity Date will be paid to the owner.

28. Endowment at age 95 Option:

You may surrender this Policy at any time after the first policy year and apply the surrender value to purchase Endowment at age 95 insurance coverage on the Insured, subject to the following:

1. Written request for this option must be made to us;

2. The maximum amount of Endowment At Age 95 Insurance that may be purchased without evidence of insurability shall be calculated as (A), minus (B), plus (C), where

    (A) Is the amount of the Insured's death benefit under this Policy on the date of surrender,

    (B) Is the surrender value of this Policy on the date of surrender; and,

    (C) Is the amount applied as the Single Premium for the option. The amount applied must not be greater than the surrender value;

3. The consideration for the Endowment At Age 95 option shall be based on the same risk classification as the Policy;

4. The date of issue of the new Policy will be the date that the Insured's coverage under this Policy terminates;

5. The Single Premium for the new Policy will be based on the 1980 Commissioners' Standard Ordinary Mortality Table, Age Last Birthday, and 5.5% annual interest, or any more favorable current Endowment At Age 95 form approved in your State.

6. Any excess surrender value over and above the amount necessary to provide the maximum amount of Insurance that may be purchased under this Option will be refunded to the owner, or may also be used to purchase Endowment At Age 95 insurance on the same basis as specified above, except that evidence of insurability may be required.

29. Table of Guaranteed Values:

This Policy's Guaranteed Values are shown in the table on the schedule page. The table assumes that the scheduled premiums have been paid to the end of the policy year indicated, and that there is no debt. This table also assumes guaranteed cost of insurance rates and guaranteed interest rates. We will determine the cash value at any time within a policy year, with allowance for the time elapsed in such year and for the period that

premiums have been paid. We will furnish values upon request for policy years not shown.

30. Basis of Computations:

Surrender charges are based on the 1980 Commissioners' Standard Ordinary Mortality Table, Age Last Birthday, with interest at 4.5% per year, compounded yearly. A detailed statement of the surrender charges under this Policy has been filed with the Insurance Department of the State in which this Policy was delivered. Cash values under this Policy are not less than the minimums required on the Policy date by the State in which this Policy was delivered.

Part VI -- Settlement Options

31. Election of Options:

You may elect to have all or part of the proceeds of this Policy applied under one of the following settlement options. You may cancel or change a previous election, but only if you do so prior to the death of the Covered Insured or the endowment maturity date of the policy, if applicable. If you do not elect a settlement option prior to the Covered Insured's death, the beneficiary may do so provided the election is made within one year after the date of death of the Covered Insured. Any settlement option election will be subject to the limitations and conditions set forth below.

Any election or cancellation of a settlement option must be in writing in a form satisfactory to us. At the time an option is elected, we will prepare an agreement to be signed which will state the terms and conditions under which payments will be made. Any change of beneficiary will cancel any previous election of a settlement option.

OPTION 1--Income for a Fixed Period

We will pay the proceeds in equal installments over a period of from one to thirty years. The amount of each installment will be based upon the period and the frequency of the installments selected from Table 1 on the following page.

OPTION 2--Income for Life

We will pay a monthly income during a person's lifetime. The monthly income may be a life annuity only--Option 2(A), a life annuity with a minimum guaranteed period of 5, 10, or 20 years--Option 2(B), or an installment refund life annuity--Option 2(C), as shown in Table 2 on the following page. Payments will be at least equal to the amount shown in Table 2. Higher payments may be made at our discretion.

OPTION 3--Income of a Fixed Amount

We will pay the proceeds in equal installments in the amount and at the intervals agreed upon until the proceeds applied under this option, with interest at 3% per annum, are exhausted. The final installment will be for the then remaining balance only.

OPTION 4--Interest Income

We will hold the proceeds on deposit and pay or credit interest at the rate of 3% per annum. Payment of interest will be at such times and for such periods as are agreeable to you and us.

OPTION 5--Joint and Survivor Income for Life

We will pay an income during the lifetime of two payees, and continuing until the death of the survivor. This option includes a minimum guaranteed period of 10 years. Payments will be at least equal to the amount shown in Table 3. Higher payments may be made at our discretion. On request, we will furnish minimum income information for age combinations not shown in the table.

OPTION 6--Joint and Two-thirds Survivor Income for Life

We will pay an income (the "original amount") during the time two persons both remain alive, and two-thirds of the original amount during the remaining lifetime of the survivor. Payments during the time both payees are alive will be at least equal to the amount shown in Table 3. Higher payments may be made at our discretion. On request, we will furnish minimum income information for age combinations not shown in the table.

Limitations/Conditions

1. The amount applied under any Settlement Option must be at least $2,000 and must be sufficient to provide a periodic installment or interest payment of at least $20.

2. An Option will be available without our consent only if the proceeds are payable to a natural person receiving for his or her own benefit.

3. We may require proof of the age of any payee under Option 2, 5, or 6. We also may require evidence that the payee is living at the time any payment is due.

4. The first payment under an Option will be due on the date proceeds are applied, except under Option 4 it will be due at the end of the first payment interval.

Death of Payee

If the last surviving payee dies while receiving payments under an Option, we will pay as follows:

1. If Option 1 was elected, an amount equal to the commuted value of any unpaid installments.

2. If Option 2(B) or 5 was elected, an amount equal to the commuted value of any unpaid installments for the guaranteed period.

3. If Option 2(C) was elected, an amount equal to the commuted value of any unpaid installments required to equal the amount of proceeds applied under the Option.

4. If Option 3 or 4 was elected, an amount equal to any proceeds still on deposit plus accrued interest.

5. If Option 2A or 6 was elected, an amount equal to any unpaid installment due prior to the death of the payee under Option 2A or the last survivor under Option 6.

Commuted values under Option 1 will be calculated by us using 3% interest per year, compounded annually. Commuted values under Options 2(B), 2(C), or 5 will be calculated by us using interest compounded annually at the rate of 3% per year, or the rate of interest used in the calculation of the amount of the monthly installments, whichever is higher. Unless we have agreed otherwise in writing, payment shall be made in one sum to the payee's estate.

Surrender of Benefits

Unless the right was reserved in the Settlement Option election, no payee is allowed to (a) assign or borrow against the proceeds of an Option, (b) receive any installment payments in advance, or (c) make any changes in the provisions elected. All benefits shall be exempt from the claims of creditors to the maximum extent permitted by law.

Additional Interest

We may pay or credit additional interest of such amount and in such manner as we determine.

Settlement Option Tables

Monthly installments are shown per $1,000 of proceeds and are calculated using an interest rate of 3% per year, compounded annually. Installment amounts under Options 2, 5, and 6

depend on the age last birthday of the payee or payees on the date the first installment is due. Installments for any age or combination of ages not shown in Table 2 or 3 (Minimum age 50) will be furnished by us on request.

TABLE 1 -- Income for a Fixed Period

(Annual, semiannual, or quarterly installments shall be determined by multiplying the monthly installment by 11.839, 5.963, or 2.993 respectively.)

Years	Monthly Installment	Years	Monthly Installment	Years	Monthly Installment	Years	Monthly Installment	Years	Monthly Installment	Years	Monthly Installment
1	$84.47	6	$15.14	11	$8.86	16	$6.53	21	$5.32	26	$4.59
2	42.86	7	13.16	12	8.24	17	6.23	22	5.15	27	4.47
3	28.99	8	11.68	13	7.71	18	5.96	23	4.99	28	4.37
4	22.06	9	10.53	14	7.26	19	5.73	24	4.84	29	4.27
5	17.91	10	9.61	15	6.87	20	5.51	25	4.71	30	4.18

TABLE 2 -- Income for Life

Age of Payee	2A Life Annuity	2B Guaranteed Period			2C Installment Refund	Age of Payee	2A Life Annuity	2B Guaranteed Period			2C Installment Refund
		5 Years	10 Years	20 Years				5 Years	10 Years	20 Years	
46	$4.36	$4.35	$4.31	$4.14	$4.14	66	$7.34	$7.16	$6.66	$5.29	6.21
47	4.45	4.44	4.39	4.20	4.20	67	7.61	7.40	6.83	5.32	6.38
48	4.54	4.52	4.47	4.26	4.27	68	7.90	7.65	7.00	5.36	6.56
49	4.63	4.62	4.56	4.32	4.34	69	8.20	7.92	7.18	5.39	6.75
50	4.73	4.71	4.65	4.38	4.42	70	8.54	8.20	7.36	5.41	6.95
51	4.84	4.01	4.74	4.44	4.49	71	8.90	8.50	7.54	5.44	7.17
52	4.95	4.92	4.83	4.50	4.57	72	9.28	8.82	7.71	5.45	7.39
53	5.06	5.03	4.93	4.56	4.66	73	9.70	9.15	7.89	5.47	7.63
54	5.18	5.15	5.04	4.62	4.74	74	10.15	9.50	8.06	5.48	7.89
55	5.31	5.27	5.14	4.69	4.84	75	10.63	9.87	8.23	5.49	8.16
56	5.44	5.40	5.26	4.75	4.93	76	11.15	10.26	8.40	5.50	8.45
57	5.58	5.53	5.37	4.81	5.03	77	11.72	10.65	8.55	5.50	8.75
58	5.73	5.67	5.49	4.87	5.14	78	12.33	11.07	8.70	5.51	9.08
59	5.89	5.82	5.62	4.93	5.25	79	13.00	11.49	8.84	5.51	9.43
60	6.06	5.98	5.75	4.99	5.37	80	13.72	11.93	8.96	5.51	9.79
61	6.24	6.15	5.89	5.05	5.49	81	14.50	12.38	9.08	5.51	10.19
62	6.43	6.33	6.04	5.10	5.62	82	15.34	12.83	9.18	5.51	10.61
63	6.63	6.52	6.18	5.15	5.75	83	16.26	13.28	9.27	5.51	11.06
64	6.85	6.72	6.34	5.20	5.30	84	17.27	13.74	9.34	5.51	11.54
65	7.09	6.93	6.50	5.25	6.05	85 and over	18.35	14.18	9.41	5.51	12.06

TABLE 3 -- Joint and Survivor Life Income

OPTION 5 — Joint Life Income with Installments Guaranteed for 10 Years

OPTION 6 — Joint Life Income with Two-thirds to Survivor

Age of Payee	50	55	57	58	59	60	62	65	70	Age of Payee	50	55	57	58	59	60	62	65	70
50	4.19	4.37	4.44	4.47	4.50	4.53	4.59	4.66	4.76	50	4.70	4.96	5.06	5.12	5.17	5.23	5.35	5.52	5.82
51	4.23	4.42	4.49	4.53	4.56	4.60	4.66	4.74	4.85	51	4.75	5.02	5.13	5.19	5.24	5.30	5.42	5.61	5.92
52	4.26	4.47	4.55	4.59	4.63	4.66	4.73	4.82	4.94	52	4.80	5.08	5.19	5.25	5.31	5.37	5.50	5.69	6.02
53	4.30	4.52	4.61	4.65	4.69	4.73	4.80	4.90	5.03	53	4.85	5.14	5.26	5.32	5.39	5.45	5.58	5.78	6.12
54	4.34	4.57	4.66	4.71	4.75	4.79	4.87	4.98	5.12	54	4.90	5.20	5.33	5.39	5.46	5.53	5.66	5.87	6.23
55	4.37	4.62	4.72	4.77	4.81	4.86	4.94	5.06	5.22	55	4.96	5.27	5.40	5.47	5.53	5.60	5.75	5.96	6.34
56	4.41	4.67	4.77	4.83	4.87	4.92	5.02	5.14	5.32	56	5.01	5.33	5.47	5.54	5.61	5.68	5.83	6.06	6.46
57	4.44	4.72	4.83	4.88	4.94	4.99	5.09	5.23	5.42	57	5.06	5.40	5.54	5.61	5.69	5.76	5.92	6.16	6.57
58	4.47	4.77	4.88	4.94	5.00	5.06	5.16	5.32	5.52	58	5.12	5.47	5.61	5.69	5.77	5.85	6.01	6.26	6.70
59	4.50	4.81	4.94	5.00	5.06	5.12	5.24	5.40	5.63	59	5.17	5.53	5.69	5.77	5.85	5.93	6.10	6.37	6.82
60	4.53	4.86	4.99	5.06	5.12	5.19	5.31	5.49	5.74	60	5.23	5.60	5.76	5.85	5.93	6.02	6.20	6.47	6.96
61	4.56	4.90	5.04	5.11	5.18	5.25	5.38	5.58	5.85	61	5.29	5.67	5.84	5.93	6.02	6.11	6.29	6.58	8.09
62	4.59	4.94	5.09	5.16	5.24	5.31	5.46	5.66	5.96	62	5.35	5.75	5.92	6.01	6.10	6.20	6.39	6.70	7.23
63	4.61	4.98	5.14	5.22	5.29	5.37	5.53	5.75	6.07	63	5.40	5.82	6.00	6.09	6.19	6.29	6.49	6.61	7.38
64	4.64	5.02	5.19	5.27	5.35	5.43	5.60	5.83	6.18	64	5.46	5.89	6.08	6.18	6.28	6.38	6.59	6.93	7.53
65	4.66	5.06	5.23	5.32	5.40	5.49	5.66	5.92	6.29	65	5.52	5.96	6.16	6.26	6.37	6.47	6.70	7.05	7.68
66	4.68	5.10	5.27	5.36	5.45	5.54	5.73	6.00	6.41	66	5.58	6.04	6.24	6.35	6.46	6.57	6.80	7.17	7.84
67	4.71	5.13	5.31	5.41	5.50	5.60	5.79	6.08	6.51	67	5.64	6.11	6.32	6.44	6.55	6.67	6.91	7.30	8.00
68	4.72	5.16	5.35	5.45	5.54	5.65	5.85	6.15	6.62	68	5.70	6.19	6.41	6.52	6.64	6.76	7.02	7.42	8.16
69	4.74	5.19	5.39	5.49	5.59	5.69	5.91	6.23	6.72	69	5.76	6.27	6.49	6.61	6.73	6.86	7.12	7.55	8.33
70	4.76	5.22	5.42	5.52	5.63	5.74	5.96	6.29	6.82	70	5.82	6.34	6.57	6.70	6.82	6.96	7.23	7.68	8.50
71	4.77	5.24	5.45	5.56	5.67	5.78	6.01	6.36	6.92	71	5.88	6.42	6.66	6.79	6.92	7.05	7.34	7.81	8.67
72	4.79	5.27	5.48	5.59	5.70	5.82	6.06	6.42	7.01	72	5.94	6.49	6.74	6.87	7.01	7.15	7.45	7.94	8.84
73	4.80	5.29	5.51	5.62	5.74	5.86	6.10	6.48	7.10	73	6.00	6.57	6.82	6.96	7.10	7.25	7.56	8.07	9.02
74	4.81	5.31	5.53	5.65	5.77	5.89	6.14	6.53	7.18	74	6.06	6.64	6.91	7.05	7.19	7.35	7.67	8.20	9.20
75	4.82	5.32	5.55	5.67	5.79	5.92	6.18	6.58	7.25	75	6.12	6.71	6.99	7.13	7.28	7.44	7.78	8.33	9.37

WASHINGTON NATIONAL INSURANCE COMPANY
ORDINARY LIFE DEPARTMENT
1630 CHICAGO AVENUE
EVANSTON, ILLINOIS 60201

FOR MORE INFORMATION ABOUT THIS POLICY PLEASE CONTACT:
HOME OFFICE
HOME OFFICE
WASHINGTON NATIONAL INS CO
1630 CHICAGO AVENUE
EVANSTON IL 60201

02/22/88
POLICY NUMBER
86-9999999-

STATEMENT OF POLICY COST AND BENEFIT INFORMATION
PREPARED FOR: DOE,JANE S
AGE BASIS: 35   ISSUE BASIS: NONSMOKER

BASIC POLICY   ADJUSTABLE LIFE INSURANCE
AT AGE BASIS SHOWN, THE DEATH BENEFIT EQUALS THE LARGER OF
1) THE SPECIFIED AMOUNT, OR 2) 250% OF THE ACCUMULATED VALUE

POLICY YEAR	ANNUALIZED PREMIUM *	GUARANTEED (4.500%)			PROJECTED **		
		+DEATH BENEFIT	+ACCUMULATED VALUE	+CASH VALUE	+DEATH BENEFIT	+ACCUMULATED VALUE	+CASH VALUE
1	1,322.91	50,000	1,253	867	50,000	1,253	867
2	1,600.00	50,000	2,789	2,185	50,000	2,915	2,312
3	1,600.00	50,000	4,393	3,790	50,000	4,722	4,118
4	1,600.00	50,000	6,070	5,466	50,000	6,686	6,082
5	1,600.00	50,000	7,821	7,218	50,000	8,822	8,218
6	1,600.00	50,000	9,650	9,047	50,000	11,145	10,541
7	1,600.00	50,000	11,557	10,953	50,000	13,672	13,068
8	1,600.00	50,000	13,546	12,942	50,000	16,423	15,820
9	1,600.00	50,000	15,622	15,018	50,000	19,422	18,818
10	1,600.00	50,000	17,789	17,789	50,372	22,690	22,690
11	1,600.00	50,000	20,055	20,055	56,426	26,244	26,244
12	1,600.00	50,000	22,424	22,424	62,906	30,099	30,099
13	1,600.00	50,549	24,901	24,901	69,581	34,276	34,276
14	1,600.00	54,144	27,484	27,484	76,448	38,806	38,806
15	1,600.00	57,623	30,169	30,169	83,498	43,716	43,716
16	1,600.00	60,974	32,959	32,959	90,721	49,039	49,039
17	1,600.00	63,831	35,860	35,860	97,560	54,809	54,809
18	1,600.00	66,483	38,879	38,879	104,427	61,068	61,068
19	1,600.00	68,914	42,021	42,021	111,287	67,858	67,858
20	1,600.00	71,112	45,294	45,294	118,109	75,229	75,229
AGE 60	1,600.00	88,286	67,912	67,912	175,300	134,846	134,846
AGE 65	1,600.00	109,590	91,325	91,325	255,313	212,761	212,761

++BASED ON GUARANTEED VALUES, POLICY MATURES ON FEBRUARY 22 2048
   BASED ON PROJECTED VALUES, POLICY MATURES ON FEBRUARY 22 2048

**CURRENTLY PROJECTED VALUES REFLECT COST OF INSURANCE CHARGES AND INTEREST RATES AT CURRENT

NON-GUARANTEED LEVELS.   PRESENTLY THE COMPANY IS PAYING 8.900% ON ACCUMULATED VALUES.

	NET PAYMENT COST INDEX *		SURRENDER COST INDEX *		EXPLANATIONS OF THE INTENDED
	PROJECTED----GUARANTEED		PROJECTED----GUARANTEED		USE OF THESE INDEXES ARE
					PROVIDED IN THE LIFE INSURANCE
					BUYER'S GUIDE.
YEAR 10	31.316	31.316	-3.045	4.377	
YEAR 20	31.576	31.576	-11.759	5.485	

* INCLUDES PREMIUM FOR RIDERS, IF ANY. PLANNED PERIODIC PREMIUM PAID QUARTERLY.

+ END OF YEAR VALUE.

++THESE VALUES ARE BASED ON THE INTEREST RATES AND MORTALITY, AND OTHER CHARGES GUARANTEED IN THE POLICY AND
THE ANTICIPATED OR ASSUMED ANNUAL PREMIUMS SHOWN IN THE POLICY SUMMARY.

POLICY LOAN INTEREST RATE IS 7.4% PAID IN ADVANCE.
THIS DISCLOSURE IS FOR YOUR PROTECTION. IT PROVIDES BASIC INFORMATION ABOUT THE COST AND COVERAGE OF THIS
POLICY. READ IT CAREFULLY. IT IS NOT AN OFFER TO CONTRACT AND DOES NOT ALTER OR MODIFY ANY POLICY OR RIDER.

WASHINGTON NATIONAL INSURANCE COMPANY
ORDINARY LIFE DEPARTMENT
1630 CHICAGO AVENUE
EVANSTON. ILLINOIS   60201

FOR MORE INFORMATION ABOUT THIS POLICY PLEASE CONTACT:
HOME OFFICE
HOME OFFICE
WASHINGTON NATIONAL INS CO
1630 CHICAGO AVENUE
EVANSTON IL 60201

02/22/88
POLICY NUMBER
86-9999999-

STATEMENT OF POLICY COST AND BENEFIT INFORMATION (CONTINUED)
PREPARED FOR: DOE.JANE S
AGE BASIS: 35   ISSUE BASIS: NONSMOKER

--WAIVER OF MONTHLY COST OF INSURANCE-- (1)

POL YR	CENTS PER DOLLAR OF MONTHLY DEDUCTION TO BE WAIVED
1	0.07
2	0.08
3	0.09
4	0.10
5	0.10
6	0.11
7	0.12
8	0.12
9	0.12
10	0.13
11	0.13
12	0.13
13	0.14
14	0.14
15	0.15
16	0.16
17	0.18
18	0.19
19	0.21
20	0.23
@ 60	0.29
@ 65	0.00

(1) WAIVER BENEFIT - COST OF INSURANCE AND MONTHLY EXPENSE CHARGES WAIVED IN THE EVENT OF TOTAL
AND PERMANENT DISABILITY OCCURING BEFORE AGE 65. COST OF INSURANCE DEDUCTED TO AGE 65.

Appendix J. Glossary of Legal Terms

absolute assignment The irrevocable transfer of all the policyowner's rights in a life insurance policy.

acceptance Assent by an offeree to the terms of an offer.

accident An unusual, unforeseeable event which happens suddenly and unexpectedly and without the insured's intent.

accidental means clause A clause requiring both means and result to be accidental if accidental death benefits are to be payable.

accidental result clause A clause requiring only the result to be accidental if accidental death benefits are to be payable.

actual authority The authority to act on the principal's behalf that an agent reasonably believes he or she has been given by the principal. Actual authority can be express or implied.

administrative officer An official belonging to the executive branch of government.

affirmative action plan A plan used to remedy the effects of past discrimination by requiring the hiring of women and members of other protected classes.

agent A person who acts for another person, the principal, especially in contractual dealings with third parties.

aleatory contract A contract in which the promise by one party is conditioned on the happening of an uncertain event.

answer A formal written statement by a defendant in which she or he explains the facts alleged by the plaintiff.

apparent authority Agency authority a person has because a principal has created the appearance of authority to a third person.

appellate court (1) An intermediate court; (2) a court where appeals are taken.

assignment (1) A transfer of an ownership right, usually a chose in action; (2) a written document used to effect such a transfer.

bilateral contract A contract under which promises are made by both parties.

bona fide occupational qualification A characteristic, such as sex or religion, upon which it is usually unlawful to base an employment decision, but upon which such a decision can lawfully be based as to the job in question.

breach of contract The failure of a party to perform a promise according to its terms, without a legal excuse.

broker   A person who brings buyers and sellers together.

burden of proof   (1) The duty of producing evidence; (2) the obligation of the plaintiff to present the court with a preponderance of evidence in his or her favor.

case law   Law laid down in reported court decisions.

center of gravity rule   A state conflict of laws rule by which a state applies the law of the state most concerned with the outcome of the litigation. Also called grouping of contacts rule, principal contacts rule, most significant relationship rule, governmental interest analysis, and paramount interest rule.

chose in action   A right that can be enforced by legal action, or by a suit in equity.

chose in possession   Something tangible of which one has actual possession, such as a chair.

civil law   (1) Law derived from Roman law; (2) the body of law which determines private rights and liabilities.

class action   A lawsuit brought by a representative member, or members, of a large group of persons on behalf of all members of the group.

code   A collection of statutes systematically arranged, indexed, revised, and reenacted by the legislature in that form.

collateral assignment   A temporary transfer of some, but not all, policy rights to a lender to provide security for a loan.

collusion   A secret agreement between two or more persons to do some act in order to defraud a third person.

Commerce Clause   A clause in the federal Constitution which reads, in part, "The Congress shall have Power . . . To regulate Commerce with foreign Nations, and among the several States, and with the Indian Tribes."

common disaster   A disaster common to two or more people in which they lose their lives, such as an automobile accident, fire, or flood.

common law   (1) A heritage of general principles and concepts involving custom, public policy and ideas of justice that are followed by courts of common-law countries, states, and provinces; (2) a system of law followed by England and by nations which derive their law from English law (as contrasted to civil law); (3) decisions of the courts.

community property   Property owned by a husband and wife residing in a community property state.

compensatory damages   The money which a court awards a plaintiff to compensate for a wrong done to her or him.

competent party   A person competent to enter into a valid contract because he or she is of legal age and without mental infirmity or other incapacity.

complaint   A formal written statement of a plaintiff's cause of action.

compromise settlement   An agreement between two or more persons to settle a matter in dispute between them, and the performance of the promises made in the agreement; accord and satisfaction.

condition precedent   An uncertain event which must occur before a right arises.

condition subsequent An event which cancels an existing right.

conflict of laws That part of the law of each state or nation which determines whether, in dealing with a legal situation, the law of some other state or nation will be recognized, be given effect, or be applied.

consideration The thing of value requested and given in exchange for a promise; any benefit to the promisor or detriment to the promisee.

constitution The general principles that form the legal foundation of a government.

construe Interpret.

contest, policy A court action challenging the validity of a policy.

contract An agreement enforceable at law; a promise or set of promises for breach of which the law gives a remedy or the performance of which the law recognizes as a duty.

conversion An unauthorized act which deprives an owner of her or his property.

corporation A legal entity authorized by law to carry on a business of a specific nature.

counteroffer A rejection of an offer and making of a new offer.

court of original jurisdiction A court where a case is first brought.

crime Conduct causing harm to the public; a felony or misdemeanor.

criminal law Law which prohibits and punishes conduct causing harm to the public.

declaratory judgment A judgment that declares the rights of the parties involved in the suit, but does not require either of the parties to take any action or pay any money to the other.

defamation A false communication which tends to harm the reputation of a person so as to lower the person in the estimation of others and deter others from associating or dealing with the defamed person. Defamation is a tort.

default judgment A judgment, usually in favor of the plaintiff, entered without the defendant's being heard in his or her own defense, because of the defendant's failure to answer the complaint or to appear at trial.

deposition The oral testimony under oath of a witness prior to trial.

discovery The determination of facts and issues by means of pretrial devices such as depositions, interrogatories, subpoenas, and medical examinations.

disparate impact discrimination The discrimination which occurs when an apparently nondiscriminatory job requirement has a disproportionately large adverse impact on the opportunities of people in a protected class, such as blacks, women, etc.

disparate treatment discrimination Discrimination in which an employer bases an employment decision on a person's race, religion, national origin, sex, age, and so forth.

district court A first level federal court.

diversity of citizenship   Domicile in different states by parties on opposite sides of a lawsuit. One of the grounds to invoke jurisdiction of a United States District Court.

dividend, policyowners'   The refund of excess premium to the owner of a participating policy; a premium abatement.

dividend, stockholders'   The money paid to the owners of corporate stock, usually out of the accumulated earnings of the corporation.

duress   An inducement to make a contract against a person's will by the wrongful act or threat of another.

election, doctrine of   The doctrine applied by the courts that a person with two or more inconsistent remedies available for the enforcement of a single right must elect one remedy and forgo the others.

employment-at-will rule   The rule that an employer can dismiss an employee who was hired for an indefinite period of time without notice or cause. This rule is being riddled with exceptions.

equity courts   The courts which arose in England because of the inadequacy of legal remedies.

escheat   The reversion of ownership of property to the state in the absence of persons legally entitled to take claim to the property.

estoppel, equitable   Words or conduct of one party which misleads a second party to act so that harm results to the second party.

executive branch   The branch of government empowered to carry out laws.

exemption   A right given by law to a debtor to retain certain property free from seizure by her or his creditors.

exoneration statutes   Statutes in community property states which make payment of a death benefit, in good faith and without knowledge of an adverse claim, sufficient to discharge the insurer of liability.

Expressio unius est exclusio alterius   A Latin phrase meaning "the expression of one thing means the exclusion of another thing."

felony   A serious crime for which the punishment can be imprisonment in the state or federal penitentiary, or even death.

forgery   The signing of another person's name to a document with the intention of deceitfully and fraudulently presenting the signature as genuine.

formal contract   A contract binding because of its form.

fraud   An intentional misrepresentation communicated to another person who is injured as a result of relying on the misrepresentation.

gift   A voluntary transfer of property to another person, made without receiving consideration in return.

gift *causa mortis*   A gift made by a person in apprehension of his or her death, when death seems imminent, on condition that, if the death does not occur as anticipated from the illness or injury then suffered, ownership of the property will return to the giver.

grantor   One who creates a trust by transferring property to a trustee.

heirs   Those persons entitled to inherit the property of a person who has no will.

incorporation by reference   A rule of contract law that permits contracting parties to incorporate into a written contract any other document by referring to it in the contract.

independent contractor   A person who has a distinct business, is hired to do a particular job, is paid for that job, rather than on a salary basis, uses her or his own tools, and follows her or his own discretion in carrying out the job.

informal contract   A contract which creates legal duties because the parties have met requirements that relate to the substance, rather than to the form, of the transaction.

insurable interest   An interest which takes an insurance contract out of the class of wager contracts. An insurable interest in another person's life is any reasonable expectation of benefit or advantage from the continued life of that person.

interpleader   An equitable action brought by a disinterested holder of property to which there are conflicting claims. The holder deposits the property with the court, and is dismissed from the case, leaving the claimants to litigate.

interrogatories   A series of written questions drawn up by one party to a lawsuit and given to the other party, or to a witness, to answer within a fixed period of time.

inter vivos trust   A trust which takes effect during the lifetime of the grantor.

intestate   A person who dies without a valid will.

issue   (1) Lineal descendants such as children, grandchildren, great-grandchildren and so forth; (2) a material point which is affirmed by one party to a lawsuit and denied by the other. Issues can be of fact or of law.

issue of fact   A material fact alleged by one party to a lawsuit and denied by the other.

issue of law   A disagreement by plaintiff and defendant as to the application of the law to the facts in a lawsuit.

joint tenancy   A form of property ownership in which two or more persons hold property with equal rights to share in its enjoyment during their lives and rights of survivorship.

judicial branch   The branch of government empowered to interpret laws.

jurisdiction of the subject matter   The power of a court to hear and make an enforceable decision in a case.

jurisdiction over the person   The jurisdiction of a court over the person sued because of compliance by the court with certain constitutional requirements.

laches   In equity, an unreasonable delay by a plaintiff which harms the defendant.

legislative branch   The branch of government empowered to make laws.

libel   Written or pictorial defamation.

loan   The transfer of money from one person, the creditor, to another person, the debtor, upon agreement that the debtor will return to the creditor an equivalent sum at a later date (usually plus interest).

master   A word used for *principal* in cases involving torts against third persons committed by an agent, usually called a *servant* in this context.

means   Cause.

misdemeanor   A crime less serious than a felony, usually punishable by fine or by imprisonment other than in a penitentiary, as, for example, in a county jail.

model law   An act or regulation proposed by experts in a particular field for adoption by the states; a uniform law.

necessaries   Things reasonably necessary for a minor's or mentally infirm person's maintenance, considering her or his social position and financial status.

offer   A proposal that, if accepted by another person according to its terms, will create a binding agreement.

operation of law   The determination of rights and obligations through the automatic effects of the law, and not by any direct act of an affected party.

parol evidence   Oral evidence (testimony) given by a witness in court.

parol evidence rule   The rule that, when parties put their contract into an unambiguous writing, all previous oral agreements merge into the written contract and that parol evidence is not admissible to add to, detract from, or alter the contract as written.

partnership   An association of two or more persons to carry on an unincorporated business.

per capita   (1) By head or by individual; (2) to share equally.

personal property   A right over that which is not land or something attached to land, such as a bracelet, a racehorse, money, or shares of stock.

personal representative   The executor or administrator of an estate.

per stirpes   By family branches. A per stirpes beneficiary designation is a method of dividing benefits among living members of a class of beneficiaries and the descendants of deceased members.

pleadings   The formal written statements of the respective claims and defenses of the parties to a court action.

precedent   A previous decision by a court, or by a higher court of the same jurisdiction, on the same question and involving the same general set of facts. A precedent will be followed unless there is a strong reason to depart from it.

presumption   A conclusion that the law requires to be drawn from a given set of facts, which conclusion will stand until adequate evidence to the contrary is presented to the court.

pretext interview   An interview in which the interviewer, in an attempt to obtain information about someone, makes a misrepresentation or refuses to identify himself or herself.

prima facie case   A set of facts, established by sufficient evidence, that entitles a person to the relief she or he is asking, in the absence of evidence to dispute those facts.

principal   One for whom an agent acts, especially as to contractual dealings with third persons.

privacy   (1) The right to be let alone; (2) in insurance contexts, the right to fair personal information practices.

privacy, invasion of   A tort taking four forms: (1) appropriation of a person's name or likeness for another's benefit; (2) unreasonable intrusion into a person's seclusion, solitude, or private affairs; (3) public disclosure of private facts about a person; (4) placing a person in a false light in the public eye.

probate   To prove the validity of a will in court.

procedural law   Rules for bringing a court action.

promissory note   A written promise to pay a stated sum of money.

property   (1) Rights of possession, use, control, and disposition; (2) popularly, that which is owned.

proximate cause   A cause that is either directly responsible for a death (or injury) or that initiates an unbroken chain of events, each causing the next, which leads to and brings about the death.

punitive damages   The damages awarded to a plaintiff to punish and make an example of the defendant; exemplary damages.

Qui facit per alium facit per se   A Latin phrase meaning "he who acts for another acts himself."

ratification   The validation by a principal of an unauthorized act done by her or his purported agent.

real property   A right over land and that which is attached to the land, such as a house and trees; real estate.

reasonable expectations doctrine   The doctrine that the reasonable expectations of policyowners and beneficiaries will be honored, even though the strict terms of the policy do not support those expectations.

rebate   Something of value, such as part of a commission, given to a prospect to induce the purchase of insurance.

reformation   An equitable remedy by which a written contract is revised or interpreted to express the original intent of the parties.

release   The giving up of a right or claim, ordinarily in exchange for consideration.

representation   A statement by an applicant of facts upon which the insurer bases its decision whether or not to issue the applied-for policy.

rescission   An equitable remedy in which a court declares a contract void because of material misrepresentation or mistake.

Respondeat superior   "Let the master answer"; the principal that a master is responsible for the wrongful act (tort) of a servant committed in the course of the servant's employment.

reverse discrimination   Discrimination against persons who are not ordinarily discriminated against, such as a young white Protestant male.

rights of survivorship   The rights of a joint tenant, or joint tenants, on the death of another joint tenant, to the deceased tenant's share of the estate.

rule against accumulations   The rule which prohibits one person from leaving property to another person to accumulate income for the other person too far into the future.

rule against perpetuities   A rule aimed at preventing remoteness of vesting. The rule is stated "No interest is good, unless it must vest, if at all, not later than 21 years after some life in being at the creation of the interest."

seal   An impression on wax, or a gummed wafer, affixed to a document, or an impression in the paper of the document, made to authenticate the document.

separation of powers   The division of a government into branches, as the executive, legislative, and judicial branches.

sexual harrassment   Unwelcome sexual advances, requests for sexual favors, and other verbal or physical conduct of a sexual nature.

slander   Spoken defamation.

sole proprietorship   An unincorporated business owned by one person.

specific performance   An equitable remedy which requires that a contract be carried out as promised.

Stare decisis   The practice by courts of following previous court decisions on the same question.

statute   An act of the legislature declaring, commanding, or prohibiting something; the written will of the legislature, expressed according to the forms necessary to constitute it the law of the state.

Statute of Frauds   A statute originally enacted in England, since enacted in the states, requiring that certain informal contracts be evidenced by a writing.

subagent   The agent of an agent.

substantial compliance rule   The rule that, where a policyholder has done everything possible to comply with the beneficiary change procedure set forth in the policy, but has failed because of circumstances beyond his or her control, the change will be effective.

summons   A notice to a defendant that an action has been filed against her or him and that a judgment will be granted unless an answer is filed within a specified period of time.

tender   An unconditional and timely offer to pay the full sum due in a medium of payment acceptable to an insurer (or other person).

testamentary trust   A trust created by a will and which takes effect at the testator's death.

testator   A person who makes a will.

tort   A violation of a duty to another person imposed by law, rather than by contract, for which the person harmed can recover money damages from the person who committed the tort.

trust   An arrangement whereby property is transferred to a trustee, who has legal title to the property, with the intention that the property be administered for the benefit of someone other than the trustee, who has equitable title (the trust beneficiary).

undue influence   The misuse of a position of confidence or dominion to overcome the will of another person.

uniform law   See model law.

unilateral contract   A contract having promises by one party only.

void contract   An unenforceable agreement. *Void contract* is a contradiction in terms.

voidable contract   A contract that is enforceable until a party who has the right to do so (such as a minor) takes some action to disaffirm the contract.

wagering agreement   An aleatory agreement which is often illegal.

waiver   The voluntary and intentional giving up of a known right. Waivers can be express or implied.

warranty   A statement guaranteed to be true in all respects. If the statement is untrue in any respect, even if it is not material, the contract of which it is a part can be rescinded.

will   A document directing the disposition of property after the death of the owner (the testator).

wrongful death statute   A statute which gives the executor, administrator, or heirs of a deceased person a cause of action for injuries to the deceased that resulted from the wrongful acts of another.

Index of Cases

Acacia Mutual Life Association, Densby
v., 422 n

Acacia Mutual Life Association v. Kaul,
393

Adair, Froelich v., 573–74

Aetna Insurance Co., Gruenberg v.,
463 n

Aetna Life & Casualty Co., Spencer v.,
465 n

Aetna Life Insurance Co. v. Bartlett, 298

Aetna Life Insurance Co., Cason v., 505

Aetna Life Insurance Co. v. Harris &
Reichard Fur Dyers, 107 n

Aetna Life Insurance Co., Hoffman v.,
118 n

Aetna Life Insurance Co. v. Hooker,
431 n

Aetna Life Insurance Co., Kowalski v.,
492 n

Aetna Life Insurance Co. v. Lavoie, 466

Aetna Life Insurance Co., Lester v.,
317 n

Aetna Life Insurance Co., Rocky Mutual
Savings & Trust Co. v., 383 n

Aetna Life Insurance Co. v. Routon,
122 n

Aetna Life Insurance Co. v. Schmitt,
231 n

Aetna Life Insurance Co., Shea v., 492 n

Aetna Life Insurance Co., Smith v.,
492 n

Aetna Life Insurance Co., Tyre v., 232 n,
234 n

Aiello v. United Airlines, Inc., 594 n

Albrent v. Spencer, 360

Allen v. Metropolitan Life Insurance
Co., 153

Allen v. Travelers' Protective Association, 208 n

All States Life Insurance Co. v. Tillman,
493 n

American Bankers' Insurance Co., Lucus
v., 185 n

American Home Mutual Life Insurance
Co. v. Harvey, 505

American Insurance Co. v. Nationwide
Mutual Insurance Co., 119 n

American Life Insurance Co. v. Stewart,
422 n

American Life Insurance Co. v. Stewart,
436

American National Insurance Co., Balyeat v., 316 n

American Surety Co., Coen v., 179 n

Ancient Order of United Workmen, Holdom v., 447 n

Angelus v. Government Personnel Life
Insurance Co., 454

Arizona Governing Committee v. Norris,
158

Associated Aviation Underwriters, Johns
v., 576

Atlantic American Life Insurance Co. v.
White, 208 n

Austero v. National Casualty Co., 463 n

Austin, Mutual Reserve Fund Life Association v., 426 n

Austin, Sears v., 501 n

Automobile Club, Riordan v., 139 n,
540 n

Avent v. National Life and Accident Insurance Co., 203

Baker, In re, 105

Bailey, Travelers Insurance Co. v., 407 n

Bailey v. Pacific Mutual Life Insurance
Co., 420 n

Balyeat v. American National Insurance
Co., 316 n

Banker's Life Association, Duffy v.,
142 n

Bankers Life & Casualty Co. v. Erenshaw, 466

Bankers National Life Insurance Co.,
Dorothy M. Deder v., 391–93

Bankers National Life Insurance Co., Smith v., 381 n

Barnes, Gulf Atlantic Life Insurance Co. v., 465 n

Barry, United States Mutual Accident Association v., 203

Barstow v. Federal Life Insurance Co., 120 n

Bartlett, Aetna Life Insurance Co. v., 298

Beacon Life Association, Witten v., 142 n

Beebe Rubber Co., Monge v., 594 n

Beeman v. Supreme Lodge, Shield of Honor, 326 n

Bekken v. Equitable Life Assurance Society of the United States, 144 n

Bennett v. National Life & Accident Insurance Co., 123 n

Bernard v. Prudential Insurance Co., 208 n

Bernier v. Pacific Mutual Life Insurance Co., 426 n

Bernier v. Pacific Mutual Life Insurance Co., 427

Bess, United States v., 239 n

Bethlehem, Myers v., 401

Betty Jackson v. Elizabeth Smith, 246–50

Bieniek, Franklin Life Insurance Co. v., 130 n

Bishop v. Capitol Life Insurance Co., 532

Blethen v. Pacific Mutual Life Insurance Co., 232 n

Blue Cross and Blue Shield, Toussaint v., 594 n

Board of Assessors v. New York Life Insurance Co., 353

Board of Trustees of Unitarian Church v. Nationwide Life Insurance Co., 339 n

Boeing Airplane Co., Johnson v., 572–73

Boggio v. California-Western States Life Insurance Co., 116, 122

Boise Dodge, Inc. v. Clark, 463 n

Bollinger, Conservative Life Insurance Co. v., 342 n

Botts v. Hartford Accident & Indemnity Co., 206 n

T. J. Bowman v. Zenith Life Insurance Co., 172

Boyer v. State Farmers' Mutual Hail Insurance Co., 142 n

Bradwell v. The State, 3 n

Brand v. Erisman, 370

Brawner v. Welfare Finance Corp., 104 n

Breeden, Sloan v., 369 n

Broderick, Union Mutual Life Insurance Co. v., 232 n

Brooks v. Louisiana and Southern Life Insurance Co., 16 n

Brown v. Gordon, 238 n

Brown, Travelers Insurance Co. v., 326 n

Browne v. John Hancock Mutual Life Insurance Co., 309 n

Bryce, Pacific States Life Insurance Co. v., 342 n

Buechler, Doering v., 270

Burch v. Mellor, 106 n

Burne v. Franklin Life Insurance Co., 210 n

Burr v. Commercial Travelers Mutual Accident Association, 205

Business Men's Accident Association, Pledger v., 202 n

Business Men's Assurance Co., Price v., 208 n

Butterworth v. Mississippi Valley Trust Co., 367

Butts, General American Life Insurance Co. v., 317 n

Byrle, Faber v., 574–76

California Life Insurance Co., Silberg v., 463 n

California, Robertson v., 98

California State Life Insurance Co., Narver v., 315 n

California-Western States Life Insurance Co., Boggio v., 116, 122

California-Western States Life Insurance Co., Moore v., 232 n

California-Western States Life Insurance Co., Schaefer v., 423 n

California-Western States Life Insurance Co. v. Sanford, 448 n

Candimat Co., Connecticut General Life Insurance Co. v., 398 n

Cannon v. Southland Life Insurance Co., 152 n

Capital Life and Health Insurance Co., Henderson v., 309

Capitol Life Insurance Co., Bishop v., 532

Capitol Life Insurance Co., Exchange Trust Co. v., 383 n

Carter, Provident Life & Accident Insurance Co. v., 447 n

Carter v. Continental Life Insurance Co., 431 n

Carter v. Kaskaskia Community Action Agency, 597–98

Cason v. Aetna Life Insurance Co., 505

Central Accident Insurance Co. v. Rembe, 209 n

Central Plains Insurance Co., Southards v., 532

Central States Life Insurance Co., Lynch v., 492 n

Charbonnier v. Chicago National Life Insurance Co., 431 n

Charter Oak Life Insurance Co., Worthington v., 310 n

Chavers v. National Security Fire Casualty Co., 465 n

Chavis v. Southern Insurance Co., 386 n

Chelly v. Home Insurance Co., 202 n

Chelsea-Wheeler Coal Co. v. Marvin, 369 n

Chicago National Life Insurance Co., Charbonnier v., 431 n

Chrysler Corp., Kot v., 363 n

Chrysler Corp., Murphy v., 492 n

Citizen's Home Insurance Co. v. Glisson, 77 n

Citizens' National Bank, Hutsell v., 362 n

City Bank & Trust Co., Starbuck v., 266

Clark and Clark, Prudential Insurance Co. of America v., 80–83

Clark, Boise Dodge, Inc. v., 463 n

Clark v. Lone Star Life Insurance Co., 221 n

Clark, Wheelock v., 140 n

Clement v. New York Life Insurance Co., 431 n

Cleveland, Liberty Mutual Insurance Co. v., 118 n

Cleverdon, Pacific Mutual Life Insurance Co., 232 n

Coen v. American Surety Co., 179 n

Coile v. Order of United Commercial Travelers of American, 326 n

Cole, Metropolitan Life Insurance Co. v., 492 n

Collister v. Nationwide Life Insurance Co., 154 n

Colorado in Urbancich v. Jersin, 302

Columbian Mutual Life Insurance Co. v. Martin, 431 n

Columbian National Life Insurance Co., Maslin v., 430

Commercial Travelers Mutual Accident Association, Burr v., 205

Commissioner, Morse v., 343 n

Commissioner v. Stern, 239 n

Commonwealth Life Insurance Co. v. Spears, 122 n

Connallon, Prudential Insurance Co. v., 179 n

Connecticut Gen. Life Insurance Co. v. Candimat Co., 398 n

Connecticut Mutual Life Insurance Co. v. Luchs, 164

Conrad, Sea v., 266

Conroy, Continental Assurance Co. v., 357 n

Conservative Life Insurance Co. v. Bollinger, 342 n

Consolidated American Life Insurance Co., Johnson v., 423 n

Continental Assurance Co., Provident National Bank v., 438-41

Continental Assurance Co. v. Conroy, 357 n

Continental Life & Accident Co. v. Songer, 142 n, 144 n

Continental Life Insurance Co., Carter v., 431 n

Conway, Metropolitan Life Insurance Co. v., 4, 426

Conway v. Minnesota Mutual Life Insurance Co., 382

Cook v. Cook, 271 n

Cook, Finnerty v., 271 n

Cook v. Lum, 303

Coons v. Home Life Insurance Co., 339 n

Cooper v. Cooper, 267

Copeland, Harris v., 268

Country Life Insurance Co., Talbot v., 104 n

Country Life Insurance Co. and Melody, Talbot v., 112–13

Counts, Woodmen of the World Life Insurance Society v., 556

Craddock v. Fidelity Life Association, 133 n

Craver v. Union Fidelity Insurance Co., 539 n

D. & P. Terminal, Inc. v. Western Life Insurance Co., 311

Dade County Consumer Advocate's Office, Department of Insurance v., 101 n

Damm v. National Insurance Co. of American, 461 n

David v. Metropolitan Life Insurance Co., 352

Davis, Kansas City Life Insurance Co. v., 131 n

Davis v. Modern Industrial Bank, 359 n

Davis, Warnock v., 163

de Almada v. Sovereign Camp, W.O.W., 317 n

Dedeaux, Pilot Life Insurance Co. v., 467

Deem, Equitable Life Assurance Society v., 432

Deer Lodge County, New York Life Insurance Co. v., 20

Densby v. Acacia Mutual Life Association, 422 n

Denton, Ping v., 266

Department of Insurance v. Dade County Consumer Advocate's Office, 101 n

Dibble, Simon v., 447 n

Dietlin, John Hancock Mutual Life Insurance Co. v., 57–59

Dixon, Kaiser v., 598

Dobbs v. Zink, 66 n

Doering v. Buechler, 270

Dooley, Progressive Life Insurance Co. v., 121 n

Dorman, John Hancock Mutual Life Insurance Co. v., 482

Dorothy M. Feder v. Bankers National Life Insurance Co., 391–93

Dotson v. McLaughlin, 573–74

Dressel v. Mutual Benefit Life Insurance Co., 339 n

Duffy v. Banker's Life Association, 142 n

Duke Power Co., Griggs v., 581–82

Duldulao v. Saint Mary of Nazareth Hospital Center, 596–600

Duldulao v. St. Mary of Nazareth Hospital Center, 594 n

Eagle Lodge, Kirkpatrick v., 574

Earl, Stevenson v., 303

Eastern Life Insurance Co. of New York, Ginsberg v., 381

Eastman, Hartford Life & Annuity Insurance Co. v., 326 n

Edwards, National Life & Accident Insurance Co. v., 210 n

Eichwedel v. Metropolitan Life Insurance Co., 422 n

Elizabeth Smith, Betty Jackson v., 246–50

Ellis v. John Hancock Mutual Life Insurance Co., 448

Ellis, Mutual Benefit Life Insurance Co. v., 298, 302

Ellis, Mutual Benefit Life Insurance Co. v., 298

Employers Casualty Co., Tix v., 209 n

Equitable Life Assurance Society, Kallman v., 381

Equitable Life Assurance Society of the United States, Bekken v., 144 n

Equitable Life Assurance Society of the United States, Hutchinson v., 323

Equitable Life Assurance Society v. James, supra, 473

Equitable Life Assurance Society v. Deem, 432

Equitable Life Assurance Society, Greer v., 493 n

Equitable Life Assurance Society, Lipman v., 342 n

Equitable Life Assurance Society, Schuler v., 127 n

Equitable Life Insurance Co. of Iowa, Sellwood v., 385

Erenshaw, Bankers Life & Casualty Co. v., 466

Erie Railway Co. v. Tompkins, 13, 326

Erisman, Brand v., 370

Evans v. Penn Mutual Life Insurance Co., 420

Exchange Trust Co. v. Capitol Life Insurance Co., 383 n

Faber v. Byrle, 574–76

Farmers Insurance Exchange, Neal v., 463 n, 465 n

Farmers Life Association, Thornburg v., 141 n

Fayman v. Franklin Life Insurance Co., 125 n

Federal Life Insurance Co., Barstow v., 120 n

Federal Life Insurance Co., Hunter v.,
401 n
Federal National Bank of Shawnee, Oklahoma, New York Life Insurance Co.
v., 363
Federal National Bank of Shawnee, Oklahoma, New York Life Insurance Co.
v., 268
Feick v. Prudential Insurance Co., 219 n
Fendler v. Foy, 319 n
Fidelity and Casualty Co., Steven v.,
460 n
Fidelity Casualty Co. v. Johnson, 208 n
Fidelity Life Association, Craddock v.,
133 n
Fidelity Union Trust Co. v. Phillips, 352
Fields v. Universal Life & Accident Insurance Co., 422 n
Finnerty v. Cook, 271 n
Finney, State Life Insurance Co. v.,
126 n
First National Bank and Trust Co. v.
Purcell, 287
Fisher v. Prudential Insurance Co., 483
Flax v. Prudential Life Insurance Co.,
407 n
Fletcher v. Western National Life Insurance Co., 464
Fore v. New York Life Insurance Co.,
426 n
Fortune v. National Cash Register Co.,
594 n
Founders Life Assurance Co. of Florida,
Smith v., 504–5
Fox v. Volunteer State Life Insurance
Co., 142 n
Franck, Mutual Life Insurance Co. v.,
266
Franklin Life Insurance Co., Burne v.,
210 n
Franklin Life Insurance Co., Fayman v.,
125 n
Franklin Life Insurance Co., Kaminer v.,
125 n
Franklin Life Insurance Co., Kampf v.,
393
Franklin Life Insurance Co. v. Bieniek,
130 n
Franklin Life Insurance Co. v. Parish,
384 n
Franklin Life Insurance Co. v. Strickland, 447 n
Frazee, Roundtree v., 357 n

Fried, Occidental Life Insurance Co. v.,
389
Fritz v. Old American Insurance Co.,
540 n
Froelich v. Adair, 573–74
FTC v. Travelers Health Association,
23 n
Fuller v. Supreme Council of Royal
Arcanum, 473

Gardner v. North State Mutual Life Insurance Co., 120 n, 122 n
Garland v. Jefferson Standard Life Insurance Co., 125 n
Garrett, Pan American Insurance Co. v.,
492
Gaudynski, Krzysko v., 71 n
General American Life Insurance Co. v.
Butts, 317 n
General American Life Insurance Co.,
Lindemann v., 209 n
General American Life Insurance Co.,
Zielinski v., 142 n
Gilby v. Travelers Insurance Co., 492 n
Giltnane, Western & Southern Life Insurance Co. v., 325
Ginsberg v. Eastern Life Insurance Co.
of New York, 381
Girard Life Insurance Co., Givens v., 415
Givens v. Girard Life Insurance Co., 415
Gleed v. Lincoln National Life Insurance
Co., 322
Glisson, Citizen's Home Insurance Co.
v., 77 n
Goldman, Massachusetts Mutual Life
Insurance Co. v., 435–36
Goldstein v. New York Life Insurance
Co., 431 n
Goodwin v. Provident Saving Life Assurance Society, 426 n
Gordon, Brown v., 238 n
Gordon v. New York Life Insurance Co.,
108 n
Government Personnel, Angelus v., 454
Grand Lodge of A. O. U. W., Rice v.,
326 n
Grant v. John Hancock Mutual Life
Insurance Co., 152
Great American Insurance Co. v. Violet
Sanders, 413–16
Great American Reserve Insurance Co. v.
Sumner, 222–24

Great American Reserve Insurance Co. v.
Sanders, 232 n, 400 n

Great Northern Life Insurance Co.,
Johnson v., 386

Greer, v. Equitable Life Assurance Society, 493 n

Gressler v. New York Life Insurance Co.,
383

Griggs v. Duke Power Co., 581–82

Grigsby, Standard Life Insurance Co. v.,
325

Grigsby v. Russell, 161, 233, 367

Gruenberg v. Aetna Insurance Co., 463 n

Guarantee Reserve Life Insurance Co.,
Reynolds v., 141 n

Guardian Life Insurance Co. of America,
Woloshin v., 308–9

Guardian Life Insurance Co., Tatum v.,
387

Guerrero v. Guerrero, 232 n

Gulf Atlantic Life Insurance Co. v.
Barnes, 465 n

Haberkorn v. Sears, Roebuck & Co.,
105 n

Hammer, Lincoln National Life Insurance Co. v., 184 n

Hanna v. Rio Grande Nat. Life Insurance
Co., 224

Hansen, supra., New York Life Insurance Co. v., 386

Harms v. John Hancock Mutual Life Insurance Co., 324

Harrington, New York Life Insurance
Co. v., 207 n

Harrison-Wright Co., Standard Accident
Insurance Co. v., 538 n

Harris & Reichard Fur Dyers, Aetna Life
Insurance Co. v., 107 n

Harris, Sovereign Camp, W.O.W. v.,
316 n

Harris v. Copeland, 268

Hart v. Hart, 245 n

Hartford Accident & Indemnity Co.,
Botts v., 206 n

Hartford Life Insurance Co., Hise v.,
241 n

Hartford Life & Annuity Insurance Co.
v. Eastman, 326 n

Hart v. Prudential Insurance Co., 121 n

Harvey, American Home Mutual Life Insurance Co. v., 505

Harvey, New England Mutual Life Insurance Co. v., 298

Hawkins v. New York Life Insurance
Co., 205 n

Hearne, Missouri State Life Insurance
Co. v., 381 n

Hearst Magazines, Valerni v., 559 n

Henderson v. Capital Life and Health
Insurance Co., 309

Henderson v. Life Insurance Co. of Virginia, 431

Hendrick, Minnesota Mutual Life Insurance Co. v., 266

Hicks, Masonic Relief Association v.,
310 n

Hill v. Philadelphia Life Insurance Co.,
316 n

Hilliard v. Wisconsin Life Insurance Co.,
238 n

Hise v. Hartford Life Insurance Co.,
241 n

Hocks, Nees v., 594

Hoffman ex rel. Keithley v. New York
Life Insurance Co., 374

Hoffman v. Aetna Life Insurance Co.,
118 n

Hogan v. John Hancock Mutual Life
Insurance Co., 388 n

Holdom v. Ancient Order of United
Workmen, 447 n

Holmes v. John Hancock Mutual Life
Insurance Co., 287

Home Insurance Co., Chelly v., 202 n

Home Life Insurance Co., Coons v., 339 n

Home Life Insurance Co. v. Masterson,
431 n

Home Sec. Life Insurance Co., Wharton
v., 431 n

Homesteaders Life Association, Pierce
v., 125

Hooker, Aetna Life Insurance Co. v.,
431 n

Huber v. New York Life Insurance Co.,
108 n

Humphrys, Praetorian Mutual Life Insurance Co. v., 202 n

Hunter v. Federal Life Insurance Co.,
401 n

Hutchcraft's Ex'r v. Travelers' Insurance
Co., 208 n

Hutchcraft's Protective Association,
Allen v., 208 n

Hutchinson v. Equitable Life Assurance Society of the United States, 323

Hutchinson v. National Life Insurance Co., 339 n

Hutsell v. Citizens' National Bank, 362 n

Ideal Food Stores, Munsell v., 572–73

Illinois Institute of Technology, Sargent v., 598

Insurance Co. of North America, Wilson v., 220 n

Insurance Corporation of Ireland, Theatre Guild Productions v., 164

International Life Insurance Co., McGee v., 496

Interstate Fire and Casualty Co., Otteman v., 107 n

Interstate Life & Accident Co. v. Jackson, 339 n

Jackson, Interstate Life & Accident Co. v., 339 n

James, supra, Equitable Life Assurance Society v., 473

Jefferson Standard Life Insurance Co., Garland v., 125 n

Jefferson Trust & Savings Bank of Peoria v. Lincoln Life Insurance Co., 373–76

Jersin, Colorado in Urbancich v., 302

JMR Electronics Corp., Mutual Benefit Life Insurance Co. v., 159

John H. Miller & Co., Oregon State Bar v., 105

John Hancock Mutual Life Insurance Co., Browne v., 309 n

John Hancock Mutual Life Insurance Co. v. Dietlin, 57–59

John Hancock Mutual Life Insurance Co. v. Dorman, 482

John Hancock Mutual Life Insurance Co., Ellis v., 448

John Hancock Mutual Life Insurance Co., Grant v., 152

John Hancock Mutual Life Insurance Co., Harms v., 324

John Hancock Mutual Life Insurance Co., Hogan v., 388 n

John Hancock Mutual Life Insurance Co., Holmes v., 287

John Hancock Mutual Life Insurance Co., Ludwinska v., 430

John Hancock Mutual Life Insurance Co. v. Mann, 315 n

John Hancock Mutual Life Insurance Co., Noble v., 332–34

John Hancock Mutual Life Insurance Co., Parsons v., 109 n

John Hancock Mutual Life Insurance Co., Szymanski v., 492 n

John Hancock Mutual Life Insurance Co., Walsh v., 319 n

Johnson, Fidelity Casualty Co. v., 208 n

Johnson v. Boeing Airplane Co., 572–73

Johnson v. Consolidated American Life Insurance Co., 423 n

Johnson v. Great Northern Life Insurance Co., 386

Johnson v. Johnson, 232 n

Johnson v. Life Insurance Co. of Virginia, 384 n

Johnson v. Life Insurance Co. of Virginia, 389

Johnson v. Schrapferman, 107 n

Johns v. Associated Aviation Underwriters, 576

Jones v. Mutual Life Insurance Co., 348 n

Jorgenson v. Metropolitan Life Insurance Co., 219 n

Kaiser v. Dixon, 598

Kaiser v. Prudential Insurance Co., 495

Kallman v. Equitable Life Assurance Society, 381

Kaminer v. Franklin Life Insurance Co., 125 n

Kampf v. Franklin Life Insurance Co., 393

Kanelles v. Lock, 67 n

Kansas City Life Insurance Co. v. Davis, 131 n

Kansas Protective Union, Somers v., 141 n

Karasek, National Life Accident Insurance Co. v., 205 n

Karl v. New York Life Insurance Co., 210 n

Karol v. New Hampshire Insurance Co., 461 n

Kaskaskia Community Action Agency, Carter v., 597–98

Katz, United Benefit Life Insurance Co.
v., 399 n

Katz v. United States, 560

Kaul, Acacia Mutual Life Association v.,
393

Keller v. North Amer. Life Insurance
Co., 184 n

Kennedy v. Occidental Life Insurance
Co., 382

Kentucky Central Life Insurance Co. v.
Willett, 266

Kenyon v. Knights Templar & M. Mutual
Aid Association, 326 n

Kewin v. Massachusetts Mutual Life
Insurance Co., 465 n

Keyes, Vorlander v., 241 n

Kievet v. Loyal Protective Life Insurance
Co., 461 n

Kimbro v. New York Life Insurance Co.,
141 n

Kings Entertainment Co., Thompson v.,
594 n

Kirkpatrick v. Eagle Lodge, 574

K Mart v. Ponsock, 594 n

Knickerbocker Life Insurance Co.,
Rohrschneider v., 538 n

Knights Templar & M. Mutual Aid Association, Kenyon v., 326 n

Knutson, Swedish-American Insurance
Co. v., 119 n

Koger v. Mutual of Omaha Insurance
Co., 207 n

Kot v. Chrysler Corp., 363 n

Kowalski v. Aetna Life Insurance Co.,
492 n

Krause v. Pacific Mutual Life Insurance
Co., 221 n

Kronjaeger v. Travelers Insurance Co.,
140 n

Krzysko v. Gaudynski, 71 n

Kuhn v. Wolf, 238 n

Kurtz v. New York Life Insurance Co.,
400 n

Kwasniewski, United States v., 448 n

Lain v. Metropolitan Life Insurance Co.,
369 n

Lakin v. Postal Life & Casualty Co., 161,
166 n

Lamme, Prudential Insurance Co. of
America v., 154 n

Landress v. Phoenix Mutual Life Insurance Co., 201

Lane v. New York Life Insurance Co.,
382

Langan v. United States Life Insurance
Co., 428 n

Larson v. Transamerica Life and Annuity
Insurance Co., 104 n

Lavoie, Aetna Life Insurance Co. v., 466

Lawrence v. Providential Life Insurance
Co., 554–56

Leal v. Leal, 319 n

Lechler v. Montana Life Insurance Co.,
141 n

Legare v. West Coast Life Insurance Co.,
537 n

Lester v. Aetna Life Insurance Co., 317 n

Lewis v. Continental Life & Accident
Co., 538 n

Liberty Mutual Insurance Co. v. Cleveland, 118 n

Liberty National Life Insurance Co. v.
Weldon, 166–67

Life & Casualty Insurance Co. v.
Wheeler, 339 n

Life Insurance Co. of Virginia, Henderson v., 431

Life Insurance Co. of Virginia, Johnson
v., 384 n

Life Insurance Co. of Virginia, Johnson
v., 389

Life Insurance Co. of Virginia, Suggs v.,
195–97

Lincoln National Life Insurance Co.,
Gleed v., 322

Lincoln National Life Insurance Co. v.
Hammer, 184 n

Lincoln National Life Insurance Co., Jefferson Trust and Savings of Peoria v.,
373–76

Lindemann v. General American Life Insurance Co., 209 n

Lineberger v. Security Life & Trust Co.,
492 n

Liner v. Penn Mutual Life Insurance Co.,
410

Linscott v. Ranier National Life Insurance Co., 465 n

Linthicum v. Nationwide Life Insurance
Co., 466

Lipman v. Equitable Life Assurance Society, 342 n

Lock, Kanelles v., 67 n

Lone Star Life Insurance Co., Clark v., 221 n

Longley v. Prudential Insurance Co., 493 n

Louisiana and Southern Life, Brooks v., 16 n

Loyal Protective Life Insurance Co., Kievet v., 461 n

Luchs, Connecticut Mutual Life Insurance Co. v., 164

Lucus v. American Bankers' Insurance Co., 185 n

Ludwinska v. John Hancock Mutual Life Insurance Co., 430 n

Lum, Cook v., 303

Lynch v. Central States Life Insurance Co., 492 n

McAllen State Bank v., Texas Bank & Trust Co., 359 n

McBride v. McBride, 267

McCurdy v. McCurdy, 231 n

McDaniel v. State Farm Mutual Insurance Co., 531–34

MacDonald v. Metropolitan Life Insurance Co., 384 n

MacDonald v. Pennsylvania Mutual Life Insurance Co., 492 n

McGee v. International Life Insurance Co., 496

McLaughlin, Dotson v., 573–74

McLean v. Metropolitan Life Insurance Co., 490

McMahan v. McMahan, 128 n

Magee v. Sun Life Assurance Co., 493 n

Magers v. Western & Southern Life Insurance Co., 328

Maloney v. Maryland Casualty Co., 556

Mann, John Hancock Mutual Life Insurance Co. v., 315 n

Markel v. Travelers Insurance Co., 320 n

Martin, Columbian Mutual Life Insurance Co. v., 431 n

Marvin, Chelsea-Wheeler Coal Co. v., 369 n

Maryland Casualty Co., Maloney v., 556

Maslin v. Columbian National Life Insurance Co., 430

Masonic Relief Association v. Hicks, 310 n

Mason, Prudential Insurance Co. v., 384 n

Massachusetts Accident Co., Pierce v., 309

Massachusetts Mutual Life Insurance Co., Kewin v., 465 n

Massachusetts Mutual Life Insurance Co., Mayers v., 340 n

Massachusetts Mutual Life Insurance Co. v. Goldman, 435

Masterson, Home Life Insurance Co. v., 431 n

Mau v. Union Labor Life Insurance Co., 317 n

Maxa v. Neidlein, 463 n

Mayers v. Massachusetts Mutual Life Insurance Co., 340 n

Mayer v. Northern Life Insurance Co., 576–77

Mellor, Burch v., 106 n

Metropolitan Life Insurance Co., Allen v., 153

Metropolitan Life Insurance Co., Baumann v., 324

Metropolitan Life Insurance Co. v. Cole, 492 n

Metropolitan Life Insurance Co. v. Conway, 4, 426

Metropolitan Life Insurance Co., David v., 352

Metropolitan Life Insurance Co., Eichwedel v., 422 n

Metropolitan Life Insurance Co., Jorgenson v., 219 n

Metropolitan Life Insurance Co., Lain v., 369 n

Metropolitan Life Insurance Co., MacDonald v., 384 n

Metropolitan Life Insurance Co., McLean v., 490

Metropolitan Life Insurance Co., Monahan v., 4, 165, 433

Metropolitan Life Insurance Co., Morticians' Acceptance Co. v., 363 n

Metropolitan Life Insurance Co., Peyton v., 492 n

Metropolitan Life Insurance Co., Reynolds v., 125 n

Metropolitan Life Insurance Co., Skov v., 267

Metropolitan Life Insurance Co., Spychala v., 220 n

Metropolitan Life Insurance Co., Still v., 453

Metropolitan Life Insurance Co., Telford
v., 422 n
Metropolitan Life Insurance Co.,
Tesauro v., 319 n
Metropolitan Life Insurance Co.,
Thomas v., 362 n
Metropolitan Life Insurance Co.,
Thompson v., 501
Metropolitan Life Insurance Co., Trapp
v., 384 n
Metropolitan Life Insurance Co., Wald-
ner v., 384
Mettille, Pine River State Bank v., 598
Michaelson v. Sokolove, 369 n
Mid-South Insurance Co., Modzingo v.,
202 n
Miller v. Union Cent. Life Insurance Co.,
104 n
Miner v. Standard Life and Accident In-
surance Co., 340 n
Minnesota Mutual Life Insurance Co.,
Conway v., 382
Minnesota Mutual Life Insurance Co.,
Smith v., 142 n
Minnesota Mutual Life Insurance Co. v.
Hendrick, 266
Minnick v. State Farm Mutual Auto
Insurance Co., 326 n
Minton, Young v., 492 n
Missouri State Life Insurance Co. v.
Hearne, 381 n
Missouri State Life Insurance Co., Wen-
dorff v., 220 n
Missouri Valley Trust Co., Butterworth
v., 367
Mitchell, Rowlett v., 232 n
Modern Industrial Bank, Davis v., 359 n
Modern Woodmen of America, Roberts
v., 469–74
Monahan v. Metropolitan Life Insurance
Co., 4, 165, 433
Mohanan v. Metropolitan Life Insurance
Co., 433
Monge v. Beebe Rubber Co., 594 n
Montana Life Insurance Co., Lechler v.,
141 n
Monumental Life Insurance Co., Pannun-
zio v., 121 n
Moore v. California-Western States Life
Insurance Co., 232 n
Morse v. Commissioner, 343 n
Morticians' Acceptance Co. v. Metropol-
itan Life Insurance Co., 363 n

Mozingo v. Mid-South Insurance Co.,
202 n
Munsell v. Ideal Food Stores, 572–73
Murphy v. Chrysler Corp., 492 n
Murphy v. Western & S. Life Insurance
Co., 204 n
Mutual Benefit Life Insurance Co.,
Nicholas v., 202 n
Mutual Benefit Life Insurance Co. v.
JMR Electronics Corp., 159
Mutual Benefit Life Insurance Co., Dres-
sel v., 339 n
Mutual Benefit Life Insurance Co. supra
v. Ellis, 298, 302
Mutual Benefit Life Insurance Co. v.
Ellis, 298
Mutual Benefit Life Insurance Co., Jones
v., 348 n
Mutual Life Insurance Co., Rose v.,
312 n
Mutual Life Insurance Co. v. Franck, 266
Mutual Life Insurance Co. v. Young's
Adm'r, 141 n
Mutual Life Insurance Co., Wilcox v.,
266
Mutual of Omaha Insurance Co., Koger
v., 207 n
Mutual Reserve Fund Life Association v.
Austin, 426 n
Mutual Reserve Fund Life Association v.
Tuchfeld, 326 n
Myers v. Bethlehem, 401

Narver v. California State Life Insurance
Co., 170
Narver v. California State Life Insurance
Co., 315 n
Nash, Sovereign Camp, W.O.W. v., 104 n
National Casualty Co., Austero v., 463 n
National Cash Register Co., Fortune v.,
594 n
National Insurance Co. of American,
Damm v., 461 n
National Life & Accident Insurance Co.,
Bennett v., 123 n
National Life & Accident Insurance Co.,
Smith v., 185 n
National Life & Accident Insurance Co.
v. Singleton, 204 n
National Life & Accident Insurance Co.
v. Edwards, 210 n

National Life & Accident Insurance Co.
v. Karasek, 205 n

National Life and Accident Insurance
Co., Avent v., 203

National Life Insurance Co., Hutchinson
v., 339 n

National Life Insurance Co. of the
United States, Wolford v., 312 n

National Security Fire Casualty Co.,
Chavers v., 465 n

Nationwide Life Insurance Co., Board of
Trustees of Unitarian Church v.,
339 n

Nationwide Life Insurance Co., Collister
v., 154 n

Nationwide Life Insurance Co., Linthicum v., 466

Nationwide Mutual Insurance Co., American Insurance Co. v., 119 n

Neal v. Farmers Insurance Exchange,
463 n, 465 n

Nees v. Hocks, 594

Neidlein, Maxa v., 463 n

New England Mutual Life Insurance Co.,
O'Brien v., 343 n

New England Mutual Life Insurance Co.
v. Harvey, 298

New Hampshire Insurance Co., Karol v.,
461 n

New Jersey, Texas v., 451 n

New York Life Insurance Co., Board of
Assessors v., 344, 353

New York Life Insurance Co., Clement
v., 431

New York Life Insurance Co. v. Deer
Lodge County, 20

New York Life Insurance Co. v. Federal
National Bank of Shawnee, Oklahoma, 268

New York Life Insurance Co., Fore v.,
426 n

New York Life Insurance Co., Goldstein
v., 431 n

New York Life Insurance Co., Gordon v.,
108 n

New York Life Insurance Co., Gressler
v., 383

New York Life Insurance Co. v. Hansen,
supra., 386

New York Life Insurance Co. v. Harrington, 207 n

New York Life Insurance Co., Hawkins
v., 205 n

New York Life Insurance Co., Hoffman
ex rel. Keithley v., 374

New York Life Insurance Co., Huber v.,
108 n

New York Life Insurance Co., Karl v.,
210 n

New York Life Insurance Co., Kimbro
v., 141 n

New York Life Insurance Co., Kurtz v.,
400 n

New York Life Insurance Co., Lane v.,
382

New York Life Insurance Co., Pitts v.,
134–37

New York Life Insurance Co., Poffenber-
ger v., 496

New York Life Insurance Co., Robinson
v., 26–28

New York Life Insurance Co., Schiel v.,
388

New York Life Insurance Co., Statham
v., 310, 326

New York Life Insurance Co., Toulouse
v., 294–304

New York Life Insurance Co., Wadsworth v., 142

New York Life Insurance Co., Walls v.,
319 n

New York Life Insurance Co., Weiss v.,
393

Nicholas v. Mutual Benefit Life Insurance
Co., 202 n

Noble v. John Hancock Mutual Insurance
Co., 332–34

Norris, Arizona Governing Committee v.,
158

North Amer. Life Insurance Co., Keller
v., 184 n

Northern Life Insurance Co., Mayer v.,
576–77

North State Mutual Life Insurance Co.,
Gardner v., 120 n, 122 n

Northwestern Mutual Life Insurance
Co., Thomas v., 310 n

Northwestern Mutual Life Insurance
Co., supra, Whitesell v., 234

Northwestern Mutual Life Insurance
Co., Pierce v., 102

Obartuch v. Security Mutual Life Insurance Co., 53 n, 430

O'Brien v. New England Mutual Life
Insurance Co., 343 n
Occidental Life Insurance Co. v. Fried,
389
Occidental Life Insurance Co., Kennedy
v., 382
Occidental Life Insurance Co., Roberts
v., 469–74
Old American Insurance Co., Fritz v.,
540 n
Oregon State Bar v. Miller & Co., 105
Otteman v. Interstate Fire and Casualty
Co., 107 n
Overton v. Washington National Insur-
ance Co., 46 n

Pacific Mills, Thompson v., 492 n
Pacific Mutual Life Insurance Co., Bailey
v., 420 n
Pacific Mutual Life Insurance Co., Ber-
nier v., 426 n, 427
Pacific Mutual Life Insurance Co.,
Blethen v., 232 n
Pacific Mutual Life Insurance Co.,
Cleverdon, 232 n
Pacific Mutual Life Insurance Co.,
Krause v., 221 n
Pacific Mutual Life Insurance Co. v.
Rhame, 127 n
Pacific Mutual Life Insurance Co. v. Wat-
son, 318 n
Pacific Mutual Life Insurance Co. v.
Bryce, 342 n
Pack v. Progressive Life Insurance Co.,
342 n
Page, Travelers Insurance Co. v., 517
Pan American Insurance Co. v. Garrett,
492
Pannunzio v. Monumental Life Insurance
Co., 121 n
Pape v. Pape, 259
Parish, Franklin Life Insurance Co. v.,
384 n
Parsons v. John Hancock Mutual Life
Insurance Co., 109 n
Paul v. Virginia, 20–21
Peddicord v. Prudential Insurance Co. of
America, 143 n
Penn Mutual Life Insurance Co. v.
Forbes, 357 n
Penn Mutual Life Insurance Co., Wil-
liams v., 401 n

Penn Mutual Life Insurance Co., Evans
v., 420
Penn Mutual Life Insurance Co., Liner
v., 410
Penn Mutual Life Insurance Co., Ransom
v., 152
Pennsylvania Mutual Life Insurance Co.,
MacDonald v., 492 n
Perry v. Perry, 319 n
Peterman v. Teamsters, 593
Peyton v. Metropolitan Life Insurance
Co., 492 n
Philadelphia Life Insurance Co., Hill v.,
316 n
Phillips, Fidelity Union Trust Co. v., 352
Phoenix Mutual Life Insurance Co.,
Simpson v., 482
Phoenix Mutual Life, Landress v., 201
Piedmont S. Life Insurance Co., Raney
v., 315 n
Pierce v. Homesteaders Life Association,
125
Pierce v. Massachusetts Accident Co.,
309 n
Pierce v. Northwestern Mutual Life In-
surance Co., 102
Pilot Life Insurance Co. v. Dedeaux, 467
Pine River State Bank v. Mettille, 598
Ping v. Denton, 266
Pitts v. New York Life Insurance Co.,
134–37
Pledger v. Business Men's Accident As-
sociation, 202 n
Poffenbarger v. New York Life Insurance
Co., 496
Ponsock, K Mart v., 594 n
Postal Life & Casualty Co., Lakin v.,
161, 166 n
Praetorian Mutual Life Insurance Co. v.
Humphrys, 202 n
Price v. Business Men's Assurance Co.,
208 n
Progressive Life Insurance Co., Pack v.,
342 n
Progressive Life Insurance Co. v. Dooley,
121 n
Providential Life Insurance Co., Law-
rence v., 554–56
Provident Life & Accident Insurance Co.
v. Carter, 447 n
Provident Life Insurance Co., supra,
Rott v., 386

Provident National Bank v. Continental Assurance Co., 438–41

Provident Saving Life Assurance Society, Goodwin v., 426 n

Prudential Insurance Co., Bernard v., 208 n

Prudential Insurance Co. v. Connallon, 179 n

Prudential Insurance Co., Corder v., 273–74

Prudential Insurance Co., Feick v., 219 n

Prudential Insurance Co., Fisher v., 483

Prudential Insurance Co., Flax v., 407 n

Prudential Insurance Co., Hart v., 121 n

Prudential Insurance Co., Kaiser v., 495

Prudential Insurance Co., Longley v., 493 n

Prudential Insurance Co. v. Mason, 384 n

Prudential Insurance Co., Savage v., 143

Prudential Insurance Co., Zuliskey v., 207 n

Prudential Insurance Co. of America v. Clark and Clark, 80–83

Prudential Insurance Co. of America v. Lamme, 154 n

Prudential Insurance Co. of America, Peddicord, v., 143 n

Prudential Insurance Co. of America, Thompson v., 203 n

Purcell, First National Bank and Trust Co. v., 287

Quick v. United Benefit Life Insurance Co., 447 n

Raney v. Piedmont S. Life Insurance Co., 315 n

Ranier National Life Insurance Co., Linscott v., 465 n

Ransom v. Penn Mutual Life Insurance Co., 152

Releford v. Reserve Life Insurance Co., 222

Reliable Life Insurance Co., Tripp v., 154 n

Rembe, Central Accident Insurance Co. v., 209 n

Republic National Life Insurance Co., Sparks v., 465 n

Reserve Life Insurance Co., Releford v., 222

Resnek v. Mutual Life Insurance Co., 362 n

Reynolds v. Guarantee Reserve Life Insurance Co., 141 n

Reynolds, v. Metropolitan Life Insurance Co., 125 n

Rhame, Pacific Mutual Life Insurance Co. v., 127 n

Rice v. Grand Lodge of A.O.U.W., 326 n

Rio Grande National Life Insurance Co., Hanna v., 224

Rio Grande National Life Insurance Co. v. Schmidt, 400 n

Riordan v. Automobile Club, 139 n, 540 n

Rittler v. Smith, 236 n

Rivers v. State Capital Life Insurance Co., 493 n

Robertson v. California, 98

Roberts v. Modern Woodmen of America, 469–74

Roberts v. Occidental Life Insurance Co., 469–74

Roberts v. Wabash Life Insurance Co., 469–74

Robinson v. New York Life Insurance Co., 26–28

Robinson v. United States Benevolent Society, 142

Robinson v. United States Benefit Society, 556

Rocky Mt. Sav. & Trust Co. v. Aetna Life Insurance Co., 383 n

Rohrschneider v. Knickerbocker Life Insurance Co., 535 n

Rose v. Mutual Life Insurance Co., 312 n

Rose v. Rose, 447 n

Rott v. Provident Life Insurance Co., supra, 386

Roundtree v. Frazee, 357 n

Routon, Aetna Life Insurance Co. v., 122 n

Rowlett v. Mitchell, 232 n

Royal Globe Insurance Co. v. Superior Court, 460

Royal Highlanders v. Wiseman, 329

Roy, Fendler v., 319 n

Russell, Grigsby v., 161, 233

Sachs v. United States, 236 n

Saint Mary of Nazareth Hospital Center Duldulao v., 596–600

Sanders, Great American Reserve Insurance Co. v., 232 n, 400 n

Sanford, California-Western Life Insurance Co. v., 448 n

Sargent v. Illinois Institute of Technology, 598

Savage v. Prudential Life Insurance Co., 143

Schaefer v. California-Western States Life Insurance Co., 423 n

Scherer v. Wahlstrom, 257 n

Schiel v. New York Life Insurance Co., 388

Schmidt, Rio Grande National Life Insurance Co. v., 400 n

Schrapferman, Johnson v., 107 n

Schuler v. Equitable Life Assurance Society, 127 n

Schwartz. In re Estate of, 351–54

Sears, Roebuck & Co., Haberkorn v., 105 n

Sears v. Austin, 501 n

Sea v. Conrad, 266

Security Benefit Life Insurance Co., Senogles v., 570–77

Security Benefit Life Insurance Co., Wyatt v., 492 n

Security Life & Trust Co., Lineberger v., 492 n

Security Mutual Life Insurance Co., Obartuch v., 53 n

Security Mutual Life Insurance Co., Obartuch v., 430

SEC v. Variable Annuity Life Insurance Co., 23

Sellwood v. Equitable Life Insurance Co. of Iowa, 385

Senogles v. Security Benefit Life Insurance Co., 570–77

Shain, State ex rel. Mutual Life Insurance Co. v., 221 n

Shea v. Aetna Life Insurance Co., 492 n

Sheets v. Teddy's Frosted Foods, Inc., 594 n

Silberg v. California Life Insurance Co., 463 n

Simmons v. Simmons, 258

Simon v. Dibble, 447 n

Simpson v. Phoenix Mutual Life Insurance Co., 482

Singleton, National Life & Accident Insurance Co. v., 204 n

Sjoberg v. State Automobile Insurance Association, 314

Skov, Metropolitan Life Insurance Co. v., 267

Sloan v. Breeden, 369 n

Smillie v. Travelers Insurance Co., 491

Smith v. Aetna Life Insurance Co., 492 n

Smith v. Bankers National Life Insurance Co., 381 n

Smith v. Founders Life Assurance Co. of Florida, 504–5

Smith v. Minnesota Mutual Life Insurance Co., 142 n

Smith v. National Life & Accident Insurance Co., 185 n

Smith, Rittler v., 236 n

Smith v. Smith, 298

Smith v. Westland Life Insurance Co., 153

Sokolove, Michaelson v., 369 n

Somers v. Kansas Protective Union, 141 n

Songer, Continental Life & Accident Co. v., 142 n

Southards v. Central Plains Insurance Co., 532

South-Eastern Underwriters Association, United States v., 20 n

South-Eastern Underwriters Association, United States v., 3, 8, 20–22

Southern Insurance Co., Chavis v., 386 n

Southland Life Insurance Co., Cannon v., 152 n

Sovereign Camp, W.O.W., de Almada v., 317 n

Sovereign Camp, W.O.W. v. Nash, 104 n

Sovereign Camp, W.O.W. v. Harris, 316 n

Sparks v. Republic National Life Insurance Co., 465 n

Spears, Commonwealth Life Insurance Co. v., 122 n

Spencer, Albrent v., 360

Spencer v. Aetna Life & Casualty Co., 465 n

Spychala v. Metropolitan Life Insurance Co., 220 n

Standard Accident Insurance Co. v. Harrison-Wright Co., 538 n

Standard Life and Accident Insurance Co., Miner v., 340 n

Standard Life Insurance Co. v. Grigsby, 325

Starbuck v. City Bank & Trust Co., 266

The State, Bradwell v., 3
State Automobile Insurance Association,
    Sjoberg v., 314
State Capital Life Insurance Co., Rivers
    v., 493 n
State ex rel. Mutual Life Insurance Co.
    v. Shain, 221 n
State Farmers' Mutual Hail Insurance
    Co., Boyer v., 142 n
State Farm Mutual Auto Insurance Co.,
    Minnick v., 326 n
State Farm Mutual Insurance, McDaniel
    v., 531–34
State Life Insurance Co. v. Finney, 126 n
Statham, New York Life Insurance Co.
    v., 310, 326
Stern, Commissioner v., 239 n
Stevenson v. Earl, 302–3
Steven v. Fidelity and Casualty Co.,
    460 n
Stewart, American Life Insurance Co. v.,
    422 n
Stewart, American Life Insurance Co. v.,
    436
Stewart v. Union Mutual Life Insurance
    Co., 131 n
Still v. Metropolitan Life Insurance Co.,
    453
St. Mary of Nazareth Hospital Center,
    Duldulao v., 594 n
Strickland, Franklin Life Insurance Co.
    v., 447 n
Suggs v. The Life Insurance Co. of Vir-
    ginia, 195–97
Sumner, Great American Reserve Insur-
    ance Co. v., 222–24
Sundstrom v. Sundstrom, 371
Sun Life Assurance Co., Magee v., 493 n
Superior Court, Royal Globe Insurance
    Co. v., 460
Supreme Council of Royal Arcanum,
    Fuller v., 473
Supreme Lodge, Shield of Honor, Bee-
    man v., 326 n
Swedish-American Insurance Co. v.
    Knutson, 119 n
Swift v. Tyson, 13
Szymanski v. John Hancock Mutual Life
    Insurance Co., 492 n

Talbot v. Country Life Insurance Co. and
    Melody, 112–13

Talbot v. Country Life Insurance Co.,
    104 n
Tatum v. Guardian Life Insurance Co.,
    387
Travelers Insurance Co., Smillie v., 491
Teamsters, Peterman v., 593
Teddy's Frosted Foods, Inc., Sheets v.,
    594 n
Telford v. Metropolitan Life Insurance
    Co., 422 n
Terkelsen, Titus v., 233
Tesauro, Metropolitan Life Insurance
    Co. v., 319 n
Texas Bank & Trust Co., McAllen State
    Bank v., 359 n
Texas v. New Jersey, 451 n
Theatre Guild Productions v. Insurance
    Corporation of Ireland, 164
Theros v. Metropolitan Life Insurance
    Co., 121
Thomas v. Metropolitan Life Insurance
    Co., 362 n
Thomas v. Northwestern Mutual Life In-
    surance Co., 310 n
Thompson, Metropolitan Life Insurance
    Co. v., 501
Thompson v. Kings Entertainment Co.,
    594 n
Thompson v. Pacific Mills, 492 n
Thompson v. Prudential Insurance Co. of
    America, 203 n
Thornburg v. Farmers Life Association,
    141 n
Tillman, All States Life Insurance Co. v.,
    493 n
Titus v. Terkelsen, 233
Tix v. Employers Casualty Co., 209 n
Toevs v. Western Farm Bureau Life In-
    surance Co., 154 n
Tompkins, Erie Railroad Co. v., 13
Tompkins, Erie Railway Co. v., 326
Toulouse v. New York Life Insurance
    Co., 294–304
Toussaint v. Blue Cross and Blue Shield,
    594 n
Transamerica Life and Annuity Insurance
    Co., Larson v., 104 n
Trapp v. Metropolitan Life Insurance
    Co., 384 n
Travelers Health Association, FTC v.,
    23 n
Travelers' Insurance Co., Hutchcraft's
    Ex'r v., 208 n

Travelers Insurance Co., Kronjaeger v.,
140 n
Travelers Insurance Co. v. Bailey, 407 n
Travelers Insurance Co. v. Brown, 326 n
Travelers Insurance Co., Markel v., 320 n
Travelers Insurance Co. v. Page, 517
Travelers Insurance Co., Woehr v., 493 n
Travelers Protective Association, Allen
v., 208 n
Travelers Protective Association of
America v. Ziegler, 393
Tripp v. Reliable Life Insurance Co.,
154 n
Trust Co. of Chicago, Van Houton v., 375
Tuchfeld, Mutual Reserve Fund Life As-
sociation v., 326 n
Tyre v. Aetna Life Insurance Co. 232 n,
234 n
Tyson, Swift v., 13

Ulrich v. Reinoehl, 236 n
Union Cent. Life Insurance Co., Miller
v., 104 n
Union Central Life Insurance Co., Wil-
liams v., 340 n
Union Fidelity Insurance Co., Craver v.,
539 n
Union Labor Life Insurance Co., Mau v.,
317 n
Union Mutual Life Insurance Co. v.
Broderick, 232 n
Union Mutual Life Insurance Co., Stew-
art v., 131 n
Union Mutual Insurance Co. v. Wilkin-
son, 128
United Benefit Life Insurance Co., Quick
v., 447 n
United Benefit Life Insurance Co. v.
Katz, 399 n
United States, Sachs v., 236 n
United States Benevolent Society, Robin-
son v., 142
United States Benefit Society, Robinson
v., 556
United States v. Bess, 239 n
United States, Katz v., 560
United States Life Insurance Co., Lan-
gan v., 428 n
United States Mutual Accident Associa-
tion v. Barry, 203
United States v. Kwasniewski, 448 n

United States v. South-Eastern Under-
writers Association, 3, 8, 20–22
Universal Life & Accident Insurance
Co., Fields v., 422 n

Valerni v. Hearst Magazines, 559 n
Van Houton v. Trust Co. of Chicago, 375
Variable Annuity Life Insurance Co. v.
SEC, 23
Variable Life Insurance Co., SEC v., 23
Violet Sanders, Great American Reserve
Insurance Co. v., 413–16
Virginia, Paul v., 20–21
Volunteer State Life Insurance Co., Fox
v., 142 n
Vorlander v. Keyes, 241 n

Wabash Life Insurance Co., Roberts v.,
469–74
Wadsworth v. New York Life Insurance
Co., 142
Wahlstrom, Scherer v., 257 n
Waldner v. Metropolitan Life Insurance
Co., 384
Walls, New York Life Insurance Co. v.,
319 n
Walsh v. John Hancock Mutual Life
Insurance Co., 319 n
Warnock v. Davis, 163
Washington National Insurance Co.,
Overton v., 46 n
Watson, Pacific Mutual Life Insurance
Co. v., 318 n
Weiss, New York Life Insurance Co. v.,
393
Weldon, Liberty National Life Insurance
Co. v., 166–67
Welfare Finance Corp., Brawner v., 104 n
Wendorff v. Missouri State Life Insur-
ance Co., 220 n
Wesley D. Corder v. Prudential Insurance
Co., 273–74
West Coast Life Insurance Co., Legare
v., 537 n
Western Farm Bureau Life Insurance
Co., Toevs v., 154 n
Western Life Insurance Co., D. & P. Ter-
minal, Inc. v., 311
Western National Life Insurance Co.,
Fletcher v., 464

Western & S. Life Insurance Co., Murphy v., 204 n

Western & Southern Life Insurance Co. v. Giltnane, 325

Western & Southern Life Insurance Co., Magers v., 328

Westland Life Insurance Co., Smith v., 153

Wharton v. Home Sec. Life Insurance Co., 431 n

Wheeler, Life & Casualty Insurance Co. v., 339 n

Wheelock v. Clark, 140 n

White, Atlantic American Life Insurance Co. v., 208 n

White, New York Life Insurance Co. v., 219 n

Whitesell v. Northwestern Mutual Life Insurance Co., supra, 234

Wilcox v. Mutual Life Insurance Co., 266

Wilkinson, Union Mutual Insurance Co. v., 128

Willett, Kentucky Central Life Insurance Co. v., 266

Williams v. Penn. Mutual Life Insurance Co., 401 n

Williams v. Union Central Life Insurance Co., 340 n

Wilson v. Insurance Co. of North America, 220 n

Wisconsin Life Insurance Co., Hilliard v., 238 n

Wiseman, Royal Highlanders v., 329

Witten v. Beacon Life Association, 142 n

Woehr v. Travelers Insurance Co., 493 n

Wolf, Kuhn v., 328 n

Wolford v. National Life Insurance Co. of the United States, 312 n

Woloshin v. Guardian Life Insurance Co. of America, 308–9

Womack v. Womack, 234 n

Woodmen of the World Life Insurance Society v. Counts, 556

Worthington v. Charter Oak Life Insurance Co., 310 n

Wyatt v. Security Benefit Life Insurance Co., 492 n

Young's Adm'r, Mutual Life Insurance Co. v., 141 n

Young v. Minton, 492 n

Zenith Life Insurance Co., T. J. Bowman v., 172

Ziegler, Travelers Protective Association of America v., 393

Zielinski v. General American Life Insurance Co., 142

Zink, Dobbs v., 66 n

Zuliskey v. Prudential Insurance Co., 207 n

Index

A. B. A. assignment form; *see* Collateral
   agreement
Absolute assignment; *see* Assignment
Acceptance of offer
  bilateral contracts, 38
  communication of acceptance, 37
  completion of contract, 38
  general rule, 36–37
  in life insurance, 139
  unilateral contracts, 37–38
Accidental death benefit, 199–200
  accidental means, 201–2
    accidental and disease, 208–9
    burden of proof, 211–12
    cases, 203–6
    defined, 202
    external and violent, 206
    harm inflicted by another, 208
    risks not covered, 210–11
    suicide, 207
    time limitation clauses, 209–10
    voluntary assumption of a known
      risk, 207
  accident and accidental defined, 200
  proximate cause, 200–201
Accident and health insurance; *see*
   Health insurance
Accumulations, rule against, 287
Advance payment of premiums, 313
Advertising
  federal regulation of, 23, 542–43
  interstate, 23
  Model Rules Governing Accident and
    Sickness, 545–52; *see also* NAIC
    Model bills, regulations and
    statutes
    applicability, 546
    benefits payable, 548–50
    definitions, 546–47
    disparaging statements, 551
    enforcements procedures, 552
    form and content of advertisements,
      548
    identity of insurer and policy, 551

Advertising—*Cont.*
  Model Rules—*Cont.*
    jurisdictional licensing and status,
      551
    method of disclosure, 548
    preamble, 545–46
    purpose, 54
    renewability provisions, 550
    special offers, 551
    statements about insurer, 551
    testimonials and endorsements, 550
    use of statistics, 551
  Model Rules Governing Advertising of
    Life Insurance; *see also* NAIC
    Model bills, regulations and
    statutes
    binding the insurer, 539–41
    disclosure requirements, 553
    definitions, 552
    direct response, 139, 538–39
    form and content of advertisements,
      552
    interstate, 541
  promotional literature, 537–38
  regulation by federal government
    by agencies, 542–43
    McCarran-Ferguson Act, 2, 22–23,
      542
  state laws governing
    all advertising, 543
    insurance advertising only, 543–44
    Model Unfair Trade Practices Act,
      544–45
  waiver and estoppel in, 538
Agency
  creation of, 65–66
  definition, 62
  indicia of authority, 68, 77
  master and servant, 77–78
  by ratification, 68–69
Agent
  accounting, premiums collected, 108
  actual authority, 65–66
  authority of, 123–24

Agent—*Cont.*
  authority of—*Cont.*
    actual, 65–66
    apparent, 63, 66–68, 77
    compared to principals, 64–65
    delegation, 69–70
    express, 63, 66
    implied, 63, 66
    limitations of, 70–71
    lingering apparent, 67–68
    termination, 76–77
  capacity to contract, 64–65
  classification of, 75–76
  to collect premiums, 66
  collusion, between applicant and,
      122–23
  commissions, 109–10
  continuing education, 95
  creation, principal-agency relationship,
      65
  defamation, 101–3
  definition, 62, 77
  disclosure, 99
  duties, 71–72
  fiduciary to principal, 71
  forgery, 103
  fraud, misconduct or negligence, 130
  general, 75–76
  implied authority, 63
  indicia of authority, 68, 77
  insured, keeping informed, 106
  and insurer, keeping informed, 120
  keeping insured informed, 107
  knowledge of, 64
  laws governing, 85
  liabilities to third persons, 74–75
  license required, 65, 88–89
  limitations of authority, 62, 70–71
  master and servant, 77–78
  misrepresentation, 98
  Model Regulation, 95; *see also* NAIC
      Model bills, regulations and
      statutes
  obedience to principal, 72
  power versus authority, 63
  premiums, collection of, 107–8
  premiums, lending funds for, 108–9
  ratification, 68
    effects of, 69
    form of, 69
    requirements for, 68–69
  ratification, unauthorized act, 68–69
  rebating, 100–101

Agent—*Cont.*
  receiving payment, 63
  receiving payment, equals payment to
      insurer, 320
  records and reports, 110–11
  remedies against principal, 73–74
  replacement, 99–100
  rights against third persons, 75
  special, 75–76
  subagent, 69–70
  termination of powers, 76–77
  timely and competent service, 103
  unauthorized practice of law, 104–6
  work of, 62–63
AIDS
  limitation on liberty of contract, 157
  and privacy, 568–69
  underwriting for, 158–59
Alabama statutes, establishing proper
      payee, 445
American Experience Table of Mortality,
      337
Annuities, variable, regulation of, 23
Appeals, when permitted, 26 n
Applicant
  collusion, between agent and, 122–23
  errors in contract, knowing of, 121
  minor as, 43
  presumed to have read contract, 122
Application
  delay in acting upon
    implied acceptance, 141
    and tort liability, 142–44
  insurer's unreasonable delay, 142–44
  invitation to make offer, 139
  nonwaiver clause in, 123
  not always an offer, 141
  policyowner elects dividend option, 317
  rejection of, 140–41
  signature on, 141
  withdrawal of, 140
Arizona statutes
  NAIC Model Privacy Act, law based
      on, 563
  punitive damages, 466
  use of gender-based actuarial tables,
      158
Arkansas statutes, contestability of rein-
      stated policy, 385
Armstrong Investigation, 179–80, 186,
      424
"Art of Readable Writing, The," 176

Assignee
 insurable interest of, 367
 notice of insurer to, 365
 rights of successive, 368–69
Assignment
 absolute, 356
  collateral, 357–58
  gifts, 356–57
  position of beneficiary under, 357
  sales, 357
 absolute assignment clauses, 361
 absolute, to secure loan, 360–61
 by beneficiary, 369
 beneficiary's rights on collateral
  assignment, 359–60
 clauses prohibiting, 362
 collateral assignment forms, 358–59
 collateral, clause, 361–62
 compliance with policy terms, 366
 consent of insurer, 362
 delivery, 366–67
 equitable, 371–72
 insurable interest of assignee, 367
 insurer's role, 361–65
 legal capacity of assignor, 366
 made in bad faith, 368
 made in good faith, 367–68
 notice to assignee, 365
 notice to insurer, 363
 reassignment after payment of debt,
  365
 requirements for, 365–66
 successive assignees to same policy,
  368–69
 validity of assignment, 363–65
 written, 366
Assignor
 delivery of policy, 366–67
 legal capacity of, 366
Automatic premium loan, 374
 established to prevent lapse of policy,
  316
Aviation hazard exclusion
 status or result clauses, 458
 types of aircraft defined, 220–21

Backdated policies, 190–91, 312
Bad faith, basis for damages, 463–65
Ballentine's Law Dictionary, 43 n, 48 n,
  62 n, 92 n, 162 n
Bankruptcy of policyowner-insured, 240
Bankruptcy trustee, duties, 240 n

Beneficiary
 community property rights, 252–53
 contingent, 254–55
 creditor, 255
 definition, 251
 designating contingent payee, 276
 donee, 255
 facility-of-payment clauses and, 265
 group life insurance restrictions, 253
 incidental, 256
 insurable interest, 252
 intended, 255
 inter vivos trust as, 262–63
 irrevocable, no positive rights, 254
 killing of the insured by, 245
 limitations on right to choose, 252
 policyowner
  as a minor, 253
  right to designate, 251
  right to change, 251
  right to choose, 252
 primary, 254–55
 revocable, rights of, 253, 349
 rights
  on absolute assignment, 357
  on collateral assignment, 359–60
  provided by policy, 252
Beneficiary, change of
 authority, contained in policy, 265
 change by will, 271–72
 community property rights, 267
 effect of divorce decree, 266–67
 endorsement, 269
 incompetency, 267–68
 limitations on right to change, 266
 methods of effecting change, 268–72
 substantial compliance, 269–71
Beneficiary designation
 children as, 258
 class, 258–59
 corporation as, 264
 fiancee as, 257–58
 guardian as, 261–62
 importance of, 256
 inter vivos trust as, 262–63
 issue and heirs as, 259–60
 minor as irrevocable, 261
 multiple beneficiaries, 264
 naming contingent beneficiary, 256
 no beneficiary designated, 264
 per capita, 260–61
 personal representative as, 262
 per stirpes, 260–61

Beneficiary designation—*Cont.*
  policyowner as, 265
  review designation frequently, 256
  sole proprietorship, 263–64
  spouse as, 257–58
  testamentary trust, 263
  time clause, 282
  trustee as, 262
Benefit amount, computation of, 458
Berg, Gertrude, 164
Bill of Rights, 6
Binding premium receipt
  illustrative form, 150
  subject to condition subsequent, 151
Black's Law Dictionary, 7 n, 103 n
Breach of conditions, where condition
    precedent exists, 421–22
Brokers
  defined, 85, 89
  licensing of, 88, 89
Burden of proof, 16–17

California statutes
  acknowledgement receipt, initial pre-
      mium, 308
  agent's license, qualifications for, 92
  community personal property; manage-
      ment and control, 230
  conclusive presumption, policy in
      force, 308
  licensing health insurance brokers, 85
  licensing of consultants, 86–87
  limited licenses, 94–95
  management, community personal
      property, 230
  misrepresentation, 98
  notice from insurer to assignee, 365
  premium receipts, 156
  presumption of payment, 308
  punitive damages, 464–65
  requirements for licensing, 92
  temporary licenses, 94
  unlicensed insurers, 98
Capacity to contract
  corporations, 45–46
  insurer, 45
  minors, 42–43
Case law, 5, 12, 17
Cash values
  cash surrender option, 338–39
  creditors of policyowner insured,
      238–39

Cash values—*Cont.*
  Elizur Wright, 336
  extended term insurance option,
      339–40
  Guertin legislation, 337–38
  nonforfeiture provisions, 336–43
  policy provision, 338
  reduced paid-up insurance option,
      340–41
  right to defer payment, 339
  source of, 336
  term policies, no cash value, 335
  treatment under state exemption laws,
      237–38
Causa Mortis gifts, 291
Center of gravity rule, 13
Chose in action, 228
Chose in possession, 228
Civil law and common law, 4–5
Civil law and criminal law, 18
Civil Rights Act, 1964, 24
Claims litigation, 461–62
  compensatory damages, 462–63
  countervailing forces, 466–67
  damage amounts, tied to defendant's
      wealth, 465
  punitive damages, 463–65
Collateral assignment, 357–59
  A. B. A. form, 358
  assignment forms, 358–59
  beneficiary rights, 359–60
  security of loan, 236
Colorado statutes, laws based on Licens-
    ing Model Act, 89
Commissions, 109–10
Common disaster, 282, 450
Common law, 229
  application of, 17
  and case law, 5
  and civil law, 4–5
  general principles of, 4
Common law marriage, defined, 258 n
Community property
  California statute, 230
  definition, 229, 233
  exoneration statutes, 235
  life policy, separate or community
      property, 231
  management of, 230–31
  policy, cash surrender value, 233
  rights, based on state statutes, 229
  states having community property
      laws, 229

Community property—*Cont.*
third person as beneficiary, 231–32
Compensatory damages, 462–63
Competent parties
definition, 41
mentally infirm persons, contractual
capacity of, 44
minors, 41–43
void and voidable contracts, 41
Compromise settlement
definition, 459
reference to unfair claim settlement
practices act, 459–60
Computers
LEXIS, 4
WESTLAW, 4
Condition
precedent, 146
receipts, court interpretation of, 151–56
receipts, subject to condition precedent, 151
renewal premium, condition precedent
to continue coverage, 331
subsequent, 146, 151
Conflict of laws rule, 12–13
Connecticut statutes
agent against insurer, 102
reinstatement, conditions of basic contract not altered, 389
Consideration, 66
adequacy, determination of, 39–40
benefit or detriment, 40
conditional promises, 40
with contract, consideration exchanged, 291
definition, 39, 40
inadequate, 40
legally adequate, 39
in life insurance contracts, 307
past, 40
preexisting legal duty, 40–41
promise for promise, 40
Constitution, 5
Contract Clause, 55
dual system, United States, 6
federal, 6–7
state, 7
Due Process Clauses, 55
protection, existing contracts, 55
purposes of, 5–6
Constructive trustee, 361 n
Consultant
covered by NAIC Model Act, 86

Consultant—*Cont.*
defined, 86
Contest of policy
definition, 422
definition of, 422
incontestable clause, 423
material misrepresentation, 418–21,
419–21
no contest, action outside court, 422
some not barred by incontestable
clause, 429–32
Contingent beneficiary contrasted with
contingent payee, 280–81
Contingent life insurance trust, 284
Continuing education, 95–96
Contract
adhesion, 51
agreement enforceable at law, 30
agreement enforceable, court of law, 48
aleatory, related, uncertain events, 49
avoiding, 42
between insurer and agent, 97
bilateral, 31, 38
binding promise, 30–31
breach of, 31, 47, 54
capacity to, 64–65
construction
definition, 50
rules of, 50–51
damages, 462–63
elements, enforceable informal contract, 32
formal, 31
freedom of will, 50
illegal agreements, 48
incomplete, 53
informal, 31–32, 39, 46
invalid, defects in information, 418
liberty of, 54–55
offer, 33
oral informal, 46
parol evidence rule, 54
printed, typed, handwritten matter, 52
promise or act, 33
protection, existing contracts, 55
reformation, 53
rights, value of, 55
unclear language, 51
unilateral, 31, 37–38
valid, void, and voidable, 41, 44, 418
valid without will, 291
wagering agreements, 49
written form, necessity, 47

Contract law, 140, 142
 general principles of, 55
 understanding, 2
Contract performance
 compromise settlement, 459
 existence of debt, compromise settlement, 459
 reasonable expectations doctrine,
   460–61
 when acts required are done, 442–43
Contract performance, determining payee
 acquitted beneficiary, 447–48
 assignee beneficiaries, 444
 beneficiary designation, 443
 common disaster, 449–50
 conflicting claimants, 451
 executor or administrator beneficiaries,
   443–44
 homicide beneficiaries, 446–47
 incompetent beneficiaries, 444–46
 justifiable homicides, 447
 lesser degrees of wrongful killing, 447
 policies procured in good faith, 448
 policies procured with intent to murder, 448–49
 suicide, 452–56
 trustee beneficiaries, 444
 unclaimed benefits, 451–52
 when no named beneficiary, 443
Contractual capacity, 41
 aliens, 45
 convicts, 44
 corporations, 45
 guardian appointed, 44
 insurance companies, 45–46
 intoxicated persons, 44
 mentally infirm persons, 44
 minors, 41–43
 no guardian appointed, 44
Contractural intent, 353
Conversion, 72
 of group coverage, 486–88
Coordination of benefits, 527–28
Corporations
 acts through agents, 62
 capacity to be agent, 65
Corpus Juris Secundum, 4
Couch on Insurance, 4
Counteroffer, 36, 140
Courts
 of appeal, 3
 appellate, 3, 10–11
   form of reference to, 3–4

Courts—*Cont.*
 common-law, 128
 dual court system, United States, 9
   federal courts, 9–10
   state courts, 10–11
 equitable benefits, 9
 of equity, 18–19
 federal court hierarchy, 10
 of law, 18–19
 original jurisdiction, 10
 rules of jurisdiction, 11
 special federal, 10
 supreme, 10
 trials, procedures, 13–17
 United States Supreme Court, 13
Covenant of good faith and fair dealing,
   breach of, 463–65
Coverage, creation of not possible by
   waiver or estoppel, 125
Creditors' rights
 exemptions from creditors' claims, 237
 insurance exemptions, 237–38
 in life insurance policies, 236
 to property of debtor, 236–37
 Uniform Exemptions Act, 238
Criminal law and civil law, 18

Damages
 amount of award, 465
 claims litigation, 461–62
 compensatory, 462–63
 countervailing forces, 466–67
 punitive, 463–65
Death
 computation of benefit, 458
 of offeror, 36
 presumption of, 456
Declaratory judgment
 an equitable remedy, 410
 claims questions, 411–12
 contract interpretation, 410–11
 declaratory judgment acts, 410
 insurance regulations, 412
 Uniform Declaratory Judgments Act,
   410 n
Defamation, 101–3
Deferred annuities, 542–43
Delay clause, 282
Delay in acting upon application; *see*
   Application
Delivery of policy, 168–70
Detriment, 40

Dictionary of Insurance, 378 n
Direct response advertising, 139
Direct response advertising; *see*
    Advertising
Disability
    benefits, 212–13
    general and occupational, 214–15
    monthly income, 212
    permanent, 215–16
    policy definition of total, 214
    risks not covered, 216
    total, 213–14
    waiver of premium, 213
Disappearance of insured
    explainable disappearance, 457
    keeping policy in force, 457
    mysterious disappearance, 456
    reappearance, 457
Disclosure to applicant by agent, 99
Discovery, 15
Discretion as to payment to beneficiary,
    288
Discrimination
    advertising for job applicants, 583
    affirmative action, 591–92
    among insureds of same class, 157
    applications and interviews, 583–85
    bona fide occupational qualifications,
        582–83
    disparate impact, 580–82
    disparate treatment, 580
    employment practices and decisions,
        582
    federal statutes, 579
    Immigration Reform and Control Act of
        1986, 585
    job performance evaluations, 585–87
    limitations on liberty of contract, 157
    mandatory unisex rates, 158
    NAIC Model Regulation (impairments),
        157
    NAIC Model Regulation (sex), 157
    New York statute, 157
    nonsmoker premium discounts, 159–60
    penalties for employment, 593
    preferences of co-workers or cus-
        tomers, 588
    pregnancy, 590–91
    retaliation by employer, 592–93
    reverse, 591
    sexual harassment, 588–90
    state statutes, 580
    underwriting for AIDS, 158–59

Discrimination—*Cont.*
    unfair handicap, 157
    unfair sex discrimination, 157
    uniform standards for job performance,
        587–88
    wrongful discharge, 593–94
Dividends
    automatic dividend option, 331
    creditors attaching, 329
    one-year term dividend option, 330–31
    options, 330–31
    other dividend privileges, 331
    paid from earned surplus, 329
    policyowner's right to, 329
    right to withdraw or direct application
        of, 228
    stock and policyowner dividends de-
        fined, 328–29
    two types, 317 n
    use of accumulation to pay up or ma-
        ture policy, 317
Divorce
    and community property, 232–34
    interpleader action, 244
    and property rights, 258
Doctrine
    of consideration, 39
    election of remedies, 127
    respondeat superior, 102

Electronic Funds Transfer Act, 318
Employee Retirement Income Security
    Act (ERISA), 106
Employment laws, 2
Endorsement method of changing benefi-
    ciary, 269
English Statute of Frauds, 47 n
Equitable principles
    clean hands, 397
    court of equity, no jury, 398
    laches, 397–98
    no adequate remedy at law, 396–97
Equitable remedies
    declaratory judgment, 410
    election of, 127
    interpleader, 399–402
    reformation, 406–10
    rescission, 402
    rescission, not available, material mis-
        representation, 406
Equity, 408–9; *see also* Equitable princi-
    ples *and* Equitable remedies

ERISA, 85, 106
  and group insurance, 497–98
  and punitive damages, 467
  recordkeeping, 111 n
Estoppel, 121
  from application process, 129
  common situations, 129
  defined, 116
  by election, 127
  equitable, 116
  forbidden, 124
  invoked, premium payments, 130
  legal doctrine, 115
  parol evidence rule, 128–29
Exemption laws
  bankruptcy of policyowner-insured,
    240
  cash values, 238–39
  creditors of beneficiary, 241–42
  creditors of policyowner-insured, 238
  federal tax lien, 239
  insurance, 237–38
  Oklahoma statute, 239
  premium payments in fraud of credi-
    tors, 240–41
  premiums paid from wrongfully taken
    funds, 241
  proceeds of life policy, 239–40
  purpose of, 237
  Uniform Exemptions Act, 237–38
Exoneration statutes in community prop-
    erty states, 235
Extended term insurance
  definition, 339
  legal questions, 339–40
Extra-contract compensatory damages,
    462–63

Fair Labor Standards Act, 24
Federal regulation of advertising; see
    Advertising
Federal statutes
  age discrimination in employment, 579
  bankruptcy, policyowner-insured, 240
  Bankruptcy Reform Act of 1978, 240
  Consolidated Omnibus Budget Recon-
    ciliation Act (COBRA), 528–29
  Declaratory Judgment Act, 410–12
  employees, protection of, 579–80
  federal employment statutes, 579
  Group Health Insurance Model Acts,
    527

Federal statutes—*Cont.*
  McCarran-Ferguson Act, 2, 22–23, 542
  Medicare and Medicare supplement
    policies, 524–25
  NAIC Model Privacy Act, 562–68
  Privacy act of 1974, 561–62
  privacy, constitutional protection of,
    560
Federal tax lien under exemption laws,
    239
Federal Trade Commission, 23
Fiduciary
  definition, 62 n
  role, 71
Filing and approval of policy, 194
Filing method of effecting beneficiary
    change, 269
Financial planners, principal business,
    87–88
Flesch, Rudolph, 176
Flesch scale readability score, 176–77
Flexibility under settlement options, 288
Forgery by agent on application, 103
Franchise health insurance, 502
Fraud(s)
  definition, 464
  fraudulent impersonation, 429–30
  fraudulent misrepresentation, 419–20
  statute of, 46–47

Gaon, Joseph, 159
Gift *causa mortis,* 291
Grace period, 181–83, 481–82, 511
Group health insurance, 502, 526–28
Group life insurance
  actively at work full time, 491
  actively at work requirement, 490
  Civil Service Commission, responsible
    informing employees of benefits,
    501
  conflict of laws, 495–96
  creditor rates, 494
  definitions, 478–79
    association groups, 480
    creditor groups, 479–80
    credit union groups, 480–81
    discretionary groups, 481
    employer-employee groups, 479
    labor union groups, 480
    trusteed groups, 480
  dependents, 489
  dividends, 493–94
  employee welfare benefit plans, 497

Group life insurance—*Cont.*
  and ERISA, 497–98
  ERISA, impact on, 497–98
  federal government
    for civilian employees, 500
    FEGLI and SGLI, 500–501
  federal taxation, impact on, 497
  group policy premiums and dividends,
    493
  history, 476–78
  increase in amount of insurance, 491
  Internal Revenue Code, Section 89
    discrimination tests, 498–99
    employees excluded, 499
    highly compensated employees, 499
    other Section 89 rules, 500
    plans, 500
    qualifications tests, 498
  master policy, 489–90
  Montgomery Ward introduced concept,
    477
  policyholder as agent, 494–95
  standard policy provisions, 481
    application, 484
    certificate, 486
    continuation of coverage during dis-
      ability, 488
    conversion, 486
    conversion at termination of employ-
      ment, 486–87
  conversion at policy termination, 487
  creditor group life insurance certifi-
    cates, 488
  evidence of insurability, 484
  extension of death benefit, 487–88
  grace period, 481–82
  incontestable clause, 482–83
  misstatement of age, 484–85
  nonforfeiture, 488–89
  settlement, 485
  supplementary bill relating to conver-
    sion, 488
  termination of, 491–92
    date of, 493
    definition, 491–92
Guaranteed insurability option, 216–17
Guardian
  beneficiary designation, 261–62
  minor's estate, 446
  payment of death benefit, 446
Guertin, Alfred N., 337
Guertin legislation, 337–38

Hand, Learned, 152
Health insurance, 507–8
  benefit provisions, 520
  cancellation and renewal provisions,
    522–24
    guaranteed renewable, 523
    noncancellable, 522–23
    optional cancellation, 522
    optionally renewable, 522
  definition of terms, 516
    hospital, 517–18
    injury, 516–17
    physician, 518–19
    sickness, 517
  exclusions and limitations, 521–22
  group, 526
    Consolidated Omnibus Budget Rec-
      onciliation Act (COBRA), 528
    continuation of, 528–29
    coordination of benefits, 527–28
    Model Acts, 527; *see also* NAIC
      Model bills, regulations and
      statutes
    overinsurance, 527
  long-term care policies, 525–26
  mandated provisions, 520–21
  Medicare and Medicare supplement
    policies, 524–25
  optional provisions, 514
    change of occupation, 514
    illegal occupation, 516
    intoxicants and narcotics, 516
    overinsurance, 514–16
    payment of claims, 514
  persons covered, 509
  preexisting conditions, 519–20
  required provisions, 509–10
    beneficiary change, 513–14
    claims, 512–13
    entire contract provision, 510
    grace period provision, 511
    legal actions, 513
    reinstatement, 512
    time limit on certain defenses provi-
      sion, 510–11
  Universal Individual Accident and
    Sickness Policy Provisions Law,
    508, 508–9
Health insurance, preferred usage, 544 n
Heir apparent, defined, 260
Holmes, Oliver Wendell, 344
Home service life policy, 265 n

Idaho statutes
  exoneration statutes, 235
  records and reports, 110
Illinois statutes
  automatic nonforfeiture benefit, 341
  dividend options, 330
  fraudulent or material misrepresenta-
    tion, 420
  lapse, of policy, 379
  less value statutes, 191–92
  minor as insurance applicant, 43
  misrepresentation, 420
  Monahan case, 434
  nonresident licenses, 93
  notice from insurer to assignee, 365
  physician, use of term, 519
  premium notices, 321–22
  records and reports, 110
  reinstatement laws, 379
  relating to premium notices, 321–22
  requirements for licensing, 92
  Revised Statutes, 3
  simultaneous death acts, 450
  spendthrift clause, 243–44
  state employment statutes, 580
  time limit on legal or equitable actions,
    190–91
  waiving need for Illinois license, 93
Illustrative policy provisions
  collateral assignment, 188
  divisible surplus, 186
  entire contract, 183–84
  free examination period, 179
  grace period, 181–82
  misstatement of age, 184–85
  policy exchange, 189
  suicide, 188–89
Income tax, 329
Incontestable clause
  breach of conditions, 421–22
  conflict with other policy provisions,
    425–29
    aviation exclusion, 426
    majority view, 426–27
    minority view, 427
    misstatement of age clause, 428–29
    model statute, 427–28
  contest, meaning of, 418
  contests
    barred by, 429–32
    meaning of, 422
  Conway case, 427, 428
  development of, 423, 423–25

Incontestable clause—*Cont.*
  disability and accidental death cover-
    age, 432–33
  disability clause phrase: "During
    lifetime of insured," 433–34
  effective date of policy, 436
  fraudulent impersonation, 429–30
  impact on other policy provisions,
    426–27
  lack of insurable interest, 431
  misstatement of age clause, 428–29
  Monahan case, 433–34
  not applicable, nonpayment of premi-
    ums, 425–26
  omitting phrase: "during lifetime . . .,"
    434–36
  policy procured with intent to murder,
    431–32
  statutory remedy, 434
Insurability
  and good health, 381
  not the same as good health, 381
  satisfactory to insurer, 382
Insurability premium receipt, 147–49
Insurable interest
  in another person's life, 162–65
  blood relationship, 163
  business relationships and, 164–65
  consent of insured, 165
  defined, 162
  English statute requiring, 160
  of fundamental importance, 418
  historical development, 160–61
  marriage relationship, 164
  in one's own life, 161
  question of fact, 165–66
Insurance
  agents and brokers; *see* Agent
  business, mismanagement, serious so-
    cial and economic consequences,
    24
  companies, contractual capacity, 45
  federal regulation, 2, 23–24
    non-insurance activities, 24
  industry
    employees, statutory protection of,
      579–80
    employment picture, 578–79
    employment practices; *see*
      Discrimination
  insurance, study of, 87, 96
  law, understanding, 2
  regulation of, 2

Insurance—*Cont.*
  regulations
    commerce clause, federal constitution, 19–20
    federal situation today, 23
    history, 19
    interstate commerce, 19–20
  state regulation, 2, 24
  variable life, regulation of, 23
  work performed, agents, 62
Insured
  definition, 192 n
  disappearance of, 456–57
  killed by beneficiary, 245
Insurer
  and agent, fraud, misconduct or negligence of, 130
  breach of condition waived, 131–32
  claims investigation, delay of, 132
  as corporation, 329 n
  delay in acting upon application, 140–44
  denial of liability, 132–33
  dishonored checks and waiver policy, 131
  election of remedies, 127
  expressly waives timely payment, 322
  failure, receive complete information, 130
  implied waiver, timely payments, 130–31
  keeping surplus for contingencies, 329
  knowing and assenting, contract contents, 120
  limitation of time to sue, waiving, 132
  and payee, debtor-creditor relationship, 289
  premium due notices and waiver policy, 131
  premiums, collection of, 307
  promise to pay, 132
  proof of loss, 132
  proof of loss and waiving breach of condition, 132
  responsible for carrying out policyowner's wishes as to dividends, 329
  tort liability of, 142–44, 166–67
  waived right, receive cash payment, 131
  when estopped from lapsing policy, 321
Interest income option
  policy permits, 277

Interest income option—*Cont.*
  right to change to another settlement option, 278
Interpleader
  an equitable remedy, 399
  claimants claiming same property, 402
  claimants in different states, 402
  defined, 50 n
  disinterested stakeholder, 401
  in divorce cases, 244
  how it is used, 399–400
  instituted by plaintiff or defendant, 401
  no adequate remedy at law, 400–401
  statutory, 400
Inter vivos trust as beneficiary, 262–63
Intestate, statutes relating to, 290
Investment Advisers Acts, 23, 87–88
Investment Company Act, 23
Investment counsel, restrictions using term, 88
Investments, return on, 288
Irrevocable beneficiary
  minor, 261
  no positive rights, 254
  policyowner, 251–52

Joint tenancy
  in lieu of will, 291
  will substitute, 291
Jurisdiction, 11

Kansas statutes, licensing of agents, 91
Kentucky statutes, divorce, 266

Laches, 397–98
Lapse, of policy
  definition, 378
  reinstatement provision, 377–79
Law
  acceptance of, 3
  administrative rules and regulations, 8–9
  agency, 63–65
  applicable, determination of, 11–12
  case
    application of, 17
    when used, 13
  civil
    and common law, 4–5
    Louisiana, civil-law state, 5 n

Law—*Cont.*
  codes, 3
  common, 4, 49
    application of, 17
  community property laws, 229–31
  computer, 3
  concept of, 2
  conflict of, 12–13
  continuing education, 96
  criminal, 18
  and equity, 19
  general contract, principles of, 30–59
  of gifts, 298
  model, 9; *see also* NAIC Model bills,
    regulations and statutes
  rule of contract, 64
  solicitation of business, 97
  sources of, 3, 24
  statutes, 7–8
  structure of, 2
  unauthorized practice of, 104–6
  of wills, 289–90
Legitimated child, defined, 259 n
LEXIS, 4
Liability of insurer
  delay in acting upon application,
    141–44
  and insurable interest, 165–66
  tort, 142–44, 166–67
Licensing
  of agents and brokers, 85–86
  agents and brokers, 90
  exemptions, 95
  interstate requirements, 90–91
  laws, all states and District of Colum-
    bia, 88
  laws, patterns among, 89
  limited, 94–95
  nonresident, 92–93
  nonresident licenses, 92
  persons who must be licensed, 90
  requirements for, 91, 92
  suspension, revocation, refusal, 96
  temporary, 94
  twisting, 96 n, 99
  unlicensed insurers, 97–98
Life and health insurance advertising; *see*
    Advertising
Life income option,
  and settlement option, 288
Life insurance
  application, Statute of Frauds, 47–48

Life insurance—*Cont.*
  beneficiary, value, insurable interest,
    49
  initial premium, collection, 67
  minor as applicant, 43
  parol evidence rule, 52–53
  trusts, valid substitute for will, 293
  and unilateral contracts, 31
  validity of, 48–49
Life insurance agent; *see* Agent
Life insurance contract
  advantages over will, 291
  competent contracting parties, 168
  consideration, 167–68
  delivery of policy
    as condition precedent, 168
    constructive, 169
    for inspection, 169–70
  effective date of, 170
  formation of
    acceptance, 139
    application, signature, 141
    binding receipt, 149–51
    competent contracting parties, 168
    consideration, 167–68
    court cases involving receipts,
      151–56
    delivery of policy, 168–69
    insurability receipt, 147–49
    insurable interest, 160–67
    offer and acceptance theory, 139
    offer by applicant, 139
    premium receipts, 144–46
    rejection and counteroffer, 140
    rejection of application, 140–41
    selection and discrimination, 156–60
    solicitation by agent, 139
    statutes and regulations relating to,
      156
    withdrawal of offer, 140
  provides dividend options, 330
  rules, formation of, 139–97
  substitute for will, 291
Life Insurance Disclosure Model Regula-
    tion, 99
Louisiana statutes
  licensing health insurance brokers, 85
  records and recordkeeping, 111
  unfair methods of competition, 103

Maine statutes, insurable interest in an-
    other person's life, 162

Malice, definition, 464
Malpractice insurance, 107
Maryland statutes, case of equity, 398
Massachusetts statutes
  first nonforfeiture law, 336
  law based on Licensing Model Act, 89
  licensing of consultants, 86
  mandatory unisex rates, 158
  nonresident licenses, 93
  requirements for licensing, 92
  requires nonresident agents have Massachusetts license, 93
  suspension, revocation, refusal of license, 96
  temporary licenses, 94
Material misrepresentation
  adequate remedy at law, 406
  and incontestable clause, 423
  what it means, 418–19
McCarran-Ferguson Act, 2, 22–23, 542
Michigan statutes
  divorce of policyowner, 266
  licensing of consultants, 86
Ministerial act, defined, 169 n
Minnesota statutes, divorce, 266
Minor
  Alabama statute, 445
  as an insurance applicant, 43
  contracts, cannot avoid, 42–43
  disaffirmance of a contract, 42
  Montana statute, 446
  policyowners, New York statute, 253
  protected by life insurance trust, 284
  release of certain rights, 458–59
Misrepresentation, 98
  agent, 98
  of intention, 405
  of material fact, 405
  of opinion, 405
  related to cause of loss, 421
  statutes relating to
    Illinois, 420
    Louisiana, 427
    Missouri, 421
    New York, 427
    Ohio, 420
    Pennsylvania, 420
Missouri statutes
  duty of agent, premiums collected, 108
  misrepresentation related to cause of loss, 421
  suicide statutes, 453

Misstatement of age provision
  and group insurance, 484–85
  policy provisions, 184–85
  and the incontestable clause, 428–29
Model regulations, 95; *see also* NAIC
  Model bills, regulations and statutes
Model Rules Governing Advertising of
  Life Insurance; *see* Advertising
Montana statutes
  establishing proper beneficiary, 446
  incompetent beneficiaries, 446
  mandatory unisex rates, 158
  punitive damages claims, 466
Montgomery Ward, introduced concept
  of group insurance, 477

NAIC Model bills, regulations and
  statutes
  accident and sickness, 508, 516–18
  advertising accident and sickness insurance, 545–52
  agents and brokers licensing, 85–86, 88–90, 94–96
  agents continuing education, 95–96
  consultant, 86–87
  disclosure requirements, 553
  discrimination, 157
  form and content of advertising, 552
  governing advertising of life insurance, 552–53
  group health definitions and provisions, 527
  group life insurance definitions, 478–81
  incontestable clause, 427–28
  individual accident and sickness policy provisions, 508–10
  lapse, 378
  mandated benefits, 520–21
  Medicare supplement insurance minimum standards, 525
  Medicare supplement, minimum standards, 525
  newborn children, 509
  persons covered, 509
  policy language simplification, 509
  preexisting condition, defined, 519
  preexisting conditions, 519–20
  simplified language, 176–77, 509
  simultaneous death, 450
  solicitation of insurance, 99–100

NAIC Model bills—*Cont.*
 unfair claims settlement practices,
  459–60
 unfair trade practices, 460
 variable life contract and regulation, 23
 war risk exclusion, 218
National Association of Insurance Commissioners (NAIC), 9
National Association of Securities Dealers, 90
National Labor Relations Act, 23
Necessaries, 42–43
New Jersey statutes
 definition, moral turpitude, 92
 limited licenses, 95
 nonresident licenses, 93
 requirements for licensing, 91, 92
New York statutes
 divorce of policyowner, 266
 divisible surplus provision, 186
 illegal contracts, 48
 insurable interest, 163
 law based on Licensing Model Act, 89
 licensing of consultants, 86–87
 minor policyowners, 253
 misrepresentation, not deemed material, 405
 misstatement of age, 184–85
 Monahan case, 434
 notice from insurer to assignee, 365
 optional methods, application of dividends, 330
 reinstatement laws, 378
 settlement option provision, 276
 settlement options tables, 180–81
 standard policy provisions law, 180
 temporary licenses, 94
 time limit on legal or equitable actions,
  191
 unfair sex discrimination, 157
Noncore coverage, defined, 499 n
Nonforfeiture provisions
 additional benefits, 343
 Armstrong Investigation, New York,
  336
 automatic nonforfeiture benefit, 341
 beneficiary's rights, 343
 cash surrender option, 338–39
 extended term, 348–49
 extended term insurance option,
  339–40
 Guertin legislation, 337–38
 historical development, 336–38

Nonforfeiture provisions—*Cont.*
 incomplete nonforfeiture transactions,
  341–43
 Massachusetts enacted first nonforfeiture law, 336
 policy loans
  amount of, 345–46
  contrasted with true loans, 344
  endorsement, 347
  historical perspective, 344
  interest rate, 346–47
  misnomer, 344
  premium, 345
  repayment of, 349–50
  using policy as security, 343
  variable policy loan interest rate
   laws, 347
 reduced paid-up insurance, 340–41
 reduced paid-up policies, 348–49
 standard policy provision laws, 336
Nonpayment of premium
 agreement by the insurer, 322
 and estoppel, 323
 excuses for, 322–27
 failure, agent to collect premium, 325
 failure, due to war, 326–27
 failure of post office to deliver, 326
 failure to send premium notice, 325
 implied waiver of timely payment,
  322–23
 refusal of tender by insurer, 323
Nonsmokers, premium discounts, 159
North Carolina statutes, contestability of
  reinstated policy, 385–86
North Dakota statutes
 contestability of reinstated policy, 386
 law based on Licensing Model Act, 89

Offer
 acceptance of, 36–38
 acceptance, unconditional, 36
 applicant, made by, 139
 for bilateral contract, 38
 choices of offeree, 33
 commitment, 34
 communication of acceptance, 37–38
 communication to offeree, 34–35
 death, offeror, offeree, 36
 duration of, 35
 incapacity of offeror or offeree, 36
 insurer's duty to act promptly on, 37
 made by applicant, 139

Offer—*Cont.*
  made by insurer, 139
  mutual assent, essential, 37
  promise or act, 33
  rejection and counteroffer, 35–36, 140
  requirements for a valid, 34
  revocation of, 35
  for unilateral contract, 37
  valid, requirements of, 34
  who may accept, 37
  withdrawal or revocation, 35
Ohio statutes, fraudulent or material mis-
      representation, 420
Oklahoma statutes
  law based on Licensing Model Act, 89
  policies procured in good faith, 448
  proceeds of life policy, 239
Oppression, definition, 464
Optional policy provisions
  assignment, 188
  collateral assignment, 188
  contract change, 189
  ownership, 187–88
  policy exchange, 189
  suicide, 188–89
Options in life insurance policies
  cash surrender, 338–39
  dividends, right to, 329
  extended term insurance option,
      339–40
  nonforfeiture, 338–41
  settlement, 275–82
Oregon statutes
  good faith policies, 448
  unfair sex discrimination, 157

Parol
  definition, 52
  evidence rule and estoppel, 52, 128
    definition, 52
    formation defects, 52–53
    incomplete contract, 53
    interpretation, 53
    reformation, 53
    subsequent modifications, 54
Participating policies, dividends, 329
Past consideration, 40
Payee
  contingent, 276, 280
  settlement agreement, 276–77
  short-term survivorship, 281–82

Payment of premium
  to agent, payment to insurer, 320
  excuses for nonpayment, 322–27
  irrelevant who pays, 317
  method of, 313–17
  presumption of, 307
  renewal of obligation, 309–11
  time of, 311–13
  waiver of timely payment, 309
Pennsylvania statutes, misrepresentation,
      98, 420
Per capita beneficiary designation,
      260–61
Personal property, 228
  chose in action, 228
  chose in possession, 228
  definition, 289 n
  disposed of by will, 289
Person, definition of, 31
Per stirpes beneficiary designation,
      260–61
Pleadings, 14–15
Policy
  backdated, 312
  cash surrender, not eligible reinstate-
      ment, 379
  cash value enhanced, payment by auto-
      matic premium loan, 316
  cash value, from level premium, 336
  caused to lapse, failure to renew, 310
  contents, 177–78
  contest of, court action, 418
  contests, material misrepresentation,
      418–21
  delivery of, 168–170
  delivery of, *prima facie,* 308
  dividends, 328–31
  drafted by insurer, 176
  face page, 178–79
  in force, payment initial premium and
      delivery of policy, 307
  home service insurance, 265 n
  language raises rebuttable presumption,
      308
  legal constraints, form and content,
      176
  nonparticipating, 329
  optional provisions
    assignment, 188
    collateral assignment, 188
    contract change, 189
    ownership, 187–88

Policy—*Cont.*
  optional provisions—*Cont.*
    policy exchange privilege, 189
    suicide, 188–89
  participating, 329
  right to surrender for cash value, 228
  simplified language, 176–77
  term, 335–36
Policy forms, approval required, 98
Policy loans, 228
  amount of maximum loan, 345–46
  automatic premium, 345
  available from level premium policy,
      336
  beneficiary's rights, 349
  cash loans, 345
  and collateral assignments, 357–58
  endorsement, 347
  interest rate, 346–47
  not a true loan, 344
  repayment of, 349–50
  secured, 344
  security for, 344
  variable policy loan interest rate laws,
      347
Policy provisions
  backdated, 190–91, 312
  divisible surplus, 186
  entire contract, 183–84
  filing and approving, 194
  forfeiture for failure to repay policy
      loan, 192
  grace period, 181–82
    interest charge, 182–83
    length of period, 182
  including settlement option, 277
  incontestable clause, 183
  introductory statutory language, 180
  less value statutes, 191–92
  misstatement of age, 184–85
  nonforfeiture, 181
  policy loan, 186–87
  reinstatement, 187, 379–90
  required, 179–80
  settlement options tables, 180–81
Premium receipts
  approval conditional, 147–56
  binding, 149–51
  conditional, 146–56
  insurability conditional receipt, 147–49
  promises of insurer are binding, 307 n
  statutes and regulations relating to, 156
  submitted with application, 144–46

Premiums
  accompanying application, 139
  almost no excuse for nonpayment, 322
  backdated policies, 312
  California Insurance Code, 308
  clause referring to initial, 308
  collection by agent, 107–8
  definition, 307
  discount, nonsmokers, 159
  extension of time, 312–13
  failure of agent to collect premium, 325
  failure of post office to deliver pre-
      mium, 326
  failure to pay premiums due to war,
      326
  failure to send premium notice, 325
  grace period, 312
  implied waiver of timely payment,
      322–23
  importance of initial, 307
  initial, payment of, 307
  insurer agrees not to lapse policy, 322
  insurer waives timely payment, 322
  level, 336
  method of payment, 313–17
  notices, not always required, 321–22
  paid in advance, 313, 327
  paid under mistake of fact, 327
  payment of
    by agent or broker, 320
    by allotment plans, 319
    by assignee, 320
    by beneficiary, 319
    conclusive presumption of, 307
    by credit, 315–16
    by dividends, 317
    by employer, 318
    by order on a bank, 318
    by personal check, 314–15
    by preauthorized check plans, 318
    by preauthorized electronic funds
        transfer, 318–19
    by premium loan, 316–17
    by promissory note, 315
    rebuttable presumption of, 307
  persons making payment, 317–20
  persons receiving payment, 320–21
  presumption of payment, 307
  refusal of tender by Insurer, defined,
      323
  renewal of, 309–11
  renewal premium due date, 311–12
  return of, 327–28

Premiums—*Cont.*
  risk not assumed, premium returned, 328
  suicide clause, 327–28
  Supreme Court of South Carolina, 309
  time of payment, 311–13
  waiver of timely payment, 308–9
  whole life renewal, 310
Presumption, 16
  applicant has read signed policy, 121
  conclusive, 307–8
  of payment, 307–9
  rebuttable, based on language, 308
  rebuttable, defined, 307
  that policy is in force, 308
Prima facie case, 16
Principal
  agent, acting on behalf of, 106
  apparent authority, 66–67
  authority compared to agents, 64–65
  control over agent, degree, 71
  creation, agent-principal relationship, 65
  duties, 73
  independent contractor, 78
  liabilities to third persons, 74
  limitation of authority, 70–71
  lingering apparent authority, 68
  master and servant relationship, 77–78
    servant status, determination of, 78
  ratification, 68
  ratification, effects of, 69
  ratification, form of, 69
  ratification, requirements for, 68–69
  remedies against agent, 72–73
  rights against third persons, 74
  rights, waived by authorized agent, 123–24
  subagent, 70
Privacy
  access to recorded personal information, 565–66
  adverse underwriting decisions, 566–67
  AIDS and, 568–69
    position papers on, 568
    public concern regarding underwriting, 569
  constitutional protection of, 560
  correction, amendment or deletion of information, 566
  definition, 558
  disclosure authorization forms, 565

Privacy—*Cont.*
  disclosure limitations and conditions, 567
  enforcement, 567–68
  Fair Credit Reporting Act, 560–61
  federal legislation on, 560–62
  history of privacy law, 559
  investigative consumer reports, 565
  NAIC Model Privacy Act, 562–68
  notice of insurance information practices, 564–65
  pretext interviews, 563–64
  Privacy Act of 1974, 561–62
  state privacy laws, 562–63
  tort of invasion of privacy, 559
Proceeds, safety of, prefer settlement agreement over trust, 288
Process of nature rule, defined, 210 n
Prohibited policy provisions, 189
  dating back, 190–91
  Illinois statute, 190, 191
  less value statutes, 191–92
  New York statute, 191
  time limit on legal or equitable actions, 190
Prohibited Transaction Exemption, 111 n
Proof of facts, 15–17
Property
  community, 229–35
  testamentary disposition of, 290
  transfer at death without will, 290–93
Property law, 226–29
Property rights, 226–50
  chose in action, 228
  chose in possession, 228
  community, 229–35
  by operation of law, 228–29
  under insurance policy terms, 228
Pro tanto, defined, 388 n
Public policy, 124–25
Punitive damages, 463–65
  California statute, 463
  countervailing forces, 466–67
  damage amounts, 465

Real property, 227
  definition, 289 n
  disposed of by will, 289
Reasonable expectations doctrine, 460–61
Rebating, 100–101
  defined, 96 n

Reformation
  burden of proof, 409–10
  grounds for, 407–9
  for misrepresentation, innocent or
      intentional, 409
  for mistake, 407
  mutual mistake, 407
  suit to reform, no contest of policy, 422
Refunds, as dividends, participating pol-
      icy, 329
Registered investment advisor, 88
Reinstatement
  addition of new contract terms, 388–89
  and adverse selection, 380–82
  contestability of reinstated policy,
      384–87
  continuation of original contract, 384
  contractural right, 384
  death during reinstatement application
      review, 382–84
  and insurability, 380–82
  law governing reinstated policy, 389–90
  North Dakota statute, 386
  payment of unpaid premiums, plus
      interest, 382
  policy, surrendered, cash value, not
      reinstated, 380
  and suicide clause, 387–88
  suicide clause in reinstated policy, 387
  West Virginia statutes, contestability of
      reinstated policy, 385
  when a new contract, 384
Release
  of a collateral assignment, 357–58
  of certain rights, 458–59
Remedies, equitable; see Equitable
      remedies
Replacement, NAIC Model Regulation,
      99–100
Replacement of Life Insurance and An-
      nuities Model Regulation, 100
Representations
  compared to warranties, 425
  true as to facts material to risk, 424–25
Rescission
  an equitable remedy, 402
  fraud, 405
  grounds for, 403–4
  how accomplished, 402–3
  important to insurers, 402
  innocent misrepresentation, 405
  and material misrepresentation, 419

Rescission—*Cont.*
  misrepresentation of material fact,
      404–5
  and Monahan case, 434
  related to incontestable clause, 403
Respondeat superior, 78, 102 n
Restatements of the Law, 4
Rhode Island statutes
  policies procured in good faith, 448
  relating to punitive damages, 465
RIA; *see* Registered investment advisor,
      88
Rights
  by operation of law, 228–29
  policyowner, to elect way dividends are
      applied, 329
  prematurity, right to transfer, 228
  for public benefit, cannot be waived,
      124–25
  of survivorship, definition, 291
  under life insurance policy terms, 228
Risk selection, 156
Rules, common-law, 128

Securities Act, 23
Securities Exchange Act, 23, 85
Securities Exchange Commission (SEC),
      87
  rules governing receipt compensation,
      88
Security Acts, 1933, 1940, 23
Security laws, 2
Selection of risks, 156
Settlement agreements
  beneficiary, naming others to receive
      funds, 292
  character, settlement option, set forth
      in, 276
  death through common disaster, 281
  discretion as to payment to beneficiary,
      287
  election of options, 276
  insurer and payee, debtor-creditor rela-
      tionship, 289
  insurer cannot act as personal counse-
      lor, 289
  no expense incurred, 288–89
  problems related to short-term survi-
      vorship, 450
  proceeds commingled for investment
      purposes, 289
  return on investment, 288

Settlement agreements—*Cont.*
  for safety of proceeds, 288
  time clauses, 282
  and trusts contrasted, 287
  trusts, more flexible than, 288
  using trusts in lieu of, 282
  valid will substitute, 291
Settlement options
  choice by beneficiary, 277
  choice by policyowner, 277
  community property, 234–35
  contingent beneficiaries, 280–81
  contingent payees, 280–81
  income for fixed period, 278–79
  income for life, 279–80
  income of fixed amount, 279
  installment payout versus lump sum
      payment, 276
  interest income, 277–78
  life income, 288
  limitations on, 280
  tables, 180–81
  and trusts, 287–89
  types of, 277–80
Sherman Antitrust Act, 21, 23
Short-term survivorship
  survivorship clause, 450
  use of settlement option, 450
Short-term survivorship of beneficiary,
      survivorship clause, 282
Simultaneous death
  definition, 281
  Illinois statute, 450
  Uniform Simultaneous Death Act, 450
  use of settlement options for, 450
  use of survivorship clause for, 450
South Carolina statutes
  acting as agent for insurer, 98
  agent for nonadmitted insurer, 98
  sharing commissions, 110
  waiver of timely payment, 309
South Eastern Underwriters
  Decision, 2
Spendthrift clause
  creditors not harmed, 242
  form of, 244
  Illinois Insurance Code, 243
  purpose, 242
  settlement agreement, 277
  special type of trust, 256
State, power to regulate insurance busi-
      ness, 88

Statute of Frauds, 48
  history, 46–47
  listing, five contract classes, 47
Straight life insurance, defined, 180 n
Subrogation, 252 n
Substantial compliance rule in change of
      beneficiary, 269–71
Suicide
  and accidental death benefit, 456
  burden of proof, 453–55
  exclusion, 452
  policies without suicide exclusion, 456
  statutes
      Missouri, 453
      Tennessee, 453
  while sane or insane, 453
Summary judgment, defined, 273 n
Survivorship clause, 282
Sweet, Judge, 160

Temporary coverage, under conditional
      receipt, 144–146
Tennessee statutes, suicide, 453
Testamentary disposition of property, in
      violation, statute of wills, 292
Testamentary intent, 353
Texas statutes
  automatic nonforfeiture benefit, 341
  commissions, 109
  definition, agent, 89
  licensing of consultants, 86–87
  persons who must be licensed, 90
  policies procured in good faith, 448
  requirements for licensing, 92
  temporary licenses, 94
Time clause, 282
Tontine system, 186 n
Tort, 72
  defined, 48 n, 101, 102
  insurer liability for delay in acting
      upon application, 142–44
Transfer of policy rights
  intestate succession, 370
  property settlement agreements,
      divorce, 370
  sale of assets, 370–71
  wills, 370
Trial procedures, pleadings, discovery,
      proof of facts, 14–17
Trust
  administrative expense incurred,
      288–89

Trust—*Cont.*
   contingent life insurance, 284
   definition, 283
   document, existence of, 285
   inter vivos, 284–86
   irrevocable life insurance, 284
   in lieu of will, 292–93
   life insurance, 283–84
   minor children, 284
   naming trustee, 283
   property, invested separately from
      other trusts, 289
   responsibilities of insurer, 284–85
   responsibility of insurer, 284–85
   return on investment, 288
   revocable life insurance, 284
   rule against accumulations, 287
   rule against perpetuities, 285–87
   rules of law, 285–87
   testamentary, 283, 285–86
   trustee, acting as personal counselor,
      289
   when created, 283
Trustee
   holds legal title to property, 283
   legal title to proceeds, 289
   premium nonpayment, breach of fidu-
      ciary duty, 319
Twisting, 96 n, 99

Unapproved policy forms, 98
Unauthorized practice of law, 104–6
Uniform Commercial Code, 47 n
Uniform laws, 9
United States Code, 3
United States Supreme Court, 20
Universal and variable insurance laws,
   192
   universal life insurance regulations,
      192–93
   variable life insurance laws, 193–94
   variable universal life insurance laws,
      194
Unsecured debt, defined, 256 n
Utah statutes, contestability of reinstated
   policy, 385

Value, determination of, 39

Waiver
   from application process, 129

Waiver—*Cont.*
   common situations, 129
   creation of coverage, 125
   defined, 116
   and estoppel in group advertising, 538
   express, 117–18
   forbidden, 124
   implied, 118–19
   intent to waive, 119–20
   invoked, premium payments, 130
   legal doctrine of, 115
   releasing right, receive money, 125–26
   revocation of, 126
   by silence, 119
War hazard exclusion, 458
War hazard exclusion rider, 217–18
   existence of war, 219
   military activities, 219
   military service, 218–19
   status and result clauses, 218–19
Warranties
   Armstrong Investigation, 424
   history, 423–24
WESTLAW, 4
West Virginia statutes
   contestability of reinstated insurance,
      385
   nonresident licenses, 93
   rules, life, sickness policies, 93
Wholesale life insurance, 502
Will
   an instrument, distribution of property,
      289–90
   characteristics of, 290
   contracts, valid without will, 291
   formerly *last will and testament*, 289
   gifts *causa mortis*, 291
   intestate, 290
   joint tenancy, 291
   life insurance contract, substitute for,
      291
   life insurance trust, valid substitute,
      293
   probate of, 290
   substitutes for, 290–93
   validity of, spelled out by state stat-
      utes, 290
Williston on Contracts, 4
Wright, Elizur, 336
Wyoming statutes
   accident and health policies, signed by
      resident agents, 93
   nonresident licenses, 93